Here's what America's top magazines, newspapers and readers are saying about Skiing America — They love it.

"...a no-holds-barred look at ski resorts. Unlike snazzy brochures that claim their respective resorts are perfect for everyone, this guide offers the lowdown on which places are better for families, singles, honeymooners, beginners and experts."
—The Gannett Newspapers

"Ski vacationers will want to look at Skiing America and Ski Europe."
—*Consumer Reports Travel Letter*

"When Leocha talks about something he finds lacking, there is no sugar coating . . . when he writes about something he likes, you know you're getting the truth." —*Wood River Journal*, Sun Valley/Ketchum

"It provides independent evaluation of the ski terrain and offers more extensive information than found in other guides."
—*Skier News*

"If you're planning a ski vacation . . . this guide should serve you well."
—*Ski Magazine*

"Up-to-the-minute info, so accurate that even ski resort personnel peruse these pages . . . The only guidebook you'll ever need. The latest edition is packed chockablock with detailed information about the ski experience at every major resort in the United States and Canada."
—*Robb Report*

"Charlie Leocha is first a skier, then a writer. He shuns the party line of the big ski corporations, preferring instead to talk to locals. *Skiing America*'s perspective is direct, credible, and no-holds-barred."
—*Daily Record*, NJ

"Detailed information on lift ticket prices, cross-country facilities, nightlife and more." —*Powder Magazine*

"The flavor, feel and personality of each resort."
—*The Boston Globe*

Thanks

*No project as complex as this can be completed by
a single person or team without help from others.*

•

*Thank you to Diane Slezak Scholfield,
the main force behind updating this massive amount of detailed
information and keeping everyone on schedule.
Thanks to Vanessa Reese for keeping
everchanging details in coherent order.*

•

*Thank you to the public relations personnel at each of the ski resorts
reviewed in these pages: they carefully check facts,
phone numbers, prices and programs
even though they don't always agree with our reviews.*

•

*Special thanks to KLM and Northwest Airlines for getting the
Skiing America and Ski Europe staff to resorts from California to the Alps.
KLM/Northwest flights serve almost every resort mentioned in this book
and Northwest World Vacations℠ offers ski and snowboard
packages to many of these resorts.*

•

*And thank you to Auto Europe who arranges automobile rentals
for the Skiing America and Ski Europe staff
whenever they travel to Canada or Europe.
If you are planning to rent a car abroad, this company is a secret all
travelers should know about—(800) 223-5555.*

SKIING AMERICA '99

by Charles A. Leocha

Diane Slezak Scholfield, executive editor

with

Steve Giordano
Karen Cummings
Andrew Bill
Glen Putman
Claudia Carbone
Katy Keck
James Kitfield
Lynn Rosen
Hilary Nangle

WORLD LEISURE CORPORATION

Hampstead, NH   Boston, MA

Help us do a better job

Research for this book is an ongoing process—we have been at it for more than a decade. Each year we revisit many of these resorts, and every winter we speak with locals from all of them.
If you find a new restaurant, hotel, bar or disco that you feel we should include, please let us know. If you find anything in these pages that is misleading or has changed, we would like to hear that too.
If we use your suggestion we will send you a copy of next year's edition.
Send your suggestions and comments to:
Charlie Leocha, *Skiing America,* World Leisure Corporation
Box 160, Hampstead NH 03841, USA
e-mail: wleisure@aol.com or visit us on the Internet at www.worldleisure.com

Copyright © 1988, 1989, 1990, 1991, 1992,
1993, 1994, 1995, 1996, 1997, 1998 by Charles A. Leocha

Cover photo: Park City Mountain Resort, Park City, Utah
back cover photo: Sharpshooter Resort Photography, Inc., Heavenly Valley, CA

Distributed to national chains, Ingram, Baker & Taylor, Bookazine in USA
by Midwest Trade Books, Inc., 27 W. 20th Street, Suite 1102,
New York, NY 10011, Tel. (212) 727-0190, fax (212) 727-0195.

Distributed to mass market, independent bookstores, regional chains, and other wholesalers by BookWorld Companies, 1933 Whitfield Park Loop, Sarasota, FL 34243
Tel. (800) 444-2524 or (941) 758-8094, fax (800) 777-2525 or (941) 753-9396.

Distributed to the trade in U.K. by
Portfolio, Unit 1c, West Ealing Business Centre, Alexandria Road, London W13 0NJ.
Tel. (0181) 579-7748, fax (0181)567-0904.

Mail Order, Catalog, Mass Market, other International sales and rights, and Special Sales contact the publisher:
World Leisure Corporation, 177 Paris Street, Boston, MA 02128.
Tel. (617) 569-1966, fax (617) 561-7654
E-mail: wleisure@aol.com; Internet: www.worldleisure.com

ISBN: 0-915009-63-3   ISSN: 1072-8988   LCCN: 93-643936

Contents

Contributors to *Skiing America '99*

Charlie Leocha has skied virtually every major international resort. He is the author of *Ski Europe,* a guidebook to the Alps' top resorts and *Travel Rights,* a guide to travelers' rights. He writes about travel and skiing for scores of magazines and newspapers. Charlie, who lives in New England, is a black-diamond skier, but a double-diamond après-skier. The rest of us bow to his energy level and dancing ability. He's also the only *Skiing America* staffer who knows which resorts have the best wine lists *and* the best bacon-and-eggs breakfasts. He is a member of the North American Snowsports Journalists Association (NASJA).

Diane Slezak Scholfield, a near-native Southern Californian, learned to ski in college and still remembers when getting off the chair lift without falling was the biggest challenge of the day. She now skis black diamonds, but only on sunny spring days. She's our best scout for accurate beginner and intermediate listings, mellow après-ski, microbrews on tap, and bagel-and-coffee breakfasts. She is the snow sports columnist for *The San Diego Union-Tribune,* edits the website SnowLink (www.snowlink.com) and has won NASJA's Excellence in Ski Writing award three times.

Steve Giordano is a veteran ski and travel journalist whose work has appeared in newspapers, magazines, books, radio and television. He used to be a ski patroller, but switched to ski journalism after pulling one too many drunks out of snowy creeks. He has written many books, one of which is *Now Hiring! Ski Resort Jobs.* A skier for more than 20 years, he switched to snowboarding a few years ago, and we rarely see him on two planks. Perhaps because he lives in the general vicinity of Seattle, he's forever searching out the best gourmet coffees at ski resorts. He is a member of NASJA and the Society of American Travel Writers.

Karen Cummings has been writing about skiing for over a decade from both the journalist and PR sides of the fence. She began skiing at the tender age of 25 and immediately discovered après-ski which became her specialty—these days her nightlife forays are "research." Karen is our expert shopper who has bought something at almost every ski resort in the Rockies and New England. She is also our cross-country aficionado who loves a workout with skating skis. She is a member of the board of directors of the Eastern Ski Writers Association.

Andrew Bill has worked as a travel journalist for more than 15 years, contributing to leading consumer magazines and newspapers on both sides of the Atlantic. Andy has written about adventure travel and alcoholic potables—he produces "The Best Bars Of The World" supplement for *Newsweek International* and so, ski writing was a natural progression. Our staff's witty Brit, who describes himself as "an avid if erratic skier," Andy contributes to both *Skiing America* and *Ski Europe.*

Glen Putman is one of those multi-sport, multi-resort kind of guys who squeezes in skiing, golf or tennis into every spare minute of the day. He once did a marathon of those three sports on the same day, and was finished by the cocktail hour. And he's one of the few people who has skied in the 49th and 50th states—Alyeska in Alaska and Mauna Kea in Hawaii (seafood's great in both states, but Hawaii wins for après-ski). Good thing Glen's job is to write about the sports he loves so much. He has written articles about skiing, golf and travel for scores of newspapers and magazines. He also is a member of NASJA.

Claudia Carbone lives in the woods, minutes from Breckenridge in her native state of Colorado. Her idea of a great day is dancing through knee-deep Rocky Mountain powder in the backcountry. Claudia writes a ski column for *The Denver Post* and national publications such as *Snow Country* and *Women's Sports & Fitness*. Her groundbreaking book, *WomenSki*, established her as a national authority on women's skiing. Claudia is a founder of Snow Sports Association for Women and is the recipient of the Lowell Thomas Award from Colorado Ski Country and NASJA's Excellence in Ski Writing award.

Katy Keck laments that when sent to resorts for research, she ends up spending more time in kitchens than on the slopes. She worked in France under chefs at Michelin-star restaurants. She owns and runs Savoir Faire Foods, a consulting company in New York specializing in food styling, recipe development and catering. She has been recognized as one of the Top 50 Women Chefs in The World. She is co-owner of a New York City restaurant, New World Grill at 329 W. 49th Street.

James Kitfield is an expert après-skier who first met Charlie Leocha dancing in a conga line through a bar in Verbier, Switzerland. Life has been downhill since, at least as often as he can manage trips to the mountains. On the slopes he points his skis down double diamonds and prides himself on making few turns. Amazingly, he has a serious side. He has been awarded the Gerald R. Ford prize twice for distinguished reporting, and the Jesse H. Neal award for excellence in reporting. His first book, *Prodigal Soldiers*, was published by Simon & Schuster.

Lynn Rosen is an Emmy award-winning broadcaster, producer and writer at "border station" KVOS-TV in Bellingham, which markets to Vancouver, B.C. That's just her day job. She's also a theater critic and travel/ski writer for publications that include *Backstage West, Ski Press* and *RV Life*. Mountain scenery is so dramatic, so it's fitting that Lynn belongs to the American Theater Critics Association as well as NASJA. She also is one of the staff champion shoppers, a pushover for unique jewelry and clothing. She's also married to Steve Giordano, and the two of them make sure our Northwest entries are up-to-date.

Hilary Nangle dropped out of grad school to work at a ski area and has stayed connected to the sport ever since. She is currently features editor for *The Times Record*, a daily newspaper in Brunswick, Maine, where she writes regularly on food, travel and skiing. Another of the many NASJA members on staff, she writes for regional and national ski and travel magazines, and has contributed to more than a dozen Fodor's Travel Guides. She has visited just about every B&B and country inn in Maine. A Mainer through and through, she believes the ideal skier's lunch is a bowl of lobster stew.

Other contributors: **Christopher Elliott** and **Kari Astrid**, Beaver Creek; **Colleen Maloney**, various Montana and Western Canada resorts; **Ed Blumstein**, Poconos; **Mike Terrell**, Midwest; **Cindy Bohl**, Jay Peak and Stratton; and **Brendan Gibbon**, Mount Snow.

How to get the most from Skiing America

You may have already done this. Pick a chapter in this book about any resort you have already visited. Read it carefully. I am sure you will agree, this is the way it is. Every chapter in *Skiing America* is just as carefully researched and described.

This is as straightforward and honest a guide to North America's top resorts as you can buy. We also include our opinions and personal observations. We detail the personality of each resort, where we found the best skiing and snowboarding, where we liked to eat and where we enjoyed the liveliest off-slope fun. And we give you the facts—hotel and restaurant descriptions, lift ticket and lesson prices, child-care programs, nightlife hot spots, and where to call, fax, e-mail or write for more information. Each skier and snowboarder has various likes and dislikes, and resorts have different personalities. Our staff includes experts and intermediates (including some who learned as adults), Generation Xers and Baby Boomers, skiers and snowboarders, egg-and-bacon breakfast eaters and gourmet-coffee-and-bagel fans. Our goal is to match you with the right vacation spot.

The resorts in this book can support four to seven days of on- and off-slope activity without becoming repetitious.

What's new in this edition

No new chapters, but just keeping up with the resort changes kept us quite busy this year. Mountain resorts used to be individually owned, but during the past three seasons, about a half-dozen resort corporations have been snatching up the bigger fish and investing millions in improvements. Keeping up with the restaurant, hotel and off-slope activity closings and

---

A note about prices

We make every attempt to include prices for the current 1998/99 ski season. Unfortunately, as of early August many resorts had not announced their new prices. Current prices have the 98/99 notation. Where there is no notation, assume the prices are from last season (97/98). The prices provided in this guidebook are in no way official and are subject to change at any time. Resorts sometimes announce one price in July and change it by November, or even change announced prices during the season. Our intention is to provide you the best possible information for planning and comparison.

Skiing America is published every fall, but sometimes bookstores have older copies in their inventory. If you are reading this book in the fall of 1999 or after, please call (800) 444-2524 to order the latest edition. International visitors should send e-mail to wleisure@aol.com, fax orders to (941) 753-9396 or call (941) 758-8094 to order with a credit card.

openings also meant a lot of copy changes. And don't even get us started on area codes! Mountain areas in North America have experienced about a dozen area-code changes in the past two years, so if you're using an old guidebook, your phone calls won't go through.

If it's been a while since you bought a copy of *Skiing America,* you'll notice the "capital improvements" we made a couple of seasons ago. We expanded the fact boxes in each chapter so you can get basic information quickly, including fax numbers, e-mail and internet addresses. If you like what you see at a glance, you can read the chapter for the details. Icons clearly indicate different sections.

Chapter organization

Each resort chapter has several sections. We begin by sketching the personality of the place—is it old and quaint, or modern and high-rise? Clustered at the base of the slopes, or a few miles down the road? Remote and isolated, or freeway-close? Family-oriented or catering to singles? Filled with friendly faces or an aloof herd of "beautiful" skiers?

We start with the basic statistics of each resort including **addresses and phone numbers**: postal, e-mail, internet, toll-free, fax—all of them that we could find.

A few important notes: The resort's **area code** is listed in the fact box and at the bottom of each even-numbered page. We don't list the local area code for every number in the chapter because you probably will use local numbers most often while you're at the resort (in the case of restaurants, for instance). But if you need it at home, that's where you'll find it. Some of the fax numbers we list are for the ski area; others are for the central reservations office; some resorts don't have public fax numbers. In almost every instance, the internet address we list is the officially sanctioned one maintained by the resort.

Next are terrain stats—the **base and summit altitudes,** important for those with altitude-related medical difficulties or for sea-level dwellers who plan to hit the slopes the same day they arrive; **vertical drop, skiable acreage** and **number and types of lifts,** all of which will give you a good idea of the resort's size.

An important note about our terrain stats: They reflect *lift-served* terrain. Examples: Breckenridge, Colorado, lists its vertical as 3,398 feet; we list it at 2,546. If you want that maximum vertical, you must hike the extra 852 feet to the in-bounds summit. Grand Targhee has two mountains totaling 3,000 acres, but half of that acreage is reserved for snowcat skiing and snowboarding. Exceptions like these are explained where they occur.

Uphill lift capacity is the number of riders the lift system can carry each hour. **Bed base** is the approximate number of people who can be accommodated overnight near the resort. If the uphill capacity is much bigger than the bed base, the result is usually shorter lift lines. (Resorts with great uphill capacity/bed base ratios may still have long weekend lines if they are near major cities—we try to identify these.)

We tell you how close the **nearest lodging** is, if the resort has **child care** and youngest age accepted, and if there are any restrictions on **snowboarding**. The **lift ticket** price in the fact box tells the per-day range of the adult lift ticket. The lower price usually is the per-day cost of the longest adult multiday ticket (or the midweek price), while the higher price is the weekend walk-up-to-the-window cost. Ticket prices in the stat box are intended as an approximation; look in the chapter for more details.

Finally, **we rate the slopes** (based on five ability levels), the **dining,** the **nightlife** and the **other activities.** One star means it's poor, two is okay, three is good, four is very good and five is outstanding. Ratings are quite subjective, but they are a general consensus of the members of the *Skiing America* staff. We're simply trying to point you in the right direction.

Following the fact box are a detailed description of the **Mountain layout** and a **Mountain rating**. The first describes various sections of the mountain best for each of five ability levels. The second is a summary of the mountain's best and worst features, such as which slopes may be too tough for the beginner or too mild for the expert.

Cross-country information will tell you which resorts have Nordic trails, as well as significant cross-country and backcountry skiing opportunities nearby, and snowshoe rental and tour information. If you'd like additional information, we can recommend two books: *Northern Michigan's Best Cross Country Ski Trails*, by Mike Terrell, published by Outdoor Recreational Press, $12.95; and *Jonathan Wiesel's Cross-Country Ski Vacations*, published by John Muir Publications, $15.95.

Snowboarding lists facilities such as halfpipes and terrain parks.

The **Lessons** section details instructional programs for adults and children, including any special programs and recreational racing. The term "never-ever package" refers to a package with half-day or full-day first-time lesson, a lift ticket (often just for the beginner lift) and use of rental equipment. Some resorts charge more for first-time snowboarders than for skiers. Though it might appear that resorts are either cashing in on the trendy sport or discriminating against boarders, they tell us that the higher price is because fewer people sign up for first-time snowboard group lessons, and snowboard rental equipment takes a greater beating.

Child care covers non-skiing nursery and day care programs, either at the resort or nearby.

Lift tickets are listed for adults, children, teens and seniors. We've organized them in a chart with one-day, three-day and five-day prices, followed by "Who skis free" and "Who skis at a discount" listed in paragraph form. Where prices are from last season, assume an increase of a couple of dollars. Be aware that resorts have various terms for children's lift tickets—"junior," "youth" and "young adult" are common.

Under **Accommodations** we list both the most luxurious places and many of the budget lodges, including features such as slopeside location, pools and spas, health clubs and intra-resort transportation. We also suggest lodging that is particularly suited to families, and our favorite B&Bs and inns.

Dining always includes the gourmet restaurants, but we don't leave out affordable places where a hungry family or a skier on a budget can chow down and relax. We have compiled these suggestions from dozens of interviews with locals and tourists, plus our own dining experiences.

Après-ski/nightlife describes places to go when the lifts close, and where to find entertainment later in the evening. We tell you which bars are loud, which are quiet, what kind of music they play and whether they have live music.

Other activities covers off-slope activities—such as shopping, fitness clubs, sleigh rides, dogsledding, ice skating and snowmobiling.

Getting there and getting around tells you how to get to the resort by air and car (and sometimes by train or bus), and whether a car is optional or necessary at the resort.

Types of accommodations

A **hotel** is relatively large, with 25 rooms or more, and comes without meals. If hotel rates include any meals, that is noted.

A **mountain inn** usually has fewer rooms than a hotel. Many have packages that include breakfast and dinner.

A **bed & breakfast (B&B)** tends to be even smaller, with just a few rooms. Most B&Bs have private baths now, so if guests must share a bath, we say so. Breakfast is included and some B&Bs also offer dinner.

Motels don't have the amenities of a hotel or the ambiance of a B&B, and often are further from the slopes. Motels are good for families and budget-minded skiers.

Condominiums have become the most affordable group lodging at American ski resorts because of their separate bedrooms and kitchen facilities. They usually have a central check-in facility. Most condominiums have daily maid service for everything but the kitchen.

When you call the resort's central reservations number, ask for suggestions. Most of the staff have been on lodging tours and can make honest recommendations based on your needs.

High and low season

North American mountain resorts have several pricing seasons. The highest prices are during the Christmas-New Year holidays in late December. Regular season usually runs all of February and March, but at some resorts March is high season. Value Season is in January after New Year at some resorts. Low Season is usually the first couple of weeks in December, and April until closing. These vary from resort to resort, so ask for more information when you call. The most noticeable change is in the cost of accommodations, but some resorts also vary the prices of lift tickets, especially in pre-season and in spring.

Ability levels

These are the terms we use in the "Mountain layout" and other sections:

Never-evers are just what the name implies. We apply the term to novices during their first couple of days on skis or a snowboard.

Beginners can turn and stop (more or less) when they choose, but still rely on snowplow turns. This group feels most comfortable on wide, fairly flat terrain.

Intermediates generally head for blue trails and parallel ski (more or less) on the smooth stuff. They return to survival technique on expert trails, and struggle in heavy powder and crud.

Advanced skiers and boarders can descend virtually any trail with carved turns, but are still intimidated by deep powder, crud and super steeps. Advanced terrain by our definition includes moguls and glade skiing.

Experts favor chutes, tight trees on steep slopes, deep-powder bowls and off-piste exploration. True experts are few and far between.

Skiing & snowboarding for everyone

Skiers and snowboarders come in all abilities, genders, interests and ages. Better equipment and slope grooming techniques mean that skiing—and we use this as a catch-all term to describe Nordic or Alpine skiing, snowboarding, snow skating and other forms of sliding on snowy slopes—is easier to learn and you never have to give it up as you age. As more people are attracted to the sport, resorts are putting more emphasis on teaching how much fun you can have with downhill, cross-country or snowboarding. These are sports that combine the best of Mother Nature with the best of friendly people out to enjoy themselves.

Snowboarders, please don't take offense. In this guide, we use the word "ski" in a general sense, meaning skiing or snowboarding. Our staff includes boarders who like to ride some days and ski on other days.

The first step is learning. We touch here on the basics of lessons, equipment and clothing, then explore learning programs for various specialized groups.

The novice's experience

When you ski or snowboard, you escape from your everyday routine. No matter your level of expertise, you find challenge, beauty and a balance with nature. This is a sport where beginners *and* experts can have fun amid clean air and stunning scenery. It's also a sport where you'll easily meet other people.

Learning is not difficult if you don't try to teach yourself. We firmly believe that lessons are the only way to go for never-evers, whatever their athletic ability. Natural athletes may quickly develop balance, but they'll also develop bad habits that will hinder later progress. Toddlers can start as young as three and you're never too old to learn—really. Learning will not break the bank: many resorts offer heavily discounted lessons for novices and advancing beginners. A few resorts even have free beginner lessons, either all the time or at certain times of the season. Where we know about these, we've noted them chapter by chapter.

After only four or five lessons, most beginners have improved enough to negotiate their way down more than half the marked ski trails in North America. For cross-country you need only a couple of lessons to begin gliding through the forests and across rolling meadows.

How do you get started? First, read the information about never-ever packages in our Lessons sections. Also pay attention to our notes on never-ever terrain in the Mountain Layout section. Some resorts are not good for a first-timer's experience. Call several resorts in advance and ask them to send you information on novice lessons. The best resorts will have a separate brochure or information sheet on the topic.

Most skiing and snowboarding websites are aimed toward those who already love these sports. One that also gives great advice for those just starting out is *SnowLink.com* (www.snowlink.com), the website of SnowSports Industries America. This website also has about 600 links to official websites for equipment and clothing companies, resorts and ski clubs, as well as a searchable database to find the ski or snowboard shop nearest your home.

While learning to ski or snowboard, rent your equipment. Renting is much less expensive than buying at this point, because as you get better you'll need more advanced gear. Ski or snowboard shop pros will help you with the correct length and type, boots, bindings and adjustments. As you improve, they can suggest how to upgrade. The two principal places to rent are shops near home or at the resort. The choice will probably be based on how you get to the resort—flying or driving—and how much time you'll spend there. If possible, rent near home or at the resort the afternoon or evening before you start. You'll get better attention if you're not part of the masses the morning of your first lesson.

Proper clothing also is important. You don't need the latest, most colorful ski fashions—what you can find in your closet should do just fine, provided you can find such basics as a pair of long johns, a sweater, a waterproof or water-resistant jacket, wool or acrylic socks and a pair of wool trousers or nylon wind pants. One warning: because your backside will be spending time in contact with the snow at first, don't wear jeans or other cotton pants. In fact, don't wear anything made of cotton, such as cotton socks or a T-shirt or sweatshirt. Cotton soaks up and holds moisture—either sweat or snow—and you will soon be cold. If you are missing any of the basics, borrow from a friend. The secret to staying just warm enough is layering. A few lightweight garments are better than one heavy one, since layers trap the air. You can remove or add layers as temperatures change.

Wear a hat—50 percent of your body heat can escape through your head! Wear gloves—they will keep your hands warm and protected. Ski and snowboard gloves are padded and reinforced in ways different from any other gloves you're likely to have on hand, so these should be a specific purchase if you can't borrow them. Though you can get by with sunglasses, goggles are *vital* for seeing trail contours on overcast days or when skiing in falling snow. Use sunscreen—at high altitudes the sun's rays are stronger and the reflection of rays off the snow increases your total dose.

Your first lessons will teach you how to walk, slide and—most importantly—stop. Then the lessons focus on how to get up after falling (you may have already practiced that lesson on your own). You will learn the basic turn, called a "snowplow" or "wedge" turn for skiers and a "falling leaf" turn for snowboarders. With this turn you will be able to negotiate almost any groomed slope. Your instructor will show you how to use the lifts, and you'll be on your way.

You don't have to start with downhill skiing. Many skiers go right to cross-country or to snowboarding. Just pick the sport that suits you best. Enjoy!

Getting in shape

How important is it to be in shape for skiing? Well, we aren't going to lie to you—the more fit you are, the more fun you'll have and the better you'll ski.

But this doesn't mean you have to devote half your life to jogging and hamstring stretches. Just realize that if you get lax about exercise at home, you'll pay for it when you're on the slopes.

A moderate exercise program—about an hour, three to four times a week—is all it takes. Here are key things to include:

• **Aerobics.** Get that heart pumping so your whole body will process oxygen more efficiently. A good portion of America's skiers—especially those who buy guidebooks—live at or near sea level. Most of the Rocky Mountain ski areas are at 8,000- to 12,000-foot elevations where the air is thin. Those who lead unathletic lives where the oxygen is plentiful will be exhausted after a short time where there's less of it. You've spent big money for your ski trip—why waste a minute?

• **Flexibility.** *Stretch* those muscles, particularly the ones down the backs of your legs. Sometimes your skis decide to head in different directions, and your feet may stay attached. If your hamstrings or inner-thigh muscles are tight, a fall like that could put you out of commission for the rest of your vacation.

• **Strength.** Most skiers, even new ones, know that strong leg muscles make skiing a lot easier. Muscles that are just as important, but ignored by many skiers, are the ones in your upper body. Have you ever had to push yourself across a long flat section of the mountain? Have you ever carried 15 pounds of equipment from your car or lodge to the chair lift? Have you ever pushed yourself up off the snow after a fall? Sure you have, and you do all of this with your arms and shoulders.

If you're snowboarding, get your stomach muscles in shape, especially if you find it's easier to get to a standing position when you're facing the hill. From time to time, you'll need to lift the board slightly off the snow from a sitting position, and if your stomach muscles are weak you may strain your back. A strong upper body is more important in snowboarding, since you don't have poles to help you get up.

Of course, consult your doctor before going from a chair-bound lifestyle to a regular exercise program. And it's best to get some professional help regarding the best program for you. Fitness centers—especially in cities that have a lot of skiers—often have ski-conditioning classes during the fall months focusing on exercises that mimic skiing movements. Such a class can give you a real head start.

If you can't find a ski-conditioning class in your area, you can take one with your VCR. Several ski-conditioning videos are on the market now, such as Patty Wade's "In Shape To Ski." Wade, a fitness instructor in Aspen, teaches a ski-conditioning class each autumn that many of the locals swear by. Her 60-minute video workout offers a thorough and tough workout. You can adjust the pace to your level by not doing the exercises as long as she does. Call (800) 925-9754 for ordering information if you can't find it at a local video outlet.

Mountain maladies

Even those skiers in the best of shape can find themselves spending their vacation in the condo if they aren't careful. These four skier maladies are easily avoidable. Here's how to keep from being a victim.

• **Altitude sickness.** Caused by a too-rapid gain in elevation, the symptoms are a bit like the flu—nausea, headaches, insomnia. The best way to avoid it is to go easy the first day or so—ski slow and easy, eat light and drink lots of water but little alcohol. If this is a persistent problem for you, go to ski areas where the base elevation is below 8,000 feet.

• **Snow blindness.** Always wear sunglasses or goggles when you ski, and be sure they protect your eyes from damaging rays. Sun reflecting off bright snow can easily "sunburn" your retinas. Your eyes will feel as if someone has dumped a load of sand in them, and the only cure is resting in a darkened room for a day or two—no reading, no TV and definitely no outdoor activity.

• **Hypothermia.** It's 10 degrees outside, the wind is howling and you don't want to wear a hat because it will flatten your hair? Your vanity could make you sick. When you lose body heat faster than you can replace it, you're risking hypothermia. Wear enough clothes so you're warm, but not so many that you're soaked through with sweat. (Cold weather and wet clothing act as a hypothermia magnet.) If you start to shiver, get inside. Add a layer of clothes. If you still are shivering, quit for the day. Better to lose a few hours than several days.

• **Frostbite.** This happens to fingers, toes, cheeks, noses and ears when body tissue starts to freeze. If any of these start to feel cold, check to see if your skin is turning white. If it is, get inside, drink something warm and non-alcoholic, and cover the affected part with extra clothing or warm it with body heat. Don't rub it or hold it near a fireplace: this could do further damage.

Programs for the silver-haired crowd

Skiing (and snowboarding) isn't just for youngsters anymore. One of the fastest growing age groups in skiing is 55 and older. By the year 2010, 37 percent of all skiers are expected to be in that age group.

Some of those skiers learned when they were young and never stopped skiing, but others started late in life. Many resorts have started programs that cater to the upper age group. Nearly every ski area in North America offers free or heavily discounted lift tickets to skiers when they reach 60, 65 or 70.

And thanks to clubs such as the Over the Hill Gang and the 70+ Club, older skiers always have companionship. The 70+ Club started in 1977 with 34 members; now it has more than 10,000—all 70 or older—in several countries.

Here is a partial list of clubs and programs for older skiers. New programs are starting every season.

Clubs: Members of the **70+ Ski Club** wear distinctive red-and-white patches that identify them as part of this elite group. A $5 lifetime membership fee, and a copy of a legal document that clearly shows date of birth (such as a passport or driver's license), is all it takes to join. Founder Lloyd Lambert was a pioneer in getting discounts for older skiers. Lambert died in 1997 (well into his 90s), but his son has taken over administration duties. For information, write to 104 East Side Drive, Ballston Lake, NY 12019.

The **Over The Hill Gang** is for skiers 50 and older. This nationwide group has local chapters all over the country whose members not only ski, but also play volleyball and tennis, go hiking and sailing and otherwise enjoy the outdoor life. Contact the Over The Hill Gang at 3310 Cedar Heights Dr., Colorado Springs, CO 80904; (719) 685-4656.

Members of the **Over Eighty Ski Club** get their names inscribed on a Scroll of Distinction at the U.S. Ski Hall of Fame. The club began in 1985, and the list has included kings (the late Olav V of Norway was a member) and commoners. To become a member of this special group, send a minimum donation of $25 to the U.S. Ski Hall of Fame, (Attn: Ray Leverton), Box 191, Ishpeming, MI 49849-0191.

Elderhostel offers learn-to-ski programs several times a year at Sunday River Ski Resort in Maine. The skiing is combined with other academic courses. This is the first Elderhostel campus to offer skiing. Call Elderhostel at (617) 426-8056.

Ski area programs: Special instruction or social programs for seniors are offered at Purgatory, Colorado; Park City, Utah; Badger Pass, California; Northstar-at-Tahoe, California; Waterville Valley, New Hampshire; Aspen, Colorado; Stratton, Vermont; and Sun Valley, Idaho, among other resorts. Some are day programs, others are week-long vacations with big-band dances and wine-and-cheese parties.

Women's instruction

Nearly every major resort, and many of the smaller ones, has some sort of program just for women.

Why segregate? Claudia Carbone, award-winning Colorado ski journalist and author of the book *WomenSki,* ($14.95; to order call 1-800-444-2524) observes, "There's more than one way to ski. The ultimate experience doesn't have to be a steep, fast, frightening run down back-bowl slopes. Some people experience exhilaration and satisfaction from a seamless sequence of perfectly carved arcs. Or a wintry waltz through fresh powder. Or smooth and easy gliding on a brilliant crisp day. You're not alone if you like to caress, rather than attack, the hill."

The goal of such seminars is not to segregate women from their male friends on the slopes permanently, but to provide an environment geared to eliminating learning barriers so that "women only" instruction ultimately becomes unnecessary.

Because lessons are usually with the same instructor each day, improvement is both dramatic and clearly recognizable.

Discussions address issues particular to women skiers and snowboarders, such developing confidence and selecting proper equipment. Most programs incorporate video sessions. Some seminars are as heavy on social fun as improving skills; others are for higher-ability skiers who want to learn to race, ski moguls or ski powder.

There are women's programs that have received very high reviews at Squaw Valley, where Elissa Slanger originated this type of program a quarter-century ago; Telluride, where Annie Vareille Savath's influence as ski-school director shows through, and Crested Butte, where Kim Reichhelm, a former ski racer who also has been the Women's World Extreme Skiing Champion, operates her Women's Ski Adventures program. Information about the Telluride and Squaw Valley programs are available from those ski areas; for Reichhelm's program at Crested Butte, call (800) 992-7700.

The Snow Sports Association for Women (SSAW) will have its second annual Take Your Daughter to the Slopes Day on Feb. 6, 1999. Ski areas and shops across the country will offer special programs and deals for those who bring a female friend or relative to the slopes that day. See the *SnowLink.com* website (www.snowlink.com) for a complete list about two weeks prior to the event. (Resorts and shops will be added as they commit, so you also can check it earlier.)

Skiing for the physically challenged

At many areas, you're likely to see a few empty wheelchairs next to the ski racks in the base area. Skiing is a great sport for physically challenged people, because gravity plays such a major role. Special equipment is available for about any type of disability. If a resort doesn't have the right equipment, they'll invent it. There is no reason why an otherwise disabled skier can't ski as fast as an able-bodied one; in fact, sometimes they're faster—a real ego boost for those who must proceed a little slower than most on dry land.

Winter Park, Colorado, has been the pioneer in this area, and still has one of the best programs. Hal O'Leary, founder and director of the **National Sports Center for the Disabled,** began with a few sets of borrowed skis and a broom-closet office. Now a full-time staff of 13 and a volunteer organization of 850 handles 2,500 participants with 45 types of disabilities, and gives 14,500 lessons yearly.

Among those who can ski are amputees, wheelchair users, the blind and those with cerebral palsy and multiple sclerosis. Write to Hal O'Leary, Director, **National Sports Center for the Disabled,** Box 36, Winter Park, CO 80482; (970) 726-5514.

Disabled Sports USA has chapters and programs in more than 60 cities and resorts, and reports that more than 12,000 individuals are in learning programs each year. Write to 451 Hungerford Dr., Suite 100, Rockville, MD 20850; (301) 217-0960.

Among the other ski schools for the disabled:

Tahoe Handicapped Ski School at Alpine Meadows; offices at 5926 Illinois Avenue, Orangevale, CA 95662; (530) 989-0402. Onsite phone: (530) 581-4161.

Bear Mountain (two-and-a-half hours east of Los Angeles) Box 6812, Big Bear Lake, CA 92315; (909) 585-2519.

Breckenridge Outdoor Education Center, Box 697, Breckenridge, CO 80424; (970) 453-6422.

New England Handicapped Sportsmen's Association. The program is at Mt. Snow/ Haystack in Vermont; offices are at 26 McFarlin Rd., Chelmsford, MA 01824; (508) 256-3240.

Ski Windham; at 1A Lincoln Ave., Albany, NY 12205; (518) 452-6095.

Park City Handicapped Sports Association, Box 680286, Park City, UT 84068; (435) 649-3991.

Clinics for advanced skiers

Advanced skiers hardly ever take lessons, and it's no wonder. Until recently, advanced skiers were taught just like beginners: groups of four to six make a few turns, then listen to the instructor give generalized tips on improvement. That format works well for lower-level skiers, all of whom need to learn the same skills. But while most skiers develop bad habits as they progress, not all develop the same ones. One skier may need to work on pole plants; another may need to keep his shoulders square to the hill and a third may be sitting too far back on her skis. Just like World Cup racers, these skiers need fine-tuning. They need a coach, not an instructor: someone who will observe the way they ski and then give very specific tips on breaking the habits that keep skiers from progressing to the next level.

Resorts have responded to advanced skiers' needs with coaching, not lessons. The terminology has changed—lessons are "workshops" or "clinics." Instructors are "coaches" or "pros." Ski school is "mountain development center" or some other politically correct term. Instead of the standard ski-stop-listen format, most of these clinics are heavy on ski, ski, ski and listening to the instructor as you go or while on the lift. Quite a few work on the "condition du jour"—powder, moguls, crud, etc. Other work on snowboard-specific skills, such as halfpipe tricks or carving. Many clinics have video feedback.

If you're at the intermediate or advanced level, look into these programs. But here are a few tips to be sure to get what you want:

• Don't use the word "lesson." Ask what type of clinics or workshops are offered for upper-level skiers or snowboarders.

• Be specific when asking about the format. How much time is spent moving on the hill? What skills will we work on?

• Insist that the instructor address each student's needs. Some instructors won't target individuals for fear of offending them. That's fine for beginners, but not for better skiers and snowboarders who need specific advice.

• If after the clinic you don't feel you got your money's worth, go to the ski school office and politely tell them why. ("I expected to actually ski moguls during the mogul clinic, not practice short turns on groomed slopes.") If the ski school is smart, they'll get you in the right workshop.

One instructional method we can recommend heartily is **Perfect Turn®**, which began at Sunday River, Maine, and has spread to Sugarloaf in Maine, Mt. Bachelor in Oregon; Sugarbush, Killington and Mount Snow/Haystack in Vermont, Attitash/Bear Peak in New Hampshire, Jiminy Peak in Massachusetts and Blue Mountain in Ontario, among other areas. Perfect Turn operates on total positive reinforcement. The ski pros (they aren't called instructors) never tell you what you're doing wrong; only what you're doing right.

Example: a non-Perfect Turn ski instructor would first tell a student, "You're sitting back too far on your skis," then illustrate how to correct that—perhaps by telling the student to push her shin against the tongue of her boot just enough to keep a hundred-dollar bill from flying away. The Perfect Turn ski pro skips the critical comment and goes right to the correctional tip. Additionally, the pro identifies what the skier does very well and compliments those skills lavishly.

Because he makes you feel confident about your current skills, you believe that you can take on a bigger challenge and do that well, too. Jump off that cornice into those igloo-sized moguls? Sure, coach, if you say I can do it, I can.

It may sound hokey, but it works. One of our contributors, halfway between intermediate and advanced, took one Perfect Turn clinic, then merrily led two companions—both advanced skiers—down a slope of cut-up powder. Throughout the season she skied black diamonds with more confidence than ever before. If you learn faster when you get positive strokes, take a trip to a resort that offers this program.

North Lake Tahoe Area

Alpine Meadows

Squaw Valley USA

Northstar-at-Tahoe

Diamond Peak

Sugar Bowl

with

Reno, Nevada

Toll-free reservations:
(800) TAHOE-4-U (824-6348), North Lake Tahoe
(800) GO-TAHOE (468-2463), Incline Village/Crystal Bay
(800) FOR-RENO (367-7366), Reno
Internet: http://www.tahoenet.com (North Lake Tahoe)
http://www.reno.net (Reno)
Dining:★★★
Apres-ski/nightlife:★★(near the lake) ★★★★(Reno)
Other activities:★★★

Few regions on the North American continent have the ski-resort diversity of the Lake Tahoe region. When you consider the elements of a perfect ski vacation—variety of terrain, good snow, comfortable lodging, beautiful scenery, a wide choice of restaurants and nightlife, a myriad of other activities, accessibility—Lake Tahoe would rank near the top in all but a couple of categories (and it would be above the median in those).

Lake Tahoe, one of the largest and most stunningly beautiful mountain lakes in the world, straddles the border of California and Nevada about 200 miles east of San Francisco. Tahoe has received accolades from travel writers for more than a century. Mark Twain was one of the first to note its beauty. In 1861, he wrote in *Roughing It*, Tahoe was "the fairest picture the whole earth affords." Because the lake is so deep and doesn't freeze, it retains its sapphire-blue color throughout the winter. Its name comes from a Washoe Indian word meaning "water in a high place"—the lake is about 6,200 feet above sea level.

Tahoe is best divided into two regions for vacation purposes. Though you can run yourself ragged by trying to visit every major area in a week, it's better to concentrate on the North Shore or the South Shore. This chapter covers the North Shore, while the following chapter concentrates on the South Shore.

The two regions provide different vacation experiences. South Tahoe is densely developed, with high-rise casino-hotels hugging the California-Nevada state line, frequent big-name entertainment, and non-stop après-ski activity. It has three ski/snowboard resorts, one of which overlooks the twin towns of Stateline and South Lake Tahoe. Speaking in general terms, South Shore tends to attract to the region first-time visitors who live outside California and Nevada, while the North Shore tends to attract fewer first-time visitors, but loads of Californians.

North Shore has history, is more spread out and a lot quieter, and has an amazing concentration of excellent skiing and snowboarding facilities. Resort skiing in California started in the North Lake Tahoe region in the late 1930s, when a group of investors, including Walt Disney, started Sugar Bowl. The 1960 Winter Olympics were staged at another North Tahoe resort, Squaw Valley. North Tahoe isn't as densely developed as the South Shore, but it covers a lot more miles of the lake shore. Its Nevada side has casinos, but they are not as prominent as the ones at South Shore. The California side of North Tahoe is dominated by

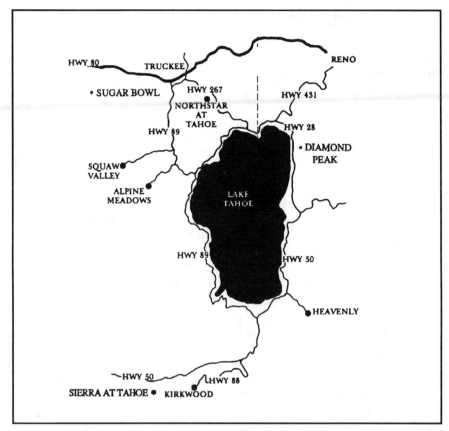

condos that are vacation homes for Northern Californians. There are restaurants and nightlife, but things get quiet once the sun goes down. If you like to collect ski pins, North Shore has nine Alpine ski facilities (the lake is visible from five of them) and seven cross-country areas. (We detail the five largest in this chapter, and give information on three others in our Regional Getaway chapter. The ninth is a very tiny area at a resort called Granlibakken, mentioned in our *Accommodations* section.)

There may be higher peaks in Colorado, quainter ski huts in the Alps, and Utah mining towns with richer histories, but it's difficult to top Lake Tahoe's unique, breathtaking beauty.

Note: Northern Nevada's area code will change from 702 to 775 starting in December, 1998. If you have trouble with some of these phone numbers, try the new area code.

Tahoe Interchangeable tickets (98/99 prices)

The Ski Lake Tahoe interchangeable lift pass is good at Kirkwood, Heavenly, Sierra-at-Tahoe, Northstar, Alpine Meadows and Squaw Valley USA. Five of six consecutive days cost about $245 ($49 a day).

Squaw Valley USA

Summit elevation:	**9,050 feet**
Vertical drop:	**2,850 feet**
Base elevation:	**6,200 feet**

Expert:★★★★
Advanced:★★★★
Intermediate:★★
Beginner:★★★
Never-ever:★★★

Address: Box 2007, Olympic Valley CA 96146
☎ **Area code:** 530
Ski area phone: 583-6985
Snow report: 583-6955
ⓘ **Toll-free reservations:** (888) 766-9321
Fax: 581-7106
E-mail: squaw@squaw.com
Internet: http://www.squaw.com

Number of lifts: 30–1 cable car, 1 funitel,
1 pulse lift, 4 high-speed quads, 1 quad,
9 triples, 10 doubles, 3 surface lifts
Snowmaking: 15 percent
Total acreage: 4,000 lift-served acres
Uphill capacity: 49,000 per hour
Snowboarding: Yes, unlimited
Bed Base: 3,500 within 3 miles
Nearest lodging: slopeside
Resort child care: Yes, 2 years and older
Adult ticket, per day: $41-$48 (97/98 prices)

Squaw Valley USA is the best-known resort in the region, having hosted the 1960 Winter Olympics. It offers some of the finest skiing in the United States. There aren't many trail-cut runs here, just wide-open snow fields—4,000 acres of them. Anything within the boundaries can be skied by anyone daring enough to challenge the mountain. All levels can be challenged here—experts and beginners alike ride side-by-side on the cable car to the top.

Access starts at the base with the Funitel lift, the fourth of its kind in the world. Or, board the 150-person cable car. Or, start with the Squaw One high-speed quad and then connect to other lifts. Six separate peaks, each with every conceivable exposure, overlook Lake Tahoe.

New for 98/99: Squaw Valley will have completed two unusual lifts it began to install last season—a Funitel and The Pulse, a custom gondola. The Funitel, which carries 15 people seated or 28 standing, replaced Squaw Valley's gondola and follows its course from the base to the Gold Coast area. The Pulse connects the resort's two mid-mountain complexes at High Camp and Gold Coast. It has five cabins that operate with the push of a button. These new lifts enable guests to take a mountain tour without putting on skis or a snowboard (of course, skiers and boarders will use them, too). They can ride the cable car to High Camp, the pulse lift to Gold Coast, then download on the Funitel to the mountain's base.

◆◆ **Expert** ◆ **Advanced:** Extreme skiers will be in heaven at Squaw. Thirty percent of the runs are either single- or double-black diamond. Two popular spots are the Palisades above Siberia Bowl and Eagle's Nest at the top of KT22. The Granite Chief, Headwall and Silverado lifts access some of the most challenging terrain in the world. Locals will take you to terrain that resembles an elevator shaft.

Experts who like to keep their skis on the snow will find plenty of challenging terrain. The entire KT22 side of Squaw Valley is expert, except for The Saddle, which is groomed. Try Chute 75, the Alternates, and the Dead Tree Chute, or the National Chute off the Palisades. At Elevation 8200, on the upper mountain, try the Funnel or the Slot, or hike to the top of Granite Chief. These are solid black diamonds.

■ **Intermediate:** Intermediate terrain (about 45 percent) has challenge and variety. Siberia Express accesses the largest intermediate bowl. Newport, Gold Coast and Emigrant lifts offer acres of open-bowl intermediate terrain. For tougher runs, take the Headwall Lift, then opt for Chicken Bowl or drop over the back of the ridge to Sun Bowl, a beauty if conditions are right. Go up Siberia Express—advanced levels turn left getting off the lift, intermediates traverse to the right, which feeds into the Gold Coast terrain and other wide-open slopes. Intermediates will like the Shirley Lake area served by a high-speed quad and a triple chair.

The Mountain Run is a crowded end-of-the-day cruise: top to bottom, it's a hefty three-mile run. Another great cruise is Home Run. Or give the Olympic High ski run a try. It follows the route of the original 1960 Olympic men's downhill, won by France's Jean Vuarnet of current sunglasses fame. It begins above the bottom shack of Headwall and heads to the base, bypassing the Mountain Run entirely.

●● **Beginner** ● **Never-ever:** Though Squaw Valley's well publicized black-diamond terrain has given it a menacing reputation, it has a little-known surprise: this is a great spot for never-evers to learn. Squaw has a gentle bowl at the top of the cable car known as Bailey's Beach, served by two slow-moving lifts. Though Bailey's Beach is not physically separated from the other terrain, better skiers rarely use it. Beginners usually long to head toward any summit just like the big boys and girls, and here they can. They just ride the cable car up to High Camp (where they'll also find restaurants, shelter and an outdoor ice rink), and at the end of the day, ride the cable car back down.

Snowboarding

Snowboarding is permitted on all sections of Squaw Valley USA. Squaw has a halfpipe, lessons, special clinics, rentals and a terrain park next to the Riviera Lift. Central Park is the freestyle area. It is fully lit until 9 p.m. and has a "pumping sound system," according to one of our sources.

Lessons (97/98 prices)

Group lessons: Lower intermediate to intermediate skier levels get instruction through a "Ski Your Pro" format where instructors are assigned to training areas on the mountain, and skiers can join in on the hour for as long as they want for $31. Higher-level skiers get two-hour workshops on specific skills, such as moguls, powder or gate training, also for $31.

Never-ever package: A First-Timer Package that includes a beginner lift ticket, equipment rental and a two-hour lesson is $59 for skiing or snowboarding.

Private lessons: $65 an hour; $25 for each additional person.

Racing: A coin-op course is at the top of the Shirley Lake Express, $1 per run.

Children's lessons: Ages 4–12 can take an all-day lesson, with lunch, lift ticket, activities and instruction for $60. The half-day price is $45 and includes a snack instead of lunch.

Call the ski school at (530) 581-7263. Squaw Valley also has programs to teach shaped ski techniques and a full-service adaptive ski school.

Child care (97/98 prices)

Ages: 2–3 years.

Costs: All-day care at the licensed Toddler Care center is $60 with lunch, activities and supervision, while half-day care is $45 (no lunch). A one-and-a-half-hour ski option for 3-year-olds is extra—call to get the price.

Reservations: Recommended; call (530) 581-7225. Parents must provide current immunization records. Children aged 4 and older enroll in ski school programs. The day care is located in the Children's World center, which is a one-stop area for kids' ski school and day care, with a special parking area for the parents.

Lift tickets (97/98 prices)

	Adult	Child (Up to 12)
One day	$48	$5
Three days	$129 ($43/day)	$15 ($5/day)
Five days	$205 ($41/day)	$25 ($5/day)

Who skis free: Ages 75 and older.

Who skis at a discount: Tickets for ages 65-74 and youth aged 13-15 are $24. Non-skiers wishing to ride the cable car, pulse lift and Funitel can do so for $14 for adults, $12 for seniors and youth, and $5 for children. All full-day lift tickets also include night skiing, offered daily until 9 p.m. Otherwise, night skiing costs $20 for adults, $10 for seniors/youth and $5 for children.

Accommodations at the resort

Olympic Valley (that's the name of the base-area town; Squaw Valley is the name of the resort) has several lodging choices. All lodges give easy access to the slopes, but evening activities are limited. If you are staying here, it is best to rent a car if you'd like to explore dining and nightlife in Truckee and Tahoe City. Plans call for a joint venture with Intrawest, a ski-village developer that built Whistler and Tremblant's pedestrian villages, for a new alpine village at the resort base. Some $30 million in mountain improvements and expansions are planned during the next three years; the eventual project—estimated at $250 million—will include 700 residential units and 110,000 square feet of commercial space. But until that project becomes reality, here are the choices. Rates fluctuate quite a bit, depending on whether it's midweek or the weekend, early or late season, and whether there's a big group in residence. Generally, though, you can expect a range of $150 to $300 per night. We've listed the hotels more or less in order from most expensive to least.

The **PlumpJack Squaw Valley Inn** (800-323-7666 or 530-583-1576) is the hottest thing to hit the valley in years. This remodeled hotel, with 61 rooms, originally housed delegates to the 1960 Winter Olympics, and is right across from the cable car building. However, it's far from the dorm accommodations it used to be. The rooms now have down comforters, hooded bathrobes and VCRs. A lap pool and two hot tubs further pamper the guest experience.

The hotel and restaurant are operated by the same team that owns the highly successful PlumpJack Restaurant and Balboa Cafe in San Francisco. The new lodging blends intimate country charm with the style and service of a grand Continental hotel. Its name honors Sir John Falstaff, Shakespeare's swaggering, high-living character. Its restaurant is excellent—details in the Dining section.

Resort at Squaw Creek (800-327-3353 or 530-583-6300) is a multistory luxury hotel that blends well with the valley. It connects with the ski area by its own lift, and is a self-contained resort, with five restaurants and three pools (one of which is open in winter), several hot tubs, a complete fitness center, cross-country skiing and an ice-skating rink.

Squaw Valley Lodge (800-992-9920; in California, 800-922-9970) is only a few yards' walk from the lifts. The lodge boasts a fully equipped health club, free covered parking and kitchenettes in the units.

The Olympic Village Inn (800-845-5243 or 530-583-1501) has five hot tubs, and all units have kitchens. Rates: About $195 a night on weekends, $165 Sunday–Thursday.

The **Squaw Tahoe Inn** (800-323-7666 or 530-583-5176) is a basic hotel, across from the gondola and cable car.

Squaw Valley USA also has **central reservations:** (800) 545-4350 or (530) 583-5585.

Alpine Meadows

It's hard not to like Alpine Meadows. For every level, particularly intermediate and advanced, Alpine Meadows has something to offer. It has expert terrain, sweeping intermediate bowls and scenic trails, and a good beginner area. The view from the base lodge suggests that Alpine is a relatively small area. Not so. You'll see just how big it is when you take the Summit Six (a speedy six-seater) and see it unfold beneath you. In the Lake Tahoe area, Alpine Meadows has traditionally been the ski area with the earliest and longest season (it's open well into May and some years, until July 4).

Alpine Meadows Facts

Summit elevation:	**8,637 feet**	
Vertical drop:	**1,802 feet**	
Base elevation:	**6,835 feet**	

Expert:★★★
Advanced:★★★★★
Intermediate:★★★★
Beginner:★★★
Never-ever:★★★
Address: Box 5279, Tahoe City CA 95730
☎ **Area code:** 530
Ski area phone: 583-4232
Snow report: 581-8374
ⓘ **Toll-free information:** (800) 441-4423
Fax: 583-0963

Internet: http://www.skialpine.com
Number of lifts: 12–1 high-speed six-person chair, 1 high-speed quad, 4 triples, 5 doubles, 1 surface lift
Snowmaking: 12 percent
Skiable acreage: 2,000 acres
Uphill capacity: 16,400 per hour
Snowboarding: Yes, unlimited
Bed base: 10,000 (N. Lake Tahoe Area)
Nearest lodging: Tahoe City, 6 miles
Resort child care: none
Adult ticket, per day: $40-$48 (97/98 prices)

New for 98/99: The oldest chairlift at Alpine Meadows, 34-year-old Weasel Chair, is being replaced with a new triple chair that is as yet unnamed. Scott Chair, which accesses expert terrain, also will be upgraded from a double to a triple. The Weasel not only takes visitors to the beginner terrain, but it also is a major access chair to the back bowls. The added weight of the triple chairs will allow the Scott Chair to run more often in bad weather, good news to experts who want to get to this area during a snowfall.

◆◆ **Expert:** This level has plenty of great bowl skiing and enough steeps to keep hearts in throats. Here's a route suggestion: take the Summit Six and descend into the expert Wolverine Bowl, Beaver Bowl and Estelle Bowl (they're to the right as you ascend), then take the Summit Six again and cruise into the upper-blue territory of Alpine Bowl. Finally, take the Alpine Bowl Chair and traverse to the Sherwood Bowls on the back side of the area or take the High Yellow Traverse to the Saddle Bowl. When you come up the Sherwood Chair, drop down Our Father—and you can say a few enroute—then head to Scott Chair and try out Scott Chute for a direct plunge, or take it easy on tree-lined roundabouts. By then your knees will have earned a cruise. The Promised Land has great tree skiing for top skiers.

◆ **Advanced:** Take your warm-up in Alpine Bowl, staying to skier's right on Rock Garden and Yellow Trail as you cruise down to the Weasel Chair (which will have a new name by the time you read this). Then head for the Back Bowls. If there's a line at the new chair, you also can reach the bowls via the Scott Chair through the blue-square Lakeview area to Ray's Rut. Depending on your mood, you can stay on the groomed Sherwood run to check out the scene, or traverse to the steeper Sherwood Face or South Face. You may want to stay here all day—our advanced-level staffer did.

■ **Intermediate:** Plenty of terrain for this level off these lifts: Alpine Bowl, Roundhouse and Lakeview. The terrain off the Kangaroo lift is a short intermediate run, but much of it is devoted to race programs and the terrain park. This activity creates a narrow descent, something many intermediates are uncomfortable with.

●● **Beginner:** Good terrain under the Meadows and Subway chairs.

● **Never-ever:** This level has a small but sheltered area close to the base lodge. The terrain is quite gentle and seldom used by better skiers.

Snowboarding

Snowboarding is fairly new to Alpine Meadows, but the resort now has many facilities for the sport, including a snowboard center called The Boardroom, which has rentals; a halfpipe called Gravity Cavity near the top of the Roundhouse lift, and a terrain park called Roo's Ride off the Kangaroo lift. Both have snowmaking and daily grooming to keep the features in top condition. Lessons also are offered. The Back Bowls are great powder runs, though the run-out back to the lift gets a bit flat at the end.

Lessons (98/99 prices)

Group lessons: $32 for two hours, $20 for each additional two-hour session (Note: Lessons officially last one hour and 50 minutes, but we're going to use "two-hour" for brevity's sake.) Alpine also offers a coupon book of five two-hour lessons for $185 ($28 each). Anyone may use the coupons, so this is a good deal for families where everyone wants to take a refresher.

Never-ever package: A two-hour adult learn-to-ski or -snowboard program includes beginner lifts, equipment and instruction for $52. Two aditional hours are $20.

Private lessons: For 1–2 people with rates that vary from $55 to $65 depending on time of day. For three or more people, add $20 a person.

Special programs: Clinics for disabled skiers, women, or those who want to try shaped-ski techniques and various advanced skills such as powder, telemark, moguls and trees. Most clinics cost $32. Five or more in a group can tailor their own program. Telemark lessons are $32, including equipment rental, and are offered Saturday, Sunday and Wednesday at noon.

Racing: Daily race-training clinics are offered at $42, or you can buy a book of five sessions for $175. There is a race every Thursday for all abilities with special prizes for $8 for two runs. Alpine Meadows also has coin-op racing.

Children's lessons: Snow school for children ages 4–6 costs $72 a full day and $68 for an additional child from the same family; $46 a half day and $44 per additional child. Reservations are recommended but not required.

Junior Mountaineers is for children 7–12, and it sounds like so much fun we want to enroll too. Kids get lessons, of course, but they also visit and learn about snow grooming, avalanche dog rescuers, ski patrol and other mountain services. Half-day cost is $46 which includes a lift ticket. A full-day program that includes a supervised lunch, lift ticket and five hours of lessons is $72.

Child care

Alpine Meadows has no child care.

Lift tickets (98/99 prices)

	Adult	Child (7-12)
One day	$48	$10
Three days	$141 ($47/day)	$30 ($10/day)
Five days	$235 ($47/day)	$50 ($10/day)

Who skis free: No one.

Who skis at a discount: Ages 65–69 ski for $26; 6 and younger and 70 and older ski for $6. Teens 13–18 ski for $36. Parents can get an interchangeable ticket which can be traded between them for $48 a day.

Accommodations at the resort

Alpine Meadows doesn't have lodging at the base, but has lodging-lift packages. Call Alpine Meadows at (800) 949-3296.

Northstar-at-Tahoe

Unlike Squaw and Alpine, Northstar is a planned resort area, designed to make ski vacationing easy. Condos line the lower slopes, and the runs are laid out for family skiing. Here an intermediate can feel like a World Cup racer. The grooming is impeccable—you'll have to look for bumps—and the entire area management and operations are squeaky clean.

You won't find bowls and cornices on Northstar's Mount Pluto, which makes the skiing here different than at Squaw or Alpine. The skiing is all trail-cut.

New for 98/99: Northstar remodeled its day lodge, built a four-story condo-retail center at the base, and a new ski/snowboard school building.

◆◆ **Expert** ◆ **Advanced:** Not much here for high-level experts, but advanced skiers or those aspiring to the upper levels of intermediate will find some challenge in the drops off the East Ridge (labeled as black diamonds, but the mapmaker was being generous). Normally most of the runs in this section are groomed and the others have moderate bumps. Tonini's is the longest, but The Plunge is the steepest. The only bad part is that it's over too soon. Chute, Crosscut and Powderbowl are also fun—short but sweet. If you're an air skier, you'll be disappointed; these blacks would be blues at Squaw.

Instead of getting your exhilaration by plummeting down some shaft, enjoy the longer rides with moderately steep and sustained pitch off the back side via Lookout Chair and the long traverse called Back Door. This run makes you feel as though you're in another mountain range, far away from any crowds; nine stretched-out swaths provide some of the longest continuous pitches in the West, all served by the Backside Express quad lift. Though they're all labeled as advanced runs, a strong intermediate will have no difficulty in good conditions.

The gem of Northstar lies between these runs, through the trees. Start down Rail Splitter, then take off into the woods to the right or left. After a storm, Northstar is one of the prime areas where you can enjoy powder through the trees long after Squaw's powder has been skied off.

Northstar-at-Tahoe Facts

Summit elevation:	**8,610 feet**
Vertical drop:	**2,280 feet**
Base elevation:	**6,330 feet**

Expert:★
Advanced:★★★
Intermediate:★★★★
Beginner:★★★★★
Never-ever:★★★★
Address: Box 129, Truckee, CA 96160
✆ Area code: 530
Ski area phone: 562-1010
Snow report: 562-1330
ⓘ Toll-free reservations:
(800) GO-NORTH (466-6784)

Fax: 562-2215
E-mail: northstar@boothcreek.com
Internet: http://www.skinorthstar.com
Number of lifts: 12—1 gondola,
4 high-speed quads, 2 triples, 2 doubles,
3 surface lifts
Snowmaking: 50% of developed acres
Total acreage: 2,420 total acres,
500 developed acres
Uphill capacity: 19,400 per hour
Snowboarding: Yes, unlimited
Bed Base: 5,500 at resort
Nearest lodging: slopeside
Resort child care: Yes, 2 years and older
Adult ticket, per day: $40–$46 (97/98 prices)

■ **Intermediate:** This group will enjoy most of the mountain, particularly the smooth blues that descend from the two ridges into Main Street, which is the intermediate run that nearly every other run on the mountain feeds into. Avoid Main Street except when you need to get to a lift. Strong intermediates should try some of the black runs here. While they are the toughest that Northstar has to offer and therefore labeled correctly, they are not the frightening steeps you'll find at Squaw or Alpine, Northstar's neighbors. They will provide a good challenge to an intermediate looking to improve.

●● **Beginner** ● **Never-ever:** Northstar is the best never-ever and beginner resort in this region because its gentlest terrain is below the gondola, while all the other runs are above it. Better skiers leave this area to the learners except at day's end, when some of them use it to practice tucks. Luckily for everyone, it is fairly flat here, so no one can keep up excessive speed.

 ## Snowboarding

Boarding is allowed on all areas of the mountain. Lessons are available and boards may be rented at the Village Ski Rental Shop. The Ground Zero terrain park has a halfpipe among its features, and the Epicenter is a boarders' gathering place with food and videos.

 ## Lessons (98/99 prices)

Group lessons: Free, 1.75-hour skill improvement clinics are held every hour between 10 a.m. and 2 p.m. for solid intermediate and better skiers and snowboarders age 13 and older. Sign up at the summit. Other group lessons are $25 for adult or child.

Never-ever package: Intro to Skiing I is a 1.75-hour lesson with beginner lift access and rental equipment for $54; Intro to Skiing II is the same program but with expanded lifts for $69. Intro to Snowboarding also is offered at the same price.

Private lessons: $65 per hour with each additional person $25. Take your private lesson at 9 a.m. and you'll save $10.

Special programs: Three-day clinics for women or men are offered a few times per year from $259.

Racing: NASTAR is offered Thursday through Sunday; coin-op course operates daily.

Children's lessons: All-day program for children 5–12 is $69 with lifts, lessons and lunch and equipment). An afternoon-only program is $59.

An introduction to skiing or snowboarding program similar to the adults' program costs $39 for the first level and $45 for the next level.

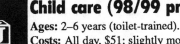 ## Child care (98/99 prices)

Ages: 2–6 years (toilet-trained).
Costs: All day, $51; slightly more for ski instruction. Half-day costs $31. The program combines skiing with other activities, including art, snow play, science, drama and language development.

Reservations: Recommended; call (530) 562-2278. Hours: 8 a.m. to 4:30 p.m.

Lift tickets (98/99 prices)

	Adult	Child (5-12)
One day	$47	$10
Three days	$127 ($42.33/day)	$30 ($10/day)
Five days	$207 ($41.50/day)	$50 ($10/day)

Who skis free: Children under age 5 with a parent ski free.

Who skis at a discount: Ages 60–69 ski for $24 a day; 70 and older ski for $5. Unlimited gondola rides for non-skiers cost $5. Ages 13–22 ski for $38 a day, $103 for three days.

Note: Northstar's parking lot sometimes fills on busy days, and cars are turned away at the entrance.

Northstar also has an electronic frequent-skier program called Vertical Plus that offers discounted lift tickets, prizes for achieving certain vertical-feet totals, and a separate chair lift entrance to help you speed through lift lines. Northstar is one of 11 resorts operated by Booth Creek, Inc. The Vertical Plus program also operates at Booth Creek's other California resorts, Sierra-at-Tahoe and Bear Mountain, the latter in Southern California.

Accommodations at the resort (98/99 prices)

This area was created for condo living. The village has a convenient lodge, with rooms from $174 a night, two-night minimum. The condo rates range from $159 a night for a studio to $289 for a two-bedroom, two-bath unit. Northstar also has full-sized homes for rent, accommodating five to eight people for $379 to $669 a night. Packages are totally flexible, and can be arranged for whatever resort amenities you need—airfare, lifts, rentals and lessons are just some of the choices. Reservations: (800) 466-6784.

Diamond Peak

Bigger is not always better, nor desirable. For skiers and snowboarders who don't want the expansive terrain of most Lake Tahoe resorts, let us recommend Diamond Peak, a medium-sized but exquisite jewel that destination vacationers too often overlook. If we were to rate Tahoe's best family resorts—meaning superb non-extreme skiing and excellent accommodations—we'd rank Northstar first, followed by Diamond Peak. For best lake views, it's Heavenly, Diamond Peak and Ski Homewood (the latter is on the west shore—see the Regional Getaway chapter for info).

◆◆ **Expert ◆ Advanced:** Solitude Canyon has the greatest concentration of advanced terrain. The rest of the resort's terrain falls from a single ridge that starts at the summit and ends at the octagonal Snowflake Lodge overlooking Lake Tahoe. These runs are gentle blacks and blues, relatively short near the bottom and longer near the summit.

The canyons and gullies off Crystal Ridge (a long blue run) are labeled advanced, but strong intermediates will have a blast on them.

■ **Intermediate:** This is a wonderful area for intermediates, especially families who don't want to worry about the kids taking a wrong turn and getting lost. The aforementioned Crystal Ridge is a long blue from the summit, with a stunning view of the lake. The lower-mountain runs off Red Fox also have a nice intermediate pitch.

Diamond Peak Facts

Summit elevation:	8,540 feet
Vertical drop:	1,840 feet
Base elevation:	6,700 feet

Expert:★
Advanced:★★★
Intermediate:★★★★
Beginner:★★★
Never-ever:★★★
Address: 1210 Ski Way
Incline Village, NV 89451
✆ **Area code: 702** (changes to 775 in Dec. 1998)
Ski area phone: 832-1177

Snow report: 831-3211
ⓘ **Toll-free reservations:** (800) 468-2463
Fax: 832-1281 **E-mail:** info@diamondpeak.com
Internet: http://www.diamondpeak.com
Number of lifts: 6–3 quads, 3 doubles
Snowmaking: 80 percent
Skiable acreage: 655 acres
Uphill capacity: 9,800 per hour
Snowboarding: Yes, unlimited
Bed Base: 6,000
Nearest lodging: about 1/4 mile away
Resort child care: Yes, 3 years and older
Adult ticket, per day: $38 (98/99 price)

●● **Beginner** ● **Never-ever:** This is a great learner's mountain more because of its friendly atmosphere and manageable size rather than its terrain (unfortunately, the amount of beginner terrain is a bit limited). Diamond Peak employs about 100 instructors—equal to much larger areas—another indication that it's a good place to learn.

Notes: This is a very friendly area, relatively uncrowded and peaceful. Take a camera—the view is beautiful. A few years ago, Diamond Peak became the first U.S. ski resort to install a "launch pad" loading system, a conveyor belt covered with a skiable felt surface. All three of its quad chairs now have this efficient, family-friendly loading system.

Snowboarding

This resort's snowboarding support and terrain features attract boarders at every skill level, from first-timers to the most advanced. Lessons and rentals are available. For more advanced boarders, Diamond Peak's terrain park provides great hits and super views of Lake Tahoe just off the mid-mountain Ridge chair.

Lessons (98/99 prices)

Group lessons: Two-hour clinics cost $23 (ski or snowboard), which includes a coupon for $8 off your next clinic.

Never-ever package: A Learn-to-Ski Special including beginner lifts, rentals and two-hour lesson is $39. Learn-to-Snowboard is $49, ages 7 and older. As an incentive to keep improving, each student receives a "Graduation Special" coupon valid for a $10 group lesson.

Private lessons: $45-$60 an hour, depending on the time you take your lesson. Private adaptive lessons are available for disabled learners. Reservations required: (702) 832-1135.

Children's lessons: All day group lessons cost $59 for skiers; $69 for snowboarders aged 7–12. Ages 4-6 have a full-day ski lesson program with rentals and lunch for $75. Three-year-olds welcome in private lessons. Reservations required for children's lessons: (702) 832-1130.

Child care (98/99 prices)

Ages: 3–6 years; must be toilet-trained.
Costs: $20 for the morning or afternoon session; $35 for full day.
Reservations: Required; call 832-1130.

Note: Diamond Peak has the Bee Ferrato Child Ski Center, named for its director, a New Zealand native every kid will want to adopt as a grandmother. Bee's Snowplay is a program costing $15 per hour that lets children play in the snow under supervision.

Lift tickets (98/99 prices)

	Adult	Child (6-12)
One day	$38	$14

Who skis free: Younger than 6.

Who skis at a discount: Ages 13–17 pay $31; ages 60–69 pay $21 and ages 70 and older pay $5. Parents can buy an adult ticket that either of them can use—a good deal for those with toddlers. Wednesdays are half-price days, except holidays.

Accommodations near the resort

Incline Village has several hotels and condo complexes. Two worthy of mention are **Hyatt Regency Lake Tahoe Resort and Casino** and **Inn at Incline Motor Lodge and Condominiums.** The Hyatt is a four-star luxury hotel with rates from $135 to $705 a night, while the Inn at Incline has more modest facilities and rates (starting around $70 a night.) The **Tahoe Biltmore Casino** in Crystal Bay has midweek ski packages with Diamond Peak, including a lift ticket, lodging, a full breakfast and transportation to and from the slopes. Last season's price was $39 per night. The **Crystal Bay Motel** (702-831-0287) is an economy property ($35–$65) near casinos and **Haus Bavaria** (800-731-6222) is a European-style guest house with five rooms. **Cal-Neva Resort** is split by the state line between California and Nevada and offers lakefront rooms from $69 to $239.

Sugar Bowl

Sugar Bowl is one of the oldest resorts at Lake Tahoe and the oldest chair-lift-served resort in California. From the moment you step out of your car and board the Magic Carpet gondola to ride *down* across a pristine valley to the lifts, you feel you're stepping back in time.

Sugar Bowl is another of Tahoe's overlooked ski areas, at least by destination skiers. That's a shame, because it has great variety. We recommend Sugar Bowl for a day's change of pace from the larger Tahoe resorts. However, remember that it's one of the first ski areas on the drive from San Francisco, Oakland and Sacramento and gets its big crowds on weekends. So visit midweek if you can.

New for 98/99: Sugar Bowl built a new day lodge at the Mt. Judah base and installed a new quad on Christmas Tree.

◆◆ Expert ◆ Advanced: Mt. Disney, one of three peaks at Sugar Bowl, has advanced runs off either side of a ridge. Mt. Lincoln is the other peak with advanced terrain. There's a very steep cliff area to the right of the Silver Belt chair which is double diamond, but the rest of the black diamonds are more advanced than expert.

Sugar Bowl Facts

Summit elevation:	**8,383 feet**
Vertical drop:	**1,500 feet**
Base elevation:	**6,883 feet**

Expert:★★
Advanced:★★★
Intermediate:★★★★
Beginner:★★★
Never-ever:★★★
Address: P.O. Box 5, Norden, CA 95724
✆ Area code: 530
ⓘ Ski area phone/reservations: 426-9000
Snow report: 426-1111

E-mail: info@sugarbowl.com
Internet: http://www.sugarbowl.com
Number of lifts: 12–1 gondola, 2 high-speed quads, 3 quads, 4 double chairs, 2 surface lifts
Snowmaking: 9 percent
Skiable acreage: 1,500 acres
Uphill capacity: 15,188 per hour
Snowboarding: Yes, unlimited
Bed Base: 460
Nearest lodging: slopeside
Resort child care: Yes, 3 years and older
Adult ticket, per day: $45 (98/99 price)

■ **Intermediate:** Lower intermediates will find the best runs off the Christmas Tree chair. Stronger intermediates should progress to the Jerome Hill Express quad on 8,238-foot Mt. Judah and the Silver Belt lift to the top of 8,383-foot Mt. Lincoln. Crow's Nest lift on Mt. Disney also serves nice blue runs.

●● **Beginner** ● **Never-ever:** Beginners have beautiful long runs off the Christmas Tree, Jerome Hill and Mt. Judah chairs. A relatively new novice area at Mt. Judah is a big improvement over the previous one at the main base.

Snowboarding

The entire mountain is open to snowboarders, with terrain parks on Golden Gate and Coldstream runs. All instruction programs offered to skiers also are available to boarders.

Lessons (98/99 prices)

Group lessons: $25 for a two-hour lesson; $45 for two lessons on the same day.

Never-ever package: The ABC package of lift, lesson and rental for ski or snowboard never-evers through intermediates is $50 for adults, $40 for children.

Private lessons: $60 an hour, with each additional person $20.

Children's lessons: All-day program for ages 6–12 is $60, which includes lifts, equipment, lessons and lunch.

Child care (98/99 prices)

Ages: 3–6 years.

Costs: All day is $60, and half day (without lunch) is $40. Sugar Bears Child Care is a licensed center with educational and recreational activities as well as skiing and quiet time. The program includes snacks, lunch and ski equipment.

Reservations: Suggested; call the ski area.

Lift tickets (98/99 prices)

	Adult	Child (5-12)
One day	$45	$10
Two days	$80 ($40/day)	$18 ($9/day)

Who skis free: Children younger than 5 and ages 70 and older.

Who skis at a discount: Ages 60–69 pay $20; ages 13–21 pay $39. Adults who turn in their all-day lift ticket by 12:30 p.m. receive a credit coupon for $15 off another day's ticket.

Accommodations at the resort

Sugar Bowl has a lodge that is certainly unusual, and possibly unique at American ski resorts: a base lodge that also is a hotel. It is reached by the same four-passenger gondola that brings skiers to this part of the mountain. In addition to the usual services on the ground floor, Sugar Bowl's base lodge also has 28 rooms on the upper two levels. Though it was built in 1939, the rooms have been remodeled for a combination of historic charm and modern convenience. The dining room preserves the grace of a former era with its decor and jacket-required dress code. Room rates, based on double occupancy, start at $115 per night. Bed-breakfast-lift packages, available Sunday through Thursday, non-holiday, are $155 single occupancy, $195 double, $245 triple and $295 quad. Five-day ski weeks with two meals a day also are available; call for prices.

Call (530) 426-9000 for reservations, well in advance.

Cross-country

The Lake Tahoe region may have the greatest concentration of large cross-country ski areas in the U.S., with more than 800 km. of groomed trails. We have listed the bigger operations; local tourist offices can direct you to smaller and less expensive centers. Many of the ones we list here also have full-moon tours and snowshoe rentals and tours; call for information.

Seven of these Nordic centers offer a **Seven Mountain interchangeable trail pass.** They are Royal Gorge, Diamond Peak, Northstar, Spooner Lake, Squaw Creek, Tahoe Donner and Lakeview. The pass cost averages about $10–$12 per day and can be bought through the North Lake Tahoe Resort Association, (800) 824-6348 or (530) 581-8724. If you use the pass at Royal Gorge, there is a $4 surcharge.

The largest private trail system in North America is in California at **Royal Gorge** (530-426-3871; 800-500-3871; e-mail: info@royalgorge.com; Web site: www.royalgorge.com) just off I-80, west of Donner Summit at the Soda Springs exit. Royal Gorge has nearly 9,000 acres of terrain, and more than 300 km. of trails with a skating lane inside the tracks. They also make snow on some trails and use modern snowcats. Adult trail fees are $19.50, for children 7–14, $8.50; with discounts for midweek, multiday tickets and skiers 65 and older.

Royal Gorge has four surface lifts to help skiers up the tougher inclines. It is a full-service ski area, with rental equipment, ski school, ten warming huts, four cafes and a full-time ski patrol. Trailside lodging is at Rainbow Lodge, an historic 1920s B&B, or at Wilderness Lodge, a rustic retreat nestled in the middle of the trail system. Book either through the ski area.

Northstar-at-Tahoe (530-562-2475) has 65 km. of groomed and marked trails. Trail fees: adults $16, children 5–12, $8. Lessons (one-and-a-half hour) with equipment, $22. Rentals and lessons are available, as are snowshoe rentals. All are located near the day lodge and downhill slopes. This is one of the gentler trail systems in the area—very good for families and those just starting this sport.

The **Tahoe Donner Cross-Country Area** (530-587-9484; e-mail: tahoedon @ix.netcom.com) also is off I-80 at Donner State Park exit. This area has 70 km. of trails, all double-tracked with wide skating lanes, and a day lodge with cafe. Tahoe Donner has California's only lighted night cross-country skiing, Wednesdays and Saturdays. Day trail fees are $16 for adults, $13 for teens 13–17 and seniors 60–69, and $9 for kids ages 6–12. Those younger than 6 and older than 69 ski free.

Squaw Creek Cross-Country Ski Center (530-583-6300) is a small area at the Resort at Squaw Creek, which has rentals and lessons. Trails cover 18 km., are groomed daily, and range from beginner to expert. Trail fees are $12 for adults, $10 for children ages 12 and younger. Child care is available starting at age 4.

Lakeview Cross-Country Ski Area (530-583-9353) is two miles east of Tahoe City. It has 65 km. of groomed skating lanes and tracks, a day lodge, cafe, lessons and rentals. A beginner package includes equipment rental, lesson and trail pass for $38 adults, $30 seniors and teens, and $25 child. Trail fees are $15 for adults, less for teens 13–17, seniors 60–69, and children 7–12. Those older than 69 and younger than 7 ski free.

Diamond Peak Cross-Country & Snow Shoe Center (702-832-1177) is located just above Incline Village, atop Carson Range, which has a panoramic view of Lake Tahoe from 9,100 feet. Snowshoers also can use the trails. Trail fees are $15 for adults. Children 6–12 and seniors 60–69 pay $9. Those older than 69 and younger than 6 ski free. Limited food and beverage is available, and don't forget your camera.

Spooner Lake Cross-Country (702-887-8844, recording; 702-749-5349, live voice) on Highway 28 about a half-mile north of the junction with Highway 50, has more than 100 km. of trails, nearly all of which are machine groomed, with one 19-km. backcountry trail. Adult trail fees are $16.50; less for ages 7–15. Younger than 7 ski free. Rentals and lessons are available.

Accommodations

The North Shore is relatively quiet. If you want to stay near one of the resorts, see the accommodations listing at the end of each resort description. Generally, prices near the resorts are above $150 per night; the accommodations in this section generally run less than $150; however, the more luxurious lodging will top out closer to $200.

The North Shore has bed-and-breakfast inns, cabins on the lake, plush or spartan condominiums, and medium-sized casino hotels—a place for everyone. Following is a small list of properties that we've toured, stayed in or had recommended to us by readers or trusted locals. **North Lake Tahoe Resort Association Lodging Information & Reservations** is at (800) 824-6348 (TAHOE-4-U) or (530) 583-3494. Its website is www.tahoe-4-u.com.That agency can also suggest private homes and condos.

The most upscale bed-and-breakfast is the **Rockwood Lodge** (530-525-5273), originally built in the mid-1930s. There are four rooms, two with private bath. It has antique furnishings, plush carpet, brass-and-porcelain bath fixtures, and down comforters on the beds. The lodge is next to the Ski Homewood Ski Area, on the west shore of Tahoe about seven miles south of Tahoe City. NOTE: This is a No-Smoking inn and does not accept children.

The **Mayfield House** (530-583-1001), another B&B, was once a private residence in Tahoe City. The atmosphere is elegant and romantic, and full breakfasts come with the rate. Each of the rooms has a private bath.

Other B&Bs that are recommended are **The Cottage Inn** (530-581-4073; 800-581-4073) in Tahoe City; **The Shore House** (530-546-7270; 800-207-5160) in Tahoe Vista; or **Tahoma Meadows Bed & Breakfast** (530-525-1553) in Homewood.

Just south of Tahoe City is the **Sunnyside Lodge** (530-583-7200, or in California only, 800-822-2754), located directly on the lake. There are 23 rooms, all with a lake view and a few rooms have fireplaces. No. 39 makes a great honeymoon suite, but reserve early because there is a four- to six-week waiting list. This is an excellent property with a lively après-ski bar and a good restaurant, the Chris Craft.

Perhaps the most luxury for the money on the North Shore is the **Tahoe Vista Inn & Marina** (530-546-1515) in Tahoe Vista. The six units here are spectacular and sited directly on the lake. The Jacuzzi tubs are big and the picture windows looking onto the lake are massive. Rates range from about $160 a night for the smallest unit to $240 for a one-bedroom suite with a panoramic lake view.

Among the casinos, the **Cal-Neva Lodge Hotel Spa Casino** (800-225-6382 or 800-CAL-NEVA) is split by the state line and once was owned by Frank Sinatra and visited by Marilyn Monroe. Every room has a lake view, the best from the deluxe suites on the top three floors. There are also honeymoon bungalows with heart-shaped tubs, round beds and mirrored ceilings.

The **Granlibakken Resort & Conference Center** (800-543-3221) in Tahoe City is a great place to stay. Lodging is in 160 privately-owned suites and townhouses and some feature a kitchen and fireplace. Sizes start at one bedroom and top out at a six-bedroom, six-bath townhouse. Two saunas and an outdoor spa are on site. The lovely complex sits on a hill among towering pines and red firs, next to the site of a former ski jump used for the 1932 Olympic tryouts. Two cross-country ski trails and a beginner's Alpine hill also are on site. Ski packages are available with Squaw Valley and Alpine Meadows.

For families or anyone looking for a great deal, **North Lake Lodge** (530-546-2731), in Kings Beach only a few feet from the shore, is one of the oldest hotels but still in great shape. Continental breakfast is included and the shuttlebuses stop just across the street.

River Ranch (530-583-4264) on Highway 89 near Alpine Meadows, is another moderately priced lodge. This historic ski lodge sits on the banks of the Truckee River and rooms are furnished with early American antiques. Continental breakfast is included, and the shuttles for Squaw Valley and Alpine Meadows are nearby.

Away from the lake in Truckee, but convenient to Northstar and Sugar Bowl, is the **Truckee Hotel** (530-587-4444), which has been welcoming guests since 1873. Mostly it housed timber and railroad workers, but one of the residents was a madam who reportedly ran a little business on the side. It has been renovated, but you'll still feel like you're sleeping in the Old West. Some rooms have baths—the old-fashioned claw-footed kind. Some rooms have private baths, some don't. Some rooms are large enough to sleep six, and there is a restaurant, The Passage, that serves lunch and dinner.

The **Richardson House** (888-229-0365; 530-587-5388) is a B&B in Truckee that was built in the 1880s as a private residence. It has been fully restored. Six of the eight rooms have private baths. A full breakfast buffet is included, as well as 24-hour access to the "refreshment center." This may be a big attraction (or not, if you have allergies): The beds and comforters are feather-filled.

Another recommended lodge is the **Best Western Truckee-Tahoe Inn** (530-587-4525) with 100 rooms and complimentary breakfast.

Accommodations—Nevada Northeast

Reno offers big-time casino atmosphere closer to the North Shore and at lower prices than you'll find at the South Shore. Reno also has a planetarium and two major museums, and is 30–45 minutes by car from the North Shore resorts. Some hotels have ski shuttles, but most visitors here probably will want a car. **Reno Central Reservations** is at (800) 367-7366 (FOR-RENO).

Incline Village is a quiet upscale community that is home to Diamond Peak ski area. It has several very fine hotels and condo units, some of which we list in the Diamond Peak section. It also has private homes that can easily sleep 12–16 people. For **Incline Village** accommodations, call (800) 468-2463 (GO-TAHOE).

Dining (530 area code unless noted)

For those not concerned with price:

PlumpJack Squaw Valley (583-1576) is an extraordinary dining experience in a medieval style that is as unique as the cuisine is delicious. The wine list is carefully selected and prices are very reasonable, given the high quality. A bar menu features wood-fired-oven pizza, grilled chicken quesadillas and fine California wines by the glass. Reservations strongly suggested; this place is fairly new and popular.

Glissandi at the Resort at Squaw Creek (581-6621) brings New York and San Francisco style and service, all overlooking Squaw Valley. Reservations suggested. **Graham's** is located in Squaw Valley at the Christy Inn (581-0454).

Captain Jon's (546-4819) in Tahoe Vista serves excellent seafood and French country specialties. Closed Mondays. **Le Petit Pier** (546-4464) in Tahoe Vista presents upscale French cuisine. Reservations needed. Open daily.

Swiss Lakewood Restaurant (525-5211), in Homewood, is Lake Tahoe's oldest and one of its finest dining experiences. Cuisine is French-Swiss and classic continental, service impeccable. Closed Mondays, except holidays.

Wolfdales (583-5700) in downtown Tahoe City has superb dining. Reservations are suggested. Closed Tuesdays.

Christy Hill in Tahoe City (115 Grove Street, reservations recommended, 583-8551) is a real find. Just on the edge of the Lake Tahoe North Shore, Christy Hill offers superb lake views in an intimate, casually elegant atmosphere. The menu, which changes several times each week, is loaded with the freshest fish and specialty produce. The restaurant is open for dinner only from Tuesday through Sunday from 5:30 p.m. Appetizers are $8–$10 and entrées range from $18 to $24.

On the other side of the lake, in Incline Village, head for **The Lone Eagle Grill** at the Hyatt Regency (702-832-3250) for some of the best food that the Nevada lakeshore offers in one Tahoe's most spectacular architectural and natural settings. The soaring stone and timber and the massive fireplace blend with magnificent views across the lake at sunset, and the cuisine and extensive wine list provide accomplished accompaniment.

For more moderate fare try:

Black Bear Tavern (583-8626) is in an historic A-frame log building with knotty-pine walls and a large stone fireplace. Just south of Tahoe City on Hwy. 89, this roadhouse features top-rate dining at moderate prices—steak, chicken, and fresh salmon and swordfish when available. Portions are large, but save room for apple crisp, an old German recipe smothered in vanilla ice cream.

The Basque Club Restaurant (562-2460) in the Northstar-at-Tahoe Golf Clubhouse serves a family-style five-course meal of traditional Basque cuisine—be sure you're hungry. There are always two entrées, as well as many side dishes you think are entrées before the real thing is served. Sleigh rides depart hourly from the clubhouse.

Sunsets (546-3640) in Tahoe Vista features Northern Italian cuisine and beautiful lake views.

In Truckee: **The Passage** (587-7619) in the Truckee Hotel has good soups and interesting salads; the bar is cozy but the dining room is uninviting and small. **OB's** (587-4164) has a pleasantly cluttered decor with old farm antiques and creative cuisine (example: potato-asparagus soup with nutmeg) at cheap prices.

Others to try closer to the lake: **River Ranch** (583-4264) at the access road to Alpine Meadows (ask for a table over the river or next to the river-rock fireplace), **Jake's on the Lake** (583-0188) in Tahoe City, **Gar Woods** (546-3366) in Carnelian Bay, **Za's** (583-1812) in Tahoe City for moderately priced Italian, and **Grazie!** (583-0233) in the Roundhouse Mall for nouveau Italian food and great lake views. **The Soule Domain** (546-7529) in Crystal Bay received consistent raves from people at both ends of the lake. For Mexican with a big dose of margaritas and a shoulder-to-shoulder crowd on weekends, a good choice is the **Hacienda del Lago** (583-0358) in Tahoe City in the Boatworks Mall. **Cafe 333** (702-832-7333) in Incline Village has been written up in *Bon Appetit* several times and is favored by Incline locals. It has French country decor and a moderately priced menu.

For lots of good food at very reasonable prices:

Bacchi's (583-3324) just outside Tahoe City or **Lanza's** (546-2434) in Kings Beach, both serving good Italian fare. **Bridgetender** (583-3342) has burgers and an extensive beer selection. **Mandarin Villa** (583-1188) on Grove Street in Tahoe City serves affordable Chinese food.

The casinos on the Nevada border all serve inexpensive breakfast, lunch and dinner specials.

For pizza, try **Pizza Junction** (587-7411) outside of Truckee, where they make their own Truckee River Beer, **Lake House Pizza** (583-2222) where you can enjoy a great view of Lake Tahoe, **C.B's Pizza** (546-4738) in Kings Beach or **Squaw Valley Pizza** (583-4787), at the entrance to the Squaw Valley resort.

Azzara's (702-831-0346) in Incline Village serves good reasonable Italian food. **Austin's** (702-832-7778) gets raves for meatloaf and homemade soups. **Stanley's** (702-831-9944) is an Incline institution for Sunday breakfast and Friday night local entertainment in the bar. **Jack Rabbit Moon** (702-832-3007) gets the nod for dinner from knowledgeable locals.

The best breakfasts are at the **Squeeze In** (587-9814) in Truckee where the list of omelets requires a speed-reading course. The Squeeze In has all the atmosphere you could want in a breakfast joint, built in a former alley and only 10 feet wide. On weekends, expect to wait a while—this place is popular. Down the street is the **Coffee And**, which also serves up a good basic breakfast. Don't miss **The Fire Sign** (583-0871) about two miles south of Tahoe

City, and where many believe the best breakfasts and lunches in the region are served. If you're further to the north, try the **Old Post Office** (546-3205) at Carnelian Bay or the **Log Cabin** (546-7109) in Kings Beach. Near Alpine Meadows, try **The Alpine Riverside Cafe** (583-6896) for breakfast and lunch.

Après-ski/nightlife

At Squaw, local hangouts include the bar at **PlumpJack, Bullwackers** at the Resort at Squaw Creek, **Bar One** and **Plaza Bar** at the Olympic House and the **Red Dog Saloon** at the Opera House. Also try **River Ranch** on the Alpine Meadows access road, which was voted top après-ski in North Lake Tahoe.

In Tahoe City, places to head include **Pete'n'Peter's, Rosie's Café, Pierce Street Annex** behind Safeway near the Boatworks Mall or **Jake's on the Lake. Sunnyside,** just a couple of miles south of Tahoe City on the lake, has a lively bar. **Hacienda del Lago** in the Boatworks has nachos till 6 p.m. For the best live music, try **Elevation** (formerly Humpty's) across from Safeway. An offbeat après-ski spot is **Naughty Dawg** on the main road in Tahoe City, where you can get munchies and speciality drinks served in dog dishes. Watch out for "shotskis," a ritual of drinks served in an unusual way.

In Truckee there is occasional music at **The Passage** in the Truckee Hotel and at the **Bar of America** and the **Pastime Club**, both at Commercial Row. The **Cottonwood Restaurant** overlooking Truckee on Hwy. 267 has jazz. The casinos on North Lake Tahoe have entertainment every night. Sure bets are the **Cal-Neva Lodge, The Crystal Bay Club, Hyatt Lake Tahoe** and the **Tahoe Biltmore.** Incline locals hang at **Hacienda de la Sierra, Rookie's Sports Grill** and **Legends.**

Child care

Child care options are listed with the resorts that offer that service, but we also wanted to let you know about this business: **Baby's Away** (530-581-3930) rents and will deliver baby items (cribs, strollers, toys, etc.) to your hotel or condo. For babysitting referrals, call (530) 587-5960.

Other activities

Ice skating: Squaw Valley's High Camp at the top of the cable car has **ice skating, bungee jumping, swimming** (yes, in winter), **tubing** and more. **Sleigh rides:** Northstar-at-Tahoe, 562-2480. There's also **snowmobiling, scenic flights, hot-air balloon rides, horseback riding, bowling, movies** and **health clubs. Snowfest** is North Tahoe's winter carnival, usually in late February/early March. Call (800) 824-6348 or (530) 583-3494 for a complete list of things to do.

For off-slope activity near Diamond Peak, check out the **Incline Village Recreation Center**, which has aerobics, basketball court, weight room and an indoor pool among its amenities. Visitors can use the facilities for $10 per day or $25 per week. Discounts are available for children, teens, seniors and families. Another spot for family fun is **Bowl Incline** with more than bowling. You'll find pool tables, other pinball gizmos, video poker built into the bar and a golf simulator where you can play seven world-class courses. Greens fees are $24 per hour and it takes about an hour to play 18 holes.

Getting there and getting around

By air: Reno-Tahoe International Airport has more than 100 nonstop flights a day from various parts of the country. The airport is 45 miles from Squaw Valley USA, 50 miles from Alpine Meadows, 35 miles from Diamond Peak and 38 miles from Northstar-at-Tahoe.

By train: Amtrak serves Truckee and Reno on the California Zephyr line, running from Oakland to Chicago. Call (800) 872-7245.

By bus: Shuttles run from almost every major hotel to each principal ski resort. Check for schedules when you arrive. Most of the shuttles that cruise around the North or South Shores are free, but when you need to go from one end of the lake to the other, take the Lake Lapper for $5 round-trip. It's really more for sightseeing, as it doesn't serve the ski areas. However, it does run at night. Call 542-5900 for more information.

Sierra Nevada Gray Lines (800-822-6009 or 702-329-1147) operates a daily ski shuttle between downtown Reno and Alpine Meadows, Northstar-at-Tahoe (except Saturdays) and Squaw Valley USA from mid-December through the end of March. Tahoe Casino Express runs 17 times daily between Reno airport and South Shore for about $15 each way.

By car: Driving time from Reno is about an hour to any major North Shore resort. San Francisco is about four hours away via I-80 to the North Shore. During storms, the California Highway Patrol doesn't let drivers come up the mountains without chains or a 4-wheel-drive vehicle, so be prepared.

Sugar Bowl is off I-80 just west of Donner Lake. Alpine Meadows and Squaw Valley are on Highway 89 and Northstar-at-Tahoe is on Highway 267 (both highways run between I-80 and Highway 28, which hugs the North Shore). Diamond Peak is on Highway 28 in Nevada on the lake's east side. Tip: If you are driving a rental car from Reno on I-80, headed west toward Northstar, Squaw or Alpine, you may pass through a California agricultural checkpoint. If you do, get off the freeway at the next stop and turn around. That checkpoint means you just missed the turnoff for Hwy. 89, just like one of our staffers did. The signs are dimly lit at night and tough to see a couple of hours before sunset.

Getting around: As much as we hate to recommend adding more auto pollution to this pristine location, rent a car. If you stay near one of the ski resorts, you could do without one, but your dining and evening options would be limited. Alpine Meadows, Squaw Valley, Diamond Peak and Northstar all have shuttles from North Tahoe towns, as does one of the areas mentioned in our Regional Getaway chapter, Ski Homewood.

South Lake Tahoe Area

Kirkwood

Heavenly

Sierra-at-Tahoe

Toll-free reservations:
(800) AT-TAHOE (288-2463)
Internet: http://www.virtualtahoe.com
Dining:★★★
Apres-ski/nightlife:★★★★★
Other activities:★★★

As we said in the previous chapter, few regions on the North American continent have the ski-resort diversity of the Lake Tahoe region. Tahoe's South Shore offers something unique—24-hour activity in its large casino-hotels that hug the California-Nevada state line. Here you'll find big-name entertainment (country star Wynonna was booked during our stay last season) nearly every week during ski season, and you can stay up all night playing blackjack or feeding slot machines.

If you're in love and looking for a no-hassle way to get married, South Lake Tahoe's the spot. Especially around Valentine's Day, Feb. 14, it is a common sight to see a wedding veil hanging from a car's back window, with the groom and best man in the front seats and the bride and maid of honor in back. We have more details in the *Other Activities* section.

Two of the largest Tahoe resorts, Heavenly and Kirkwood, are here. Heavenly is the most popular Tahoe resort with out-of-towners, probably because you can see its runs rising above town, almost close enough to touch from South Lake Tahoe Boulevard. Kirkwood is gaining a well-deserved reputation for awesome terrain and nassive amounts of snow. A lesser-known resort, but one you shouldn't miss, is Sierra-at-Tahoe.

A word on phone numbers: Last season, the California side of Tahoe got a new area code, 530. This year, the Nevada side of the lake gets a new area code, 775, which begins in December 1998. The grace period lasts until May 1999, so we've left the phone numbers as is. If you have trouble getting through, try the new area code. Though the South Shore appears to be one big town, it's two towns in two states. If you're staying on the Nevada side, you'll need to dial the area code before all California phone numbers, and vice versa.

Heavenly Resort

Heavenly is big. It ranks Number One at Lake Tahoe for highest elevation (10,040 feet), greatest vertical rise (3,500 feet) and longest run (5.5 miles). Heavenly has some good expert terrain—Mott Canyon on the Nevada side and its famous face run, Gunbarrel, on the California side. Other than that, however, the resort is most appropriate for intermediates and advanced skiers.

Heavenly is also the only two-state ski resort—you can start out from either California or Nevada. Though the California base is better known because it's in clear view of South Lake Tahoe's casinos, skiers and snowboarders also can start from the Nevada side by driving on the Kingsbury Grade to either the Stagecoach or Boulder bases. Most visitors start from California, so beginning in Nevada is often a good way to avoid the crowds.

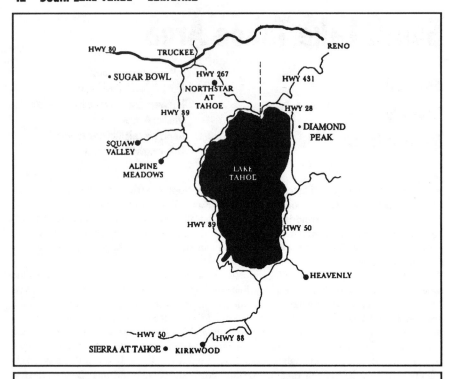

Tahoe Interchangeable tickets (98/99 prices)

The Ski Lake Tahoe interchangeable lift pass is good at Kirkwood, Heavenly, Sierra-at-Tahoe, Northstar, Alpine Meadows and Squaw Valley USA. Five of six consecutive days cost $245 ($49 a day).

But mostly, Heavenly is the view. The most spectacular view of Lake Tahoe—perhaps the most awesome view from a ski area summit anywhere—is at the top of the Sky Express. A photographer is stationed up there to take visitor photos, and often, there is a waiting line. From here on a sunny day just after a storm, the lake looks a brilliant blue sapphire, nesting in soft folds of white velvet. As you traverse into Nevada, you'll see the muted browns, greens and yellows of the Nevada winter desert. Pack a camera. You'll be glad you did.

Heavenly is now part of the American Skiing Company family of resorts, a corporation that owns several New England areas, plus The Canyons in Utah and Steamboat in Colorado.

New for 98/99: Heavenly plans to replace the Gunbarrel triple chair and the Stagecoach double chair with high-speed quads. The resort also is adding a daycare center, which will accept ages 6 months to 4 years; a new mid-mountain day lodge on the California side; and a winch cat and a Pipe Dragon to their grooming fleet. A winch cat allows the resort to groom very steep slopes, while the Pipe Dragon grooms terrain-park halfpipes.

◆◆ **Expert:** The California base, on Ski Run Boulevard from Highway 50, strikes awe in all but the best skiers because the world seems to drop straight down into Lake Tahoe.

Gunbarrel and East Bowl are straight ladders of bumps 1,700 vertical feet high, often with dangerous-looking rocky protrusions in early winter or late spring.

On the Nevada side (see the advanced section for directions on crossing the state line), experts have their own playgrounds, Mott Canyon and Killebrew Canyon. These north-facing walls are peppered with pines and have half-a-dozen expert chutes. This lift-served area can only be entered through designated gates.

◆ **Advanced:** If the bumps on the California face look too menacing, leap over them by taking either the Gunbarrel Chair or the aerial tram. Then head down Patsy's (unfortunately a horrible bottleneck on weekends) to the Waterfall Chair, which gives access to superb advanced runs off Ridge, Canyon and Sky Express Chairs. From the top of the Sky Express, the best of the California side opens up. After you have admired the inspiring view of Lake Tahoe, drop down Ellie's if you are looking for bumps. Sometimes you can catch Ellie's when it's groomed, and then it's a screaming cruiser.

When you have had enough of California, strike out for Nevada, where 50 percent of the terrain is located. You get to the Nevada side from the top of Sky Express; go left along the Skyline Trail, which requires a bit of pushing. Here's a trick for advanced intermediates who want the best of the Milky Way Bowl: the Skyline Trail dips a bit after you get off the Sky Express Chair. You then make a small climb and the trail starts down again. Just as you begin dropping, look to your right for tracks leading into the trees and follow them. After a short traverse you will end up at the top of the Milky Way Bowl, with about twice the vertical you would have found had you stayed on the trail. Those coming off the Dipper chair on the Nevada side can use the same traverse. From the top of Milky Way to the bottom of Mott Canyon in one long run covers over 2,000 vertical feet through black and blacker terrain.

On the Nevada side, advanced sliders with moguls on their minds can bump down Big Dipper Bowl or traverse a bit further and try the Little Dipper.

Heavenly Resort Facts

California Side—

Summit:	10,040 feet
Vertical drop:	3,500 feet
Base:	6,540 feet

Nevada Side—

Summit:	10,040 feet
Vertical drop:	2,840 feet
Base:	7,200 feet

Expert: ★★★★
Advanced: ★★★★
Intermediate: ★★★★
Beginner: ★★ **Never-ever:** ★
Address: Box 2180, Stateline, NV 89449
✆ **Area code:** 702 (changes to 775 in 12/98)
Ski area phone: 586-7000
Snow report: (530) 541-7544

ⓘ **Toll-free reservations:**
(800) 243-2836 (2-HEAVEN)
E-mail: info@skiheavenly.com
World Wide Web: http://www.skiheavenly.com
Number of lifts: 27–1 aerial tram, 1 six-passenger high-speed chair, 5 high-speed quads, 8 triples, 5 doubles, 7 surface lifts
Snowmaking: 69 percent of trails
Total acreage: 4,800 patrolled acres (1,084 skiable trail acres)
Uphill capacity: 29,000 per hour
Snowboarding: Yes, unlimited
Bed Base: 22,000 in S. Lake Tahoe
Nearest lodging: about a mile away
Resort child care: Yes, 6 months and older
Adult ticket, per day: $45-$52 (98/99 prices)

■ **Intermediate:** If you want long smooth cruising, head to the right from the Sky Express when you get off the chair and steam down Liz's, Canyon, Betty's or Ridge Run.

The Nevada side has even better cruises. From the top of the Dipper Express are the Big Dipper and Orion. The Galaxy Chair is a good spot for low intermediates to gain confidence. For a cruise that seems to take forever, take Olympic Downhill to Stagecoach Base.

●● **Beginner** ● **Never-ever:** Though Heavenly is exactly that for intermediates and up, never-evers should pick another resort for their skiing or snowboarding baptism. Except for a tiny learning section at the California base, Heavenly's green terrain is smack in the middle of a place where four lifts have their boarding areas. People dart in every direction, making a most intimidating scene. However, everyone—non-skiers included—can ride the tram to admire the view of the lake. If you must take your first lesson here, go to the Boulder base area on the Nevada side, where there is a gentle slope and more room to spread out.

Note: If you've been skiing in Nevada, here's how to get back to the California base: take the Dipper Express to the top and traverse right to the California Trail, or take Comet and then cruise the 49er run. The runs meander into a small depression where the three-mile winding Roundabout trail down the face gets most of the intermediate traffic at the end of the day (beginners will want to ride the tram back down). Advanced sliders who want to descend The Face should board Patsy's or Groove, two short lifts that return you to the top. Tram riders should board Patsy's.

Snowboarding

Snowboarding is allowed on both sides of the mountain. This season, Heavenly will have halfpipes and terrain parks on both sides, as well as additional terrain features on various runs. Heavenly also bought a Pipe Dragon this season to keep the pipes in top shape. Lessons and rentals are available on both sides.

Lessons (98/99 prices)

Group lessons: American Skiing Company's Perfect Turn program is now practiced at Heavenly. (For a description, see our *Skiing for Everyone* chapter.) For levels higher than advanced beginner, ski and snowboard clinics (called Mountain Adventure Clinics) cost $29. If you also need rentals and/or a lift ticket, ask about packages. You also can buy a three- to five-day clinic booklet at a discount. The booklet does not have to be used on consecutive days.

Never-ever package: A two-hour Perfect Turn clinic, rentals and access to the beginner lifts is $56, ski or snowboard. Ask about multi-day savings.

Private lessons: $75 per hour. Discounts offered for multiple hours and for early-morning or late-afternoon lessons. Reservations suggested. Call (702) 586-7000, Ext. 6244.

Special programs: Heavenly has special theme clinics, such as Mott and Killebrew guided tours for experts, carving clinics, and clinics for women. Call for prices and dates.

Racing: A coin-op course operates daily on the Rusutsu run on the California side, at $2 per run.

Children's programs: Full day for ages 4–13 is $76, including instruction, equipment, lunch, snacks and lift access. Ages 7-13 can take snowboard lessons for the same price. The afternoon session costs $52, and does not include lunch. A Tag-A-Long private lesson allowing the parent to participate with their child is 75 minutes long and costs $85.

Child care

Ages: 6 months to 4 years.
Costs: Not available; call resort.
Reservations: A good idea. Heavenly has had quite a demand for child care services, and was planning to offer this service starting with the 98/99 season. Call the resort at (702) 586-7000 or check its Web page (www.skiheavenly.com) for an update.

Lift tickets (98/99 prices)

	Adult	Child (6-12)
One day	$52	$24
Three days (of 4)	$147 ($49/day)	$66 ($22/day)
Five days	$230 ($46/day)	$100 ($20/day)

Who skis free: Children ages 5 and younger ski free with a paying adult.
Who skis at a discount: Youth (ages 13–15) ski for $38 a day, $105 for three days, $165 for five days. Ages 65 and older ski for children's prices.

Kirkwood

After the bustle of Heavenly and its casino-laced hometown, Kirkwood is like taking a trip back into the wilderness. The lovely drive through Hope Valley to Kirkwood from South Lake Tahoe takes only about 45 minutes, but it is light-years away in altitude and ambiance. There are no bright lights, no ringing jackpots, no wide blue lake, no high-rise buildings and no urban noise. Instead, you have the feeling that you are entering a special secret place, known to a select few.

Kirkwood is a superb area for skiing and snowboarding; but not so great for off-slope socializing and activities. Terrain-wise, Kirkwood is the most balanced resort in the Tahoe region. It has one of the best learning areas in the country—several gentle runs that are off to one side, away from the main traffic and served by their own lift. Kirkwood will thrill any

Kirkwood Facts

Summit elevation:	**9,800 feet**
Vertical drop:	**2,000 feet**
Base elevation:	**7,800 feet**

Expert:★★★★
Advanced:★★★★
Intermediate:★★★★★
Beginner:★★★
Never-ever:★★★★
Address: Box 1, Kirkwood, CA 95646
Area code: 209
✆ Ski area phone: 258-6000
Snow report: 258-3000

ⓘ Toll-free reservations: (800) 967-7500
Fax: 258-8899
World Wide Web: http://www.skikirkwood.com
Number of lifts: 12—1 quad, 7 triples, 2 doubles, 2 surface lifts
Snowmaking: 2 percent
Skiable acreage: 2,300 acres
Uphill capacity: 15,600 per hour
Snowboarding: Yes, unlimited
Bed Base: 10,500 in S. Lake Tahoe
Nearest lodging: slopeside
Resort child care: Yes, 2 years and older
Adult ticket, per day: $40-$43 (97/98 prices)

expert, even super-expert, with its steeps and dozens of chutes. And it offers great terrain for all ability levels between those extremes. Kirkwood's northeast exposure in a snow pocket gives light, dry conditions and produces storms that linger and dump more. Kirkwood frequently stays open into May with good late-season conditions.

For the past decade natural snow has often arrived late in the California mountains, so Kirkwood recently added snowmaking on four of the most popular runs—Hay Flat, Buckboard, Race Course and Zachary— top to bottom, as well as the beginner tow, No. 8. Kirkwood has both named and numbered its lifts. Locals and staff tend to use the numbers, so we list those in parentheses in the following terrain description.

◆◆ **Expert:** Wagonwheel/The Wall (Chair 10) and Cornice (Chair 6) rise from the base area to serve the toughest terrain. The resort cut an entry at the top of Wagonwheel to eliminate the leap formerly required to get into the double-black runs below the Sisters. Some of the best skiing is further west (right on the map), below False Peak through chutes and trees. Cornice serves single-diamond runs, including Palisades Bowl, to the far right on the trail map. Because getting here requires a bit of a traverse, you can find some good powder shots.

On the far left of the trail map, Sunrise (Chair 4) serves an area called The Wave because it gets a cornice that looks like a giant ocean breaker. On the right (west) side of the chair the half dozen runs of Thunder Saddle keep powder for three days after a snowfall because it takes three chairs to get there. Watch your step along the ridge. When you get toward the bottom of the steeps, after dropping down One Man Chute, Bogie's Slide or Corner Chute, tuck and keep your speed up for the flat run back to the Wagonwheel (Chair 10) or Cornice (Chair 6) lifts.

◆ **Advanced:** Part of Sentinel Bowl is groomed every day and is beautiful for anyone looking for super-smooth steeps. If you want bumps, try Olympic, Look-Out Janek, Zack's (Zachary on the map) or Monte Wolfe, which drop to either side of the Cornice Chair. The Reut (Chair 11) has some great cruisers—marked black on the map, but a solid intermediate could handle them.

■ **Intermediate:** Intermediates can stay on the lower sections of the face, using Hole'n'Wall (Chair 7) and Solitude (Chair 5), or work their way over Caples Crest (Chair 2) to the Sunrise section. Here is plenty of groomed intermediate terrain to the east (left on the map) of Sunrise (Chair 4). The entire lower mountain, with just a couple of exceptions, is perfectly suited for intermediates. When you're ready to test your black-diamond skills, try the runs off Chair 11. If you can handle those, you're probably ready for a groomed run in Sentinel Bowl.

●● **Beginner:** Beginners will find gentle trails served by Snowkirk Chair (Chair 1) to the east, and Bunny Chair (Chair 9) and Hole 'n' Wall (Chair 7) at the far west.

● **Never-ever:** Never-evers should head straight for the Timber Creek Lodge, a right hand turn before you reach the main parking lot (there's a sign). There novices will find a rental shop and ticket window, plus Chairs 9 and 7 (Bunny and Hole'n'Wall) that serve novice and low intermediate terrain. Experienced skiers and snowboarders park in the main lot and get their tickets in the main lodge farther down the road, but if there's a novice in your group, you can get to the main area using Chair 7. Kirkwood has—by far—the best setup for novices in the South Tahoe region.

 ## Snowboarding

Boarding is permitted on all areas of the mountain. The area has numerous naturally occurring halfpipes and quarterpipes. Boards may be rented at the Red Cliffs Lodge (main lodge) at the base, and the ski school has lessons. Kirkwood has a freestyle terrain park, reached by Chair 2, and a halfpipe, reached by Chair 7.

Lessons (97/98 prices)

Group lessons: Kirkwood's Ski School offers Pro Turn Ski Clinics for all levels except beginners. These are 90 minutes long, cost $15, and are designed to smooth out rough edges, rather than teach the basics from scratch. Skiers can learn how to use the Elan shaped skis.

Never-ever package: A Learn To Ski package including a four-hour lesson, beginner lift ticket and rental equipment costs $43. The ski school guarantees that a never-ever will be able to ski the beginner area by the end of the day, or return for a free lesson. Kirkwood offers two follow-up sessions that include rentals, a Pro Turn clinic and intermediate lift ticket for $43 each day. (The follow-up days do not have to be used consecutively, and the ticket gets you on Chairs 1, 2, 3, 5, 7 and 9.) Kirkwood is using shaped skis to teach never-evers.

Learn to snowboard packages with a 2.5-hour lesson, beginner lift ticket and rental equipment are $60. As it does with the ski program, Kirkwood offers novice snowboarders two follow-up lessons with the same benefits for $60 per day.

Private lessons: $60 for an hour, $25 each additional person.

Special programs: Kirkwood has programs for women, skiers aged 40 and older, and others. Call for dates and prices.

Racing: Self-timed courses are open daily for $1 per run, $2 for three runs and $7 for an all-day pass.

Children's lessons: Ages 4–12 have a program with equipment, lessons and lifts for $60 for a full day with lunch, $50 for a half day. Kirkwood's children's center is located in the Timber Creek novice area, the first right-hand turn before you reach the main parking lot.

Child care

Ages: 2–6 years, toilet-trained.
Costs: All day is $55 including lunch, a half day $45.
Reservations: Recommended; call (209) 258-6000. Licensed child care for infants can be arranged with an outside agency at (209) 258-8783.

Lift tickets (98/99 prices)

	Adult	Child (6-12)
One day	$45	$7
Three days	$129 ($43/day)	$21 ($7/day)
Five days	$210 ($42/day)	$35 ($7/day)

Who skis free: Ages 5 and younger.

Who skis at a discount: Ages 60 and older ski for $23; young adults 13–24 ski for $35.

The Avid Skier Card provides a free day of skiing or boarding for every four full-day lift tickets purchased. The full-day lift tickets need not be on consecutive days.

Sierra-at-Tahoe

Sierra-at-Tahoe often is overlooked by destination skiers to the South Shore. What a shame. If Heavenly gets a little crowded, or the previous night's partying has made the drive to Kirkwood unthinkable, point yourself west and drive 12 miles to this fun, little resort.

Oops. Did we say "little?" Our mistake. Sierra-at-Tahoe has more than 2,000 vertical feet and 2,000 acres. That's not little. So let us rephrase: Drive 12 miles west to this fun, big resort with an intimate feel. Better yet, ride the free shuttles that pick up at 43 locations in Stateline and the Highway 50 corridor.

◆◆ **Expert** ◆ **Advanced:** Sierra-at-Tahoe has a good collection of bumped-up black-diamond trails under the Grand View Express and Tahoe King chairs. Castle, Preacher's Passion and Dynamite all cascade roughly 1,300 vertical feet.

■ **Intermediate:** This is a wonderful area for intermediates. West Bowl will fast become the favorite area of the mountain for this level, especially the terrain park (or "Fun Zone," as the resort calls it) on Pyramid. Lower Main is a steep, groomed run that rises above the day lodge. It's gotta be the toughest blue run here. If you see this trail and gulp, don't worry. Fun awaits in West Bowl. The Backside is another good spot for intermediates.

●● **Beginner:** Sugar 'n' Spice is a 2.5-mile, easy cruise from the summit. Ride the Grand View Express chair and take a moment to look at the view of the lake (much better on the roof deck of the Grand View Grill). As you descend Sugar 'n' Spice, stay a good distance from the snowbank on the left edge of the run, especially when it gets to be head-high. Hot shots like to shoot out of the trees between this run and Upper Snowshoe. Fortunately, Sugar 'n' Spice is plenty wide. Stay to the middle or the right and give the idiots some room.

Upper Snowshoe is another good beginner run, but be sure to turn right at Marten to meet up with Sugar 'n' Spice, or you'll be on Lower Snowshoe, a blue run. Another chair that serves good beginner terrain is Rock Garden.

● **Never-ever:** This is a great learner's mountain. Sierra-at-Tahoe has a super learning slope called Broadway, right at the day lodge and served by its own quad chair.

Sierra-at-Tahoe Facts

Summit elevation:	**8,852 feet**
Vertical drop:	**2,212 feet**
Base elevation:	**6,640 feet**

Expert:★★
Advanced:★★★★
Intermediate:★★★★
Beginner:★★★★
Never-ever:★★★★
Address: 1111 Sierra-at-Tahoe Rd.
Twin Bridges, CA 95735
✆ **Area code:** 530
Ski area phone: 659-7453
Snow report: 659-7475

ⓘ **Toll-free reservations:** no lodging on site
Fax: 659-7749 **E-mail:** sierra@sierra.net
Web site: www.sierratahoe.com
Number of lifts: 9–3 high-speed quads,
1 triple, 5 doubles
Snowmaking: 22 percent
Skiable acreage: 2,000 acres
Uphill capacity: 14,921 per hour
Snowboarding: Yes, unlimited
Bed Base: in S. Lake Tahoe
Nearest lodging: about 12 miles away
Resort child care: Yes, 2 years and older
Adult ticket, per day: $35-$43 (97/98 prices)

Snowboarding

Snowboarding is allowed everywhere. Sierra-at-Tahoe has four terrain parks open to snowboarders and skiers. All four are marked with pink highlighting on the trail map. Rentals and lessons are available.

Lessons (98/99 prices)

Group lessons: Skill Improvement Clinics for levels 6 through expert are offered twice a day midweek and four times a day on weekends and holidays. The clinics are free on a first-come basis for ages 13 and older. For advancing beginners through lower intermediates, 1.75-hour lessons cost $27.

Never-ever package: A First Tracks package including beginner lifts, rentals and 1.75-hour lesson is $45 for skiers, $55 for boarders. The second-day package is $65 for skiers and $74 for boarders and includes access to more lifts.

Private lessons: $60 an hour, with discounts for additional hours or early-bird lessons.

Children's lessons: All day instruction (including lunch) is $67 for ages 4–12; $57 for half day (with lunch included for the morning session).

Child care (98/99 prices)

Ages: 2–5 years.

Costs: $47 for a 3.5-hour session; $57 for full day (full day includes lunch).

Reservations: Recommended; call (530) 659-7453 Ext. 276. You also can register on the resort's website (www.sierratahoe.com).

Lift tickets (98/99 prices)

	Adult	Child (6-12)
One day	$45	$7
Two days	$75 ($37.50/day)	$14 ($7/day)
Three days	$112 ($37.33/day)	$21 ($7/day)

Who skis free: Younger than 6.

Who skis at a discount: Ages 70 and older ski at child prices. Ages 60–69 ski for $22, and young adults aged 13-22 ski for $35. Both age groups get multiday discounts.

Cross-country (97/98 prices)

The Lake Tahoe region may have the greatest concentration of large cross-country ski areas in the U.S., with more than 800 km. of groomed trails. Most of that is on the north end of the lake, but South Shore has a good network of trails, too. Most also allow snowshoes. Trail fees generally are $8 to $16 for adults and about half of that for kids and seniors.

Spooner Lake Cross-Country (702-887-8844, recording; 702-749-5349, live voice) on Highway 28 about a half-mile north of the junction with Highway 50, has more than 100 km. of trails, nearly all of which are machine groomed, with one 19-km. backcountry trail. Rentals and lessons are available.

Kirkwood Cross-Country (209-258-7248) has 80 km. of machine-groomed tracks, skating lanes and three interconnected trail systems with three warming huts, including the

Hope Valley Cross-Country Ski Center (530-694-2337) is near the junction of Highways 89 and 88. It has about 100 km. of marked trails, a quarter of which are groomed, as well as lessons and rentals. Trail fees are by donation.

Camp Richardson Resort (530-542-6584) in South Lake Tahoe has a cross-country ski center with lessons, rentals and trails along the Lake Tahoe shoreline.

 ## Accommodations (97/98 prices)

South Shore accommodations divide into four categories: the multistory casinos hugging the Nevada border for great views and nonstop nightlife; the top of Kingsbury Grade, near the base of Heavenly's Nevada side, for upscale condominiums and top-quality hotels; along the California lake shore for moderately priced motels, and at Kirkwood to escape the hustle and bustle. We list just a tiny slice of what's available.

Central Reservations for South Lake Tahoe is at (800) 288-2463 (AT-TAHOE). If you plan to do all your skiing at Heavenly, Heavenly Central Reservations can arrange an entire ski vacation including airfare, transfers, lessons, rentals, non-ski activities, skiing and lodging. Call (800) 243-2836 (2-HEAVEN) or (702) 588-4584.

If you can stay here Sunday through Thursday nights, you can get extremely good deals. Lodging and lift packages can run as low as $55 per person, per night, double occupancy. If you're here Friday and Saturday, however, prices double or sometimes triple. South Shore has a wide variety of lodges and prices, however, so tell the reservationist how much you want to spend.

The lodging and general look of South Lake Tahoe takes many visitors by surprise. They expect to see Rocky Mountain-style luxury. Instead, they find a lot of '50s- and '60s-style budget motels, cabins and shopping strip malls lining a very traffic-heavy main street. If we can be frank (and we can—it's our book), much of South Shore is not very attractive.

However, this is about to change. Several beautiful new hotels have been built in the past few years, and several more will be built in connection with Heavenly's plan to put a gondola right at the state line, within walking distance of hundreds of hotel rooms.

Nevada allows casino gambling, California doesn't. Most of the visitors to this region come from Northern California's urban areas. Keep that in mind and you'll realize why the high-rise casino-hotels were built inches from the state line.

Many destination visitors like to be smack in the middle of the action. If you're in that group, try Harvey's (800-648-3361 from outside Nevada or 702-588-2411 from Nevada) and Harrah's (800-648-3353 or 702-588-3515), which have everyone's highest ratings, from AAA to Mobil. Other casino-hotels within walking distance of the state line are Caesars Tahoe (800-648-3353 or 702-586-2000) and the Horizon Casino Resort (800-648-3322).

We like to be near the casinos, but don't want to hear that constant ringing of the slot machines when we come downstairs for breakfast. One of our favorite places to stay—in fact, our staff spent a few days together here a couple of seasons ago—is the Embassy Suites Resort (800-362-2779; 530-544-5400; www.embassytahoe.com). Just 50 feet from the nearest casino, this property was chosen No. 1 in the 108-hotel Embassy Suites chain in a survey of 40,000 guests. It has received AAA's Four Diamond award each year since it opened in 1991. It has an indoor atrium, indoor pool and spa, an exercise center, wedding chapel and on-site restaurants and nightclub. Cooked-to-order breakfast and a free happy hour is included in the rates, which start at about $95 for midweek packages.

For the Nevada side of Heavenly accommodations, there are scores of condos at Stage-coach Base and Boulder Base areas. At the base of Kingsbury Grade on Highway 50 you'll find the **Lakeside Inn & Casino** (800-624-7980; 702-588-7777), which offers some of the best deals. The rooms are simple and motelish but access to the mountain is excellent.

The California side of South Lake Tahoe has many small motels lining Lake Tahoe Boulevard for miles.

Among the best of the motel bunch are two Best Western properties—**The Timber Cove Lodge** (800-528-1234 or 530-541-6722), located on the beach; and **Station House Inn** (800-822-5953 or 530-542-1101), within walking distance of the casino area, on the California side of the border.

Inn By The Lake (800-877-1466; 530-542-0330) is less than 100 feet from the shore and two miles from the casinos. It has 100 guest rooms (including nine suites with kitchens), free continental breakfast, heated pool, bi-level spa, sauna and free shuttles to the slopes. Midweek and AAA rates available.

Lakeland Village (800-822-5969; 530-544-1685) has a hotel and collection of condo-miniums right on the lake with convenient shuttlebus service to the bases of Heavenly and Kirkwood. The units range in size from studios to a lakefront four-bedroom, three-bath unit. For those who want a room just across from Heavenly's lifts on the California side, the **Tahoe Seasons Resort** has received good reviews from everyone locally (530-541-6700). Another possibility is the **Holiday Inn Express** (800-544-5288; 530-544-5900).

One more, for couples only: The **Fantasy Inn** (800-367-7736, 530-541-4200) has about 60 rooms designed for romance. Tahoe had another Fantasy Inn a while back that was quite tacky, but this one is very tastefully done. Each room has one bed in a choice of several shapes (round, heart-shaped, water or regular mattress, king-size), a private spa for two, an in-room music system with 30 channels, adjustable peach-colored lighting and showers with double shower heads. Sixteen of the rooms are theme or theme deluxe suites, such as Rain Forest (plants and rattan decor), Caesar's Indulgence (a sexy black decor), and Romeo and Juliet (the honeymoon suite we didn't see because it was continually booked during our visit). A wedding chapel is on the premises. Per-night rates start at about $185. Theme suites are in the $245–$295 range. Ask about special ski and/or wedding package rates. If are there with a special someone and you can swing it financially, rent a theme room—you won't forget it.

Kirkwood: If you want big-mountain skiing and a get-away-from-it-all location, stay here. Kirkwood is working on a slopeside village with about 300 condos and many new shops and services. Phase One is now complete: **The Lodge at Kirkwood**, 19 units from one to four bedrooms. It's so new, we haven't seen it, but the plans looked luxurious. Of the other condo complexes the top choice is **Sun Meadows**, which is across from the Solitude and Cornice chairs and about as centrally located as you can get in Kirkwood. The second choice is **The Meadows**, between Timber Creek and the Cornice Chair. Rates range from $110 for a studio to about $325 for a three-bedroom condo. Packages—particularly midweek stays—bring down the cost. Reservations: (209) 258-7000 or (800) 967-7500.

Dining

For the best restaurants in the higher priced category (all area codes are 530 unless noted):

Evan's American Gourmet Café (542-1990) on State Route 89 has become one of the best-liked restaurants on the south shore. The chef prepares California Cuisine with an unusual flair. Expect to pay for his efforts, but they are reported to be well worth it. **Primavera Restaurant** (702-586-2000) in Caesar's Hotel & Casino serves Italian poolside in an atmosphere reminiscent of quaint European cafes with excellent service, quality and wine list. For an excellent meal, great wine list and attentive service—with a beautiful view—head to **Friday's Station** (702-588-6611) at the top of Harrah's casino-hotel.

For good reasonable restaurants, try:

Fresh Ketch (541-5683) for fish, **The Cantina Bar and Grill** (544-1233) for Mexican, **Scusa** (542-0100) for Italian, **Dixon's Restaurant and Brewery** (542-3389) for microbrews and home-style cuisine, or head to one of the casinos' great buffets or fixed-price dinners. **Dory's Oar** (541-6603) was recommended by locals. **Harvey's** (702-588-2411) has a reasonably priced seafood buffet with large portions. **Zackary's Restaurant** (544-5400) in the Embassy Suites hotel has delicious blackened salmon, among other dishes. **Bennigan's** (702-588-5977) is in Bill's Tahoe Casino across from the High Sierra. Others to try are **Beacon** (541-0630), on the lake with blackened prime rib a specialty; and **Nephele's** (544-8130), which serves California cuisine in a cozy setting and has private hot-tub rentals. Next door is an outstanding restaurant called **Café Fiori** (541-2908). It doesn't seat many, so reservations are a must. The food is superb, the wine list extensive and the prices reasonable (under $20 for most entrées).

For great breakfasts head to **The Red Hut** (541-9024), where you can pack into a small room and listen to the talk of the town. A new branch opened on Kingsbury Grade (702-588-7488), handy for skiers heading to the Nevada side of Heavenly. At **Heidi's** (544-8113), get anything from dozens of types of Belgian waffles to chocolate pancakes. The other two locals' spots for morning gossip and breakfast, **Frank's** (544-3434) and **Ernie's** (541-2161), just about face each other on Route 50 south. And just in case you crave a malt "so thick it holds the straw up," head to the **Zephyr Cove Resort**. Try the banana-chocolate shake.

At Heavenly, table linen lunch service is offered at **Top of the Tram** restaurant. Heavenly also has a gourmet picnic service, **Heavenly Mountain Caterers** (542-5153). Place your reservation by 10 a.m. and enjoy a steak or chicken picnic in a secluded outdoor location with great views. It's about $45 per person, two people minimum.

If you're staying at Kirkwood, you'll probably discover the places to eat on your own—not a big selection, but all pretty good, especially the **Cornice Cafe Restaurant and Bar**, for slopeside dining with gourmet cuisine and an extensive wine list (and a sushi happy hour once a week); **Kirkwood Inn**, built in 1864 by Zachary Kirkwood and in operation ever since, featuring hearty meals such as steaks and seafood; and **Caples Lake Resort**, fine dining overlooking scenic Caples Lake, a mile east of Kirkwood on Hwy. 88.

The best on-mountain lunch was at Sierra-at-Tahoe, however. We had a totally delicious Thai chicken wrap (kind of like a burrito), washed down with a Sierra Nevada Pale Ale at **The Sierra Pub** in the day lodge. The pub serves several microbrews and wine by the glass, as well as non-alcoholic beverages. The resort also has a grill-style restaurant at the summit, and fresh-ground coffee and fresh-baked goods in the day lodge.

 ## Après-ski/nightlife

Head to **Chevy's** immediately after skiing or stop in the **California Bar** at Heavenly's Base Lodge. If you want quieter après-ski with a flickering fireplace, stop in at **Christiana Inn** across from the Heavenly ski area. Later in the evening, **Turtle's**, a Tahoe institution which relocated to the Embassy Suites, has good dancing. **Nero's 2000** in Caesars Casino has dancing seven nights a week, and live music on the weekends. They have reggae on Mondays and Alternative Night on Wednesdays. On our most recent visit here, we had a long list of places we were intending to check out. However, we ended up at **McPee's**, a great Irish pub near the state line, on the first night and just kept coming back. Great live music (listenable rather than danceable), a pool table in back, and packed every night. Other spots that had been recommended to us were **Mulligan's, Hoss Hogs, Bumper's, Ellis Island, The Brewery, Dixon's** and **Lake Tahoe Pizza Company**.

And of course, the casinos have musical reviews that are extravaganzas of sight and sound. Some shows run through the season; others are top-name singers and comedians who do one or two shows.

 ## Child care

Child care options are listed with the resorts that offer that service, but we also wanted to let you know about this business: **Baby's Away** (530-544-2229 or 800-446-9030) rents and will deliver baby items (cribs, strollers, toys, etc) to your hotel or condo.

 ## Other activities

South Tahoe has tons to do, but space doesn't permit us to list all the options. Ask your hotel concierge for suggestions. **Ice skating** is at the South Tahoe Ice Center, also called STIC. Figure and hockey skates are available for rent, and the Tahoe Lakers pro hockey team plays on Friday and Saturday nights. Call 530-542-4700.

Weddings aren't your everyday optional ski activity, but if you're thinking of getting married with little fuss, this is one of the best spots to do it. As we said earlier in the chapter, Valentine's Day (Feb. 14) is the most popular winter day to be married, so plan well ahead if this is your intention. More than 20 wedding chapels dot the area, but probably the nicest ones are in the big hotels. These have features such as discreet video cameras that record the happy moment from several angles and lighting that changes with the music. Most have wedding concierges to plan every detail. You also can be married outdoors, either by the lake or on the slopes. California marriage licenses cost about $50; Nevada licenses are a bit less, plus no blood test is required. For more information, contact the Lake Tahoe Visitors Authority at (800) AT-TAHOE (288-2463).

 ## Getting there and getting around

By air: Reno-Tahoe International Airport has more than 100 nonstop flights a day from various parts of the country. The airport is 55 miles from Heavenly, 67 miles from Sierra-at-Tahoe and 70 miles from Kirkwood.

The Lake Tahoe Airport, near South Lake Tahoe and 10 minutes from Heavenly, has limited service from California. Buses and hotel shuttles take skiers to the resorts from both airports.

By train: Amtrak serves Truckee and Reno on the California Zephyr line, running from Oakland to Chicago. Call (800) 872-7245.

By boat: The Hornblower Tahoe Queen, an authentic Mississippi sternwheeler, double-decked and heated, has had some recent ups and downs, but the latest info we have says she'll continue to take South Shore skiers and boarders across Lake Tahoe to the big North Shore resorts (buses take skiers from the dock to the ski areas). The phone number is (530) 541-3364, and the round-trip fare has been about $20.

By bus: Shuttles run from almost every major hotel to each of the three ski resorts. Check for schedules when you arrive. Most of the shuttles that cruise around the North or South Shores are free, but when you need to go from one end of the lake to the other, take the Lake Lapper, which runs from 8 a.m. to 11 p.m. and costs about $5. Call the ski areas or hotels for more information.

Sierra Nevada Gray Lines (800-822-6009 or 702-329-1147) operates a daily ski shuttle between downtown Reno and Alpine Meadows, Northstar-at-Tahoe (except Saturdays) and Squaw Valley USA from mid-December through the end of March. Tahoe Casino Express runs 17 times daily between the Reno airport and South Shore for about $17 each way.

By car: Driving time from Reno is about an hour to any major resort except Kirkwood, which is approximately 90 minutes. San Francisco is about four hours away (that's the way Californians describe driving distances), by Hwy. 50 to South Lake Tahoe or Hwy. 88 to Kirkwood. During storms, the California Highway Patrol doesn't let drivers come up the mountains without chains or a 4-wheel-drive vehicle, so be prepared.

Heavenly is right off Hwy. 50 in South Lake Tahoe, Sierra-at-Tahoe is 12 miles west of the lake on Hwy. 50 and Kirkwood is on Hwy. 88 (follow signs from South Lake Tahoe).

Getting around: Bring a car if you intend to move frequently from south to north; otherwise, a car is optional. We'd say have one if you like to roam far afield at night. If not, you can walk to restaurants and nightspots near your hotel and use the ski shuttles during the day.

Mammoth Mountain
June Mountain

California

Summit elevation: **11,053 feet**
Vertical drop: **3,100 feet**
Base elevation: **7,953 feet**

Address: Mammoth Mountain, Box 24; Mammoth Lakes Visitors Bureau, Box 48; both Mammoth Lakes, CA 93546
☎ **Area code:** 760
Ski area phone: 934-2571
ⓘ **Toll-free snow report/information:** (888) 4-MAMMOTH (462-6668)
Toll-free reservations: (888) GO-MAMMOTH (466-2666)
Fax: 934-7066
E-mail: mammothmtn@aol.com
Internet: http://www.visitmammoth.com(town); http://www.mammoth-mtn.com (ski area)

Dining:★★★
Apres-ski/nightlife:★★★
Other activities:★★★

Expert:★★★★★
Advanced:★★★★★
Intermediate:★★★★★
Beginner:★★★★
Never-ever:★★★

Mammoth Mountain Facts
Number and types of lifts: 29–2 gondolas, 5 high-speed quads, 3 quads, 7 triples, 11 doubles, 1 surface lift
Skiable acreage: 3,500+ acres
Snowmaking: 20 percent
Uphill capacity: 53,000 per hour
Snowboarding: Yes, unlimited
Bed base: 30,000
Nearest lodging: slopeside
Resort child care: Yes, newborns and older
Adult ticket, per day: $42-$49 (98/99 prices)

June Mountain Facts
Summit elevation: 10,135 feet
Vertical drop: 2,590 feet
Base elevation: 7,545 feet
Number and types of lifts: 8–2 quads, 5 doubles, 1 surface lift
Skiable acreage: 500+ acres
Uphill capacity: 10,000 per hour
Bed base: 2,000 local

When you stand at the base lodge and scan the mountain you can't even see a quarter of the ski terrain. The encircling ridge, all above treeline, promises dramatic skiing, but what you can't see is even better. This is what remains of a massive, 700,000-year-old volcano at the edge of two wilderness areas. Even now with most of the cone missing, it gives access to half a dozen wide bowls with the largest, once the interior of the cone, a whopping 13,000 feet across. Lower peaks such as Lincoln Mountain, Gold Hill and Hemlock Ridge, all with groomed swaths and moguled canyons, stretch six-and-a-half miles in width. Mammoth is one of the nation's largest ski areas in size, and is at times the nation's busiest, with more than 14,000 skiers swooping over its slopes on an average weekend.

Its season runs from early November through June—legitimately. Mammoth often relies on its 300 acres of snowmaking to be open by Thanksgiving, but not always. During the 1994/95 season, Mammoth ran its lifts 305 days—from Oct. 8 through Aug. 13—taking five days off in July to dig out a mountain bike trail for an annual race. Skiing here on the Fourth of July happens enough years to be a well-loved tradition among the diehards who haven't had enough. And yet, outside of California, it is not well known.

Here, you come to ski—at the top of the mountain road there's not much to distract you. There is a labyrinthine base lodge with ski school, lift ticket windows, rental shops and hundreds of lockers for locals and visitors. Across the parking lot is the Yodler chalet, brought piece by piece from the Alps and rebuilt to house a restaurant and bar. Slopeside is the Mammoth Mountain Inn.

At the bottom of the mountain road lies the small but spread-out town of Mammoth Lakes. Here is just about all you need for a ski vacation short of luxury hotels. Don't expect a cozy, picturesque atmosphere, though. As the town grew to support the ski area's success, newcomers haphazardly transplanted Southern California sprawl and mini-malls to the mountains. Most visitors come by car from Southern California, but the few who don't will feel the need for wheels—not much is within easy walking distance. However, there is a free town bus that runs day and night.

New for 98/99: At press time in June, construction crews were waiting for the 14-foot snow depth to melt enough to start work on $21 million of capital improvements, mostly new lifts. Plans are to replace Mammoth's upper gondola with a new high-speed, eight-passenger gondola; replace Chair 4 with an express quad; add a new express quad between Stump Alley and Chair 10 that will unload at the saddle between Lincoln Mountain and the top of Chair 5; build a new restaurant at the base of the Stump Alley Express chair and remodel The Canyon Lodge.

Coming attractions: Mammoth is now owned in part by Intrawest, a ski and golf resort company based in Vancouver. Intrawest plans to build a large, slopeside pedestrian village with 1,000 residential units and 140,000 square feet of retail stores over the next 10 years. The first part of this extensive plan is the Juniper Springs Lodge, consisting of 174 resort condominiums, with architecture inspired by the timber-and-rock construction of The Ahwahnee Lodge in Yosemite.

If size intimidates you, Mammoth's little sister June Mountain, a half-hour drive from Mammoth Lakes, will appeal to you. Its Old-World village atmosphere in a sheltered canyon is on a more human scale. That is not to say it's a puny resort: it has eight chair lifts and a 2,590-foot vertical rise (as opposed to 3,100 feet at Mammoth).

 ## Mountain layout

First-time visitors cannot help but smile at the size of the mountain. Forget knowing the names of peaks at this resort— almost everything goes by number. The mountain is crisscrossed with a network of chair lifts numbered in the order they were built. Chair 22, for example, is not anywhere near Chair 23. It makes perfect sense to visitors who grew up with the mountain, but it's confusing to the first-time visitor who hears regulars planning their day football-quarter-back style, "Take one to three, then back side to 23, down the ridge to 14, then to 13 and lateral to 19."

With massive weekend crowds the lines at the base lifts can be long, but since the area is so expansive you can easily avoid them if you avoid the main base area. (Also, the lines move very fast, thanks to express lifts in key spots.) From left to right on the trail map, try Chairs 9, 18, 25, 22, 21, 10, 5, 12, 13 and 14.

The chair most likely to be crowded on weekends is Broadway Express (Chair 1), an express lift that takes off from the Main Lodge. It is especially popular because experts can either plunge down Gravy Chute or weave through The Wall, a panel of bubbly moguls, while their intermediate friends can coast down wide, smooth Broadway and meet them at the bottom. You can board lifts at four different base areas—from left to right, Chair 15, Canyon Lodge, Stump Alley Express (Chair 2) and the Main Lodge. Never-evers should go to Canyon Lodge or Main Lodge, beginners also can start at Chair 15.

◆◆ **Expert:** Expert yaa-hoo skiers and snowboarders will strike out for the ridge, reachable by the gondola or a series of chairs. From the ridge, any chute or path will open into a wide bowl. Mammoth's signature run, a snarling lip of snow called The Cornice, looms large in every expert's memory bank. Other runs dropping from the ridge are considered steeper and more treacherous. Reached from the gondola, Hangman's—Mammoth's toughest—is an hour-glass-shaped chute hanging from the summit and bordered by wicked rocks. At its narrow part there's space for only one turn—a perfect one. Other expert shots can be found off Chair 22, and on powder days you can often find untracked or less-tracked snow on the far east Dragon's Back off Chair 9, or the far west Hemlock Ridge above Chair 14.

◆ **Advanced:** One of the most popular advanced areas is the group of bowls available from Face Lift Express (Chair 3). They're great warm-up runs for experts, but plan to get here early on weekends. By 9:30 or 10 a.m., the line can be outrageous (that's our term; one of our favorite Mammoth employees describes it as "healthy"), although it diminishes at lunch time. Midweek, no problem. This express quad was new mid-season last year, and we weren't able to ride it. We suspect it will help reduce the line, but cause a bottleneck on the initial narrow descent down the back side on busy days.

A slightly less busy alternative is triple-Chair 5, the next chair to the left on the trail map, or Chair 14, to the far right on the map. At busy times, skiers in the know head for Chair 19, which gives them half a dozen runs hidden in a glen that keep their grooming late into the day. Also, Chairs 22 and 25, which provide access to Lincoln Mountain and its intermediate runs and advanced chutes, rarely have lines.

When you feel like attacking the ridge, head to Dave's Run. Off the gondola, traverse the ridge to trail-map left, then drop down when the pitch isn't sheer vertical. Dave's is still pretty steep, but of the single-black options off the ridge, it's usually the least crowded. If you have any doubts, ride the gondola back down to Mid-Chalet.

■ **Intermediate:** The mid-to-lower mountain lets the intermediate traverse vast expanses and crisscross runs. Hidden canyons like Lower Dry Creek are full of swoops and surprises, and require tighter turns. For long cruising, head to Chairs 15 and 24. Other intermediate playgrounds are served by the tree-lined runs from Chairs 8, 4, 16, 20, 21, and 10 between the Canyon Lodge and the Stump Alley Express (Chair 2) Outpost. At the other edge of the area is Chair 12 and the drop over to Chairs 13 and 14.

●● **Beginner:** If you aren't a first-timer, but still practicing turns, the runs near Canyon Lodge are best. Trails such as Hansel and Gretel weave gently through evergreens. There are sheltered slopes for learning, tucked away from the paths of speed demons shooting down from the top (look out for this breed on Stump Alley, a crowded raceway down to Chair 2). When you're ready for the next step, Christmas Tree, a long run under Chair 15, is pretty gentle. This part of the mountain gets soupy in the afternoon on warm days, however.

● **Never-ever:** The never-ever slopes are off Chairs 11 and 27 at the Main Lodge and Chair 7 from the Canyon Lodge, separated from the hot shots.

June Mountain: Beginners and intermediates will find June Mountain challenging, though it has none of the high broad bowls that make Mammoth Mountain famous. The steepest terrain at June, The Face, is as steep as anything at Mammoth. Because it is on the lower mountain, it unfortunately doesn't keep the snow as long as the upper runs—intermediate cruisers and expert chutes like Dave's Drop and Pro Bowl. Since June is more sheltered than Mammoth and none of its slopes is above the tree line, June tends to hold powder longer than Mammoth's more exposed bowls and the snow doesn't crust up so quickly. There's a great view of June Lake from the upper runs.

Mountain rating

No matter what level you're at, you won't be shortchanged. If you are visiting for the first time, take a trail map. (Seriously. Our executive editor has skied here for two decades, but she still carries a trail map—and occasionally needs to use it.) If you're with a group, decide where to meet if you get separated. We usually pick a centrally located short chair, such as Chair 20, rather than Mid-Chalet or the Main Lodge, which are usually loaded with bodies looking for other bodies. We just stay on the runs under that chair and watch from the lift until we all hook up. This is a huge mountain, and because of the crazy lift numbering system, it's hard for first-time visitors to figure out how to get back to the starting point without the map.

June doesn't have quite Mammoth's range of terrain, but most skiers and boarders will enjoy it. The pace at June is slower and the crowds considerably fewer and sometimes non-existent (locals come here on weekends and holidays).

Cross-country

Twenty to 25 miles of groomed trails, actually summer roads, wind around four of the dozen or more high Alpine lakes for which the town of Mammoth Lakes is named. **Tamarack Lodge,** (934-2442; 800-237-6879) a 50-year-old summer hunting and fishing lodge, maintains these trails and charges $15 for access ($10 for those ages 11–17, free younger than that). The Lakes Basin includes many trail heads into the backcountry, where no fee is charged. Rentals and lessons are available. On weekends it's advisable to reserve.

Snowboarding

Both Mammoth and June host national competitions, and each has a halfpipe and a snowboard park featuring steep jumps, a quarter pipe, table jumps, and other treats. Mammoth also has a boardercross course set up on Forest Trail. Snowboarding lessons and rentals are available.

Lessons (97/98 prices)

Programs are the same at Mammoth or June unless otherwise noted. At Mammoth, lessons are available at both the Main Lodge and the Canyon Lodge. Reservations are not necessary, but questions can be answered at 934-0685 for Main Lodge, 934-0787 for The Canyon Lodge. For June Mountain Ski School call 648-7733.

Group lessons: All day for six to eight is $46 per person, half day $32. A transferable book of five all-day group lessons is $230.

Never-ever package: Rentals, lift ticket and four hours of lessons are $60 per day for skiers or snowboarders.

Private lessons: For adults or children, $75 for one hour, $10 for each additional person. Discounts are offered at 9-10 a.m. and 12:30-1:30 p.m.

Special programs: There are many, including three-day camps for seniors ($150), women and advanced skiers ($210 for either). Two-day clinics cover mogul improvement and extreme skiing, either for $170. Call the ski school for dates.

Racing: Mammoth has a well-established racing heritage. It has hosted World Cup races, and several U.S. Ski Team coaches and executives call this resort home. Self-timed courses at Mammoth or June cost $1 per run.

Children's lessons: The Woollywood Ski School teaches kids 4–12. Full-day lessons for skiing or snowboarding (minimum age for the latter is 7), including a supervised lunch, are $70 per child. Half-day sessions are $32, full day without lunch $46.

Child care (98/99 prices)

Ages: Newborn to 12 years.

Costs: Care for newborn to 2-year-old children is $56 per day, $40 for a half-day. Care for kids 2–12 years is $49 for a full day and $35 for a half day. Additional children in a family get a $5 reduction for full day; $3 for half day. Fees include snacks and lunch, except for infants.

Reservations: Strongly advised, six to eight weeks ahead. Day care is located at both The Small World Day Care Center at Mammoth Mountain Inn (934-0646), just across the street from the Main Lodge, and the child care center at June Mountain (648-7609).

Day care can be combined with ski school for ages 4–12 (ages 7–12 for snowboarding). They get supervised activities from 8 a.m. to 5 p.m., including a lesson from 10 a.m. until noon. Rate is $78, including lunch. Mammoth has helmet rentals for the kids ($5), and pager rentals for the adults ($2).

Lift tickets (98/99 prices unless noted)

	Adult	Child (7-12)
One day	$49	$25
Three days	$133 ($44+/day)	$68 ($22+/day)
Five days	$214 ($42+/day)	$109 ($21+/day)

Who skis free: Children aged 6 and younger ski free, as do never-evers taking a ski school lesson.

Who skis at a discount: Ages 65 and older ski for child prices. Ages 13–18 are charged $37 for the day, $100 for three days; $161 for five days. A beginner lift ticket costs $20 and is valid on Chairs 7, 11 and 27.

Lift tickets may be used at either Mammoth or June; however, if you just ski June Mountain it's $37 for adults, $27 for ages 13–18, $20 for kids (97/98 prices).

Ticket offices are at the Main Lodge, the Canyon Lodge and Chair 15 areas, as well as June Mountain. Additional satellite offices at Chairs 4, 10 and 2 (Chair 2 is now called Stump Alley Express) are open weekends and holidays.

Note: The multiday rates listed here are non-holiday. During holidays, regular per-day rates apply, though you still can buy a multiday ticket. Anyone who skis Mammoth more than six days in a season should buy a Mammoth Club Card. It costs $60 for adults, but allows you to buy lift tickets for $37. (Club Cards are available also for teens, children and seniors.)

Accommodations (97/98 prices)

One of the nicest places to stay, **Mammoth Mountain Inn** (800-228-4947; 934-2581), is also the most convenient—a very short walk to the lifts. Lodging is deluxe to moderate, including hotel units with room service, motel and condominium units. Weekend 97/98 rates (midweek is cheaper) are $115 for rooms to $445 for a condo that sleeps eleven.

We list just a few of the places to stay. As a starting point, call **Mammoth Lakes Visitors Bureau** (800-466-2666), or for condos only, call **Mammoth Reservation Bureau** (800-527-6273). Generally, condos start at about $100 per night, while hotel accommodations—we use the term loosely, as Mammoth currently has more motels than true hotels—can be found for less than $70 per night. Sunday through Thursday stays are quite a bit cheaper than Friday and Saturday.

Mammoth Lakes has been called Condo City of the Sierras. Just beyond the central part of town, **Snowcreek** (934-3333; 800-544-6007) is huge and wooded with an athletic club that includes racquetball and basketball. It's actually a neighborhood. Units are spacious one-, two- and three-bedroom loft style, $110–$400.

Closer to the slopes, in fact next to The Canyon Lodge, two other large condominium complexes have a range of units. Try **Sierra Megeve** (934-3723; 800-227-7669), **Mountainback** (934-4549; 800-468-6225) **1849 Condominiums** (934-7525) and **Aspen Creek** (934-3933; 800-227-7669), located next to Chairs 15 and 24.

In the middle of town, only a walk to restaurants and a shuttle to the lifts, you'll find **Sierra Nevada Rodeway Inn** (800-824-5132, 934-2515) has hotel rooms and chalet units. **The Snowgoose Inn** (800-874-7368; 934-2660) is one of five bed-and-breakfast inns in town. Decorated with antiques, with breakfast served communally in a friendly atmosphere, its approximate rates are $80–$170.

The least expensive private rooms are at **Motel 6** (934-6660). One place offers dorm rooms—**Ullr Lodge** (934-2454) has rooms with private baths, rooms that share baths and some dorm bunks for about $16–$58 per night. **Alpenhof Lodge** (934-6330) rooms go for $75–$135. **Mammoth Thriftlodge** (800-525-9055; 934-2416; $65–$99) is located in North Village across from the **Mammoth Travelodge** (800-578-7878; 934-8576; rates $95–$158).

June Mountain: June has two large condominium complexes, with prices starting around $100 midweek and $135 weekends. **Interlaken** has studios to three-bedroom units. **Edgewater** has only one size unit, suitable for six to nine people. All other lodgings at June are small and quaint, even funky. **The Haven** has studios for about $70. Call **June Lake Properties Reservation** at (800) 648-5863 (648-JUNE) or **Century 21 Rainbow Ridge** at (800) 462-5589 for condominium reservations.

Also try **Fern Creek Lodge** (800-621-9146), **Whispering Pines** (800-648-7762), or **Boulder Lodge** (970-648-7533), all of which have rooms and cabins in the $50 to $145 range.

 **Dining**

Mammoth Lakes has nearly 60 dining options, from gourmet French cuisine to delicatessen sandwiches and quick take-out. A relatively new entry into the fine dining category is **Aspen Grill** (934-2537). This restaurant, formerly known as The Rafters, has excellent meats and fish, such as mahogany-smoked baby back ribs, a good wine list and a comfortable bar separate from the dining room. Other top choices are **Skadi's** (934-3902), with a romantic atmosphere, or **O'Kelly and Dunns Restaurant** (934-9316), which leans toward American country with dried flowers, grasses and quilts gracing the walls.

For the most romantic (and expensive) dining, head out to **Lakefront Restaurant at Tamarack Lodge** (934-3534) where the menu is basic but the presentation excellent. The atmosphere is Old World in a small dining room decorated with photos of movie stars who used to hang out here. After dinner wander into the lodge and have after-dinner drinks in front of the fireplace. On a night with a full moon, make plans to head out to **The Restaurant at Convict Lake** (934-3803), four miles south of Mammoth Lakes on Route 395. With the moon reflecting on the lake, there is no prettier setting for dining in front of a flickering fire. **Cervino's** (934-4734) serves Northern Italian cuisine and received a 1996 Wine Spectator Award of Excellence (as did The Restaurant at Convict Lake).

Nevados (934-4466) receives good recommendations, but expect to pay handsomely for continental cuisine with unusual dishes. For the best steaks and prime rib head to **Whiskey Creek** (934-2555), or try **The Mogul Restaurant** (934-3039) and the **Chart House** (934-4526) which also serves fish dinners.

Families (or anyone with limited funds) will want to stop in at **Berger's** (934-6622) for big, big portions. The tuna salad is massive and you can have not only burgers but also chicken, salad or Canadian stew. Another family spot is **Angel's** (934-7427) with great ribs, beans and barbecue.

The **Old Mammoth Pasta House** (934-8088) dishes out huge plates of fresh pasta and friendly service. Locals consider **Nik-N-Willie's Pizza** (934-2012) the best in town. Pizzas also appear at **Giovanni's** (934-7563) or **Perry's Italian Cafe** (934-6521). The best Mexican food is at **Roberto's** (934-3667) with homemade tortillas and authentic big servings. Other Mexican-food choices are **La Sierra's** (934-8083), **Gringo's** (934-8595), known for its "almost world famous Rotisserie Chicken," or **Gomez's** (924-2693).

Grumpy's (934-8587) holds the distinction of the town's best fried chicken and big steaks, also the best cole slaw, all presented in a big-screen TV, No Smoking, sports-bar atmosphere.

Shogun (934-3970) has Japanese cuisine and a sushi bar. Try **Matsu** (934-8277) for inexpensive Chinese-American. **Austria Hof** (934-2764) and **Alpenrose** (934-3077) serve German and Austrian specialties.

Ocean Harvest (934-8539) is the prime seafood restaurant, offering fresh fish caught from the owner's boat.

The best breakfast in town is served at **The Stove** (934-2821) with biscuits 3 or 4 inches high, though it could be challenged by **The Breakfast Club** (934-6944) at the intersection of Old Mammoth Road and Highway 203. We visit Mammoth every year, midweek, and for two years running, we couldn't get a parking space here (next year, a 5:30 a.m. wake-up call!). Coffee lovers, your choices are **Looney Bean** (934-1345) on Main Street next to the Chevron station or **World Cup Coffee** (924-3629) on Old Mammoth Road across from the movie theater. Both have in-house bakers for rolls and muffins. For very good baked goodies and good gourmet coffee, try **Paul Schat's Bakery and Cafe** (934-6055) on Main Street, which serves breakfast on weekends, fresh-baked goodies every day.

For dining on the mountain for lunch or dinner the best bet by far is the **Mountainside Grill** (934-0601) in the Mammoth Mountain Inn. Surprisingly, the prices are not much more than the base-lodge cafeteria, which is crowded and serves so-so food. Or head over to the more crowded **Yodler** (934-0636).

In June Lake, try the **Fern Creek Grill** (648-7897) for breakfast, burgers, steaks and chicken. The **Sierra Inn Restaurant** (648-7774) has a slightly more upscale menu, but the best dining is in Mammoth Lakes.

 ## Après-ski/nightlife

Lively après-ski gets under way across the parking lot from the Main Lodge at the **Yodler** or in the **Thunder Mountain Bar** in the Main Lodge, decorated with photos of early Mammoth days. At the Canyon Lodge base area, try **Grizzly's**, Mammoth Mountain's newest hot spot. **Slocum's** in town is the après-ski hangout for ski patrol and instructors. At **Austria Hof**, there's usually live entertainment after the lifts close. Entertainment is also at the **Ocean Club** and Mammoth Mountain Inn's **Dry Creek Bar**.

Mammoth's longtime meet market (you may meet someone whose parents used to party hardy here in their younger days) is **Whiskey Creek,** which serves six microbrews. Another equally packed hangout is **The Stonehouse Brewery** on Old Mammoth Road. The **Aspen Grill** has an older clientele and a quieter atmosphere.

There's plenty of nighttime hoopla at **Grumpy's**. Featured are five giant-screen TVs, pool, foosball, inexpensive chili and burgers. Visiting Brits like this place, and also hang out at the **Clock Tower Cellar** at the Alpenhof Lodge.

Shogun has karaoke sing-along on Tuesday and Saturday nights with a sushi bar, tempura, sukiyaki and teriyaki, which you can wash down with sake and imported beer.

 ## Other activities

Shopping: Mammoth's shopping is oriented as much for the local population as for tourists. You won't find many trendy boutiques here, though there is a factory outlet center on Main Street, and many small shopping malls scattered throughout town. A favorite store with an eclectic inventory of jewelry, soothing CDs, nature books and mountain survival supplies is The Great Outdoors on Old Mammoth Road.

Snowmobiles can be rented from DJs Snowmobile Adventures (935-4480); Center Street Snowmobile (934-6888); or Mammoth Adventures (934-9645). The area has about 300 miles of snowmobile trails, some signed and groomed, others not. **Bobsledding or tubing** down a designated track is available through Sledz (934-7533). **Dogsled rides** are offered by Dog Sled Adventures (934-6270).

Hot-air balloon trips with High Sierra Ballooning Company (934-7188) take off from Mammoth Meadow. **Snowcreek Athletic Club** (934-8511) has a variety of indoor and outdoor facilities. **The Monkey Bar** (924-1082) offers an indoor climbing wall and **Golf 'n' Stuff** (924-1082) has indoor miniature golf and an arcade for kids of all ages.

Mammoth Lakes also has two **movie theaters** (one with two screens), Minaret Cinemas and Plaza Theater (both at 934-3131). The Mammoth Times, a free weekly newspaper, is a good source for special events listings.

Getting there and getting around

By air: Mountain Air Express (800-788-4247) serves Mammoth from Long Beach, Fresno and San Jose airports, and select charter companies fly regularly from the Los Angeles area. The nearest major airport is Reno. It's best to rent a car for the drive south, but ground transportation is usually available. Mammoth's air service information changes frequently, so for the latest news, call the Mammoth Lakes Visitors Bureau, (888) 466-2666 or consult the MLVB website (www.visitmammoth.com).

By car: Mammoth is 325 miles north of Los Angeles on Hwy. 395 and 165 miles south of Reno on the same road. June Mountain is also off Hwy. 395, 20 miles north of Mammoth Lakes.

Getting around: The resort operates a free shuttle that runs throughout the town and to Mammoth's Main Lodge (four miles out) and to the Canyon Lodge and Chair 15. A nightly shuttle makes loops around town until midnight during the week, 1 a.m. on Friday and Saturday nights, or call Mammoth Shuttle (934-3030) or Sierra Express (924-TAXI; 924-8294). Most visitors have a car.

Colorado

⌁ Steamboat

⌁ Winter Park

Vail/Beaver Creek ⌁   ○ Denver

Aspen/Snowmass ⌁   ⌁ Summit County

⌁ Crested Butte

⌁ Telluride

⌁ Purgatory

Telephone area code: 970

Aspen Area

Colorado

Aspen Mountain
Buttermilk Mountain
Aspen Highlands

Address: Aspen Skiing Company,
P.O. Box 1248, Aspen, CO 81612
Area code: 970
✆ **Ski area phone:** 925-1220
or (800) 525-6200
Snow report: 925-1221 or 888-ASPEN-SNO (277-3676)
ⓘ **Toll-free reservations:** (800) 262-7736
Fax: 925-9008
E-mail: acrone@rof.net (reservations)
or aspenint@rof.net (ski info)
Internet: http://www.skiaspen.com

Bed Base: 9,000
Nearest lodging: slopeside, hotels, condos
Resort child care: See Child Care section
Snowboarding: Yes, but not at Aspen Mountain
Adult ticket, per day: $39-$59 (97/98 prices)

Dining:★★★★★
Apres-ski/nightlife:★★★★★
Other activities:★★★★

Ask a crowd of non-skiing Americans to name a ski resort, and you can bet a bundle that Aspen will be one of those they name, though they'll probably know more about the rich and famous who frequent the resort than about its equally notable skiing. With four mountains within a 12-mile radius (one of those, Snowmass, is detailed in its own chapter), offering 40 lifts, 270 trails and more than 4,000 skiable acres, a trip to Aspen just for the skiing would be well worth it. But Aspen has much more.

Aspen fits a niche unique among North American ski resorts. Sure, other resorts attract wealth, but Aspen's wealth glitters and sparkles with a "look-this-way" flamboyance. Sophisticated New York and Hollywood fashions shimmer against turn-of-the-century brick façades. Lear jets wait for their owners on the airport tarmac. The newest ski outfits are beyond being *de rigueur;* they're commonplace. And paparazzi aim their lenses at every celebrity in town so that supermarket tabloids can keep their pages filled.

Don't head to Aspen purely to observe celebrities, however. You may not find any. They are most common during the Christmas-New Years holidays and March's sunshine days, but sometimes hard to spot when in ski clothes. If you want to mix with the upscale crowd, stay close to the Aspen Mountain gondola base, where the fanciest hotels and shops are clustered. You'll find a mixed crowd in the heart of the pedestrian mall, which combines expensive and reasonably priced restaurants and bars. Beyond downtown, the outward signs of wealth disappear, and residents and tourists who reside here probably wouldn't look twice if Goldie Hawn were seated at the next table.

If all your information about Aspen comes from *People* magazine, you probably think you can't afford to ski there. True, the single-day lift ticket is one of the priciest in America, but it's a little-known fact that lodging and restaurants have a huge price range, starting out with inexpensive dorm accommodations and topping out at stratospheric luxury suites.

At heart, Aspen is a Victorian mountain town, albeit one of the larger ones. There's a side to Aspen where perfectly painted lips, careful coiffure and cosmopolitan style are not the rule. Aspen has women and men who exude a natural freshness, whose smiles are spontaneous rather than reserved for photo sessions. Aspen has restaurants where one can eat without taking out a loan and bars that have never seen a fur coat. Children play tag, parents attend PTA meetings and folks go out for a beer after work.

Aspen also draws skiers and snowboarders who could care less about the off-mountain scene. They come for the slopes, which have received rave reviews for decades. The region has four separate ski areas, all operated by Aspen Skiing Company. Aspen Mountain, or Ajax as it's often called, challenges intermediate and advanced skiers (no snowboarders allowed on the lift-served terrain). Buttermilk is the perfect beginner and cruising mountain. Aspen Highlands is the most varied, with skiing for experts and beginners, cruisers and bumpers. Snowmass, larger than the other three combined, is several miles farther down the road. Though it is one of the four Aspen Skiing Company areas and included in that lift ticket, it also has its own lodging, restaurants and shops, and is covered in the next chapter.

Take your choice: If you want glamour and you don't mind paying for it, you can find it here. If you don't, there are ways to avoid it.

New for 98/99: Aspen Skiing Company will begin new development at the Aspen Highlands base area and install a new double chair from the base to the top of Golden Horn, which replaces a chair-and-poma-combination ride to get to the same spot. They are also adding more snowmaking to improve coverage of Ruthie's. World Cup ski races also return November 27–28 1998 with a men's Super G and Slalom

Mountain layout

Aspen's four mountains are close to each other, but not interconnected (a free shuttle runs from base to base). This chapter covers Aspen Mountain, Aspen Highlands and Buttermilk. Snowmass is described separately.

Free, daily mountain tours at 10 a.m. and 1:30 p.m. orient guests. Aspen-area residents volunteer to assist guests at on-mountain Concierge Centers. They wear dark blue ski suits with silver "Ambassador" lettering on the back. They also conduct the tours, which last 90 minutes.

Here's a little known freebie: grab a free postcard at the ticket offices or Concierge Centers to let the folks back home know how much fun you're having. Give it back to the staff and ASC will pay the postage.

◆◆ **Expert: Aspen Highlands** is the best-balanced mountain of the three with slopes for every level, and it's the locals' favorite. No need for fur-trimmed outfits here; you can be comfortable if you appear for lunch at mid-mountain in jeans and gaiters. The vertical rise is one of the highest in Colorado. Aspen Highlands has two high-speed quads that dramatically cut the time needed to reach the summit.

From the top of Loge Peak, the run back to the base is an uneven series of steeps, catwalks and gentle runouts. This mountain has some fantastic long cruises. The ridge, knifing directly to the summit, has thrilling pitches down both sides.

Aspen Mountain Facts
Summit elevation: 11,212 feet
Base elevation: 7,945 feet
Vertical drop: 3,267 feet
Number of lifts: 8–1 gondola, 1 high-speed quad, 1 high-speed double, 2 quads, 3 doubles
Snowmaking: 33 percent **Skiable acreage:** 675 acres
Uphill capacity: 10,775 per hour **Snowboarding:** Not allowed
Expert:★★★★ **Advanced:**★★★★★
Intermediate:★★★★ **Beginner:**★ **Never-ever:**★

Buttermilk Mountain Facts
Summit elevation: 9,900 feet
Vertical drop: 2,030 feet
Base elevation: 7,870 feet
Number of lifts: 7–1 high-speed quad, 5 doubles, 1 surface lift
Snowmaking: 27 percent **Skiable acreage:** 410 acres
Uphill capacity: 7,500 per hour **Snowboarding:** Unlimited
Expert:★ **Advanced:**★★ **Intermediate:**★★★★
Beginner:★★★★★ **Never-ever:**★★★★★

Aspen Highlands Facts
Summit elevation: 11,675 feet
Vertical drop: 3,635 feet
Base elevation: 8,040 feet
Number of lifts: 6–2 high-speed quads, 4 doubles
Snowmaking: 20 percent **Skiable acreage:** 651 acres
Uphill capacity: 9,145 per hour Snowboarding: **Unlimited**
Expert:★★★★ **Advanced:**★★★★★ **Intermediate:**★★★★
Beginner:★★★ **Never-ever:**★★

Other than a few short blacks, such as Suzy Q and Limelight, the terrain makes a pronounced jump from intermediate to double-diamond expert. Experts should head for the steeps at the top of Loge Peak in the Steeplechase (sunny in the morning) and Olympic Bowl (sunny in the afternoon) areas. These are very steep with no bail-out areas, so be sure you want to be here. Both areas have long cat trails leading back to the lifts. Last season, new terrain was opened on the periphery of the infamous Highlands Bowl called Y-Zones.

Also check out the lower mountain. The new double chair will take you from the base to the top of Bob's Glades or Upper Stein, or you can drop into double-black territory at several points along blue-square Golden Horn. Powder Bowl, a black run at the top of Thunderbowl lift, has great double-black bumps. Ski the Golden Horn/Thunderbowl area early—at day's end, it's a popular route home.

The basic guideline for **Aspen Mountain** is that the intermediate terrain is on the top knob around the summit and in the gullies between the ridges. The expert stuff drops from the ridges into the gullies. Of the blacks, take your pick and be sure you're up to it. These runs are very black. Take a trail map as you ride the lifts, and you'll be able to pick out what you'd like to ski. Guided "Powder Tours" are offered on the back side of Aspen Mountain, and these are open to snowboarders, too. Call (800) 525-6200 for more information

◆ **Advanced:** If you consider yourself a very confident advanced skier, read the expert section. If you feel you have recently reached advanced status, read the intermediate section. In our experience, there's a big jump from intermediate to expert terrain at Aspen Highlands and Aspen Mountain. Buttermilk's marked advanced terrain is really more advanced intermediate. Or, head to Snowmass. Lots of true advanced stuff there.

■ **Intermediate:** If you're hovering between intermediate and advanced status and would like to say you skied a black run on **Aspen Mountain,** Upper Little Percy or Red's Run are among the blacks that are groomed occasionally. Stop at the ticket office or the on-mountain Concierge Center at the summit and pick up a grooming report (you can do this at all the mountains, by the way).

Unsure if you can handle the terrain? If you can ski blues at other areas, do this: Ride the gondola to the top and ski the gentlest terrain, at the summit—runs such as Dipsy Doodle, Pussyfoot and Silver Bell. Keep riding the Ajax Express (formerly Chairs 3) and Gentlemen's Ridge (formerly Chair 7). If any of those blue runs presents a challenge, ride back down in the gondola (the last one down is at 3:45 p.m.). The alternative to riding down is Copper Bowl or Spar Gulch, two gullies that can get packed as skiers funnel into them toward the base. Both runs join at Kleenex Corner, a sharp and narrow turn, then dump into Little Nell, a fairly steep blue just above the gondola base. It's known as "Little Hell," because at day's end, it's in the shade, crowded, often a little slick and/or moguled, and smack in view of the entire world.

The blue cruisers in sight of Bonnie's outdoor deck, led by North American, are a delight. If you're a confident intermediate, don't pass up skiing at Ajax. The experts shouldn't have all the fun.

At **Buttermilk,** intermediates with confident turns will have fun on Jacob's Ladder and Bear, which drop from the Cliff House to the main area, but the real playground is under the Tiehack chair. Much of this area is colored black on the trail map, but don't get too excited—it's only black on the map. You'll discover good solid intermediate trails that make inspiring cruisers. In one day you can ride the Upper Tiehack chair a dozen times, taking a different cruise on each run. Buckskin, Ptarmigan, Sterner, the Glades, Tiehack Parkway and Racer's Edge (where the Mahre brothers trained) all offer 1,500 feet of dipping and sweeping curves. Javelin is the best of the lot—a couple of tree islands to keep you awake and a lot of good dips and rolls. Smile in the evening when you overhear others scoffing about what a waste Buttermilk is for real skiers, and savor memories of 15,000 feet of vertical in just one afternoon.

At **Aspen Highlands**, intermediates will want to take these lifts: Cloud Nine, Olympic and Loge Peak. (The easiest of the intermediates are off Cloud Nine.) Don't miss Golden Horn and Thunderbowl on the lower mountain, very wide cruisers.

●● **Beginner: Aspen Mountain** may be the only ski mountain in America that has no designated green-circle runs. Don't try it if you're at this level.

Buttermilk Mountain is all that Aspen Mountain isn't. Beginners can experience top-to-bottom runs as soon as they master snowplows or halting stem christies. The beginner terrain concentrates under the Buttermilk West chair. Tom's Thumb, Red's Rover, Larkspur, Westward Ho and Blue Grouse will keep beginners improving. The Homestead Road turns back to the Savio chair and lazily winds its way to the Main Buttermilk area.

At **Aspen Highlands,** beginners are best served by the trails from the Exhibition II chair—Prospector, Nugget, Exhibition, Red Onion and Apple Strudel.

● **Never-ever:** Take your first few lessons at **Buttermilk.** Of Aspen's four mountains, this is by far the best for a first day on skis or a snowboard.

Mountain rating

Everyone gets something at Aspen. Beginners will have the most fun at Buttermilk. Intermediates probably will have a more varied day at Aspen Highlands than on Aspen Mountain, but the longest runs sweep down Ajax, and it's hard to beat the exhilarating cruising on Buttermilk. Experts have a tossup between Aspen Highlands and Aspen Mountain.

Snowboarding

Unlimited snowboarding is permitted at Aspen Highlands, Buttermilk Mountain and Snowmass (see the Snowmass chapter for specifics on that mountain). Boarding is not allowed on the front side of Aspen Mountain (the side shown on the trail map); however, boarders are welcome on the Powder Tours offered by the Aspen Skiing Company on the back side of Aspen Mountain. Call ASC at (800) 525-6200 for more information.

Buttermilk and Aspen Highlands have terrain parks and Buttermilk has a halfpipe, but much of Aspen Highlands also is a natural terrain park. Pick up the "Ride Guide," a snowboarder's version of the trail map. Lessons and rentals are available at Aspen Highlands, Buttermilk Mountain and Snowmass.

Cross-country (97/98 prices)

Aspen/Snowmass has the most extensive free Nordic trail system in America, more than 80 km. of groomed trails called "Aspen's fifth mountain." The **Aspen Nordic Council's** free system is accessible from Aspen or Snowmass and includes easy golf-course skiing as well as more difficult trails rising up to Snowmass.

In addition to the free trails provided by Aspen's Nordic Council, **Ashcroft Ski Touring Unlimited** (925-1971) has 30 km. of groomed and set trails, and backcountry skiers can use summer hiking trails. Trail fees are $15 per day, and lessons and rentals are available.

Hut systems connect Aspen with Vail on the Tenth Mountain Trail and with Crested Butte over the Pearl Pass. Guides are available and recommended. Call **Tenth Mountain Trail Association** for more information, 925-5775.

Other cross-country centers are the **Aspen Cross Country Center,** 925-2145; **Ute Mountaineer,** 925-2849; **Braun Hut System** (information on trails to Crested Butte), 925-6618; and **Snowmass Club Cross Country Center,** 923-3148.

Snowshoeing is quite popular in town, so ask about those programs at any of the cross country centers mentioned here. Aspen Skiing Company has tours for $35 each day on Buttermilk Mountain and Snowmass Ski Area. Tours leave at 12:30 p.m. from Buttermilk Sports and the Two Creeks Ski Shop, respectively, and the $35 cost includes equipment, applicable lift and shuttle tickets, guides and fanny packs with water and sunscreen. Call 923-3148 for reservations.

Lessons (98/99 prices)

Group lessons: Adult beginner group lessons cost $62 a day, $52 for half day, are offered at Buttermilk and Snowmass, and are limited to six per class for all beginner levels (up to those just starting to tackle blue runs). Intermediate and higher ability levels take semi-private lessons, offered at all four mountains, no more than three students per group, for $92 for a half day; $142 for a full day. If you sign up for three full days of semi-private lessons at $365, you'll get the same instructor.

Never-ever package: Three-day first-time skier packages, including shaped-ski equipment rental, run $199 and are offered at Buttermilk and Snowmass. (Without equipment, it's $169.) The snowboard package is $345 for three days and $119 for one day, offered at Buttermilk, Snowmass and Aspen Highlands.

Private lessons: $159 for 90 minutes for one to five people. Multihour discounts available, and reservations are required. Languages offered are Spanish, Portuguese, French and German.

Special programs: Numerous, including clinics and/or Ski Weeks for women, bumps, powder, disabled skiers, video analysis, equipment assessment, shaped skis, and many more. Call ASC at (800) 525-6200 and ask for a ski school brochure.

Racing: NASTAR is offered for $5 for two runs ($6 for two runs at Snowmass). Courses are located at Silver Dip Swing at Aspen Mountain (daily), Exhibition at Aspen Highlands (daily) and Cabin Trail at Snowmass (daily except Saturdays). Clinics also are offered. Snowmass has a speed course on Fridays for skiers and snowboarders on Slot, including use of a helmet and some basic instruction. Call for prices.

Children's lessons: Aspen Skiing Company has a completely different program for each mountain. Ages, per-day costs and phone numbers: Buttermilk (ages 3–6, $99, 920-0935), Snowmass (ages 3 1/2–4, $99, 923-0570; ages 5–6, $99, 923-0580) or Aspen Highlands (3 1/2–6, $75, 544-3025). These programs include instruction and lunch, but rentals are extra. Ages 5–7 can learn to snowboard at Snowmass with Bears on Board; cost for full-day is $160 and includes equipment, instruction, lunch and indoor activities; call 923-0580.

Ages 7–12, skiing; ages 8–12, snowboarding: Lessons at Buttermilk, Aspen Highlands or Snowmass are $69 a day (with lunch and lift ticket). Ages 13–19 have classes at Snowmass for $64 per day. Three- and five-day programs add fun races and picnics, and run $189 (three days) or $289 (five days) for younger children and $174/$264 for teens.

For brochures and information, or to make reservations for ski school programs, call 925-1220 or (800) 525-6200.

Child care (98/99 prices)

Ages: 6 weeks to 4 years.
Costs: $85 full day, with multiday discounts; or $14 per hour.
Reservations: Recommended; call (970) 925-3136. Child care in Aspen is offered by Kids' Club in the Yellow Brick Building, 315 Garmisch St. The state-licensed program offers indoor and outdoor (non-skiing) activities.

Other options: Also try **Supersitters** (923-6080), **Aimee's Angels** (923-2809) and **Aspen Day Trippers** (920-1769) for child care needs. **Baby's Away** (800-948-9030; 970-920-1699) rents and will deliver baby needs to your lodge, such as crib, stroller, car seat and toys. Reservations are recommended for all of these services.

Children from fifth through 12th grade can mingle with local kids at the **Aspen Youth Center** in downtown Aspen. The center has games, ping-pong, pool tables, movies and a dance room. The center does special programs depending on the season. Admission is free and a hotline gives weekly activities information, 925-7091.

Lift tickets (98/99 prices)

	Adult	Young Adult (13-27)	Child (7-12)
Three days	$177 ($59/day)	$135 ($45/day)	$111 ($37/day)
Five days	$285 ($57/day)	$205 ($41/day)	$170 ($34/day)
Six days	$330 ($55/day)	$235 ($39.17/day)	$197 ($32.83/day)

Who skis free: Ages 6 and younger and 70 and older.

Who skis at a discount: Ages 65 to 69 can buy these tickets for $165 for three days, $260 for five and $305 for six. "Young adult" is more than a euphemism here—it covers ages 13–27. Beginners can buy a lower-lift ticket at Snowmass or Buttermilk for a big discount; inquire about this before you pay full price. The RSVP program allows skiers to return unused portions of tickets within 14 days for credit toward future lift tickets and lessons.

Early season (November 21-29) rates are $49 a day for adults to $37 a day for children.

The Aspen ski areas offer a 14-day advanced purchase program that provides about a ten percent discount. Call (800) 525-6200 to order lift tickets in advance.

The four Aspen-area mountains are far from any other ski resorts and far from metropolitan areas. Consequently, just about all the visitors ski for more than one day. All tickets are valid at all four mountains.

Accommodations

Accommodations in Aspen range from luxurious to inexpensive. Reservations for virtually all properties are available through **Aspen Central Reservations,** (800) 262-7736 or 925-9000. Multiday lift-and-lodging packages are the best deal; ACR can suggest some.

Seventeen of the moderate- and budget-priced lodges have banded together as the "Treasures of Aspen." ACR represents this worthy group, and we were favorably impressed with the ones we inspected on our visit. Three-night packages, with two days of lift tickets, start at around $200 per person—hardly the stereotypical expensive Aspen vacation.

Top of the line ($300 or more per night in regular season):

Hotel Jerome, 330 East Main Street, (800-331-7213 or 920-1000) is on the National Register of Historic Places, and it has been restored to more elegance than the silver barons ever knew. The lounges are furnished with overstuffed chairs and framed in etched glass. Rooms are filled with antiques, and each has a brass or carved wooden bed. Baths feature Jacuzzis and marble counters.

The **Sardy House** (920-2525 or 800-321-3457) on East Main Street is a restored Victorian mansion. A modern addition has been tacked onto the rear, but we suggest you try to get one of the original rooms.

The **Little Nell** (920-4600 or 888-843-6355) has 92 rooms and suites, only steps from the Silver Queen Gondola at the base of Aspen Mountain. It has received the highest rating (five on a 1–5 scale) from several rating services, such as AAA and Mobil. All rooms have fireplaces, sofas, oversized beds with comforters, and marble bathrooms. There is a spa and a heated outdoor pool.

The St. Regis, Aspen (970-920-3300 or 800-241-3333) is the new name of what used to be the Ritz-Carlton. It is richly appointed, with a tasteful decor that brings to mind an exclusive hunting club. It has a fitness center and various ski packages, and its restaurants are top-flight.

The Residence (970-920-6532) has world-class European suites in an historic downtown landmark building. Also luxurious are the Aspen Club Lodge (800-882-2582) and the small Hotel Lenado (800-321-3457).

In the moderate category ($125–$250 a night, generally):

The Snowflake Inn, a block from the transportation center on East Hyman Avenue (970-925-3221 or 800-247-2069) is clean, roomy and is walking distance from the Aspen Mountain gondola, the buses to the other areas, and the downtown area. And it has a very friendly staff, laundry facilities, a heated pool and spa, and a free continental breakfast and après-ski snacks. What more does one need?

Our favorite place in Aspen, a lodge of a kind that's disappearing all too fast, is The Mountain Chalet (970-925-7797 or 800-321-7813). This place is just plain friendly to everyone, including families. If you can't stand a 3-year-old crawling over a lounge chair in the lobby or families howling over a game of Monopoly, then don't stay here. Rates are reasonable and include a hearty breakfast served family-style. It's a few blocks from the Aspen Mountain gondola, and across the street from the transportation center (ideally situated, in other words). Call early for rooms, because folks reserve space here well in advance. Package deals can get the price under $75 per person per day in December and under $105 in January and March with lodging, lift tickets and full breakfast included.

Other places that treat guests very well are the Mountain House Lodge (970-920-2550), The Beaumont (970-925-7081 or 800-344-3853), the Hotel Aspen (800-527-7369) and the Molly Gibson Lodge (800-356-6559).

Also try Skier's Chalet (970-920-2037) across from the Shadow Mountain Lift (formerly Lift 1-A) with a heated outdoor pool, the Limelight (970-925-3025 or 800-433-0832), the Christiana (970-925-3014) at 501 West Main Street and the St. Moritz Lodge (970-925-3220), a hostel only five blocks from the center of town.

We will observe a one-year mourning period for the Little Red Ski Haus, which we have been told has closed. Clean and fun dorms like it are getting hard to find in ski country, and we mourn its loss. You can still find inexpensive rooms at the Christmas Inn (970-925-3822), Innsbruck Inn (970-925-2980), Ullr Lodge (970-925-7696) and budget champion Tyrolean Lodge (970-925-4595 or 800-321-7025).

The Maroon Creek Lodge at Aspen Highlands has closed, but the Heatherbed Lodge (970-925-7077; 800-356-6782) is still a good place to stay beyond Aspen's bustle. Rates are about $110 per night, depending on season.

Several management companies rent condominiums. For luxury condos right on the slopes, try Mountain Queen Condominiums (970-925-6366); all are three-bedroom units. The Gant (800-345-1471) is another choice in condo lodging.

Coates, Reid and Waldron, 720 East Hyman Ave. (970-925-1400 or 800-222-7736), is the largest management company in the area, with condos and homes. Chateau Eau Claire and Chateau Roaring Fork are two of their popular units. Shadow Mountain is not so luxurious, but has a ski-in/ski-out location.

Condominiums directly on the slopes are the Fasching Haus (970-925-5900), Fifth Avenue (970-925-7397) and Durant Condominiums (970-925-7910). They are available through Aspen Central Reservations.

# Dining

Let's start with *the* place to eat breakfast, **The Wienerstube** at 633 E. Hyman and Spring. Come here for Eggs Benedict, Austrian sausages and homemade Viennese pastries. **Main Street Bakery**, 201 E. Main St., has homemade baked goods, granola, fruit, eggs and great coffee for reasonable prices. Another recommended breakfast spot is **Poppycock's Cafe**, 609 E. Cooper. For the best coffee in town, according to some locals, head to **Aspen Bagel Bites**, next to Clark's Market; or **Café Ink**, inside the D&E Snowboard Shop in the Ajax Mountain Building.

Dinner recommendations: **Cache Cache** (925-3835) on the lower level of the Mill Street Plaza is highly recommended by locals for Mediterranean and French provincial cuisine, and it has half-price early-bird specials. The polenta niçoise, wild mushroom cannelloni and perfectly grilled yellowtail were favorites.

Carnevale Ristorante (920-4885) located at 430 E. Hyman, may be the tops in a crowded Italian-cuisine field. Prices there are on the high side, but locals and tourists give it consistently high marks. Other outstanding gourmet Italian restaurants are **Mezzaluna** at 600 E. Cooper (925-5882), **Farfalla** at 415 E. Main (925-8222) and **Campo de Fiori** at 205 S. Mill (920-7717).

Matsuhira (544-6628) is the latest don't-miss restaurant in town, we're told, and some other recommended new restaurants we haven't yet had the chance to try include **Vihn Vihn** (920-4373), for Vietnamese food; **Blue Maize** (925-6698), featuring Southwest and Latin America foods, and **Baang Bar & Cafe** (925-9969), which blends French cuisine with Asian. Some eateries recommended by locals and visitors: **L'Hostaria** (925-9022), with furniture, paintings and recipes direct from Italy; and **The Big Wrap** (544-1700), which features the latest healthy-food trend, wraps. These are like a burrito, but with non-Mexican fillings.

La Cocina (925-9714), 308 E. Hopkins, is a very popular Mexican place with locals (they call it "Lah-co"), and after eating there on our last visit, we know why—great food, low prices (no credit cards accepted). **The Cantina** (925-3663) at the corner of Mill and Main is a trendier alternative.

Boogie's Diner at 534 E. Cooper (925-6610) is a real '50s diner with oldies like Elvis' "Hound Dog," blue plate specials and meatloaf (great milkshakes, too). The **Flying Dog Brew Pub** at 424 E. Cooper (925-7464), which gets its name from a Sherpa guide's interpretation of the term "bird dog," has home-brewed beers and affordable menu selections. It's downstairs at 424 E. Cooper. **Little Annie's Eating House** (925-1098) at 517 E. Hyman is still the ribs, chicken, hamburger and potato pancake champ. **The Skier's Chalet Steak House** (925-3381) at 710 S. Aspen has been around since 1951 and is very inexpensive. **The Steak Pit** (925-3459), at the corner of Hopkins and Monarch, also has some of the best steaks in Aspen and a great and cheap salad bar. **Little Ollie's** (544-9888), 308 S. Hunter, is recommended for Chinese food. It has free delivery, or you can dine at the restaurant.

The T-Lazy-7 Ranch (925-7254) organizes a Western night every Wednesday and Thursday. It includes sleigh rides, cooking your own steak and chicken on an open grill and a Country & Western band cookin' up some footstompin' music.

Dining with Katy

Katy Keck, our gourmet expert, has repeatedly visited Aspen and has these recommendations for finding the best of the town. Entreés typically are in the $20s, with some lower and some higher. Here are Katy's dining recommendations, in her words:

In town: Aspen has enjoyed an unparalleled culinary revolution that has bypassed sole meunière for a more exotic "beach party" shellfish. Exotic ingredients and foods are definitely trendy. Over the past few years, we've seen black trumpets and white truffles, edible nasturtiums and a veal dish called "@*#?&!." Aspen is a place where you can enjoy the fine restaurants thoroughly, knowing that the next day you'll ski off those calories.

One of Aspen's long-time favorites had a culinary rebirth a few years back. **The Restaurant at the Little Nell** at 675 E. Durant (920-6330) specializes in contemporary American Alpine cuisine, and was voted tops in Colorado by the readers of *Gourmet*.

Syzygy's menu combines French, southwestern, Oriental and Italian cuisines. Don't be put off by the hard-to-pronounce name (Siz i je) or the obscure explanation of its meaning on the menu. At 520 E. Hyman Avenue (925-3700, reservations required); the atmosphere is intimate yet casual. Open daily 6 to 10 p.m.

Go to **Piñons** (second floor at 105 S. Mill; 920-2021) to dine in a cozy western ranch decor, with stucco walls, a leather bar and huge brass bowls. All meats and fish are grilled over mesquite and cherry wood. Desserts vary daily. Open daily 6 to 10 p.m.; reservations recommended.

If you think that at these prices, you should be entertained and have your apartment cleaned for a year, one man will at least do the former. Mead Metcalf has been playing to **The Crystal Palace** sellout crowds each evening at 6 and 9 p.m. for nearly four decades. At 300 East Hyman Avenue (925-1455; reservations may be necessary several weeks in advance), the Crystal Palace adds wit and satire to the old notion of barbershop quartets. Amid stained glass and crystal chandeliers, the talented staff not only cranks out a full dinner and bar service, but then belts out a cabaret revue spoofing the media's latest victims. You can choose from perfectly pink beef tenderloin with Madeira sauce, roast duckling, rack of lamb or prime rib. The food doesn't have to be good, but it is.

On the outside chance there's still a platinum card burning a hole in your parka, try **Renaissance,** 304 East Hopkins (925-2402). Chef-owner Charles Dale (who grew up in the palace in Monaco with Caroline and Albert) claims his is one of three restaurants in the world to have a daily changing degustation or tasting menu (five courses), as well as offering course-by-course, by-the-glass wine pairings. Wine gets special attention at Renaissance. The list has won the Wine Spectator Award of Excellence. Reservations recommended.

For a real adventure, head out to the **Pinecreek Cookhouse,** (925-1044) for a casual evening and solid fare. At an elevation of 9,725 feet, this rustic log cabin is in the midst of towering pines beneath Elk Mountain peaks some 12 miles from Aspen. It is accessible by a one-and-a-half-mile cross-country trek or by a sleigh drawn by a team of Percherons. Views are outstanding. Reservations are essential (at times two to four weeks in advance), as the logistics of running a kitchen not reached by road in winter is no small matter. The Cookhouse feeds several hundred people each day, and all that food comes in by snowmobile. Meals are prepared right in front of you in the open kitchen and will be served by one of your cross-country guides.

On the mountain: Unlike the majority of U.S. resorts, the Aspen Skiing Company puts restaurant contracts up for public bidding, so real restaurateurs end up with them, and the food is a far cry from the usual stacked-trays and steam-table fare.

A good example of this phenomenon is **Bumps** at the Buttermilk base area. The menu features foods from a wood-fired rotisserie, brick ovens and a pit smoker. The same managers operate the **Ajax Tavern,** the menu at which boasts Mediterranean influences in a clubby room. Lunch is a hearty selection of pastas, salads, and sandwiches with outdoor seating.

While not a sit-down restaurant, **Bonnie's,** just above Lift 3 on Aspen Mountain, feeds some 1,500 hungry skiers per day between 9:30 a.m. and 2:30 p.m. Go before noon or after 2 p.m., unless you love lines. Owner Bonnie Rayburn's gourmet pizza on freshly made crust is a huge crowd pleaser. Homemade soups, such as the Colorado white-bean chili, are served with large crusty pieces of fresh French bread. Save room for apple strudel.

At the top of the Shadow Mountain Lift (formerly Lift 1A) on Aspen Mountain is **La Baita** (920-0728). The innovative buffet cafeteria features traditional Italian fare with gourmet pizzas, panini and a variety of lasagnas. A sit-down restaurant with the best views of town, it has relaxed dining over such dishes as white polenta with wild mushrooms, grilled pheasant, creative pastas, and Aspen's best tiramisu.

Après-ski/nightlife

Ajax Tavern, adjacent to The Little Nell, draws a big crowd as the lifts start to close. If you don't find what you want there, the crowd spreads out to **The Little Nell Bar, Mezzaluna, the Aspen Club Lodge, Little Annie's, Cooper Street Pier,** the **Red Onion** and **O'Leary's.** Après-ski comes in all varieties here, from **The Cantina,** with its very happy hour (have a margarita in the compadre size) to the quiet and genteel **Hotel Jerome Bar.** Après-ski also gets lively at the **J-Bar.**

At night, the music and dance beat begins to take over. Earlier in the evening, the high-energy place to find out who's in town is **Mezzaluna,** with its brassy horseshoe-shaped bar. **Planet Hollywood** and the **Hard Rock Cafe** attract a lot of tourists looking for celebrities, but few celebs—and few locals.

For dancing, head to **Club Soda,** where a DJ pumps out the tunes. Another place to dance are **The Tippler,** with its '70s night every Tuesday. **St. Regis** has live music in the lounge, and **The Little Nell** bar has jazz.

For a good singles bar, head to **Mezzaluna** for the best in upscale people-watching. **Eric's Bar, Cigar Bar** and **Aspen Billiards** also attract singles, and have lots of microbrews on tap (great scotch, too). Another upscale beer spot is **McStorlie's Pub.** A relatively mixed crowd with normal pedestrian tastes congregate in the **Red Onion, Little Annie's** and **O'Leary's.**

Cooper Street is very much a local and college student hangout. **Shooter's,** on Hyman Avenue, is a very dark and smoky Country & Western bar with great deals on shooters and beer and great dancing. **Flying Dog Brew Pub** has live bluegrass. **J-Bar** has live music Sundays and Wednesdays during the ski season. For the best "last call," try **Mother Lode.**

Other activities

Shopping: This town is a shopper's heaven. A longtime favorite is **Boogie's,** which has many unique clothing and accessories items. Part of the decor is a 1955 red Corvette that Elvis Presley bought for $3,500 (you can easily blow that much in this entertaining store). A newer favorite is **The Omnibus Gallery,** which specializes in antique full-color posters. And we always enjoy prowling through the racks at Aspen's two **secondhand stores,** Susie's and Gracy's, where you can buy a seldom-worn designer outfit for a fraction of its original price.

Arts lovers will enjoy Aspen's 40-plus galleries, its two resident theater groups, three movie houses (including art films) and its winter classical concert series. The Aspen Chamber Resort Association has more information, 925-1940.

For winter **fly-fishing** trips call Aspen Outfitting Co. (925-3406), Oxbow Outfitting Co. (925-1505) or Aspen Sports (925-6332).

The Aspen Center for Environmental Studies (925-5756) has daily self-guided Hallam Lake **snowshoe touring,** and daily two-hour naturalist-guided snowshoe walks atop Aspen Mountain twice a day for about $40. Free guided environmental interpretive ski tours are offered on one or more of the Aspen Skiing Company's four mountains each day. For the schedule, call 925-5756. Snowshoeing is very popular here, and several other companies offer tours and rentals. See the Cross-Country section for more.

Go for a **hot-air balloon ride** with Unicorn Balloon Company (925-5752) or Above It All Balloon Company (970-927-9606; 888-927-9606), or go **ice skating** at the Silver Circle rink across from the transportation center.

Sleigh rides take place at the T-Lazy-7 Ranch. Call 925-7040. The Aspen Carriage Company (925-4289) offers one-hour **carriage rides**.

The **Aspen Athletic Club** (925-2531) is open to the public from 7 a.m. to 10 p.m. on weekdays and 8 a.m. to 8 p.m. on weekends for a $15 daily fee.

Getting there and getting around

By air: Aspen/Sardy Field is served by 250 flights per week from five cities: Denver (United, American and Frontier), Phoenix (America West), Dallas/Ft. Worth (American), Minneapolis/St.Paul (Northwest) and Los Angeles (United). Aspen/Snowmass has a concierge at United Gate B-60 at Denver International Airport to help passengers connecting there.

Delta, United, Northwest and American fly into the Eagle County airport, about 70 miles away. Colorado Mountain Express takes skiers from Eagle to Aspen. Regular ground transportation also leaves the Denver International Airport for Aspen, but it's a very long drive on I-70, about 150 miles away.

By train: Amtrak has service to Glenwood Springs, where skiers can get ground transportation the rest of the way.

By bus: Greyhound has bus service between Glenwood Springs and Denver International Airport.

Getting around: Aspen has a free bus system, RFTA, with several routes in town and to Glenwood Springs. There also is a separate, free shuttle between the various ski mountains. Downtown is enjoyably walkable. Not only is a car unnecessary, parking is a pain.

Snowmass

Colorado

Summit elevation: 12,510 feet
Vertical drop: 4,406 feet
Base elevation: 8,104 feet

Address: Aspen Skiing Company
P.O. Box 1248, Aspen, CO 81612 or
Snowmass Resort Association,
P.O. Box 5566, Snowmass Village, CO 81615
✆ **Area code:** 970
Ski area phone: 925-1220 or
(800) 525-6200
Snow report: 925-1221 or (888-ASPEN-SNO, 277-3676)
ⓘ **Toll-free reservations:** (800) 598-2005
Fax: 923-5466
E-mail: info@snowmassvillage.com
Internet: http://www.snowmassvillage.com

Expert:★★★★ **Advanced:**★★★★
Intermediate:★★★★★
Beginner:★★★ **Never-ever:**★★

Number of lifts: 18–7 high-speed quads,
2 triples, 6 doubles, 3 surface lifts
Snowmaking: 3 percent
Skiable acreage: 2,850 acres
Uphill capacity: 23,869 per hour
Bed Base: 6,000 rentable units
Nearest lodging: slopeside, condos
Resort child care: Yes, 6 weeks and older
Snowboarding: Yes, unlimited
Adult ticket, per day: $39–$59

Dining:★★★ (at resort)
★★★★★ (in the region)
Apres-ski/nightlife:★★ (at resort)
★★★★★ (in the region)
Other activities:★★★

Though it is lumped into the Aspen experience by geography, Snowmass can stand on its own as a ski destination. Measuring by skiable acreage, Snowmass is one of the top ten resorts in America in size, and it's the second-largest in Colorado (after Vail). It covers more than 2,800 acres—more than Aspen Mountain, Buttermilk Mountain and Aspen Highlands combined. And thanks to a brand-new surface lift to the top of the Cirque (formerly reached by a hike or snowcat), Snowmass lays claim to the highest lift-served skiing in North America, and the longest vertical drop in the United States, 4,406 feet. (Big Sky, MT, has a 4,180-foot vertical; Jackson Hole, WY, 4,139 feet. Now you have your après-ski bar conversation opener.)

Snowmass has a relatively new base area called Two Creeks, with a new high-speed lift, a day lodge, parking for 200 cars, a mass transit terminal and 155 acres of intermediate ski trails. The Two Creeks quad connects to the Elk Creek high-speed quad lift, getting you to the top of Elk Camp in less than 20 minutes. This newer base area is the most convenient entrance if you're staying in Aspen.

Snowmass is a wonderful intermediate and advanced area. The Big Burn allows you to activate your autopilot, and the run from the top of Elk Camp to Fanny Hill is a four-mile-plus cruise. But Snowmass has steeps such as Hanging Valley that pucker up intermediates and delight expert skiers.

Snowmass village seems to stretch forever. Like Keystone or Copper Mountain, this is a purpose-built ski resort. A village mall has shops, restaurants, bars and ski administration facilities. Hundreds of condos line the lower part of the ski area, and about 90 percent of the lodging is ski-in/ski-out. It doesn't get much more convenient than Snowmass.

Mountain layout

◆◆ **Expert:** Experts will get an adrenaline rush by dropping through the trees in the Hanging Valley Glades or into steep open-bowl skiing on the Hanging Valley Wall. Both are labeled double black diamonds. To get there quickly on powder mornings, take Wood Run, Alpine Springs and High Alpine Chairs. The ski school offers guided tours back here. Check at their desk at High Alpine.

Another extreme playground is the Cirque, a scooped-out place between Sheer Bliss and High Alpine lifts. This now is served by a surface lift, at the top of which you'll find the "Rocky Mountain High" run, named in memory of the late singer John Denver. Don't try this area unless you're comfortable on Hanging Valley Wall: you'll have to be deft of foot on Rock Island and KT Gully. Even more challenging is AMF at the top. A local says it stands for "Adios, My Friend."

◆ **Advanced:** Advanced skiers and snowboarders ready to burn up steep-pitched cruising will think they've found nirvana when they make the first descent into the Campground area, to the far right on the trail map. Here is a wonderful long run for solid intermediates or advanced skiers: to come off the top of Big Burn on Sneaky's, schuss to avoid the uphill stretch at Sam's Knob, cut south around the Knob and head into the blacks of Bear Claw, Slot, Wildcat or Zugspitze to the base of the Campground lift. All offer great cruises and patches of moguls normally of the mellow sand-dune variety.

■ **Intermediate:** In addition to its black runs, Sam's Knob also is a great intermediate area, as are Elk Camp and the new Two Creeks area. The Big Burn is legendary cruiser fun. It's an entire side of a mountain that was allegedly set aflame by Ute Indians in the 1880s as a warning to advancing white settlers. The pioneers settled anyway, but the trees never grew back thickly, so the run, dotted by a few spruces, is a mile wide and a mile and a half long. On low visibility days, though, watch out. Those sparse trees appear out of nowhere when you can't see very far ahead.

If the pitch at Big Burn is not quite to your liking, head over to High Alpine, which is perhaps five degrees steeper. If you ride the new surface lift to the Cirque and find it isn't to your liking, ski the intermediate ridge back to the Big Burn.

●● **Beginner:** Beginners have a wide gentle area parallel to the village. Fanny Hill eases down by the mall, Wood Run lift opens another easy glide around the Wood Road side of the village, and further to the left a long straightaway, Funnel, will give beginners the feeling they're really covering terrain.

Beginners who want to see more of the mountain can head up to Sam's Knob, eat lunch, enjoy the view and head down a meandering trail bearing the names Max Park, Lunchline and Dawdler, which turns back to Fanny Hill. (Avoid the blue runs on the face of Sam's Knob because they are not for beginners.) The next step up would be Elk Camp, labeled blue but very gentle. By the way, Assay Hill is a good spot for beginning snowboarders.

● **Never-ever:** We would give the beginner terrain here a higher rating but for one important fact: Many of the ski in/ski out condos are along the green runs, so at the beginning and end of the day, they often are used by skilled skiers and snowboarders in a hurry to get to either the lifts or the hot tub. If you're just starting out, we recommend a trip to Aspen's Buttermilk Mountain.

Mountain rating

This is an intermediate mountain, even though it has pockets of advanced terrain and beginner smoothies. Skiers who love to cruise will think they have arrived in heaven. Few competent skiers who have returned from Snowmass have been heard complaining. That's the best recommendation of all.

Snowboarding

Snowboarding is allowed all over the mountain. Just below the Naked Lady chair on the Funnel trail is a 500-foot-long, 50-foot-wide halfpipe with eight-foot sides. The resort also has two new halfpipes and a new terrain park that can be accessed by the Coney Glade lift. D&E Snowboards in the village and the Two Creeks rental shop have equipment.

Cross-country

See the Aspen chapter.

Lessons

See the Aspen chapter. Snowmass has a unique kind of recreational racing—a speed course on Slot, for $5 for three runs or $15 for the whole day (97/98 prices) on Fridays. The fee includes use of a helmet and basic instruction.

Child care (98/99 prices)

Ages: 6 weeks to 3 1/2 years.
Costs: $55 half day, $85 a day with multiday discounts. Child care combines snow play, indoor activities and ski lessons for the 3-year-olds.
Reservations: Required; call 923-0563 or (800) 525-6200.
Other options: Little Red School House (923-3756) offers licensed day care for children ages 3–5 years; Aimee's Angels (923-2809) has day care for kids ages 12 months to 3 years; and The Agency (923-3773) is another childcare program based in Snowmass. Nighthawks is an evening child care program (923-0470) for ages 3–10. For other suggestions, see the Aspen chapter.

Lift tickets

See the Aspen chapter.

Accommodations

There are few hotels but thousands of condominiums. You can't beat their slopeside positioning or soaring cathedral ceilings and wide-open, glassed-in living rooms. Hotel and lodge prices generally start at $150 and up a night (condos about $50 more), though you can find some for some for a whole lot more. For other recommendations, and reservations, call **Snowmass Central Reservations** (800-598-2004).

Hotel accommodations are relatively limited: **The Snowmass Lodge and Club** is below and outside the village, but upscale. It serves as the Nordic center and has a deluxe athletic club. There are regular shuttles to the slopes, including the Two Creeks area, which is a couple of minutes away. Rates, including lift tickets: $225–$430 a night. Midweek package deals here are as low as $54 per person per day in early season; ask about other packages.

These two are the class acts in Snowmass Village. The contemporary **Silvertree** has been open since the ski area began in 1967 and is the largest property in the area. Across the street is the **Wildwood Lodge**, with slightly lower rates. Both are comfortable with beautiful rooms, and close to everything in Snowmass.

Mountain Chalet includes a full breakfast and soup lunch, and slopeside convenience. The **Pokolodi** offers good value for the money. **Snowmass Lodging Company** (800-365-0410 or 923-3232) books some of the most upscale condos, including **Woodrun V** and **Chamonix.**

The **Top of the Village** and the **Timberline** condos are a good five- to ten-minute climb above the village mall. The **Stonebridge** is in the center of the village. The **Terracehouse, Willows** and **Lichenhearth** are two levels below Village Mall. The Willows are unusual because they are separate buildings, either cozy studios with kitchenettes or two-bedroom units. Above the village is the **Sonnenblick**, which has only large units, three to five bedrooms ranging from about $300 to $800.

 # Dining

Snowmass claims some of the best restaurants in the area. **Krabloonik** (923-3953) is a formal dining experience featuring wild game and seafood amid spectacular views and the howling of sled dogs in the kennels outside. With a bit of imagination you're in Doctor Zhivago or Jack London country. The specialty is wild game, including boar, caribou, elk, moose and pheasant.

The chef at **La Boheme** (923-6804), Maurice Couturier, was once the chef for the King of Jordan. His specialties include lamb, pheasant, deer and caribou. He also oversees the cooking at the less expensive **La Brasserie** (923-6803), which specializes in pasta and fish dishes and has live jazz performances.

The Snowmass Lodge & Club bistro, **Sage** (923-5600), offers distinctive food—highly recommended by our dining expert, Katy Keck—with a casual unpretentious atmosphere and at more moderate prices. The hottest place in Snowmass and one of Katy's favorites is **Cowboys** (923-5249) in the Silvertree Complex, which is open for lunch, après-ski appetizers, and dinner. The menu would thrill even the boldest cowboy. Katy's experience included Colorado loin of lamb stuffed with achiote and roast garlic pesto served with a rosemary tomato cream, and mesquite-grilled T-bone. Come for the food and stay for the live music.

Other quality spots are **Il Poggio** (923-4292) and **The Conservatory.**

Midrange dining can be found at **The Tower, The Stonebridge, Cottonwoods** (with live jazz on weekends), **Pippins Steak and Lobster, Butch's Lobster Bar** (formerly Moguls), **Brothers' Grille** (which reportedly has the best hamburgers in the valley) and **Mountain Dragon** (for Chinese).

Every restaurant in Snowmass has children's menus, but **The Stewpot** features soups, tasty and unusual stews and sandwiches. For soups and sandwiches, try **Paradise Bakery** in Silvertree Plaza. Or go to **S'noBeach Café** (featuring "eggs S'noBeach" for breakfast). A popular hangout is **La Piñata** for fair Mexican food at fair prices, where sombreros and wild art line the walls and locals play darts and table shuffleboard.

Families might like the **Burlingame Dinner Rides** (925-1220), a 20-minute sleigh ride followed by a hearty southwestern meal and Western entertainment.

For a quick breakfast on the way to the slopes, try **Moondogs Cable Car. Café Ink** serves gourmet coffee from inside D&E Snowboard shop.

Dining on the Mountain—According to Katy, our gourmet specialist, Snowmass excels with mountaintop cookery. **Café Suzanne** is at the bottom of Elk Camp Lift 10 at Snowmass and specializes in French Country Cuisine. Although it's a cafeteria, the food is a pleasant surprise, with a daily assortment of entrée crêpes, such as buckwheat crêpes with spinach, mushroom or chicken, and dessert crêpes. Suzanne McPherson has taken her classical French training and customized it to the fast-food needs of the mountain. There is a daily entrée special, generally a Provençal or Norman dish, and a special soup with a homemade sourdough boule. You won't find a Parisian hot dog with gruyère and Dijon in any other mountain restaurant here. Open daily 9 a.m. to 3:30 p.m.

Also at Snowmass, try **Gwyn's High Alpine Restaurant,** at the top of Alpine Springs (Lift 8), for fine dining. Gwyn offers a sit-down breakfast daily from 9:30 to 10:30 a.m. Lunch is served from 11:30 a.m. to 2:30 p.m. Reservations are essential (923-5188). If you take the first chair up, but aren't ready to brave the cold, relax with an orange blossom and enjoy breakfast with a cup of Kona coffee. At noon, warm up with the elegant lunch offerings.

Krabloonik (923-3953), mentioned earlier, is also open for lunch. It is located at the base of Campground off the Dawdler Catwalk.

 ## Après-ski/nightlife

The **Cirque Cafe** and the **Brothers' Grille** are the hubs of après-ski. The Cirque Cafe tends to be more crowded and rowdier. Brothers' has five different draft beers and almost a dozen hot drinks for quick warmups. **La Piñata** is another popular après-ski hangout. **Zoom's Saloon** is a sports bar with après-ski drink specials. **Cottonwoods** and **La Brasserie** have live jazz on weekends.

At night Snowmass is quiet. The best action in town is in the **Tower,** where Doc Eason performs magic throughout the night. At **Cowboys** they strike up C&W.

Other activities

 The **Anderson Ranch Arts Center** (923-3181) in Snowmass Village exhibits work by visiting and resident artists throughout the winter. The center also offers a series of workshops in ceramics, woodworking and photography from January through April. Call for current events. **Krabloonik Kennels** in Snowmass (923-3953) has dogsled rides. Two-hour rides cost about $185 and include lunch.

Also see the Aspen chapter.

 ## Getting there and getting around

See the Aspen section.

Summit County

Colorado

Some winter vacationers aren't satisfied with skiing at just one place. When they return to the office, they want to drop resort names and compare the black-diamond plunges. For these skiers, we suggest Summit County.

Summit County, about a 90-minute drive from downtown Denver, has four well-known ski areas—Breckenridge, Copper Mountain, Keystone and Arapahoe Basin. Each resort—except A-Basin—has its own village with lodging, shopping and restaurants.

If you plan to do most of your skiing at just one area, stay at that resort, but if you want to experience them all and save some money, then set up your base camp in Dillon, Frisco or Silverthorne, three small towns that surround Dillon Reservoir off I-70.

This tri-town area is smack in the center of the ski action. Breckenridge is about nine miles in one direction, Copper Mountain five miles in another, Keystone seven miles away in a third, and A-Basin just a little farther than Keystone. Having a car is nice, but not really necessary. The reliable Summit Stage, the free bus system subsidized by sales tax revenue, runs between the towns and the ski areas all day.

Summit County deserves its lofty name. Each of the ski areas, and each of the three mountain towns, has a base elevation above 9,000 feet. (If you have problems with high altitudes, take note. If you like spring skiing, also take note: high elevations usually mean a longer ski season.) Each of these areas stays open at least until late April in normal snow years, and Arapahoe Basin—with its base lodge above 10,000 feet—often stays open until July 4.

Vail Resorts Inc. owns Keystone and Breckenridge. It has an interchangeable lift ticket that includes Vail, Beaver Creek, Keystone and Breckenridge. You'll have to buy separate tickets to ski at Copper Mountain and A-Basin, although we keep hearing Vail Resorts may start some sort of ticket-exchange policy with the latter area, so keep that in mind when you buy your tickets.

This chapter lists accommodations, dining, nightlife and non-ski activities in the tri-town area of Frisco, Dillon and Silverthorne. You can pick up information and helpful brochures at two Summit County Chamber Visitors' Centers, one at 150 Tenderfoot (off Lake Dillon Drive) in Dillon and another in Frisco on South Summit Boulevard on the lake side. Or call the chamber at (800) 530-3099 or (970) 668-0376. They'll act as matchmaker for you and your lodging needs.

Separate chapters detail the skiing, lodging, dining and nightlife at Breckenridge, Copper Mountain and Keystone. For information on skiing at A-Basin, refer to the Regional Getaway chapter at the end of the book.

The area code for local numbers is 970.

Accommodations

Frisco: This is our first choice for a home base, for several reasons. One, it is the closest town to Breckenridge and Copper Mountain, and Keystone isn't far away. Two, its downtown area along Main Street has lots of funky shops and restaurants, perfect for a late afternoon or evening stroll. And three, we like friendly mountain inns, and found three good ones.

The **Galena Street Inn** (800-248-9138 or 970-668-3224), First Avenue and Galena Street (one block off Main Street), was built just a few years ago. Its 15 rooms have private baths, televisions and phones, and all are nicely furnished. A hot tub and sauna are among the amenities. A full breakfast with hot entrée is included, as are après-ski refreshments. No Smoking, no pets. Room rates, based on double occupancy, are about $105–$135 during February and March, $95–$115 in January (it depends on the specific room). For each extra person in the same room, it's $20 each.

Hotel Frisco (800-262-1002 or 970-668-5009; www.hotelfrisco.com; email: rmoreno@csn.net), formerly called the Twilight Inn, has been completely remodeled during the past year. Located at 308 Main Street, it is no longer a B&B, and now has 16 rooms instead of 12. Rates range from $70-180.

The gurgling of Ten Mile Creek is the wake-up call for guests at **Creekside Inn** (800-668-7320 or 970-668-5607). Innkeepers Ed and Arlene Housley found this quiet setting at the west end of Main Street the ideal spot to build a quintessential mountain inn with a touch of the Old World. Afternoon snacks, special-diet and early-bird breakfasts, ski storage and wheelchair access are a few of the amenities. The seven guest rooms each have a private bath, and a fireplace in the great room and deck hot tub make this a tempting home away from home. Rates are in the $79-to-$160 range, depending on room size and season. No Smoking, no pets, no children younger than 12.

Dillon/Silverthorne: Lodging here is mostly chain hotels and motels. Rooms usually cost between $100 and $160.

The **Best Western Ptarmigan Lodge** (800-842-5939 or 970-468-2341) in the Dillon town center is one of the best bargains, particularly during the early and late seasons and in January.

Off the interstate in Silverthorne are side-by-side chain hotels—**Hampton Inn** (800-321-3509 or 970-468-6200) and **Days Inn** (800-329-7466 or 970-468-8661). The Summit Stage stops at their doors, and they are convenient to the Factory Stores (see *Other Activities*).

Budget travelers should stay at the **Super 8** motel (800-800-8000; 970-468-8888) in Dillon, across from the Summit Place Shopping Center. Most of the best cheap restaurants are in this center. Or, try the **Alpen Hutte** (468-6336), 471 RainbowDrive. Both the Greyhound bus from Denver and the Summit County shuttle buses stop there, and for about $20, you get a bed in an eight-person dorm room. It has a nice kitchen, is clean and it's walking distance from restaurants (especially the brewery) and shopping.

The towns have many more B&Bs, chain hotels, private homes and condos. For reservations, call **Summit County Central Reservations** (800) 365-6365 or **Reservations for the Summit** at (800) 999-9510.

 ## Dining

Frisco: One of the newest and arguably the best restaurant in Frisco is **Uptown Bistro** (668-4728) next to the Daily Planet bookstore on Main Street. A '90s bistro atmosphere complements an uptown á la carte menu. Main courses include such delights as pumpkin squash ravioli with sage brown butter and garlic-ginger-flavored seared ahi with a spicy mushroom spring roll. Great desserts and wood-oven-baked gourmet pizzas. Make reservations and ask to be seated in the back, away from the front-door draft.

A longtime favorite is the **Blue Spruce Inn** (668-5900) in a historic log cabin at the corner of Madison and Main. Entrées include such dishes as filet béarnaise, vegetables en croûte, grilled venison and scallops dijonaise. The food is good, though a little sauce-heavy, and the atmosphere and service are excellent. Reservations recommended.

More moderate fare is found at **Charity's** (668-3644), 307 Main St., which features Mexican and Southwestern dishes with pasta, chicken and seafood for variety. Another Southwestern-styled restaurant is **Golden Annie's** (668-0345) on the corner of 6th and Main. Prices are $8–$15 at both; the difference is atmosphere. Charity's is historic saloon, while Golden Annie's is yuppie faux-adobe. **El Rio Cantina & Grill** (668-5043), 450 W. Main, has the most complete Mexican menu and a lively happy hour, and **Barkley's** (668-3694) at 620 Main St. serves good prime rib and Mexican food.

Budget eats: Locals recommended **Ge-Jo's** (668-3308), upstairs at 409 Main St., for inexpensive Italian fare and **Szechuan Taste** (668-5685) at 310 Main St. for Chinese food (dine in or take out)

Frisco also has many fast-food chain restaurants, most along Summit Boulevard. Influence from the Lone Star State shows in the newest chain eatery direct from Austin, **Tex's Star Cafe** (668-2010) on North Summit Boulevard near Wal-Mart. Family fare here is pure Americana.

Halfway between Frisco and Breckenridge, in an area called Farmer's Korner, are neighboring restaurants that are quite different. **The Blue River Inn** (547-9928) is a no-frills local hangout with great burgers, inexpensive draft beers and a 10-ounce sirloin that is probably still less than $10. **The Swan Mountain Inn** (453-7903) offers a nightly four-course meal in a seven-table dining room with a fireplace. The inn also has a weekend brunch.

Dillon & Silverthorne: Locals and visitors alike rave about **Silverheels Southwest Grill** (468-2926) 81 Buffalo Drive in Silverthorne. Fine Southwestern fare and a Spanish tapas bar are the specialties here. The restaurant, in a hacienda-style building in the Wildernest area, is a bit off the main drag but worth the search. When you call for reservations ask for directions.

Another choice for finer dining is **Ristorante Al Lago** (468-6111) in the Dillon town center. It serves Northern Italian meals.

For slightly more casual dining in Dillon, try **Antonia's** (468-5055) in the same building as Christy's Sports on Highway 6, **Pug Ryan's** (468-2145) in the Dillon town center, or **Wild Bill's Stone Oven Pizza** (468-2006), also in the Dillon town center. In Silverthorne, you can cook your own meat over an open grill at **The Historic Mint** (468-5247) or enjoy Tex-Mex food at **Old Dillon Inn** (468-2791).

Budget diners: the Summit Place Shopping Center on Highway 6 on the Dillon-Silverthorne border has several great restaurants, including **Sunshine Cafe** (468-6663), jammed with locals; and **Nick-N-Willy's** (262-1111) for very good bake-your-own take-out pizza.

Breakfast: The best breakfast in the tri-town area is **Claimjumper** (668-3617), on Summit Boulevard in Frisco across the street from Wal-Mart. Not only does it have an extensive omelet-and-pancake menu, it has breakfast specials that taste great and fill the plate.

A close second is the **Arapahoe Cafe** on Lake Dillon Drive in the Dillon town center (468-0873), a huge favorite with locals. The cafe building used to stand in the old town of Dillon, but was moved in the 1960s when the new reservoir flooded the area. The service is great, the menu names are creative (Arapahuevos Rancheros, Hans and Franz Power Breakfast, etc.) and eavesdropping on the other tables will fill you in on local politics. Both restaurants also have inexpensive lunch and dinner menus.

Definitely in the running for the Best Breakfast title are **Sunshine Cafe** in the Summit Place Shopping Center and **Log Cabin Cafe** (668-3847) on Main Street in Frisco.

For those who prefer a lighter breakfast, head for the **Butterhorn Bakery** (668-3997), 408 W. Main Street in Frisco. Across the street is **Pika Bagel Bakery** (668-0902), and in the Summit Place Shopping Center in Silverthorne, **Blue Moon Baking Company** (468-1472).

Après-ski/nightlife

Mountain resorts and brew pubs seem to go hand in hand. Summit County has five, three of which are in the tri-town area. **Backcountry Brewery** is on the corner of Summit and Main in Frisco, **Pug Ryan's** is in the Dillon Town Center and **The Dam Brewery** is behind Antonia's in Dillon. (The others are in Breckenridge and Keystone; read about them in those chapters.) The current trend is to end a day on the mountain with a freshly drawn Colorado specialty brewski. Both places also serve food and have lively happy hours.

Barkley's West in Frisco varies its entertainment from live music to dance classes to Under 21 nights. This new upscale nightclub opened in 1998.

The leading sports bar is **High Mountain Billiards,** an upscale game room with pool tables, dart boards, shuffleboard, chess, checkers, backgammon and sports TV. This No Smoking, richly decorated bar serves a mostly over-30 clientele. It's next to the Backcountry Brewery in Frisco.

Old Dillon Inn has live Country & Western music on weekends, and the best margaritas in town. Its 120-year-old bar definitely has authentic Old West atmosphere. The building was pieced together from bits of defunct establishments, and the whole thing was moved in 1961 when the old town of Dillon disappeared under the aforementioned lake.

Other popular choices are the **Pub Down Under,** underneath the Arapahoe Cafe in Dillon, or the **Corona St. Grill,** in the Dillon Town Center. For a smoky, low-key locals' hangout with pool and darts, try the **Virgin Islands Lounge** in the Summit Place Shopping Center on the Dillon-Silverthorne border.

Child care

Services of the Summit, Inc. (668-0255) in Frisco has professional babysitters aged 18–65 who are insured, bonded and child-care trained. They will come to your hotel or condo anywhere in the county. **Baby's Away** (800-571-0077) rents and will deliver baby needs to your lodge, such as crib, stroller, car seat and toys.

Other activities

Shopping and services: Pack an extra suitcase. Better yet, buy a bag at one of the four luggage stores in the **Silverthorne Factory Stores.** Then start filling it with bargains at nearly 80 brand-name stores. This is probably the largest factory outlet center in Western ski country. Among the stores are Carole Little, Anne Klein, Liz Claiborne, Levi, Nike, Great Outdoor Clothing Co., Pfaltzgraff, Dansk, Corning/Revere, Bass Shoes, Capezio Shoes, American Tourister and Samsonite.

Collectibles and antiques lovers will go nuts at **Junk-Tique,** 313 Main St. in Frisco. It has an excellent inventory of collectible housewares, clothing and furniture at very attractive prices. The store also stocks some new jewelry and knickknack items. Kids will love the huge black locomotive that is the centerpiece of the store. Cigar lovers can stop by **Antler's Liquor Store** in Frisco, which has what the owner claims is the largest humidor room in Colorado.

Companies that offer **snowmobiling** and/or **sleigh and dogsled rides** are Tiger Run Tours, 453-2231; Good Times Tours, 453-7604; and Two Below Zero Dinner Sleigh Rides, 453-1520. In the Dillon/Silverthorne area, call Eagles Nest Equestrian Center, 468-0677.

Cross-country skiing is available at the Frisco Nordic Center on Highway 9 about one mile out of town toward Breckenridge. Trail passes are less than $10, with discounts for those aged 55 and older or 12 and younger. Rentals and instruction are available. Call 668-0866.

Getting there and getting around

By air and car: Frisco, Dillon and Silverthorne are just off I-70, about 75 miles west of downtown Denver. Resort Express vans transport from Denver International Airport, (800) 334-7433 or (970) 468-7600. The airport is about two hours away.

Getting around: Frisco is laid out nicely for walking along Main Street or you can take the free Frisco Flyer from 7 a.m. to 7 p.m. Otherwise, take the Summit Stage, the free bus system that links the towns with each other and the ski areas. Ridge Taxi (453-TAXI) operates into the wee hours if you miss the bus.

A car is an option here; most distances are too far for walking, but the Summit Stage is reliable. Call 668-0999 for route info, or pick up a route map and schedule from the Chamber of Commerce or the stores that carry them. If you really enjoy nightlife and want to do extensive exploration of the restaurants and bars, we recommend a car. For car rental once you get to Summit County, call Michael Tamborello at Summit Car Rental (970-453-8212 or 888-677-1949).

Breckenridge

Colorado

Summit elevation: 12,146 feet
Vertical drop: 2,546 feet
Base elevation: 9,600 feet

Address: Box 1058
Breckenridge, CO 80435
✆ **Area code:** 970
Ski area phone: 453-5000 or
(800) 784-7669
Snow report: 453-6118
ⓘ **Toll-free reservations:**
(800) 221-1091; (800) 800-BREC
Toll-free foreign fax numbers:
UK: 0800-96-0055
Brazil: 000811-715-5559
Germany: 0130-82-7807
Netherlands: 06-022-6653
Fax: 453-7238
E-mail: eagle@vailresorts.com (ski area) or
cenres@brecknet.com (lodging)
Internet:
http://www.breckenridge.snow.com (ski area)
or http://www.gobreck.com (visitors' bureau)

Expert:★★★★
Advanced:★★★★★
Intermediate:★★★★
Beginner:★★★★
Never-ever:★★★★
Number and types of lifts: 22–6 high-speed
quads, 1 triple, 7 doubles and 8 surface lifts
Skiable acreage: 2,043 acres
Snowmaking: 25 percent (504 acres)
Uphill capacity: 30,625 per hour
Snowboarding: Yes, unlimited
Bed base: 23,000+
Nearest lodging: slopeside
Resort child care: Yes, 2 months and older
Adult ticket, per day: $27–$51 (98/99 prices)

Dining:★★★
Apres-ski/nightlife:★★★★
Other activities:★★★

Breckenridge has become one of the snow sports industry's giants, attracting more than a million visits each season. A good number are what is called Front Range skiers, who live in Denver and its suburbs. Another large portion are destination skiers from the U.S. And a third fast-growing group are skiers from Great Britain, Mexico and other countries.

Breckenridge has a split personality, but it's been that way from the beginning. It was named for a man who became a Confederate brigadier general, but its streets are named for Union heroes—Lincoln, Grant and Sherman. The Victorian buildings lining the streets witnessed wild revelry during gold and silver booms and the discovery of Colorado's largest gold nugget—the 13-pound "Tom's Baby" in 1887 — but they also stood silent over windswept, vacant streets when Breckenridge joined the list of Colorado ghost towns.

Though the closest Breckenridge comes to being a ghost town these days is the mud season in May, it still displays its inherited division. Modern architecture around the base area is a contrast to the Victorian downtown, which houses hundreds of boutiques, scores of pubs and dozens of restaurants packed into brightly colored restored 19th-century buildings in one of Colorado's largest historic districts.

Because Breckenridge is so close to Denver, weekend skiers stream into the town, packing lift lines. With the purchase of this resort by Vail Resorts, Inc., look for some major capital improvements on the mountain (more high-speed quads, for instance) during the next few years—something the previous owners promised but never delivered. Some improvements were made last season, such as two high-speed quads and snowmaking on Peak 8.

You'll find your fellow skiers and snowboarders are a mixed bag. Though the general atmosphere is still more down-to-earth than at some other Colorado resorts, Breckenridge also attracts society's upper crust. New shops and restaurants tend to cater to the upscale crowd; now, with Vail's ownership, this trend probably will continue. Restaurant and ski-area workers remain as friendly as ever, and long-time Breckenridge locals still retain much of the devil-may-care attitude of their 19th-century predecessors, which helps balance out any stuffiness that the tourists may bring with them. For now, the Breckenridge crowd is not as free-spending as that of Aspen or Vail, nor as laid back as Crested Butte. It's middle-of-the-road and comfortable with plenty of great skiing.

New for 98/99: A big new mid-mountain restaurant, Ten-Mile Station, will open this season. It's between Peak 9's Beaver Run high-speed quad and Peak 10's Falcon high-speed quad. The resort also made major improvements to The Great Divide Hotel, formerly the Breckenridge Hilton.

Mountain layout

Breckenridge encompasses four interconnected mountains covering 2,031 acres. Skiers and boarders can load lifts from four base areas: the Quicksilver high-speed quad from The Village at the bottom of Peak 9 (the most crowded of all in the morning); the Super Chair at Beaver Run, also on Peak 9; the Colorado SuperChair at Peak 8 (this was the original ski area that opened in 1961); and the Snowflake, a new double chair off Four O'Clock Road that accesses Peaks 9 and 10 on the left and Peaks 8 and 7 on the right. Free shuttles to these lifts run continuously from town. (Note: A close-in pay lot at Peak 8 fills by 9:30 a.m. most days.)

◆◆ **Expert:** Years ago Breckenridge was known as an excellent beginner and intermediate resort, but the opening of the bowls of Peak 8, the North Face of Peak 9, and Peaks 7 and 10 added hundreds of acres of expert, steep terrain. Today, Breckenridge boasts a very high percentage of black-diamond terrain (60 percent overall) and some of the highest inbounds skiing in North America, but still maintains its wide-open well-groomed runs for beginners and intermediates.

Imperial Bowl, crowning Peak 8, tops out at nearly 13,000 feet, creating a total vertical that's only two feet shy of 3,400. If you noticed that our statistics show a much smaller vertical, it's because we list the highest *lift-served* terrain. Imperial Bowl is in bounds but not lift-served. If you want to ski it, you must hike first. Same with the highest bowls on Peak 7. You can ski from the 12,677-foot summit, but only if you hoof it to the top. Locals love it; visitors from sea level often pass up the opportunity to ski some of the best snow in the country (which is another reason why the locals love it).

The North Face on the back of Peak 9 is expert territory. Plenty of good skiers have begged for a rest after playing with Tom's Baby, and even prayers won't help lower intermediates who accidentally find themselves in Hades, Devil's Crotch or Inferno—once you drop down the face from Chair E, there is no escape.

◆ **Advanced:** Peak 10 is evenly split between black and blue runs. In the black-diamond category you'll find Mustang, Dark Rider and Blackhawk boasting monstrous bumps.

Telephone area code: 970

Cimarron, marked black on the map, often is groomed. The Burn, dropping to the left of the high-speed lift, offers limited short-but-sweet tree skiing.

■ **Intermediate:** For the best cruising, head to Peak 10 and alternate between Centennial and Crystal. Runs here are slightly easier than those on Peak 9, but the pairing of a high-speed lift and mostly expert-marked terrain keeps crowds down.

On Peak 9, intermediates should take Lift B to the summit and ski down Cashier, Bonanza and Upper Columbia. More advanced intermediates enjoy American, Gold King and Peerless, which might be rated black at a smaller resort.

Peak 8 offers great intermediate terrain alongside the high-speed Colorado lift down Springmeier, Crescendo and Swinger; if those feel good, try the black-diamond slopes in this area, such as Callie's and Rounders.

●● **Beginner:** Peak 9 has the best trails for beginners who have had a little experience (stick to the Quicksilver lift; the Beaver Run lift will take you higher to intermediate terrain).

● **Never-ever:** Peak 8 has the best terrain for a first ski or snowboard day.

Mountain rating

Breckenridge has many ingredients for the perfect winter vacation: lots of good terrain for all levels, plenty of slopeside lodging and a charming town. It's urban enough to have a good variety of restaurants and shops, yet not so urban that you'll feel as if you never left home. And if you don't find enough here to keep you busy, Copper Mountain and Keystone are nearby.

Snowboarding

This was one of the first major resorts to allow snowboarding. It has rentals, lessons, special clinics and a halfpipe and terrain park on the Gold King Run on Peak 9.

There is a wonderful snowboard terrain garden and an Olympic-specification halfpipe on Peak 9. This season the resort has added another snowboard terrain on Peak 8 on the Freeway trail. A new Pipe Dragon grooming machine will be keeping the terrain gardens tuned up. The snowboard school has been grouped into "learning zones."

Beginning snowboarding lesson including a lift ticket is $59. All other level teens (13–17) pay $46 a day; adults (18+), $50.

Cross-country

The **Breckenridge Nordic Ski Center** (453-6855), near Peak 8 base on Ski Hill Road, has 28 km. of double-set trails for all abilities. Trail passes also are valid at the Frisco Nordic Center. Equipment rentals, lessons, and guided backcountry tours are available. You can also rent snowshoes.

Lessons (98/99 prices)

Group lessons: Adults, $50 for a full day (five hours), $42 a half day; teens (13–17), $46 for a full day, $38 for a half day; children (3–12), $62 for a full day and $54 for a half day.

Never-ever package: None. Lessons, lifts and rentals must all be purchased separately.

Private lessons: $80 per hour; multihour discounts available.

Special programs: Many, including daily programs and multiday programs offered a few times a season. Among the topics are women's clinics, racing, telemark lessons, bumps, 50-plus age group, and lessons for disabled skiers.

Women's seminars are available January 22–24, February 5–7 or 25–27, and March 11–13. The cost is $385 and includes three days of lunch, video analysis, a group dinner, wine and cheese party, and a guest speaker.

The Women's Workshop series offers a single full day of instruction each week for three weeks starting December 4th, 11th and 18th. Cost is $150 including video analysis, instruction and lunches.

A 50-Plus program takes place February 3–4 or 24–25 and March 10–11. This program costs $195 and includes lift tickets, instruction, video analysis and a group dinner. A special Over the Hill Gang seminar takes place February 15–18 and costs $370.

Racing: NASTAR and self-timed courses are set up on Country Boy on Peak 9. NASTAR fees are $6 for two runs and $1 for additional runs. The self-timed course is $1 a run.

Children's lessons: These operate from two children's centers at the bases of Peak 8 and Peak 9. Ski instruction starts at age 3 with a special ski-school morning program and afternoon care for $62 (morning only lessons without care is $54).

Ages 4 and 5 also have a combination of ski lessons and day care. Half day (no rentals) is $54; all day is $62 (with lunch). Kids this age ride the lifts for free.

Children 6–9 have their own classes for $62 a full day, and $54 a half day. Lift ticket is extra. Ages 10–13 also have their own classes at the same price as ages 6–9.

Child care (98/99 prices)

Ages: 2 months to 6 years (first grade) at the Peak 8 Children's Center; ages 3 to 6 years at the Peak 9 or Peak 8 centers.

Costs: $62 a full day, $52 a half day. Parents must provide diapers, formula, change of clothes, and so forth for infants. Child care for 3- to 5-year-olds (must be toilet-trained) includes a snow play program to build snowmen, go sledding and do other outdoor activities. Full day programs include lunch.

Reservations: Required; call (800) 789-7669 well in advance.

Other options: Another possibility for child care and instruction is **Kinderhut** (800-541-8779 or 970-453-0379) a privately owned children's ski school and licensed day-care center. It accepts children 6 weeks to 6 years. **Baby's Away** (800-571-0077; Web site: http://www.csd.net/~babyaway) rents and will deliver baby needs to your lodge, such as crib, stroller, car seat and toys. This Breckenridge-based company has several locations in resort communities, and we've listed them in each appropriate chapter.

Lift tickets (98/99 prices)

	Adult	Child (5-12)
One day	$49	$19
Three days	$132 ($44/day)	$57 ($19/day)
Five of six days	$210 ($42/day)	$95 ($19/day)

Who skis free: Ages 4 and younger and 70 and older.
Who skis at a discount: Ages 65–69 pay $30 per day.

Note: These are "off-peak" prices. Peak season is Dec. 26 to January 2 and March 13–27. During those times, tickets are a couple of dollars more per day. Any ticket may be used at Breckenridge or Keystone. With a three-day ticket, one day may be exchanged for a day at Vail or Beaver Creek; two days may be exchanged on a five-day ticket. Lift tickets are only $27 for adults and $15 for kids before Thanksgiving and April 11–17, then only $19 through the end of the season.

Accommodations

Breckenridge boasts extensive ski-in/ski-out lodging, and an assortment of B&Bs and private chalets, both in town and in the woods. Most lodging is moderately priced, but luxury and dorm rooms are available for those on both ends of the affordability spectrum. Early December, January and April-May are the most affordable times. Breckenridge's lifts keep running into May some years, but one caveat: many of the town's shops and restaurants start closing down at the end of April. Some restaurants that do stay open offer two-for-one meals.

Double rooms in all these accommodations are about $130-$225 depending on the time of the season and the lodge you select. **Breckenridge Central Reservations** (phone numbers and e-mail addresses are in the stat box on this chapter's lead page) handles 98 percent of the resort's lodging. It's your best starting point, though we also give you individual phone numbers in case you know the lodge you want to stay at.

The Village at Breckenridge (800-800-7829; 970-453-2000) surrounds the Peak 9 base area. Try to get into Plaza 1, 2 or 3, which are the most spacious units. The three-bedroom units here are giant. Many amenities are available: on-site health club facilities, indoor/outdoor pools, hot tubs, racquetball, steam, sauna and exercise room.

Beaver Run Resort and Conference Center (reservations and information: 800-525-2253; 453-6000). This complex is slopeside on Peak 9. It has restaurants, outdoor hot tubs, indoor/outdoor swimming pools, a giant indoor miniature golf course and a great game room for kids. The Kinderhut child-care center, in the hotel, will take children from the ages of 1 to 3; kids 3 to 6 can take ski lessons.

You won't recognize the old Hilton, now called **The Great Divide Lodge** (800-321-8444; Denver: 303-825-3800; local: 453-4500). New owners, Vail Resorts, poured $4 million into remodeling each guest room, the entire lobby and pool/spa area—a remodel that is looking like four-star material. But they kept one of its best amenities—it's only 50 yards from the slopes.

The River Mountain Lodge (800-325-2342; UK direct 0800-897-497; local 453-4121) This group of studio to four-bedroom suites is in the heart of town, only steps away from Main Street. The ski bus stops across the street. This is one of the town's most reasonable accommodations.

Distinctive inns have found an instant audience with guests who appreciate the genteel side of Breckenridge. Four such places—specifically built as B&B accommodations—range in price from $95–$250 per night. All are within walking distance of town, on the ski bus route, wheelchair accessible and do not permit smoking or pets.

The Wellington Inn (800-655-7557 or 453-9464) at 200 N. Main St. captures Victorian romance in its four spacious and beautifully decorated rooms. All have outside decks and bathrooms with spa-jet tubs. A German restaurant on the main floor serves lunch and dinner. One drawback: its Main Street location is not for light sleepers.

Hunt Placer Inn (800-472-1430 or 453-7573) off Ski Hill Road near Peak 8 is named for the gold mining claim on the property. The decor in its eight rooms (all with balconies, three with fireplaces) evokes various times and places in history.

Little Mountain Lodge (800-468-7707 or 453-1969) is anything but little. This white-washed log home has an intimate staying-at-a-friend's-home feeling. Innkeepers Lynn and Truman Esmond add nice touches, such as placing a silver tray of coffee and tea at each guest-room door (there are 10) a half hour before breakfast.

Allaire Timbers Inn (800-624-4904 outside Colorado; 453-7530) at 9511 Hwy. 9/South Main St. has great views. Hosts Jack and Kathy Humph are very hospitable. Each of the eight guest room and two suites—all named after Colorado mountain passes—have private decks.

Several 19th-century homes in town have been converted into B&Bs: **Evans House** (453-5509; request the Colorado Room), **Bed & Breckfast** (formerly The Williams House, 800-795-2975), **Fireside Inn** (453-6456), **Ridge Street Inn** (800-452-4680 or 453-4680), **Swiss Inn** (453-6489) and **The Walker House** (453-2426).

The Lodge and Spa at Breckenridge (800-736-1607, 970-453-9300) underwent an extensive remodeling for its inclusion in the distinguished Small Luxury Hotels of the World by spring of 1998. The hotel—which perches on a cliff at 10,200 feet with a magnificent view of the Breckenridge mountain range—houses Summit County's only full-service spa.

 **Dining**

At one time in the not-too-distant past, Breckenridge didn't have many restaurants that would set a Michelin scout's tongue to quivering, Breckenridge gradually is emerging from the dining doldrums. With more people with discriminating tastes building fabulous homes and vacationing from over-seas, we expect the trend to continue.

For now, **Pierre's Riverwalk Cafe** (453-0989), 137 S. Main, stands alone in the field of excellent and expensive restaurants (entrées $18-$29). Owner/chef Pierre Luc prepares French dishes with a California twist, consisting mostly of fish and game delicacies such as ostrich, pheasant and rabbit. Desserts are deliciously French.

Top of the World Restaurant (453-9300) in the Lodge and Spa at Breckenridge prom-ises to rival Pierre's with an enticing fine-dining menu created by a nationally acclaimed chef, Ken Frank, and an expensive vintage wine list.

Cafe Alpine (453-8218), 103 E. Adams St., has an eclectic mix of cultural entrées, such as Greek spanekopeta, Thai curried pork, Italian tortelloni, American trout and Spanish tapas. This Victorian-home-turned-restaurant is a consistent winner in The Taste of Breckenridge annual contest. Prices are reasonable.

The Swiss Haven (453-6969), 325 S. Main, has melt-in-your-mouth cheese fondues, raclette, Fondue Chinois, and four types of rösti (a potato dish). Plan to spend the evening and linger over a cappuccino-and-kirsch (or two). As in Europe, they won't bring the bill until you ask for it, which can be pricey ($20+) if you order soup, salad and the homemade apple tart.

The Hearthstone (453-7028), 130 S. Ridge Street, is in a stunning blue-and-white Vic-torian house that has undergone many facelifts over the years. The Old-World ambiance, moderately priced selection of meat, chicken and seafood and the killer desserts make this a very popular spot with locals and visitors. The old **Brown Hotel** (453-0084), 208 S. Ridge, is another historic site that's heavy on atmosphere and light on the wallet.

Other mid-priced recommendations on Main Street: **The St. Bernard Inn** (453-2572); **Poirrier's Cajun Cafe** (453-1877); **Adams Street Grill** (453-4700) for Southwest American food; or **Blue River Bistro** (453-6974). For traditional Mexican and great margaritas, head for **Mi Casa** (453-2071), 600 S. Park Ave. Other ethnic dining options are **Ghandi** for Indian, **Red Orchid** for Chinese; and **Sushi Breck** for Japanese. **Noodle & Bean's** (453-8966), on the river bank, is a delightful new gourmet vegetarian eatery with a super friendly staff.

Some suggestions for good cheap eats (less than $10):

Beer lovers should try the **Breckenridge Brewery** (453-1550), 600 S. Main St. The menu has good variety, and the micro-brewed beer is excellent. Or try **Rasta Pasta** (453-7467) for whimsical Jamaican-flavored pasta, **Giampietro Pizzeria & Pasta** (453-3838); **Bubba's Bones BBQ** (547-9942) and **Fatty's Pizzeria** (453-9802), a town favorite since 1975.

Breakfast: The hands-down winner is **The Prospector** (453-6858) at 130 S. Main Street. The Huevos Rancheros will test your facial sweat glands. A pancake's width behind is **The Blue Moose** (453-4859), 540 S. Main St., for its egg specialties. Healthy eaters flock to **Love Bagels** (547-1115). For lighter fare and gourmet coffee, try **Mountain Java** (453-1874) upstairs at 118 Ridge St. or **Clint's** (453-1736), 131 S. Main St. The best bargain breakfast is at the **Copper Top** in Beaver Run.

 ## Après-ski/nightlife

Breckenridge's liveliest après-ski bars are **Tiffany's** and **Copper Top** in Beaver Run, the **Village Pub** in the Bell Tower Mall, and **Mi Casa**, with great margaritas by the liter.

Tiffany's at Beaver Run rocks until the wee hours, but after dinner most of the action moves into town. **Downstairs at Eric's**, 109 Main Street, and **The Underworld**, across the hall, have raucous younger crowds with loud live music and long lines on weekends. A slightly older group with plenty of locals gathers at **Shamus O'Toole's**, 115 S. Ridge Street, a wide-open roadhouse with live music on most evenings and an eclectic crowd, ranging from absolute blue-collar to those yuppied-up for the evening. Some nights the mix is intoxicating, and on others it's merely intoxicated, which often sets off fireworks. **Dirck's** youngish customers party to live music in a huge upstairs room on South Park Avenue.

The Alligator Lounge on Main Street has become the hot spot for live music and dancing, with an eclectic lineup of bands playing blues, jazz, funk and reggae, plus local musicians' nights, all in an unfinished-sheet-rock atmosphere. This places really rocks, so if you packed your dancin' shoes, head here.

For a non-dancing, quieter time, try the **St. Bernard** on Main Street; a cozy bar in the back is often packed with business-class locals; or **The Breckenridge Brewery & Pub,** which has live music specials, but in our experience, the atmosphere is pleasantly tame for chatting.

Salt Creek, 110 E. Lincoln, is the only Country & Western place in town, and a guaranteed good time. **The Dredge**, which is a replica of the dredge boats that churned the Blue River for gold in the early 1900s, has a classy bar.

The old **Gold Pan**, 103 N. Main Street, is the oldest continuously operating bar west of the Mississippi and was one of the wildest places in the Wild West, with a miner or two known to be thrown through the saloon doors. A long century-old mahogany bar presides over a now worn, dimly lit room with a pinball machine tucked into the back corner and a couple of well-utilized pool tables frequented by a crowd of truckers, pool sharks sporting earrings, and the temporarily unemployed.

A slightly more mature clientele gathers at the **Wine Cellar** below the Wellington Inn for brandy next to a roaring fire. If you don't mind the smoke, **Cecelia's Cigar Bar** makes great martinis and plays swing music.

Other activities

Exploring the old town of Breckenridge is great fun, either with a formal **historical tour** (435-9022) or on your own armed with a free guidesheet.

Shopping: Downtown has scores of boutiques, many replacing the T-shirt shops that used to dominate storefronts. Some of our favorites on Main Street: Adornments, Vintage West, LiftOff Sportswear, Alpen Collections, Tom Girl, The Sheepherder and Goods, all for clothing and accessories. Browse The Quiet Moose, 326 S. Main, even if you aren't furnishing a mountain home. Peek inside Creatures Great & Small if you're an animal lover.

Breckenridge isn't quite an art community like Aspen, but more and more collectors are discovering its galleries, six of them fine art. We recommend The Village Gallery, Ole Moon and Paint Horse Gallery (western); and Skilled Hands for handcrafted goods by Colorado artisans. Quandry Antiques is another fun browsing spot.

Breckenridge Nordic Ski Center (453-6855) near Peak 8 base on Ski Hill Road, has evening **horse-drawn sleigh rides** (with dinner). The Breckenridge Recreation Center (547-3125) on Airport Road north of town offers an array of indoor activities for non-ski days, such as **swimming, tennis, racquetball, wall climbing, exercise machines** and **basketball.** Also check the Summit County chapter for other activities. Breckenridge also has bloomed as a mecca for weddings, both summer and winter. For a wedding and honeymoon guide, call 453-6018.

Getting there and getting around

By air: Breckenridge is 98 miles west of Denver International Airport. Resort Express has regular vans connecting the resort with the airport. Telephone: (970) 468-7600 or (800) 334-7433.

By car: From Denver, take I-70 to Exit 203, then south on Highway 9.

Getting around: Nearly everything is within walking distance. The town trolley and buses cruise the streets regularly. The Summit Stage provides free transportation between Dillon, Silverthorne, Frisco, Breckenridge and Copper Mountain. Call 668-0999 for route information. Keystone and Breckenridge also operate a free inter-resort shuttle, the Ski KAB Express, at varying times according to demand. To check the schedule, call 496-4200. All transportation is free.

Keystone

Colorado

Summit elevation:	**11,980 feet**
Vertical drop:	**2,680 feet**
Base elevation:	**9,300 feet**

Address: Box 38, Keystone, CO 80435
✆ Area code: 970
Ski area phone: 496-2316
Snow report: 496-4111
ⓘ Toll-free reservations: (800) 404-3535
Toll-free foreign numbers:
UK (fax): 0800-89-6868
Germany (fax): 0130 82 0958
Netherlands (fax) 060 22 3972
Mexico (fax) 95-800-936-5633
Brazil: (fax) 000811-712-0553
Fax: (970) 496-4343
E-mail: eagle@vailresorts.com
Internet http://www.keystone.snow.com
Bed base: 5,000
Nearest lodging: walking distance
Resort child care: Yes, 2 months and older
Adult ticket, per day: $27–$51 (98/99 prices)

Number and types of lifts: 20–2 gondolas, 4 high-speed quads, 1 quad, 3 triples, 5 doubles, 5 surface lifts
Skiable acreage: 1,755 acres
Snowmaking: 49 percent
Uphill capacity: 27,273 skiers per hour
Snowboarding: Yes, unlimited

Expert:★★★★
Advanced:★★★★
Intermediate:★★★★★
Beginner:★★★★★
Never-ever:★★★

Dining:★★★★★
Apres-ski/nightlife:★★
Other activities:★★★

Many winter vacationers associate Colorado skiing with 19th-century Victorian mining-town charm. You won't find that here, because Keystone was built to be a smoothly humming community with buses shuttling to every corner, foot-of-the-mountain child care, the Rockies' largest snowmaking system and one-number central reservations. Keystone's employees also deliver Service—with a capital S and a smile. Even late in the season, when personnel at many resorts get snappy from too many long days, Keystone workers are cordial and helpful. The resort is perfect for families, couples or small groups of friends who want to spend time with each other.

Keystone is a superb intermediate playground, but it has good terrain at either end of the ability scale, too. It has one of the nation's best summit-to-base beginner runs (Schoolmarm), and advanced skiing on North Peak and The Outback.

Keystone now belongs to Vail Resorts, Inc., which made many improvements last season. Among the plans for 98/99 are a new high-speed quad to replace the Santiago lift, which will provide quick access to the bumps on North Peak; a mountaintop recreation area with tubing and access to cross country skiing; 80 acres of new terrain between Keystone Mountain and North Peak; terrain-park features on blue-square Jackwhacker; and a much-needed beginner-level trail leading to the base of River Run.

Mountain layout

Unlike other areas that have peaks side by side, Keystone has three peaks one behind another. In front is Keystone Mountain, with beginner and intermediate terrain. In back of that is North Peak, and finally, the Outback. Other than one snaking green-circle trail, these latter peaks have just blue and black terrain.

This unusual arrangement lends an exploratory quality to the day. As you get farther from the base area, the skiing feels a little wilder, a little more off-piste.

◆◆ **Expert:** Head to the farthest peak, the Outback. The 889-acre Outback is a mix of open-bowl skiing, natural chutes and tree-lined glades. The quartet of Timberwolf, Bushwacker, Badger and The Grizz are visible from North Peak and allow tree fans to pick how tight they want their forest to be. Two black-diamond bowls are accessible by a short uphill hike from the top of the Outback Express high-speed quad. (This in-bounds terrain tops out at 12,200 feet, giving Keystone a 2,900-foot vertical descent, slightly more than is listed in the stat box, where we list lift-served terrain.)

◆ **Advanced:** North Peak, the middle mountain, also has good advanced terrain, though it is generally tamer. From the top of Keystone Mountain, advanced skiers and snowboarders can reach the North Peak base down Mineshaft or Diamond Back. North Peak is a great spot for working on technique and steeps. Star Fire, rated blue, is a superb steep, groomed run, and a good warmup for this area. Black diamonds that plunge off this run are Ambush, Powder Cap or Bullet. On the other side of the lift, Cat Dancer and Geronimo offer a challenge, and experts can break their own tracks through the trees directly beneath the Santiago lift, which serves this area and which will be upgraded to a high-speed quad.

On Keystone Mountain, there's only one section that develops pitch—Go Devil and The Slot, which drop down the far right edge of the area as you look at the trail map.

■ **Intermediate:** This level has the run of the three sections, with appropriate terrain on each. Keystone Mountain has runs such as Paymaster, the Wild Irishman, Frenchman and Flying Dutchman that play with God-given terrain. The twists and natural steps on these cruisers represent a trail at its best—they obviously did not have their character bulldozed out of them. Snowmaking covers 100 percent of the trails, and the slope grooming ranks among the best in the country. The Mountain House base area has three chair lifts taking skiers up the mountain, and the other base area, River Run, is the lower station of the River Run Gondola. The gondola serves the night-skiing area until 9 p.m. The resort says it's the largest single-mountain night ski operation in the United States, covering 17 runs.

Intermediates also can head to North Peak down Mozart, a wide blue run. Its width is essential, because it's the main pathway to the two rear peaks. On North Peak, Prospector and Last Alamo are the easier of the blues, with Star Fire a good test for the Outback. If you think Star Fire is fun, not scary, head down Anticipation or Spillway to the Outback and play on the intermediate runs under the Outback Express chair. The advanced intermediate glades to the far right of the map—Wolverine, Wildfire and Pika—are not as tough as the glades of the Black Forest, but also not a spot for timid intermediates.

●● **Beginner:** Stay on Keystone Mountain. Trails cutting across the mountain are principally for beginners. You can take most of them traversing from the top of the Peru Chair, or take Schoolmarm along the ridge and drop down Silver Spoon or Last Chance. You can—and you should—ride the Outpost gondola to the gorgeous Outpost Lodge on North Peak. There, you can try Fox Trot, a gentle trail. If you're up for a blue, head down on Prospector and

Mozart for the ride to the Keystone Mountain summit; otherwise, ride the Outpost gondola back to Keystone Mountain.

Keystone has plans for 98/99 to cut a beginner trail to the River Run area. If this was completed, ignore this paragraph and take that trail to get back to River Run. But if the project was delayed, you're staying at River Run and you're still a tentative skier, do one of two things to get home: either ride the River Run Gondola down to the base, or take Schoolmarm to the Mountain House base and ride the free bus to River Run. The last portion of the River Run intermediate trail—up to now the only route to the base—is an absolute madhouse at the end of the day. At the bottom, everyone (gondola riders, too) must walk down a slippery pathway in ski boots while toting his or her equipment. Intermediates will have a tough enough time with this run; we wouldn't wish this experience on any beginner.

● **Never-ever:** Last season, Keystone added a learning center at the top of the Diamond Back trail on Keystone Mountain, with two learning runs and a triple chairlift. Keystone Mountain also has plenty of gentle terrain to practice on.

Nearby **Arapahoe Basin**, long a legend with die-hard skiers, is a good side trip while you're at Keystone. Though Vail Resorts doesn't own A-Basin, it has arranged for Keystone/ Breckenridge lift tickets to be valid at A-Basin, too. You'll find brief information on A-Basin in the Regional Getaway chapter in the back of this book.

Mountain rating

These mountains divide easily into categories, with some exceptions as noted above. Keystone is great beginner and cruising terrain. North Peak is for advanced skiers with expert tendencies. The Outback is for upper intermediates and experts.

Snowboarding

Keystone now allows snowboarding on all runs, and has added several snowboarding features in Packsaddle Bowl—Area 51, a 20-acre terrain park; and two halfpipes. All are serviced by the Packsaddle II lift, and the terrain park is lit for night-snowboarding. The resort also has a special learning area for boarders, and offers clinics and rentals.

Keystone has extensive snowboarding lessons. Beginners pay $67 for a ful day lesson. The more experienced pay $79 for the full day that includes rentals as well.

Cross-country

Keystone has an extensive cross-country touring area, with 18 km. of groomed trails around the resort, and an additional 57 km. of ungroomed backcountry skiing trails to ghost mining towns in the Montezuma area. Lessons and rentals are available from the touring center (496-4275).

Cross-country activities include moonlight tours. Snowshoe rentals also are available.

Lessons (98/99 prices)

Group lessons: These meet daily at 10:30 a.m. and 1:30 p.m. for a 2.5-hour session. An intermediate instruction, called "Parallel Breakthrough," costs $85 for 2.5 hours with lifts and rentals. Advanced skiers can take "Mountain Masters" for a full day for $50 ($91 with lifts and $107 with lift and rentals).

Never-ever package: A 2.5-hour lesson, lift ticket and equipment rental is $63 for skiing. An adult snowboard lesson-lift-rental package is $80.

Private lessons: $85 for one hour, $120 for 90 minutes, $155 for two hours, $230 three hours, and $360 for six hours.

Special programs: Clinics are held for women skiers, upper-intermediate to advanced skiers who want to crossover to snowboarding, snowboarders who want to learn halfpipe freestyle jumps, and more. Most are $50 for a 2.5-hour lesson. The Mahre Training Centers are held here exclusively. These are five- and three-day sessions conducted in part by either Phil or Steve Mahre, Olympic medal winners. The skiing, for all levels, teaches fundamentals. Evening classroom sessions review on-slope activities and techniques, and one of the Mahre brothers is available to answer questions. The three-day program is $375 and the five-day program costs $600. Both include six hours of instruction daily, video, races and time for fun. Lodging and lifts are not included. The Mahre programs run in December and January.

Racing: NASTAR racing, clinics and a self-timed course are located on Keystone Mountain.

Children's lessons: The programs for ages 4–kindergarten include rental equipment, lift ticket, lesson and lunch for a full-day rate of $76; half-day, $65. Keystone puts a big emphasis on families and children's lessons. It has parts of the mountain that are designated Children Only, and they try to keep classes small, usually no more than five students.

For ski school, call (800) 255-3715; at the resort, 496-4170.

Child care (98/99 prices)

Ages: 2 months and older. (Keystone doesn't specify an upper age limit, but most kids older than 6 or 7 want to be on the mountain.)

Costs: Child care is $59 for a full day and $49 for a half day, either morning or afternoon. Both include lunch. Children age 3 and older get outdoor snow play as part of the fun. Babysitting at night costs $8 per hour.

Reservations: Required; call 496-4182 or (800) 255-3715.

Other options: Baby's Away (800-571-0077) rents and will deliver baby needs to your lodge, such as crib, stroller, car seat and toys.

Lift tickets (98/99 prices)

	Adult	Child (5-12)
One day	$49	$19
Three days	$132 ($44/day)	$57 ($19/day)
Five of six days	$210 ($42/day)	$95 ($19/day)

Who skis free: Ages 4 and younger and 70 and older.

Who skis at a discount: Ages 65–69 pay $30 per day.

Note: These are "off-peak" prices. Peak season is Dec. 26 to January 2 and March 13–27. During those times, tickets are a couple of dollars more per day. Any ticket may be used at Breckenridge or Keystone. With a three-day ticket, one day may be exchanged for a day at Vail or Beaver Creek; two days may be exchanged on a five-day ticket. Lift tickets are only $27 for adults and $15 for kids before Thanksgiving and April 11–17, then only $19 through the end of the season. Keystone's season is one of the longest in the country, and it strives to be the first resort in Colorado to open for the season, often in October.

Keystone also has one of the largest night-skiing operations in the country. Prices are $38 from noon to 9 p.m., $35 from 2–9 p.m., $29 for 4–9 p.m. and $21 for 6–9 p.m. If you buy a full day ticket, night skiing is also included.

 ## Accommodations

Vail Resorts Central Reservations (800-404-3535) can book lodging and arrange for air transportation, lift tickets and other needs. Keystone is mostly a condominium community, but it also has two hotels and a quaint mountain inn. Unless you're booking very early or late in the season, room or condo rates start at about $200 per night. Midweek discounts bring the price down a bit, too.

One hotel is the modern **Keystone Lodge**, which also houses the main restaurants and conference rooms for business meetings. The Lodge underwent major renovation recently, including enlarged bathrooms with upscale fixtures, and telephones with dual data ports. Another hotel is **The Inn**, with 103 rooms within walking distance of Keystone Mountain.

The quaint **Ski Tip Lodge**, which was a stagecoach stop in the late 1800s, is a near-perfect ski lodge. Rooms are rustic (in the best sense of the word) with true ski history, the dining room elegant and the sitting room warm and inviting. The Ski Tip Lodge rents rooms with breakfast included. Private rooms have baths, and the dorm rooms share one. The rooms are not huge but are comfortable and the food is very good. Private rooms in regular season are approximately $210 per person a night; dorm rooms cost roughly $75 per person a night.

Keystone divides its **rental condominiums** into six "neighborhoods," with each group having a central swimming pool, shops and restaurants, and serviced by excellent shuttle-bus access. Generally, the closer the condo group is to the lifts, the nicer it is and the more interior amenities it has.

The newest lodging at Keystone is in the attractive **River Run area**, which is walking distance from the River Run Gondola. The condos are spacious and convenient to the slopes and the best shopping in Keystone.

Slopeside condominiums are virtually ski-in/ski-out—they are right across the street from the Keystone Mountain Base Area. The **Chateaux d'Mont** condos are spectacular, luxurious and worth every penny. We strongly recommend trying to get one of these units. Farther from the slopes, **The St. John** units have spectacular views and were built with just about every amenity. We also highly recommend the **Pines** condominiums.

Kids ages 12 and younger stay free with their parents, provided minimum occupancy is met and maximum occupancy not exceeded.

 ## Dining

Keystone's fine dining does not have the widespread reputation that other Colorado resorts such as Aspen or Crested Butte have, but it should. Let us be at the head of the parade on spreading the word. Keystone has three dining experiences not to be missed—**The Keystone Ranch**, the **Ski Tip Lodge** and the **Alpenglow Stube**, the latter perched at 11,444 feet at the top of North Peak.

All are sophisticated gourmet restaurants in charming settings, perfect for romantic dinners or groups of adults (and not at all suitable for noisy young children). The chefs at each have a friendly rivalry, which helps to keep the standards high. Save room for dessert and appetizers.

All require reservations, which you can make before leaving home by calling the activities/dining toll-free number, (800) 354-4386 (354-4FUN). If you're staying at a resort property, dial extension 4FUN (4386). If you're staying elsewhere in Summit County, call 496-4386 for all but the Ski Tip Lodge, which is 496-4202. Use these numbers for all the restaurants we list here.

The **Keystone Ranch** is a restored log ranch house, built in the 1930s as a wedding present to Bernardine Smith and Howard Reynolds. Reportedly, the only completely original part of the house is the fireplace, yet you feel as if you are dining at the home of an intimate friend. Chef David Welch prepares American regional cuisine with Rocky Mountain indigenous ingredients—piñon-encrusted lamb or elk with wild mushrooms, for instance.

The **Ski Tip Lodge** (reservations: 496-4202) exudes a homey, rustic flavor. It was an 1800s stagecoach stop turned private residence for Arapahoe Basin founders Max and Edna Dercum. Chef Mark Martin follows that country inn theme in his elegant but down-home menu. The lodge serves a prix-fixe four-course meal for adults and a three-course meal for children age 12 and younger.

The **Alpenglow Stube** is located in The Outpost, which features rough-hewn timbers, massive fireplaces, vaulted ceilings and expansive windows. It is reached by a ride on the River Run and Outpost gondolas. The restaurant, a large but cozy room that looks as if Martha Stewart's Swiss cousin were the decorator, features a six-course menu (for a fixed price of about $75 per person) of such non-traditional skiing fare as wood-grilled salmon, grilled wild game and slow-roasted duck. Ask to sit at the chefs' counter; only eight people get to do it each seating. You'll see the chefs preparing the meal on open grills, get to taste dishes they're working on for future menus, and receive a little more attention than the other diners. Chefs Chris Rybak and Chris Wyant do an incredible job, even more so when you realize that every bit of fresh food on your plate was transported via gondola or snowcat.

You say your kids want to ride the gondolas for dinner, too? Take the family to **Der Fondue Chessel,** also at The Outpost. Ride the gondola to the top of North Peak and then enjoy fondue, raclette and wine by candlelight with music by a Bavarian band.

In the Keystone Lodge, the **Garden Room** offers fanciful gourmet fare. However, the setting is a notch below the impeccable level of the Ski Tip Lodge, Keystone Ranch and Alpenglow Stube. It's convenient, but for our money, we'd book reservations at one of the latter three.

Keystone Village and River Run have several restaurants for more casual dining, such as **Kickapoo Tavern** at the River Run base; **Out-of-Bounds Restaurant and Sports Bar**, in Keystone Village; **The Bighorn**, in Keystone Lodge; or **RazzBerrys**, in the Keystone Inn, serving grilled items and pastas. For truly casual dining, we got a tasty individual-sized pizza and a draught beer sitting at the bar in the **Snake River Saloon.**

New to Keystone is **Su Casa** (262-9185), which serves the same high-quality Mexican dishes as its sister restaurant, Mi Casa in Breckenridge.

Après-ski/nightlife

Keystone's nightlife is limited, at least in the categories of leaning on a bar, knocking back a few brews and dancing.

The best bet for a good night out dancing and meeting the other nightlife denizens is **Out-of-Bounds** or **Bandito's**. Across the highway from Bandito's you will find the **Snake River Saloon**, which has good action with a slightly older crowd. **Keysters** in River Run Plaza offers karaoke.

For immediate après-ski activity, try the **Last Lift Bar** in the Mountain House at Keystone Mountain base or the **Snake River Saloon**. **Tenderfoot Lounge,** in Keystone Lodge, has piano entertainment and a 15-foot fireplace. Locals give high marks to après-ski at **China Café.** At River Run, **Kickapoo Tavern** draws a crowd on its patio on sunny days, and inside on snowy ones.

Other activities

Shopping: You'll find a few of the standard souvenir and T-shirt shops in Keystone Village, but nothing memorable. River Run has some very good shops, mostly selling upscale costume jewelry, Native American pottery and crafts, and elegant clothing. Nearby good shopping is in Breckenridge or the Silverthorne Factory Stores.

If you aspire to be a gourmet chef in your home kitchen, sign up for the Thursday night **cooking class** taught by the Keystone Conference Center chef Bob Burden. Students, no more than 20 per class, help to prepare a six-course meal in the conference center kitchen. While Burden explains how it's done, students at the Keystone Culinary Institute assist. The meal and the instruction cost $50 per person—after you've cooked, you get to eat take home the recipes.

Keystone has a good **athletic club** with two indoor tennis courts.

Sleigh rides to the Soda Creek Homestead include a dinner with all the fixins. Call (800) 354-4386 or (970) 496-4386.

Ice skating in the middle of Keystone Village is open every day and night. The outdoor lake, reportedly the largest maintained outdoor skating lake in North America, is smoothed twice a day. Fees are $6 for adults, $5 for ages 13-17, $3.50 for children 5–12, and $1 for 4 and younger, not including skate rental.

Getting there and getting around

By air: Keystone is 90 miles from Denver International Airport via I-70. Transportation between the airport and the resort can be booked with the central reservations number, (800) 404-3535. Several ground transportation companies provide connections from the airport to the resort. Ask when you book your trip, or check in with one of the companies when you arrive in Denver.

By car: Take I-70 west from Denver, through the Eisenhower Tunnel, to Dillon at Exit 205. Head east for six miles on Hwy. 6.

Getting around: Within Keystone an excellent free shuttle system runs continuously from 7:30 a.m., passing every 15 minutes. In the evenings the shuttles run every 20 minutes until midnight on weeknights, until 2 a.m. on Fridays and Saturdays. Bartenders and hotel doormen will call the shuttle to ensure pickup in the evenings and late at night, 496-3273. If you are staying and skiing mostly at Keystone, you won't need a car.

The Summit Stage provides free transportation between Dillon, Silverthorne, Frisco, Breckenridge and Copper Mountain. Call 668-0999 for route information. Keystone and Breckenridge also operate a free inter-resort shuttle, the Ski KAB Express, at varying times according to demand. To check the schedule, call 496-4200.

Copper Mountain

Colorado

Summit: 12,313 feet
Vertical: 2,601 feet
Base: 9,712 feet

Address: P.O. Box 3001,
Copper Mountain, CO 80443
☎ Area code: 970
Ski area phone: 968-2882
**ⓘ Toll-free information
& reservations:** (800) 458-8386
For reservations outside the U.S.:
(970) 968-2882
Fax: 968-2711
E-mail: cmr-gs@ski-copper.com
Internet: http://www.ski-copper.com
Expert:★★★★ **Advanced:**★★★★
Intermediate:★★★★
Beginner:★★★★
Never-ever:★★★★

Lifts: 20—1 high-speed 6-passenger
chair lift, 4 high-speed quads,
5 triple chairs, 6 double chairs,
and 4 surface lifts
Skiable Acreage: 2,433 acres
Snowmaking: 16 percent
Uphill capacity: 30,630 per hour
Snowboarding: Yes, unlimited
Bed base: 2,800
Nearest lodging: walking distance, condos
Child care: Yes, 2 months and older
Adult ticket, per day: $40–$50 (98/99 prices)
Dining:★★
Apres-ski/nightlife:★★
Other activities:★

If ski resorts were people, Copper Mountain Resort would be the ultra-organized type—the kind of guy whose sock drawer has navy dress socks neatly folded on the left side, black dress socks stacked on the right, and white athletic socks nesting in the middle. Copper's trail system and base village are similarly arranged in a logical, easy-to-find manner.

As you face the mountain, the beginner slopes are to the right, the intermediate trails are in the middle and advanced runs are on the left. The most difficult stuff is at the summit, where several lifts serve primarily expert and advanced terrain. The base village, built from the ground up a couple of decades ago, has clusters of restaurants and shops surrounded by multi-story condo buildings, with an efficient free shuttle system connecting the whole thing. Even getting there is a snap. Drive about an hour and a half west of Denver on I-70, and the resort and its base village appear on the left side of the freeway.

This is not to imply that Copper Mountain is a dull place for a ski vacation; the bowls at the top of Copper and Union peaks have plenty of chutes, cornices and powder stashes. Copper's layout makes for a convenient vacation. Just as Mr. Neat doesn't waste time finding a matching pair of socks, you won't waste it consulting the trail map or riding endless lifts to find your type of terrain.

Don't expect to find any old copper mines or even a miner's turn-of-the-century saloon—Copper is strictly a creature of modern-day master plan. Its condominium villages are divided into three sections. The heartbeat of the resort thumps from the Village Center, where you'll find the high-speed American Eagle and American Flyer quads, as well as most of Copper's dining and nightlife. The condos in this section tend to be more elegant. The East Village, centered at the base of the new Super Bee lift, offers less expensive accommodations, plus a few bars and restaurants. The West Village, close to the Union Creek area, is home to Club Med, some upscale properties and the cross-country center.

New for 98/99: Copper Mountain is spending $66 million to upgrade much of the East Village during the summer of 1998. The plans are extensive: a new six-passenger high-speed chair, the Super Bee, which replaces chairs B and B-1 and covers 2,300 vertical feet; a three-story day lodge and conference center called Copper Station; the Copper Springs Lodge, which will have 108 privately-owned units; the Excelerator, a new express quad to replace the E lift; new snowboard facilities and more.

If you want to be sure you're skiing or snowboarding terrain appropriate to your level, you like to be within walking distance of everything and you don't need a huge variety of restaurants or nightlife, Copper Mountain is an excellent choice. Copper Mountain belongs to the Intrawest ski resort family, which also includes Whistler/Blackcomb, Tremblant, Mammoth, Stratton and others.

Mountain layout

◆◆ **Expert** ◆ **Advanced:** The 700-acre Copper Bowl, on the back side of Union Peak, provides above-treeline skiing as well as excellent glades. All three runs that parallel the new Excelerator express quad are short and steep, and Brennan's Grin in particular will bring a smile to a serious bump skier's face. Bear far right off the Excelerator lift and you can find serious tree skiing on Enchanted Forest (even more serious tree skiing, albeit unmarked, is available if you bear left about halfway off the Collage run).

If you take the Storm King surface lift instead of heading down Enchanted Forest, you'll come to the toughest terrain at Copper: Spaulding Bowl. Lose a ski here and you'd better hope to have an uphill friend. If you survive the bowl, you can choose from several very worthy expert runs to the bottom of the Resolution lift. To get back to the top of the bowl, you have to take the Storm King lift again. All the lifts mentioned here (except Excelerator) serve only expert runs, so there's rarely a wait.

■ **Intermediate:** Exit to the right of the American Flyer quad and try the American Flyer, I-Beam and Windsong runs under the Timberline Express lift. Better yet, take the American Eagle quad chair from Village Center and dart down any of the runs under this lift.

If you're patient enough to continue up the mountain on the Excelerator lift, you'll have the best intermediate runs of the resort at your feet. Both Collage and Andy's Encore are worthy challenges for the intermediate, offering good grade without the heavy moguls or tight funnels that can turn a blue run black (and an unwary intermediate black and blue).

●● **Beginner:** Hop on the high-speed American Flyer lift, the G lift next to American Flyer, or the H lift in the Union Creek area. Nearly the whole side of the mountain under Union Peak consists of sweeping runs lined by trees, perfect for the advanced beginner and lower intermediate.

For a long run to the bottom, beginners should bear left when getting off the high-speed American Flyer and take Coppertone for an easy cruise. From the H lift, head right down

Woodwinds to the Timberline Express quad chair, ride to the top and ski the sweeping Soliloquy to Roundabout connection to the bottom.

● **Never-ever:** The K lift, at the far right border of the resort, serves a super gentle, isolated area. When you have these runs conquered, the next step is the nearby L lift, another chair with only beginner runs beneath it.

Note: In the midst of all this order is a confusing lift-naming system, though it is getting much better than it used to be. Copper used to letter all of its lifts: A, B, C, D, E and so forth. But then they added B-1 and C-1, skipped a few letters in the middle, and finally, only the locals could figure it out. But as older lifts are replaced, Copper is giving the new ones names, a change we welcome. If you use lifts as meeting places, pay attention to the American *Eagle* and American *Flyer* chairs. If you're meeting someone at the top of one of those chairs, be very specific: they start in the same general area but unload on different peaks.

Mountain rating

Various skill levels are kept separated so that no one needs to feel intimidated or slowed down by fellow skiers or snowboarders.

Snowboarding

Boarding is permitted on all sections of the mountain. Copper Mountain is planning to move its snowboarding park sites from their 97/98 locations, but the destinations were unknown at press time. Riders can expect two competition-quality halfpipes, a mini-halfpipe, and at least two terrain parks, one geared toward beginners and the other for more accomplished riders. Copper has hosted several top snowboard competition events.

Cross-country (98/99 prices)

Copper Mountain has an excellent cross-country trail system. About 25 km. of set tracks and skating lanes fan out from the Union Creek cross-country center. The center offers rentals, lessons and clinics. Track fees for adults are $10; children 5 and younger and 70 and older ski free. A package for cross-country first-timers, including half-day lesson, track pass and equipment rental is $40. The never-ever telemark package includes a half-day lesson, equipment rental and beginner lift ticket for $60. Group lessons are $36 for a half day. The telemark program costs $56 and includes all lifts and a lesson. Private lessons are $48 an hour per person including trail pass; $22 per hour for each additional person. Overnight hut tours, a gentle ski tour with a four-course progressive meal and various telemark camps are among the Nordic programs. Skiers with multiday lift tickets may trade a day of downhill skiing for the Newcomer Track Package. The **Copper Mountain Cross-Country Center** phone is 968-2318, Ext. 6342.

Lessons (98/99 prices)

Group lessons: $48, 2.5 hours; never-evers through near-intermediates meet at the Union Creek area; upper-ability levels meet in front of the Center Building. Package includes lessons, lifts and rentals for seasoned skiers for $75.

Never-ever package: $65, including lesson, beginner lift and rentals.

Private lessons: $95 for one or $110 for two to four skiers, 90 minutes. Discounts available for multiple hours.

Special programs: Examples include Women's Skiing Seminars, two- and three-day seminars offered several times a season; snowboard camps for adults or children; an Advanced Skiing Seminar and the Copper Mountain Adaptive Ski Program.

Children's lessons: Full day (lunch, rentals, lesson, lifts) are $75; additional days are $67; half-day, $45 (half-day doesn't include lunch); without rentals, $69. Ages are 4–12 for Alpine skiing and 8–12 for snowboarding.

Child care (98/99 prices)

Ages: 2 months to 4 years.

Costs: Full day with lunch costs $57; half day is $47. Parents should provide diapers, a change of clothing, a blanket and a favorite toy. In-room babysitting services require 24-hour advance reservations or cancellations, and cost $8 per hour, plus $1 for each additional child.

Reservations: Required; call 968-2318, Ext. 6345; or (800) 458-8386. Copper Mountain long has received high marks for its children's care and learning programs.

Lift tickets (98/99 prices)

	Adult	Child (6-14)
One day	$50	$17
Three days	$126 ($42/day)	$39 ($13/day)
Five days	$202 ($40.40/day)	$65 ($13/day)

Who skis free: 70 and older, 5 and younger. Copper Mountain has Kids Ski Free/Stay Free packages that allow children age 14 and under to ski and stay free when accompanied by parents. Children always stay free. Check with the resort for the ski free part of the bargain. There is a Seniors Ski Free program for those 62 and older when they stay at Copper Mountain at certain times. Beginners can ride the K & L lifts free on many weekdays during the season; ask before you buy a ticket.

Who skis at a discount: Skiers aged 60–69 pay $34 per day.

Note: Multiday tickets are valid over a 14-day period (children's multiday tickets are valid the whole season). Also, discounted Copper lift tickets are sold at hundreds of ski shops, grocery stores and convenience stores in Denver and the rest of the Front Range. Call the resort to find out where to buy these tickets.

Accommodations

All Copper Mountain Lodging Services properties include membership in the Athletic Club (see Other Activities).

Lodging is designated according to the village—Village Center, East Village and West Village. All condos are in the same general price range; those managed by Copper Mountain Lodging Services are newer, concentrated in the Village Center and West Village area. Top condo choice is the **Spruce Lodge** because it's so close to the lifts. The **Telemark Lodge** in West Village has a small bar and crackling fireplace, and sits equidistant from the downhill lifts and the cross-country area. Next door are the **Beeler Place Townhomes** with glass-enclosed patios (and creaky floors; if you're a light sleeper, pick the bedroom on the top floor). The **Mountain Plaza** has some hotel rooms.

Westlake Lodge and **Bridge End**, both costing the same as Spruce Lodge, are significantly farther from the lifts. The Lodging Services properties are $120–$190 a night for a hotel room, $130–$245 for a one-bedroom condo, $219–$415 for a two-bedroom unit, and $279–$480 for three-bedroom units. These prices are higher at Christmas.

The East Village condominiums are a bit older, slightly less expensive and convenient to the intermediate and expert lifts. However, they will be out of the way if your group includes beginners. Of these properties, the **Peregine** is perhaps the most luxurious and **Anaconda** follows. These Carbonate Property Management units start at $99 for a hotel room, $139–$170 for one-bedroom units, $169–$239 for two-bedroom condos, and $230–$300 for three-bedroom units. The **Best Western Foxpine Inn** is the distant poor cousin of Copper Mountain properties.

Excellent packages combine lodging and lifts. From early January through mid-February, packages start around $107 per day per person, double occupancy. In early or late season, packages start at $59 per person, a virtually unbeatable deal. Copper Mountain also has one of the few single-occupancy packages, which start at $98 in early December and mid-April to closing, rising to $195 in February and March.

Club Mediterranée is the first Club Med built in North America and still is its only U.S. winter club. Rooms are small. Programs and activities are nonstop, and everything is included in the price except drinks. There are ski lessons, dancing, and sumptuous spreads for breakfast, lunch and dinner. In fact, Club Med guests rarely venture outside the Club Med world except to ski—and even then they are still lesson-wrapped in the Club Med cocoon. For reservations, call (800) 258-2633 (CLUB MED).

Dining

Copper Mountain's range of restaurants is fair for a resort of modest size. **Pesce Fresco** (968-2318, Ext. 6505) in Mountain Plaza is the most upscale restaurant. Reservations are suggested. **O'Shea's** in the Copper Junction building has great bargains, and the best breakfast buffet for miles. **Salsa Mountain Cantina** is a new Mexican restaurant.

Rackets Restaurant (968-2318, Ext. 6386) located in the Racquet and Athletic Club has a Southwestern menu and a great salad bar.

The East Village has the best restaurants. Virtually everyone's favorite was **Farley's** (968-2577) in the Snowflake building, which serves up heaping portions of prime rib, steaks and fish. Reservations are a good idea—don't hesitate to ask for the table next to the fireplace.

Another favorite for light fare and great burgers is the **B-Lift Pub**, which has a lunch and dinner menu and is by far the best bar in town.

The **Village Square** shopping area has some specialty choices: **Imperial Palace** for Chinese food; **Lizzie's Bagelry**, in the same building but facing toward West Village, has bagels, muffins and other items for a light breakfast. The **Corner Grocery** is in Village Square, for those who prefer to dine in their condos. However, it has typical resort prices; skiers with cars may wish to stop along I-70 to stock up.

Dinner sleighrides cost $55 for adults; $35 for children aged 5-12. A horse-drawn sleigh takes diners to a heated cabin for a gourmet meal. Call 968-2232 for more information or reservations.

Après-ski/nightlife

This is one of Colorado's better immediate après-ski resorts. The **B-Lift Pub** rocks from 3–5 p.m. It's a great spot to meet avid skiers, because the bar anchors the mountain's expert and intermediate sections. **Kokomo's Bar** in the Copper Commons gets overflow après-ski, and **O'Shea's** hums as well.

Later in the evening, **O'Shea's, Farley's** and the **B-Lift Pub** are always a good time. If you like to dance, though, you'll have to head for other parts of Summit County or perhaps to Vail.

Other activities

Shopping: Copper Mountain's shopping opportunities are limited to a few souvenir and clothing shops. The Copper Collection, in the Village Square center, has some nice upper-end sweatshirts and T-shirts, plus elegant knick-knacks, some handcrafted by Colorado artisans. The new Copper Station in the East Village also will have shops.

The **Copper Mountain Racquet and Athletic Club** is the primary nonskiing activity. Membership is included when you stay in Copper Mountain Lodging Services properties. Amenities include a lap pool, sauna, steamroom, exercise classes and two indoor tennis courts (these for an extra fee). Call 968-2826 for information.

For more activities see the Summit County or Vail chapters. Copper is about 20 miles from Vail and about 10 miles from the tri-town area of Dillon, Frisco and Silverthorne.

Getting there and getting around

By air: Copper Mountain is 90 miles west of Denver International Airport on I-70. **Resort Express** runs vans between the airport and your lodge, with many daily departures. You can make arrangements when you reserve lodging, or call Resort Express at 468-7600 or (800) 334-7433.

By car: Right off I-70 at Exit 195. You can see the trails from the freeway.

Getting around: Copper Mountain will buy five new "low-entry" buses for 98/99 that have an easy-entry design similar to the buses used on Denver's 16th Street Mall. This will improve an already superb (and free) shuttle service within the Copper Mountain village. You also can easily walk between the outlying condos and the village center. The free Summit Stage buses can take you to three nearby ski areas—Breckenridge, Keystone and Arapahoe Basin—as well as the towns of Dillon, Silverthorne and Frisco.

If you plan to head over to Vail or to the other Summit County areas frequently, you'll probably want a car, otherwise you don't need one. If you are not staying at Copper, one warning about parking: the two lots nearest the center lifts cost money ($10 per day last season). There are several free lots; try the B Lift lot for upper-level skiers, or the Union Creek lot for lower-level.

Crested Butte

Colorado

Summit elevation: **11,875 feet**
Vertical drop: **2,775 feet**
Base elevation: **9,100 feet**

Address: P.O. Box A
Mt. Crested Butte, CO 81225
✆ Area code: 970
Ski area phone: 349-2333
Snow report: 349-2323
ⓘ Toll-free reservations: (800) 544-8448
Toll-free foreign numbers:
U.K.: 0800 894085, ext. 2286
Mexico: 95-800-417-2772, ext. 2286
Australia: 0014-800-127-665, ext. 2286
Fax: 349-2250
E-mail: info@cbmr.com
Internet: http://www.crestedbutteresort.com
Expert:★★★★★
Advanced:★★★★★ Intermediate:★★★★
Beginner:★★★ Never-ever:★★★★

Number of lifts: 14–3 high-speed quads,
3 triples, 3 doubles, 5 surface lifts
Snowmaking: 35 percent
Skiable acreage: 1,162 acres
Uphill capacity: 17,440 per hour
Snowboarding: Yes, unlimited
Bed Base: 5,750
Nearest lodging: slopeside
Resort child care: Yes, infants and older
Adult ticket, per day: $42–$47 (97/98)

Dining:★★★★★
Apres-ski/nightlife:★★★★
Other activities:★★★

Great skiing and snowboarding—especially for advanced and expert levels—and down-home western friendliness make Crested Butte one of our favorite resorts.

Many Colorado resorts cater to the well-to-do celebrity or CEO visitor, and that's fine. But this is one place you can come if you want to avoid that scene. Crested Butte has a laid-back attitude and the locals have a way of looking at the better side of life.

The town has been designated a National Historic District, and its charm is impossible to convey in words. More than 40 historic structures are tucked in and around the town. A walk down Elk Avenue, the main street, takes you past the old post office, built in 1900; and The Forest Queen, reputed to have once been a brothel. New businesses have moved into buildings that have been lovingly restored, and others have been built to look as though they've been there for 100 years. In contrast, the ski area, about three miles away, is surrounded by modern condominiums and a couple of hotels, with more in the planning stages. With the shuttlebus system you won't need a car after you arrive.

Crested Butte has also made a major commitment to snowmaking, which has ensured excellent coverage for early season skiing. The snowfall statistics speak for themselves. Crested Butte has one of the highest average snowfalls of any ski town in Colorado.

In 98/99: The ESPN Winter X Games will return to Crested Butte January 14–18, 1999, with 200 extreme-sport athletes competing for $200,000 in prizes.

Mountain layout

◆◆ **Expert:** The Crested Butte skier likes the terrain just as nature left it. You'll notice that named trails cover only about half the terrain. Looking at a trail map, on the left is a huge area called the North Face with a series of double diamonds punctuating the mountainside, and on the far right is another grouping of double diamonds hard against the area boundary. Both areas are tough, offering what experts claim is Colorado's best extreme terrain, comparable to Utah steeps. If you want to ski this terrain, plan to arrive mid-January or later, or you might find it closed.

A couple of random notes: The resort has free mountain tours for all levels, including the extensive expert terrain. Our stats reflect lift-served terrain—you can hike to the 12,162-foot level for a 3,062-foot vertical descent. (Also, our base elevation is at the point of the lowest lift. The base area where the facilities are is about 200 feet higher.)

◆ **Advanced:** Crested Butte's single blacks are long, bumpy and fun. Most will be found under the Silver Queen and Twister lifts, but don't miss the Double-Top Glades served by the East River Lift.

■ **Intermediate:** Those in search of long cruising runs should go up Keystone or Silver Queen, and head down Treasury, Ruby Chief, Forest Queen, Bushwacker, Gallowich and variations of the same. Runs under the Paradise and Teocalli lifts are the best cruisers on the mountain—long and fast. The Paradise Bowl at the top of the Paradise lift gives intermediates a taste of powder on good days.

Advanced intermediates can manage most of the runs down from the Silver Queen high-speed quad. The short and steep Twister and Crystal both have good bail-out routes about halfway down.

●● **Beginner:** Crested Butte has extensive green-circle terrain, served by the Keystone lift. However, this is not stuff you want to attempt with the skiing ability you learned from a book on the plane. Houston probably is the most gentle of the greens, but we'd color the rest turquoise—greens leaning into blues.

● **Never-ever:** Head to the Peachtree lift, take a couple of lessons and practice for a day or two before attempting the Keystone lift. When you're ready for Keystone, get off at the second stop and try Houston.

Mountain rating

Crested Butte has terrain for every level of skier. It needs it, because there are no alternatives in the near vicinity, with the notable exception of 2,000 acres of snowcat powder skiing at nearby Irwin Lodge, the largest such operation in North America.

Irwin Lodge (97/98 prices)

Irwin Lodge at Lake Irwin, 12 miles west of Crested Butte, is Colorado's most exclusive and remote ski area. It stretches over 2,200 acres with an overall 2,100-foot vertical drop, but you won't find a chair lift or a snowmaking gun anywhere, and only 50 or so skiers and snowboarders can use the area at a time. Irwin Lodge specializes in snowcat skiing.

The 25-room lodge was built in 1974 by an eccentric millionaire. The only way in is by snowmobile, snowcat or cross-country skis. There are no phones (the only contact with the outside world is two-way radio), no network television, and one massive wooden lodge, perched on a ridge. Its isolation has presented special challenges to several owners, but its special magic keeps them trying. Irwin Lodge was taken over last season by a group of ten investors from California, Colorado, Washington and New Mexico (called The Irwin Ten,

LLC). Irwin Ten bought new snowcats, renovated the lodge's interior and bought new rental equipment—fat powder skis, cross-country skis, snowboards, snowshoes and emergency avalanche locating beacon transceivers, a precaution supplied to all guests and guides.

Mornings begin with breakfast, then snowcats make their first climb to the ridge, loaded with skiers and snowboarders, and cross-country skiers take off on organized tours. Skiing is available for every level of ability. We don't recommend this for a first-time ski experience, but we do recommend it for a first time in powder. Two groomed slopes serve the needs of intermediates and beginners, one slope for each. Of course, there's plenty of untracked, steep slopes for those with more experience.

Skiing normally starts at 9:30 a.m. and continues until 4:30 p.m. From 12:30 to 1:30 p.m. everything stops for the lunch buffet while the snowcats are serviced and the skiers fuel up for the afternoon. Irwin also offers snowmobiling, guided cross-country skiing, ice fishing and snowshoeing.

Packages combine lodging, three meals, activities and round-trip transportation from Crested Butte. Per-person, per-day prices in the prime season (generally, Christmas through March) are $315 for single occupancy, $275 double, or $255 triple or quad. Savings in the early or late season are about 20 percent, and there's a 10 percent savings for stays of three days or longer. Guests who don't participate in the activities pay lower prices, which we aren't listing here because we can't imagine why anyone would come here and not go outdoors. Day trips from Crested Butte are $175–$200 per person, depending on how many people sign up, including transportation, activities and lunch. Ask about renting powder skis when you make reservations.

Contact Irwin Lodge, PO Box 457, Crested Butte, CO 81224, (970) 349-9800, or (888) 464-7946 (888-GO-IRWIN). The fax number is (970) 349-9801.

Cross-country

Crested Butte is linked with one of the most extensive cross-country networks in Colorado. The **Crested Butte Nordic Center** is located at the edge of town, on 2nd Street between Sopris and Whiterock Streets. There are about 30 km. of Nordic tracks, which begin a few yards from the Nordic Center. The center also has hot tubs and racquetball courts for après-Nordic activity. There are more than 100 miles of backcountry trails. Call 349-1707 for pricing on lessons and rentals. Group lessons, half-day and all-day tours are scheduled several times each week, but private lessons and special tours must be requested two days in advance.

Crested Butte Mountain Resort was the pioneering resort in the rediscovery and popularization of telemarking. It has long had more of these skiers per capita than any other big-time ski resort. In April hundreds of free-heel skiers scramble up the North Face and drop 1,200 vertical feet through deep snow to compete in the Al Johnson Memorial Uphill/Downhill Race. Johnson used to deliver mail on Nordic skis to 1880s mining camps.

Snowboarding

Snowboarding is allowed everywhere, including the double-diamond areas. Crested Butte has a snowboard park with slides, quarterpipes and other features, reached by the Keystone Lift.

Lessons (98/99 prices)

Group lessons: Adult group lessons are $45 for a 2.5-hour lesson, including a lift ticket.

Never-ever package: A one-day novice ski or snowboard lesson with lift ticket (rent equipment separately) is $55.

Private lessons: $120 for two hours. Multihour and multiperson discounts available.

Special programs: Many, including clinics for seniors, halfpipe tricks, bumps, telemark, shaped skis, powder, and turning fundamentals cost $65 for 2.5 hours. There's a four-person minimum for these clinics.

Kim Reichhelm, a renowned extreme ski champion and former U.S. Ski Team member, teaches several four-day women's workshops here. We know Kim personally and can vouch for her ability to improve women's technique and confidence without scaring them to smithereens. These Women's Ski Adventures cost $850, but include clinics with video analysis, daily off-slope fun, gift bags, product demos, welcome and award dinners, breakfasts and lunches, lift tickets and more. Call (888) 444-8151 for more information on this program.

Racing: NASTAR races cost $5 for two runs and $1 for each additional run. Race clinics are offered for adults and children.

Children's lessons: The programs for ages 3–7 include ski rental and supervised daycare after the lesson, and cost $69 for a full day (with lunch) or $59 for half-day (no lunch). More experienced child skiers have classes separate from beginners. For ages 8–12, half-day lessons are $54; a full day is $64. These prices do not include lift tickets or rental equipment. Lunch is included on the full-day program. Snowboard lessons for this age group are $79 for a full day and $59 for half day, including board rental. Crested Butte also offers a teen ski program for ages 13–15 for $64 full day, $54 half day.

Registration and reservations for all programs are at the ski school desk in the Gothic Center, 349-2251, or (800) 444-9236.

Child care (98/99 prices)

Ages: 6 months to 7 years.

Costs: $69 per full day; or $11 per hour. The program includes crafts, games, snow play and other activities, but no ski lessons, and toddlers have separate programs from the older children.

Reservations: Strongly recommended; registration and information are in the Kid's Ski & Snowboard World in the Whetstone Building at the base of the Silver Queen Lift; (970) 349-2259 or (800) 444-9236.

Lift tickets (97/98 prices)

	Adult	Child (0-12)
One day	$49	Pay their age (see below)
Three days	$147 ($49/day)	
Five days	$225 ($45/day)	

Who skis free: Crested Butte doesn't charge for lift tickets in its low season. That's right: FREE SKIING November 20 through December 19, 1998, and again April 5–18, 1999. Call (800) 754-3733 for more information (800-SKI-FREE). Ages 70 and older always ski free.

Who skis at a discount: Ages 65-69 ski for half the adult price.

Note: When children ages 12 and younger ski with one full-paying adult, they pay their age per day. This program has no blackout periods, nor any limits to the number of children, but proof of age may be required.

 Accommodations

Most of the accommodations are clustered around the ski area in Mount Crested Butte. The historic town has a handful of lodges, but they are not as modern nor as convenient to the slopes. They are less expensive and closer to the nightlife however; and offer a taste of more rustic Western atmosphere. A free bus service takes skiers right to the slopes, so the primary inconvenience of in-town lodging is the short bus ride.

Crested Butte Vacations can take care of everything from your plane tickets to hotel room, lift tickets and lessons with one phone call. It also offers some of the best packages available. Before you make any arrangements, call (800) 544-8448 and ask for the best possible deal. The fax number is listed in our fact box.

The Sheraton Hotel at Crested Butte (formerly the Mountainlair Hotel) is 225 yards from the Silver Queen high-speed quad. It recently doubled in size, adding 127 suites, meeting space, an indoor/outdoor pool, hot tubs, a restaurant and bar, and two shops. It also has 125 large rooms with two king-sized beds in each, two outdoor hot tubs and a coin-operated laundry. Rates are $108–$272 per night.

The Crested Butte Marriott Resort (formerly the Grande Butte Hotel, 349-4000), has ski-in/ski-out lodging with a tasteful decor and 260 nice-sized rooms, all with private balconies and whirlpool tubs. Mountain hotels don't get much better than this, at least in this price range. Room rates are $135–$800 per night, depending on room size and season.

Crested Mountain Village is perhaps the top luxury group of properties at the mountain. It has a series of spectacular penthouse suites that open onto the slopes.

The Buttes are well-appointed condos close to the lifts. Rooms range in size from studios to three bedrooms; prices are $138–$501 per night.

The Gateway, across from the Peachtree lift and about a two-minute stroll from the Silver Queen, may be the best value of any condo on the mountain when you trade price for space and amenities. One-, two- and three-bedroom units range from $195–$570 per night. Gateway units are managed by High Country Resorts (800-451-5699; 349-2400).

The Plaza, only 80 yards from the Silver Queen superchair, is one of the most popular condos. It gives excellent value and is especially popular with groups because special functions can be arranged. Two- and three-bedroom units cost $212–$626 per night.

Wood Creek and **Mountain Edge** are convenient to the lifts, and the **Columbine** is a more moderate ski-in/ski-out property. These three, together with nine others within shuttlebus distance of the lifts, are managed by several agencies, so it's best to book through Crested Butte Vacations (800-544-8448). Rates are $140–$495 per night.

The Crested Butte Club (349-6655) on Second Street in town, is the upscale old-world elegance champion of the area. Though the lifts are a bit far, this place is worth the inconvenience. Seven suites have been individually furnished with Victorian furnishings including double sinks and a copper-and-brass tub, as well as beautiful four-poster or canopied beds and a fireplace. The amenities include the fitness club, with heated swimming pool, two steam baths, three hot tubs, weight room, and massage and weight trainer. This is a No-Smoking property. Room rate is about $75–$225.

The **Claim Jumper** (349-6471), at 704 Whiterock Street, is a historic log-home bed-and-breakfast and the class act in town. Jerry and Robbie Bigelow run it and have filled it with a collection of memorable antiques. Bedrooms have themes and are furnished with brass or old iron beds. There are only five rooms, four with private bath. Room rates are $99–$149 per night including a full breakfast. Children are not encouraged; No-Smoking. The Claim Jumper can arrange catered special-occasion wedding receptions.

The **Christiana Guesthaus** (800-824-7899; 349-5326) 621 Maroon Ave., is only a block from the ski shuttle and a five-minute walk from downtown. This has a mountain inn atmosphere and most of the guests manage to get to know one another. The rooms are small, but guests spend a good deal of time in the hotel's living rooms so this doesn't really matter. Let the owners know if you need quiet, because some rooms get quite a bit of traffic from the owner's family and folk using the washers and dryers. Rates are $67–$91.

The **Forest Queen** (349-5336), corner of Elk and 2nd, is inexpensive, with a double with bath for $45–$70.

The **Elk Mountain Lodge** (349-7533) around the corner from the Forest Queen on 2nd Street has simple but comfortable rooms, all with private bath, for $69 to $118 per room per night. Ask for Room 20 on the third floor with lots of space, a balcony and a great view.

Other B&Bs in town (which we have not inspected) are **Elizabeth Anne** (349-0147; 703 Maroon Ave.); **Purple Mountain Lodge** (349-5888; 714 Gothic Ave.) and the **Last Resort** (349-0445; 213 3rd St.)

Crested Butte Property Management (349-5354), at 214 6th Street, has rentals in private homes as well as in many special condominiums. For something out of the ordinary, check with them for help.

 ## Dining

Crested Butte is blessed with more excellent, affordable restaurants than any other resort in the West. You can dine on gourmet French cuisine in an intimate setting, or chow down on platters of family-style fried chicken and steaks. We sent our chef-in-residence, Katy Keck, on a return visit to Crested Butte last season. One new restaurant she was unable to visit, but about which we've heard good reports, is **The WoodStone Grille** (349-8030), open for breakfast, lunch and dinner at the Crested Butte Sheraton Resort at the ski area's base. Here's Katy's report:

At the far end of Elk Avenue is **The Timberline Restaurant** (349-9831). Chef Tim Egelhoff spent five years as sous-chef at Creme Carmel in Carmel, California, before opening Timberline a few years ago. He combines seasonal products to create a Café French Cuisine, whose roots are classic French, with a pinch of California and a dash of the Rockies. The menu changes often. Open nightly from 5–10 p.m.

At the other end of Elk Avenue, near the four-way stop, Timberline has opened a new bakery and casual restaurant called the **Timberline Café.** Open from 7:30 a.m. to 11 p.m. (no reservations), it offers a fast, tasty alternative to long restaurant waits. It has creative wrap sandwiches—such as ahi tuna and Thai vegetable—pastries, and a full coffee menu for the serious coffee drinker. Heartier dinner choices include osso bucco and cassoulet.

Also near the four-way stop at 435 Sixth St. is **Backcountry Gourmet** (349-6733), a relaxed, global dining experience. It has a tapas menu, but if you're used to the small plates used in Spain, get ready. You can easily make a meal from just a couple of Backcountry's tapas menu offerings. Circle the globe with their selection: Jamaican wontons are served with sweet 'n' sour cherry sauce; Moroccan chicken b'stella is chock-full of curried chicken and almonds. Thailand, Indonesia, India, Szechuan China and Senegal are all represented in this United Nations palate salute. The restaurant has a wide selection of beer and wine by the glass. Tapas are less than $10, while entrées are in the low $20s.

Le Bosquet (349-5808), a former fixture on Elk Avenue, has popped up in the Majestic Plaza at Sixth and Bellview. Signature dishes still include Colorado roast rack of lamb, hazelnut chicken, and salmon with a ginger glaze. This is possibly Crested Butte's finest in formal French cuisine. Le Bosquet also has added a bistro menu at its bar.

Soupçon Restaurant (349-5448) is hidden in the alley behind Kochevar's Bar. This log cabin started at half its current size in 1916 as a private residence to the Kochevars. Soupçon dates back almost a quarter of a century. Current owners Maura and Mac Bailey have created an innovative French cuisine, with menu items posted daily on a chalkboard. Reserve two to three days ahead for one of two seatings, 6 and 8:15 p.m.

The **Idle Spur Steakhouse and Microbrewery** (349-5026) is always crowded and noisy. It offers the finest hand-cut steaks in town plus burgers (including vegetable and elk—sounds better than it is), Mexican entrées and a selection of fresh fish, all reasonably priced. Six beers are brewed in-house from the White Buffalo Peace Ale to the full-bodied Rodeo Stout. Brewery tours 2–5 p.m. daily during happy hour.

Next to the Old Town Hall bus stop (130 Elk Avenue) is the **Powerhouse Bar Y Grill,** known for its Mexican specialties, like cabrito, fajitas, tamales, and tacos. Prices are quite reasonable and portions are huge. Be prepared for a wait though—this popular restaurant doesn't take reservations, and the line for tables can be more than an hour.

For hard-to-beat group and family dining, head to **The Slogar** (349-5765). It used to be the first bar the miners hit when returning from the mines and is decorated in old bordello decor. Slogar's offers a skillet-fried chicken dinner with mashed potatoes, biscuits, creamed corn, ice cream and even some other extras for a flat price. It also offers a family-style steak dinner. Reservations recommended.

For other substantial meals, head down Elk Avenue to **Donita's Cantina** (349-6674), where the margaritas are giant and strong and Mexican food comes in heaping portions. Be early or be ready to wait. No reservations. For a quick meal, try **Angello's** (349-5351) for pizza and Italian food. **The Gourmet Noodle** (349-7401) has many pasta dishes prepared fresh daily, espresso and cappuccino and tempting desserts, such as peanut butter pie and chocolate mousse.

The best breakfast by far is served in the **Forest Queen**. The atmosphere is Old West and turn of the century. Ask for the "baggins." You won't find it on the menu—it has developed as a specialty for most of the locals. The Forest Queen also serves lunch and dinner.

For breakfast on the mountain head to **The Avalanche**, in the Treasury Center. Or meet at 8:15 a.m. at the Keystone lift for first tracks on the mountain and an all-you-can-eat breakfast buffet. Call 349-2378 for information.

For a good lunch, try **Rafters** or **The Avalanche**. For a more elegant setting, go to **The Artichoke,** and start off with artichoke soup. The **Swiss Chalet** serves Alpine fare, such as fondue and raclette, plus a good selection of European beer.

Crested Butte has several outdoor dining experiences, such as the **Twister Fondue Party**, every Sunday, Wednesday and Friday when at 4:30 p.m., diners board the Keystone Lift for a three-course on-mountain fondue dinner, followed by a gentle ski to the base by torchlight. **Paradise Sleigh Ride Dinners** are every Tuesday, Thursday and Saturday via snowcat-drawn sleigh. Call 349-2211 or 349-2378 for either of those. Another company offering dinner sleigh rides is **Just Horsin' Around** (349-9822).

Après-ski/nightlife

Here nightlife means wandering from bar to bar. The immediate après-ski action is centered in **Rafters** at the base of the lifts, or **The Dugout Sports Bar and Grill** in the Marriott. Then it begins to move downtown to the **Wooden Nickel**, with some wild drinks, and **The El Dorado**, known around town as "The Eldo," which has a "smokin' dance floor," said one local. **Talk of the Town** is a smoky locals' place with video games, shuffleboard and pool tables. **Kochevar's** is another local favorite. **The Idle Spur** is a microbrewery with live music on weekends. Cover charges are $3 to $8, depending on the talent, and it has dancing, such as Friday's Wild Disco Night.

Rafters has dancing and good singles action most nights in Mount Crested Butte, and it's within stumbling distance of most of the lodging. Those staying in town can take an inexpensive town taxi service if they miss the last bus of the night.

For a dinner and show, try the **I-Bar Ranch** Western barbecue and show, advertised as family-style fun with dancing. Call 641-4100.

The **Princess Wine Bar** at 218 Elk Avenue is the place to finish your night on the town. Serving a limited menu of mostly soups and salads, there are a few tempting desserts to enjoy with cappuccino or a fine dessert wine. With no doubt the best selection of quality wines by the glass, Princess also carries a full list of cognacs, ports, and single malts. Come relax by the fire. Open daily from 10 a.m. to "whenever."

Other activities

Shopping: Lots of great shops at the resort and in town. Among them: Diamond Tanita Art Gallery, for jewelry, glass, ceramics, paper, forged iron and other functional art pieces; Cookworks, Inc., a gourmet kitchen shop; Book Cellar, with local maps, Western art and collectibles; and Minor's Closet, out-of-the-ordinary children's gifts.

Crested Butte has several more active things to do. These include **snowmobiling, winter horseback riding, sleigh rides** with and without dinners, and **ballooning**—weather permitting. Call Crested Butte Chamber of Commerce at 349-6438 for brochures and information. For resort activities, call 349-2211.

Getting there and getting around

By air: Despite its seemingly isolated location, Crested Butte is quite convenient to reach. American Airlines has nonstop daily jet service from Dallas/Ft. Worth, Delta has daily nonstop jets from Atlanta and United Express offers several flights daily from Denver. The nearest airport is Gunnison, 30 miles from the resort.

Alpine Express (970-641-5074 or 800-822-4844) meets every arriving flight and takes you direct to your hotel or condo for about $36 round-trip. For reservations, call Crested Butte Vacations or directly to the company.

By car: Crested Butte is at the end of wintertime Hwy. 135, about 30 miles north of Gunnison. It's about 230 miles from Denver via Hwys. 285, 50 and 135.

Getting around: No need for a car. Crested Butte's free town-resort shuttle is reliable and fun to ride, thanks to some free-spirited and friendly drivers.

Purgatory

Colorado

Summit elevation: 10,822 feet
Vertical drop: 2,029 feet
Base elevation: 8,793 feet

Address: One Skier Place
Durango, CO 81301
✆ **Area code:** 970
Ski area phone/Snow report: 247-9000
ⓘ **Toll-free reservations:** (800) 525-0892
Fax: 385-2107
E-mail: through the Web site
Internet: http://www.ski-purg.com

Expert:★★
Advanced:★★★
Intermediate:★★★
Beginner:★★★★
Never-ever:★★★★

Number of lifts: 11–1 high-speed quad,
4 triples, 4 doubles, 2 surface lifts
Snowmaking: 34 percent
Skiable acreage: 1,200 acres
Uphill capacity: 13,600 per hour
Snowboarding: Yes, some limits
Bed base: 3,120 near resort, 7,000 in Durango
Nearest lodging: slopeside
Resort child care: Yes, 2 months and older
Adult ticket, per day: $43 (98/99 price)

Dining:★★★
Apres-ski/nightlife:★★★
Other activities:★★★

If you ever are banished to Purgatory, consider yourself lucky—if your exile is to this resort in southwestern Colorado, 25 miles north of Durango.

Purgatory is a ski area that feels comfortable right from the start. It draws heavily from Texas, Arizona, and New Mexico, and to a growing extent Southern California and the Southeast. Its clientele includes skiers and snowboarders who take one trip a year, or even one every other year. What draws them are low prices (winter is off-season in Durango), great weather and a welcoming attitude. When we last visited, scores of buses from Texas church groups were stacked up in the parking lot.

Purgatory attracts families, college students and people turned off by ostentatious displays. Flaunting one's wealth in Durango is not looked upon with favor. And though Purgatory has challenging terrain that attracts many talented skiers, there are quite a few folks doing the flying snowplow—skis in pizza position, arms akimbo, big smiles on their faces, barreling downhill while flirting with control. No one makes fun of them or makes them feel unwelcome, not even the other visitors.

The descents are fun, thanks largely to the area's undulating terrain. Thousands of years ago glaciers scraped this valley, leaving narrow natural terraces on the mountainside. Purgatory's runs plunge downward for a bit, then level off, then plunge, then level off—all the way to the bottom. The effect is rather like a roller coaster ride. It's super for those who love to get air. Those who don't can use the flat spots to rest before the next drop off.

The resort is 25 miles from town. For years skiers stayed in Durango and drove the 50-mile round trip, but with the growth of Purgatory Village at the base area you now have a choice. There's little going on nightlife-wise in the village, but it has the big advantage of being slopeside. Durango has lots to do and a very charming setting, but it's far from the slopes. Rent a car if your group stays in town. If you are alone, or a couple that doesn't want the hassle of driving, you can ride a shuttle. (See "Getting Around").

Purgatory owes its name, indirectly, to a 16th-century Spanish explorer who drowned in the river that flows through Durango. His companions christened the river "Rio de las Animas Perdidas," River of Lost Souls. A witty 19th-century mapmaker named a brook that flows into the river Purgatory Creek. The ski area was built along the creek and adopted its name. The trail names were inspired by the Divine Comedy, Dante Alighieri's 14th-century epic poem that described a journey through Hell, Purgatory and Paradise.

 ## Mountain layout

At Purgatory, skiers and snowboarders enjoy a nice progression from beginner to expert terrain.

● **Never-ever:** First-timers have their own learning area, Columbine Station. An intra-area shuttle bus takes never-evers here after they have acquired their rentals and lift tickets. After a couple of lessons on the terrain under the Columbine Lift, they are ready to board Graduate Lift, which takes them back to the base area.

●● **Beginner:** Start with the runs under the Twilight Lift. The easiest of these is Pinkerton Toll Road, a gently winding cat track trail. Divinity and Angel's Tread are wide gentle runs, and Columbine winds through stands of trees, giving beginners the feeling of being deep in the woods. As they progress, they may want to head down Salvation toward the Hermosa Park Express, the high-speed quad that goes straight to the summit. From there they can descend The Bank or Silvertip to West Fork, where they have many choices for getting back down.

■ **Intermediate:** The next step is the intermediate runs off the Engineer Lift. Snowmaking on these runs ensures a good surface. After skiers feel comfortable on What, Limbo, and West Fork, they should head for Peace and Boogie, two wide intermediate runs off the Hermosa Park Express. Still not enough of a challenge? Head down blue-square The Legends toward Dead Spike, the widest of Purgatory's runs, or continue on The Legends to the mid-loading station on the Legends Lift. From the top of this lift, Sally's Run is not as steep as Chet's, but both are challenging blues.

◆ **Advanced:** Still not enough to make your heart leap into your throat? Go for Wapiti, a black run under the Grizzly Lift where the moguls grow to small igloo size. Or try Catharsis or No Mercy, two short black runs under Spud Lift and Needles Lift. Or try Pandemonium, a long black diamond under the Spud Lift that gets steeper and bumpier the farther down you go. When Pandemonium is groomed it's really a blast. Other advanced areas include the short steep runs at the bottom of the Legends Chair, which sometimes are winch-cat groomed, and Styx and Lower Hades off the Spud and Needles lifts.

◆◆ **Expert:** If you have Pandemonium wired, then you're ready for Bull Run, a double-black trail that starts just below Dante's Restaurant off the Grizzly Chair. It has a tough pitch as well as funnels and moguls (and once you're on it, you're on it).

Note: Purgatory's trails are quite long. Most stretch from summit to base, and have lots of dips, twists and turns to keep them interesting. The gentler runs wind around stands of pine, passing islands of aspens and picnic tables. The more difficult runs make a beeline for the bottom.

A tip for powder hounds and other natural-terrain fans: the vast majority of Purgatory's skiers like groomed terrain, so after a storm the powder between the timber is often still fresh long into the afternoon. Tree fans might like the aspens between Pandemonium and Lower Hades. Beginning adventure skiers can try the easier powder stashes between Peace and Boogie or should try Snag for a bit steeper terrain. Paul's Park, below the Legends Lift, has chutes for gladed skiing.

Mountain rating

Purgatory may be a place where souls suffer before being allowed into Paradise, but that's in Dante's poem. Intermediates head straight for the blessed abodes, such are the variety and plenitude of trails for this level. This resort also is an excellent place to learn, because of a completely separate learning area and a half-price program for first-time skiers and snowboarders. Advanced skiers will have a great time, too. Only super-experts looking for extremes will be disappointed.

Cross-country

The **Purgatory Nordic Center**, just north of the Alpine ski area across Highway 550, is maintained by the Durango Nordic Ski Club. It has 16 km. of trails groomed for skating and diagonal skiing. Nordic skiers will find the same undulating terrain as the downhill ski area, with appropriate terrain for various ability levels.

Rentals and lessons are available. As part of Purgatory's Total Ticket program, one Alpine ski day can be exchanged for the Nordic package.

Snowboarding

Purgatory has welcomed snowboarders since 1985. It has a new nine-acre snowboard park called Pitchfork with a halfpipe, wave wall, table tops and more. Boarding is permitted on all runs, except the Family Ski Zone, a beginner area below the Twilight lift, and Vincent's, a beginner run in the Legends area (intended to offset the snowboard-only park). However, you won't find many snowboarders in the Legends area, because the only way to return to the base is BD&M Expressway, a very long, very flat run (locals say the initials stand for Boring, Dull, and Monotonous; actually, the run is named for three of Purgatory's pioneers).

The Purgatory Village Center Mall houses the **Pandemonium Sports**, which sells equipment and clothing, rents equipment, and does tuning and repairs.

Lessons (98/99 prices)

Group lessons: $40 for a half day and $48 for a full day.
Never-ever package: The program is called First Things First. It offers never-ever skiers and snowboarders half-price half-day group lessons ($20 per session). Never-evers (ski or snowboard) need to rent equipment, buy a lift ticket and sign up for First Things First.

Private lessons: $120 for two hours.

Special programs: Throughout the season, Purgatory offers lessons for snowboarding, racing, telemark skiing, and mogul techniques. Call ahead for details, or check with the

Resort Concierge desk, a handy service that can explain services and provide the events calendar. Free clinics and daily events are also announced on the daily snow report and posted with the list of groomed trails throughout the resort.

For nature lovers, Purgatory offers a free guided nature tour of the mountain every Sunday morning. Naturalists from the U.S. Forest Service and local experts guide the two-hour tour covering winter ecology and native wildlife.

Racing: NASTAR racing occurs daily at the Paradise Events Arena at the top of the Needles and Spud lifts, or skiers can opt for self-timed race training gates. Purgatory also stages other competitions from time to time that are open to resort guests, such as SuperCarve contests.

Children's lessons: Kids in lessons receive a lift ticket for the day of their class. The full-day program for ages 3–4 is $70, which includes lunch, indoor activity, and an introduction-to-ski lesson with special kids' skis, the use of which is included. The half-day program ($55) includes either a morning or afternoon ski session with snacks but no lunch. Slightly older children (ages 4–5) have lessons with full Alpine equipment for the same price as the 3–4 ages. Prices for ages 6–12 are $70 full day, including lunch, and $55 half day, for skiing or snowboarding.

Note: Reservations are required for children 3–5 in ski school programs. For information on any of the ski school programs, call 247-9000 or (800) 525-0892.

One of the country's outstanding instruction programs for **disabled skiers** is here. Programs include lift ticket, adaptive equipment and private lessons. For information, call 970-259-0374.

Child care (98/99 prices)

Ages: 2 months to 3 years.
Costs: $70 for a full day with lunch and $55 for half day. Toddlers (2-3) get outdoor snow play, arts and crafts, games, movies and story time.
Reservations: Required; call 247-9000 or (800) 525-0892.

Note: The day care staff also can recommend a babysitter who can watch your kids while you enjoy a night out. If you're not sure whether to put your child in day care or lessons, Purgatory's Kids Central, located on the second floor of the Village Center, will help assess your child's abilities and interests, then escort him or her to the appropriate spot.

Other options: Baby's Away (800-785-9030; 382-9838) rents and will deliver baby needs to your lodge, such as crib, stroller, car seat and toys.

Lift tickets (98/99 prices)

	Adult	Child (6-12)
One day	$43	$21
Three days	$129 ($43/day)	$63 ($21/day)
Five days	$215 ($43/day)	$105 ($21/day)

Who skis free: Ages 5 and younger and 70 and older.
Who skis at a discount: Ages 62–69 ski for $25.

Note: Purgatory has adopted an "everyday low price" philosophy in regard to lift-ticket pricing. The per-day price is the lowest of the major Colorado resorts. The resort has an unusual program called Total Ticket™. Skiers with four-day or longer multiday tickets may exchange a day of downhill skiing for cross-country skiing or one of several vacation activities in southwest Colorado, examples of which are the Durango & Silverton Narrow Gauge Railroad train, a soak and massage at Trimble Hot Springs, a dinner sleigh ride, or a tour of Mesa Verde National Park, a collection of ancient cliff dwellings that have been named a World Heritage site. Call the resort for complete details on this program.

Accommodations

Purgatory has three lodging areas. The condos at the base are the most expensive; hotels and condos within 10 miles of the ski area are a little less so—and lodging in Durango can be dirt cheap, but 25 miles away.

Base-area lodging is at the **Purgatory Village Hotel, Best Western Lodge at Purgatory** and the following condo complexes: **Angelhaus, Brimstone, East Rim, Edelweiss, Graysill, Sitzmark** and **Twilight View**. Condos have full-service units (kitchens, fireplaces, common-area hot tubs and laundry facilities) from about $110 for a studio to $595 for larger suites. Prices vary slightly for similar-size units in the various complexes. Hotel costs are about $90–$275.

Several other complexes are one to ten miles from the ski area. The prices at **Cascade Village, Needles, Silver Pick** and **Tamarron** are $110–$435. Most of the outlying condo complexes have free shuttles to and from the ski area. (Even if you brought your own car, leave it behind and take the shuttle: it will get you closer.) And many of them, such as Tamarron, have their own restaurants and sundries shops, so you can get just about anything you need.

Durango, like Banff, Jackson, and Lake Tahoe, considers winter low season with prices below the summer rates. Winter rates are as low as $29 a night for a one-bed unit in a clean but frills-free motel, and several motels have this price. At other Durango lodging, prices go as high as $175 per night, but the average is about $55–$70.

Four historic lodging properties are worth mentioning. **The Strater Hotel** (800-247-4431) and the **General Palmer Hotel** (800-523-3358) are multistory, brick hotels that date back over 100 years. Both are in the heart of the walkable downtown and run $70–$215. The Strater has a great Victorian-style hot tub area that would be the envy of many larger, more sophisticated properties and the Diamond Belle Saloon is a classic. You might find an antique rolltop desk in your room. Sometimes the drawers stick and the wood in the antiques gives off a musty odor, but that's because the furniture is authentic.

Leland House Bed & Breakfast and **The Rochester Hotel,** (800-664-1920 for both) across the street from each other on East Second Avenue, were bought by the same family and completely renovated. The Leland House has a Durango history theme, with the rooms named after local historic figures. The Rochester Hotel has a Hollywood theme, with each room named for a film shot at least in part in Durango. "Butch Cassidy and the Sundance Kid," "Around The World in 80 Days" and "City Slickers" were all filmed in this region, and you can read about how they were made in framed narratives researched and written by one of the owners, Frederic Wildfang. Rates at these two historic properties run about $90–$150.

All Durango and Purgatory lodging can be booked through **Durango Central Reservations**, (800) 525-0892.

 ## Dining

Purgatory base area offers **Purgatory Creek** (nice food and atmosphere), **Double Diamond Grill** (upgraded cafeteria food and atmosphere) and **Farquahrt's** (bar food and atmosphere) and the **Columbine Cabin** (lunch items and local brews at the base of the beginner hill). For some of the best fish in Colorado, flown in daily, and for local game, try the **Cafe Cascade,** two miles north of Purgatory (259-3500), which has elegant dining in a rustic setting; everyone who has eaten here raves about it. **Sow's Ear** (247-3527), just north of the Purgatory entrance, is famed for its large, hand-cut steaks.

Café de los Piños, at the midway loading station of the Grizzly Chair, offers sit-down gourmet dining at lunch, accessible only by skis or snowboards. **Dante's**, in the same building, offers a quick bite to eat as does **The Powderhouse** near the Engineer Lift.

Durango is where you'll find most of the restaurants. Two things to know when trying to find a Durango street address: One, nearly all of Durango's streets have numbered names. The streets parallel to Main Avenue are called "avenues" and the numbers usually are spelled out (Second Avenue, for example). The streets that intersect Main all are "streets" and the number is seldom spelled out. Most tourists hang out between 5th Street and 11th Street, and occasionally venture onto Second or Third Avenue, but if you're directed to "the corner of Second and 8th," you'll know it isn't a mistake. Second thing to know: 6th Street was renamed College Drive a few years ago.

Seasons (382-9790), 764 Main Ave., a newer fine-dining spot in town, features rotisserie-roasted dinners (sea bass, trout, chicken, lamb) and fine wines by the glass in a spiffy bistro atmosphere. Make sure you try the garlic mashed potatoes, but save room for the apple crisp for dessert. This will cost $20-25 per person, excluding drinks. Our favorite casual, and cheap, dinner was at **Milan's** (382-8865) at 1150 Main, where the "Build Your Own Pizza" by the slice concept works like a dream. We had duck sausage on one and Thai chicken on the other. Washed down with a local microbrew, you can't go wrong. Lots of families and kids fill up the tables, but the friendly bar is perfect for a couple or single in a hurry. Prices are very reasonable. **Ariano's** (247-8146), 150 East College Dr., serves northern Italian cuisine.

The Ore House (247-5707), 147 College Dr., is an Old West steak house, rustic and casual with entrées in the $10–$20 range; **The Red Snapper** (259-3417), 144 East 9th St., also has fresh seafood, wonderful vegetables and salads, and saltwater-aquarium decor. Entrées are $11–$16.

Capers (247-1510), 160 E. College Dr., is for families and those looking for a bargain, and features gourmet wood-fired pizza and sandwiches. **Gazpacho** (259-9494), 431 E. Second Ave., has northern New Mexican cuisine that can get very spicy.

Olde Tymer's Cafe (259-2990), 1000 Main Ave., is top choice for a good hamburger and huge margaritas. Daily specials include $2.95 burgers Monday nights, $1.25 taco night on Friday, when locals jam the place. **The Golden Dragon** (259-0956), 992 Main Ave., serves Chinese food in huge portions.

Carver's Bakery and Brew Pub (259-2545), 1022 Main Ave., is the best place in Durango for breakfast; muffins and bagels are fresh daily. It's a hangout for locals, who joke that the place serves baked grains and brewed grains. If you prefer the eggs-and-bacon-type breakfast, head for the **Durango Diner** (247-9889), 957 Main Ave. Sunday brunch at the **Doubletree Hotel** is outstanding and a good choice for mountain visitors departing on Sunday, since the inn is between the ski area and the airport.

 ## Après-ski/nightlife

Skiers congregate at the bottom of the hill in three places after the lifts close: **Farquahrt's**, where the music is the liveliest; **Purgatory Creek**, slightly more sedate; or **Double Diamond Grill**, which is the quietest. Nightlife at the ski area is limited to Farquahrt's, which has live bands Thursday through Sunday.

Most ski areas have a "locals" spot, and at Purgatory it's the **Olde Schoolhouse Cafe**, a small and friendly hangout located two miles south of the resort, across the road from the Needles Country Square on U.S. Highway 550. This is where the lift operators, ski patrollers and other insiders go for beer and calzones the size of footballs. The music rocks, and pool shootin' is free. If you don't have a car, make friends with your ski instructor or other friendly local. **Steamworks**, a brew pub on the corner of 8th Street and East Second Ave., has good beer and good company.

A popular après-ski spot is the **Trimble Hot Springs**, about 20 miles from the ski area toward Durango. Natural mineral springs bubble into two outdoor therapy pools, one heated to 90 degrees and the other to 105. Private tub rentals and massages are available.

If you really want to tango, go to Durango. Depending on the time of year, Durango is either jumping or mildly hopping. Spring Break, which goes on for several weeks in March, brings thousands of college students and the bars schedule lots of entertainment.

Durango has quite a variety of musical entertainment. Try **The San Juan Room** (formerly the Sundance Saloon) downtown for dancing.

Lady Falconburgh's Barley Exchange has live jazz and some 20 microbrews on tap, 80 different bottles. It serves dinner as well and has become a local hangout.

Carver's Bakery and Brew Pub has strong and tasty locally brewed beers accompanied by fresh rolls from the bakery, or choose from the full dinner menu. To tourists who ask why a bakery is also a brewery, locals quote the sage who said, "Beer is just a modified form of bread." In warmer weather (and Durango can get pleasantly warm in winter), diners can sit on the patio.

The bar on the second floor of **The Pelican's Nest** restaurant on Main Avenue has live jazz on the weekends and a jam session on Thursdays—bring your own instrument and join local amateur jazz musicians. Other nights, talented entertainer Ron Urban sings a variety of music. On football Sundays, the best big screen in town is **A.J.'s Grill & Sports Bar** on College Dr., with pool tables, pinball and other games. Live bands and comedians play here occasionally.

Solid Muldoon is worth a visit just for the decor. Everything imaginable—typewriter, kayak, bubble gum machine (with gumballs), and the kitchen sink—hangs from the ceiling. They spin a wheel of fortune every so often, setting the price of drinks for the next few minutes. Over at the **Diamond Belle Saloon** in the Strater Hotel, a ragtime piano player plunks out hit tunes from the Gay '90s—1890s, that is.

 ## Other activities

Shopping: Durango has great stores. Among our favorites: New West Galleries between 7th and 8th; Toh Atin's Art On Main, 865 Main Ave. and Toh Atin Gallery, 145 W. 9th Street, for Western, Southwestern and Native American clothing and art; The Bookcase, 601 E. Second Ave., with a fine inventory of used and collector books; and O'Farrell Hat Company, on

Main near the General Palmer Hotel, where you can buy a custom-made cowboy hat. You can check out several antique stores in the area, too.

Durango has a couple of off-slope activities unique in the ski industry. One of America's finest national parks is nearby **Mesa Verde.** Anasazi Indian cliff dwellings dating back more than 800 years have been preserved here. Another unique activity is the **Durango & Silverton Narrow Gauge Railroad.** Until a few years ago, this historic train ran only in the summer. Now, in winter, it goes halfway to Silverton, then returns to Durango, a five-hour trip. The fare is about $50 for adults, $25 for 11 and younger. Though the cars are enclosed, warm clothing is recommended.

Sleigh rides, snowmobiling and other activities can be booked through the Purgatory Ski Concierge in the Village Center. An attraction which was new last year is tubing. The beginners' surface lift at the Columbine Station was relocated and it now hauls tubers up in the afternoon and evening.

Getting there and getting around

By air: The Durango-La Plata County Airport (DRO), is 42 miles south of Purgatory and about 18 miles from Durango, American Airlines has daily nonstop jet flights from Dallas-Ft. Worth, from mid-December through the end of March. Other airlines are United Express (Mesa Airlines) connecting from Denver, America West Express from Phoenix, and MAX (Mountain Air Express) from Colorado Springs, connecting with Western Pacific Airlines. An alternative airport is Albuquerque, N.M. (Southwest has 50 flights per day there), but then you must drive three and a half hours.

By car: Purgatory is 25 miles north of Durango, 350 miles southwest of Denver, 232 miles northwest of Albuquerque and 470 miles northeast of Phoenix. There are no major mountain passes from the south or west. Nevertheless, if you don't have four-wheel drive, carry chains.

Getting around: Transportation from Durango to Purgatory has been a perennial challenge for the skier or boarder without a car. Last season, the resort started a continuously running bus service, Mountain TranSport, between town and the slopes for day and evening. We weren't at Purgatory last season to try it, so we haven't heard how successful it was.

Otherwise, visitors have three ground transportation options: (1) The larger hotels offer free or low-cost shuttle service to and from the slopes. Others have free or low-cost airport shuttles. Some lodges on the north end of town even offer free nightlife shuttles for guests. Ask about transportation when making a reservation. (2) Rent a car. The Durango airport has a number of rental agencies as do some of the hotels. (3) **Durango Transportation** (259-4818) provides on-call taxi service as well as airport pick-ups. One-way fare from the airport to Purgatory is about $65 for one person, or $25 each for five or more passengers. From the airport to Durango, the fare is about $15 per person.

Steamboat

Colorado

Summit elevation:	**10,568 feet**
Vertical drop:	**3,668 feet**
Base elevation:	**6,900 feet**

Address: 2305 Mt. Werner Circle
Steamboat Springs, CO 80487
✆ **Area code:** 970
Ski area phone: 879-6111
Snow report: 879-7300
ⓘ **Toll-free reservations:** (800) 922-2722
Fax: 879-4757
E-mail: steamboat-info@steamboat-ski.com
Internet: http://www.steamboat-ski.com
Expert:★★★
Advanced:★★★★
Intermediate:★★★★★
Beginner:★★
Never-ever:★★

Number and types of lifts: 22–1 gondola,
4 high-speed quads, 1 quad, 6 triples,
6 doubles, 4 surface lifts
Skiable acreage: 2,939 acres
Snowmaking: 15 percent
Uphill capacity: 32,158 per hour
Snowboarding: Yes, unlimited
Bed base: 17,218
Nearest lodging: slopeside
Resort child care: Yes, 6 months and older
Adult ticket, per day: $47-$52 (98/99 price)
Dining:★★★★
Apres-ski/nightlife:★★★
Other activities:★★★★

Steamboat's ad campaign would have you believe that horses outnumber the cars in its parking lot, that cowboy hats and sheepskin jackets are the preferred ski wear and that you trip over Lone Star longnecks on the dance floors. In reality, this is a big, sleek, modern ski area with more microbrews and gourmet coffees than spittoons.

Steamboat Mountain Village, the cluster of condos, shops and restaurants next to the ski mountain, is unpretentiously upscale. Boutiques offering elegant high-priced goods are intermixed with T-shirt shops; gourmet restaurants are within steps of ribs-and-hamburger eateries. You will see an occasional socialite swathed in fur, but right behind her will be someone wearing a 15-year-old ski parka. Everyone looks right at home.

In the village, the only cowboy hats you're likely to see grace the heads of Steamboat's resident celebrity, Billy Kidd, and the ticket punchers in the gondola building. Venture into downtown Steamboat Springs, though, and you may see cowboys sauntering down Lincoln Avenue. Northwest Colorado still has many cattle ranches, so they'll probably be the real thing.

The downtown area—about five minutes by car and 15 minutes by a free shuttlebus from the village—squeezes into its dozen blocks a hodgepodge of old Victorian buildings, 1950s storefronts and a gas station or hardware store here and there. Good restaurants and nightlife hideouts are at the village, downtown, and on the highway linking the two. The bus runs between slopes and town every 20 minutes, making it easy to enjoy the village, town and everything in between.

Steamboat is also a great place for non-skiers. In addition to great shopping, it has activities that go beyond the usual sleigh rides and snowmobile tours (see Other Activities).

New for 98/99: Steamboat will add a new lift, additional trails and snowmaking. A new express quad chair lift will service Pioneer Ridge's 260 acres of terrain, which opened for skiing and riding in 97/98. Eleven new intermediate and advanced trails will be added in this area, which will have 770 acres of trails and terrain when fully completed. The resort's new snowmaking will ensure top-to-bottom coverage, a blessing for early-season visitors.

Mountain layout

◆◆ **Expert** ◆ **Advanced:** Expert descents here mean trees and lots of them. Steamboat has only a few extreme steeps, but the runs from the Sundown Express chair are tree skiing and riding developed to an art. These trails have been expertly thinned, both by humans and Mother Nature. Some trees are only about 10 feet apart, so stay alert. Such trails—natural slalom courses where the poles ain't spring-loaded—produce gallons of adrenaline even for the best skiers and snowboarders.

Other good areas for advanced and expert skiers and riders are off of The Ridge to the north of Storm Peak. There, Chutes 1, 2 and 3, No Name Chutes, the Christmas Tree Bowl, and other descents provide great challenges. The top of Morningside lift opens up first-rate expert skiing. The short hike required to reach these knee-knockers keeps away all but the truly dedicated.

Morningside Park consists of 179 acres of intermediate and advanced terrain on the back side of Storm Peak. Pioneer Ridge also challenges advanced skiers and riders. Arrowhead Glade, between Concentration and Vagabond on the lower part of the mountain, is another advanced playground.

■ **Intermediate:** Among the great cruisers are all the blue trails from the Sunshine Chair (locals call this area "Wally World"), Sunset and Rainbow off the Four Points lift and Vagabond and Heavenly Daze off Thunderhead Express. The Sunshine Chair blues also have spots where beginning tree skiers can get some practice. If the crowds build in any of those areas, head for the intermediate runs reached by the Bashor and Christie chairs, which often are deserted.

Longhorn, one of Steamboat's newest runs off Pioneer Ridge, has quickly become a locals' favorite. It offers unparalleled views of the Yampa Valley. Skiers and riders can duck in and out of the lodgepole pines that border both side of this run as they cruise to the Storm Peak Express lift.

Many of the black-diamond runs aren't as intimidating as intermediates might think. Though the terrain gets steep in spots and the moguls pretty high, the trails are generally wide, allowing ample room for mistakes and recoveries. Westside, a black trail below Rendezvous Saddle, is steep but usually groomed. It's a good starting point for intermediates who wonder if they can handle the other black runs. If you're learning to do moguls, head for Concentration, marked black on the map, or Surprise, marked blue. Often half of these runs is groomed, while the other half is left to build bumps.

●● **Beginner:** With the exception of some gentle terrain served by the Bashor and the two Christie chairs, most of the green trails above the base area are cat trails. Although they have a gentle grade, they also have very narrow spots, intersect higher-ability runs (where bombers sometimes use the intersection as a launching pad for the next section), and they have some very intimidating dropoffs on the downhill side. If beginners are part of your group, encourage them to enroll in a clinic so they will have a pleasant experience.

● **Never-ever:** Mixed reviews here. A successful first-time experience—especially for adults—depends on two things: great instruction and suitable, uncrowded terrain. Steamboat rates highly on the former, but not on the latter. The resort allows novices to repeat the first lesson at no charge until they've learned to descend from the Preview lift in a controlled manner. However, the learning area at the base gets crowded at the end of the day, and the slope's natural contours are opposite to the route back to the lifts. Steamboat records more than a million skier-days a year, so that's a lot of people whizzing by. If you don't get rattled easily, you'll probably do fine. But for everyone else, we recommend you learn elsewhere, then come here when you've had a little experience.

Mountain rating

Excellent tree skiing for experts, nice mogul runs for advanced, great cruisers for intermediates. Passable for beginners and never-evers. Though this isn't exactly slope-related, this section seems like a good place to add this rave review: Steamboat's Website (www.steamboat-ski.com) is one of the best in the snow sports industry. Loads fast, looks nice, it's updated regularly, and we have yet to need a piece of info that wasn't there.

Cross-country (97/98 prices)

The **Steamboat Ski Touring Center** (879-8180) at 2000 Clubhouse Drive has about 30 km. of groomed set tracks winding along Fish Creek and the surrounding countryside. The touring center has group and private instruction, rentals at $11 for a full day or $9 half day, a restaurant, and backcountry guided tours. Trail fees are $10 for a full day, $8 half day after 1 p.m. Snowshoeing also is available on 8 km. of trails.

Track skiing also is available at **Howelsen Hill** in downtown Steamboat Springs (879-8499) and at **Vista Verde** (879-3858; 800-526-7433), **High Meadows Ranch** (736-8416; 800-457-4453) and **Home Ranch** (879-1780), all guest ranches 18–25 miles from Steamboat Springs. The latter trio cater to overnight guests, but day visitors also are welcome. Vista Verde's 30-km. system is especially good for beginners, because most of the terrain is quite gentle. High Meadows grooms about 12 km., with additional trails groomed as needed. Home Ranch has 40 km. of groomed track, and it offers cross-country, backcountry and telemarking opportunities.

For a real thrill, take a tour to **Rabbit Ears Pass** (guided tours available through Steamboat Touring Center and Ski Haus, 879-0385); you'll be skiing on the Continental Divide. The marked backcountry ski trails range from 1.7 to 7 miles, from relatively gentle slopes to steep and gnarly, but on a clear day you can see forever. Call or visit the U.S. Forest Service (29587 W. US 40 in Steamboat Springs, 879-1722) to get current ski conditions and safety tips. Other popular backcountry areas are **Buffalo Pass, Pearl Lake State Park, Stagecoach State Recreation Area** and **Steamboat Lake State Park.**

Snowboarding

Steamboat has several terrain parks—Dude Ranch is a competition halfpipe and Sunshine Reef has various jumps, slides and obstacles. A terrain park just for kids is called the Beehive, on the Giggle Gulch trail off Christie Peak.

Lessons are offered daily; children must be 8 years or older for snowboard lessons. Steamboat also offers Learn-To-Ride weekends with a two-hour lesson, a lower mountain lift ticket and rental equipment the first two weekends in December.

Lessons (98/99 prices)

Group lessons: $38 for two hours; $57 for all day, with multiday discounts and lift-lesson packages available. Snowboard clinics cost $45 for a half day and $63 for a full day with lunch.

Never-ever package: Steamboat has two Learn-to-Ski/Ride Weekend packages early in the season for $15 per day for a lower-mountain lift ticket, a two-hour lesson and rental equipment. But from Christmas vacation on, novices sign up for a group or private lesson.

Private lessons: $80 for one hour, $150 for two and $200 for three. Semi-private rates (2–5 people) are $120, $225 and $300 respectively. Reservations required.

Special programs: Many, including race clinics, telemark skiing, bumps, powder, first tracks, skiers 65 and older, women, disabled skiers—even a style clinic to teach grace. Group clinics last from 1.5 to 3 hours and cost $30 to $52.

A Ski Week package for adults is available Monday–Friday including five two-hour lessons, video analysis, NASTAR racing and a Ski Week ball cap and pin, for $167.

Racing: Steamboat is the home to 43 Olympic and world medalists, so it's natural that the resort has many programs for racing and competition. Steamboat has three courses, a NASTAR course, a self-timed course on the Bashor run and another self-timed course on Spike near Rendezvous Saddle. Two runs cost $5, with each additional run $1. NASTAR clinics are Monday and Wednesday, and cost $52 for two hours of coaching, video analysis and two runs down the course.

Steamboat also has the Billy Kidd Performance Center, which offers two- and three-day camps for adults, teens and kids who are at least of intermediate ability. The camps refine technique in the bumps, through race gates and on tough terrain (Olympic bronze medalist Nelson Carmichael headlines the bump series). The cost is $170 per day for adults, $155 for ages 13–18, $140 for kids.

Children's lessons: $63 for an all-day lesson (including lunch), or $45 for a 2.5-hour afternoon lesson for ages first grade through 15. (Side note to readers outside the U.S.: First grade usually is age 6.) Classes are grouped according to age and ability. Ages 13–18 who are at the intermediate level or higher have separate lessons Monday–Friday during the Christmas holidays and from mid-February through March for $63, all day with lunch.

Ages 2 to kindergarten (again, a side note: that's usually age 5) can opt for a one-hour private lesson and all-day child care for $130, including lunch.

Children and teens also have a Ski Week program for $285, but unlike the adult version, their lessons are all day and all lunches are included. Kids stay with the same instructor the entire week. Lift tickets are extra.

Child care (98/99 prices)

Ages: 6 months to kindergarten (usually age 5).

Costs: $63 all day (lunch included) or $45 half day. Multiday discounts are available. Parents must provide a lunch for children younger than 2.

Reservations: Required for all care programs, and must be prepaid. Cancellations must be 24 hours in advance to avoid being charged. Call the Kids Vacation Center, 879-6111, Ext. 469 or make reservations through Steamboat Central Reservations, (800) 922-2722.

Note: Steamboat's children's programs are rated tops in the West by *Snow Country* magazine. The resort offers numerous, supervised evening programs for children and teens, ranging in cost from $9 per hour to $35. Call or visit the Website for specific details.

Other options: Baby's Away (800-978-9030; 970-879-2354) rents and will deliver baby needs to your lodge, such as crib, stroller, car seat and toys.

Lift tickets (98/99 prices)

	Adult	Child (Up to 12)
One day	$52	$29
Three days	$156 ($52/day)	$87 ($29/day)
Five days	$235 ($47/day)	$145 ($27/day)

Who skis free: One child up to age 12 skis free the same number of days as his or her parent when the parent buys a 5-day or longer lift ticket. Two kids, two parents, both kids ski free. Three kids, two parents, the third kid buys a ticket. No blackout periods, even during Christmas. Children must bring proof of age. Ages 70 and older ski free; photo ID required.

Who skis at a discount: Teens 13–18 ride lifts for $40 per day the same number of days as their parents when parents buy a 5-day or longer ticket. The rules are the same as for the Kids Ski Free program. Ages 65–69 ride for $33 per day. Adult and teen tickets are less (adults $42–$47 per day, depending on number of days, teens $35) very early and very late in the season, usually before mid-December and the first week in April.

Accommodations

In general, lodging in Steamboat Mountain Village is more expensive than in town. Condos outnumber hotel and motel rooms. Many properties have rates that vary throughout the season. Before mid-December and after March 31 are the cheapest; January comes next, and Christmas and Presidents' Weekend are most expensive.

Steamboat Central Reservations will make suggestions to match your needs and desires. Let the reservationist know the price range, location and room requirements (quiet location, good for families, laundry or other special amenities). The number is (800) 922-2722 or (970) 879-0740, fax (970) 879-4757, or you can submit a reservations inquiry from the resort's Website.

The **Sheraton Steamboat Resort**, (800-848-8878, 800-848-8877 in Colorado, 970-879-2220) a luxury full-service hotel, sits 60 feet from the Silver Bullet Gondola. Rates are about $99–$385.

Nearly all the other lodging at the ski area is in condominiums—hundreds of them surrounding the base.

Torian Plum (970-879-8811 or 800-228-2458) is one of the best, with spotless rooms and facilities, an extremely helpful staff, the ski area out one door and the top bars and restaurants out the other. Prices start at about $165 a night for the smallest units and top out close to $1,000 for the largest ones at prime times.

Torian Plum's sister properties, **Bronze Tree** and **Trappeur's Crossing,** have similar prices. Bronze Tree has two- and three-bedroom units. Trappeur's Crossing is about two blocks from the lifts, but offers a free private shuttle from 7 a.m. to 11 p.m.

Generally, prices are based on how close the property is to the lifts. Among those in the expensive category ($170 per night and up for hotel rooms and small condo units) are the **Best Western Ptarmigan Inn** (800-538-7519 or 970-879-1730) at the base of the Silver Bullet gondola, **Storm Meadows Townhomes** (800-262-5150 or 970-879-5151), **Norwegian Log Condominiums** (800-525-2622 or 970-879-3700) and **Thunderhead Lodge and Condominiums** (800-525-5502 or 970-879-9000).

Others in this price category are **Timber Run Condominiums** (800-525-5502 or 970-879-7000) with three outdoor hot tubs of varying sizes); **the Harbor Hotel** in downtown Steamboat (800-543-8888, 800-334-1012 in Colorado, 970-879-1522) which includes a free bus pass; **The Lodge at Steamboat** (800-525-5502 or 970-879-6000); **The Ranch at Steamboat** (800-525-2002 or 970-879-3000) with great views of the ski hill and the broad Yampa Valley; and the **Ski Town Inn** (formerly the Ramada; 800-754-8696 or 970-879-9300), about half a mile from downtown and two miles from the lifts.

Economy lodging ($109 and lower for hotels/motels and $65–$265 for condos) includes **Alpiner Lodge** (800-538-7519 or 970-879-1430) downtown, **Shadow Run Condominiums** (800-525-2622 or 970-879-3700) only 500 yards from lifts, **Alpine Meadows Townhomes** (800-525-2622 or 970-879-3700, a bit further at 800 yards) and **The Rockies** (800-525-7654 or 970-879-7654), half a mile away.

The Steamboat Bed and Breakfast (970-879-5724) just a few years old, is located at 442 Pine St. This B&B has rooms filled with antiques. Winter rates are about $95–$135 per double room with breakfast. No children, no pets. **Caroline's Bed and Breakfast** (970-870-1696), 838 Merritt St. is another good choice for those who like B&Bs.

Travelers who enjoy remote rural elegance will be delighted by a stay at **The Home Ranch** (970-879-1700) in the nearby town of Clark. This is one of only a handful of Relais et Chateaux properties in the U.S. Eight individual wooden cabins are nestled in the aspens of the Elk River Valley with a view of Hahn's Peak and the surrounding mountains, each distinctly decorated and with a hot tub on the porch and a wood stove inside. The main lodge also has six guest rooms, and is where everyone is served three gourmet meals per day (the dining room is exclusive to ranch guests). Rates of $450–$550 per double-occupancy room also include lift tickets and a shuttle to the ski area, though many people will be happy exploring the cross country and snowshoe trails at the ranch.

 # Dining

Steamboat has a great variety of restaurants—varied menus, varied atmosphere and varied prices. The area has more than 70 restaurants, including one or more Cajun, Chinese, French, Italian, and Scandinavian. Look for the Steamboat Dining Guide in your hotel or condo—it has menus and prices.

If you're looking for fine dining, our staff dining expert, Katy Keck, suggests these:

Without a doubt, the most impressive evening in Steamboat starts at Gondola Square at the Silver Bullet terminal. Here, you set off on the journey into the stars on the Silver Bullet to **Hazie's** (879-6111, ext. 465; reservations required) at the top of Thunderhead. Hazie's offers exquisite nouvelle continental cuisine, with unbeatable views. The Steamboat executive chef,

Danish-born Morten Hoj, has created a menu that will intrigue any palate. Hazie's also serves lunch (reservations recommended) from 11:30 a.m. to 2:30 p.m., featuring an assortment of soups and salads, entrées and burgers.

Ragnar's (879-6111, Ext. 465; reservations for lunch suggested) at Rendezvous Saddle features Scandinavian and continental cuisine. Start with the baked Camembert tivoli or gravlax with mustard dill sauce. Entrées include daily specials. Lunch costs about $9–$14.

Three nights a week (Thursday through Saturday), Ragnar's offers a prix-fixe Scandinavian menu at $69 for adults. This evening also starts at Gondola Square, but once off the Silver Bullet at the top of Thunderhead, you climb into a sleigh to continue your journey to Rendezvous Saddle. We recommend a mug of hot spiced glögg before relaxing to music and enjoying the meal. Reservations are required at night.

For Steamboat's pinnacle of French dining, try **L'Apogee** (911 Lincoln Avenue, 879-1919). Chef-owner Jamie Jenny has created a casually elegant ambiance where he serves some of the area's finest French food. While the food cannot be too highly praised, it is the wine list that is truly impressive. There are more than 500 wines, ranging from $12 to $1,000 a bottle, all maintained in three temperature-controlled cellars. L'Apogee also features Steamboat's only cruvinet system, serving over 30 wines and ports by the glass.

This crew also services the more casual **Harwig's Grill** (same address, no reservations). Here, the menu reflects a passion for Southeast Asian flavors. Prices range from $3.95 for appetizers to $7–$11 for entrées with a list of 60 very affordable wines. Daily from 5 p.m.

Another fine-dining choice is **Antares** (57 1/2 Eighth St., 879-9939). Not coincidentally, all the principals are alums from L'Apogee. Serving new American cuisine, this restaurant—named for a star in the Scorpio constellation—is housed in the historic Rehder building, built in the early 1900s. Open daily 5:30 to 10:30 p.m.

For more than Mex, don't miss **La Montaña**, (879-5800) located at 2500 Village Drive. Chef Michael Fragola has created an inventive menu that goes way beyond tacos and fajitas. Appetizer prices are about $9 and entrées about $15 for Tex-Mex dinners and $7 to $25 for the Southwestern specials.

The **Steamboat Smokehouse** at 912 Lincoln Ave has a no-credit card, no-reservations, no-nonsense atmosphere, with some of Colorado's best Texas-style hickory-smoked barbecued anything—you name it—brisket, sausage, turkey, chicken, ham and more.

A popular seafood restaurant is the **Steamboat Yacht Club** (879-4774) at 811 Yampa Avenue. The dining room overlooking the river is perfect for watching night skiing or Wednesday night ski jumping on Howelsen Hill. Its menu is designed to mix and match fish, cooking techniques and sauces to suit your tastes. The Yacht Club also serves meat and poultry.

Here are some that have moderate prices ($15–$20 per meal, including drinks) and a casual atmosphere:

At the ski area or close by:

Dos Amigos (879-4270) serves Tex-Mex food and sandwiches and is part of the infamous "Steamboat Triangle" après-ski circuit along with **Tugboat** and **Mattie Silks'** bars, and **The Cathouse Cafe**. Grubstake (879-4448) serves hamburgers and steak sandwiches.

Downtown:

Old West Steakhouse (879-1441) is somewhat expensive, but packs in the crowds for steaks and seafood.

Giovanni's (879-4141) has not only Brooklyn-style Italian fare, but also what may be the largest collection of Brooklyn memorabilia this side of the borough. For more moderate

Italian, head to **Riggio's** (879-9010) on Lincoln. Seafood and veal are especially good, and be sure to leave room for their homemade desserts.

Ore House at the Pine Grove (879-1441) is a Steamboat tradition serving steaks, seafood, elk and buffalo for more than a quarter-century. **Yama-Chans** (879-8862) is Steamboat's first Japanese restaurant. **The Cantina** (879-0826) is downtown's equivalent of Dos Amigos. **Cugino's** (879-5805) has the best pizza.

If you're in town for breakfast or lunch, try the **In-Season Bakery and Deli** (879-1840). Homemade soup, sandwiches and salads are served along with soothing classical music. For some quiet-time and a light lunch (sandwiches, homemade pasta salads and soups) head to the **Off The Beaten Path** bookstore and coffeehouse (879-6830) across from the Harbor Hotel. We like the bookstore (especially because it stocks *Skiing America*), the great gourmet coffees and the linger-as-long-as-you-want attitude.

Good breakfast spots are **Winona's** or **The Shack Cafe** downtown, or **The Tugboat** at the base area. Also try **Market on the Mountain**, in the same complex as La Montaña, for homemade muffins, cinnamon rolls and bagels for breakfast and deli sandwiches; or **Mocha Molly's**, with muffins, bagels and fancy coffees at two locations at the ski area base and downtown. Avid skiers can board the gondola at 8 a.m. and have breakfast at **The Early Bird Breakfast Buffet** at the top of the gondola until the slopes open. Biscuits and gravy are a specialty, with other high-fuel fare also served, cafeteria-style.

Après-ski/nightlife

For immediate, relatively rowdy après-ski, the place to go is the **Inferno,** just behind the base of the Silver Bullet gondola. People pack into the bar, where each hour the bartender spins the shot wheel, setting prices from 35 to 95 cents. When 35 cents comes up, revelers buy shots by the tray.

Dos Amigos, as noted, is one leg of the "Steamboat Triangle." Have margaritas here, then head for the **Cathouse Cafe** and **Tugboat** for beer or mixed drinks. Friday is Zoo Night at the Cathouse, where any beer that has an animal on the label or in the name is $2.50.

Downtown, the **Old Town Pub** and **The Steamboat Yacht Club** have great après-ski.

Quieter après-ski locations on the mountain include **HB's** in the Sheraton or **The Slopeside Grill**. Steamboat also has two brew pubs, **Heavenly Daze**, in Ski Time Square at the ski area, and **Steamboat Brewery & Tavern** downtown.

Late-night places include **Inferno, Dos Amigos, Heavenly Daze** and **Tugboat**, all with live music and lots of people. Downtown, the lively spots include **BW-3, The Steamboat Smokehouse** and **The Old Town Pub**.

Steamboat has a movie theater downtown and one at the mountain. A night trip to Strawberry Park Hot Springs is great fun (see Other Activities).

Other activities

Steamboat has so much to do off the mountain, it's tempting to skip the skiing. Here is a mere sampling:

Soak in the natural thermal waters at **Strawberry Park Hot Springs** (879-0342), about 10 miles north of the ski area. Admission to the hot springs is $5–$10; a tour (transportation and admission) is $25. Unless you have four-wheel drive, spend the extra for the tour—the road to the springs is narrow, slick and winding. It's open from 10 a.m. to 10 p.m. during the week and stays open a little later on weekends.

Helpful info: after dark, many bathers go without suits (unless it's a moonlit night, you won't see much). The only place to change is an unheated teepee, so wear your swimsuit under your clothes. Many people bring a plastic bag to store their clothes; otherwise steam from the pools combined with the cold air may freeze them. Water shoes will protect your feet from the rocky entry. Beverages are OK as long as they aren't in a glass container. Families might prefer the Steamboat Health and Recreation Center, with hot springs pools and a water slide that kids enjoy. Call 879-1828.

Learn to drive on slick roads at the **Bridgestone Winter Driving School** (879-6104 or 800-WHY-SKID). Half-day ($115), full-day ($225) and multiday lessons on a specially constructed course are a unique experience, one that could save your life. Two of our contributors have taken the course, and both give it their highest recommendation.

Steamboat introduced **on-mountain snowshoe tours** during the 97/98 season, meeting each Wednesday from the top of the Silver Bullet gondola and guided by the Mountain Hosts, Steamboat's cadre of on-mountain information specialists. Bring your own shoes or rent from Steamboat Ski Rentals (879-6111, Ext. 345).

Shopping opportunities are many and varied, both in the village and downtown. Other activities include weekend **theater** from the Steamboat Community Players (879-3254), **dogsled rides** (879-4662), **snowcat skiing/boarding** (879-5188), **ice skating** at Howelsen Ice Arena (879-0341), **ice climbing** (879-4857), **indoor climbing** (879-5421), **horseback riding or hot-air balloons** (several businesses offer these activities; ask when you get into town), **indoor tennis** (879-8400), and far too many more to list.

You can make reservations for activities through **Steamboat Central Reservations** (879-0740 or 800-922-2722), or **Windwalker Premier Tours** (879-8065; 800-748-1642).

 ## Getting there and getting around

By air: Yampa Valley Airport at Hayden, 22 miles away, handles jets. American, Continental, United, TWA and Northwest have direct or non-stop flights from more than 100 North American cities. Three ground transportation companies provide service from the airport and from Denver International Airport—(all 970 area codes) Alpine Taxi/Limo, 879-2800; Western Coach 4x4 Limo, 870-0771, and Mountain Luxury Limousine, 879-0077. Avis, Budget and Hertz have cars available at the Yampa Valley Airport.

By car: Steamboat is 157 miles northwest of Denver via I-70 west through the Eisenhower Tunnel to exit 205 at Silverthorne (allow extra time if you want to stop at Silverthorne's huge factory outlet mall), north on Hwy. 9 to Kremmling, then west on Hwy. 40 to the resort.

Getting around: A car is optional. Steamboat has an excellent free bus system between town and ski area running every 20 minutes. Call 879-5585 for information.

Telluride

Colorado

Summit elevation: 11,890 feet
Vertical drop: 3,165 feet
Base elevation: 8,725 feet

Address: P.O. Box 11155, Telluride, CO 81435
✆ **Area code:** 970
Ski area phone: 728-6900
Snow report: 728-7425
ⓘ **Toll-free reservations:** (800) 525-3455
Fax: 728-6475
E-mail: skitelluride@telski.com
Internet: http://www.telski.com (ski area)
http://www.telluridelodging.com (lodging)
http://www.telluridegateway.com (visitors guide)
Expert:★★★★★
Advanced:★★★★★
Intermediate:★★★
Beginner:★★★★★
Never-ever:★★★★★

Number and types of lifts: 12—1 gondola,
2 high-speed quads, 2 triples, 5 doubles,
2 surface lifts
Skiable Acreage: 1,050 acres
Snowmaking: 15 percent
Uphill capacity: 12,076 per hour
Snowboarding: Yes, unlimited
Bed base: 4,600
Nearest lodging: slopeside
Resort child care: Yes, 2 months and older
Adult ticket, per day: $34-$53 (98/99)

Dining:★★★
Apres-ski/nightlife:★★★
Other activities:★★★

When Butch Cassidy robbed the Bank of Telluride more than 100 years ago during the town's celebrated mining heyday, he left the best treasure behind.

But then, it would be difficult to fit the town of Telluride and its slopes into a pair of saddle bags. Nestled in a box canyon 8,725 feet high in the jagged San Juan Mountains of southwestern Colorado, the town of Telluride is a neat pattern of streets six blocks wide and 14 blocks long, miniaturized by massive 14,000-foot peaks tumbling into neighborhoods. Author John Naisbitt has described it as "the most beautiful place on earth."

Telluride is in a delightful time warp—a nostalgic blend of the Old West captured in Victorian buildings you'd swear were a movie set, and all the civilized pleasures of a modern resort. When skiing replaced the dying mining industry in the early 1970s, it saved the tiny community from becoming a ghost town and opened the way for careful preservation of the entire town—designated a National Historic District—and an orderly five-phase development plan for a world-class ski resort.

Telluride Ski & Golf Company is a quarter-century old now. Though its early reputation was built as a place dedicated to steeps, it has added terrain that has transformed it into an all-around area with some of the best beginner slopes in the nation.

In addition to its historic town, Telluride also has a different face, built on the opposite side of the ski mountain. This hamlet, called Mountain Village, offers excellent access to the mountain, but is quite different in look and feel. Mountain Village is a master-planned community anchored by what is considered the most luxurious hotel in the area, The Peaks at Telluride.

A 2.5-mile gondola links the town of Telluride with Mountain Village. This free "gondola transportation system"—as the resort calls it—replaced an eight-mile, 20-minute drive by car or bus with a 12-minute ride. It operates 16 hours a day, 7 a.m. to 11 p.m. (midnight on Fridays and Saturdays) during winter and summer and makes commuting between the two towns for shopping or dining a snap. It also is used as a lift to the slopes, but you'd better have a lift ticket if you're using it for that purpose.

 ## Mountain layout

◆◆ **Expert:** Start with what put Telluride on the skiers' map—The Plunge and Spiral Stairs. This duo, when left ungroomed, is as challenging a combination of steep bumps as you can find anywhere. If you manage to get down without too many bruises or sore spots, you can savor a sense of accomplishment. Mammoth is an alternate trail but not any easier.

Another good area for experts is the 450 acres of glade and above-timberline skiing in the Gold Hill area. These double-diamond runs require a hike to the 12,247-foot mark (if you want to go to the top of in-bounds skiing), which makes Telluride's legal vertical drop 3,522 feet. If it's a clear day after a powder dump, take a nanosecond to admire the view from the summit before you plunge in. It is magnificent. Someday in the not-too-distant future, Telluride plans to put a lift up here.

◆ **Advanced:** Telluride occasionally uses a winch cat to groom some of the runs on the front face. (Some of the runs are "split-groomed," meaning half is smooth and half is left to build bumps.) On our most recent visit, The Plunge had been recently groomed, creating one of the steepest and most daringly exciting snow highways we've seen. Bushwacker's normally monstrous bumps were merely huge, thanks to a grooming a few days earlier. While some highly accomplished skiers and snowboarders may mourn this development, the face still has plenty of terrain that mere advanced skiers won't touch, and at least now there are enough bodies riding Chair 9 to justify the electric bill.

■ **Intermediate:** Telluride is one of the few resorts that has an hourglass shape to its ability chart—lots to offer at either end, but comparatively slim in the middle. Intermediate trails here tend to be short. See Forever is the exception—nearly three miles top to bottom. True intermediate terrain is under Chairs 3, 4 and 5, but the Telluride Face with its occasional grooming is now acceptable for strong intermediates looking to rise to the next level. In fact, even without adding terrain, increased grooming has made more runs available to intermediates each year.

The most fun for an intermediate would be repeated trips up Chair 4, and down Peek a Boo, Humboldt Draw, Pick and Gad and Tomboy. The black-rated runs off Chair 6 are short and you can assess from the chair whether you can handle them. If not, just head toward See Forever.

Just learning moguls? Head for the top of Misty Maiden or Palmyra, where you can practice, practice, practice before trying out The Face.

Eventually, intermediates will get their due reward. The U.S. Forest Service is in the process of approving an expansion plan for Telluride that will add a tremendous amount— nearly 700 acres—of fine expert and intermediate terrain.

●● **Beginner:** Sunshine Peak is a perfect spot to develop confidence, because the runs are long and very gentle, and none of the high-speed, high-ability skiers or snowboarders come here. This is simply one of the top spots on the continent for this ability level.

For those looking to improve: Telluride divides its runs into six categories instead of three or four. One green circle is easiest, then double greens, then single blues, then double blues, single black and double black. This allows an easier progression for those still developing their skills.

● **Never-ever:** The Meadows, served by a Chondola (a hybrid high-speed quad with gondola cars also on the cable), has for years been considered a perfect novice area.

Mountain rating

Telluride is a rite of passage for experts. It's a chance to test oneself against consistent steeps and monstrous bumps. Telluride makes a serious effort to groom formerly expert slopes to make them advanced, and advanced slopes to put them within reach of intermediates trying to graduate to the advanced level. If you are an intermediate whose trademark trails are long, mellow cruising terrain, head elsewhere. For never-evers and beginners, there are few better places to be introduced to snow sports.

Snowboarding

Snowboarding is allowed on the entire mountain. The East and West Drains are natural halfpipes, and the gentle terrain in the Meadows and Sunshine Peak make this a great place to learn this sport. The Air Garden terrain park is one of the largest in the Southwest, with more than 800 vertical feet of berms, gaps, hits and tabletops, plus a 110-meter-long, 15-meter-wide halfpipe that mimics the specs of the one built for the 1998 Winter Olympics in Japan. Several other small terrain parks are scattered around the mountain.

Cross-country

Here again the spectacular scenery makes cross-country a joy to experience. For high-mesa cross-country skiing this area is difficult to beat. The **Telluride Nordic Center,** 728-7260, offers a 55-km. network of groomed trails around town and the ski area.

Lessons are also available; call (800) 525-2717 or locally, 728-6265 to book lessons. If you use the groomed trails on the valley floor, there is no cost; if you'd like to ski the 30 km. of intermediate and advanced groomed trails at the top of Lift 10, buy a $12 ticket at the downhill ski area ticket windows. Adult and children's group lessons are priced at about $30; $38 with rentals. Full day backcountry tours cost approximately $65. Equipment rentals—skis, boots and poles—for a full day are about $15 for adults or children.

Guided tours wind through the San Juan Mountains and a five-hut, 68-mile network of intermediate and advanced trails. Huts are approximately six miles apart and each is equipped with padded bunks, propane cooking appliances and a big potbelly stove. The same rates apply to all programs: about $22 per person cabin fee and $25 a day for provisions, which covers breakfast, lunch and dinner. Guides are available for groups, which are held to a maximum of eight skiers. Call the **San Juan Hut System** for rates: 728-6935.

Nearby is the **San Juan Guest Ranch** (626-5360; 800-331-3015), which acccommodates overnight visitors. Day visitors also may use the trails. Usually, at least 12 km. are groomed, but sometimes additional kilometers are groomed if guests' needs warrant it. The home of the Ouray Mountain Guides, the ranch also offers ice climbing, backcountry touring, and all forms of winter mountaineering, including avalanche awareness training.

Lessons (98/99 prices)

Telluride's 200-instructor ski school, run by Annie Vareille Savath for the past 20 years, has a good reputation. A successful learning experience requires two main ingredients: good instruction and appropriate terrain. Telluride has both. Ski school operates out of the Mountain Village Activity Center, a one-stop-shopping facility that has lift tickets, lessons, a full-service rental shop, overnight equipment storage, children's ski school and child care. A computer system links Telluride Sports' six rental shops and stores client information permanently so future rentals can be paperwork-free. Scanable disks track equipment so it can be returned at any of the rental locations. Nearby is the Rossignol Test Center where specialists can match you with the latest demo gear for alpine skiing, telemarking or snowboarding.

Group lessons: Small-group lessons—four people or fewer—are offered in afternoons only for advanced beginners through experts for $70. All-day group lessons cost $63 with more than four to a group.

Never-ever package: For Alpine skiers, telemarkers, Nordic skiers or snowboarders; $85 for skiers or snowboarders includes a full day of lessons, lifts and rentals. Nordic and telemark are offered only on certain days; call for specifics.

Private lessons: $95 an hour, with discounts for each additional skier. A full day is $420.

Special programs: Many, including a highly acclaimed Women's Week program that offers lifts, races, video analysis, seminars, and wine and cheese parties. Perhaps because Telluride's ski school is run by a woman, this program is one of the best and longest-running of this type. A five-day session is $500, while a four-day session is $440.

Other programs include the Triple Threat Snowboard Camp, a four- or five-day camp for intermediate or higher-ability riders that covers free riding, park tricks and carving. Another program, Primary Movements, incorporates biomechanical alignment and equipment fitting to shorten the learning curve. More information is available on the Harb Ski Systems Website (http://www.harbskisystems.com).

Racing: NASTAR two-hour clinics cost $35, day camps are $130, or practice on your own for $5 (two runs) and $1 for each additional run. The course is near Lift 4. Also, a self-timed dual course is $1 per run.

Children's lessons: The Children's Adventure Center (728-7533) takes ages 3–12. Lessons, lift and rentals are $93 a full day, with multiday discounts. Half-day lessons are available. Snowboard lessons are offered for kids aged 6–12. A supervision program called Adventure Club is available before and after ski school programs; it's free for those enrolled in ski school.

Child care (98/99 prices)

Ages: 2 months to 3 years.

Costs: $55 for a full day with lunch, $45 for a half day (8 a.m.–12:30 p.m. or 12:30–5 p.m.).

Reservations: Required; call 728-7533 or (800) 801-4832 at least 24 hours in advance. Children's ski and day-care programs are in the Village Nursery and Children's Center in the the Mountain Village Activity Center.

Telephone area code: 970

Lift tickets (98/99 prices)

	Adult	Child (6–12)
One day	$53	$26
Three days	$153 ($51/day)	$78 ($26/day)
Five days	$230 ($46/day)	$130 ($26/day)

(a $2 surcharge is added to all tickets 12/19/98 to 1/3/99)

Who skis free: Ages 70 and older and 5 and younger.
Who skis at a discount: Ages 65–69 ski for $31. Telluride's early-season discounted rates, good from the opening to December 18, are $34 per day for adults, $17 for children 6–12, and $26 for seniors 65–69.

Accommodations

In Telluride you can stay down in the old town or in the Mountain Village. We start with some of our favorite spots in town; lodging in the mountain village is listed at the end of this section. Some lodging prices include lift tickets. You can "see" many of the lodges on the town of Telluride's Web site (http://www.telluridegateway.com). For more information on these and other places to stay, call **Telluride Central Reservations**, (800) 525-3455.

The **San Sophia Bed & Breakfast** (800-537-4781) is near the Oak Street lift. Rates are $185–$295. This cozy B&B is considered one of Telluride's best, with exceptional service. The direct Web address is http://www.sansophia.com

Another wonderful bed & breakfast is **Alpine Inn Bed & Breakfast** on Colorado Avenue, (800-707-3344 or locally 728-6282; website: http://www.alpineinn.com/telluride). The eight rooms are varied in size and in beds, so that just about any type of small group (couples, friends, singles) can stay here. The location is central, the breakfasts are superb and hosts John and Denise couldn't be more helpful. Rates are from $60 to $210 per night, depending on the season and size of room.

One of the newest luxury spots to stay is **The Hotel Columbia** (800-201-9505; 970-728-0660) right at the Telluride base of the new gondola. The hotel was built to look historic, but with the space and amenities of modern hotel rooms, such as fireplaces, big beds and luxurious bathrooms. The hotel has an office for guests' use, equipped with fax, copier and computer. Rates are $160–$425, the latter for the penthouse with kitchen during the Christmas and President's Weekend holiday periods.

The historic **New Sheridan Hotel** (800-200-1891; 970-728-4351) is a step back in time. It's on Colorado Avenue close to everything, with a skiers' shuttle stop outside the front door. Rates: $85–$285, depending on time and season.

The **Johnstone Inn** (970-728-3316 or 800-752-1901; http://www.johnstoneinn.com) is a B&B with eight small quaint rooms with private bath and a full breakfast every morning for $125–$145 per night. **Bear Creek Bed & Breakfast** (970-728-6681 or 800-338-7064), in a brick building on Colorado Avenue, has ten rooms with private bath and TV, roof deck, sauna and steam room for $60–$155 per night.

The **Ice House Lodge** (800-544-3436; 970-728-6300), a block from the Oak Street lift, has 6-foot tubs, comforters, balconies, custom furniture, a continental breakfast and après-ski goodies. Rates are $175–$650 a night. The **Camel's Garden** (888-772-2635; 970-728-9300) was opened in 1998 in the gondola plaza. In stark contrast to the town's prevalent Victorian theme, this contemporary luxury property has underground parking and a small conference space. Rates run $210 for a hotel room to $1,100 for a three-bedroom condo.

The **Manitou Bed & Breakfast** is decorated with country fabrics and antiques. It is near the Oak Street lift and a two-minute walk from the town center. Each room has a double bed. Rates are $145–$197. **The Riverside Condos** are perhaps the nicest in town and near the base of the Oak Street lift. **The Manitou Riverhouse** is just as close to the lifts but be ready for lots of stairs if you rent here. Around the Coonskin Base check into **Viking Lodge, Etta Place** and **Cimarron Lodge**, where you can almost literally fall out of bed and onto the lifts, and the **Tower House** about two blocks from the lifts. More moderately priced units are **West Willow** and **Coronet Creek**. All the properties in this paragraph (and others not listed) are managed by **Telluride Resort Accommodations,** (800) 538-7754 (LETS-SKI). The central check-in desk can get backed up at times—you may have to wait a couple of hours before you can get into your unit after check in. The town bus has a pickup spot close to the office; ask the desk clerk to direct you, and you can browse around town while you're waiting. If you are traveling with young children, or want to get into your condo right away for other reasons, discuss that with the reservations agent at the time of booking.

In the Mountain Village

The most luxurious property is the **The Peaks at Telluride** (970-728-6800 or 800-789-2220). This ski-in/ski-out resort hotel boasts one of the largest full-service spas in the country. Rates with daily spa access are $200–$1,250 per night.

Pennington's (800-543-1437; 970-728-5337) is the B&B of choice for the utmost in elegance. The rooms are giant and the views magnificent. The only problem is that you are quite a way from restaurants and nightlife, because Pennington's is just inside the entrance gate to the Mountain Village (too far to walk to its core). Prices are $150–$260 per room with breakfast. **The Inn at Lost Creek** (888-601-5678; 970-728-5678) and **Aspen Ridge** (800-324-6388; 970-728-4217) are Mountain Village's newest luxury properties.

Mountain Village has many condos, some of which start at $180 per night (double that for the ones closest to the lifts) and top out around $800. Call Telluride Resort Accommodations (800-538-7754) for more information.

Telluride has a **Regional Half-Price Program** with seven neighboring towns. If you stay in one of these spots, you can get half-price lift tickets throughout the season. The towns, their distance from Telluride and the number to call are: Cortez/Dolores/Rico/Mancos, four towns 25–70 miles away, (800) 253-1616; Montrose, 65 miles, (800) 348-3495; Ouray, 47 miles, (800) 228-1876; and Ridgway, 37 miles, (800) 754-3103. Durango, which is nearer to Purgatory Resort, also is part of this program, (800) 228-1876. Durango is 125 miles from Telluride and just 25 miles from Purgatory. If you want to do both resorts on one trip, it might be worth a call to this program.

 **Dining**

Telluride has about 30 restaurants in town and the Mountain Village. Dining is getting better every visit—with several fine restaurants, all with entrées in the $15–$28 range. **La Marmotte** (728-6232) near the Ice House Lodge serves French cuisine. **221 S. Oak** (it's both the name and address; 728-9507) is in a Victorian house with regional American specialties that vary daily in response to the freshest products available.

The **Powderhouse** (728-3622) on Colorado Avenue is another good choice for good food. **The Cosmopolitan** (728-1292), in the Hotel Columbia at the gondola base, serves eclectic American fare. **Rustico** (728-4046), on Telluride's main street, is run by Italian natives and has good food at good prices. It got rave reviews from the Italian-heritaged *Skiing America* staffer who visited here in 97/98, and she doesn't use the word "authentic" very often when it comes to the food of her homeland. **Campagna** (435 W. Pacific, 728-6190), serves Italian specialties. It's directly behind The Alpine Inn.

In the Mountain Village, **Legends** at The Peaks (728-6800) is open for breakfast and lunch only, while **Sundance** serves Southwestern fare for dinner.

Back to town for more casual and moderate dining: **Leimgruber's** (728-4663) serves German cooking and beer imported from Munich. It's a hot spot when the lifts close, too. **The Floradora** (728-3888) claims the best burgers. **Excelsior Cafe** (728-4250) has good-value and excellent-tasting North Italian cuisine.

The T-ride Country Club and Sports Bar (728-6344) offers cook-your-own steaks and seafood. **Sofio's** (728-4882) serves good Mexican cuisine but be prepared for a wait. It's worth it—have a margarita.

Coffee houses have hit Telluride, and visitors have six to choose from: **The Steaming Bean, Maggie's, Bad Ass Coffee Company** and **Between the Covers.** All are on Colorado Avenue. In the Mountain Village, **The Java Shack** is the coffee spot. **Skiers Union,** which is new and located at the bottom of Chairs 3 and 4, has great juices and coffee. **Wildflour** is a new gourmet bakery in Camel's Garden by the gondola, and **Baked in Telluride** is a 20-year-old bakery in a century-old warehouse. The locals call it by its acronym, BIT, and it's great for deli sandwiches, pizza and inexpensive dinners, washed down by their own brews.

Plan one evening for a magical sleigh ride dinner at **Skyline Guest Ranch**, even if you aren't staying there. Call (970) 728-3757 far in advance for reservations and information.

Après ski/nightlife

For immediate après-ski, stop at **Leimgruber's Bierstube** near the Coonskin Lift (Lift 7) for a selection of great beer and a sure shot at meeting folks. **Swede Finn Hall** on Pacific Street is another locals' favorite for an après-ski beer. **Eagle's Bar and Grille** on Colorado Avenue has a huge bar and seems to be the baby boomer meeting place.

For live music go to the **Fly Me to the Moon Saloon** with entertainment Thursday through Saturday. **The Last Dollar Saloon** has the best selection of imported beer in Telluride, plus pool tables and dart boards. It's a bit of a manly-man beer bar—not many women hang out. The old Victorian **New Sheridan Bar** is one of the "must sees" in Telluride to experience the essence of the Old West. The 20-something crowd likes **The House**, a tavern at 131 N. Fir St.

Other activities

Shopping: Telluride has some great shopping now, a far cry from a decade ago when your souvenir choices were either a large or extra-large T-shirt. Some of our favorites, all on Colorado Avenue: **Lizard Head Mining Co.**, for its extraordinary custom-made jewelry; **At Home in Telluride**, with distinctive housewares; **North Moon**, with handcrafted jewelry and crafts; and **Picaya**, above Telluride Creamery, with some nice and inexpensive jewelry and clothing.

Helicopter skiing is run by Helitrax for downhill and cross-country enthusiasts. Box 1560, Telluride CO 81435; 728-4904.

Telluride also has **sleigh rides** from Deep Creek Sleigh Rides, 728-3565; **gliding** with Telluride Soaring, 728-5424; **horseback riding** with Roudy, Telluride Horseback, 728-9611; **hot-air ballooning** from San Juan Balloon Adventures, 626-5495; **snowmobile tours** from Telluride Outside, 728-3895 and a pond in Mountain Village for **ice-skating**. It isn't every town that has a colorful past like Telluride's, so the **Historic Walking Tour** is well worth the time. Call 728-6639 for information.

Getting there and getting around

By air: Telluride has a small, weather-plagued airport five miles from town, served by United Express from Denver and America West Express from Phoenix. Montrose, 65 miles away, is where most visitors arrive, either by plan or by a weather diversion from Telluride. Continental has daily, nonstop jet service to Montrose from Houston, and nonstop service from Newark on Saturdays. United has daily jet service from Denver and often, from other cities as well.

If you fly into the Telluride airport, no matter what the weather, pack a carry-on with enough essentials to get you through 24 hours. These small planes fill with people, then add as much luggage as they can safely transport. This is a sound policy, but it also means that your bags may be delayed. Ways around the problem: 1) Fly to Montrose. The drive is farther, but you'll have your bags with you. 2) Send your bags early via UPS or Federal Express to Mail Boxes Etc. That business will arrange for your bags to be delivered to your lodging for about $8 per bag (inbound and outbound). Call (800) 557-EASY (557-3279) for complete details.

Ground transport is provided by **Telluride Transit** (728-6000); **Skip's Taxi** (728-6667); and **Mountain Limo** (728-9606). Call 24 hours in advance for Montrose airport pickups. Several other companies also are available with 48-hour advance reservations; ask central reservations about these when you call.

By car: Telluride is 335 miles from Denver via I-70 west, and Hwys. 50, 550, 62 and 145. From the southwest, it is 125 miles from Durango via Hwys. 160, 184 and 145.

Getting around: A car is unnecessary. The town is just eight blocks long—you can walk anywhere. If you have them, bring boots with at least an ankle-high cuff. During warm spells, the snow melt on the side streets can get quite deep. A free bus service runs in town, and the free gondola makes the commute between town and the Mountain Village a snap.

Vail

Colorado

Summit elevation: 11,450 feet
Vertical drop: 3,330 feet
Base elevation: 8,120 feet

Address: P.O. Box 7
Vail, CO 81658
☎ **Area code:** 970
Ski area phone: 476-5601
Snow report: 476-4888 or (800) 427-8308
ⓘ **Toll-free reservations:** (800) 427-8308
Toll-free foreign numbers:
U.K. (fax): 0800-891-675
New Zealand (fax): 0800-44-0415
Australia (fax): 0014-800-128-088
Mexico (fax): 95-800-010-1028
Brazil (fax): 000811-515-5557
Fax: 845-2609
E-mail: eagle@vailresorts.com
Internet: http://www.vail.snow.com

Expert:★★★★ **Advanced:**★★★★★
Intermediate:★★★★★
Beginner:★★★ **Never-ever:**★★★
Number and types of lifts: 30–
10 high-speed quads, 1 12-person gondola,
1 quad chair, 3 triple chairs,
5 double chairs, 10 surface lifts
Skiable acreage: 4,644 acres
Snowmaking: 10 percent
Uphill capacity: 46,161 per hour
Snowboarding: Yes, unlimited
Bed base: 41,305 within 10 miles
Nearest lodging: slopeside, condos & hotels
Resort child care: Yes, 2 months and older
Adult ticket, per day: $38-$61 (98/99 prices)
Dining:★★★★★
Apres-ski/nightlife:★★★★
Other activities:★★★★

In survey after survey, Vail is usually found near the top—never, it seems, lower than two or three. It is a *complete* area, lacking none of the essential ingredients that form the magical stew of a world-class ski resort. Vail has an ersatz Old World village and condominium convenience, raucous nightlife and quiet lounges, fine dining and pizzeria snacking. Its offslope activities are unsurpassed—shopping, skating, movies, museums, sleigh riding and so much more—everything money can buy. Bring lots of money—temptations abound, and bargains are few.

But village and expenses aside, there is above all The Mountain. Vail Mountain is a single stoop-shouldered behemoth so massive that every crease and wrinkle in its cape becomes another entire section to explore. Though it does not have the ultra-steeps or deeps of some of its Rocky Mountain cousins, what it has is a huge front face of long and very smooth cruisers, and an enormous back-bowl experience of wide-open adventure unlike anything this side of the Atlantic.

Vail's network of 10 high-speed quads is also the largest in the country. Combined, the mountain and its system of 30 lifts let you do more skiing and less back-tracking than almost any other resort you can name.

As important as it is, skiing only constitutes part of the total ski-vacation experience. A true world-class resort has to have amenities and atmosphere, and Vail is one of a kind in both areas. You'll find city conveniences such as 24-hour pharmacies (which you don't appreciate until you need medication in a more rural ski resort), but you won't find the typical Colorado mining-town atmosphere: Vail never was a mining town. About 35 years ago, it was a sheep pasture. Developers who saw the potential of the mountain built a village styled after an Austrian ski town. Vail gets a lot of ribbing about its Europe-in-the-USA look, but lots of people apparently like it—Vail consistently gets about 1.6 million skier visits each year, far more than any other American mountain resort.

Vail is what we call "urban skiing." This city-town just doesn't feel rural. It bustles with traffic and people jams in peak periods. You won't see too many stars at night—too many streetlights. But no stoplights, thanks to the adoption of European-style traffic roundabouts. If you head into one, don't panic. Just keep going and follow the signs.

But for many of the urban guests, Vail is just rural enough to let them feel they are getting away from it all. They find the well-lit streets comforting, they want the amenities of big-city life and they don't mind paying for it. Vail is their kind of place.

 ## Mountain layout

Vail Mountain is the biggest single ski mountain in North America. But it is segmented: you can concentrate on separate bowls and faces for a morning or afternoon, always having the choice of a new path down the mountain. And none of these runs seems intimidating, although there is plenty of challenge for every level of skier.

One suggestion: If you're skiing with a group, arrange a meeting place in case you get separated. This is one big mountain.

◆◆ **Expert** ◆ **Advanced:** Head to the far left of the mountain face to a trio of double black diamonds named Blue Ox, Highline and Rogers Run. The straight-down-the-lift waist-high mogul-masher Highline is the stiffest test of the three. Nearby Prima is almost as tough, and the short drop of Pronto down to the Northwoods chair lets you strut your mogul-mauling stuff in front of the lift lines. The only authentic gut-suckers on the front face are the tops of South and North Rim off the Northwoods lift, leading to a tight but nice Gandy Dancer.

Experts can drop down the Northeast Bowl or come off Prima Ridge through the trees on Gandy Dancer, Prima Cornice or Pronto to the Northwoods area.

Solid skiers, of course, will also want to explore Vail's famous Back Bowls. Stretching seven miles across, they provide more than 2,600 acres of choose-your-own-path skiing. On a sunny day, these bowls are about as good as skiing gets. Skiers who have skied Vail for years say they now ski the front side only when they come down at the end of the day. The bowls also are an excellent way to escape crowds that may have built up on the front side of the mountain.

■ **Intermediate:** These folk will run out of vacation time before they run out of trails to explore. Few other mountains offer an intermediate expansive terrain and seemingly countless trails. Especially worthy cruising areas include the long ride down the mountain under and to the right of the Eagle Bahn gondola, almost any of the runs bordering the Avanti express chair, the Northwoods run, and the relatively short but sweet trio down to Game Creek Bowl—The Woods, Baccarat and Dealer's Choice. Our vote for best run on the mountain, and one available to advanced intermediates (though parts are rated black), is the top-to-bottom swath named Riva Ridge.

Confident intermediates also can enjoy the Back Bowls, but should stick close to smoothed trails in China Bowl and Tea Cup Bowl that the grooming machines make most nights. That way, if you get tired or frustrated with the natural conditions, you can bail out easily.

●● **Beginner:** Best areas are at Golden Peak and Eagle's Nest, and a group of short green runs under the Sourdough Lift on the top left of the trail map. Unfortunately, Vail doesn't have a large area of concentrated green runs. Most lifts on the front face have one or two green-designated trails, a bunch of blue trails and one or two blacks. Take a trail map and pay attention to the signs.

A series of crisscrossing cat tracks, some of which are named Cub's Way, Gitalong and Skid Road, allow beginners to work their way down the mountain. If cat tracks make you nervous, Vail's trail map marks them with dotted lines. However, it's tough to avoid them here, unless you stay in the Eagle's Nest area and ride that gondola back down.

● **Never-ever:** There are small learning areas in the Golden Peak base area and the top of the Eagle Bahn gondola at Eagle's Nest.

Mountain rating

Vail is one of the best ski mountains in the world for all but the extreme fringes of the skier ability chart. Super experts will miss the extreme skiing of a Snowbird, Jackson Hole or Squaw Valley, and frankly, Vail is a little overwhelming for a first-timer's adventure. But for ability levels 2-9 (on a scale of 10), Vail offers a wide array of options.

Cross-country

Two cross-country centers serve Nordic skiers, one at Golden Peak and one at the Vail Golf Course. Both offer lessons, tours and rentals. Call 845-5313.

Snowboarding (98/99 prices)

Boarders are welcome anywhere on the mountain. Snowboarders will want to head for the halfpipes at Eagle's Nest and Golden Peak. Vail has picked 12 runs for adventurous boarders, with gullies, jibs, jumps and slides. A special trail map shows where they are.

A full-day Get on Board package (lift, lesson) is $95 off-peak; $100 peak (See Lift Tickets for peak times). Lessons are $70 for a full day ($75 peak), and Vail can package lift tickets and/or rentals if you need them.

Lessons (98/99 prices)

The ski school has offices and meeting places at Vail Village near the base of the Vista Bahn Express, at Lionshead next to the gondola, at Golden Peak next to Chairs 6 and 12, at Mid-Vail next to Chairs 3 and 4, and at Eagle's Nest at the top of the gondola. Private lessons meet at Vail Village. Lessons are taught in more than 30 languages. Call the Ski School at 476-3239.

Skiers watch a video that displays nine levels of skiing skills the school uses to form classes, then place themselves accordingly in classes ranging from never-evers to advanced.

Group lessons: $70 for a full day (10 a.m. to 3:30 p.m.) for any level skier ($75 at peak times). Vail offers a wide variety of lesson-lift-and/or-rental packages too detailed for us to list here, so ask about them. Half-day lessons also are available, but the savings aren't much.

Never-ever package: Lesson and lift cost $95 ($100 peak) for skiers. (See Snowboarding section for information on the Get on Board program.) If you need just lessons and lift, or lesson and rentals, you can get it.

Private lessons: One to six people cost $110 for an hour, $215 for two hours, up to $425 for the day ($435 at peak times). One- and two-hour lessons are booked based on availability.

Special workshops: Focus on specific skills or snow conditions, such as parallel skiing or bumps. Most are morning or afternoon three-hour sessions for $60 off-peak, $65 peak.

A free Ski Tips program meets at 11 a.m. daily at Mid-Vail. The session gives you a chance to ski down a gentle slope alongside an instructor who will provide a critique and suggestions on which lesson program will offer the best benefits.

Kenny's Double Diamond Ski Shop in Vail hosts one of the best women's programs in the country. Owner Heidi Friedman brings equipment guru Jeannie Thoren to Vail in December and January to teach women the importance of properly fitted equipment. Participants demo the latest brands that Thoren modifies and custom-fits to each woman's specific bio-mechanics. Then they go skiing—better than ever. We know Jeannie well, and can heartily recommend this program. Call (800) 466-2704 or 926-5936 for more information.

Pepi's Wedel Weeks were created in the European tradition, which allows skiers to start off the ski season with an inexpensive lesson package. These are held for three weeks only, in November and early December. It's a seven-day program with breakfast, lessons every morning and afternoon, races, a welcome reception, an evening party, a fashion show and a farewell dinner. Call (800) 445-8245.

Racing: Vail has quite a recreational racing complex near the bottom of the Avanti Express lift with two NASTAR courses, two coin-operated courses, two courses reserved for groups, a course for teaching clinics and a Sybervision area. A surface lift serves the courses.

Children's lessons: Vail provides a real adventure for kids, starting outside the high walls of Fort Whippersnapper atop the Golden Peak lift. Here children enter a magical land and follow in the tracks of the little Indians Gitchee and Gumee, as they accompany Jackrabbit Joe and Sourdough Pete on a quest to find the treasure of the Lost Silver Mine. This adventure is just part of the program offered by the Children's Ski and Snowboard Centers at Golden Peak and Lionshead, which have extensive facilities for children of all ages. There are also special Kids Nights Out programs featuring dinner, theater and special games.

Registration starts at 8:30 a.m., or preregister the day before. Special children's rental shops are available at both centers. Call 476-3239 for information and reservations.

Children ages 3–6 have a supervised playroom and non-skiing programs. Full-day prices are $76 off-peak, $79 peak. Prices include lesson, lift and lunch.

Children 6–14 can spend their day on the mountain, be entertained with videos and have supervised meeting rooms. Group lessons, ski or snowboard, are $76 off-peak, $79 peak a day for lessons, lunch and lifts. Information on Kids' Night Out and Family Night Out dinner theater programs is available by calling the Family Adventure line, 479-2048.

Ages 13–18 have daily all-day classes during peak times for $90.

Child care (98/99 prices)

Vail has an excellent overall program for children. Together with Ft. Whippersnapper they are adding a new mid-mountain kids' area called Chaos Canyon and enhancing their mountaintop Adventure Ridge family area. Their child care programs are state of the art.

Ages: 2 months to 6 years.

Costs: $78 per day off-peak; $84 peak (see Lift Tickets for peak times). Toilet-trained 3-year-olds can take lessons for $78 off-peak, $84 peak.

    Reservations: Required; call 479-2044 or fax to 479-4449. Small World Play School is run by the ski school and is in the Golden Peak base area.

    Other options: For babysitters call 479-2292 or 476-7400. **Baby's Away** (800-369-9030; 926-5256) rents and will deliver baby needs to your lodge, such as crib, stroller, car seat and toys.

Lift tickets (98/99 prices)

	Adult	Child (5-12)
One day	$59	$37
Three days	$177 ($59/day)	$111 ($37/day)
Five days	$285 ($57/day)	$185 ($37/day)

Who skis free: Ages 70 and older, and 4 and younger.

Who skis at a discount: Ages 65–69 years ski for $47 per day.

    These are "off-peak" prices. Peak season—when tickets are generally $2 per day more—is a 10-day (or so) period after Christmas and March 13–27. Vail/Beaver Creek's multiday rate tops out at $59 per day for adults and $37 a day for kids. Lift tickets are also valid at Vail, Breckenridge and Keystone.

Accommodations

Vail's premier properties are clustered in Vail Village at the base of the Vista Bahn Express. Selecting the best place in town is a virtual toss-up between four hotels.

    The Lodge at Vail (476-5011 or 800-331-5634) is the original, around which they built the rest of the resort. It is only steps away from the lifts, ski school and main street action. **Gasthof Gramshammer** (476-5626) is located at the crossroads of Vail Village. Our favorite and the most economical within this group of hotels is the **Christiania** (476-5641; 800-530-3999). **Sonnenalp Resort** (476-5656 or 800-654-8312) is a group of buildings that exude Alpine warmth and charm.

    At the Lionshead end of town the **Marriott's Mountain Resort at Vail** (476-4444; 800-648-0720) is the top of the line and has an excellent location only three minutes' walk from the gondola. **Lion Square Lodge** (476-2281) is steps from the new gondola and Born Free express lift.

    The Vail Cascade Hotel (476-7111) in Cascade Village is luxurious. The Cascade Club, across the parking lot from the hotel, is available without extra charge to hotel guests. The hotel has a dedicated ski lift, which makes getting to the slopes a pleasure.

    Condominiums are plentiful in the Vail region. The most reasonable for those who want to be on the shuttlebus route are in Lionshead, clustered around the gondola, and in East Vail at **Vail Racquet Club** (476-4840; 800-428-4840).

    The **Vailglo Lodge** (476-5506) is a 34-room Best Western hotel that operates like an elegant B&B. In Lionshead, it has easy access to the slopes and town. For other relatively more affordable lodging, try **West Vail Lodge** (476-3890) in West Vail; **Antlers** (476-2471) in Lionshead; **Manor Vail** (476-5000; 800-950-8245) in Gold Peak; the **Holiday Inn at Vail** (476-5631) and **Vail Village Inn** (476-5622).

A recommended B&B is the **Black Bear Inn** (476-1304) in West Vail.

Vail's lodging choices are so vast we can't even begin to list them here. Before you call Central Reservations, know your price range, what amenities you need and which ones you want, how close you'd like to be to the lifts and how close you'll settle for if you find nothing in your budget within that distance.

Prices dip from 25 to 40 percent before Christmas and in April. But if you come at that time, be sure the bus system is in full operation or that you're within walking distance of necessities; otherwise rent a car.

 ## Dining

Eating out in Vail is as much of a tradition as skiing the Back Bowls. Always make reservations. Walk-ins have a slim chance of being seated. More than 150 bars and restaurants offer the spectrum of options from pizza to fine gourmet dining.

In the expensive category, **La Tour** (476-4403) and **The Left Bank** (476-3696), both French, have long been considered Vail's best. Another standby, **Sweet Basil** (476-0125), is consistently good with creative dishes. **The Tyrolean Inn** (476-2204) specializes in wild game and is a favorite among visiting Europeans. **Terra Bistro** (476-6836) in the Vail Athletic Club serves organic vegetables and free-range meats and poultry in unique pairings. We like **Lancelot** (476-5828) for prime rib, **Montauk** (476-2601) for seafood, **Alpenrose** (476-3194) for German and its wonderful breads and pastries, **Alfredo's** (476-7014) in the Vail Cascade Hotel for Northern Italian, and **Wild Flower** (476-5011) in The Lodge for contemporary American. **Michael's American Bistro** (476-5353) is worth a try.

Less expensive but just as scrumptious is the legendary **Pepi's** (476-5626) for the best goulash and white veal bratwursts; and **Camp di Fiore** (476-8994), which replaced Ambrosia's with fine Italian fare, an extensive wine list and a friendly staff. **Cucina Rustica** (476-5011) took over Cafe Arlberg and now serves Tuscan-style Italian in The Lodge. **Uptown Grill** 9476-2727) calls its cuisine "Colorado Classic." **Blu's** (476-3113) fixes great classics, and if you're willing to drive west to a local's favorite in Eagle Vail, **Ti Amo** (845-8153) won't disappoint.

Those on a budget should try **Pazzo's** (476-9026), which offers pasta for less than $10 and create-your-own-pizza. **Bart and Yeti's** (476-2754) in Lionshead is great for lunch or light dinner. Locals love **The Jackalope Cantina** (476-4314) in West Vail and **Clancy's** (476-3886) in Cascade Village.

Visitors with a car should head to nearby Minturn. Here the **Minturn Country Club** lets you grill your own meat or fish steak. Just across the street, the area's best Mexican food is dished out at the raucous **Saloon**—a favorite of World Cup racers—or **Chili Willy's.** Stop by **Bonjour Bakery** (827-5539) to pick up several loaves of to-die-for bread, but call for winter hours before you make the trip.

On the mountain, lunch at the beautiful **Two Elk Restaurant** above China Bowl. Go early or late, because finding a seating at prime time is tough. If you get squeezed out, backtrack a few yards to **Camp 1**, a cabin alongside the platter pull. It serves a variety of "wraps," which are tortilla-wrapped sandwiches. **Mid-Vail's** food court has moderate (for Vail) prices—$10 buys a huge potato with toppings, a local beer and a piece of fruit, for example.

We heard very good reports about the **Game Creek Club** (479-4275), a snowcat ride from the top of the Eagle Bahn. It's a private lunch club in Game Creek Bowl, but it's open to the public at night. For $75 per person, sans alcohol and gratuity but including the transportation, you get a six-course gourmet meal and a gorgeous view of the valley below. Make your reservation to coincide with sunset. Another memorable Vail dining experience is a night at **Beano's Cabin** at Beaver Creek Resort. See that chapter for details.

Après-ski/nightlife

Après-ski is centered in the Village or in Lionshead. In the Village, try **Sarah's** in the Christiania for squeezebox music with Helmut Fricker on Tuesdays and Fridays; and **Vendetta's**, which normally has live music. **Mickey's** at the Lodge at Vail has the top piano bar. Several restaurants have house entertainers who are long-time career musicians. In Lionshead, **Sundance Saloon** fills up with locals and probably has the best drink prices in town, especially at happy hour in the late afternoon. **The Hong Kong Café** is also a hot locals' bar.

In Lionshead, Oktoberfest happens daily at **Katlenberg Castle**, the latest brewhouse of the 700-year-old royal brewing family of Prince Luitpold of Bavaria. Its massive dining room, built in the likeness of an authentic Bavarian castle, serves traditional German food, but we preferred the sun-splashed porch for end-of-the-day relaxing. Three specialty beers on tap and oom-pah-pah music create post-slope fun fit for a (Bavarian) king.

For later nightlife, **Club Chelsea** on Bridge Street caters to the over-30 crowd with three rooms—a DJ dance area, a piano bar and a sealed-off cigar bar, while a few doors away, **Nick's** attracts a young crowd with loud rock'n'roll. Another cigar-and-cognac spot is **Palmos** in the Gateway Plaza. **The Club** normally offers acoustic guitar music. **Garton's Saloon** has live alternative music. On weekends the **Sundance Saloon** in Lionshead and the **Jackalope** in the West Vail shopping center have live music.

Other activities

Shopping: Vail's unique boutiques and shops, mostly upscale, can keep your credit card active for days. Late March is the best time to find bargains in ski wear and winter clothes. Vail has an unusual ski clothing shop we wish was more common—hard-to-fit men and women (small, tall, big, etc.) can find their sizes in ski and outdoor clothing at T. Lamé on Meadow Drive (476-4536).

Adventure Ridge at Eagle's Nest is a relatively new on-mountain activity center, open from noon to 10 p.m.. Though ski purists call it a travesty and liken it to Disneyland, tourists seem to enjoy this addition in the Eagle's Nest area at the top of the gondola. It includes an ice skating rink, snowboard halfpipe, tubing hill, sledding park, snowbike equipment and terrain and other activities. Three restaurants serve dinner. The gondola cabins are heated and lighted.

Vail has a number of **athletic clubs.** The Vail Cascade Club and Spa (476-7400) has indoor tennis courts, squash and racquetball courts, weight room, indoor track, outdoor heated pool and spa facilities. The Vail Athletic Club (476-7960) also has fitness facilities in Vail Village. The Vail Racquet Club (476-3267) in East Vail has indoor tennis, squash and racquetball courts, swimming pool and weight room.

Steve Jones Sleigh Rides on the Vail Golf Course can be booked by calling 476-8057.

The **Colorado Ski Museum** in the Vail Transportation Center traces the history of skiing in the state. Admission is free. Vail also has two **movie theaters,** an indoor **ice skating** rink, several **hot-air balloon companies** and many other things to do. Call the Vail Activity Desk at 476-9090 for the complete list.

 ## Getting there and getting around

By air: Flights land at the Vail/Eagle County airport, about 35 miles west of Vail, and the Denver International Airport 110 miles east. Eagle County airport is served by American, Northwest, Delta, Continental and United.

Ground transportation between Denver and Vail is frequent and convenient. Contact Vail Valley Transportation at (800) 882-8872; Colorado Mountain Express at (800) 525-6363; Airlink Shuttle at (800) 554-8245; or Vail Valley Taxi (Eagle airport only) at (970) 476-8294. Though flights into Denver may be a bit less expensive than Eagle, also consider the cost of ground transportation, which is about $60 per person round trip from Eagle and $100 or more from Denver.

By car: Vail is just off I-70, 100 miles west of Denver and 140 miles east of Grand Junction.

Getting around: Most parts of Vail are very self-contained, and the free, reliable bus service runs throughout town from East to West Vail. Visitors and locals ride the bus, because parking is very limited and expensive. Shuttles between Beaver Creek and Vail cost $3 one way and depart from the Transportation Center above the parking structure in Vail Village.

During most times of the season, you won't need a car. But if you come in early or late season (early December or April), be sure to ask the person making your reservations whether the bus schedule will be cut back during your visit. In past seasons, this has been the case. If so, rent a car.

Beaver Creek

Colorado

Summit elevation: 11,440 feet
Vertical drop: 4,040 feet
Base elevation: 7,400 feet

Address: P.O. Box 7
Vail, CO 81658
☎ **Area code:** 970
Ski area phone: 949-5750
Snow report: 476-4888 or (800) 427-8308
ⓘ **Toll-free reservations:** (800) 427-8308
(see Vail chapter for foreign toll-free numbers)
Fax: 845-5729
E-mail: info@vailresorts.com
Internet: http://www.beavercreek.snow.com
Expert:★★★
Advanced:★★★★
Intermediate:★★★★
Beginner:★★★★ **Never-ever:**★★★

Number and types of lifts:
14—6 high-speed quads, 3 triples, 4 doubles,
1 surface lift
Skiable Acreage: 1,625 acres
Snowmaking: 43 percent
Uphill capacity: 24,739 per hour
Snowboarding: Yes, unlimited
Bed Base: 4,700 in resort, 4,000 in Avon
Nearest lodging: slopeside, hotels
Resort child care: Yes, 2 months and older
Adult ticket, per day: $38-$61 (98/99)
Dining:★★★★
Apres-ski/nightlife:★
Other activities:★★

Looking for a ski experience where nothing is left to chance—not even the snow? Master-planned Beaver Creek Resort, a high-flying getaway owned by Vail Resorts, is a good choice. Beaver Creek is a complex of condominiums, hotels, two small shopping malls and excellent base facilities. Its purpose, quite simply, is to plop those with a taste for being pampered squarely in the lap of luxury. More upscale than big brother Vail, better-planned than Aspen, Beaver Creek is unlike few other mountain resorts, maybe because everything about it is so carefully scripted, and maybe because of the A-list guests it draws.

Beaver Creek began as a monument to the excesses of the '80s. The initial marketing concept came across as something like, "If you aren't worth a million dollars, don't even bother coming here." That pretentiousness has been toned down quite a bit, but remnants still linger. Beaver Creek sometimes projects an air of country-club-style exclusivity. Some say that if your appearance isn't that of a corporate CEO, you may receive the occasional withering glance from a concierge, shopkeeper or wealthy guest who wonders how you snuck through the guarded entrance at the bottom of the enclave. Others say this is never a problem. However, here's fair warning: If you want to blend in, you may want to leave the mismatched ski clothes at home.

You'll find very good skiing and snowboarding for most ability levels, especially now that the Beaver Creek-Arrowhead expansion is finished. Vail Resorts connected these two areas with the opening of terrain in an area called Bachelor Gulch, which created an inter-connected village-to-village experience, where visitors can ski or snowboard between the three base villages. If you do this, be aware of the time it involves so you don't get stuck at Arrowhead after the lift closes when your car or lodge is at Beaver Creek (or vice versa). Shuttle buses make the loop, but not as frequently as you might like.

To be sure, Beaver Creek is nowhere near the celebrity magnet that Aspen and Vail are. It attracts much the same type of visitor as Deer Valley in Utah: the Fortune 500 crowd is right at home here and many of the condominiums are corporate-owned. An exclusive air still pervades Beaver Creek, with prices as upscale as its visitors. It won't be everyone's cup of tea, but Beaver Creek serves its chosen niche well.

Vail Resorts, the parent company, owns Vail, Beaver Creek, Breckenridge and Keystone, all quite close to each other. Multiday lift tickets are available that allow skiing at each of these resorts.

New for 1998–99: Beaver Creek and Vail will host the 1999 World Alpine Ski Championships from Jan. 31 through Feb. 14, featuring more than 300 athletes from 50 nations. Beaver Creek will host three of the 12 races, including the downhill. That most thrilling of the ski races will be on a new course in the Birds of Prey area, starting at the top of Chair 8 and finishing at the bottom of Red Tail.

 ## Mountain layout

If there's one characteristic that sets Beaver Creek apart from other mountain resorts, it's the extent to which its slopes are groomed. An enthusiastic fleet of snowcats patrols the mountainside 20 out of every 24 hours, looking for an opportunity to plow over a chunk of ice or a patch of powder. To ski at Beaver Creek is "to ski on corduroy." Other distinguishing features: a conspicuous absence of lift lines and copious snowmaking abilities.

◆◆ **Expert** ◆ **Advanced:** When Beaver Creek opened in 1980, its first runs were mostly beginner and intermediate. Some still think of it—mistakenly—as a cruiser mountain. Not so: advanced skiers and experts should spend at least a day here, maybe more. Our advice is to choose a Saturday or Sunday, when the lines can climb over the 15–20 minute barrier at Vail, yet be nonexistent here.

What's surprising is the amount of truly tough stuff. The Birds of Prey runs rival anything Vail offers—all long, steep and mogul-studded. While somewhat shorter, Ripsaw and Cataract in Rose Bowl, and Loco in Larkspur Bowl, are equally challenging. Grouse Mountain is strictly for black-diamond types, no matter what the trail map may suggest. Only in spring, when slushier snow slows skiers down, should such runs as Screech Owl, Falcon Park and Royal Elk Glades be attempted by thrill-seeking intermediates.

■ **Intermediate:** Intermediates should turn their equipment loose down one of America's best unheralded cruisers, Centennial, which dips and turns down the lower half of the mountain under the Centennial Express lift. Harrier, to the skier's left of Centennial, is a locals' favorite where you'll often find yourself skiing or boarding solo. All of the runs under the Strawberry Park lift are great for intermediates, as is just about every run under the Centennial Express. Bachelor Gulch and Arrowhead also offer solid intermediate skiing, with just the right pitch and pockets of trees that are perfect for wannabe powder pigs.

●● **Beginner:** The mountain is laid out upside down, with the easiest skiing at the top, down the Stump Park lift. You get back to the bottom on a long, clearly marked beginner run called Cinch. One thing beginners should watch out for: Beaver Creek has sudden shifts from beginner to expert terrain. The trails are well-marked, but when you're moving fast and trying to concentrate, the signs can fly by. The Arrowhead section also is good for beginners, with a winding run called Piece O' Cake.

● **Never-ever:** Beaver Creek's learning area is at the base, served by two lifts.

Mountain rating

There is a bit of everything for all levels of skier. Beaver Creek, with the Birds of Prey and Grouse Mountain runs, is the spot for aggressive, bump-hungry experts. Intermediates will also be happy at Beaver Creek Resort with its long runs and virtually no lift lines. Beginners can ski at the summit and see the view, a rare treat.

Cross-country (97/98 prices)

For a truly different Nordic experience at an Alpine ski area, head to the McCoy Park cross-country center at the top of the Strawberry Park Lift. Instead of skiing on the flats (usually a golf course) at the base of a ski area, you'll be on a 32-km. system at the summit at 9,840 feet, with spectacular views in every direction. Groomed and tracked for both skating and diagonal skiing, the trail system has one advanced (and exciting) loop, the Wild Side trail, but is basically beginner and intermediate. An ungroomed single track for snowshoers is called the Upper Atlas Traverse. Skiers can either download on the Strawberry Park Lift or take the very gradual Home Comfort trail (6 km.) all the way down. It's great fun if there's some new snow to slow you down but a little too speedy if there isn't.

Adult fees are $18 for an all-day pass, $12 for a half day beginning at noon; $9 and $6 for children and seniors.

All-day cross-country tours cost $59; afternoon tours cost $39. The park also has snowshoe rentals and tours. One such tour includes a gourmet lunch and costs $73. Tours alone cost $39 for 2.5 hours. Snowshoe tours include rental equipment.

For more information on Nordic skiing, call the Beaver Creek Cross-Country Center at 845-5313; or Paragon Guides, 926-5299.

Snowboarding (98/99 prices)

Beaver Creek has a snowboard park called Stickline, located off the Centennial Express chair on the Moonshine run. The resort has designated seven runs that feature gullies, jibs, jumps, slides and a halfpipe as being especially good for adventurous snowboarders. Special maps show where to find them. A full-day "Get on Board!" lesson is $95 ($100 during Peak season) for lessons for lifts and lessons (you'll need to rent equipment or have your own).

This is one of the top spots to learn, especially if you are an adult. Brian and Kevin Delaney, who are national and world snowboarding champions, teach two- or three-day learning camps here with a staff of excellent instructors. Call this school at (800) 743-3790 or visit the Website (www.delaneysnowboard.com).

Lessons (98/99 prices)

Lessons meet at One Beaver Creek next to Chair 1 (Haymeadow Lift) and at Spruce Saddle atop the Centennial Express lift. Instruction is available in nearly 30 languages. Call the Beaver Creek Ski School at 845-5300 or send a fax to 845-5321.

Lessons are priced for peak and non-peak times. We list High Season prices, which apply during the Christmas season and mid-February to April. Non-peak prices are normally about $5 less.

Group lessons: Day-long instruction is $100. Adult lessons are offered à la carte (the prices we list) or packaged with lift tickets. A semi-private lesson, offered in the afternoon, is $100, with a guarantee of no more than five students.

Never-ever package: Lesson and lifts for a half day costs $80.

Private lessons (for one to six people) cost $215 for two hours, $305 for a half day (three and a half hours) and $435 for a full day (8:30 a.m.–3:30 p.m.). One-hour lessons, when available, are $110. Booking in advance ensures the off-peak rate (about $15 less) on full- and half-day lessons. Call the Private Lesson Concierge at (800) 354-5630.

Special programs: Special clinics, called Signature Programs, concentrate on specific skills or snow conditions. One employs the Feldenkrais method of neuromuscular re-education to help you break bad habits. Prices vary, so call or consult the website.

A free Ski Tips program meets at 11 a.m. daily at Spruce Saddle. The session gives you a chance to ski on a gentle slope with an instructor who provides a critique and suggests which ski school program will be best for you. Another free program is Meet the Mountain, a tour at 1 p.m. on Sundays through Tuesdays for intermediate and higher-level skiers.

Racing: Two NASTAR courses and a coin-op course are next to the Centennial run.

Children's lessons: Offered for ages 3–14. Groups are arranged by age and ability, and run from 9:15 a.m. to 3:30 p.m., with registration beginning at 8 a.m. Lessons include lunch and lift tickets for $90. The Children's Ski and Snowboard School has doubled its capacity this season.

Child care (97/98 prices)

Ages: 2 months to 6 years.

Costs: $60 per day in peak season; $57 non-peak; includes lunch (see Lift Tickets for peak times). Half-day is $45, peak and non-peak.

Reservations: Required; call 845-5325 or 479-2044, or fax 479-4449.

Note: The Small World Play School, is open from 8 a.m. to 4:30 p.m. Free parent pagers are available.

Other options: Baby's Away (800-369-9030; 970-926-5256) rents and will deliver baby needs to your lodge, such as crib, stroller, car seat and toys.

Lift tickets (98/99 prices)

	Adult	Child (5-12)
One day	$59	$37
Three days	$177 ($59/day)	$111 ($37/day)
Five days	$285 ($57/day)	$185 ($37/day)

Who skis free: Ages 70 and older, and 4 and younger.

Who skis at a discount: Ages 65–69 years ski for $47 per day.

These are "off-peak" prices. Peak season—when tickets are generally $2 per day more— is a 10-day (or so) period after Christmas and March 13–27. Vail/Beaver Creek's multiday rate tops out at $59 per day for adults and $37 a day for kids. Lift tickets are also valid at Vail, Breckenridge and Keystone.

Accommodations

Beaver Creek lodging is expensive. It's tough to find a room for less than $200 per night, unless you want to vacation in the early season. **Hyatt Regency Beaver Creek** (800-233-1234; 970-949-1234) is the resort's central and largest hotel, with 300 rooms, a health club, outdoor pool and spa and two excellent restaurants. Decor is elegant but not excessive, and service is top-notch. Rates are $245–$695, depending on room and time of year. The hotel also features an unusual program that matches up singles who want to take advantage of the double occupancy rates.

The **Inn at Beaver Creek** (800-859-8242), ski-in/ski-out lodging on a far smaller scale than the Hyatt, has 37 rooms and eight suites with a free continental breakfast. Cocktails and cappuccinos are served après-ski. Guests also have a sauna and steam room.

The **Beaver Creek Embassy Suites** (800-732-6777) is the only all-suite resort in the Vail Valley. The 71 units have living rooms, fireplaces, and TVs with VCRs. Once guests find the lobby to check in, the rest is easy.

The **Centennial Lodge** (800-845-7060) and **Creekside Lodge** (800-677-7071; 970-949-7071) are just about 300 yards from the base of the Centennial Lift. **The Poste Montane** (800-497-9238; 970-845-7500) is located directly in Beaver Creek Resort Village as is **St. James Place** (800-859-8242; 970-845-9300). **The Pines Lodge** and **Inn at Beaver Creek** are near the Strawberry Park Lift and can be booked through Central Reservations, (800) 243-8053.

Many corporate- or privately-owned condominiums are available for weekly rentals. Note that restrictions are more severe than for a hotel reservation. Hefty cancellation fees apply, so read the fine print before booking.

Units at the **Kiva** (800-228-7306; 970-949-5474) are larger than at a comparable hotel. Continental breakfast and après-ski goodies are included in the rates. Amenities include a full kitchen, dining room, fireplace, television and morning newspaper delivery.

Park Plaza Condominiums (800-528-7275; 970-845-7700), near Village Square, are a bit more generous with space. Chandeliers replace lamps, marble replaces wood. Large windows overlook an enclosed pool, and in-room hot tubs are standard.

The **Charter** (800-525-6660; 970-949-6660), which bills itself as having "all of the conveniences of a condominium with all of the luxuries of a world-class hotel," gives guests more of the typical Beaver Creek amenities—wonderful wood-paneled interiors, European decor, fireplaces and stunning mountain views. One- through five-bedroom units are available. Three restaurants offer menus to suit anyone's tastes.

If your budget won't support accommodations inside Beaver Creek's gates, head to nearby town of Avon for the valley's best condo deals at the **Christie Lodge** (800-551-4320; 970-949-7700), about $99–$199 per night for a one-bedroom unit.

Dining

Beaver Creek is infatuated with the term "gourmet." Everything, right down to the garden-variety burger, is designated gourmet. Plus, these Colorado chefs do love their spices. The dishes we tried featured gratuitous amounts of onions, garlic and exotic flavors.

The **Patina** (949-1234), in the Hyatt, is a noteworthy Italian and seafood dining experience. The wine list is first-rate, the atmosphere is exciting, and the staff is helpful. Ask for a seat by the window and watch children roasting marshmallows over an enormous fire. The bill, including wine and dessert, will be roughly $55 per person, moderate to expensive by Beaver Creek standards.

SaddleRidge (845-5450) is decorated with impressive antiques the like of which might only be found in a museum. It is open for dinner with a game-dominated menu. After dessert take a look at the saddle with Buffalo Bill's sketch impressed into the leather. The image is his own handiwork. Expect to pay about $70 per person.

The **Golden Eagle** (949-1940) is a less costly, though not less exotic, place to dine. With entrées such as Medallions of Australian Kangaroo and Roast Loin of Elk on the menu, guests can take a culinary world tour without leaving their seats. Decorations are Bavarian and desert Southwest, exactly the unlikely mix you'd expect from a restaurant that serves a Blue Corn Elk Quesadilla and other odd but tasty treats. You'll probably part with $40 per person here.

Legends (949-5540) in the Poste Montane dishes out Colorado cuisine against the backdrop of Western-themed paintings and paraphernalia. Try the fish, said to be the best in the valley. Dinner runs about $60 per person. **Mirabelle** (949-7728), a longtime local favorite at the bottom of the resort access road in an old farmhouse, serves well-prepared nouvelle cuisine.

TraMonti (949-5552), at the Charter, is one of the less expensive places to dine. Dinner per person will run about $30. Another reason to make reservations: on a clear night, the view of the mountain through the restaurant's cathedral-like windows is unbelievable. Another inexpensive place is **Toscanini** (845-5590), with prices $4.50–$6 for kids and $10–$17 for adults. Its children's menu doubles as a coloring book. Follow your nose to the aromas wafting from this Italian eatery in Market Square.

Rendezvous Bar and Grill (845-5500) in Beaver Creek Village rolls all of the 1990s favorites into their offerings: brasserie-style food, wine by the glass and a martini bar. Oh, and a children's menu, too.

In Avon try **The Brass Parrot** and **Cassidy's**. **Masato's Sushi Bar** (between Wal-Mart and City Market) has great sushi chefs and reasonably priced Japanese food. **Gratzie** is Avon's best for good-value Italian. Or try the town of Edwards, just west of Avon. In the River Center, **Zino's** (same owners as Vail's Sweet Basil) is the "in" place to be. Try the roasted mussels served in an iron skillet before diving into entrees that include pasta, risotto, and creative meat and fish dishes. The **Gore Range Brewery**, another hang-out, has outrageous salads, wood-fired thin-crust pizza, and peel-and-eat shrimp.

Beaver Creek has a memorable dining experience, a night at **Beano's Cabin**. Groups are bundled onto a 40-person sleigh (don't even begin to think romantic, this is purely utilitarian) and pulled up the mountain under the stars by a snowcat. The cabin (a bit of a misnomer, since the building is fairly large) is upscale-rustic on the outside and elegant inside, with a roaring stone-hearth fire, log beams and well-prepared cuisine (it is certainly worth the ride). The six-course meal concludes with remarkable desserts. The cost is $85 per person, including the sleigh ride but not the wine. Reservations (book early), 949-9090.

 ## Après-ski/nightlife

Asked what nightlife was worth a look, one worker first told us, "There isn't anything," then after a bit of thinking, amended her response to, "Well, there are some meeting places."

The Coyote Cafe would surely qualify as one. This Mexican cantina/watering hole caters to locals, and prices are reasonable. Bartenders can whip up a Luper to get you in the aprés-ski mood, and the staff is intentionally informal—in contrast with the rest of Beaver Creek. Don't plan on staying out late—it closes at 11 p.m. Slopeside **Rendezvous Bar and Grill** holds aprés-ski from 3–6 p.m., live entertainment begins at 7:30, and from 10–11, late-night tidbits and desserts take center stage. **Blue Moose Pizzeria** has great pizza and a fun atmosphere, and the lowest prices in Beaver Creek Village.

At the **Players Pub** in the Beaver Creek Lodge, visitors can shoot pool, play darts or watch sports on the big-screen TV. Ask about the Bald Spot if you're looking for either a spicy drink or the locals' extreme ski hideout (it's the name of both). The Hyatt Regency's **Crooked Hearth** bar, which stays open until 2 a.m., features entertainment from local musicians. At night, when the stars are out, it's a dazzling display for tired skiers and snowboarders.

Other activities

Shopping: This used to be the only option to skiing. Beautiful boutiques still line the pedestrian walkway in the heart of the resort. But in 1998, the Vilar Center for the Arts opened. This 528-seat **performing arts center** was fashioned after a turn-of-the-century theater in Munich and no doubt will become the premier cultural venue in the Colorado mountains. A stone wall surrounds the new **ice rink**, and a nearby fire pit warms skaters and spectators. Ice skating exhibitions are held here in the winter. **Snowshoe** trails wind through scenic aspens and firs. If you need more, head to Vail.

Getting there and getting around

By air: Flights land at the Vail/Eagle County airport, about 35 miles west of Vail, and the Denver International Airport 110 miles east. Eagle County airport is served by American, Northwest, Delta or United.

Ground transportation between Denver and Vail is frequent and convenient. The trip to Vail takes about two and a half hours. Contact Colorado Mountain Express at (800) 424-6363; Vail Valley Taxi (476-8294); or Airport Transportation Service (476-7576). Though flights into Denver may be a bit less expensive than Eagle, also consider the cost of ground transportation, which is about $60 per person round trip from Eagle and $100 or more from Denver.

By car: Beaver Creek and Vail are right on I-70, 100 miles west of Denver and 140 miles east of Grand Junction. Beaver Creek is 10 miles west of Vail.

Getting around: Beaver Creek is very self-contained. Shuttles between Beaver Creek and Vail cost $2. If you plan to commute frequently between Vail and Beaver Creek, you may want to rent a car. If you are not staying at Beaver Creek, you must park your car in the town of Avon (at the base of Beaver Creek) and ride shuttles to the village and lifts. Allow extra time for this.

Winter Park

Colorado

Summit elevation: 12,060 feet
Vertical drop: 3,060 feet
Base elevation: 9,000 feet

Address: P.O. Box 36,
Winter Park, CO 80482
✆ **Area code:** 970
Ski area phone: 726-5514
Denver line: (303) 892-0961
ⓘ **Toll-free reservations:** (800) 729-5813;
(970) 726-5587 outside the U.S. and Canada
Fax: (970) 726-5993
E-mail: cenres@rkymtnhi.com (lodging) or
wp@mail.skiwinterpark.com (ski resort)
Internet: //www.skiwinterpark.com
Expert:★★★★ Advanced:★★★★
Intermediate:★★★★
Beginner:★★★★
Never-ever:★★★★★

Number of lifts: 20—7 high-speed quads;
5 triple chairs, 8 double chairs
Snowmaking: 20 percent
Skiable acreage: 2,886
Uphill capacity: 34,910 per hour
Snowboarding: Yes, unlimited
Bed Base: 12,500
Nearest lodging: close by, but none slopeside
Resort child care: Yes, 2 months and older
Adult ticket, per day: $35-$46 (97/98 prices)

Dining:★★★
Apres-ski/nightlife:★★
Other activities:★★

Early this century, when the Moffat Tunnel through the Rockies was completed, Denverites began to ride the train here. The shacks first built for the tunnel construction crews made perfect warming huts for hardy skiers who climbed the mountains and schussed down on seven-foot boards. Eventually the ski area became part of the Denver public parks system, which explains its name. Today Winter Park ranks as one of the largest ski areas in Colorado.

Winter Park doesn't have the glamour of Aspen or Vail, nor the quaint Victorian charm of Telluride, Breckenridge or Crested Butte. What it has is a great mountain, and a wonderfully easy-going atmosphere. Winter Park has no massive condo complexes lining the roads, and no built-up center of town. The ski area and most of the lodgings are tucked into the woods off the main highway. A traveler might well ride through Winter Park and never realize that the town can sleep more than 12,500 in some 100 properties, including bed & breakfasts and traditional mountain inns. Traditional mountain inns—the kind with large common rooms where people can read, talk or play board games—are tough to find these days. We like them, and you'll find descriptions in the Accommodations section.

Lodging is designed with families in mind, the ski school is one of Colorado's most respected and the children's programs are among the biggest and most advanced.

Although Winter Park has maintained a great family reputation, it is surprisingly a good destination for singles. The town benefits from having only a few, but good, nightlife centers, meaning that you get to meet most of the other skiers in town if that's what you desire; and the mountain inn lodging gives singles a great opportunity to meet other vacationers over dinner and drinks, or while enjoying the hot tubs. If you are looking for a solid good time without the fanfare, Winter Park presents you with one of the best.

Mountain layout

Though the mountain is completely interconnected by lifts, it has separate base areas: Mary Jane and Winter Park. So in this section, "the Winter Park side" refers to the portion of the resort to the trail-map right of the Zephyr Express chair lift.

◆◆ **Expert:** Visitors who have read about Winter Park arrive expecting a good intermediate resort with plenty of lower-intermediate and beginner trails. Yes, that's all here—what is surprising is the amount of expert terrain. During the 97/98 season, Winter Park opened another 435 acres in the Vasquez Cirque, which features primarily expert and extreme slopes accessed by the Timberline chair lift. For 98/99, Winter Park will open up another 250 acres here, with steep chutes and gladed powder stashes.

Mary Jane is where you'll find the super-steeps. Try the chutes accessible only through controlled gates: Hole in the Wall, Awe Chute, Baldy's Chute, Jeff's Chute and Runaway, all reached by the Challenger lift.

◆ **Advanced:** For advanced skiers, the most popular lift on the Winter Park side probably will be the Zephyr Express. It follows the central ridge line of the resort, providing access to Mary Jane (via Outhouse), or many of the advanced runs on the Winter Park side—Bradley's Bash, Balch, Mulligan's Mile and Hughes. From the top of Zephyr, bump fanatics can bop down Outhouse and end up at the base of Mary Jane.

On the Mary Jane side, head for the black runs off the Iron Horse chair, and if you're still standing, then you're ready for the runs off the Challenger chair—all black-diamond, all ungroomed, and all tough as a bag of nails.

There's great skiing in Parsenn Bowl, more than 200 acres of open space. If you can hit Parsenn on a good day, you're in for a treat. The upper part is wide open and medium-steep, while the gladed bottom is a delight, especially if you're just learning to ski between trees. Though rated blue and blue-black on the trail map, wind and weather conditions can make the bowl a workout. Winds often close the Timberline lift, which provides the only access.

■ **Intermediate:** The Vasquez Ridge area on the Winter Park side has an excellent collection of cruising runs and is served by a high-speed quad. (The only drawback to Vasquez Ridge is a long runout down the Big Valley trail; the Buckaroo trail lets you avoid it.) If you find yourself on the other side of the ridge, keep up your speed and tuck for the run back to the Pioneer Express lift. To change mountains, green-circle Gunbarrel takes skiers to the High Lonesome Express high-speed quad for a drop into the Mary Jane area.

The Sunnyside lift on the Mary Jane has excellent runs for intermediates. If you can handle these with no trouble, try Sleeper, one of Winter Park's "blue-black" designated runs that help intermediates improve to advanced.

●● **Beginner:** The Winter Park base area serves most of the beginner trails. Beginners can ride to the top of the mountain to Sunspot and then ski down Allan Phipps or March Hare, or they can ski all the way back to the base using the Cranmer Cutoff to Parkway. When these become easy, try Cranmer, Jabberwocky, White Rabbit and Cheshire Cat.

● **Never-ever:** Winter Park is one of the best ski areas in the nation for never-evers. Groswold's Discovery Park is 25 acres of gentle, isolated learning terrain for beginners, served by a double, triple and a high-speed chair lift, which slows down for loading and unloading.

Winter Park also has two wonderful devices for first-time skiers—"Magic Carpet" conveyor belts that transport adults and children up the learning slope, eliminating the need for side-stepping.

Mountain rating

Winter Park is one of the few mountain resorts that can truly serve the needs of all ability and interest levels. Very few mountains have both the nearly flat, isolated terrain that never-evers need, and the precipitous plunges that experts adore. Winter Park is lucky enough to have both, plus plenty at every stage in between.

Snowboarding (98/99 prices)

Snowboarding is allowed on the entire mountain. There are several terrain parks especially for boarders, such as Mad Hatter's on the Winter Park side and Stone Grove on Mary Jane. The Rolls, also on the Winter Park side, serves as a boardercross course during competitions. The halfpipe, Knuckledragon, is just above the Snoasis mid-mountain restaurant.

Winter Park Resort has a rental shop at the base, plus there are more in town. Instruction starts with a three-hour first-time lesson for $20 with the purchase of a full-day ticket. More advanced boarders can get 2.5-hour lessons for $35 with the purchase of a full-day, all-lifts ticket. Private lessons are $90 for an hour and a half.

Cross-country (97/98 prices)

Devil's Thumb Cross-Country Center (726-5632) has great views of the mountains and 105 km. of trails groomed for both skating and gliding. National-level competitors race and train here. The center is near Tabernash on County Road 83. Trail fees are $12 a day for adults and $8 for children and seniors; those aged 6 and younger ski free. Private lessons are $30 an hour. A learn-to-ski package is $28 including rentals and trail fee; children and seniors, $23.

Snow Mountain Ranch (887-2152), eight miles west of Winter Park on Highway 40, offers 100 km. of groomed trails through a variety of terrain—open, wooded, hilly and flat. The system includes a lighted 3-km. loop for night skiing. The instruction staff includes national-level coaches and racers. Ski lessons, rentals, lodging, dining and child care are available. The trail fee is $9 a day, and children younger than 12 pay $5. Group lessons are available for $15 and private lessons are $30 an hour. Snow Mountain Ranch is also a YMCA with inexpensive dorm lodging.

Snowshoeing: Redfeather Snowshoe Tours is a $25, two-hour guided tour of the hidden glades on the mountain that includes a chair lift ride to the tour starting point.

Winter Park's extensive mountain biking trails are used in winter for snowshoeing. The trails are easy to follow and often packed down by snowmobile riders. The Winter Park/Fraser Chamber of Commerce has maps and information.

Lessons (98/99 prices)

"Skier & Rider Improvement" desks are at the Balcony House at the Winter Park base, the Mary Jane Center and the Lodge at Sunspot. Teaching is Winter Park's forté, so a large variety of clinics and lessons are offered. Here are the basics:

Group lessons: $35, 2.5 hours, for intermediate and higher; $20 for beginner levels. Quick Tips Learning Lane is a 15-minute session for advanced beginners to experts for $5. This program is located at the Winter Park Video Arena above the Snoasis mid-mountain restaurant.

Never-ever package: A half-day lesson with full-day rental is $30. The snowboard package is $35. Lift tickets are required and are extra.

Private lessons (for one or two people): $90 for 90 minutes. A First Tracks private lesson gets you on the mountain 30 minutes before the lifts open to the public; Last Tracks is from 2:30 to 4 p.m. Either is $70 for a 1.5-hour lesson, though a one-hour First Tracks is $55.

Special programs: Many. An example: In the three-hour Performance Lab, instructors will analyze your skiing and your ski equipment, then combine equipment adjustments with private lessons to enable most skiers to advance beyond their previous level. The cost is $200 plus lab fees. The relationship between proper equipment alignment and ability improvement is only beginning to be addressed, particularly with women, so Winter Park is quite cutting-edge with this program.

Winter Park's National Sports Center for the Disabled, the world's leading such skiing instruction program, also has a full-time race training program for disabled skiers. Instruction is available for all levels, and the race program is open to advanced intermediates or above.

The resort also has special multiday clinics at various times during the season, usually listed on its website.

Racing: NASTAR, daily on the Cranmer Trail above Snoasis Restaurant. $5 for the first run; $1 for each additional run.

Children's lessons: Tots aged 3 and 4 don't ride the chair lift in their all-day lesson; $73 with rentals. All-day programs for older children, including lifts and lunch, cost $65 without rentals; $73 with; discounts for additional days. Snowboard lessons start with third-graders (in American schools, that's usually age 8) to age 13 through the Children's Center. Snowboard and boots rental is $20 per day.

Child care (98/99 prices)

Ages: 2 months to 5 years.

Costs: Including lunch, $50 a day; $35 half day. Parents can rent beepers for $5 per day. Half day does not include lunch.

Reservations: Reservation forms are required and may be obtained from Winter Park Central Reservations or the Winter Park Children's Center. A $5 non-refundable fee is charged. Call 726-1551.

Note: Winter Park has always been a leader in creative children's ski programs and its commitment is evident in the multistory Children's Center built for the purpose. On some days the program handles more than 600 children—anyone who has organized anything for a group that size (of whatever age) knows what an undertaking this is. The center is open from 8 a.m. to 4 p.m.

Lift tickets (98/99 prices)

	Adult	Child (6-13)
One day (97/98 price)	$46	$15
Three days	$120 ($40/day)	$45 ($15/day)
Five days	$185 ($37/day)	$75 ($15/day)

Who skis free: Kids younger than 6; seniors 70 and older.

Who skis at a discount: Ages 62–69 ski for $25. Disabled skiers pay $27 (97/98 price). Winter Park also offers early- and late-season discounts, and has discounts through Denver businesses. Half-day tickets are offered for mornings or afternoons. Beginner lift tickets on the Galloping Goose lift at Mary Jane cost $5 per day. Try to ski here at least two consecutive days. The per-day cost drops significantly for a two-day or longer ticket.

 ## Accommodations

Winter Park Central Reservations can book 150 different lodging properties, plus air transportation, lift tickets and special activities. Call (800) 729-5813. This resort has a group of mountain inns unique in Colorado: they are like small bed & breakfasts but with dinner, as well. They all serve meals family-style so that guests get a chance to meet one another easily. Most inns have transportation to and from the slopes. The food is usually fantastic and plentiful, and the inn owners go out of their way to please their guests. Per-person double-occupancy rates at these vary, starting about $55 per night and topping out about $160.

There are eight mountain inns in Winter Park. Perhaps the most upscale is the **Gasthaus Eichler** (726-5133). The inn is very European and the rooms are well decorated with down comforters on the beds. Each bathroom is equipped with a Jacuzzi tub. It's perfect if you want quiet elegant lodging in the center of town within walking distance of restaurants and nightlife. Prices include breakfast and a massive dinner.

Arapahoe Ski Lodge (726-8222 or 800-338-2698) also downtown, is a pleasant, friendly, No-Smoking mountain inn that feels like home. The rooms have private baths. It features a large spa and indoor swimming pool. Prices include dinner, breakfast and transport to the slopes.

The Woodspur Lodge (726-8417 or 800-626-6562). The living room is massive with a fireplace, soaring roof and plenty of space. This central area makes a perfect meeting place for the guests. The rooms here are of two types—newly restored and old style. Ask for one of the updated rooms if you are staying as a couple and one of the older rooms for larger groups. The lodge is served by local buses as well as lodge vans that shuttle skiers to the area and the town. Rates include breakfast and dinner.

The Timber House Ski Lodge (726-5477 or 800-843-3502) is tucked into the woods at the edge of the area. A private trail lets you ski directly back to the lodge. You'll meet other guests in the giant living room with its stone fireplace, sitting at long tables with food served family style, or soaking in the outdoor hot tub. Rates include breakfast and dinner.

The other mountain inns are outside of town toward Tabernash. **The Outpost Inn** (726-5346), a B&B, is the most comfortable and homey. Here Ken and Barb Parker serve nonstop hospitality. Vans shuttle skiers to and from the ski area. A spa attached to the building becomes a social center in the evenings. A maximum of 20 guests at a time stay at the inn. Rates include breakfast, but no dinner.

The next lodges are not part of the Mountain Inn Association, but offer similar accommodations at less than $85 per person.

The Pines Inn (726-5416) is a B&B just around the corner from the Timber House with a personality of its own. It is accessible from the ski area by the Billy Woods Trail, which also ends at the Timber House.

Beau West B&B (726-5145 or 800-473-5145) is only 500 yards from Winter Park base and features gourmet breakfasts. It has a hot tub and great views.

The **Engelmann Pines Bed & Breakfast** (726-4632), in the nearby town of Fraser in a mountain-style home, has some rooms with fireplaces and Jacuzzi tubs for about $110–$125. Other rooms without fireplaces range from $75 to $100.

The **Grand Victorian Bed & Breakfast** (726-5881) has luxurious rooms and suites. Colorado wines, beers and cordials are served every evening in the library, and breakfasts are imaginative and huge. Rooms are about $150–$225 per night.

Devil's Thumb Ranch is at a cross-country area in Fraser, and charges about $80 per person for two sharing a room, including breakfast.

The condos of Winter Park are the mainstay accommodations for most skiers. The most luxurious is the **Iron Horse Resort Retreat** (726-8851), the closest that Winter Park has to true ski-in/ski-out, though that stretches the definition a bit. It has a swimming pool and a fitness center. The condos range from studios to two-bedroom suites at rates ranging from about $170 to $500. Iron Horse is slightly outside of the town center, but has excellent shuttle service if you want nightlife.

The Vintage (726-8801) is also slightly out of the center of town but right next to the ski areas. It features a restaurant, fitness room, swimming pool and good shuttle service into the town. The owner admires Winston Churchill and has Churchillian memorabilia throughout the hotel. The beautiful wooden bar came from a London pub. One of the finest properties in Winter Park, the Vintage has studios from $89–$225, two-room suites for $245–$435, and three-room suites for $345–$535.

For condominiums in town, try either the **Snowblaze** (726-5701) or **Crestview Place** (726-9421). Both are across the street from Cooper Creek Square. Snowblaze has a full athletic club with racquetball court, swimming pool and fitness center, which are included in the price of the condo. Studio units normally come with a Murphy bed, and two- and three-bedroom units have baths for each bedroom, private saunas and fireplaces. Costs are about $150–$500. Crestview Place does not have an athletic club or private saunas, but has fireplaces and full kitchens.

One of the most popularly priced condominiums is the **Hi Country Haus** (726-9421). These condos are spread out in a dozen buildings and share a recreation center with four hot tubs, sauna and heated swimming pool. They are within walking distance of town and are on the shuttlebus routes. Costs are about $190–$325.

Dining

Winter Park isn't packed with high-priced restaurants; instead, the emphasis is on good solid cooking.

The **Gasthaus Eichler** (726-5133) in the center of Winter Park has an Austrian/German-influenced menu. Locals all raved about **The Last Waltz** (726-4877), which is in the King's Crossing Shopping Center on Highway 40. One resident claims the Last Waltz has the best breakfast in town and the others give unanimous thumbs up to the American and Mexican menu, which features homemade dishes with very fresh ingredients. Save room for dessert.

The Divide Grill (726-4900) in the Cooper Creek Square serves Northern Italian dishes and has a good salad bar. **Deno's** (726-5332), a local's favorite, has excellent pasta dishes as well as chicken, steak and shrimp selections. And surprisingly, **The Slope** (726-5727), also known as one of the town's top nightlife spots, gets excellent marks for its table.

Fairly new is **Smokin'Moe's** (726-4600) in Cooper Creek Square, where you can load up on spicy barbecued ribs, hot links, chicken and "Okie baloney." For family fare try the **Crooked Creek Saloon** in Fraser for basic steaks and down-home cooking. The Fat Boy burger is a local tradition.

Hernando's Pizza & Pasta Pub with its central fireplace is highly recommended by locals, but is often crowded—you can opt for free delivery though. Also try the **Winter Park Pub**, located downtown on Hwy. 40, which offers traditional pub fare, 15 beers on tap, and "Mystery Beer Night." A lot of 20-somethings here.

For the best eggs-and-bacon breakfast in town head straight to **The Kitchen. Carver's Bakery & Café** behind Cooper Creek Square serves hearty breakfasts and healthy lunches and dinners.

On the slopes, the best lunch is in the **Club Car** restaurant at the Mary Jane base area. The **Lodge at Sunspot** atop the mountain is a spectacular setting for a gourmet lunch. Winter Park has a "pizza hot line" at the top of the Winter Park section of the mountain. Use it to call **Mama Mia's Pizzeria** in Snoasis and your pizza will be waiting when you arrive.

For fine food *and* a great view, head to the **Lodge at Sunspot** for dinner. The Zephyr Express converts to a gondola for a comfortable ride to this spectacular mountain restaurant. A five-course menu is $39–$59 without alcohol and gratuity. A twilight snowmobile tour with dinner at the lodge also is available. Call 726-5514 for info and reservations.

Après-ski/nightlife

For après-ski, the **Derailer Bar** in the West Portal of the Winter Park Base area is the place to be. **The Slope**, close to the base area on the road leading out to Hwy. 40, gets a good crowd at happy hour. If that's too crowded, **Adolph's**, where the locals hang out, is across the street.

For sports events, go to **Deno's Mountain Bistro** with half-a-dozen TVs, plus more than 100 types of beer and 200 wines. **The Shed** serves Mexican fare and exotic margaritas.

The dancing nightlife centers in two spots: **The Slope**, which has live music most nights, and **Rome on the Range**, which has Country & Western dancing and live music. For a quiet drink without the loud music head down to **Hideaway Bistro & Pub**. It has a fondue evening every Wednesday with live music from 7 to 10. The **Iron Horse** often has a guitar player in the bar, and a Comedy Club every other Wednesday in ski season.

The Crooked Creek Saloon in downtown Fraser also has food and music. Diehards using public transportation, take note: After midnight, you're on your own (try Tipsy Taxi at 726-5060, or hope you made a friend in the bar).

Other activities

Shopping: There are a few shops, especially for sports equipment and clothing, but this is not Winter Park's forté.

Sleigh rides: Jim's Sleigh Rides in Fraser (726-0949) and Dashing Through the Snow (726-5376) have old-fashioned sleigh rides with a stop for refreshments around a roaring campfire. Dinner at the Barn Sleigh Rides (726-4293) offers a ride to a 90-year-old ranch, gourmet dinner and old-time entertainment.

Dogsled rides: Grand Adventures (726-9247), with spirited Siberian huskies, takes tours through miles of spectacular backcountry.

Snowmobile tours: Trailblazer (726-8452) or Grand Adventures (726-9247). Snowmobile tours run about $35 for one hour, with multihour discounts.

Other fun: Snoscoots are scaled-down snowmobiles that drivers aged 9 and older can operate around a marked, flat track next to the highway between Winter Park and Fraser.

Tubing—sliding down a hill upon an inflated inner tube—is gaining popularity at ski resorts, but Winter Park has had this for a very long time. The Fraser Valley Tubing Hill (726-

5954) has a hill, rental tubes and two rope tows to pull you back to the top. Cost is $11 per hour after 6 p.m. and $10 per hour before 6 p.m.

Getting there and around

By air: Denver International Airport is a hub for several major airlines. Home James vans take skiers from the airport to Winter Park. The fare each way is about $34. Reserve through central reservations, or contact the van lines directly. Home James: (970) 726-5060 in Colorado; or (800) 525-3304.

By car: Winter Park is 85 miles northwest of Denver International Airport on Hwy. 40. Take I-70 west to Exit 232, then head toward Granby on Hwy. 40.

By train: Amtrak's California Zephyr, which runs between Chicago and San Francisco, makes a stop in Fraser, only a few miles from the ski area. Check with Amtrak on current schedules. Skiers from Chicago board the train in the afternoon and arrive in Winter Park the next morning. West Coast skiers board in the morning and arrive by the next afternoon.

Sleeper cars are available, but sleeping in the coaches is not as bad as one might think. There's lots of leg room, and the seats recline nearly all the way. Special packages make the trains very affordable. Call Winter Park Central Reservations for details. Call Amtrak for information and train-only reservations: (800) 872-7245 (USA-RAIL).

The Ski Train is an unusual treat. This special train leaves Denver's Union Station on weekends from mid-December to April, but adds a Friday departure from late February to early April. Operating for more than 50 years, it brings 800 passengers from Denver directly to the Winter Park base area, chugging along 56 miles and climbing 4,000 feet. The train snakes through 28 tunnels and across canyons, ravines, and ice-crusted rivers. The scenery is as gripping as any we have seen in the Swiss and Austrian Alps. The train leaves Denver at 7:15 a.m. and departs Winter Park at 4:15 p.m. Paid parking is available in surrounding lots for about $4, but it varies.

Two classes of train service are available; club car includes a continental buffet. Round-trip rates are about $60 club and $40 coach. For Ski Train information and reservations, call (303) 296-4754.

Getting around: Rent a car for any extensive restaurant or bar hopping. If you plan to stick close to your lodging at night and your lodge transports you to the slopes, you won't need a car. The Tipsy Taxi operates between all bars and lodging on Friday and Saturday. Book through Home James, 726-5060.

Utah skiing

and staying in Salt Lake City

If a corporation could build the perfect ski resort, it would have lots of feathery snow yet frequent sunny weather, a nearby major airport yet no airplane noise, and a variety of lodging and nightlife to appeal to a broad section of the skiing public. No ski corporation built Salt Lake City, but it fits that description.

Eleven downhill ski areas, three Nordic ski areas and the only North American facility with public ski-jumping instruction and bobsled rides are within an hour's drive of the Salt Lake City International Airport, one of the country's major air hubs. Utah's snow is legendary—light, fluffy and abundant. But that's not all. These resorts don't feel the need to be carbon copies of their neighbors. Each of the 11 nearby ski areas has a distinct personality. If you think variety is the spice of life, get ready for a well-seasoned feast. Seven of the 11 resorts are detailed in the next three chapters, and we offer capsule descriptions of two others in Regional Getaways chapter.

If you still think you can't get a drink in Utah, you're way behind the times, my friend. In most places you won't notice any difference between buying a beer here and at home (we explain the liquor laws later in the chapter). Salt Lake City claims more microbreweries per capita than any other western metropolitan city. Though we can't verify that claim, we can verify through firsthand experience that the breweries serve a very tasty product. Salt Lake City is unsurpassed in evening entertainment variety. Pro basketball or hockey, theater, comedy clubs and high-energy dance clubs are among the options.

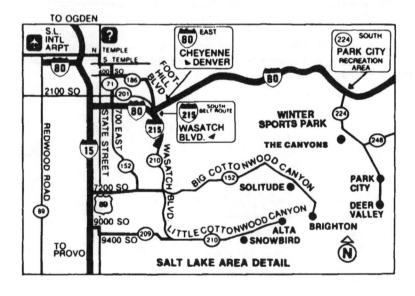

SALT LAKE AREA DETAIL

Salt Lake City will host the 2002 Winter Olympics, and will be the third U.S. site to have that honor (Lake Placid in 1932 and 1980; Squaw Valley in 1960.) Except for the downhill and Super G, which will be at Snowbasin, all of the ski events—Alpine and Nordic—will be in and around Park City.

Salt Lake City

Salt Lake City is a great spot to stay for several reasons. One, you're centrally located to sample all the major ski areas. Two, hotels are relatively inexpensive, perhaps a result of having more than 10,000 rooms available for nightly use. Three, Salt Lake City has a ton of fun stuff to do at night.

The **Utah Transit Authority** (287-4636) has a very efficient ski bus system serving Brighton and Solitude in Big Cottonwood Canyon and Snowbird and Alta in Little Cottonwood Canyon. The buses are clean, pleasant and inexpensive, and go directly from downtown to the ski areas. UTA has a free fare zone downtown, convenient for sightseeing and evening activities. **Lewis Brothers Stages** (800-826-5844 or 359-8677) has a SkiExpress service that picks up skiers and snowboarders from downtown hotels and takes them to one of seven ski areas. Many of the hotels include the service in their rates.

 ## Accommodations

Although rates are a little higher downtown than in outlying parts of the city, it is worth the extra few bucks to be close to Salt Lake City's major attractions. Here are some recommendations for per-night rates in the $90 to $170 range (unless otherwise noted):

Salt Lake Marriott (531-0800 or 800-345-4754) is across from the Salt Palace Convention Center and is connected to the Crossroads Plaza shopping mall. **Howard Johnson Hotel** (521-0130 or 800-366-3684) is across the street from Temple Square.

Doubletree Hotel (801-328-2000) is a few blocks farther south on West Temple, but it's within stumbling distance of the Zephyr Club (see *Après-ski/nightlife*). Another choice in this area is the **Peery Hotel** (521-4300; rates are about $65–$115), historic, nicely elegant, but subject to street noise.

Little America Hotel and Towers (363-6781) has some of the largest rooms we've ever seen in a hotel—great for spreading out all the junk that skiers bring.

Also recommended are **Embassy Suites Hotel** (359-7800) and the **Salt Lake Hilton** (532-3344).

The **Marriott University Park Hotel** (801-581-1000) is near the University of Utah, farther from downtown but closer to the resorts. It is at a higher elevation than downtown, so it has a dandy view of the city from its glassed-in hot tub.

Less expensive (starting at $55–$90 per night) are:

Salt Lake City Center Travelodge (531-7100), **Travelodge Temple Square** (533-8200), **Deseret Inn** (532-2900) or **Cavanaughs Olympus Hotel** (521-7373).

Those looking for the coziness of an inn can try **The Brigham Street Inn** (364-4461), on East South Temple near the university. Three B&Bs in historic buildings are clustered about seven blocks from Temple Square: **The Anniversary Inn at Kahn Mansion** (363-4900), **Anton Boxrud Bed & Breakfast** (800-524-5511) and **The Armstrong Mansion B&B** (800-708-1333). Call for rates.

For additional lodging, contact the **Salt Lake Convention and Visitors Bureau**, (800) 541-4955 or 521-2868.

Dining

Downtown Salt Lake City has many restaurants in nearly every food category you can name, including Peruvian and Thai. You may want to dress up a bit (meaning a buttoned shirt and khakis instead of a T-shirt and jeans) for the finer establishments. See our nightlife section for an explanation of "private clubs," which some of these restaurants are. All these restaurants have the 801 area code.

We're told **Metropolitan** (173 W. Broadway, 364-3472) has world-class gourmet cuisine that rivals some of the best of any other major city, but be prepared to pay for it.

Casually elegant Italian dining can be found at **Baci'Trattoria** (134 W. Pierpont Ave., 328-1500), **Ferrantelli Ristorante Italiano** (300 Trolley Square, 531-8228) with its New York atmosphere and **Ristorante della Fontana** (336 S. 400 East, 328-4243), which is in a converted church with stained-glass windows and a waterfall cascading from the ceiling. A Tuscan restaurant we haven't tried, but which has been recommended, **Il Sansovino** (299 S. Main; 533-9999).

For Asian dining, **Charlie Chow** (277 Trolley Square, 575-6700) has the most interesting atmosphere, but **Pagoda** (26 E St., 355-8155) has been around the longest, since 1946. **Mikado** (67 W. 100 South, 328-0929) has fresh fish and sushi, and has been in business for four decades.

Cafe Pierpont (122 W. Pierpont Ave., 364-1222) and **Rio Grande Cafe** (270 S. Rio Grande, at the Amtrak Station, 364-3302) are downtown's best bets for Mexican food.

American and steak and seafood restaurants abound. **New Yorker** (60 Post Office Place, 363-0166) has an elegant atmosphere in the dining room. Its more casual neighbors, **Market Street Grill** (322-4668) and **Oyster Bar** (531-6044) emphasize seafood, but also serve steaks and chicken. (Market Street Grill has great breakfasts, by the way.)

Lamb's (169 S. Main, 364-7166) is Utah's oldest restaurant, dating to 1919 and still packed today. A spectacular night view awaits diners at **Room at the Top** (150 W. 500 South, 532-3344), the Salt Lake Hilton's fine restaurant. **Piña's Restaurant** (327 W. 200 South, 355-7462) has a fun, Caribbean-influenced atmosphere.

At the base of Little Cottonwood Canyon is **La Caille** (942-1751) which gets rave reviews for its French cuisine, serving staff and setting, the latter built to look like a French chateau and surrounded by gardens filled with swans, peacocks, rabbits and other animals.

These are just a tiny portion of what's available in Salt Lake City. A great resource for finding restaurants—particularly if you like certain kinds of food—is the website City Search (www.citysearchutah.com), which has a searchable database.

Après-ski/nightlife/other activities

Utah's liquor laws: Baby-boomer skiers remember when getting a glass of wine meant a trip to the state liquor store before going to a restaurant, then paying a setup fee before you could consume your own brown-bagged bottle. Now it's much easier, but here are a few tips:

Restaurants that have liquor licenses (not all do) can serve alcohol from noon to midnight "to customers intending to dine." However, you won't find the wine list at the table. Your server will ask if you'd like "a beverage," at which point you can ask for the alcohol menu. Some restaurants are designated as private clubs, which means you'll have to pay a temporary membership fee to get in.

Telephone area code: 801

Bars don't exist in Utah, at least not by that name. If you are planning just to drink, not eat, you'll do so at a **private club.** Don't be deterred by restaurant or nightclub advertising that has phrasing like this: "A private club for the benefit of its members." You, too, can become a member. Utah residents buy an annual membership costing up to $35 for each club. Visitors pay $5 for a two-week membership, valid for two weeks for the visitor and five guests. Annual members can bring guests, too.

To avoid the charge, ask outside if someone will be your "sponsor." Once you're inside, thank your sponsor and split for separate tables. (Unless, of course, you think you might like to get to know him or her a little better, in which case, offer to buy the drinks.) Legally, you're supposed to leave with your sponsor, but no one watches that closely (and once inside, you can always find a new sponsor to leave with). If you lack such audacity, just think of the membership as a cover charge. But don't be shy about asking. Utahns are accustomed to this method of staying within the law; in fact, some single Utahns use "Need a sponsor?" as a handy pickup line.

Taverns may or may not serve food, depending on the establishment. The only alcohol served at taverns is 3.2-percent beer.

For an unusual happy hour, stop by the **Cotton Bottom Inn** (273-9830) at the base of Big and Little Cottonwood Canyons. This is a raucous, sawdust-on-the-floor tavern with great garlicburgers and an earthy crowd. The address is 2820 E. 6200 South, but it's a little hard to find. Ask a local to direct you.

For lively après-ski downtown, try the **Dead Goat Saloon** (Arrow Press Square, 165 S. West Temple). A quieter, pleasant location is **D.B. Coopers** (19 E. 200 South), which Salt Lake City's career crowd seems to favor.

Salt Lake City has brew pubs, **Squatter's Pub** (147 W. Broadway, 363-2739), **Desert Edge Brewery at the Pub** (Trolley Square, 521-8917) and **Red Rock Brewing Co.** (254 South 200 West, 521-7446). All brew their own beer on the premises and serve excellent pub fare.

If you like movies *and* microbrews, head to **Brewvies** (677 South 200 West; 322-3891). This year-old establishment combines second-run (movies that already have been shown but aren't yet in video stores), independent and classic films with a gourmet-pizza-and-beer restaurant. Many people come to eat or drink, then decide whether to hang around for the movies being shown on four screens. You must be 21 years old.

This isn't the typical ski-town nightlife activity, but classical music lovers shouldn't miss the free 8 p.m. Thursday night **rehearsals of the Mormon Tabernacle Choir** at Temple Square. You can drop in and leave as you wish.

One of our contributors describes herself as a "double-diamond après-skier," and one of her top five ski-town dance nightclubs is **Zephyr Club** (301 S. West Temple; 355-5646). She says it surpasses its billing as "Salt Lake City's premier showcase for local and national entertainment."

One place we're planning to try the next time we're here is **Club Manhattan** (5 E. 400 South; 364-7651). We're told it's in the "everything-old-is-new-again" genre, with cocktails, overstuffed chairs and a live piano-and-strings band for swing and ballroom dancing. We've been known to enjoy a little cheek-to-cheek dancing on our trips, but the right atmosphere and music is hard to find.

You can go shopping at **Trolley Square,** shops and boutiques in a restored trolley barn (you can buy Olympic souvenirs at the Olympic Spirit store); attend a **Utah Jazz** (355-DUNK) basketball game, or attend theater, symphony, dance or opera performances. Now what other ski town can offer all that?

For a more complete list of restaurants, nightlife and other activities, pick up a free copy of *This Week Salt Lake*. This excellent guide tells you what is happening within a two-week period (sports, theater, etc.) and is a handy reference guide to the city's ongoing attractions. Another great guide is *Utah After Dark*, which rates the private clubs and taverns throughout most of the state, and tells which ones have live music, pool tables, sports TV and more. A third information option is the Internet, either the Salt Lake Convention & Visitors Bureau website (http://www.saltlake.org) or City Search (www.citysearchutah.com).

The Interconnect Adventure Tour

Experienced skiers can ski to as many as five different resorts via backcountry routes on this all-day tour. Six to 14 skiers are led by mountain guides. Some traversing and walking are necessary, so you need to be a confident skier and in condition. The four-area tour (Solitude, Brighton, Alta and Snowbird) is offered three days a week, while the five-area tour (those four and Park City) goes the other four days. Each tour costs $125 (98/99 price), including return transportation and lunch. Reservations are required. Call (801) 534-1907 and have a credit card.

Getting there and getting around

Getting there: Salt Lake City is one of the country's major airports. Delta has one of its major hubs here, but several other major airlines fly here. Fares from Southern California are particularly good, thanks to ongoing competition between Delta and Southwest Airlines.

Getting around: Rent a car if you want to cover a lot of ground in the evening; otherwise, use public transportation. Getting to the resorts is a snap: several ground transportation companies operate shuttles to the ski areas from Salt Lake City hotels. We have found **Lewis Brothers Stages** (800-826-5844; 801-359-8677 in Salt Lake City) to be very reliable. Round-trip from the airport to the Cottonwood Canyon or Park City resorts is about $22 per person; reservations required; minimum of three people. Don't worry too much about the minimum; in our experience, the vans are fairly full during winter.

Lewis Brothers also will pick up at downtown hotels. Or take the Utah Transit Authority Ski Bus, $4 each way (exact fare required) to the four Cottonwood Canyon resorts (Alta, Snowbird, Solitude, Brighton). We take the UTA bus whenever we're at a hotel that's near the bus stop. The buses are clean, convenient and best of all, cheap. The UTA buses run at night downtown until about 11:30 p.m., but only about once per hour. Call UTA at 287-4636 for more info.

Park City
Utah

Park City
Deer Valley
The Canyons

Walk outside the Alamo Saloon at dusk, just as the lights of Main Street begin to twinkle seductively and the sidewalks fill with après-ski traffic, and you can almost hear the clank of spurs. Squint your eyes and the strolling figures become the miners and cowboys who roamed this same street a hundred years ago, swaggering through 30-odd saloons in what was once one of the country's largest silver mining towns. Soon the vision is gone, and the people are once again modern-day funseekers. Yet the flamboyant atmosphere of the silver rush remains.

This town originally was founded by soldiers who had been sent west to discourage Brigham Young from ending the Utah Territory's association with the Union. Park City boomed during the mining era, then almost became a ghost town during the Depression and World War II. Now Park City can be counted among the world's top winter resorts.

This is the most accessible destination resort of its caliber in the country. Just 30 miles from Salt Lake City by a major freeway, it is a 45-minute drive from the airport, door to door. Skiers and snowboarders from either coast can get one-and-a-half extra days on boards per trip because they don't have to devote two entire days to getting here and back. Accessibility was one of the key factors that helped Salt Lake City get the 2002 Olympic Winter Games. Park City, which is headquarters for the U.S. Ski and Snowboard Team, will host a number of the Olympic events. Park City Mountain Resort and Deer Valley Resort will host the slalom, combined slalom, giant slalom, aerials, moguls and snowboarding, while bobsled, luge, Nordic combined and ski jumping will be at the nearby Utah Winter Sports Park.

New for 98/99, Park City Mountain Resort: McConkey's Bowl will get its first lift, a six-passenger high-speed chair, plus four new runs in the bowl. The resort also plans to do quite a bit of regrading or realigning of existing runs, such as the beginner area at the base; CB's run, site of the Olympic alpine and snowboarding giant slaloms; and Treasure Hollow, a popular route back to the base area.

New for 98/99: Deer Valley Resort: Four new lifts and 16 new runs will be added here. A four-passenger, high-speed gondola, a fixed-grip quad and eight new runs will be added in the Deer Crest area, which is to the left and below the Snow Park Lodge base area. Empire Canyon—northwest of Flagstaff Mountain, and bordering McConkey's Bowl at PCMR—will get a high-speed quad chairlift, a fixed-grip quad and eight beginner and intermediate runs, as well as some advanced chute and bowl skiing.

The Canyons, Park City's third resort, has completed its first season under the ownership of the American Skiing Company, which owns resorts in New England, Colorado and California. You may have heard of The Canyons under one of its previous names: ParkWest or Wolf Mountain. However, it's beginning to look a bit different than it used to. Last season, the new owners installed a new gondola, four new lifts (most of which replaced aging double

Park City Mountain Resort (PCMR) Facts

Summit elevation: 10,000 feet
Vertical drop: 3,100 feet
Base elevation: 6,900 feet
Address: P.O. Box 39, Park City, UT 84060
✆ **Area code:** 435
Ski area phone: 649-8111
Snow report: 647-5449
ⓘ **Toll-free information:**
(800) 453-1360 (Park City Chamber)
Toll-free reservations:
(800) 222-7275 (Park City Ski Holidays)
Fax: 649-0532 (lodging)
Internet: http://www.pcski.com (PCMR);
http://www.netpp.com/parkcity/ (town)

Expert:★★★★ Advanced:★★★★
Intermediate:★★★★
Beginner:★★★ Never-ever:★★★
Number of lifts: 14–3 high-speed six-person chairs, 1 high-speed quad, 1 quad, 5 triple chairs, 4 double chairs
Snowmaking: 22 percent
Skiing acreage: 2,200
Uphill capacity: 26,600 per hour
Snowboarding: Yes, unlimited
Bed base: 12,000
Nearest lodging: Slopeside, condos
Resort child care: None; lessons start at age 3
Adult ticket, per day: $46-$53 (98/99 prices)
Dining:★★★
Apres-ski/nightlife:★★★
Other activities:★★★

chairs), an on-mountain restaurant, new telephone and ticketing systems, and more. The company intends to continue the improvements for 98/99, but unfortunately could not provide details by our summer deadline.

A note about the fact boxes in this chapter: If you're looking for phone numbers, websites or bed-base information on the town of Park City, check the Park City Mountain Resort box on the top of this page. "Nearest lodging" means nearest to that particular ski area. When we talk about the town and surrounding area, it's "Park City." When we talk about the ski/snowboard area, we will use its acronym, PCMR. Sorry 'bout that, but there's too much room for confusion otherwise.

Park City Mountain Resort—

Mountain layout

◆◆ **Expert:** Start off with a trip to the top of Blueslip Bowl. Reportedly, when this was the boundary of the ski area, resort workers regularly slipped under the ropes, made tracks down the bowl and then skied back into the resort. The management passed out blue (you're fired) slips to anyone caught floating through this powder bowl. If you can ski Blueslip with confidence, then try Jupiter Bowl and its neighbors—McConkey's, Puma and Scotts Bowls.

Jupiter Bowl has every type of steep expert terrain. To reach the Jupiter lift, take the Jupiter access road from the top of the Pioneer or Thaynes lifts. To the left as you get off the Jupiter lift are wide-open faces, especially on the West Face, which is the easiest way down (a relative term). Narrow gullies and chutes, such as Silver Cliff, 6 Bells and Indicator, drop vertically between tightly packed evergreens. Head to the right as you get off the chair and try Portuguese Gap, a run more akin to having the floor open below you, or traverse to Scotts Bowl, which is just as steep.

Telephone area code: 435

The adventurous (and those with parachutes) will find definite thrills in the McConkey's Bowl and Puma Bowl areas. When open, these are reached by a long traverse across Disco Ridge and some hiking on the backside of Jupiter Peak. The cornice at the top of both bowls deposits skiers and riders into steep faces and chutes, which empty out into the Pioneer lift area. These bowls used to be a wild and untamed reward for those willing to make the hike, but since many vacationing skiers and snowboarders come from sea level and aren't too excited about hiking more than an few steps at oxygen-deprived 10,000 feet, we regard the new lift in McConkey's Bowl as great news.

◆ **Advanced:** If you're looking for steeps or moguls, try the blacks off the Motherlode triple or the neighboring Thaynes double. Glory Hole, Double Jack and the like offer a good challenge. Or, ski the front face of PCMR on the runs off the Ski Team chair. Most of the deliciously long trails here are left *au naturel*, but Willy's is on the occasional grooming list. Hit it on the right day, and it's *fun*. For a steep cruiser that is groomed daily, head down nearby Silver Queen.

■ **Intermediate:** Intermediates have mind-boggling choices. If you want to start with a worthy cruiser, take PayDay from the top of the lift by the same name. The views are spectacular, and at night it becomes one of the longest lighted runs in the Rockies. This run also has a halfpipe.

Probably most popular for intermediates are the 11 trails served by the King Consolidated high-speed quad (called "King Con" by just about everyone). These runs have a steep, wide, smooth pitch.

Both intermediates and advanced skiers will enjoy the runs under the Silverlode chair. To avoid crowds, try the four blues under the Pioneer chair.

●● **Beginner:** Even those just getting into their snowplow turns can take the Pay Day and Bonanza chairs to the Summit House and descend a very long, easy, multi-named run. This trail starts with Claim Jumper, shifts to Bonanza, then finishes at the base area on Sidewinder. For an adventure and a chance to see a different part of the mountain, take the Mid-Mountain Run to the Pioneer chair, where you can have lunch at the Mid-Mountain Restaurant and watch experts head down the face of Blueslip Bowl.

The only complaint about the beginner runs here is that more advanced skiers use them too. The upper parts of the green-circle trails are used as access routes, while the bottoms are the end runs for skiers coming off more advanced terrain. The greens here are wide and gentle, but they wind in and around tougher stuff. If you're just starting out and concerned about getting in above your head, carry a trail map and pay attention to the signage. And head to the bottom well before day's end if you like plenty of room.

● **Never-ever:** At the base area, the Three Kings and First Time lifts service good learning terrain.

Note: The Town triple chair lift transports from the lower part of Main Street to the base of the Bonanza lift. Even on holidays or peak periods, the Town lift is often empty, so those faced with a long line at the bottom of the mountain may want to take the free shuttle here and avoid the crowds. If Bonanza has a long line, ski down Sidewinder a tad, catch the Crescent chair, ski down King Con to the Silverlode chair and it'll take you to the Summit area. If Pay Day has a line, try the Eagle chair (to the far right of the base area) and head down blue-square Temptation to the King Con chair.

Mountain rating

Most reviews of PCMR characterize it as a cruising paradise for intermediates, which is true enough. While it may not have as much steep and "gulp!" as Snowbird or Alta, its bowl skiing and chutes are serious—even on the expert scale. PCMR doesn't have a huge amount of lower-end terrain, but what it has allows beginners to get up on the mountain to see the views—something they can't do at every resort.

Snowboarding

Snowboarding was allowed here for the first time two seasons ago. Knowing that PCMR has some long traverses that require a bit of skating on skis, we asked a boarder-journalist friend to assess the resort. His report: He's not fond of the traverses, but likes the advantage that boarders have in the bowls, because they get to do the hike to the best stuff in soft boots, while the skiers hike in rigid boots.

Our friend mentioned Jupiter Access as an example of a traverse where you sometimes have to release your back foot and skate. However, if we could "steepen-up" one run at PCMR, it would be Thaynes Canyon, a very long and nearly flat run that connects the bottom of Jupiter Bowl with the base of the King Con chair, passing a couple of other chairs along the way. But alas, that's geography. If you just hate the flats, study a trail map to see which runs will deposit you closest to the base of a lift along that route. You can avoid the worst traverses with advance planning.

PCMR has a halfpipe on Pay Day. Rentals and lessons also are available.

PCMR—Lessons (98/99 prices)

Group lessons: $57 for four hours (two sessions) and $45 for two hours. Multiday discounts available.

Never-ever package: PCMR does not have packaged first-time instruction; novices enroll in group lessons and ride the First Time chair free during their lesson.

Private lessons: $89 per hour (an early-bird private lesson, 8:45 to 9:45 a.m. is $60). Additional skiers can be added for $15, and multihour discounts are available.

Special programs: Park City Mountain Adventure classes, four hours long for $57, are for advanced intermediate and higher-ability skiers. The classes explore Jupiter Bowl, off-trail skiing and deep powder. Women's Ski Challenge three-day camps cost $295 for instruction, skiing, seminars and continental breakfast daily.

Racing: NASTAR is on the Lost Prospector trail Wednesday through Saturday. Two runs cost $6; each additional run is $1. Park City Dual Challenge is set up on Clementine nearly every day. The cost is $1 per run; $5 for seven runs.

Children's lessons: Ages 4–6, $83 for a full day including two 90-minute lessons, hot lunch, snack and indoor activities. PCMR advises prepaid reservations for this age group, as available spaces often sell out. Ages 7–13, $79 for six hours of lessons and lunch. Half-day sessions, private and semi-private lessons and multiday discounts are available for both age groups.

Call for details on any of the ski school programs, (800) 227-2754. PCMR does not have non-skiing child care.

PCMR—Lift tickets (98/99 prices)

	Adult	Child (Up to 12)
One day	$53	$24
Three days	$150 ($50/day)	$69 ($23/day)
Five days	$230 ($46/day)	$105 ($20/day)

Who skis free: Skiers 70 and older on the entire mountain, and children ages 6 and younger on the First Time chair lift. (Kids need a ticket to ride that lift; ask at the ticket window.) Some lodging properties offer free skiing here with a booking of four days or longer; call the toll-free number in the facts box for more information.

Who skis at a discount: Ages 65–69 ski for half the adult price, $26.50.

Note: PCMR has night skiing and riding from 4–9 p.m. for $19 for adults and $9 for children.

Deer Valley—Mountain layout

Deer Valley is renowned for pampering its guests with top-flight gourmet meals, palatial accommodations, attentive service and impeccable slopes. Some of the many amenities include guest service attendants who help get skis off car racks as you pull up to unload, tissues at every lift, restaurants to make a gourmet salivate, a free ski corral service where you can safely leave the best equipment, and grooming crews who comb the snow so pool-table smooth it will make any beginner into an instant intermediate. Experts who sneer at the daily slope manicure can go somewhere else, as far as we're concerned. Deer Valley fills a marvelous niche in the ski world, satisfying those who want to be pampered and are willing to pay a little more for the privilege.

◆◆ **Expert:** Request an Experts Only trail map (it has a white cover), which points out the toughest runs and several gladed and chute areas. One of the best areas is Mayflower, to the far left on the trail map. Here you can find moguls on Morning Star, Fortune Teller,

---

Deer Valley

Summit elevation: 9,570 feet
Vertical drop: 3,000 feet
Base elevation: 6,570 feet

Address: P.O. Box 1525, Park City, UT 84060
✆ **Area code:** 435
Ski area phone: 649-1000
Snow report: 649-2000
Fax: 645-6939
ⓘ **Toll-free information:** (800) 424-3337
ⓘ **Toll-free reservations:** (800) 558-3337
Internet: http://www.deervalley.com

Expert:★★★★
Advanced:★★★★
Intermediate:★★★★ **Beginner:**★★
Never-ever:★
Number of lifts: 18–1 gondola, 4 high-speed quads, 2 quads, 9 triples, 2 doubles
Snowmaking: 27 percent
Skiable acreage: 1,750 acres
Uphill capacity: 34,800 per hour
Snowboarding: None
Nearest lodging: Slopeside
Resort child care: Yes, 2 months and older
Adult ticket, per day: $49-$57 (98/99 price)

Paradise and Narrow Gauge. These are long trails bordered by glades, perfect for darting in and out.

Flagstaff Mountain has both moguls and cruising runs; it's easy to see from the lift which is which. For experts, a short traverse to the left off the top of this lift will open up an entire mountain face called Ontario Bowl, with challenging tree skiing.

Empire Summit also will be a draw for experts. Though it borders McConkey's Bowl at PCMR, we haven't heard whether cross-resort skiing will be allowed.

◆ **Advanced:** Mayflower and its neighboring chair Sultan have ungroomed runs, but with so little traffic the bumps rarely grow monstrous. Orient Express and Stein's Way are perfect cruisers with good advanced pitch, and Perseverance, coupled with the initial steeper sections of Thunderer, Blue Ledge and Grizzly, are just right for those just entering advanced status.

■ **Intermediate:** If you want to have plenty of company and beautiful scenery, the best runs are Sunset, Birdseye (both on Bald Mountain) and Success (on Bald Eagle Mountain). The areas with the most intermediate runs are served by the Wasatch Express, Sterling and Northside Express chairs. Run after run down trails such as Legal Tender, Wizard, Nabob, Sidewinder and Hawkeye are a blast. We're starting to like the runs under the Northside Express, too, mainly because they're farther from the base areas, so they're not as crowded as the Wasatch Express area.

Don't overlook Flagstaff Mountain's short enjoyable cruisers, as well as Big Stick and Solid Muldoon on Bald Eagle Mountain, known as the "lower mountain." Last Chance passes by a lot of homes on the lower mountain, but on our last trip here, we made several runs completely alone.

If you are a timid intermediate, stick to Deer Valley's green-circle runs at first. We find the greens here to be a bit turquoise, just a shade easier than the true blues.

●● **Beginner:** If you are a timid beginner, read the Never-Ever advice. If you're a brave soul who just needs some practice, we especially recommend Sunset, a gentle, scenic route that descends from the top of Bald Mountain—but head back to the base before day's end or you'll find yourself in the role of a human slalom pole, being passed at close range by more proficient skiers.

● **Never-ever:** We recommend other resorts for a first ski experience. The novice area is gentle enough, but it's a big step to the next level. Deer Valley's green runs (most on Bald Eagle Mountain) are also access runs that better skiers use to reach the base area. A beginner will feel as though he or she is riding a scooter on a freeway.

Daily complimentary mountain tours leave from the Carpenter Express, Snow Park Lodge, at 9:30 a.m. for advanced skiers and 10 a.m. for intermediates. An intermediate tour also leaves from the Silver Lake ski corral at 1:30 p.m. and features the new Deer Crest area. Another tour leaves at the same time and place, but takes advanced and expert skiers into the new Empire Summit area.

Mountain rating

Deer Valley has built a reputation for pampering at a price, but its slopes include tougher trails than it gets credit for. On a scale of one to ten, one being a never-ever and ten being a top-flight expert, we'd say that Deer Valley is best for levels three through eight (maybe a nine with the new Empire Summit terrain). And that's no slam: the vast majority of skiers fit that profile.

Snowboarding

Not allowed. Head for The Canyons or Park City Mountain Resort.

Deer Valley—Lessons (98/99 prices)

Group lessons: (11:15 a.m.–4 p.m.) for those age 18 and older cost $65. Teens 13–17 have lessons with their own age group.

Never-ever package (lifts, lessons, rentals): None. Never-evers take group or private lessons.

Private lessons: $72 an hour for one or two skiers.

Special programs: Women have daily clinics for $65. Women also have three- and four-day clinics at certain times in the season for $300 and $360 respectively, hosted by Heidi Voelker, Deer Valley's ambassador of skiing.

Racing: Races are held on the Race Course above Silver Lake Lodge, reachable by the Sterling or Wasatch Lifts. Medalist Challenge is Deer Valley's equivalent of NASTAR. The cost is $9 for two runs and the daily chance to earn a medal. On Fridays, Deer Valley's Director of Skiing, Stein Eriksen, an Olympic gold medalist and World Champion, runs the course so you can compare your time to his. Heidi Voelker, a U.S. Ski Team veteran, will do the pacing on Saturdays. A self-timed dual slalom is $2 per run.

Children's lessons: Full day, ages 6 (first grade) to 12, is $90 for lessons, lift ticket and lunch. Ages 4 1/2 through kindergarten get a full-day program, also for $90.

Deer Valley—Child care (98/99 prices)

Ages: 2 months to 12 years.

Costs: Full day, with lunch, ages 2–12 years, $58. Half day, $45 without lunch. Full-day infant care (2 months-2 years), including lunch, $70. Half day without lunch, $55.

Reservations: Recommended at all times but essential in holiday periods. Call 645-6612 or make reservations when you book lodging.

Deer Valley—Lift tickets (98/99 prices)

	Adult	Child (Up to 12)
One day	$57	$30
Three days	$159 ($53/day)	$81 ($27/day)
Five days	$250 ($50/day)	$125 ($25/day)

Who skis free: No one.

Who skis at a discount: Skiers 65 and older ski for $40 for a single day, $108 for three days and $170 for five days.

Note: For seven days between Christmas and New Year's (Dec. 26–Jan. 1 this season), Deer Valley sells a pass for $413 ($59 per day) for adults, $231 ($33 per day) for children and $301 ($43 per day) for seniors. (You also can buy single-day tickets at the rates listed in parentheses.) Ticket sales are limited, so on holidays the extra few bucks to ski Deer Valley are worth it. You can make advance ticket reservations when you book your lodging, and this is highly recommended during the Christmas period and the February President's Holiday week.

The Canyons

The Canyons became a part of the American Skiing Company family in 1997. ASC began with several large resorts in New England, then bought The Canyons, Steamboat in Colorado and Heavenly in California/Nevada the same summer. We sent a staffer to Park City last season for an update, but on the day we came here, it was one of the those "if-you-could-see-it, over there-would-be-Square-Top-mountain" days, so we confess we didn't explore as much as we wanted to. However, we saw the major improvements in lifts and buildings. Wow. ASC has done wonders in just one season to spiff up a resort that was really showing its age. The improvements continue this season, with two additional lifts, including one that will make The Canyons' lift-served vertical more than 3,000 feet.

We plan to send our staffer back here this season (she really won't mind, trust us), but until then, our too-brief report:

Mountain layout

The first resort you pass on the way into Park City, The Canyons is a few miles away from the historic downtown, though it is connected by a free shuttle service from many points in town. When this was ParkWest, all the lifts and runs had Wild West names. As Wolf Mountain, all of the trails and lifts were named for threatened or endangered species. The Canyons kept a little of both heritages (runs such as Silver Horse and Broken Arrow, and lifts named Red Hawk and Golden Eagle), but decided to put a little testosterone into the black-diamond run names. No more "Gazelle" or "Wombat." Now it's The South Side Chutes, G Force and Super Fury.

Expert/Advanced: Most of The Canyons's terrain is not visible from the base area. What you can't see are chutes and gullies as extreme as any in Utah. The Condor chair takes you to terrain that is very steep, such as the South Side Chutes, or the dense glades of Canis Lupis. You can hike a few hundred feet to the top of Murdock Peak for ungroomed bowl descents. (Our stats reflect lift-served terrain; with the hike, the total vertical is 2,580 feet.) Another black-diamond playground is under Tombstone Express, an area to the left on the trail map that opened during The Canyons' first season.

Intermediate: There are blue runs from every chair, but sometimes only one or two descents per chair. The best trails for this level are in the center of the resort, under the Saddleback Express (Snow Dancer is quite nice), The Snow Canyon Express (wide paths

---

The Canyons

Summit elevation: 9,990 feet
Vertical drop: 3,190 feet
Base elevation: 6,800 feet

Address: 4000 ParkWest Drive
Park City, UT 84060
✆ **Area code:** 435
Ski area and snow report phone: 649-5400
ⓘ **Toll-free information:** (800) 754-1636
Fax: 645-6939
Internet: http://www.thecanyons.com

Number of lifts: 11–1 gondola, 5 high-speed quads, 3 quads, 1 triple, 1 double
Snowmaking: 6 percent
Skiable Acreage: 2,700 acres
Uphill capacity: 24,000+ per hour
Snowboarding: Yes, unlimited
Nearest lodging: About 1/2 mile; condos

here) and the lower mountain. Blue runs are marked under the Condor and Tombstone chairs, but these were parts of the mountain we didn't get to explore.

Beginner/Never-ever: There's a nice learning area at the top of the gondola, but The Canyons doesn't have a tremendous amount of gentle terrain. We suggest this level enroll in lessons, in order to have a guide to keep them out of trouble.

Snowboarding

ParkWest was the first Park City ski area to allow snowboarding, and the policy never changed, even though the area's name did. Utah boarders are very loyal because of that support. The Canyons has four natural half-pipes and one constructed pipe. Lessons and rentals are available.

Lessons, child care, lift tickets (98/99 prices)

Group lessons: American Skiing Company has an outstanding learning program called Perfect Turn®, which it offers at The Canyons. Refer to our Skiing For Everyone chapter for a description of the program. Perfect Turn clinics run about $29.

Never-ever package: Skiing or snowboarding, a three-day packagewith half-day lesson, rentals and lift access while in the clinic is $134.

Private lessons: $65 per hour.

Children's lessons: Four hours of lessons and all-day supervision is $70.

Child care: Kids Central is a program that has survived this resort's many owner changes. It's easy to see why. The "Skiers in Diapers" program puts toddlers on skis at age 18 months with a specially trained children's coach. It's the only resort we know of that starts children that young. All day care, lunch, one-hour private lesson and lift ticket for this program is $85; $75 for half-day. If you just want child care, all day with lunch is $50.

Lift tickets: Adults, $46–$48 per day, depending on how many days you buy; ages 6–12, and ages 65 and older, $24–$26; younger than age 6, free.

Cross-country

White Pine Touring (649-8701 or 649-8710) offers 18 km. of track skiing, lessons and tours at the Park City golf course. Rates are about $8 daily; those 12 and younger and 70+ ski free. Full- and half-day snowshoe and ski tours in the Uinta mountains are also available.

Accommodations (97/98 prices)

In and around the Park City Area are bed-and-breakfasts, country inns, hotels and condominiums. At Deer Valley the lodging has a decidedly upscale flavor and tariffs to match.

Park City's lodging is roughly grouped either in the old town surrounding the Resort Center Complex or in the Prospector Square area. All is served by the free shuttlebus system. In general, low rates reflect early- and late-season prices in the smallest unit; high rates are the holiday rates for the largest unit.

Downtown and at the Park City Mountain Resort base:

In old Park City the best is the **Washington School Inn** (800-824-1672 or 435-649-3800). This is a very elegant country inn built in a former schoolhouse. Each room's name honors a former Park City teacher and everything is definitely first class. It has a hot tub and steambath, and is steps away from the center of the old town. If you are on your honeymoon, ask for the Miss Urie Room. Room rates range from about $135 to $350 and include breakfast and afternoon tea. No children under age 12 or pets.

The **Blue Church Lodge & Townhouses** (800-626-5467 or 435-649-8009) are constructed around an old church a block from Main Street. It is a grouping of seven condominiums ranging from one to four bedrooms in the church, with four additional townhouses across the street. Again, this is rated as a B&B because breakfast is provided in a common area each morning, though it doesn't fit the category of B&B in the classic sense. It has indoor and outdoor spas and laundry facilities. Rates are about $105 to $570.

If the key to lodging, as in real estate, is location, location, location, then **Treasure Mountain Inn** (800-344-2460) at the top of Main Street is a winner. These are studio and one- and two-bedroom condos with kitchens. Each of the three buildings has a coin-operated laundry, and there is a hot tub in the courtyard. Rooms are quiet, but step outside and you are smack dab in the middle of the nighttime action. Rates are about $110–$425.

The bargain spots are dormitory digs and rooms in the **Chateau Après Lodge** (435-649-9372) with room rates of about $75. The lodge also has dorm beds for $25. Another choice is **Budget Lodging** (435-649-2526 or 800-522-7669), with hotel rooms to four-bedroom units for $100 to $900. College students should head to the **Main Street Dorms** (800-453-5789) to save money and be close to all the best nightlife. Rooms with two bunk beds go for about $70; if all four beds are filled, that's $17.50 per night each. Bathrooms, a lounge and a kitchenette are shared, but there are private ski lockers.

Near the Resort Center you'll find another cluster of hotels and condos. The best is the **Silver King Hotel** (800-331-8652 or 435-649-5500). This condominium hotel is about 100 yards from the lifts and at the hub of the transportation system. Amenities include an indoor/outdoor swimming pool and underground parking. Some units have private hot tubs. Rates: $140–$630.

The **Lodge at the Resort Center** (800-824-5331 or 435-649-0800) is the second choice for luxury. It literally surrounds the base area lifts. Lots of amenities—spas, health club, pool, steamroom and concierge. Rates for hotel rooms to four-bedroom units: $100–$1,600.

Shadow Ridge (800-451-3031 or 435-649-4300) is the other top property near the lifts; It has a sauna, hot tub and laundry. Hotel rooms to three-bedroom condos: $120–$750.

Snow Flower (800-852-3101 or 435-649-6400) is 100 feet from the beginner area. Each unit has single-person jetted hot tubs, plus there are outdoor pools and underground parking. Studios to five-bedroom units go for $120–$925.

For more economical condos, try the renovated **Edelweiss Haus** (800-438-3855 or 435-649-9342) across the street from the lifts and the Silver King Hotel. Extras are a heated outdoor pool and hot tub. Rates for hotel rooms to two-bedroom condos are $95–$360.

In and around Prospector Square:

The **Inn at Prospector Square** (888-870-4386 or 435-649-7100) is a group of condos that includes use of its athletic club in the rates, $90–$460. **The Yarrow Hotel** (800-327-2332 or 435-649-7000) is considered good family lodging. Children under 12 stay free and the hotel sits amid shopping, movies and restaurants. It is on the shuttlebus route, about a five-minute ride from Park City's Main Street. Rates: $215–$475. The 200-room **Olympia Park Hotel** (800-754-3279 or 435-649-2900), with swimming pool and exercise room, has hotel rooms and suites: $119–$349.

The Homestead (800-327-7220 or 435-654-1102; e-mail: homeut@aol.com) is a rambling country resort 25 minutes from Park City in the town of Midway. This 110-year-old restored country inn is charming, with cross-country skiing and snowmobiling. This is one of the Great Inns of the Rockies, rated Four Diamond by AAA. Ski packages are available that include a skierized rental car and lift passes at several Utah resorts among the amenities.

For luxury condos and houses at affordable prices as well as a chance to get some last-minute or off-peak bargains in the entire Park City area, call **Accommodations Unlimited**, (800) 321-4754.

Accommodations —Deer Valley

All lodging in Deer Valley is costly. Even in the value season the least expensive starts at about $175 per night. Accommodations have the same high quality one finds at the resort itself, and much of it is slopeside. If it's in your budget, book it. If not, stay in Park City. The skiing is only a short ride away on a frequent shuttlebus.

Top dog is the **Stein Eriksen Lodge** (800-453-1302 or 435-649-3700). Think of any luxury or service and you will probably find it—heated sidewalks between buildings, fireplaces in the rooms, fresh terrycloth robes, floor-to-ceiling windows. Room rates start at $450 a night and one-bedroom suites top out at about $950 except at Christmas.

After Stein's the places to stay on the mountain are the **Stag Lodge Condominiums** (800-453-3833 or 435-649-7444) and the **Goldener Hirsch Inn** (800-252-3373 or 435-649-7770), offering the elegance and service of a top Austrian hotel at midmountain in Deer Valley. Rates start at about $330 during the regular season.

The **Pinnacle Condominiums** with three- and four-story living rooms are spectacular inside and out. Closer to the lifts—actually ski-in/ski-out properties—are the **Pine Inn** and **La Maçonnerie**. All units have private spas. Rates start at $595.

The most economical Deer Valley condos are the **Snow Park** units, where a one-bedroom without hot tub is $300 in the regular season.

For reservations for these properties and others, call **Deer Valley Lodging** (800-453-3833 or 435-649-4040) or **Deer Valley Central Reservations** (800-558-3337 or 435-649-1000).

Dining —Deer Valley

Deer Valley has great dining, day or night. To get there in the evenings from Park City if you don't have a car, take the free Park City Transit buses, which run until 10 p.m. To make advance dinner reservations from anywhere in the United States (recommended), call (800) 424-3337 (424-DEER).

The **Mariposa** (645-6715) at Silver Lake Lodge is the gourmets' top choice and is highly rated in many restaurant surveys. **The Glitretind Restaurant** (649-3700) in Stein Eriksen Lodge offers meals with a Norwegian flair. This is not the place to come if pinching pennies, but well worth the cost. Entrées range from $25 to $35. Don't expect to leave for less than $100 for two.

Glitretind's all-you-can-eat skier's lunch buffet for $27, however, rates as a more affordable and thoroughly unforgettable eating experience. A chef cooks made-to-order pasta dishes, and there's a carving table, various salads, cold meats and delectable desserts. Unless you are more disciplined than we were, forget trying to ski for at least an hour after leaving this banquet.

The Seafood Buffet (645-6632) at Snow Park Lodge, spread out Mondays through Saturdays, is magnificent. Every type of seafood you can think of is available, and it's all you can eat. Next time, we're just going to gorge on the chef's Chilean sea bass, glazed with a soy sauce-and-honey topping. Adults pay $42 and children $20.

McHenry's in the Silver Lake Lodge serves moderately priced lunches and dinners in a casual atmosphere.

For breakfast, head to the buffet at the **Snow Park Restaurant** and for lunch go to the **Silver Lake Restaurant**. The food is laid out like a magazine photo, a spectacular presentation. These cafeteria-style restaurants glisten with shiny brass and sparkling glass. P.S. You gotta have the turkey chili. Then ask someone to direct you to the shop where you can buy the dry ingredients to take home and make your own huge pot of this delicious stuff.

 **Dining—Park City**

One restaurant that vies for best-in-town honors is **Adolph's** (649-7196) next to the U.S. Ski and Snowboard Team office on Kearns Blvd. It serves Swiss and American cuisine for about $20 per entrée. Farther from the center of town is the **Snowed Inn** (647-6-3311; reservations required), which has gourmet food in an elegant old Victorian setting. There are two seatings each night: a four-course meal at 6:30 p.m. and a seven-course dinner at 8:30 p.m. You'll need your own transportation. For its inventive Southwestern cuisine, many locals recommend **Chimayo** (649-6222), with entrées in the $17–$25 range.

Mileti's (649-8211) serves the town's best Italian food, followed closely by **Cisero's** (649-5044). Both are on Main Street. Asian restaurants are popular, with **Mikado** (655-7100) the choice for Japanese, **Bangkok Thai** (649-8424) for Thai, and **Taste of Saigon** (647-0688) for Vietnamese food. Park City also has four Chinese restaurants.

Zoom Roadhouse Grill (649-9108), at the foot of Main Street, is owned by Robert Redford, whose Sundance Film Festival is here each January. The menu is hard to describe. We call it "plain-folks food with a gourmet twist." (For example, the lunch menu includes "French Fries with Smoked Ketchup.") Zoom also serves wild game.

More recommendations are: **Nacho Mama's** (645-8226) for highly recommended Southwestern/Mexican food; and **Baja Cantina** (649-2252) at the Resort Center and the **Irish Camel** (649-6645) on Main Street for good drinks and acceptable Tex-Mex food. If not everyone in your group likes Mexican food, head to **Borderline** (649-8172) on Main Street for a menu that also includes steak, burgers and sandwiches. **Lakota** (658-3400) serves various entrées at prices in the $10 vicinity.

The **Eating Establishment** (649-8284) is a locals' cheap-eats favorite, as is the **Park City Pizza Company** (649-1591). **Texas Red's Pit Barbecue** (649-7337) is the red-meat-eater's choice. The **Grubsteak** (649-8060) gets high marks from families. Finally, the **Riverhorse Café** (649-3536) on Main Street is a can't-miss choice for anyone who enjoys a no-fuss, low-key-elegant atmosphere.

For breakfast, **The Eating Establishment** on Main Street is the leader for hearty-meal fans, while **Ziggy's** is the egg-and-pancake choice for those staying at the Park City Mountain Resort base. **Off Main Cafe and Bakery** does omelets and pancakes in the Prospector Square area. For a lighter breakfast, try **Einstein Brothers Bagel Bakery** in the Prospector Square area for a huge variety of bagels and spreads, as well as great coffee, or **Wasatch Bagels** on Kearn's Boulevard next to Dan's Grocery Store.

Après-ski/nightlife

Despite rumors of Utah party blahs, Park City has some of the best nightlife of any ski town. For the lowdown on Utah's liquor laws, including the "private club membership" you'll need for most of these places, see the Salt Lake City chapter.

Immediate après-ski centers are **Steeps** and the **Baja Cantina**, located in the Resort Center, and downtown at **Cisero's** where the happy hour can get very lively. **Bistro 7000** in the Resort Center attracts a quieter crowd—at least, it was pleasantly quiet when we were there. Others say it's on the lively side. Also try the **Wasatch Brew Pub** at the top of Main Street, where you can watch the brewing process even as you reap its yeasty rewards, or ski to the **Town Lift Brew Pub** at the base of the Town Lift.

A hot nightspot is **The Cozy**, re-opened on Main Street after a fire a couple of seasons ago. It has a large dance area with live bands every weekend and most other nights, too. Other spots are **Jammin' Salmon** on Main Street, also with live entertainment, and **Mileti's**, also on Main.

The Club caters to a fairly young crowd and is a good place for singles. The dance floor upstairs is a place to see and be seen. **The Alamo** next door is your basic saloon, with pool tables, loud music and louder conversation. **Cisero's** on Main Street is one of the best spots to meet other singles and dance a bit with a mixed crowd ranging from 20s to 40s. **The Down Under** normally has acoustic guitar. **Adolph's**, with piano music, has been recommended for quieter evenings.

When the **Egyptian Theater** has plays, it makes a nice evening's entertainment. It's Summit County's only live theater.

Child care

The Park City Chamber of Commerce can refer visitors to child-care facilities or babysitting services. Call (800) 453-1360 or locally, 649-6100. **Baby's Away** (800-379-9030; 435-645-8823) rents and will deliver baby needs to your lodge, such as crib, stroller, car seat and toys.

Other activities

Shopping: Park City's shopping is quite good now. It now boasts 20 art galleries, which sell jewelry, Native American crafts and housewares in addition to paintings.

Silver Junction Mercantile, on Main Street, is worth a look if you like inexpensive collectibles: Coke bottles, Elvis and Beatles memorabilia, old license plates and political buttons are among the treasures. The old Z Place nightclub has been transformed into Z Treasure Trove, a crafts cooperative with more than 200 crafters represented. Deer Valley has several very upscale boutiques. Just off I-80 at the Park City exit is a factory outlet center with 50 stores.

Park City offers some rare sports treats: **ski jumping, luge and bobsled** at the Utah Winter Sports Park (649-5447). Yes, you can fly off the end of a ramp just like the Olympians do (you'll be on much smaller ramps, but it will feel like the 120-meter jump, let us assure you). The park was built for the 2002 Olympic Winter Games, and it will host the Olympic competition in those events. Jumping lessons are $27 for adults; $17 for ages 12–17 and $13 for kids 11 and younger (required rental helmets included). You also can speed down the Olympic luge/bobsled track using modified equipment. Luge "ice rocket" rides are $27; a ride on the four-person bobsled is $125. (They supply the driver and brakeman, so two paying passengers ride each time.) Schedules are different each day, and not every activity is offered every day, so call for specifics. Definitely call in advance for a spot in the bobsled. This activity sells out long in advance, at least it did its inaugural season. The park is closed Mondays and Tuesdays. It's worth a tour even if you don't participate in the sports.

Park City's history is celebrated with the **Park City Silver Mine Adventure** (655-7444 or 800-467-3828). Visitors tour a museum, then take an underground tour of an actual silver mine. This tour is fascinating, but not for the claustrophobic. Thirty-two visitors at a time descend 1,500 feet in an elevator, then ride a specially designed mine train for about two-thirds of a mile. At that point, you walk around to see how the miners worked. Children must be at least 4 years old to go underground. Cost is about $18 for adults, $13 for seniors and children aged 4–12; you get a hard hat and plastic poncho to protect you from drips. You also can buy exhibit-only tickets.

Park City's calendar has some unusual events. The **World Cup** ski racing tour kicks off each year at Park City Mountain Resort in mid-November. The **Sundance Film Festival** is in late January, showcasing new films from around the world.

Many companies offer **sleigh rides, snowmobile tours** and **hot-air balloon trips.** If you need the information in advance, call the Park City Chamber of Commerce for references, (800) 453-1360; when you're in town, check the Yellow Pages or ask your hotel concierge.

The **Park City Museum** on Main Street is open Monday–Saturday, 10 a.m.–7 p.m., Sundays noon to 6 p.m. The museum tour is by donation, details local history, and is excellent.

Getting there and getting around

By air: The drive from the Salt Lake City International Airport to Park City takes 45 minutes. Ground transportation makes frequent trips from the airport for $32–$36 round-trip. Providers include Lewis Brothers Stages, (800) 826-5844 or 649-2256 in Park City, (801) 359-8677 in Salt Lake City; Park City Transportation, (800) 637-3803 or (435) 649-8567; and All Resort Express (800) 457-9457 or (435) 649-3999. If you arrive without reservations, go to the transportation counter at the airport and a representative will put you on the next available van. Call 48 hours in advance for Park City-to-airport reservations.

By car: Park City is 32 miles east of Salt Lake City, by I-80 and Utah Hwy. 224.

Getting around: To rent or not to rent a car? Our recommendation: If you're staying close to the town center or near a stop on the free bus line, do without. The town bus system has four routes with buses that come by about every 20 minutes from 7 a.m. to 1 a.m. If you plan to take a side trip to one of the Cottonwood Canyons ski resorts, the airport transportation companies have vans that will take you for about $22 round-trip.

Alta

Utah

Summit elevation: 10,550 feet
Vertical drop: 2,020 feet
Base elevation: 8,530 feet

Address: P.O. Box 8007
Alta, UT 84092-8007
✆ **Area code:** 801
Ski area phone: 742-3333
Snow report: 572-3939
ⓘ **Reservations:** (801) 942-0404
or (888) STAY-ALTA (782-9258)
Internet:: http://www.altaskiarea.com
Expert:★★★★★
Advanced:★★★★★
Intermediate:★★★★
Beginner:★★★
Never-ever:★★★

Skiable Acreage: 2,200
Snowmaking: 3 percent
Number and types of lifts: 12–2 triple chairs,
6 double chairs, 4 surface lifts
Uphill capacity: 10,750 skiers per hour
Snowboarding: No
Bed Base: 1,247
Nearest lodging: slopeside, inns
Resort child care: Yes, 2 months and older
Adult ticket, per day: $31 (98/99 price)
Dining:★★
Apres-ski/nightlife:★
Other activities:★

At the very end of Little Cottonwood Canyon lies the ski land that time forgot. Entering Alta is like stepping back into an earlier, less hurried era of skiing. Instead of sky-rise hotels and flashy new condos visitors find a handful of rustic lodges. There are no giant billboards screaming advertising messages at skiers, no faux ski villages built in Swiss gingerbread style, and no snowboarders. Even the all-day lift-passes costing only $28 are decidedly retro.

There are also no high-speed quads.

How first-time visitors feel about the essential dichotomy of an absolutely world class ski resort with unsurpassed snow and beauty but no hyper-speed lifts to whisk them up the mountain will prove critical to how they view Alta. Skiers and families who long for a less hurried, more communal skiing experience where folks eat dinner together in the lodge and swap stories around woodsy bars and roaring fires at night will find kindrid spirits in Alta.

It's not that Alta isn't feeling the pressure created by high-speed expectations or the rapid surge in popularity of snowboarding. Rather, Alta officials have opted for lines and occasional crowds at the bottom of the mountain rather than on the slopes, and they choose to retain their world famous powder for skiers.

"We had to make a decision in terms of lift-capacity whether we wanted to crowd the mountain or risk having people sometimes wait in lines, and we decided that it was better to have the guests get to the top of our mountain and not face massive crowds," said Bill Levitt, long-time mayor of Alta and owner of the Alta Lodge. "So in a sense Alta is old-fashioned, but a lot of people tell us they're tired of the corporate-feel of many newer ski resorts. Eighty percent of my customers at Alta Lodge are return customers, and they hunger for skiing as it used to be, with lodging in small inns where people eat together at the same table and share that camaraderie, and where there are a lot of little kids running around. That's our future."

Alta will celebrate its 60th anniversary during the 98/99 season. Its low-key attitude is rooted in its history. In half a century of mining, Alta went from obscurity to boom, followed by outrageous scandal when the mines suddenly collapsed in the early 1900s. At a time when glamorous international figures were being courted by the new Sun Valley, Alta was born from the simple desire of Salt Lake residents to have a place where they could ski without having to climb uphill. Beginning in 1939 using its old ore tram, Alta has pulled nearly four generations of skiers up to its ridges. It still bears a modest name: Alta Ski Area, without the word "resort" anywhere in sight. One other thing: it's pronounced AL-ta, like the name Al, not AHL-ta.

Alta provides a fine contrast to its neighbor Snowbird, just a mile down the road in Little Cottonwood Canyon. Where Snowbird with its high-occupancy tram and multistory hotel is high-tech, Alta with its serviceable lifts and multitude of mountain inns is homey. The common areas of the lodges provide a great way to meet new buddies. You may find yourself returning the same week each season and seeing the same faces.

Alta has resisted another trend: snowboarding. This is one of the few resorts that doesn't allow it. Skiers may forgive Alta for not keeping up with the trends. Of the skiers we know who have been here, the vast majority plan to return. Must be that no-fuss, home-baked warmth.

Mountain layout

The ski area has a front and back side, and two base stations. Wildcat Base is the first one you reach. It has basic facilities—ticket office, restaurants, restrooms, ski patrol. The Albion Base houses the Children's Center, Ski School, restaurant and retail and rental operations. Albion is where you find the beginner slopes, but it has intermediate and expert terrain at higher elevations. Albion and Wildcat are connected by a long, nearly level, two-way transfer rope tow, the only "lift" of this type we've ever seen. Just grab the rope and let it pull you to the other side.

◆◆ **Expert** ◆ **Advanced:** Powder is what Alta is all about. Not just because it gets a lot, but because, with its terrain of trees and sheltered gullies, it tends to keep it longer. While most skiers are swishing down groomed runs a couple of days after a storm, the Alta cognoscenti are secretly diving into snow pockets in side canyons and upper elevations. Alta, like Snowbird, is a what-you-see, you-can-ski resort, with many ways down that aren't named on the trail map. Be individual. Be creative. That's the spirit of Alta.

Uphill from the Wildcat Ticket Office, Wildcat and Collins lifts serve advanced runs on the right side of the trail map—narrow trails, bump runs, and many glades—with intermediate and more advanced runs on the left.

From the left of these two lifts, skiers can get to an entirely different ridge, West Rustler, by taking the Germania lift. That means more steep and deep at Eagle's Nest and High Rustler for experts. The line at Germania may appear daunting on powder days but rarely averages more than ten minutes, although if there's powder on weekends, it can crank up to twenty.

If you head down the back side under the Sugarloaf chair, you'll find expert bowls as far as the eye can see. Swooping down into a gully to the left of the lift as you descend usually gives you powder pockets. A day or two after a storm try Devils' Castle, the steeps under the rocks accessible from Sugarloaf.

To the far left of the trail map experts can take Supreme lift to Point Supreme, the 10,550-foot summit, and from there have plenty of steep tree skiing to the left in an area near the boundary called Spiney Ridge. Some sections are known as Piney Glades and White Squaw. It's all known as steep, and tremendously popular with Salt Lake skiers. Up here you can ski all day without ever going the same way twice.

Experts in search of a unique Alta experience should reserve the last run of the day for Alf's High Rustler, named after one of the founding fathers of Alta who just recently passed away. Getting to the run is adventure enough for some. Ride the Germania lift and take the high traverse. Stay on the traverse as it crosses the ridge toward Greeley Bowl, and keep right traversing. The height and width of the traverse at this stage are not for the faint of heart. Eventually the traverse will spill around the top mountain knoll to High Rustler, a beautiful, steep run that is little skiied, enjoys breathtaking views of the valley, and spills right out into the lodges at the bottom.

■ **Intermediate:** This group can start at either Wildcat or Albion. From Wildcat, stay to the left as you leave the Collins chair, then head down to the base on Meadow or over to Germania, where you'll find Ballroom and Mambo to the right as you leave the chair. On the Albion side, intermediates also have appropriate terrain under the Sugarloaf and Supreme chairs.

Intermediates have wonderful slopes here, plus a few very gentle pitches off to one side in the Albion area that don't get groomed—a super place to take your first powder turns. Alta doesn't skimp on grooming—we found the intermediate and beginner runs quite negotiable.

●● **Beginner:** ● **Never-evers:** From the Albion base station, Sunnyside and Albion lifts are slow riders across gentle terrain, a wide rolling beginner playground. Given a choice between Snowbird and Alta, beginners should definitely start here. Not only are the slopes less intimidating, but so are the skiers (we're talking fashion and attitude here, not ability). The mile-long beginner run serviced by the Albion lift can make a newbie feel like a real skier—and that's what the sport is all about.

Note: From the top of Germania Pass the runs down the front side return you to Wildcat base area; runs down the back return you to Albion, or give access to the Sugarloaf and Supreme lifts. Skiers wishing to cross back into the Germania/Wildcat area have two choices: a traverse from the top of the Sugarloaf lift or at the base on the transfer tow.

To follow the sun, start the morning on Sugarloaf, then move to Germania on the front side at midday, and finish on Supreme.

Mountain rating

Alta is a great place for any level of skier. Teamed with neighboring Snowbird, it's especially hard to beat. Snowbird has the edge in continuous vertical drop—the Snowbird tram opens almost 3,000 feet of continuous expert vertical, versus the maximum expert drop of about 1,000 at Alta. However, Alta is much better for groups of mixed abilities.

Snowboarding

Not permitted. Head to Snowbird.

Lessons (98/99 prices)

Bearing the name of Alf Engen, the Norwegian ski jumper who came to Utah in 1930, the ski school is recognized in the industry for its contributions to the development of professional ski instruction.

Group lessons: Two hours, $30.

Never-ever package: None; novices can ride the learning tows without charge and rentals are available.

Private lessons: $116 for two hours. Alta recommends a two-hour lesson as a minimum. Additional persons can join the lesson for $40 each.

Special programs: Afternoon workshops focus on specific skills and are $40 for two-and-a-half hours; meet at the blue and white signs below the base of Germania lift. Silver Meisters is a three-hour lesson for intermediate and higher seniors. It is not offered every day, so call the ski school for information and to reserve a spot. A telemark workshop is offered Tuesdays, Thursdays and Sundays for $40, and Diamond Challenge is a three-hour clinic for Level 9 (true expert) skiers for $50. The instructor gives pointers, but mostly acts as a guide to Alta's steep powder stashes.

Racing: Alta's race course is at the Sunnyside lift; Friday and Saturday from noon to 3 p.m. The $5 ($7 for unlimited runs) race fee is payable at the race arena or at the ticket office.

Children's lessons: Two-hour lessons for ages 4–12 cost $30. All-day packages with lunch, four hours of skiing and extended care when not in lessons are $70 for ability levels 1–2, $87 for levels 3–9.

Note: Lower-level ski lessons meet at the base of the Albion lift, while upper skill levels meet at the base of the Germania lift. All children's programs meet at the Albion base. For all ski school programs, call 742-3333.

Child care (98/99 prices)

Ages: 3 months to 12 years.
Cost: All-day infant care by reservation only is $65. All-day child care (3 and older) with lunch is $45. Multiday discounts available.
Reservations: Requested. Alta's child care center is a state-licensed facility owned and operated by Redwood Pre-School, Inc. (742-3042).

Lift tickets (98/99 prices)

	Adult	Child (Up to 12)
One day	$31	$31
Three days	$93 ($31/day)	$93 ($31/day)
Five days	$155 ($31/day)	$155 ($31/day)

Who skis free: Ages 80 and older.

Who skis at a discount: Skiers pay $22 to use the beginner lifts in the Albion area. If you aren't too sure about the conditions, buy a single-ride ticket for any lift for $6.

Note: Alta skips all the discount gimmicks, figures out what it will take to run the place, and charges everyone the same low price. They figure everyone—adults, children and seniors—occupies one spot on the lifts, hence a single price.

Accommodations (97/98 prices)

Something very important to know: some of Alta's lodges do not accept all major credit cards; some don't accept any. Ask whether your room has a private bath—some rooms do not.

Rates are lower in value season, which is prior to mid-December, most of January, and April to closing.

Rustler Lodge (742-2200, 888-532-2582) is newly remodeled, and is midway between the Albion and Rustler/Wildcat base areas. It has an outdoor pool, saunas and hot tubs. The new restaurant and bar with picture windows looking right out onto the mountain should not be missed. Prices include breakfast and dinner, per person double occupancy, starting at $115 per night for a room without private bath, $145 to $275 for rooms with bath. No credit cards are accepted here; pay by personal check, travelers checks or cash.

Alta Peruvian (800-453-8488 reservations only; 742-3000) has similar amenities, features movies each night, and is a short walk from the Wildcat base (or you can take the lodge's free shuttle). The rates include breakfast, lunch, and dinner (food's great, by the way). Dorm rooms are $81; double rooms with private bath are $120–$129 (per person, double occupancy). One- or two-bedroom suites also are available, as are multiday discounts and single rooms starting at $129. Alta Peruvian accepts credit cards.

The Alta Lodge (800-707-2582, reservations only; 742-3500) is a 57-room mountain inn with saunas, hot tubs, and several common areas, including a library. Skiers grab a rope tow at the end of the day to get back up a small hill to the lodge. The Alta Lodge has the homey feel of a pair of well-worn slippers, not surprising since many of the guests are repeat customers who return each year and know each other on a first-name basis. Alta Mayor Bill Levitt is the proprieter, and he will be happy to regale guests with tales from Alta's storied past (and present). Our favorite is how a comely ski instructor once caught the eye and changed the life of the East Coast boy who would be mayor of Alta. Breakfast and dinner are included in the price, and the food is excellent. Daily room rates (per person, double occupancy) are $157, and every room has a private bathroom. Single-occupancy rates start at $186; dorm rates are $103. No credit cards; use personal or travelers checks, or greenbacks.

Goldminer's Daughter (742-2300 or 800-453-4573 for reservations only), named after a huge mining claim, is closest to the Wildcat lift. You can step out your door into the lift line, and drop by your room between runs for a hat or neck gaiter. All rooms have private bath, except the dorms. Per-person double occupancy rates with breakfast and dinner are $94–$134. Dorm rooms are $79. Visa and MasterCard accepted here.

Snowpine Lodge (742-2000) is Alta's oldest and smallest. It was extensively renovated a few years ago, and has an outdoor hot tub, Scandinavian sauna and a warm and homey atmosphere. Rates (per person, double occupancy) are $111–$135 for a room with private bath, $93–$111 for a shared-bath room, and $79 for a bed in the men's or women's dorm. Visa and MasterCard accepted here.

Two large condominiums, **Hellgate** (801-742-2020) and **Blackjack** (801-742-3200) are located between Alta and Snowbird, with Blackjack better situated for skiing between the two resorts and therefore slightly higher-priced. Both have van service to the ski areas. Studios range from $185–$205; one-bedrooms sleeping four, $200–$275; two-bedrooms sleeping six, $250–$320; three-bedrooms, $230–$320. There is no service charge.

Canyon Services (800-862-2888) rents luxurious condos and homes with fully equipped kitchens, washers and dryers and cable TV.

Dining

At Alta you eat in your condo or your lodge, and if you're headed for a condo, stop in Salt Lake for groceries. On the slopes, **Chic's Place** has a good view. **Shallow Shaft**, on Alta's main road, has salmon, steak, pasta and chicken entrées in the $13-$25 range. Check its Web site at www.shallowshaft.com

Après-ski/nightlife

Bring your own. There's nothing going on but what visitors cook up—either in their condo or the lodge's common rooms. That said, the best nightime gatherings we found were at the bar at the Alta Peruvian Lodge, where guests and locales from around town gather (with a cover charge on weekends) for drinks at a lively bar or around the fire. The dog curled around the couch is the local mascot. The Sitzmark Bar at the Alta Lodge is also good for après-ski story swapping.

If your ski vacation is not complete without a vigorous night of dancing, stay in Salt Lake City and take the ski bus up here. (See the Salt Lake City chapter for details.)

Other activities

Shopping: A few shops in the Little Cottonwood Canyon area have local handicrafts, artwork and books, but skiers don't come to Alta for the shopping. They come for a four-letter S word. If you must, you can always take a bus or drive down to Salt Lake City for a day of heavy-duty shopping.

Heliskiing is available in Little Cottonwood Canyon from Wasatch Powderbird Guides, 742-2800 or Skiwasatch@aol.com.

Getting there and getting around

By air: Salt Lake City is a major airline hub, so flights are numerous from every corner of the continent. See the Snowbird chapter for ground transportation information.

By train: Amtrak's California Zephyr also stops here. Call (800) USA-RAIL (872-7245).

By car: Alta is 25 miles southeast of Salt Lake City in Little Cottonwood Canyon on State Highway 210. Drive east on I-80, south on I-215, Exit 6 to Wasatch Blvd., then follow the signs to Alta and Snowbird.

Getting around: Ground transportation from the airport or the city is frequent and plentiful. If you fly in, don't bother renting a car. Most of Alta's lodges have shuttles to get you to the slopes or to visit neighboring restaurants. If you are staying in Salt Lake City, take the Utah Transit Authority bus ($4 from downtown, $1.50 from the bottom of the canyon; exact fare required) or a Lewis Brothers SkiExpress van to Alta (about $15 roundtrip from downtown; 359-8677 from Salt Lake City). Bus service links Alta and Snowbird for $1.

Snowbird

Utah

Summit elevation: 11,000 feet
Vertical drop: 3,240 feet
Base elevation: 7,760 feet

Address: P.O. Box 929000
Snowbird, UT 84092-9000
✆ **Area code:** 801
Ski area phone: 933-2222
Snow report: 933-2100
ⓘ **Toll-free reservations:**
(800) 453-3000
Fax: 947-8227
Internet:: http://www.snowbird.com
Expert:★★★★
Advanced:★★★
Intermediate:★★★
Beginner:★★★ **Never-ever:**★★★★

Number of lifts: 9–1 aerial tram,
1 high-speed quad, 7 double chairs
Snowmaking: Minimal
Skiable acreage: 2,500
Uphill capacity: 11,150 per hour
Snowboarding: Yes
Bed Base: 1,800+
Nearest lodging: slopeside, hotel
Resort child care: Yes, 6 weeks and older
Adult ticket, per day: $39–$49 (98/99 prices)
Dining:★★
Apres-ski/nightlife:★
Other activities:★★

Practically every devout skier has a mecca for annual pilgrimmages to rekindle the skiing flame and commune once again with the snow spirits. The choices for skiing meccas are deeply personal. When the winds of November bring the year's first snowfalls, however, many devoted skiers find themselves drawn almost irresistibly up the winding ascent to the brawny splendor of Snowbird Ski Resort.

The initial allure is the snow, but it is much more than that. Suffice to say that Utah's little disputed claim to the "greatest snow on earth" is based largely on the slopes and bowls of Little Cottonwood, a canyon whose steep sides and craggy beauty are more reminscent of the Alps than much of the Rockies. Snowbird itself receives an annaul average of 500 inches of light, champagne powder that typically arrives early and stays around long enough for the area to enjoy 200 days of skiing. Indeed, Canadian heli-ski guides have been heard measuring their snow by Snowbird standards: "Ayuh, it's good, but it's not quite Snowbird powder." Among powder aficionados Snowbird is spoken of in the hushed tones of the truly reverent.

Snowbird's sleek, modern high-rise hotel and condo complex that seems to spring out of the mountain's roots—Iron Blossom Lodge, The Cliff Lodge, the Lodge at Snowbird—also speak to the soul of the serious skier. There are luxurious accomodations and fine dining at Snowbird, but no one comes here for the nightlife or the shopping. The rock-solid but unobtrusive design of the resort takes nothing away from the looming mountains, leaving no doubt of that their majestic appeal is what truly draws skiers back year after year.

Governed by strict laws regulating development, Snowbird has not been particularly aggressive in expanding its realm over the years. Recently, however, there have been subtle signs of promising change. Last year for the first time Snowbird opened the backside of the mountain with snowcat skiing on 400 acres in Mineral Basin, south of the Hidden Peak summit. Look for two future lifts in the basin. The old Gad 1 double chair was also replaced last year with GadZoom, the resort's first high-speed quad. Let's hope it's not the last.

In recent years, Snowbird has also begun trying to amend its reputation as a mecca primarily for the steep-and-deep skiers and powder monkeys. By adding the Baby Thunder lift in 1995, the resort opened a largely protected area that has gentle slopes great for less experienced skiers. Two additional slopes are also being regularly groomed to the corduroy smoothness favored by cruisers. Snowbird is truly becoming a resort where the whole family will want to go to ski, but with an emphasis on skiing or snowboarding.

New for 98/99: Snowbird is adding a terrain park in the Gad Valley and an ice skating rink at the Cliff Lodge. It also will offer several guided backcountry tours.

 ## Mountain layout

First-time visitors should explore the mountain with the Host and Hostess Program, a free introductory tour of the mountain that meets on the plaza level of Snowbird Center daily at 10 a.m. and 1 p.m. The hosts sort out the groups by skill level and then move to appropriate terrain, so faster skiers aren't held back and slower skiers aren't terrified. It's also a great way to meet people.

If you want to avoid crowds, ski Gad 2 and Little Cloud until 11. Then work the Gad Valley chairs. Between 12:30 and 1:30 the lines lighten up and you can go back to the top. For sunshine—the Gad Valley lifts get morning sun; in the afternoon, head to Little Cloud.

◆◆ **Expert:** No gut-wrenching decisions here. The most experienced skiers and boarders head for The Tram. Hanging across a cirque and rising to the 11,000-foot summit, it brings 125 skiers at a time to Hidden Peak, unseen from the base lodge. When the first tram arrives on powder days there's a dash for the slopes. Skiers and snowboarders hurl their equipment and then themselves over the railings to make the first tracks. After this thrill, things calm down a bit and you can decide whether to get equipment on quickly and be the first down The Cirque, or wait a bit, let others dash, and then go where they don't.

Drop under the tram into Peruvian Gulch, with intermediate, advanced and expert routes down, or to head left into the Little Cloud area. Most tram riders opt for Peruvian because of its zigzag intermediate run, Chip's. Experts can go either way. On the Peruvian side, experts tackle The Cirque, a plunge that drops into almost 3,000 vertical feet of expert slopes. You can choose a run about as steep as you want, some with chutes that hold only enough powder to slow your virtual freefall. Anyone who has dropped down Upper Silver Fox, Great Scott or Upper Cirque deserves to be treated with reverence—they're using up the extra lives they were blessed with. From the tram ridge, Primrose Path is an unrelenting black diamond, normally the choice of those who think twice about tiptoeing around the Cirque. Here at Snowbird what you can see, you can ski. So pick your own way.

Should you decide to drop over to the Little Cloud side of Hidden Peak, the skiing is somewhat tamer—by Snowbird standards. You reach the toughest stuff on this side—Gad Chutes, Barry Barry Steep and others—by taking the Cirque Traverse from the tram.

◆ **Advanced:** Before you tackle the tram blacks at the top, take a test run on Chip's on the Peruvian side, or Regulator Johnson or Road to Provo on the Little Cloud side. Regulator Johnson, which is marked black on the map, now has a wide groomed swath down the center. Some of our staff think this descent is easier than Chip's sharp switchbacks, even though Chip's is rated blue.

Another good spot for advanced skiers is the Gad 2 chair, which is skiers-only. Gad 2 opens narrower trails through the trees and over megabumps. Gadzooks, Tiger Tail, Black Forest and Organ Grinder are equal challenges.

■ **Intermediate:** Do not board the tram without a test run elsewhere. A good tryout run is Big Emma from the top of Mid-Gad. Big Emma is rated green on the trail map, but many a beginner has halted along its upper rim, asking passing skiers and boarders, "Is there an easier way down?" On cold hardpacked days, Big Emma is a challenge even for intermediates.

If you can ski Emma with ease, you have several options for the next test. Any of the blue-square runs off the three Gad chairs will be fun, and if you can handle them, you should be ready to tackle the easiest runs off the tram.

Snowbird's newest terrain is under the Baby Thunder chair. This wonderful area helps to bridge the steepness gap between Snowbird's novice slope and Big Emma. You can also work on technique on the greens under the Wilbere chair.

●● **Beginner:** A couple of years ago we would have given Snowbird one star (or maybe none) for a severe lack of beginner terrain. But the Baby Thunder area is great for lower-level skiers and snowboarders. It's gentle and isolated from faster traffic. Terrain between the runs is left ungroomed, great for practicing powder or tree skiing. Because it's a little off to one side, the initial access is a bit tricky to find. Ask a host at the base area to advise you, because directions may vary depending on the day's conditions. We recommend lessons for beginners, if only to have a guide to keep you out of trouble.

If it's a gorgeous day and you'd like to see the view, buy a tram ticket and ride back down. (And don't let any of the hot-shots shame you into skiing down—nothing from the top is easy by beginner standards.)

● **Never-ever:** Chickadee, out the door from the Cliff Lodge, is a near-ideal novice slope. (Our only gripe is the chair lift height is set for children, but we can work around that minor inconvenience.) At the very beginning of the day, skilled skiers use Chickadee to get to the other chairs, but aside from that, novices have it all to themselves.

Mountain rating

Experts, you have arrived. A healthy half of Snowbird terrain is for you. These are not public-relations black diamonds, either—they really are tough. You will leave exhilarated or frustrated, depending on whether you attack them or they attack you.

Everyone else, expect to be pushed. Owner Dick Bass, who has climbed the highest mountain on every continent, affirms, "What we gain too easily, we esteem too lightly." Let that be your rallying cry. You will improve, a phenomenon you may not recognize until you ski those home slopes you thought were a challenge. If Snowbird exhausts you or you're here for a week and know all the routes in your comfort zone by heart, go next door to Alta, which has more mellow intermediate and beginner trails.

Snowboarding

Snowboarding now is permitted everywhere on the mountain, and Snowbird recently has added many attractions for boarders. A new terrain park will be built in the Gad Valley, and the resort will offer halfpipe camps and women's snowboarding camps. Snowbird has a few flat stretches; ask a mountain host how to avoid them.

Lessons (98/99 prices)

Group lessons: $65 for all day; $50 for half-day, afternoon-only classes. **Never-ever package (ski or snowboard):** $48 includes rentals, half-day lesson and access on the Chickadee lift.

Private lessons: $80 per hour ($65 between 9 and 10 a.m.); two to five people can split a $90 charge. Multihour discounts are available.

Special programs: Mountain Experience allows advanced or expert skiers to join a guide and launch an assault on the entire mountain for $85 for one day. Silver Wings presents skiers older than 50 with the opportunity to ski with people of the same ability and age group for $48 a day. Other 2.5-hour clinics teach style, bump skiing and snowboarding. A four-day women's seminar also is offered several times a season, which covers everything except lifts and lodging. This year, a women's snowboarding camp will be added. Call for current prices.

Racing: NASTAR and/or coin-operated courses are open each day, weather permitting. The course is to one side of Big Emma, accessible by the Wilbere or Mid-Gad chairs. A racing clinic is offered daily, 10:30 to noon for $25, including two runs on the NASTAR course.

Children's lessons: Full day (lunch and lessons) is $75. Half day for beginner and lower intermediate skiers is $50. Ability levels are separated. Ages 3 and 4 get 90-minute lessons for $52. Two children per instructor means this is very popular, so sign up in advance.

Note: Snowbird Ski School has three one-stop locations for ski school registration and buying lift tickets (tickets are not included in the lesson price). The offices are on Level 1 of the Cliff Lodge, the Plaza Deck of the Snowbird Center and the Alpine Room on Level 2 of the Snowbird Center. For more information or reservations, call 933-2170.

Child care (98/99 prices)

Ages: 6 weeks to 12 years.
Costs: $65 a day, with lunch, for ages 6 weeks to 3, and $50 for ages 3–12. Half-day and multiday discounts are available. Evening babysitting is $12 an hour, a little more for an additional child.

Reservations: Required. Call Camp Snowbird at 933-2256, or reserve when you book your vacation. A non-refundable $25 registration fee is applied toward your final day.

Lift tickets (98/99 prices)

	Adult	Child (6-12)
One day	$49	Free (see below)
Three days	$129 ($43/day)	
Five days	$195 ($39/day)	

Who skis free: Two children younger than 12 ride the chairs free when an accompanying adult purchases a lift ticket. (Tram access costs $10.) Children of lodging guests ski the entire mountain free, and there's no limit on the number of children as long as they are Snowbird lodging guests.

Who skis at a discount: Ages 65 and older ski for $36, including tram access. A ticket for the Chickadee chair only is $10.

Note: These are the prices with tram access. For chairs only, the one-day prices are $39 for adults; $27 for seniors. Don't buy tram access if you aren't skiing there; you can always upgrade a day's ticket to include the tram for $10.

Accommodations (98/99 prices)

All lodging at Snowbird is within walking distance of the base lifts, and can be reserved by calling (800) 453-3000, or sending a fax to (801) 947-8227. Winter season is Dec. 18 through April 3; value season is before and after those dates. Snowbird also has added a January value season, where rates are between the high and low seasons. Snowbird's season is a long one, lasting well into May most years. Additional lodging is plentiful in Salt Lake City.

The Cliff Lodge spreads like an eagle's wings at the base. Inside there's an 11-story atrium, a renowned spa, and a glassed-in rooftop with a heated pool that overlooks the slopes. A new pool complex with a trio of hot tubs recently was added. Mountain-view rooms have picture windows from the shower that peer into the sleeping area and the view beyond (there's a shower curtain you can pull for modesty). The lodge's walls and floors also feature the largest private collection of rugs of any private facility in Utah. Last year the Cliff also added a new outdoor heated swimming pool and three new hot tubs, all serviced by a fruit-juice bar. Room rates start at $249 a night in winter season, $159 in value season, and $199 in January value season. The Cliff Lodge also has suites ranging from $379 to $959. Children younger than 12 stay and ski free with adults.

The 27,000-square-foot Cliff Spa, on the top floor of the hotel, has 20 treatment rooms and a variety of treatments for body, face, hair and nails, as well as an exercise facility. Call 933-2225 for the spa, 933-2268 for the salon.

The Lodge at Snowbird, The Inn, and **The Iron Blosam** are three condominium complexes with similar layouts. Not as elegant as the Cliff Lodge, they are well maintained, roomy and comfortable. Amenities include outdoor swimming pools, indoor hot tubs and saunas. Rates start at $119 for an efficiency or studio during value season, and top out at $689–$729 for a one-bedroom with loft during winter season.

Dining

The Aerie on top of the Cliff Lodge is considered one of the three best restaurants in Utah, for good reason. The decor is elegant and tasteful, the views from the large picture windows spectacular, and the food and house piano player are excellent. The **Cliff Express** at lobby level serves cocktails and hefty buffet breakfasts and lunches. **The Junction Keyhole** offers Mexican and Southwestern fare. The **Summit Cafe** on Level 10 of the Cliff Lodge has light and healthy cuisine such as smoothies and vegetarian meals. At the Iron Blosam Lodge, **Wildflower Ristorante & Lounge** serves outstanding Northern Italian cuisine. **The Lodge Club** in the Lodge at Snowbird has a good light dinner.

Other restaurants are in the base facility, Snowbird Center. **The Steak Pit** serves steak and seafood. There's usually a wait, but it's worth it. **The Forklift** is a breakfast and lunch spot with easy access to the slopes yet with a carpeted restaurant atmosphere. For cafeteria service, **The Rendezvous** has the usual, plus a well-stocked salad island. It also serves breakfast. **Pier 49 San Francisco Sourdough Pizza** has pizza with lots of toppings, and **Birdfeeder** has gourmet coffees and light snacks.

Après-ski/nightlife

Snowbird's nightlife is very quiet. For the liveliest après-ski, try **Tram Club**, on the bottom floor of the Snowbird Center, with space-age decor and a picture-window view of the tram's huge operating gears. **Wildflower Lounge** is mellow. In the evening, **The Aerie** has a bar with quiet piano music. At night, Tram Club is your best bet for dancing.

Remember: you are in Utah, so the nightspots are "private clubs" that charge a $5 two-week membership fee. At night, you can take the free Snowbird shuttle to and from the Snowbird Center and the various restaurants and night spots at the lodges. If you're staying at the Cliff Lodge, you can walk across the Chickadee novice slope to get to the Snowbird Center; however, we recommend the shuttle, which runs until 11 p.m. (sometimes later). The walking route is slippery, and you'll be dodging lugers who use that slope at night.

Other activities

Snowbird is not a good place for non-skiers unless they plan to spend considerable time at the Cliff Spa (see Accommodations). The only other diversion is **shopping,** and a champion browser will finish off the dozen or so shops in half a day. An actors' troupe stages a **Murder Mystery Dinner Theatre** once a month from January through March; call the resort for information on that and other entertainment special events.

Snowbird will introduce three types of **guided backcountry** programs this season. One is an introduction to backcountry skiing and snowshoe touring, another is lift-assisted backcountry tours, and the third is mountaineering and couloir skiing. Another guided tour will be skiing to yurts located in Mineral Basin where guests can enjoy day ski trips and evening dinners. Call 933-2182 for information and reservations.

During the day, Snowbird operates a tubing hill, and at night, you can go luging on the Chickadee novice slope outside the Cliff Lodge. Last season's fee for the latter was $20.

Little Cottonwood Canyon has no cross-country skiing or snowmobiling, but spectacular **helicopter skiing** is available from Wasatch Powderbird Guides; 742-2800, or Skiwasatch@aol.com.

The Snowbird Canyon Racquet Club, at the mouth of the canyon, has indoor **tennis, racquetball and squash** courts, as well as aerobics classes and an indoor climbing wall. The resort owns it; ask about rates.

Getting there and getting around

By air: Salt Lake City is a major airline hub, so flights are numerous. Ground transportation is well organized—Lewis Brothers Stages charges about $40 per person, round-trip, between the airport and Snowbird or Alta. Call (800) 826-5844 or head to the Lewis Brothers counter at the airport when you arrive.

By train: Amtrak's California Zephyr stops in Salt Lake City (at 4 a.m., but the fare is cheap). Call (800) USA-RAIL.

By car: Snowbird is 25 miles southeast of Salt Lake City in Little Cottonwood Canyon. The most direct route from the airport is east on I-80, south on I-215, Exit 6 to Wasatch Blvd., then follow the signs.

Getting around: If you fly in, don't bother renting a car—Snowbird is entirely walkable. If you plan to ski a lot of other Utah areas, stay in Salt Lake City (see Utah Skiing chapter). Utah Transit Authority ski buses are $4 from downtown or $1.50 from the park-and-ride at the canyon's mouth (exact fare is required). A Lewis Brothers SkiExpress van to Snowbird is about $15 roundtrip from downtown (call 359-8677 from Salt Lake City). Lewis Brothers also has the Canyon Jumper between Park City and Snowbird for $20.

Bus service links Alta and Snowbird for $1.25. A free Snowbird shuttle will get you to various points within the resort complex, both day and evening.

Big Cottonwood Canyon

Utah

Solitude Ski Resort
Brighton Ski Resort

Of any group of skiers waiting at a bus stop in downtown Salt Lake City for the Utah Transit Authority ski express, it used to be easy to tell who was headed to Little Cottonwood Canyon and who was headed for Big Cottonwood Canyon.

Popular myth held that those with late-model skis that extended far above their heads were headed for Snowbird or Alta in Little Cottonwood Canyon. Those with the tell-tale rental-shop stickers at the bindings were on their way to Big Cottonwood Canyon for a few snowplow turns at Solitude or Brighton. But every so often, a skier would deposit his 205cm Salomons in the ski rack of the Big Cottonwood bus, leaving the Steep and Deep crowd to wonder, "What does he know that we don't?"

Big Cottonwood Canyon's reputation as the place to learn has had more to do with prices than terrain. The adult lift tickets at Solitude and Brighton are still less than $40. Neither area is as vast as the ski areas in the neighboring canyon, but that's like saying the Empire State Building isn't as tall as the World Trade Center. To dismiss them as playgrounds where beginners whet their appetites for the real thing is to woefully underestimate the terrain. Solitude's Honeycomb Canyon and Headwall Forest will bring out the adrenaline in the best of skiers. Brighton's expert offerings are fewer, but when the Snowbird crowd is waiting in line for the tram, Brighton skiers and boarders are often cutting up the powder.

Both areas have made steady improvements during the last decade. At Solitude, first came a complete redesign of the trail and lift system that won a *Snow Country* magazine design award. Then came a gourmet on-mountain restaurant. Three seasons ago, the resort's first overnight lodging opened, the first phase of a base village. Two seasons ago, it added a full-service hotel—The Inn at Solitude—a new restaurant and shops. Brighton refurbished many of its aging buildings and built a huge Brighton Center to house lift ticket sales, rental and retail shops and more restrooms and lockers.

 ## Mountain layout

Solitude's lift layout has a logical progression from beginner to expert areas. We're going to reverse our usual order of ability levels to show you how skiers and snowboarders can progress here by a choice of terrain.

◆◆ **Expert:** Our second suggested route off the Summit Chair (see the previous paragraph) starts with the intermediate Back Door trail. You can head down Corner Chute, a cleared but steep black diamond clearly visible from the Summit chair. You might instead go into Headwall Forest, where you can pick your own line through the trees, or jump into a

Solitude Ski Resort

Summit elevation:	10,035 feet
Vertical drop:	2,047 feet
Base elevation:	7,988 feet

Address: 12000 Big Cottonwood Canyon
Solitude, UT 84121
☎ Area code: 801
Ski area phone: 534-1400
Snow report: 536-5777
ⓘ Toll-free reservations: (800) 748-4754
Fax: (435) 649-5276
E-mail: info@skisolitude.com
Internet: http://www.skisolitude.com

Expert:★★★★ **Advanced:**★★★★
Intermediate:★★★★
Beginner:★★★★ **Never-ever:**★★★★
Number of lifts: 7—1 high-speed quad,
2 triple chairs, 4 double chairs
Snowmaking: 80 acres
Skiable acreage: 1,600
Uphill capacity: 11,200 per hour
Snowboarding: Yes, unlimited
Bed base: 216, plus 12,000 in Salt Lake City
Resort child care: For lodging guests only
Nearest lodging: slopeside, condos & hotel
Adult ticket, per day: $34-$36
Dining:★★★
Apres-ski/nightlife:★
Other activities:★

couple of long, steep, narrow chutes. You also can head over to Evergreen, rated a single black diamond, but it looks mighty tough from the lift.

The third option will take you into Honeycomb Canyon, a wonderful playground for high-level skiers and boarders. Woodlawn is a marked run that follows the canyon floor. On the map it's rated black and blue. Check the grooming report before you head in: when groomed, it's a great advanced-intermediate run—otherwise, it's advanced all the way, with some gigantic mogul fields and a short but extremely steep section that looks like it might be a small waterfall in the summer.

The canyon sides are an expert's delight. From the top, traverse until you find a line you like, then go for it. Honeycomb Canyon also can be reached from the Eagle Ridge run in the main part of the ski area, but this entry is strictly double-diamond through trees. Speaking of trees, you'll find others to the left as you exit the Powderhorn chair and head down Milk Run, Middle Slope, Parachute or Cirque.

◆ **Advanced:** The Powderhorn chair has some single-black groomed screamers, such as Diamond Lane. Another lift advanced skiers and boarders will like is the Summit chair. From its top, you can go one of three ways. The first takes you back down to the Summit chair base on upper-intermediate runs like Dynamite and Liberty. Eventually you'll meet the runs off the Sunrise chair, which head back to the base.

■ **Intermediate:** The next level is the Powderhorn or Eagle Express chairs, where there are no green runs, just blue with a few black. If you can handle these, then you're ready for the Summit chair.

●● **Beginner:** When skiers conquer Link, the next step is the Moonbeam II chair, where Little Dollie, Pokey Pine and Same Street will take them back down gently. Next is either the Apex or Sunrise chair, where one green trail is surrounded by lots of blue.

● **Never-ever:** Novices start on the Link chair, a slow-moving lift that serves a nearly flat, very wide, isolated run, Easy Street.

Mountain rating

Solitude is one of the few resorts in the United States that has excellent terrain for all levels. The trail layout has one disadvantage (and it won't apply to everyone): If you have skiers or boarders in your group at the opposite ends of the ability scale, you'll likely spend your day on different parts of the mountain. Intermediates can ride lifts with beginners or experts, choose different trails and meet at the bottom, but not beginners and experts.

Snowboarding

Snowboarders can go anywhere skiers can. Lessons and rental equipment is available.

Cross-country

Located at 8,700 feet between Solitude and Brighton, the Solitude Nordic Center's Silver Lake Day Lodge is a spectacular setting for cross-country skiing or snowshoeing. It has 20 km. of prepared trails for both classic and skating styles, plus ski and snowshoe rentals, lessons (including telemark), light snacks and guided backcountry tours.

Trail passes are $12 for those aged 11 to 69, and free for older or younger skiers. A half-day pass is $8; a two-day pass is $16. For other information about the Nordic Center, call 536-5774.

Lessons (98/99 prices)

Group lessons: $40 for two hours. All-day lessons starting at 10:15 a.m. are $60.

Never-ever package: Rentals, lift ticket and a lesson is $65.

Private lessons: $75 per hour for one to three skiers; $130 for four to six persons.

Special programs: For women, snowboarding, Nordic and racing, offered at various times. Call for details, (801) 536-5730.

Racing: Solitude has an electronically timed, side-by-side dual course on the Main Street trail, open every day, weather permitting, $1.50 per run.

Children's lessons: Full day with lunch for ages 4-12 is $65; a half day without lunch is $45. An all-day never-ever kids' package is $75.

Child care: Available only to hotel and condo guests for any age child at $10 per hour. Reservations are required; make them at the front desk or when you book your lodging.

Lift tickets (98/99 prices)

	Adult (11-59)	Senior (60-69)
One day	$36	$29
Additional days	see "Note" below	

Who skis free: Two children ages 10 and younger with a paying adult (with some fine print; see "Note" below). If your party is one paying adult with more than two kids 10 or younger, the third child pays $29 to ski. Also ages 70 and older ride the lifts for free, but need a ticket. Obtain it at the ticket window.

Who skis at a discount: A beginner lift ticket, valid on the Link and Moonbeam II chairs, is $26.

Note: Solitude has Access, an electronic ticketing system that allows skiers to pay by the run, get future discounts or share a ticket with someone else. The reuseable card costs $4, then you pay for individual rides, sold in increments of 10, or an all-day ticket. Ten rides cost $36. The day ticket costs $36 the first day and $34 for following days. Put the card in your pocket and forget about it. Radio-frequency beams detect the card's presence, let you through a gate at the lift base, and deduct one ride from the card. If you reach 10 rides on the same day, the rest of the day you ski free. If not, you can use the remaining lift rides another day.

Two people can share the same card as long as they are skiing at different times. Parents who have young children can always have someone to watch the kids—with Mom out on the slopes in the morning and Dad in the afternoon. Skiers can load up the card with as many days as you like, then bypass the ticket window and head straight for the lifts. Adults who use the Access card can get a matching number of rides or days for two children 10 and younger without charge.

Whew! Armed with this information, here's our recommendation: If you are vacationing in Salt Lake City, skiing at several resorts one day each, have no children 10 or younger, and don't plan to return to Utah for several seasons, skip the Access card and buy a one-day paper ticket. If you are in the 60–69 age category, buy a one-day paper ticket to get the $29 rate.

Everyone else should use the Access system. We recommend buying by the ride rather than all-day, because the system is designed so you never pay more than the all-day ticket, but you might pay less. However, if you ski all day no matter what, then buy the all-day ticket to get the subsequent $34-per-day price. The card can be used year after year (so if you ski in Utah annually, just remember where you put it).

Accommodations (98/99 prices)

Solitude finally has base-area lodging—not much, but what it has is beautiful. If you like to be first on the lifts, stay here. There are slightly more than 200 beds at the moment, so most everyone else still will be on the road from Salt Lake City when the lifts start running. All lodging can be booked by calling (800) 748-4754.

The Inn at Solitude has 46 rooms that are spacious, most with two queen beds (though kings and suites are available). All have terry-cloth robes to wear to the pool and spa, hair dryers, mini-refrigerators, TV with VCR, daily newspaper delivery and continental breakfast. Rates are $160–315.

Solitude also has 18 condo units (one to three bedrooms) in a development called Creekside. The condos are spacious and well-appointed, and share an outdoor spa. Each unit has a private deck and fireplace, full kitchen and TV with VCR. The three-bedroom units have a jetted tub and four bathrooms, so the person sleeping on the living room sofa has a bathroom, too. Rates range from $195 to $620 per night, including continental breakfast.

Dining/après-ski/other activities

Dining: A very popular program is the **Solitude Yurt.** Twenty people ski to a yurt for a five-course gourmet meal and ski back (it's a beginner trail both ways and the equipment is included in the cost). Reservations are a must for this, and don't be too disappointed if you can't get in. Salt Lake City residents really enjoy it and hog many of the available spaces. Coffee and water are the only provided beverages, but guests may bring their own corked wine (probably other beverages, too; we forgot to ask). The cost is $65, and no children younger than 8 are allowed. **The**

Roundhouse is on the mountain, and serves lunch with a 300-degree view. At night, a snowcat-drawn sleigh brings guests to dinner Wednesday through Sunday, the cost of which is $55. Call 536-5709 for dinner reservations for either the Yurt or the Roundhouse.

St. Bernard's is in the Inn and has a menu that leans toward Swiss and German entrées, such as Wild Boar Stew, Wiener Schnitzle and fondue. **Creekside,** which is on the first floor of the Creekside condos, serves breakfast, lunch and dinner with much of the cooking done in the wood-burning oven. Pasta and pizza—large enough for two to split—are its specialties.

Solitude also upgraded its cafeteria, **Last Chance Mining Camp,** to two levels that can seat about 400 skiers (previously, Solitude had precious little space for indoor eating on inclement days). **Sunshine Grill** is open for breakfast and lunch.

Après-ski: Everyone heads to **The Thirsty Squirrel,** a full-service bar that scores big points with us because it serves microbrews by the pitcher. Oops, it's Utah, so cross out "bar" in that last sentence and substitute "private club." Be sure to ask a local to sponsor your admittance (see the Salt Lake City chapter for the full scoop on the Utah liquor laws). There's a pool table, TV with sporting events and munchies. **St. Bernard's** occasionally offers mellow live music at night, and the Inn has wine tastings and nightly movies for its guests.

Other activities: The Inn at Solitude has a full-service **health and fitness spa** with a workout room, sauna, facials, massages and more. During full moons, you can do **moonlight cross-country skiing** at the Nordic Center.

Brighton Ski Resort
Mountain layout

◆◆ Expert ◆ Advanced: Brighton regulars refer to the "Majestic" side, served by the Majestic and other chairs, and the "Millicent" side, served by the Millicent and Evergreen chairs. If avoiding lower-level skiers and boarders is your goal, stay on the Millicent side with fewer greens and blues than Majestic.

But don't miss the Majestic side, either. Experts should try a short but heart-stopping run called Hard Coin off the Snake Creek chair. The trees are so thick you can hardly pick a line, but it's a marked trail. Most of the advanced runs are concentrated under the Great Western quad. From its summit one can see the Great Salt Lake as well at Mt. Timpanogos, home of the Sundance Ski Resort. For moguls, try Rockin'R under Great Western, or Ziggy under Snake Creek. Clark's Roose and Rein's Run, off the Great Western lift, are the toughest in-bounds descents.

Brighton's has an open-boundaries policy, which means experts can head into the backcountry as they wish. But let us quote directly from a Brighton press release: "The backcountry...is for expert skiers and snowboarders (this doesn't mean people who think they're experts). An expert...has taken avalanche and mountaineering courses...has an equally prepared buddy, is familiar with the terrain, and is properly equipped to deal with any situation (i.e., beacon, shovel, maps, probe, etc.)..." You can—and should—get more information from the ski patrol.

■ **Intermediate:** Intermediates have the run of practically the whole area. The Snake Creek chair is a little less crowded than the Crest Express high-speed quad and the Majestic chairs. The Majestic side is more heavily wooded but with gentler pitches, while the Millicent side is a bit steeper, but with fewer trees. The Elk Park Ridge run descends 1,745 feet, summit to base, from the Great Western chair.

Brighton Facts

Summit elevation:	10,500 feet	
Vertical drop:	1,745 feet	
Base elevation:	8,755 feet	

Address: Star Route
Brighton, UT 84121
☎ Area code: 801
Ski area phone: 532-4731
Snow report: 943-8309
ⓘ **Toll-free information:** (800) 873-5512
Internet: http://www.skibrighton.com
Expert:★★ **Advanced:**★★★
Intermediate:★★★★
Beginner:★★★★
Never-ever:★★★★

Number of lifts: 7–2 high-speed quads;
2 triple chairs, 3 double chairs
Snowmaking: 25 percent
Skiable acreage: 850
Uphill capacity: 11,000 per hour
Snowboarding: Yes, unlimited
Bed base: About 50;12,000 in Salt Lake City
Resort child care: No
Nearest lodging: walking distance
Adult ticket, per day: $33 (98/99 price)

Dining:★★
Apres-ski/nightlife:★
Other Activities: ★

●● **Beginner:** Good beginner runs descend from the Majestic chair, and from the Snake Creek chair, which goes to the top of the mountain. Beginners should keep an eye out so they don't get onto an intermediate trail: greens and blues do a lot of intertwining here.

● **Never-ever:** Brighton has a stellar reputation as the place where Utah skiers and snowboarders learn. The Explorer chair serves a gentle slope apart from general skier traffic.

Mountain rating

Good for beginners, excellent for intermediates and very good for advanced skiers and snowboarders. Brighton has a bit of true expert terrain, but it is not nearly as extensive as the other Cottonwood Canyons resorts. We don't recommend that out-of-state visitors head into the backcountry unless they are with a local guide.

Snowboarding

O.K. everywhere. Rentals and lessons are available. Brighton has two halfpipes and a snowboard park. Because Brighton supported snowboarding early (and other Utah resorts did not), this is a very popular spot with boarders.

Lift tickets (98/99 prices)

Skiers aged 11 to 69 ski for $33. Brighton does not sell multiday tickets, but twilight tickets are available when lifts are running into the evening. Brighton also has about 200 acres of night lift operation every day except Sunday.

Who skis free: Ages 10 and younger, two children per paying adult with no restrictions or blackout dates. Skiers 70 and older also ski free.

Who skis at a discount: A beginner lift pass, good on two lifts, is $22. A single-ride ticket is $10. Night skiing costs $20–$31, depending on the number of hours you ski. Last season, on holidays and weekends, any car with five or more occupants received a $1 per day ticket discount. Brighton was undecided at our press time whether they would continue that program, but it's worth keeping in mind for large groups.

Lessons (97/98 prices)

Group lessons: $20 for two hours, also offered at night (at night, the lift ticket is included). "The Works" package includes a group lesson, all-day ticket and all-day rentals for $48 for skiers and $61 for snowboarders.

Never-ever package: Includes a full day of rentals, beginner lift ticket and a group lesson—$40 for skiing and $52 for snowboarding.

Private lessons: $50 per hour, with each additional person $20.

Special programs: Includes clinics for women, seniors, telemark, adaptive and advanced technique. Inquire at the ski and snowboard school.

Racing: None, except for club programs.

Children's programs: Ages 4 to 7 get 1.75-hour lessons for $25 without equipment, $33 with. A full day with lunch is $57.

Accommodations (97/98 prices)

The Brighton Lodge (800-873-5512 or 801-532-4731) is small, cozy, has two hot tubs and is at the base of the lifts. Rates are $91 per night for a room, $115 for a suite and $61 for an economy hostel.

Das Alpen Haus (801-649-0565) is a charming B&B near the foot of Brighton. Each of the four suites is named for a Swiss ski resort, and the atmosphere is Swiss Alpine. Prices are about $115–$185 for two.

Getting there and getting around

By air and train: Salt Lake City is a major transportation hub, so flights are numerous and Amtrak also serves the city.

By car: Solitude and Brighton are about 23 miles southeast of Salt Lake City in Big Cottonwood Canyon on State Hwy. 190. The most direct route from the airport is east on I-80, south on I-215, Exit 6 to Wasatch Blvd., then follow the signs to Solitude and Brighton.

Getting around: You can ride the Utah Transit Authority ski buses for $4 from downtown or $1.50 from the park-and-ride at the canyon's mouth (exact fare is required). Or, take a Lewis Brothers SkiExpress van ($22 roundtrip from downtown; call 801-359-8677). During the day, UTA buses run between Solitude and Brighton for $1.

If you don't like to eat at the same place twice, or you like nightlife, we recommend staying in Salt Lake City. There is no public transportation at night between Salt Lake City and the canyon.

Schweitzer Mountain

Idaho

Summit elevation: **6,400 feet**
Vertical drop: **2,406 feet**
Base elevation: **3,994 feet**

Address: P.O. Box 815
Sandpoint, ID 83864
✆ **Area code:** 208
Ski area phone: 263-9555
ⓘ **Snow report and reservations:**
(800) 831-8810
Fax: (208) 263-0775
Internet: http://www.schweitzer.com
Expert:★★★★
Advanced:★★★★
Intermediate:★★★★
Beginner:★★★★
Never-ever:★★★

Number and types of lifts: 6–1 high-speed quad, 5 double chairs
Acreage: 2,350 skiable acres
Snowmaking: Beginner runs only
Uphill capacity: 7,092 per hour
Snowboarding: Yes, unlimited
Bed Base: About 1,000 at base, 5,200 in Sandpoint
Nearest lodging: slopeside, hotel & condos
Resort child care: Yes, 3 months and older
Adult ticket, per day: $30 (98/99 prices)
Dining:★★
Apres-ski/nightlife:★★★ (in Sandpoint)
Other activities:★★

Here's a 30-year-old "overnight sensation" among destination ski areas. In recent years, this Idaho resort has received ski-magazine raves for its slopeside services, superb scenery and "greatest potential." But even with all the positive press Schweitzer has had in recent years, it's still very uncrowded. One skier per acre (2,350 acres) is a good-sized crowd here. Its acreage is second biggest in Idaho (Bogus Basin is slightly larger), and its vertical drop of 2,406 feet is second only to Sun Valley's 3,400.

Schweitzer continues its plans for the future. The resort has one slopeside hotel and a collection of condo units. A European-style village with shops, restaurants and lodging is planned for the future. Until then, many visitors stay in Sandpoint, 11 miles away on the shore of beautiful Lake Pend Oreille. This is the sort of place that people visit, then try to figure a way to move there. The town reportedly has more real-estate agents per capita than the national average, and a steady stream of building permits being filed.

Compared to Rocky Mountain resorts, Schweitzer's elevation (6,400 feet) is not high, but it gets plenty of snow from its position in the Selkirks. When the storms come from the north, the snow is dry and fluffy but more often it is wet and dense. It's drier than the Cascade Concrete that falls on Washington and Oregon areas, but still wet enough to have earned the local term, Panhandle Premix.

Fog and/or clouds can be a problem at any Northwest ski area, especially one close to a body of water like Lake Pend Oreille. If the day's ski report says, "Fog levels moving up and down," believe it.

However, when the skies are clear, the vistas are outstanding: from the top of Schweitzer, skiers can look east into Montana's Cabinet Range and north to the Canadian Selkirks. The view of big Lake Pend Oreille is memorable.

Mountain layout

◆◆ **Expert** ◆ **Advanced:** Schweitzer's runs and chutes are steepest at the top of its two broad ski bowls, North and South. The bowls are separated by the Great Divide run, a long wide ridge that gives you a continuous option to drop into either bowl.

Chutes await advanced skiers in the South Bowl, reached by either Chair 1 or The Great Escape Quad. There are so many they're lettered A Chute, B Chute, and so forth. Upper Stiles and the adjacent Headwall Chutes are gonzo favorites.

There is some double-black skiing from the rim of South Bowl, but most experts will head up the Great Escape and turn right to North Bowl. Patient trekkers will be rewarded by the Siberia Chutes.

■ **Intermediate:** Skiers at this level can wend their way down from the South Bowl summit, but are advised to unload midway on the Snow Ghost chair heading toward the summit of North Bowl. The runs under the Timber Cruiser chair, Cathedral Aisle and Zip Down, are intermediate favorites.

●● **Beginner:** This group won't be able to get to the top, but can get a view by unloading midway up Chair One and heading down Gypsy.

The Enchanted Forest and Happy Trails are perfect for children. Both run the length of the Musical Chairs Chair, which goes right by the windows of the 40,000-square-foot Headquarters Day Lodge. The Enchanted Forest, with kid-high, widely-spaced mounds that children can go over or around, is barred to adults and jealous snowboarders.

● **Never-ever:** Schweitzer has a wonderful learning area, served by a separate chair and completely isolated from other traffic. Better yet it is below the base area, so that never-evers can start out skiing, rather than sidestepping up the hill or riding a lift.

Mountain rating

Schweitzer offers a lot for most ability levels, especially intermediate to expert.

Cross-country

The resort maintains 24 km. of groomed Nordic trails that leave directly from the village area; beginners shouldn't attempt them, however. The resort rents cross-country gear and snowshoes. Trail fee is $5 a day.

Snowboarding

Snowboarders have been welcomed by Schweitzer since the sport began. A youth club, the Schweitzer Stormriders Club, works with adults to develop a racing team.

Boarders can reach the Schweitzer halfpipe by unloading at the Chair 1's midway station and riding down Midway trail to Jam Session, below the NASTAR course. Lessons and rentals are available.

Lessons (98/99 prices)

Schweitzer offers lessons for snowboarders, Alpine skiers, telemarkers and cross-country skiers.

Group lessons: $20, 90 minutes, maximum eight people per class.

Never-ever package (lifts, lesson, rental equipment): $38 for skiing; $42 for snowboarding, ages 6 and older.

Private lessons: $60 per hour ($50 at 9 a.m.).

Special programs: Workshops for women and technique clinics that cater to the day's snow conditions.

Racing: NASTAR, to the left of the midway station on Chair 1, afternoons on weekends and holidays, $5 for two runs. Coin-operated course, Wednesday through Friday, 50 cents per run.

Children's lessons: Full day (lunch, lesson, lifts): $50 for ages 7-11 and $45 for ages 5-6. Ages 3 1/2 through 6 can opt for a half day of child care and two ski lessons for $60.

Child care (98/99 prices)

Ages: 3 months to 11 years.

Costs: For children still in diapers, $40 a full day, $25 for half day. Out of diapers it's $30 and $20 respectively. Lunch is $5 extra.

Reservations: Ski area toll-free number, (800) 831-8810.

Lift tickets (98/99 prices)

	Adult	Child (7–12)
One day	$30	$20
Three days	$90 ($30/day)	$60 ($20/day)
Five days	$150 ($30/day)	$100 ($20/day)

Who skis free: Children 6 and younger. In many of the lodging packages, children 12 and younger stay and ski free.

Who skis at a discount: Seniors 65 and older ski for $25 ($63 for three days and $90 for five).

Note: Students at the upper end of the 7–12 age range should bring student ID. Night skiing, 3 to 9 p.m. Thursday through Saturday, mid-December through mid-March, is $15 for adults and $10 for students and seniors, but is free with a day ticket.

If snow conditions do not meet your expectations, return your lift ticket within one hour of purchase and get a coupon good for another day.

Accommodations

At the ski area: The **Green Gables Lodge** (800-831-8810) has 82 rooms, 28 with kitchenettes and eight with Jacuzzis, and a pool with three hot tubs and a heated deck and cabana. Children 12 and younger stay free with their parents, and ski free with a minimum four-night package. Lodging-for-two packages start at $114 per night.

About 40 condos are also for rent at the ski area, ranging in price from $98 to $370.

In Sandpoint: Lodging here is inexpensive (many rooms less than $100 a night) and fairly basic, ranging in size from the four-room lakeside **Whitaker House B&B** (208-263-0816) to the 60 rooms of the **Lakeside Inn** (800-543-8126) and **Super 8 Motel** (208-263-2210; 800-800-8000). The **Quality Inn** (800-635-2534) has the region's only indoor pool. **Connie's Best Western** (208-263-9581; 800-282-0660) has a hot tub and heated outdoor pool, and a location right in town. The **Edgewater Resort Inn** (800-635-2534) also is on the lake. Several Sandpoint hotels offer ski packages.

Dining

Jean's Northwest Bar & Grill, in the Green Gables Lodge, is best for fresh seafood and game. The pastas are good, too.

On Highway 200 in Hope at the north end of the lake, diners are well rewarded for the drive to **Trestle Creek Inn** (555 Highway 200 E. 264-5942). The accent is on fresh ingredients, including the home-baked breads. You'll find pastas, jumbo Florida shrimps, New York Strip steak, and the house specialty Hollandse Biefstuk. Cozy **Swan's Landing** (265-2000) at the south end of Long Bridge also has fine meals and great views.

For serious northern Italian food, go to **Ivano's** (124 S. Second, 263-0211) in Sandpoint. House specialties are veal, chicken, fish and pasta. **Eichardt's Pub, Grill and Coffee House** (formerly The Donkey Jaw Restaurant & Lounge, 212 Cedar St., 265-2243) is a hot new hangout with microbrews and reasonably priced food. For Mexican, try **Jalapeños** at 109 Cedar (263-2995) or **Jalapeños Express** on First Avenue or head to the **Power House** (Sandpoint Marina 265-2449) for burgers and wraps.

Après-ski/nightlife

Jean's Bar is a very happy place for après-ski with an excellent wine list. **Taps** has live entertainment on weekends and a game room upstairs. In Sandpoint, **Roxy's** (215 Pine St., 263-6696) has live bands Wednesday through Saturday.

Other activities

The **Sandpoint Winter Carnival** (800-800-2106), usually held the third week in January, has snow sculpture extravaganzas, ice skating parties, a "Taste of Sandpoint" on the Cedar Street Bridge, a Parade of Lights and a host of special events on Schweitzer Mountain.

The Green Gables Lodge activities desk can arrange Norwegian Fjord horse-drawn **sleigh rides** through an old-growth hemlock forest and **snowmobile tours** from one hour to all day.

Shopping includes Annie's Gifts in the Green Gables Lodge, The Company Store at 218 Cedar St., the Dann Hall Studios at 202 1/2 S. First St. for its astounding turn-of-the-century photographs of Idaho. Coldwater Creek is a shopping "happening" on the covered Cedar Street Bridge. Cabin Fever at 113 Cedar has truely unique Northwestern design and clothes.

Getting there and getting around

By air: Five major airlines serve Spokane International Airport, where four-wheel-drive cars can be rented.

By car: Schweitzer is a seven-hour drive from Calgary or Seattle. It's 86 miles northeast of Spokane via Highway 95. From Sandpoint drive north on 95 for two miles and left on Schweitzer Cutoff Road. After half a mile, go right at Boyer Avenue, then left after about three quarters of a mile onto the Schweitzer access road. The resort is eight miles from here.

By train: Sandpoint is on the Amtrak Empire Builder route. The train comes through at 1 a.m., but it can be an inexpensive option for Seattle and Portland skiers.

Schweitzer will arrange ground transportation from the airport and Amtrak depot.

Getting around: Some Sandpoint hotels offer ski shuttlebus service, but most people will want their own wheels—the town is a little too spread out for walking. North Idaho Community Express (NICE) runs daily shuttles to Schweitzer from Sandpoint.

Silver Mountain Resort

Idaho

Summit elevation: 6,300 feet
Vertical drop: 2,200 feet
Base elevation: 4,100 feet

Address: 610 Bunker Ave.
Kellogg, ID 83837-2200
✆ **Area code:** 208
Ski area phone: 783-1111
Snow report: (800) 204-6428
ⓘ **Toll-free reservations:** (800) 876-8921
Fax: 783-2901 **E-mail:** info@silvermt.com
Internet: http://www.silvermt.com
Expert:★★★★ **Advanced:**★★★★
Intermediate:★★★
Beginner:★★★
Never-ever:★★★★

Number and types of lifts: 7–1 eight-
passenger gondola, 1 quad, 2 triples,
2 doubles, 1 surface tow
Skiable acreage: 1,500 acres
Snowmaking: 10 percent
Uphill capacity: 8,200 skiers per hour
Snowboarding: Yes, unlimited
Bed Base: 1,500 within 35 miles
Nearest lodging: walking distance
Resort child care: Yes, 2 years and older
Adult ticket, per day: $23-$29 (97/98)
Dining:★★★
Apres-ski/nightlife:★★
Other activities:★★

Silver's original name was Jackass Ski Bowl, and you can still buy patches bearing that name for $5 at the local museum. The name honored the discoverer of the metal that brought riches to the valley more than a century ago. Local legend says a donkey got away from its owner, scampered up a hill, and was standing on a rock with a silvery glint when the owner caught up with it. Bunker Hill Mine, which also took lead, zinc and copper from the hillsides, ran the ski area for employee recreation and changed the name to Silverhorn. But in the early 1980s the price of silver plunged and Bunker Hill closed.

What the company left behind was a white-knuckle road up to the ski area (later condemned by the city) and a cleanup site of astounding proportions. The town decided to build a four-season resort, serviced by an aerial gondola to take skiers from the valley floor to the slopes. In late 1987, Kellogg got a federal grant to fund the gondola's construction; however, it had to be matched with private money. Part of it came from Kellogg residents, who taxed themselves $2 million to build the 3.1-mile lift. Silver Mountain began ski operations in 1990. In 1996 the Von Roll Tramways' interest in the mountain was bought by Eagle Crest, a Redmond, Oregon, company that plans more development of the area.

The gondola descends low over the houses and yards of the town of Wardner before climbing to Silver's "base area," called Mountain Haus, at 5,700 feet. (A hefty portion of

Silver's terrain is below the Mountain Haus, which gives the area its 2,200-foot vertical drop.) The gondola is the only way in and out of the ski area.

Silver has been the subject of quite a few glowing magazine articles recently, but because it's nowhere near a major airline hub, it's tough to reach for anyone outside the Pacific Northwest. But that disadvantage also is a big plus: Silver is an uncrowded and inexpensive ski vacation with lift ticket prices $10–$20 lower than most Colorado and California high-end resorts. Lodging is reasonable too.

Mountain layout

Silver has two connected peaks, Kellogg and Wardner. The gondola deposits skiers and snowboarders at Mountain Haus on the Kellogg side. From here they can fan out in several directions.

◆◆ **Expert** ◆ **Advanced:** Silver has a lot of serious terrain, including monster glade skiing. For advanced skiers, the run rating always depends on snow conditions. On fresh powder days, take Silver Belt to Rendezvous on the Kellogg side. For great thrills on the Wardner side, cut down anywhere from the early section of the Wardner Peak Traverse. The best skiing on powder days is off the slopes between the tops of Chairs 4 and 2.

Experts love Silver Mountain. They can take the Wardner Peak Traverse to an inspirational knob with a stupendous view of the Silver Valley below. Some nice black-diamond runs go back down to the Shaft and Chair 4.

Terrible Edith, reached by green-circle Noahs which descends from Mountain Haus, is one of those runs that makes you feel like you're skiing down a globe. It's like Dave's Run at Mammoth Mountain—the farther down you go, the steeper it gets, until finally you see the cat track below. At that point, you're only halfway down.

■ **Intermediate:** Silver Belt, from the triple Chair 2, is a wide and terrific intermediate warmup run. At the Junction you can turn down Saddle Back for a bumpier ride, or take a hard left on the Cross Over Run to the Midway load station on Chair 4 for a ride to Wardner Peak. From the top there are several trails back to Midway. Only advanced skiers pass Midway and keep going down through the Shaft to the Chair 4 base.

● **Beginner:** As good as Silver is for experts, it also offers a lot for beginners. Chairs 1, 2, 3, and 5 at the Mountain Haus base area all serve beginner terrain. Below the lodge, Ross Run is a wide beginner favorite, allowing crossover to Noahs and back again, ending on Dawdler with a choice to return to Chair 5 or Chair 3.

Note: Most skiers ski the Kellogg side, so to avoid even a mirage of crowds, ski the Wardner side. Lift lines are rarely a problem, but the gondola queue can back up for downloading at closing time (remember, you can't ski to the gondola base). To avoid morning clog, ride up a half hour early for breakfast at Mountain Haus.

Day fog can cause night ice when the thermometer dips. Until it softens up, stay on the groomed runs (most on the Kellogg side). Centennial and Tamarack are safe bets on the Wardner side.

Silver has some nice surprises. One is the free ski wax, right by the free ski check at Mountain Haus. Another is the guarantee: If snow conditions don't please you, return your lift ticket to the gondola base within an hour and a half and get a pass for another day.

Mountain rating

All levels will have fun here. Experts will like Wardner Peak's runs and the North Face Glades on Kellogg Peak. Intermediates have most of Kellogg and quite a bit on Wardner, while beginners have a mostly isolated section under the gondola and around Mountain Haus.

Cross-country

Silver has no cross-country skiing, but telemark lessons are given at the ski school.

Snowboarding

Boarders are welcomed on all runs.

Lessons (97/98 prices)

Group lessons: For ages 12 and older are $12.95 for two hours for Alpine ski, telemark or snowboard lessons.

Never-ever package: Learning programs for skiing or snowboarding are $36, including lift tickets, lessons and rental equipment.

Private lessons: These cost $19.95 per hour, with each additional student for $15.

Racing: NASTAR is offered on weekends for $1 per run and $10 for a daylong pass. The course is open from 10:30 a.m. to 2 p.m.

Children's lessons: The SKIwee lesson program is for ages 5–11. Full day costs $35 for lifts, lesson and lunch. Half days cost $22.

Child care (97/98 prices)

Ages: 2–6 years.

Costs: $30 for a full day and $20 for additional siblings. It includes lunch, a snack, snowplay and ski and snowboard equipment. Half day, which also includes lunch, is $20 ($15 for additional siblings).

Reservations: Recommended; call 783-1111.

Note: Children in Minor's Camp Daycare who want to ski can get a one-hour private lesson, equipment included, for $20. The instructor will pick up and drop off the child in Minor's Camp.

Lift tickets (97/98 prices)

	Adult	Child (7–12)
Weekends/holidays	$29	$19
Weekdays	$23	$17
2-day, weekends/holidays	$54 ($27/day)	$34 ($17/day)
2-day, weekdays	$42 ($21/day)	$30 ($15/day)

Who skis free: Children ages 6 and younger.

Who skis at a discount: Juniors (ages 13–21) and seniors (65 and older) ski for $23 on weekends and holidays; $21 weekdays. The two-day prices are $42 and $38.

Accommodations

The closest lodging is in Kellogg, where the gondola starts. So although Silver Mountain doesn't have slopeside lodging per se, some accommodations are within walking distance to the gondola. Skiers can also stay in Coeur d'Alene, about 35 miles away. The toll-free number listed in our stat box applies to all of Northern Idaho.

The gondola base **Super-8 Motel** (783-1234 or 800-785-5443), with indoor pool and spa, is new and has a midweek package of lift and lodging for $50 each, including continental breakfast.

Kellogg also has one- and two-bedroom condos at **Silver Ridge Mountain Lodge** (800-979-1991) and homes (call 800-435-2588 or 784-1166) and the **Silverhorn Motor Inn** (783-1151 or 800-437-6437), all of which have ski packages.

Ten miles east on I-90 is the mining town of Wallace. The **Best Western Wallace Inn** (800-643-2386) has Silver Mountain and Lookout Pass ski packages available from $49.95 per person per day, including round-trip shuttle to the ski area, based on quad occupancy. The Wallace Inn has 63 rooms, an on-site restaurant, heated indoor pool with Jacuzzi, sauna, steam rooms and a fitness center. The Best Western management also runs the **Jameson Hotel**, a historic and delightful lodge. Call the same 800 number if historic digs appeal to you.

The **Coeur d'Alene Resort** (800-688-5253), a hugely popular summer golf resort on the shore of Lake Coeur d'Alene, has a ski package where children ages 17 and under stay and ski free. Two-day packages start at $148 per person double occupancy on weekdays and $168 on weekends, and include lodging, lift tickets, continental breakfast and round-trip shuttle to Silver Mountain, about 35 miles away. On Fridays through Sundays, the resort also shuttles skiers to Schweitzer Mountain, which is about an hour's drive. Advantages to staying here include more to do at night (including an indoor mall attached to the hotel), a lower elevation and the resort itself, which is quite luxurious and a huge bargain in winter.

Dining

Good family fare is found at the gondola base, second floor, in the **Jackass Bar & Grill**, which has a full range of Mexican and Southwest food, plus steaks, chicken sandwiches and burgers.

The **Enaville Resort** (682-3453), Exit 43A off I-90, is always a happy discovery for skiers new to the Kellogg area. Known locally as the Snake Pit, it's more of a destination dinery than a resort. Over its 115-year history, the Snake Pit accommodated a lot of people for a lot of purposes, but sleeping through the night was never one of them. Enjoy an appetizer of Rocky Mountain oysters before moving on to buffalo burgers and barbecue.

Après-ski/nightlife

Not a strong point. At the end of the day, hang around the food court or go up to **Moguls Lounge** for some après-ski. Moguls is open until 5 p.m.

The **Jackass Bar & Grill** at the gondola base is open with live music on the weekends. It closes at 8 p.m. weekdays and at 10 p.m. Friday and Saturday.

Other activities

Snowmobiling is very big in Wallace (where it's legal on city streets), ten miles east of Kellogg on I-90, and also at Lookout Pass, ten miles past Wallace on the Montana border. Lookout has a snowmobile camp and access to 600 miles of snowmobile trails. There are several special events and rides January through April every year. Phone (800) 643-2386 for more information. (Best Western Wallace Inn is a headquarters of sorts for snowmobiling with free, secure snowmobile storage.)

Perhaps symbolic of the new Kellogg spirit are the life-size sculptures-from-scrap on view downtown—they were made by Dave Dose, a high school teacher and county commissioner with a sense of humor. **Shopping** in Kellogg is sparse. We recommend Bitterroot Stoneware and Pottery if you are looking for handmade gifts by Idaho artists.

At Cataldo, five miles west of Kellogg and 24 miles east of Coeur d'Alene on I-90 (Exit 39), sits the **Mission of the Sacred Heart**, Idaho's oldest building, finished in 1853. It was all hand built without nails, and the walls are a one-foot-thick mixture of mud, twigs and straw, covered with boards inside and out. Tours are available, and the mission is open year-round, 9 a.m.–5 p.m. in winter, admission $2 per vehicle.

Getting there and getting around

By air: Silver Mountain Resort is, as the crow flies, 70 miles east of Spokane Airport. Its regional airport is served by Horizon, Delta, Northwest, Continental, United and Southwest Airlines.

By car: Silver Mountain is at Kellogg, Exit 49 of I-90. The interstate is well maintained, and Silver Mountain's parking lot is a block off the freeway, so a four-wheel-drive car isn't necessary. However, you can rent one at the airport for $45–$85 per day. The Coeur d'Alene Resort will shuttle guests from Spokane Airport with prior arrangement. Silver Service (800-686-6432) operated through the McKinley Inn, picks up passengers headed to Kellogg; reservations are required.

Getting around: It's possible to survive without a car, especially if you stay at the Coeur d'Alene Resort, but you will probably want one.

Sun Valley

Idaho

Summit elevation:	9,150 feet
Vertical drop:	3,400 feet
Base:	5,750 feet

Address: Sun Valley Resort,
1 Sun Valley Rd., Box 10, Sun Valley, ID 83353
✆ **Area code:** 208
ⓘ **Toll-free reservations:** (800) 786-8259
(for Sun Valley properties)
or (800) 634-3347 (Central Reservations)
Snow report: (800) 635-4150
Fax: 726-4533 or 622-3700
E-mail: sunval@micron.net or
svcmktpr@sunvalley.com
Internet: http://www.sunvalley.com or
http://www.visitsunvalley.com
Expert:★★★★ **Advanced:**★★★★★
Intermediate:★★★★★
Beginner:★★★ **Never-ever:**★★★

Number of lifts: 17–7 high-speed quads,
5 triple chairs, 5 doubles
Snowmaking: 29 percent
Skiable acreage: 2,067 acres
Uphill capacity: 28,180 per hour
Snowboarding: Yes, unlimited
Bed Base: 6,000
Nearest lodging: walking distance, condos
Resort child care: Yes, 6 months and older
Adult ticket, per day: $52–$54 (98/99 prices)

Dining:★★★★★
Apres-ski/nightlife:★★★★
Other activities:★★★★

Sun Valley may provide America's perfect ski vacation. It has a European accent mixed with the Wild West. It is isolated, yet comfortable; rough in texture, but also refined; Austrian in tone, cowboy in spirit.

Ageless would be the one word to describe Sun Valley Village, America's first ski resort, built in 1936 by Union Pacific tycoon Averell Harriman. It exudes restrained elegance with the traditional Sun Valley Lodge, walking village, steeple, horse-drawn sleighs and steaming pools.

In contrast, the town of Ketchum is all-American West, a flash of red brick, a slab of prime rib, a rustic cluster of small restaurants, shops, homes, condos and lodges. It's the town of Ketchum that actually curls around the broad-shouldered evergreen rise of Bald Mountain, known as Baldy to locals. Each snow ribbon dropping from the summit into the valley leads to the streets of Ketchum.

This is Hemingway country. When he wasn't hobnobbing with Ingrid Bergman, Gary Cooper and Howard Hawks, he wrote most of *For Whom The Bell Tolls* in the Sun Valley Lodge, where photos show Hollywood celebrities who first made the place famous. Sun Valley has developed many famous winter-sport athletes: the late Gretchen Fraser, who was the first American Olympic ski champion in 1948; Christin Cooper, a 1984 silver Olympic medalist; Picabo Street, who won a silver at the 1994 Olympics, a gold in the 1998 Olympics, and a World Cup downhill title; and ice skaters Peggy Fleming, Dorothy Hamill and Scott Hamilton, Olympic champions all. Fraser, Cooper and Street have ski runs named for them.

The Sun Valley Company keeps the skiing as up-to-date as any in America with a large computerized snowmaking system; seven high-speed quads, including one that rises a whopping 3,144 vertical feet in 10 minutes; and three new lodges on the mountain since 1992—Seattle Ridge, Warm Springs and River Run—that have won raves from skiers and architectural awards from the ski industry.

And yet, it is the celebration of its history that makes Sun Valley stand out from the rest of America's ski areas. If you enjoy history, you must stay at the Sun Valley Lodge, a beautifully kept-up property with a pronounced mid-20th-century feel. The elegance of a bygone era is in the details—uniformed doormen; a formal dining room; a large second-floor "drawing room" with the piano in the center, overstuffed chairs and sofas in the middle, and fireplaces at either end; an immense "hot tub" swimming pool that dates to the early days of the resort; and continual showings on the lodge's in-room televisions of *Sun Valley Serenade*, a 1941 movie starring Sonja Henie and John Payne that is as corny as can be when you see it at home, but is lots of fun when you see it in Sun Valley. Then later, try to track down the exact filming locations on the mountain and in the lodge.

America's oldest ski resort has managed to age gracefully without losing any of the magic it had in its youth. Sun Valley's magic is in its fresh powder and vacation ambiance. It's the American version of the European ski week.

Mountain layout

The main drawback to Sun Valley is the split in the ski areas. Bald Mountain (called "Baldy") is best suited for intermediate and advanced skiers, while beginners and never-evers should stick to Dollar/Elkhorn.

◆◆ **Expert** ◆ **Advanced:** Baldy's terrain is best known for its long runs with a consistent pitch that keeps skiers concentrating on turns from top to bottom, rather than dozing off on a flat or bailing out on a cliff or wall. Mile-long ridge runs lead to a clutch of advanced and intermediate bowls.

Limelight is a long, excellent bump run for skiers with strong knees and elastic spinal columns. Of the other black descents, the Exhibition plunge is one of the best known. Fire Trail, on the ski area boundary, is a darting, tree-covered descent for those who can make quick, flowing turns. The Seattle Ridge trail with hypnotic views curves around the bowls. The bowl area below, rarely mentioned by most ski writers, is a joy. The downhill skier's right is a little easier; skier's left a little tougher, and you can catch the sun throughout the day. There are sections where you can do 50-yard wide turns, but there is no easy terrain where you can relax your quads. The only flats are on top.

■ **Intermediate:** Baldy is good for this level, too. Trails are not apt to be quite so wide as at other Rocky Mountain resorts, but they're a lot wider than the ones in New England, and these trails are for the most part long, very long.

The best warm-ups are either the Upper and Lower College runs leading to the River Run area, or the Warm Springs run. Both descend from the top and head to the base (College takes a little jog and joins with River Run near the bottom). Warm Springs is labeled blue-square, while College is labeled green. Frankly, we didn't observe that much of a difference. Both are long, moderately steep, very well groomed and loads of fun. Other good spots are Cozy, Hemingway and Greyhawk in the Warm Springs area, often less crowded because the trail map shows a black-diamond entry (there's a cat-track intermediate entrance a little farther down that isn't as obvious on the map); and the Seattle Ridge runs, marked green, but definitely intermediate level.

If you want to follow the sun, start your day in the River Run area, then shift to the runs dropping off Seattle Ridge and finish up cruising the Warm Springs face.

●● **Beginner:** Do not be fooled by the green-circle markings on the Baldy trail map. Beginners should not ski Baldy. The runs are seriously underrated for difficulty. Yes, yes, we're well aware that the green-blue-black ratings system reflects the relative difficulty of the trails at each individual resort. Sun Valley followed the rules and marked the "easiest" runs on Baldy with green circles. Compared to other resorts, however, these runs are blue—royal blue. If you are at all tentative about your skills, start out at Dollar/Elkhorn. However, this means you'll be isolated for lunch and après-ski from family and friends who are skiing Baldy. When you feel you're ready for Baldy, try the Upper and Lower College run first.

● **Never-ever:** Skiing parents can enroll their children in ski school at the River Run Lodge and Skier Services building at the base of the River Run trail on Baldy. The ski school will transport children enrolled in novice lessons to Dollar. Adult never-evers should head directly to Dollar. The terrain here is perfect for learning and good for intermediates perfecting technique or starting out in powder. Skiing on the Dollar side of this mountain is shorter and more limited than on the Elkhorn face, which offers a small bowl with greater pitch and more challenging runs.

Mountain rating

If your ski group is solid intermediate to expert, you will thoroughly enjoy skiing together on Baldy. If your group is entirely never-ever to intermediate, you also will enjoy skiing together on Dollar/Elkhorn. (When the intermediates are ready for Baldy, the lower-level skiers may be ready for a day off to explore town.) Mixed-ability groups may not be as thrilled, unless they truly don't mind being separated.

Cross-country (97/98 prices)

The Sun Valley/Ketchum area has about 210 km. of trails overall. The closest facilities are at the **Sun Valley Nordic Center** (622-2250 or 622-2251), near the Sun Valley Lodge, where 40 km. of cross-country ski trails are groomed and marked for difficulty. They range from easy two-way trails on the golf course to isolated forest escapes. There is a half-track width for children as well as a terrain garden. The daily trail fee is $11, with discounts for half day, children and seniors. Group and private lessons are available. There is also an Atlas snowshoe center, along with 6 km. of snowshoe trails, the use of which are free.

The Blaine County Recreation District grooms the **North Valley Trails,** which have more than 100 km. of groomed trails in the Sawtooth National Recreation Area supported by set trail fees or donations. The largest is **Galena Lodge** (726-4010; grooming report: 726-6662) with 50 km. of trails, a full restaurant and a ski shop. It also has a 4 km. snowshoe trail and snowshoe rentals. A popular event is dinner, followed by moonlit skiing. Adult trail passes are $7; children ages 16 and younger ski for $2. Rentals and lessons are available, and every Thursday you can ski with a ranger and learn about natural history or wildlife. These tours are free with trail pass. Galena is 24 miles north of Ketchum on Highway 75.

Wood River Trails features 30 km. of trails stretching north of Ketchum to Hailey and Bellevue. **Lake Creek** has 15.5 km. of trails, and three other areas have less than 10 km. each. The **Boulder Mountain Trail** stretches 30 km. from the Sawtooth National Recreation

Area headquarters eight miles north of Ketchum to Easley Hot Springs and Galena, and is groomed all winter, snow conditions permitting.

Avalanche and snow conditions are available 24 hours a day from the Ketchum Ranger District at 788-1200, ext. 8027, while North Valley Trails maintains a grooming hotline, 726-6662.

For backcountry tours through the largest wilderness area outside Alaska, contact either **Sun Valley Trekking** (788-9585) or **Sawtooth Mountain Guides** (774-3324). Both feature hut-to-hut skiing and the opportunity to stay in yurts as well.

Snowboarding

Private lessons for all abilities are available on Dollar and Bald Mountains, with reservations required and made through the Sun Valley Ski School. Clinics cost $44 for two hours.

Lessons (97/98 prices)

Group lessons: $47 for three hours, with multiday discounts.

Never-ever package: None. Never-evers will need to sign up for lessons, rent equipment and buy lift tickets separately.

Private lessons: $79 per person for one hour. Discounts are available for multiple hours (cheaper in the afternoon).

Special programs: Racing clinics run three hours per day for $58. A women's clinic for upper intermediates is held five times each season—call for exact dates.

Children's lessons: A four-hour session, including lunch, is $65. Discounts are available for multiple days. SKIwee programs are available for children.

Call the Sun Valley Ski School (622-2248 or 622-2231) for more information on any of these programs.

Child care (97/98 prices)

Ages (Sun Valley's Playschool on the Sun Valley Mall): 6 months to 6 years, but the upper age limit is not strictly enforced, should you have a 7-year-old who doesn't ski.

Costs: Ages 6–18 months, $80 full day, $55 for four hours. Toddlers in diapers: $60 full day, $42 for four hours. Toilet-trained and older: $52 full day, $40 for four hours.

Reservations: Required, and priority is given to guests in Sun Valley company hotels and condos. Call 622-2288.

Note: Super Sitters (788-5080) has screened sitters trained in CPR and first aid who do in-room babysitting. **Baby's Away** (800-327-9030; 208-788-7582) rents and will deliver baby needs to your lodge, such as crib, stroller, car seat and toys.

Lift tickets (98/99 prices)

	Adult	Child (Up to 12)
One day	$54	$30
Three days	$156 ($53/day)	$84 ($28+/day)
Five days	$260 ($52/day)	$135 ($27/day)

These are prices for tickets valid both at Baldy and Dollar.

Telephone area code: 208

Who skis free: Children ages 15 and younger ski and stay free when they are with a parent in a Sun Valley Resort hotel or condo or any participating property in Ketchum, Elkhorn or Warm Springs. Unfortunately, blackout periods for this offer are the Christmas/New Year holiday, most of February and half of March.

Who skis at a discount: Skiers ages 65 and older (the price was not available at our deadline; call the resort). Prices for those who ski only at Dollar/Elkhorn are: one-day adult $25, three-day adult $65, one-day child $15, three-day child $40. Sun Valley lowers ticket prices in early and late season.

 ## Accommodations

For information or reservations for Sun Valley and Ketchum, call (800) 634-3347. Per-night rates for hotel rooms and inns range from about $50 at the low end to $400 at the high end. As always, the closer you get to the lifts and the larger the room, the more expensive it is. Some of the nicer places to stay (rates of $125 a night or higher during most of the season):

The **Sun Valley Lodge** is the heart of the resort, though it is not slopeside. You can relax on terraces and in grand sitting rooms beneath coppery chandeliers. Gleaming outside is a skating rink once ruled by ice queen Sonja Henie. The village is a 3,000-acre Alpine enclave of pedestrian walkways, wall paintings, snow sculptures, and spruce foliage. Because the Lodge was built well before the time of group tourism, each room is unique: pricing depends on room size and such added factors as view and balcony. **The Sun Valley Inn,** about a hundred yards from the Lodge, is a bit less expensive but shares most amenities. Packages are available. Condos and suites are available. Call (800) 786-8259 (800-SUN-VALY) for information on the Sun Valley Lodge or the Sun Valley Inn.

Elkhorn Resort (622-4511 or 800-355-4676), near Dollar Mountain, provides its own resort hotel world away from Ketchum and Sun Valley. Name performers play during the winter season and the health club is well outfitted.

Knob Hill Inn (726-8010 or 800-526-8010) is one of the Ketchum area's most luxurious, recently accepted into the exclusive Relais et Chateaux group. The building is so Austrian you feel as if you've stepped out of your car into the Tyrol. The inn is No Smoking throughout.

The Idaho Country Inn (726-1019 or 800-250-8341) is on a knoll halfway between Ketchum and Sun Valley. Each of the ten rooms is individually decorated to reflect the Idaho heritage—the Shoshone Room, Wagon Days Room, and Whitewater Room. Breakfasts are fabulous and the hot tub sits on a hill behind the inn with a wonderful view.

River Street Inn (726-3611 or 800-954-8585) resembles a charming New England B&B. It is within walking distance of the center of town. Rooms feature Japanese soaking tubs, which are very deep, one-person tubs.

Pennay's at River Run (726-9086 or 800-736-7503) is a cluster of family-perfect condos within walking distance of River Run lifts. There is a big outdoor hot tub and units have VCRs.

Among the accommodations with per-night rates in the $75–$125 range are:

Best Western Tyrolean Lodge (726-5336 or 800-333-7912), only 400 yards from the River Run lift, has an Alpine atmosphere with wood-paneled ceilings and downy comforters dressing the beds. A champagne continental breakfast is served.

Best Western Kentwood Lodge (726-4114 or 800-805-1001) is in the middle of town, convenient to everything.

Best Western Christiania Lodge (726-3351 or 800-535-3241) has 38 rooms that vary in type and size. They have microwaves, refrigerators, and some have fireplaces. Roomside parking, cable and sports TV are offered, and there is a year-round, outside hot tub. Pets are allowed. A complimentary continental breakfast is served in a sunny coffee area. The location is near Ketchum's restaurants, shops and night life.

Clarion Inn (726-5900 or 800-262-4833) is a basic hotel with a large outdoor Jacuzzi and full breakfasts. Room doors open to outdoor walkways and the decor is simple.

Christophe CondoHotel (726-5601 or 800-521-2515) features roomy condos with underground parking. A fire truck helps out the town bus racing guests back and forth to the lifts.

Tamarack Lodge (726-3344 or 800-521-5379) is smack in the middle of town with a hot tub and indoor pool. Good for families, the lodge is equipped with microwaves, refrigerators and coffee makers. It doesn't get any more convenient than this for nightlife and dining. Rooms with fireplaces cost more.

Least expensive lodging, with most rooms starting at less than $70 per night:

Povey Pensione (128 W. Bullion St., Hailey; 788-4682) is a 108-year-old residence maintaining the original character and fine workmanship of its builder, John Povey, a carpenter from Liverpool, England, who built and lived in the house when Hailey was a mining town. Pastel wall coverings and antique furnishings give the four spacious bedrooms and two full shared baths an Old West character. This Pensione is about 13 miles south of Ketchum and Sun Valley. Children under 12 are not allowed.

Ski View Lodge (726-3441) has eight rustic individual cabins with open space before them and woodland and Bald Mountain views behind located near downtown Ketchum. The cabins have kitchens and phones, pets are welcome and there is a senior citizen discount. Rates drop 40 percent during slow seasons.

Lift Tower Lodge (726-5163 or 800-462-8646) gets its name from a section of an old ski lift. All rooms have two beds, a refrigerator, TV and phone. This lodge has a jacuzzi outside in back. Complimentary breakfasts include bagels, coffee and orange juice. The free bus stops in front. During value season the price of a room can be halved.

If you have a large group and need to rent a private home, call **Base Mountain Properties** at (800) 521-2515 or 726-5601, or visit its website at www.basemountain.com. It has rentals near the lifts, downtown Ketchum, out at Elkhorn Village near the Dollar Mountain lifts, and homes that offer privacy and isolation.

 **Dining**

On the mountain: With the recent additions of the Warm Springs, Seattle Ridge and River Run lodges have come excellent restaurants. Skiers can settle down to a lunch of prime rib, salmon, stone-fired pizza and many other delights, all while enjoying panoramic views. The deck at Seattle Ridge is gorgeous. Deli and gourmet cafeteria-style clusters are the latest in on-mountain dining, and Sun Valley has this, too.

In Sun Valley Village: The **Sun Valley Lodge** dining room has old-time elegance and is the only spot in the area with live music and dancing with meals. Specialties include Steak Diane, Chateaubriand Béarnaise Bouquetière, and fresh Idaho trout or poached salmon.

The Ram attached to the Sun Valley Inn serves basic fare ranging from pasta to chops and steaks. **Gretchen's** in the Lodge has a fine dinner menu, and serves breakfast and lunch.

The **Konditorei** has an Austrian flavor and excellent lunches, such as hearty soups served in a bread bowl next to a mountain of fruit.

In Ketchum: Sun Valley has some of the best restaurants in any ski resort in America; anyone with fine dining on his or her mind will not be disappointed. The region's real gourmet action takes place here. The price ranges we give here are a rough guide.

Entrées in the $15–$25 range:

These restaurants all vie for "best of Ketchum." **Michel's Christiania** (726-3388) run by Michel Rodigoz, serves fine French cuisine. **Felix** (726-1166) in the Knob Hill Inn has a continental menu in a very Austrian setting. **Evergreen Bistro** (726-3888) has an elegant setting of wood, crystal and glass and quite possibly the town's best wine list.

Both location and atmosphere make these last two restaurants our favorites. **Soupçon** (726-5034) has creative and elegant continental cuisine cooked in a tiny rustic house. **Chandler's** (726-1776) serves gourmet meals in a series of tiny rooms. Ask to be seated near the fireplace if you are with a group; couples should ask for the small alcove off the main fireplace room. The three-course "prix fixe" meals at Chandler's and Soupçon are some of Ketchum's best bargains.

Entrées $10–$15:

The **Sawtooth Club** (726-5233) has a great bar with cozy couches in front of a fireplace and small dining rooms tucked above and behind the bar. The food is excellent and reasonable.

The **Pioneer Saloon** (726-3139), a local hangout going back into Ketchum history, is known for its prime rib and baked potatoes. **Ketchum Grill** (726-4660) has a daring, innovative menu with flavor mixtures that will keep your tastebuds tingling, and **China Pepper** (726-0959) is the place to head for spicy Thai and Chinese food. Few restaurants enjoy such rave reviews from visitors. **Otter's** (formerly Peter's; 726-6837) serves Pacific Northwest specialties. **Globus Noodle** (726-1301) has good Chinese/Thai food according to locals.

Most entrées less than $10:

Locals rave about **Smoky Mountain Pizza** (622-5625) for great, very affordable Italian fare and massive salads. **Piccolo Pasta** (726-9251) has slightly more expensive Italian cooking in a cozy dining room, with fine light homemade pastas. **Sushi** (726-5181) has full meals in the mid to high teens, but its sushi is priced at $2–$6. **Panda Chinese Restaurant** (726-3591) serves Chinese meals from several regions.

The **Warm Springs Ranch Restaurant** (726-2609) serves a wide-ranging menu including children's specials, and features mountain trout you can see swimming in pools near the cozy cabin.

The spot for excellent and inexpensive Mexican food is **Mama Inez** (726-4213) at the start of Warm Springs Road, or head to **Desperado's** (726-3068) just behind the visitor's center on Fourth Street. For slightly more expensive Mexican that is more Tex than Mex try **Tequila Joe's** (622-4511, Ext. 1157) in the Elkhorn Resort and Golf Club. **Grumpy's** (no phone, we're told) is the locals' favorite for great burgers and beer; it's across the street from Mama Inez.

Breakfast is important with most skiers. At the Sun Valley Lodge **Gretchen's** (622-2144) has plentiful fare with moderate prices and **Konditorei** (622-2235) in the Sun Valley Village has good breakfasts. The **Lodge Dining Room** (726-2150) serves an excellent Sunday brunch.

The best breakfasts, however, are downtown in Ketchum. Locals seem split on the question, but they center on the **Buffalo Café** and the **Kneadery**. Both are open for lunch as well. The **Kneadery** (726-9462) on Leadville Street has a cozy woodsy atmosphere. The champion bargain breakfast is found at the **Buffalo Café** (726-9795) with its Baldy Breakfast Special featuring pancakes, eggs, bacon and sausage for $3.95. **The Kitchen** (726-3856) has a dozen varieties of omelets, with pancakes, waffles and a selection of specials served in an airy southwestern pale-colored room. Don't expect any bargains here—prices just about match Sun Valley Lodge.

One more eatery we should mention: Directly across the street from the Warm Springs Lodge at the base of Baldy is a Ketchum institution, **Irving's Red Hot** stand, where you can get great hotdogs. "The Works" (a dog smothered in fixings and chips) for only $2 is a lunch bargain that can't be beat.

Special Dining Experiences

One evening dining adventure that should not be missed is the horse-drawn sleigh ride dinner at **Trail Creek Cabin**. The cozy rough-hewn cabin dates from 1937 and can be reached by sleigh, car or cross-country skis. For the sleigh ride, make reservations 72 hours in advance, but you can always check for open space; call 622-2135. The sleigh ride costs $15. Dinners are $16–$24, more or less. **Galena Lodge** (726-4010) also offers moonlight dinners in the warmth of a rustic lodge.

 ## Après-ski/nightlife

The **Boiler Room** at Sun Valley has the Mike Murphy comedy show for an $8 cover every afternoon at 5 p.m. A free jazz concert is every Friday at the **Galleria**. Check the schedule for *Sun Valley Serenade* and Warren Miller movies at the **Opera House** in Sun Valley starting at 5 p.m. And the **Duchin Room** in the Lodge has music starting at 5 p.m.

If you are staying in Warm Springs, wander over to the **Baldy Base Club** or **Apples** for good après-ski crowds.

At the western-bar-themed **Whiskey Jacques,** patrons can listen to live music and dance inside an authentic log building. **The Pioneer Saloon** is famous for its steaks, prime rib, and decorations (mounted elk and moose). The saloon gets very crowded very early on weekends.

Another popular spot is **The Casino**, so named because there used to be slot machines where the tables now stand (gambling is now illegal in this part of the country). It's something of a departure from the more intense nightclubs in the area, with the dance floor replaced by pool tables.

For more sedate and elegant night action try the **Duchin Room** at the Lodge, which features the Joe Foss Trio until 1 a.m.

The Sun Valley Wine Company has a wine cellar, reportedly the largest wine selection in Idaho and offers a light lunch and dinner menu. It is above the Ketchum state liquor store on Leadville Street. Choose a bottle of wine from its large inventory, then enjoy it in a quiet, conversation-oriented environment next to a fireplace.

The Mint belongs to none other than Bruce Willis, an occasional resident of this resort town. It opened in 1995 on Main Street in Hailey, 11 miles south of Sun Valley, and became an instant magnet because of Willis' ability to draw world-class bands to the establishment.

Remember—if you are staying in Sun Valley or Warm Springs and plan on partying in Ketchum, the KART bus system stops running at midnight, but A-1 Taxi and Baldy's Express Taxis are available until closing.

Other activities

Shopping: Opportunities are extensive. A few shops worth highlighting: The Toy Store, for unique and educational toys from around the globe; Barry J. Peterson Jewelers, for Limoges collectors' boxes, Lesäl ceramics and unique jewelry; The Country Cousin for low-priced accessories and gifts; and T. D. Bambino, where you can have fleece clothing custom-made.

You can pick up some great bargains on secondhand items at the Gold Mine Thrift Shop, 331 Walnut Ave. Because this supports the The Community Library in Ketchum, residents give their (sometimes barely) used clothing and sporting goods to this store. By the way, the library is a gem. It has an amazing regional history section

Art galleries are another center of Ketchum's cultural life. Twelve galleries are members of the Sun Valley Art Gallery Association (726-2602). They provide a beautiful brochure with a map and offer guided evening gallery walks about a dozen times during the year.

Snowmobiling is available through Mike Mulligan (726-9137). **The Sun Valley Athletic Club** (726-3664) is open to visitors with daily, weekly and monthly rates. It is a full club with child care, massage, aerobics, weights and swimming. **Ice skating** is available year-round on the Sun Valley Resort outdoor rink.

Sun Valley Heli-Ski (622-3108) offers backcountry ski adventures for all levels of skiers. **Soaring** or winter glider rides are available through Sun Valley Soaring (726-3054). **Ice fishing/fly fishing** is offered by Silver Creek Outfitters (726-5282) and Lost River Outfitters (726-1706).

Sun Valley Center For Arts and Humanities has performances and showings during the ski season. Call 726-9491 for a schedule or the Chamber of Commerce, 726-3423.

Getting there and getting around

By air: The closest airport is Friedman Memorial, 12 miles south in Hailey, served by Horizon Air and Delta's SkyWest Airlines. Weather sometimes closes it (the reliability rate improves nearly every season; last year, it was nearly 90 percent), but it cannot handle big jets. Most guests arrive by jet at Twin Falls, about 90 minutes away, or Boise, about 155 miles and 2.5 hours away.

Several properties provide transportation, or you can use one of the following companies, most of which will pick you up in Hailey, Twin Falls or Boise: A-1 Taxi, 726-9351; Baldy's Express Taxi, 720-2650; Mike Mulligan Luxury Limo, 726-5466; Town and Country Tours, 788-2012; or Sun Valley Express (800) 634-6539 or 342-7795.

By car: Sun Valley/Ketchum is 82 miles north of Twin Falls on Hwy. 75.

Getting around: You don't really need a car if you're staying near the KART bus routes, which link Sun Valley, Ketchum and Baldy about every 20 minutes. For schedule information, call 726-7140.

The Big Mountain

Montana

Summit elevation: **7,000 feet**
Vertical drop: **2,500 feet**
Base elevation: **4,500 feet**

Address: P.O. Box 1400
Whitefish, MT 59937
✆ **Area code:** 406
Ski area phone: 862-1900
Snow report: 862-7669
ⓘ **Toll-free reservations:** (800) 858-4157
E-mail: bigmtn@bigmtn.com
Internet: http://www.bigmtn.com

Expert:★★★★
Advanced:★★★★
Intermediate:★★★★★
Beginner:★★
Never-ever:★★★★

Number and types of lifts:
10—2 high-speed quads, 1 quad,
4 triples, 1 double and 2 surface lifts
Skiable acreage: 3,000 acres
Snowmaking: 3 percent
Uphill capacity: 13,800 per hour
Snowboarding: Yes, unlimited
Bed base: 1,500 on mountain
Nearest lodging: slopeside, hotels and condos
Resort child care: Yes, infants and older
Adult ticket, per day: $34-$40 (98/99 prices)
Dining:★★★
Apres-ski/nightlife:★★★★
Other activities:★★★

True ski-resort discoveries are getting harder to find. If you live in a state or province along the U.S.-Canadian border west of the Great Lakes, you probably already know about this spot with skiing that stretches on forever. You probably don't want us to tell anyone in the rest of either country about it. We understand, and of course we'll keep your secret.

If you are a skier who wants lots of terrain to explore and a no-fluff off-slope atmosphere, you should head for this aptly named ski resort tucked into the far northwest corner of Montana.

This is an area popular with Seattle, Calgary and northern Midwest skiers. Many hop on Amtrak's Empire Builder, which on its every-other-day run between Seattle and Chicago dumps a load of eager skiers in the town of Whitefish within sight of The Big Mountain's trails.

Though sometimes the resort and the community business leaders long to see their name in the various annual listings of top ski resorts (acreage-wise, it ranks in the top ten, maybe even top five, depending on how you count), most other times, they'd rather just keep it the Northwest's little secret. Many folks here are expatriates from other ski areas that were once as laid-back and unpretentious as The Big Mountain is now.

Everything is clean and comfortable, but you won't find concierges and valet parking. This is a down-home, comfortable place where a fur coat would look out of place except on a grizzly-bearded mountain man.

The ski area is eight miles from the town of Whitefish, up a winding road that can be a bit scary in bad weather. At the ski area base is a cluster of hotels and condo properties and a few restaurants and bars. In Whitefish there are more hotels, the best restaurants, shopping and the biggest variety of nightlife.

The weather here is a mix of the Rockies and Pacific Northwest maritime, called "inland maritime." It creates spectacular "snow ghosts," trees encased in many layers of frost and snow, at the summit. It also produces plenty of fantastic light powder, but without the sunshine you'll find in the southern Rockies. If you forget your sunscreen you'll probably survive, but don't forget your goggles. Pack your sunglasses too—sunny days do occur, and when they do, the skiing is spectacular. You'll want those sunglasses to see the seemingly endless view of the mountains of Glacier National Park as well as the Flathead Valley and the huge lake that dominates it.

Mountain layout

◆◆ **Expert** ◆ **Advanced:** If you can see it, you can ski it! Within the boundaries are 3,000 acres of sprawling terrain; another 1,000 acres is in the U.S. Forest Service permit area. The Big Mountain ski school offers free tours of the mountain at 10 a.m. daily (open to intermediates, too).

The main access to The Big Mountain is the high-speed quad, The Glacier Chaser, which moves skiers up 2,200 feet to the summit. If you ski straight ahead when you get off the chair you'll drop down the north slope, a mostly intermediate series of runs alternating with tree-studded steeps.

If you make a U-turn when you get off the Glacier Chaser you'll reach wide, well-groomed intermediate trails, surrounded by fields of powder and thousands of trees beckoning to advanced and expert skiers. Throughout this entire Good Medicine area skiers and boarders can choose how tight they want their trees, and they have plenty of opportunities to bail out onto the groomed trails. Locals also can direct you to Movie Land, which starts with dense trees and then opens for great steep tree skiing before ending on Easy Street.

For big-air fans, The Big Mountain has a cornice next to the Summit House. Runs from this cornice, and almost all skiing to the left of the high-speed quad, end up on Easy Street.

■ **Intermediate:** Go straight off The Glacier Chaser for the groomed runs under Chair 7, or make a U-turn to reach Toni Matt, The Big Ravine or MoeMentum (formerly North Bowl; named for Olympic downhill champ Tommy Moe, who trained on the run in his younger years), all perfect for power cruising with wide GS turns. Toni Matt, Inspiration and the Big Ravine provide top-to-bottom cruising.

Lower intermediates should make a few runs off Chair 2 or the T-bar before they try The Glacier Chaser. Chair 2's runs are equivalent in pitch to the blue runs off the front of the summit, but much shorter. This lower-mountain area is also lighted for night skiing. When you're ready to try the summit runs, try the ones down the North Slope first. The toughest part will be the upper part of MoeMentum, which can build formidable moguls by afternoon.

●● **Beginner:** Chair 3 is the best bet for beginners, though they may be frustrated at not being able to ski from the summit. (There's a green trail from the summit called Easy Street, but it has a few intermediate pitches.)

● **Never-ever:** Never-evers have an excellent learning area, separate from other skiers, on the gentle trails under Chair 6 (which costs nothing to ride, by the way).

Mountain rating

The ski patrol's generous out-of-bounds policy and the abundance of tree skiing make this a delight for expert and advanced skiers. Intermediates will like the resort's superb grooming and long cruisers. The learning area is one of the best. Where the mountain is a bit lacking is in advanced beginner and lower intermediate terrain. There's a little, but perhaps not enough to keep skiers and boarders at this level happy for four or more days.

Cross-country (98/99 prices)

The **Big Mountain Nordic Center** is adjacent to the Outpost Lodge (bottom of Chair 6) and has 15 km. of groomed trails (862-2946). Trail fees are $5 for ages 7 and older and free for anyone younger than 7. Downhill ski pass holders can use the cross-country trails free. Trail passes, maps and rentals are available at the Outpost Lodge or the Big Mountain Ski Shop in the base village. There is also lighted cross-country skiing and snowshoeing at this center.

Grouse Mountain Lodge (862-3000) in Whitefish has 15 km. of groomed cross-country trails and night skiing with 2.4 km. lighted.

The **Izaak Walton Inn** (888-5700), 62 miles east on Highway 2 (also an Amtrak flag stop), has 30 km. of groomed trails as well as guides who take skiers into the Glacier National Park wilderness. Guides for groups of two to four or more cost $60–$95 per person.

Glacier National Park provides a natural cross-country paradise. Here the unplowed park roads and trails provide kilometer after kilometer of ungroomed passages into the heart of the mountains. Check with the communications center (888-5441) or the park rangers for weather and snow conditions.

Snowboarding (98/99 prices)

Many magazines rate this area highly for snowboarding. Four members of the U.S. Snowboard Team call Whitefish home. The snowboard park has new hits, jumps and wave boxes. A halfpipe groomed with a Pipe Dragon is 350 feet long. Note: Boarders may have difficulty on powder days negotiating the cat track that leads back to the Glacier Chaser chair.

The rental shop (862-1995) has board and boots for $23 for a full day; $18 for half-day; $15 when you enroll in a two-hour group lesson (ages 8 and older) for $23.

Lessons (98/99 prices)

Group lessons: Half day, $23; full day, $38. Seniors 62 and older receive a 50 percent discount on group lessons.
Never-ever package: Lift ticket (Chairs 3 and 6), two-hour lesson and rentals, $33.

Private lessons: $55 per hour ($16 for each extra person); reservations required (862-2909). Discounts offered for multiple hours. Beginner private lessons are $95 for two hours.

Special programs: You can design your own 2.5-hour clinic with four friends—anything but aerials, the resort says. Cost is $32 per person. Daily two-hour afternoon lessons for bumps, steeps and powder (conditions permitting) are $23. Telemark and Nordic lessons are by appointment only, $23 each for two or more. A women's workshop and advanced skiing seminar are taught at select times. Call the ski school at 862-2909 for dates and prices.

Racing: A NASTAR course is open off Chair 3 Thursdays through Sundays 11 a.m.–2 p.m. Cost is $5 for two runs and $1 for each additional run.

Children's lessons: For ages 3–4, private "fundamentals" lessons are required. Cost is $22 for a half-hour lesson. Ages 5–6 have a one-hour lesson that costs $13.

Full day for older children includes five-hour lessons for $38 and half-day lessons for $23. Lift tickets are $15 (though a ticket is not needed on the novice lifts) and gear rental is $10. Lunch is optional and is an additional $7.

Child care (98/99 prices)

Ages: Newborns to 12 years.

Costs: Full day, 14 months and older, $36.50 including lunch. Full day for younger than 14 months is $50 ($26 for half day), not including lunch. The day-care facility, in the Alpine Lodge at the base of Chair 3, also is open three nights a week until 10 p.m. for babysitting at $6.25 per hour; $7.50 for infants up to 14 months. The facility has room for just three infants at a time, so make reservations far in advance.

Reservations: Required for infants and recommended for toddlers, 862-1999.

Lift tickets (98/99 prices)

	Adult	Junior (7-18)
One day	$40	$27
Three days	$114 ($38/day)	$81 ($27/day)
Five days	$170 ($34/day)	$135 ($27/day)

Who skis free: Children 6 and younger. Night skiing costs $12 for everyone, but is free with a day or multiday ticket. Chair 6 and the platter lift, which serve novice terrain, are free.

Who skis at a discount: Skiers 62 and older and college students pay the junior price.

Note: Day and multiday ticket holders may ride the Glacier Chaser to the Summit House for dinner without charge on select nights (the Glacier Chaser turns into a gondola for night riding). Other passengers headed for the summit at night pay $6.

A "Lower Lift" ticket valid on the lower mountain costs only $23 per day and may be upgraded to a full mountain lift pass if skiers change their minds.

Punch cards are available that allow skiers to pay only for lifts used. They are transferable. Ten runs cost $30. Fifteen runs are $40.

The Big Mountain frequent skier card costs $40—the first day is free and every additional day costs $28. But it must be purchased by October 31st.

Accommodations

The properties located at The Big Mountain village may all be reserved by calling (800) 858-4157. Lower rates are available before Christmas, in January and in April; higher rates apply in the last two weeks of December.

The following properties are at the mountain:

Anapurna Properties (406-862-3687 or 800-243-7547) is The Big Mountain's premier condominium facility, with studio to four-bedroom condos and chalets close to the lifts; most are ski-in/ski-out and have fireplaces. There's a hot tub and the mountain's only indoor pool, plus a grocery store. Rates range from about $120–$375.

Big Mountain Alpine Homes is the area's other condo and home management company, offering 28 units with kitchen facilities. Rates range from about $125–$425.

The **Kandahar Lodge** (406-862-6098) at the ski area looks like a mountain lodge should—log decor, spacious public areas and a soaring stone fireplace. The rooms are large and the food outstanding. A free shuttle takes guests to the base area and at the end of the day skiers can glide right to the door. Rates vary from $139 per night to $275.

The **Alpinglow Inn** (406-862-6966) lies at the center of the village. This lodging has beautiful views from the restaurant and perhaps the most convenient location for skiers. A recent remodeling stripped the rooms "down to the studs," which has made the Alpinglow rooms very attractive. Sauna, two outdoor hot tubs overlooking the valley, laundry facilities and gift shop on site. Rates start at $116 per room for two people. The American plan includes lodging, lifts and meals, and the Alpinglow is the only one on the mountain to offer such an all-inclusive plan that lets you know your vacation costs before you leave home.

The **Edelweiss** (406-862-5252 or 800-228-8260) is centrally located in the base area and has studio condos for about $133 a night and two-bedroom, two-bath condos going for about $265. Complimentary ski waxing and wine-and-cheese reception are offered to guests.

The **Hibernation House** (406-862-3511) is touted as the "friendliest lodge on the mountain." It is the least expensive, and has queen beds, private baths, large indoor Jacuzzi, laundry and a clean and inviting lobby. Rates start at $85.

A new group of condominiums, **Kintla Lodge** (800-858-5439), in now renting at the base of the mountain with outdoor hot tubs, sauna and underground parking.

Eight miles away in Whitefish is a variety of lodging. Many properties offer free transportation to and from the mountain, but be sure to ask when you make your reservation.

The **Quality Inn Pine Lodge** (406-862-7600 or 800-305-7463) boasts an indoor-outdoor pool with connecting swim channel, hot tub and free continental breakfast. Rates range from $57 to $180.

The **Grouse Mountain Lodge** (406-862-3000 or 800-321-8822) is the most comfortable and convenient hotel. Its rooms are spacious and a free shuttlebus takes guests to the mountain every morning. Cross-country skiing is right out the back door and downtown is within easy walking distance. Regular season double room rates are $92–$162.

Good Medicine Lodge (406-862-5488) is built of cedar timbers and has a rustic informal atmosphere. Rooms are decorated in a Western-Native American motif with fireplaces and solid wood furnishings. Rates for two people are $85–$135, including breakfast.

The **Garden Wall Inn** (406-862-3440 or 888-530-1700; website: http://www.wtp.net/go/gardenwall) is an antique-filled B&B only a block from the city shuttle. Rates are $85–$115, though winter specials begin at $79 per night with a full gourmet breakfast.

The **Best Western-Rocky Mountain Lodge** (800-862-2569) includes breakfast with rates starting at $65 per room. Another budget choice in town is the **Super 8 Motel**, beginning at $42 per room, double occupancy.

 **Dining**

The **Summit House** (862-2900) serves dinners on the top of the mountain on Wednesday and Saturday nights (days of the week may change for 98/99) from 6 to 8 p.m. The high-speed quad Glacier Chaser chairs are replaced by gondola cars to whisk diners up the mountain. Discount dinner coupons are available at the information center.

At the base of the ski area, the best food and service is at **The Hellroaring Saloon** (862-6364). This 50-year-old log-decor building served as the original base lodge. All food on the menu is homemade. It serves lunch and dinner.

Moguls Bar and Grill (862-1980) is at the base of Chair 2 and serves breakfast, lunch and dinner. For a special evening in the base village, try **Café Kandahar** (862-6098) where chef Andrew Topel serves fine French Provincial fare in an intimate setting. The restaurant has an extensive wine list.

The **Alpinglow Restaurant** (862-6966) has the best view of the Flathead Valley, while the **Bierstube** is an inexpensive spot for lunch or dinner. Try a Back Door Burger on the outdoor deck on a sunny day.

Old West Adventures (862-2434 or 862-2900) offers a 30-minute sleigh ride and dinner in an old roadhouse on Thursdays and Fridays. Family-style dinners, live music and cowboy poetry (far more entertaining than it sounds) top off the evening.

The bulk of restaurants are found in Whitefish. The finest dining in the area is at **Logan's** (862-3000) in the Grouse Mountain Lodge or across the street in the **Whitefish Lake Restaurant** (862-5285) at the golf course. The Szechuan shrimp pasta is marvelous. **Jimmy Lee's** (852-5303) is the recommended Chinese restaurant, but for local color, wood-fired pizza and great steaks try **Truby's** (862-4979). **The Glacier Grande** (862-9400) combines nightlife with Southwest dinners. **Dos Amigos** (862-9994) is a basic Tex-Mex spot with a fine selection of imported beers.

Locals and tourists sip espresso at the **Swiftcreek Café** (862-8186) or **The Buffalo Café** (862-2833). If you can get a seat and listen a bit you'll hear about everything happening in town. At the latter spot, try the Buffalo Pie, layers of hashbrowns, ham, cheese and poached eggs, or order the Cinnamon Swirl French Toast. It's open for lunch as well. Two spots to try for a lighter breakfast are **Whitefish Bagel Company** (862-6383) or the **Trailhead Deli & Coffee House** (862-9599). Microbrew fans can head for the new **Great Northern Brewing Company** on Main Street. It also serves food.

 ## Après-ski/nightlife

If you enjoy a let-it-loose style of après-ski and nighttime fun, The Big Mountain has one of the continent's best après-ski bars, **The Bierstube** at the ski area base. Hundreds of ski-club T-shirts (some quite risqué) hang from the rafters; owner Gary Elliott has boxes of 'em and rotates them every so often. Among the various pranks and ceremonies is the Frabert Award, presented each week to the employee or visitor who commits the biggest goof-up. Other pranks are legendary, but why ruin the fun for those of you who are Bierstube virgins? Ask for your souvenir ring, in gold or silver. When ski clubs are in town and The Bierstube has a live band, the dancing goes full-blast until closing.

The Hellroaring Saloon serves some of the best après-ski nachos anywhere. Best deal: if you buy a Hellroaring baseball cap you get free beer every day you wear it to the bar. Also on the mountain, **Moguls Bar and Grille** has entertainment nightly.

It's worth a visit to the **Palace Bar** on Central Avenue in Whitefish just to see its turn-of-the-century carved mahogany bar. **The Great Northern Bar and Grill** on Central Avenue offers live music from Thursday to Saturday and acoustic open-mike on Tuesday. Locals come for the burgers and wide selection of microbrewery beers and stay for the music.

Having all the Central Avenue bars lined up makes it easy to check out the scene and decide where you want to set up camp. Choose from **Glacier Grande, The Remington, Bulldog Saloon, Casey's** or **Truby's,** all notable in their own way, and a good time when you're cruising for rock or country music and drinks.

For more mellow evenings try the drinks and the band at **Logans** in the Grouse Mountain Lodge. For a real cowboy evening, complete with live foot-stomping music and longneck beer bottles you can slip in your back pockets, head to the **Blue Moon Nite Club** in Columbia Falls at the intersection of Highways 2 and 40.

Other activities

Shopping: Quite limited at the base area. Whitefish's Central Avenue has many art galleries and stores that stock Western clothing, jewelry and crafts. Montana Coffee Traders, on Highway 93 south of town, has many Montana food gift items, such as huckleberry syrup.

Near the ski area, Old West Adventures has **sleigh rides** Tuesday through Sunday, 5 to 7 p.m. You ride through the forests to an Old West roadhouse where hot drinks are served. Call 862-2900 for reservations. Downtown in Whitefish sleigh rides leave the Grouse Mountain Lodge for a 20-minute ride to a camp near Lost Coon Lake. Call 862-3000 for reservations.

Snowmobiling is a favorite pastime of Montanans, so a variety of guide services are available. Canyon Creek Cat House (800-933-5133) is in the nearby town of Columbia Falls and offers direct access to more than 200 miles of groomed trails. Contact the Flathead Convention and Visitors Association at (800) 543-3105 for additional guide services. Snowmobiles also may be rented at the summit of The Big Mountain, from which several trails leave.

Snowcat powder skiing is also offered in areas of the mountain not yet served by lifts. Snowcat tours are four hours and cost $40 per person (that's on top of the regular lift ticket) with four or more people; call 862-2909 for more information.

Tubing is offered off Chair 6.

The Big Mountain has a terrific information center in the base village where you can find out more about other activities. Call 862-2900 (you also can make dinner reservations through this number).

Getting there and getting around

By air: Glacier Park International Airport is in Kalispell, 19 miles south of the resort, served by Delta, Horizon Air and Northwest airlines. Call Flathead Glacier Transportation (892-3390) for ground transportation.

By car: The Big Mountain, eight miles from the town of Whitefish, at the junction of Hwys. 2 and 93. Whitefish RV Park is on Hwy. 93 south.

By train: Amtrak's Empire Builder stops in Whitefish four times a week from Seattle and Portland to the west and from Chicago and Minneapolis to the east. Kids ride free. Call (800) USA-RAIL (872-7245) for information.

Getting around: If you stay and play at the mountain, you won't need a car. Whitefish Area Rapid Transit (WART), has five daily runs between town and the mountain. That works if you're staying in Whitefish and riding the bus to ski, but it's impossible for mountain lodgers who want to party late at night in town (the last run back to the mountain is about 5:30 p.m.). Taxi service is available, however.

Telephone area code: 406

Big Sky
Montana

Summit elevation: **11,150 feet**
Vertical drop: **4,180 feet**
Base elevation: **6,970 feet**

Address: P.O. Box 160001
Big Sky, MT 59716
✆ **Area code:** 406
Ski area phone (hotel guest calls and switchboard): 995-5000
Snow report: 995-5900
ⓘ **Toll-free reservations:** (800) 548-4486
Fax: 995-5002
Internet: http://www.bigskyresort.com

Expert:★★★★★
Advanced:★★★★
Intermediate:★★★★
Beginner:★★
Never-ever:★★

Number and types of lifts: 15–1 aerial tram, 1 four-passenger gondola, 3 high-speed quads, 1 quad, 3 triples, 3 doubles and 3 surface lifts
Acreage: 3,500 skiable acres
Snowmaking: 10 percent of trails
Uphill capacity: 18,000 per hour
Snowboarding: Yes, unlimited
Bed base: 4,250
Nearest lodging: slopeside, hotel
Resort child care: Yes, infants and older
Adult ticket, per day: $44-$48 (98/99)
Dining:★★★
Apres-ski/nightlife:★★
Other activities:★★

Big Sky, with its impressive Matterhorn-shaped peak scraping the heavens at 11,166 feet, is a serious skier's mountain, bare bones and low on frills. Don't expect valet service from the parking-lot attendant, luxury day lodges or other fancy amenities. You can expect spectacular scenery, friendly locals, a laid-back atmosphere, and plenty of challenging terrain.

A seven-year building boom has seen Big Sky transformed from an intermediate mountain into one that also will challenge high-ability skiers. Big Sky has more than doubled its lift capacity in the last four years, which has opened a lot of variable expert terrain.

In 1995 Big Sky added an aerial tram with two 15-passenger cars to the 11,150-foot level on Lone Peak. The Lone Peak Tram opened terrain that is tough, with pitches averaging 28 degrees. If you get to the top and find that the chutes, couloirs and steeps are over your head, no problem—admire the views of the nearby Spanish Peaks Wilderness area and ride back down.

Big Sky is a true destination resort, far from large urban areas, yet an hour from the nearest jet airport. It has a very European feel. Ski school director Hans Schernthaner is from Austria, and each year he brings in English-speaking Europeans to teach. And lift tickets work just like computerized systems in the Alps.

Big Sky now attracts more than a quarter of a million skier visits. However, they are all swallowed by the 3,500-acre terrain. A big daily turnout is 4,000, meaning short lines for the lifts. And nearly every visitor spends at least a day in Yellowstone, only an hour away.

Mountain layout

◆◆ **Expert** ◆ **Advanced:** Ever since the Lone Peak Tram went in, the runs from its summit have become the test of who is an expert and who wants to be. Fortunately, if you decide once you're on top that you're in the latter category, you can ride the tram back down. Every run from the top is rated double-black diamond.

Just below the peak's chutes and steeps is the expansive bowl area, in the heart of Lone Peak. Above-treeline slopes beckon advanced skiers and snowboarders for untouched powder. You'll find steep pitches and wide-open terrain on the bowl's South Wall.

The more adventurous can register with the ski patrol and test their skills in A-Z Chutes, the Pinnacles and the Big Couloir, all out of bounds. Out-of-bounds skiing is permitted, but only with the right rescue equipment. If you want to try this terrain, you have to take a transceiver, a shovel and a partner.

Experts also should head to the vast area on Lone Mountain's north side, where many locals ski. The Challenger chair climbs 1,750 steep vertical feet to open hair-raising in-bounds terrain—some of the toughest in-bounds skiing in the country. Steep, long pitches drop down Big Rock Tongue, north-facing bowls greet skiers in Nashville Basin and trees pepper narrow chutes on Little Tree and Zucchini Patch.

Bump enthusiasts may be a little disappointed. Except for Mad Wolf and Africa, both on Andesite, Big Sky doesn't get enough skiers to carve big moguls.

■ **Intermediate:** As recently as eight years ago, Big Sky was considered an intermediate mountain. Some of the blue trails are kind and rolling, but others—such as the blues in the Shedhorn area—lean toward black. Not all the blue trails are groomed, and some have cat-track runouts or are simply too short.

On Lone Mountain, try the runs under the gondola and new Swift Current high-speed quad (which replaced the second gondola). Also try the terrain off the Iron Horse Quad.

On Andesite, skis run fast and long on Big Horn, Elk Park and Ambush. Fine-tune your techniques on the manicured slopes of Tippy's Tumble or Silver Knife on Andesite, or Lobo Calamity Jane or Upper Morning Star on Lone Mountain.

●● **Beginner:** The south side of Andesite Mountain is great for beginners because of the wide, gentle slopes and because it gets a lot of sun. They can enjoy runs such as Sacajawea, El Dorado and Ponderosa from Andesite's Southern Comfort triple chair. Fewer hot shots ski on Andesite, a comfort to those who get unnerved when someone passes closely at high speed.

On Lone Mountain, gentle rollers such as Mr. K, White Wing and Lone Wolf are reached via the gondola or the Explorer Lift. Mr. K is one of two runs (the other is blue-square Calamity Jane) that get high traffic as the lifts close down for the day.

● **Never-ever:** Big Sky has two surface lifts, a tow and a Poma lift, at Lone Mountain's base. Though not physically isolated from the rest of the terrain, the learning area is away from the high traffic pattern until the end of the day.

Mountain rating

Big Sky is excellent for most skiers and snowboarders. However, it doesn't have vast beginner terrain. Skiers we've talked to rate Big Sky a half-trail-rating higher than what's on the map: greens tilt toward blue, blues get a little navy, and blacks are solid black. Big Sky gets high marks for no lift lines, magnificent scenery and grooming that isn't overdone.

Cross-country

Nationally acclaimed **Lone Mountain Guest Ranch** (995-4644; 800-514-4644) offers 65 km. of international-caliber Nordic skiing for all levels, with groomed and skating lanes. The trail system winds through open meadows and forested canyons.

Lone Mountain Ranch teams with Alpenguide Tours of West Yellowstone to offer a variety of backcountry skiing, including snowcat tours into the interior of Yellowstone, America's most beloved national park, to view its winter wonders. Tours also are available into the Spanish Peaks.

Deluxe cozy cabins with fireplace and full bath can be rented for a week, with all meals, trail pass and evening programs for $1,250–$2,500, based on the group and cabin size. The Ranch has a Nordic shop with apparel, equipment and mementos. Trail pass is $10 for adults; children 12 and younger ski free; half-day tickets available, as are lessons.

You can rent **snowshoes** from the Lone Mountain Guest Ranch or Grizzly Outfitters (995-2939) for $8–$10 per day.

Snowboarding

No restrictions, and the resort has group and private lessons, rentals, repairs, a natural halfpipe and a terrain park.

Lessons (98/99 prices)

Group lessons: Half-day, $31, ski or snowboard, with discounts for multiple half-day sessions.

Never-ever package: Tow ticket, rentals, lesson, $46.

Private lessons: $77 per hour, with additional skiers paying extra and multiple-hour discounts. A private snowboard or telemark lesson is $55. Guide services are $165 for half-day; $275 for a full day.

Special programs: Advanced clinics concentrate on Lone Peak's steeps and tackle moguls, powder or other conditions du jour.

Racing: The race course, located on Ambush, is $5 for two runs; $2 each additional run.

Children's lessons: For ages 4-14. Full day is $63 without lunch, which is available at an extra charge. Half-day is $40.

For information on lessons, call 995-5743.

Child care (98/99 prices)

Ages: 6 months and older.

Costs: $65 for a full day, $50 a half day for ages 6-18 months; and $55 for a full day, $40 for a half day for 18 months and older. A full day of skiing and day care for ages 4-6 is $80.

Reservations: Call 995-2335. Hours are 8:30 a.m. to 4 p.m. Immunizations records are required. Reservations are suggested for all child care services and parents will need to bring some things, so call ahead.

Lift tickets (98/99 prices)

	Adult	Juniors (11-16)*
One day	$48	$40
Three days	$138 ($46/day)	$120 ($40/day)
Five days	$220 ($44/day)	$200 ($40/day)

Who skis free: Two children (up to age 10) ski free per paying adult, good every day of the season.

Who skis at a discount: 70 and older ski for half price. Also, college students with ID can ride lifts at the junior rate.

Accommodations

Big Sky is divided into three areas spanning nine miles—the Mountain Village, the Meadow Village and the Canyon. The farther you are from the lifts, the less you generally pay. These areas are serviced by a free shuttle system during the winter. A good starting point is **Big Sky Central Reservations,** (800) 548-4486.

In the Mountain Village:

At the center of the Mountain Village are the **Huntley Lodge** and **Shoshone Condominium Hotel** (800-548-4486 or 406-995-5000). The Shoshone is a luxury ski-in/ski-out hotel with condo-type units, lap pool, health club, steam bath and more. Rates are $264–$554. The lodge has an outdoor pool, two Jacuzzis, sauna, workout room, game room and more. Rates are $160–$350.

Condos are available through Big Sky Central Reservations, too. If you want luxury, try **Snowcrest, Beaverhead and Arrowhead** with three and four bedrooms at $362–$938. Moderate two- and three-bedroom units are at **Skycrest** (underground parking, rates $306–$521) and **Stillwater** (studios and two-bedroom units, $117–$383).

Golden Eagle Condominium Rental (800-548-4488) has units at Skycrest (on the shuttle system), Bighorn (slopeside two-bedroom units at $250) and Hill (an eight-minute walk from the lifts; $105–$130 for a studio, with or without loft).

In the Meadow Village (six miles away):

River Rock Lodge (800-995-9966) is a "boutique-style European hotel" with stone and log construction and beautiful interior decor. Its 29 rooms have rates of about $95–$120, including continental breakfast.

The Golden Eagle Lodge (800-548-4488) offers budget-minded travelers clean, basic rooms that have been renovated and expanded, and a full restaurant and bar. Rates are about $40–$65.

Triple Creek Realty and Management Co. (800-543-4362) manages several condo complexes here, including Hidden Village, units set in the forest with in-house Jacuzzis and garage at $275–$350; Park, with head-on views of Lone Peak at $185–$280; and several others. **Golden Eagle Condominium Rental** (800-548-4488) has many condos on the cross-country trail system, and private homes, for $150–$400.

Also contact **Big Sky Condominium Management** (406-995-4560) or **River Rock Accommodations Management** (800-995-9966) for slopeside or Meadow Village accommodations.

Telephone area code: 406

In the Canyon (three miles from the Meadow Village, nine miles from the lifts, in the beautiful Gallatin River Canyon):

Buck's T-4 Lodge (800-822-4484), Big Sky's Best Western hotel, has two pool-size outdoor Jacuzzis, a large stone fireplace and a restaurant that specializes in wild game (see *Dining*). Rooms are about $69–$99; kitchenettes for $125–$150.

The Rainbow Ranch Lodge (406-995-4132), is a stone's throw from the Gallatin River. A luxurious lodge with a western-ranch style, it has 12 rooms with private baths, and an excellent bar and restaurant. Breakfast and dinner included in the $45–$75 rate (for two people).

Budget accommodations ($65 or less) include the **Corral Motel** (406-995-4249) and the **Cinnamon Lodge** (406-995-4253), the latter with RV hookups for $15–$20.

 ## Dining

In the Mountain Village:

Huntley Lodge (995-5783) is known for its fine dining—breakfast and dinner—and one of Montana's largest wine selections. In the Mountain Mall, **Dante's Inferno** has tableside slope views and Italian cuisine, and **M.R. Hummers** is known for its baby back ribs. **Black Bear Bar 'n' Grill** is a casual spot for breakfast or dinner. It has a full bar and is popular with the younger budget-conscious crowd. Other lunch or snack spots: **Mountain Top** for pizza, **Scissorbills Bar and Grill** at the base of Silverknife ski run, or **Sun Dog Cafe** for espresso and a muffin.

In the Meadow Village:

Intimate candlelight, linen service and sunset views of Lone Peak await at **First Place** (995-4244), behind the post office. It features American and Continental cuisine and famous desserts. **Edelweiss** (995-4665) has excellent Austrian and German food. **Rocco's** (995-4200) has Mexican and Italian food with a full bar.

Lone Mountain Ranch Dining Room (995-2782) has a quiet, smoke-free environment in rustic elegance. Sleigh-ride dinners are offered here for about $50 per adult and $45 for kids. Call ahead as space is limited (995-2783). In the Westfork meadow, there's Guinness on tap and terrific pesto pizza at **Uncle Milkies Pizza and Subs** (995-2900). Across the road, **Allgoods Bar and Grill** (995-2750) serves up hickory-smoked baby back ribs, chicken and pork, along with homemade stews and burgers. Breakfast and dinner daily and a pool table, darts and poker.

In the Gallatin Canyon:

Buck's T-4 Restaurant (995-4111) is the area's oldest and most popular dining establishment. Its specialties are wild game, Montana beef, veal and seafood. There's an extensive wine list and an original rustic bar built in 1946. If you're staying at the mountain or the meadow, ride the free shuttle. **The Rainbow Ranch Lodge** (995-4132) has intimate dining overlooking the Gallatin River. Steaks, seafood, pasta and terrific salads at $15 and up for entrées. This is a No Smoking facility.

Après-ski/nightlife

First check Big Sky's local newspaper, *The Lone Peak Lookout*, which has entertainment listings.

The hub of night activity is the Mountain Village. Happy hour kicks off in **Chet's Bar** in the Huntley Lodge, with the Crazy Austrian show (just go see it). Chet's also has poker games (legal in Montana). You can find a nice atmosphere and live music on weekends at **Lolo's**, downstairs in the Mountain Mall.

In the canyon, check out the **Buck's T-4** game room, with pool tables, foosball and video games. Locals like the **Corral** and **The Half Moon Saloon**, with darts and pool.

Other activities

Shopping: The Mountain Mall has shops and boutiques. Plum Logo has Montana-made gifts and Big Sky T-shirts and souvenirs. The Lone Spur in the Shoshone Condo complex is a good spot for high-quality western clothing, jewelry and gifts. In the Meadow Village, shop at Tick Ridge Traders, Grizzly Outfitters, Willow Boutique and By Word of Mouth (which has a great wine selection and prices). Moose Rack Books has new, out-of-print and rare books in two locations, one at the mountain and another in the canyon.

Poker is legal gambling in Montana, and nightly games are available. Ask around if this is your kind of fun. Just about all of the other activities are of the outdoor variety:

Snowmobiling in Yellowstone National Park is a major attraction. Most snowmobile shops offer a 10 percent discount with a Big Sky lift ticket and provide bus service from the resort and West Yellowstone. For information, Rendezvous Snowmobile Rentals, (800) 426-7669 or 646-9564; Snowmobile Yellowstone, (800) 221-1151; Yellowstone Adventures, (800) 231-5991 or 646-7735; West Yellowstone, (800) 541-7354 or 646-9695. To snowmobile closer to Big Sky call Canyon Rentals (995-4540) a half a mile south of the Big Sky entrance.

Dogsled rides are offered by Spirit of the North Dog Adventures (995-4644). **Sleigh rides** with dinner are available from Lone Mountain Ranch (995-2783) or 320 Ranch (995-4283). **Snowshoe tours** are available through Walking Stick Tours (995-4265).

Winter fishing on the Gallatin River is available through Gallatin Riverguides (995-2290) or East Slope Anglers (995-4369), who have licenses, equipment rentals and supplies.

Yellowstone National Park is a big attraction, and yes, it's open in winter. The drive south along Hwy. 191 follows the Gallatin River, where much of the fly-fishing, coming-of-age movie, "A River Runs Through It," was filmed.

Getting there and getting around

By air: Northwest, Horizon Air, Aspen Mountain Air, SkyWest and Delta fly into Bozeman Gallatin Field Airport, an hour from the resort. The 4X4 Stage shuttles passengers between the airport, the resort and West Yellowstone. Call 388-6404.

By car: The resort is 45 miles south of Bozeman (and 50 miles north of West Yellowstone) on Highway 191 along the Gallatin River.

Getting around: If you stay at the Mountain Village, a car is unnecessary unless you plan to do a lot of sightseeing. A free shuttlebus runs between the Big Sky villages 7 a.m.–11 p.m. starting in mid-December through the winter. In the past, visitors we checked with complained that the shuttle took an hour to complete its circuit; however, we're told that the service improved quite a bit in the 97/98 season.

Ski Santa Fe

New Mexico

Summit elevation: 12,000 feet
Vertical drop: 1,650 feet
Base elevation: 10,350 feet

Address: 1210 Luisa, #5
Santa Fe, NM 87505
✆ **Area code:** 505
Ski area phone: 982-4429
Snow report: 983-9155
ⓘ **Toll-free reservations:** (800) 776-7669
Within New Mexico: (505) 983-8200
Fax: 984-8682
E-mail: info@skisantafe.com
Internet: http://www.skisantafe.com
Expert:★★
Advanced:★★★
Intermediate:★★★
Beginner:★★★★
Never-ever:★★★

Number and types of lifts: 7–1 high-speed quad, 1 triple, 2 doubles and 3 surface lifts
Acreage: 550
Snowmaking: 30 percent
Uphill capacity: 7,300 skiers per hour
Snowboarding: Yes, unlimited
Bed base: 4,500 in Santa Fe
Nearest lodging: About 15 miles away
Resort child care: Yes, 2 months and older
Adult ticket, per day: $33–$40 (98/99 prices)

Dining:★★★★★
Apres-ski/nightlife:★★
Other activities:★★★

Here in The Land of Enchantment you can ski on a 12,000-foot peak just 16 miles from the margaritas and blue corn enchiladas at Maria's Restaurant in Santa Fe. When you take the bright sunlight of the high desert, fresh powder snow and a skier-friendly mountain, then add pre-Columbian Indian Pueblos, Spanish architecture, art galleries, and top it with a unique regional cuisine, you have the savory mix that is Santa Fe.

Santa Fe (elevation 7,000 feet) offers interesting contradictions. It is old and new, high mountains and flat desert, with cool winters that surprise out-of-staters who think of New Mexico as hot and dry. Skiing in this state is unlike anywhere else on the continent. To get a more foreign-feeling ski vacation, you'd need a passport.

Some skiers think Taos Ski Valley is the only New Mexico ski area worth a long plane ride—not so. If your main interest is racking up vertical feet, then by all means head for Taos, but Santa Fe (just an hour north of Albuquerque) is a better destination for those who prefer a balanced ski-and-sightseeing vacation. Santa Fe is one of the most culturally fascinating cities in the United States. It is loaded with great restaurants, superior art galleries and things to do, and the ski area is a lot bigger than most people imagine.

Founded by Spanish conquistadors in 1610, 10 years before the pilgrims landed in Plymouth, Santa Fe is North America's oldest capital city. It is rich in history and culture, but of a different kind from mining-town ski areas.

When the Spanish arrived, the area was already populated with 100,000 Native Americans, who spoke nine languages and lived in some 70 multi-storied adobe pueblos, some still inhabited today. For the next 150 years Santa Fe grew as a frontier military base and trading center, where Spanish soldiers and missionaries, Anglo mountain men and Native Americans mixed. In 1846, during the Mexican War, New Mexico was ceded to the United States. Santa Fe, at the end of the Santa Fe Trail, became a frontier town, hosting the likes of Billy the Kid and Kit Carson.

In the early part of this century, Santa Fe took on a new flavor. It became a magnet for men and women of the arts and literature. D.H. Lawrence, Ezra Pound, Willa Cather, Jack London and H.L. Mencken either lived or vacationed here. Artists Edward Hopper and Marsden Hartley spent time here, and Santa Fe was home to Robert Henri, George Bellows, Randall Davey, and Aaron Copland. Today this city of 60,000 is home to one of the world's premier art colonies, and it boasts a renowned opera company, which only plays in the summer.

Mountain layout

Ski Santa Fe sits 16 miles north of the city. Though the mountain is known as a day-area destination for Santa Fe and Albuquerque skiers, out-of-town visitors will find a surprising amount of terrain.

All the mountain amenities such as restaurants, ski rentals, child care, ski school and ticket sales are at the base of the mountain just a few steps from the parking lot.

◆◆ **Expert** ◆ **Advanced:** For the most part, the mountain's expert terrain is to the left of the Tesuque Peak chair. With fresh snow, locals go first to Columbine, Big Rocks and Wizard. These runs all check in as very steep, for advanced skiers only. Roadrunner is the expert bump run directly under the Tesuque chair. Tequila Sunrise and Easter Bowl have the best glade skiing.

On the far side of the mountain, reached by the Santa Fe Super Chief quad, Muerte and Defasio have isolated trail skiing for advanced skiers. Middle and Lower Broadway give the same thing to intermediate skiers.

While there are hopes to overcome environmental objections and put in a lift in the Big Tesuque Bowl, for the moment the intrepid ski into this area via Cornice (once skiers leave Cornice, they are outside the ski area's permitted boundary). Big Tesuque skiers find natural powder, bowl skiing and trees. The bowls empty onto the area's entrance road, three miles below the base area. You must then hitchhike back up to the base area. First-timers should go with a local who knows this area: it's genuine backcountry, it's big and people occasionally get lost.

■ **Intermediate:** On a fresh powder day (once a week on average), local intermediates and advanced skiers head straight for the Tesuque Peak triple chair, to 12,000 feet and the top of the mountain. To the right of the lift (as the trail map reads) is Gayway, a glorious groomed pitch with several spicy turns, that gives new meaning to the term spectacular scenery. On a clear day, you almost get the feeling of flying, thanks to the 150-mile vista as the trail drops away. Parachute, which parallels Gayway, is a groomed black diamond with a somewhat steeper pitch.

●● **Beginner:** This level will be happiest on the lower part of the mountain, on the wide boulevard of Easy Street. Lower intermediates will find more challenges and a slightly steeper pitch on Open Slope and Upper and Lower Midland; if they're feeling adventurous, they should try Lower Burro for an exhilarating, winding trip through the trees on a mild pitch that even lower intermediates can handle.

● **Never-ever:** Good terrain at the mountain's base. Our only complaint is that the same runs are used by everyone else who is trying to get back home at day's end. Our advice: Take a morning lesson (or a series of them), practice in the afternoon and quit early.

Mountain rating

Many people think Ski Santa Fe is a small, gentle day area. It's not. It definitely has enough terrain to keep a skier of any level happy for two to three days. Its gladed runs are great, though short; and Big Tesuque Bowl when skiable, is an adventure. Santa Fe could use an isolated beginner area; as noted, its green-circle trails are right in the line of traffic coming back to the base. The ski area realizes this shortcoming and would very much like to add a 75-acre beginner area; however, environmental activists are fighting Ski Santa Fe's master plan, which now is moving slowly through the U.S. Forest Service approval process.

Combined with Santa Fe's outstanding sightseeing opportunities, this is an excellent destination for skiers who don't want to be on the mountain every day (or all day). One warning: Ski Santa Fe has one of the highest lift-served elevations in the nation—12,000 feet on top, 10,350 at the base. If you're susceptible to altitude problems, take note.

Cross-country

Santa Fe has no groomed or tracked trails. However, there are maintained backcountry trails in the surrounding Santa Fe National Forest. Aspen Vista Road, two miles below the ski area, is a popular and moderately difficult seven-mile trail. Black Canyon Campground, eight miles up the ski road, is a popular area for beginners. Maps and specific information on trail and snow conditions in the Santa Fe National Forest are available from the National Forest Service at 988-6940. For ski area information only, call 984-0606.

Snowboarding

Depending on conditions, Santa Fe opens an "alternative terrain" area for snowboarders. The area also hosts workshops, daily lessons and competitions.

Lessons (98/99 prices)

Group lessons: Adult lessons cost $27. An upgrade to two sessions is $17.

Never-ever package: Two group lessons, beginner lift and rentals is $56 for skiers, $73 for snowboarders.

Private lessons: $63 per hour; discounts for multiple hours.

Special programs: Among them are a women's program, segregated classes for those 50 and older, mogul clinics, telemark lessons and powder workshops. Prices vary, and not all are offered every week. Check with the ski school at 982-4429.

Racing: Coin-op and NASTAR are each Thursday through Sunday. Racing clinics are offered through the ski school.

Children's ski school: Ages 3–9, all day including lunch, $59 (add $12 for rental equipment). Half-day programs are $43. Four-year-olds have half-day lessons, with play activities in the afternoon, while the older children have morning and afternoon ski lessons.

Child care (98/99 prices)

Ages: 3 months to 3 years.
Costs: All-day program costs $48; $36 half day.
Reservations: Required; call (505) 988-9639. Only full-day packages for child care are sold during holiday periods. Ages 3 and 4 who are completely toilet-trained can register for Snowplay, a program that is "an introduction to the skiing environment." This program, which includes indoor and outdoor activities, is $55 all day and $39 half day.

Lift tickets (98/99 prices)

	Adult	Child (Up to 12)
One day	$40	$27
Three days	$112 ($37+/day)	$75 ($25/day)
Five days	$178 ($35+/day)	$120 ($24/day)

Who skis free: Skiers aged 72 and older and kids shorter than 46 inches in ski boots.
Who skis at a discount: A ticket valid only on the beginner lift is $20. Ages 62–71 pay the child rate.

Accommodations

Ski Santa Fe has no base lodging, but even if it did, you'd want to be in Santa Fe for dining, shopping and the museums. More than 70 hotels, motels, inns, condominiums and B&Bs serve Santa Fe visitors. Winter is low season in this region, but visitors seem to be catching on to this, and prices have risen from bargain to a moderate level during the past few years. Expect to pay about $75–$110 a day, per person, for a ski-stay package at one of the many hotels on Cerrillos Road; and 25 to 50 percent more downtown. Basically, the closer to the Plaza you are, the more you'll shell out for lodging.

Lift-and-lodging packages are the best deal; call **Santa Fe Central Reservations** at (800) 776-7669 or 983-8200 or the **Santa Fe Visitors Bureau** at (800) 777-2489 (800-777-CITY). Downtown is where the best restaurants, shopping and nightlife are concentrated, although we do recommend a few great dining options outside the Plaza area.

La Fonda Hotel (800-523-5002; 982-5511) is the historic place to stay. An inn of one sort or another has been on this site for 300 years (Billy the Kid worked in the kitchen here washing dishes). The current La Fonda incarnation was built in the 1920s. If you don't stay, at least stroll through and take a look—they don't make them like this anymore.

The way they make them now is across the Plaza from La Fonda. **The Inn of the Anasazi** (800-688-8100 or 988-3030) is the politically correct place to stay. Before building, the owner consulted with Native American holy men. The hotel's restaurants use vegetables grown by local organic farmers. Leftovers are given to a homeless shelter and everything is recycled. The Southwestern decor and furnishings are immaculate. The dining room is very pleasant and the menu selections enjoyable. However, this is also a very expensive place to stay ($200 and up).

Next door, the **Hotel Plaza Real** (800-279-7325 or 988-4900) is convenient and comfortable. Of the 56 hotel units, 44 are suites with fireplaces. An ample continental breakfast is included. We also enjoyed the adobe **Inn on the Alameda** (800-506-9206 or 984-2121) which is handy to Canyon Road and offers a continental breakfast. In a village of adobe cottages,

Telephone area code: 505

most featuring their own Indian kiva fireplaces, **La Posada** (800-727-5276 or 986-0000) is a short walk from the Plaza. On the grounds is the Staab House, a Victorian mansion serving as the restaurant.

Excellent B&Bs are **Adobe Abode** (983-3133), **Alexander's Inn** (986-1431), the spacious **Dancing Ground of the Sun** (800-645-5673 or 986-9797), the **Grant Corner Inn** (983-6678), the intimate **Inn of the Animal Tracks** (988-1546) and the classy **Water Street Inn** (984-1193).

Other accommodations to consider are the historic **Hotel St. Francis** (800-529-5700 or 983-5700) and the **Hotel Santa Fe** (800-825-9876 or 982-1200), partly owned by the Picuris Pueblo. Families should try the **El Rey Inn** (800-521-1349 or 982-1931), **Garrett's Desert Inn** (800-888-2145 or 982-1851), the **Campanilla Compound** condominiums (800-828-9700 or 988-7585), and the **Otra Vez** condos (988-2244). There is also a **Hilton** (800-336-3676 or 988-2811), although it is not very interesting. **El Dorado** (800-955-4455 or 988-4455) is the city's largest hotel with 219 rooms.

Many of the chain hotels, such as **Comfort Inn, Days Inn, Holiday Inn** and **Hampton Inn,** have adopted the local adobe architectural style and are a little less expensive and conveniently located on Cerillos Road, handy for getting to the ski area but out of walking range for downtown. The El Rey Inn, one of our previous recommendations for families, is in this area.

 ## Dining

On the mountain, skiers have two choices. **La Casa Cafeteria** in the base lodge called La Casa Mall, and **Totemoff's Bar and Grill** at the base of the Tesuque Peak Chair. La Casa, with a French chef, offers a variety of options including a pasta bar and a daily special such as fresh salmon with lemon tarragon. Its breakfast burrito is wicked good, but only for brave palates. Totemoff's features burgers, salads, pasta, cocktails and a sun deck.

Back in the city, Santa Fe cooks and you're in for a treat. Including fast food, Santa Fe has nearly 200 places to strap on the feed bag. From traditional New Mexican cuisine to steaks and seafood, Santa Fe has more food variety than you could consume in a year and far more good restaurants than we have room to recommend. Per capita it's one of the greatest dining cities in the country.

Pasqual's (121 Don Gaspar; 983-9340) is highly recommended for breakfast, but it's good anytime for delicious and beautifully presented New Mexican cuisine. Call for dinner reservations or expect to wait a long time. If you want to meet people, ask to be seated at the communal table. Locals also recommended the **Coyote Cafe** (132 W. Water St.; 983-1615). The main dining room has a fixed-price menu and modern Southwestern cuisine; those in the bar can order à la carte. Expensive.

La Casa Sena (125 East Palace Ave.; 988-9232) is tastefully Continental. Don't miss the adjacent Cantina, where waiters and bartenders sing caberet between serving drinks. If you want to nibble tapas instead of dinner, this is the place to do it.

Some moderately priced restaurants are **Maria's New Mexican Kitchen** (555 W. Cordova Rd.; 983-7929), where you'll probably meet affable owner Al Lucero, who wrote *The Real Margarita Book* featuring history and recipes of the more than 50 "real" margaritas served in the restaurant. Robert Redford, a frequent customer when he's in town, wrote the foreword. The food is wonderful also, especially the posole and green chile stew.

The Pink Adobe (406 Old Santa Fe Trail; 983-7712) is a local favorite and sometimes difficult to get in. They specialize in New Mexican and Creole foods, and reservations are necessary. Prices are moderate to expensive. Next door, **The Dragon Bar** is a favorite of locals and visitors alike.

It may sound strange to recommend an East Indian restaurant in the Southwest, but a local friend took us to **India Palace** (227 Don Gasper; 986-5859); you would be hard pressed to find better Indian cuisine anywhere this side of Bombay. **Zia Diner** (326 South Guadalupe; 988-7008) is an easy 15-minute walk from the Plaza and features All-American favorites (New Mexican style, of course) such as meat loaf stuffed with piñon nuts.

Tomasita's Cafe (500 S. Guadalupe; 983-5721) is fast food with a twist. Portions are large, service is friendly, and it's a favorite of Santa Fe families, so be prepared to wait. It is inexpensive, and has some of the best New Mexican fare in town.

Don't hestitate to join the tourists at **The Ore House** (upstairs at 50 Lincoln Ave.; 983-8687) on the Plaza. Known for its seafood, its bar features big sink-in chairs and free après-ski snacks. Next door, at the **Plaza Restaurant** (54 Lincoln; 982-1664), regulars swear everything is good.

If you are in town at lunch time, go stand in line with the locals at **Josie's Casa de Comida** (225 E. Marcy; 983-5311). The regional dishes are excellent and its homemade desserts are legendary (one piece of her hot pear pie is enough for two). Josie's is very inexpensive, but closed on weekends.

On Canyon Road, **Celebrations** (613 Canyon Rd.; 989-8904) is in the heart of gallery row and is jammed at lunchtime.

Après-ski/nightlife

Santa Fe has the usual live bands, bars and places to dance. But it has some unusual off-slope activities as well.

To work out the kinks of a fresh powder day, stop at **Ten Thousand Waves** (988-1047, 982-9304) for a relaxing hot tub under the stars. About three miles from the Plaza and on the road from the ski area, Ten Thousand Waves is a Japanese-style hot tub resort, with kimonos, sandals, massage, facials, herbal wraps and gender-segregated dressing rooms. There are eight private tubs and two communal tubs. Soaking in a tub in the foothills above the city, you gaze out over the pinon and juniper forest. At night only the moon and stars look down on your bliss.

For elegant après-ski (you can go in ski clothes), head for **Inn of the Anasazi** or **La Posada**, both close to the Plaza. At the latter, ask the bartender about the resident ghost, featured on the TV show "Unsolved Mysteries."

In Santa Fe, a wonderful place to mix dinner with entertainment is at **La Casa Sena** (988-9232) in the historic Sena Plaza, a stately adobe built as a family home in the 1860s. The restaurant features New Mexican specialties—and singing waiters and waitresses. For about $20, you can eat, drink and hear an exceptional dinner theater show, belted out between courses. Children are welcome, reservations a must.

Another dinner theater is the **Santa Fe Music Hall** (800-409-3311 or 983-3311) where they perform everything from Southwest vaudeville to Phantom of the Opera. Like La Casa Sena, the actors also are your waiters.

The **Catamount Bar & Grill** (125 E. Water St.; 988-7222) is a sports bar teeming with locals and tourists featuring big-screen TV, pool tables and specials like "Jägermeister Night."

Other activities

Shopping: An initial warning: It will be much cheaper to ski all day than venture into Santa Fe's many tempting shops and galleries. That warning given, more than 100 **galleries** feature Native American crafts and art, as well as fine art on a par with galleries in New York, Florence or Paris. On weekends you can find bargains and excellent workmanship when local artisans sell their wares on blankets in front of the 480-year-old Palace of the Governors, a long-standing Santa Fe shopping tradition.

Canyon Road is the world-famous strip of galleries featuring wonderful art of all styles, for all tastes. The walk from the Plaza area is pleasant. The **Waxlander Gallery** features wonderful pastel still-life works of J. Alex Potter. Our favorite is **Nedra Matteucci's Fenn Galleries,** 1075 Paseo de Peralta, just south of Canyon Road. The day we visited, we counted four Zuniga sculptures starting at $80,000 each. Don't miss the garden.

The **museums** in Santa Fe are first rate. Buy a three-day pass for $5, which will admit you to four of the best: the Museum of International Folk Art (strong in Spanish art of the area), the Palace of the Governors (for local history), the Museum of Indian Arts and Culture and the Museum of Fine Arts (with several Georgia O'Keeffe paintings).

Exercising: For about $10 a day, the 19,000-square-foot Santa Fe Spa, 786 N. St. Francis Dr. (984-8727), has state-of-the-art exercise equipment, a heated indoor lap pool, massage staff, free child care and more. Also check out Fitness Plus, for women only, at 473-7315.

Touring: Eight Indian pueblos are near Santa Fe. The San Ildefonso Pueblo, famous for its distinctive pottery style, is the most scenic. Its annual festival to honor its patron saint is in late January and features traditional clothing and dances.

If you have a car, and especially if you are driving north on U.S. Hwy. 84/285 to Taos, be sure and take the Highway 503 turnoff at Pojoaque and drive east to Chimayo, site of the Santuario de Chimayo, famous for the dirt thought to have healing powers. At the end of the church parking lot, you'll find Leona's, a funky little walk-up where the tamale pie and burritos are exceptional. On the way to Taos you wind through foothills and into high mountain Hispanic villages like Truchas and Las Trampas. For beautiful woven blankets, stop at Ortega's in Chimayo, where family members still practice a craft brought to New Mexico in the 1600s by their ancestors.

Call the **Santa Fe Visitors Bureau** (505-984-6760; 800-777-2489) for more information on these and other activities.

Getting there and getting around

By air: Albuquerque has the nearest major airport, 60 miles away. Private pilots can use the Santa Fe Regional Airport.

By car: Santa Fe is north of Albuquerque on I-25, an easy hour's drive. The ski area is 16 miles from town on Highway 475.

Getting around: Getting around Santa Fe and to and from the ski area is difficult without a car, though a shuttle service is available from the airport to major hotels and to the ski area. The airport in Albuquerque has the leading rental car agencies. For shuttles from the airport in Albuquerque to Santa Fe, call 982-4311. For information on the Santa Fe Ski Shuttle from the town to the ski area, call 820-7541.

Taos
New Mexico

Summit elevation: 11,819 feet
Vertical drop: 2,612 feet
Base elevation: 9,207 feet

Address: Box 90,
Taos Ski Valley, NM 87525
✆ **Area code:** 505
Ski area phone: 776-2291
Snow report: 776-2916 **Fax:** 776-8596
ⓘ **Toll-free reservations:** (800) 776-1111;
(800) 821-2437
E-mail: tsv@taoswebb.com
Internet: http://taoswebb.com/nmusa/skitaos/
Expert:★★★★★
Advanced:★★★★★
Intermediate:★★★★
Beginner:★★ **Never-ever:**★

Number of lifts: 11–4 quad chairs,
1 triple chair, 5 double chairs, 1 surface lift
Percent snowmaking: 46 percent
Uphill capacity: 15,000 per hour
Total acreage: 1,096 acres terrain, 687 acres trails
Snowboarding: No
Bed Base: 3,705 at base and in town
Nearest lodging: slopeside; hotels, condos
Resort child care: Yes, 6 weeks and older
Adult ticket, per day: $39-$42 (98/99 prices)
Dining (Including town):★★★★
Apres-ski/nightlife:★★
Other activities:★★★

Taos Ski Valley is a little piece of the Alps, founded by a Swiss native and surrounded by hotels and restaurants built by Frenchmen and Austrians. It's near the town of Taos, which is a rich mix of Spanish and Indian cultures, blended over the centuries to produce the Southwestern style. This style, in art, cuisine and architecture, isn't trendy here; it's the way things have always been.

Taos Ski Valley holds another distinction: while many resorts walk a delicate marketing tightrope, touting whatever expert terrain they possess while trying not to scare anyone off, Taos seems to enjoy its tough reputation. Its marketers don't play up that image (word gets around among skiers), but they make no effort to refute it either. Instead they wisely advise visitors to meet the challenge by enrolling in Ski-Better-Week, a package of lessons, accommodations, meals and lift tickets.

Just about everybody at Taos enrolls in ski school. If you aren't part of a class, you feel like the kid that didn't get chosen for the baseball team. Après-ski talk centers on Ski-Better-Week anecdotes, leaving independents to sit at the bar with little to add to discussions.

In the four decades since Taos opened, traditions have developed. One is the quest for hidden *porrons*, hand-blown Mexican glass flasks filled with martinis and buried in the snow under trees for classes to discover. Another is free hot chocolate in winter (lemonade in spring) in lift lines if they get too long (this happens most often at the base, where two non-high-speed quads must transport everybody in the morning). And the family-like ski classes make everyone feel right at home.

Mountain layout

Taos' skiing is on two sides of a ridge marked by blue-square Bambi at the top and black-diamond Al's Run at the bottom. To the left of the ridge, as you look at the mountain, are wider, gentler runs such as Shalako Bowl, Honeysuckle, and Upper and Lower Totemoff. To the right of the ridge are narrower, steeper runs like the dense tree-filled Castor and Pollux, and upper-intermediate trails such as Lower Stauffenberg and Powderhorn Bowl.

◆◆ **Expert:** For tree skiers, Taos has a special challenge, the twin runs Castor and Pollux. They hardly look like runs, just steep wooded parts of the mountain, unskiable, where some joker put a sign that looks just like a trail marker. The trees are two to 15 feet apart, and advanced classes regularly train here.

Powder skiing lasts on Highline Ridge and Kachina Peak, for two reasons: they are double black diamonds and Kachina Peak is reachable only after an hour-and-fifteen-minute hike from the top chair at 11,800 feet to the ridge at 12,500 feet. You can, however, ski off Highline Ridge and West Basin Ridge after only a 15-minute hike. Skiers are advised to go with an instructor or a patrolman; at the very least, they must check in with the patrol at the top of Chair 6. The ski patrol will give you a rough screening to see if you can handle the double-diamond terrain. In any case you must ski the ridge with a partner.

◆ **Advanced:** If you consider yourself an advanced but not expert skier, start off on the blue-square runs. Several of the blues here have moguls (Lower Stauffenberg, for example) that would give them a black rating elsewhere. If that's no problem, then pick out a short black before you head down a long black with no escape outlet. The least crowded bowl is Hunziker, named after a Swiss lift engineer, kept isolated by a short climb to its entrance. The Hunziker Bowl entices you with a mild concave slope, but just when you feel confident and relaxed, it drops off with the steepness of a waterfall and narrows down to force you into precision skiing in short turns.

■ **Intermediate:** Smooth intermediate bowls can be found off the Kachina quad chair, the widest being Shalako. Other good intermediate terrain is under Chairs 7 and 8. Taos may push you, but stick with it: you'll find plenty of terrain that true intermediates can handle. If you're having trouble, go ski the greens for a while and keep your head held high.

●● **Beginner:** Taos has some nice beginner terrain, such as Honeysuckle, which descends the left side of the ridge (looking at the mountain) from the summit. Unfortunately, once you're there, you have to get back down.

The only ways off the mountain are straight down the infamous Al's Run or a couple of other tough black-diamond routes, or on one of two green-circle cat trails, Whitefeather on the right and Rubezahl on the left. There's usually plenty of room on Al's Run, but not on Whitefeather and Rubezahl. Despite the slow-down efforts of ski hosts stationed every 20 feet or so, both runs resemble the Hollywood Freeway at rush hour, except that the faster skiers aren't stalled in traffic. They zip around the slower ones, who are gingerly wedging their way home. On busy days it's a mess. Timing is important: come down early, or better yet, be one of the last to descend.

We recommend that lower-level skiers take lessons—not only to improve their skills but also to find the best part of the mountain for them.

● **Never-ever:** Only athletic novices should attempt to learn here. Despite the highly regarded ski school, the jump from the tiny learning area to the mountain is enormous. Better learning terrain is at nearby Angel Fire or Red River (see *Regional Getaways*).

Note: We are not trying to scare you away from Taos. We just want you to be aware that the trail ratings here are a half to a full notch above what they'd be at another ski resort. Our staffers are unanimous in their enthusiasm for this place, and that includes our resident terminal intermediates.

Two factors make Taos' intimidating topography approachable: a staff eager to help the newcomer and an outstanding instruction program. Every morning a crew of blue-jacketed hosts is stationed at the ticket area base, and at the tops of all lifts to answer questions about lift lines and appropriate trails. Here, it is no disgrace to warm up on a green run—it's a good idea.

Taos is rarely crowded: ticket sales are cut off at 4,800 although the mountain can accommodate many more. If you're looking for no people at all, the farthest run west, Lower Stauffenberg running into Don't Tell, probably will be empty. You definitely will find crowds twice a day: once in the morning as you board the two base lifts, and again in the afternoon as everyone heads for home, mostly on the two cat trails we mentioned earlier.

Mountain rating

While experts will adore Taos for its challenge (a whopping 51 percent of the runs are rated expert, and 19 of those 36 runs are double black diamonds), intermediates may be frustrated and beginners may be downright terrified. Most of the green-circle trails are narrow, high-traffic access runs to more challenging terrain. Many of the blue-square runs start off wide, but then get quite narrow in spots. Those narrow portions can build some menacing bumps.

Rise up to meet Taos' challenge. If you normally ski blue runs at other resorts, you can ski Taos. It may be tough at first, but persist—you'll catch on. Taos can be an extremely rewarding ski experience *because* of its challenge. The runs demand you give it your best. If you ski well here, you deserve to strut into the bar at the end of the day. Few highs in skiing top a successful day on this mountain. And if you don't, the mountain provides a convenient excuse. The more you ski it, the more you'll like it.

Last suggestion: take a trail map and consult it often.

Cross-country

Bonnie Golden, a personal fitness trainer, runs **Taos Fitness Adventures** (751-5977), offering guided cross-country skiing and snowshoeing in the winter, plus hiking and custom programs in warmer weather. **Southwest Nordic Center** has cross-country lessons, tours and yurt trips, 758-4761.

Enchanted Forest Cross-Country Ski Area (754-2374) is 40 miles northeast of Taos by Highways 522 and 38. It has 34 km. of backcountry trails, some groomed, and an elevation of 10,300 feet, from which you have great views of the Moreno and Red River valleys. Trail rates are $10 for adults, with discounts for teens, seniors and children. At the headquarters at Miller's Crossing in downtown Red River, you can rent equipment (including pulks, which are sleds that allow adults to pull small children as they ski) and pick up trail maps.

Snowboarding

Not permitted. Monoskis and telemark skis are allowed.

Lessons (98/99 prices)

Group lessons: Two hours, morning or afternoon, $32. Some group lessons concentrate on specific skills, such as moguls or telemarking.

Never-ever package: Novice-lift ticket, lessons, and rentals for $54.

Private lessons: $80 a person for an hour, $110 for 2–5 people.

Special programs: Ski Better Weeks are the core of the Taos ski experience, developed by former French junior Alpine champion and ski school technical director Jean Mayer. Participants are matched for five or six mornings of intensive lessons, and they ski with the same instructor all week. Sixty-five percent of the participants are intermediate or higher.

Ski Week costs $269–$390, depending on season, lifts and lessons. Many lodging properties offer the Ski Better Week as a package with meals and accommodations.

Super Ski Week is an intense course for adults who wish to focus seriously on improving their skills. Skiers are analyzed, videotaped and put through what amounts to a mini ski-racing camp every morning and afternoon for a total of five hours. This is not a program for the timid or late-night party types—most participants have no energy left for anything but a quick bite to eat and then to bed. But most will find their skills much improved by the end of the week. It's offered at selected times for $580–$640, depending on the season.

Ski Week also is offered for women, teens and for ages 50 and older, each at select times during the season.

Taos Ski Valley also has shorter programs that concentrate on specifics, such as Moguls or Extreme Weekends, designed to aid advanced and expert skiers; and Women's Weekends.

Children's programs: These operate out of the Kinderkäfig children's center, which is unfortunately an inconvenient distance from the main base area. A two-hour morning lesson, lunch and afternoon supervised skiing for ages 3–12 is $68 a day. (Ages 3–5 get a program that combines lessons, snow play and indoor activities.) Reservations are recommended; call 776-2291.

Child care (98/99 prices)

Ages: 6 weeks to 2 years.

Costs: Full day including lunch and snacks is $57. Multiday discounts are available, as is an hourly rate of $15.

Reservations: Required. Call 505-776-2291. There is one staff member for every two infants. Toddlers get indoor activities and snow play.

Lift tickets (98/99 prices)

	Adult	Child (Up to 12)
One day	$42	$26
Three days	$117 ($39/day)	$72 ($24/day)
Five days	$195 ($39/day)	$120 ($24/day)

Who skis free: Ages 70 and older.

Who skis at a discount: Ages 65–69 ski for $25. Ages 13–17 ski for $34 a single day; $31 multiday. Taos reduces its ticket prices in January value season and the early and late seasons. Prior to Dec. 19 (except Thanksgiving weekend), tickets are $29 for adults and $18 for children. Jan. 3 through Feb. 5, 1999, adults and children save a couple of bucks off the multiday rate, but not on single-day tickets. Add $5 to all rates between Dec. 27–31.

 ## Accommodations

The **Ski-Better-Week** packages include up to seven nights lodging (Saturday to Saturday), six lift tickets and six morning lessons. In some cases, meals are included, too. Prices range from about $586 to about $1,600 per person, double occupancy. If price or specific amenities are concerns, call **Taos Valley Resort Association** (800-776-1111 or 776-2233) or **Taos Central Reservations** (800-821-2437) to book lodging or ski-stay-air packages. Also, the Taos Ski Valley website (http://taoswebb.com/nmusa/skitaos/) has a convenient lodging search feature, where you can plug in what you want and it will suggest lodging.

More expensive lodging ($150 per night and higher):

The Inn at Snakedance (800-322-9815 or 776-2277) has 60 ski-in/ski-out rooms. Amenities include a spa with hot tub, sauna, exercise and massage facility; a glass-walled bar and a restaurant serving continental cuisine with a Southwest flair. Owners Mary Madden and Dan Ringeisen saved the fireplace from the old Hondo Inn, which used to occupy the space. The Inn offers the Ski-Better-Week packages with an optional meal plan.

The **Hotel St. Bernard** (776-2251) managed by Jean Mayer, Taos ski school technical director, offers the flavor of a European retreat. The cuisine and ambiance are both legendary and French. This hotel also offers the Ski-Better-Week packages with meals.

The **Hotel Edelweiss** (800-458-8754 or 776-2301) also is right at the base of the village. The charming hotel has an outdoor hot tub and large sundeck. It has a restaurant, and offers the Ski Week package, including meals.

Moderate lodging (generally $100–$150 per night):

The **Austing Haus** (800-748-2932 or 776-2649) is 1.5 miles from the base of Taos Ski Valley, and is an unusual structure. It is the tallest timber frame building in the United States and owner Paul Austing is justifiably proud of the 24-unit lodge he helped build himself. The food in the glass dining room is very good.

Between the ski area and town is a bed-and-breakfast inn, the **Salsa del Salto**. Formerly the residence of Hotel St. Bernard owner, Jean Mayer, it's now run by Jean's brother, Dadou, a French-trained chef who cooks Salsa del Salto's gourmet breakfasts. We also enjoyed three other B&Bs in Taos, which seems to have an unusual number of fine choices: **Hacienda del Sol** owned by John and Marcine Landon, the **Old Taos Guesthouse** owned by Tim and Leslie Reeves, who are fun to ski with, and **Inn on La Loma Plaza**, owned by Peggy Davis and her husband, Jerry, both former mayors in Vail and Avon, CO. B&Bs can be booked through the Taos B&B Association, (800) 876-7857.

The town of Taos offers a wide range of accommodations. Prices are generally less expensive than staying at Taos Ski Valley. At the northern edge of town, **Quail Ridge Inn** (776-2211 or 800-624-4448) is a fully appointed condominium complex at a tennis ranch, including indoor and outdoor courts. Looking much like a pueblo, it exudes the Southwestern atmosphere.

The **Historic Taos Inn** (800-826-7466; spells TAOS-INN) is the cultural center of Taos. The lobby, built around the old town well, is a gathering place for artists. Rooms feature adobe fireplaces, antiques and Taos-style furniture built by local artisans.

The **Sagebrush Inn** (800-428-3626 or 758-2254) is an historic inn with a priceless collection of Southwestern art in the lobby and some of the best nightlife in town.

Least expensive lodging (generally $85 or less):

At the lower end of the price range are **El Pueblo Lodge** (800-433-9612), **Indian Hills Inn** (800-444-2346), and often, rooms in the chain hotels, such as Holiday Inn or Ramada.

The least expensive is the skiers' hostel, **The Abominable Snowmansion** (776-8298) in Arroyo Seco, nine miles from the Village, where the rates are about $25–$60. Another bargain choice is the **Fraser House Hostel** (776-5753) in nearby Valdez.

 ## Dining

Because so many properties at Taos Ski Valley offer Ski-Better-Week packages, which include meals, most restaurants are operated by the lodges. The best independent eateries in the village are **Rhoda's Restaurant, Dolomite** and **Tim's Stray Dog Cantina.** Rhoda's has many New Mexican specialties. Dolomite features Northern Italian pasta and pizza, but it's not a pizza joint—owner Karen Lubliner is a classically trained chef. At Tim's Stray Dog, owner Laurie Harter continues the tradition established by her late husband, Tim, who left the St. Bernard to start his own business (hence the name). Try the Tequila Shrimp.

The **Hondo Restaurant** at The Inn at Snakedance is also open to non-guests for breakfast, lunch and dinner and features winemaker dinners with California vintners. **Hotel Edelweiss** also serves three meals daily to the general public.

On the road into the valley, the **Casa Cordova** (776-2500) specializes in American and continental cuisine (entrées are $15–$22). **Tim's Chile Connection** (776-8787) is known for its chicken chimichanga and Pollo Borracho; entrées run $8–$12. **Renegade Cafe** at the Quail Ridge Inn (776-8319) specializes in Mediterranean-style food.

The town of Taos has great variety when it comes to restaurants. **Jacquelina's** (751-0399), on S. Santa Fe Road (also known as Paseo del Pueblo Sur), specializes in Southwestern cuisine. The pork loin, marinated in honey and chipotle chili, is outstanding. For the best burger in town, locals recommend the not-so-Southwest-sounding **Fred's Place** on S. Santa Fe Road (758-0514). The menu at the intimate **Apple Tree Restaurant** (758-1900) lists Southwestern dishes and continental cuisine.

On the historic plaza, **The Garden Restaurant** (758-9483) offers New Mexican as well as American, Italian and French entrées. **Doc Martin's** (758-1977) in the Taos Inn has creative Southwestern cuisine. **The Trading Post** (758-5089) has a bit of everything—Cajun, New Mexican, Italian, steaks.

Michael's Kitchen (758-4178) gets raves from locals for its breakfasts.

 ## Après-ski/nightlife

Yawn. That is the sound of Taos' bone-tired skiers heading off to dreamland after dinner. The nightlife will never make any Top 10 lists.

When lifts close, skiers will be found on the deck of the **Hotel St. Bernard**, the **Martini Tree Bar** at the Resort Center, or the **Twining Tavern** at the Thunderbird Lodge. The St. Bernard has live music every night—a mix of reggae, country, jazz, and acoustic guitar. The Thunderbird Lodge has live music in spurts. The Martini Tree has live music après-ski. **The Inn at Snakedance** has entertainment nightly.

It's livelier in town. **The Sagebrush Inn** has C&W dances. The Kachina Lodge's **Cabaret Room** has a dance floor and occasional acts such as Arlo Guthrie, and **Ogelvie's Bar and Grill** in Taos Plaza hops. For microbrew fans, **Eske's Brew Pub** off the Taos Plaza is the spot.

Skiers and local artists mix at the **Adobe Bar** of the Taos Inn, called the living room for artsy locals. Order a margarita and watch the beautiful people. The *Taos News* has a weekly entertainment guide.

Other activities

Shopping: Georgia O'Keeffe and R.C. Gorman have made Taos legendary with art lovers. About 80 galleries are here, and the Quast Gallery has a Meet the Artist series in winter. You will find extensive specialty shops around the plaza. Get a list from Taos Chamber of Commerce, 758-3873 or (800) 732-TAOS.

Taos is quite historic. The Martinez Hacienda, built in 1804, is a monument to the Spanish Colonial era in Northern New Mexico. Kit Carson is buried in Taos and his home and museum are open to the public.

Adventure Tours has **sleigh rides** and **snowmobile tours,** 758-1167. **Taos Ice Arena** is open Thanksgiving through February, 758-8234. **Fly fishing** tours are offered in winter on the Red River by Los Rios Anglers, 758-2798.

Visit the **Taos Pueblo,** the 700-year-old home of the Tiwa Indians. Visitors are welcome to the pueblo, workshops, ceremonies and sacred dances, except for a four- to six-week period each winter when the pueblo is closed for religious reasons. For exact dates, call the Taos Chamber of Commerce (800-732-8267). The pueblo is open from 9 a.m. to 4:30 p.m.

Getting there and getting around

By air: Albuquerque is the nearest major airport, 135 miles south. Rental car agencies are at the airport. For ground transportation, contact Faust's Transportation, 758-3410 in Taos or 843-9042 in Albuquerque; or Pride of Taos, 758-8340.

By car: I-25 north to Santa Fe, then Highways 285, 84 and 68 to Taos. Taos Ski Valley is 18 miles farther north on Hwy. 150.

Getting around: If you stay in Taos Ski Valley village and have no desire to go into the town of Taos 18 miles away, you won't need a car. If you want to visit the town, or aren't staying at the ski area, you'll need one.

Mt. Bachelor

Oregon

Summit elevation: 9,065 feet
Vertical drop: 3,365 feet
Base elevation: 5,700 feet

Address: P.O. Box 1031
Bend, OR 97709-1031
✆ **Area code:** 541
Ski area: 382-2442
Snow report: 382-7888
ⓘ **Toll-free reservations:**
(800) 800-8334
E-mail: MTB@bendnet.com
Internet: http://www.mtbachelor.com
http://www.empnet.com/cova (lodging)
Expert:★★★ **Advanced:**★★★
Intermediate:★★★★★
Beginner:★★★★
Never-ever:★★★★

Number of lifts: 13—7 high-speed quads,
3 triples, 1 double, 2 surface lifts
Snowmaking: none
Skiable acreage: 3,686 lift-served acres
Uphill capacity: 21,000 per hour
Snowboarding: Yes, unlimited
Bed Base: 7,500
Nearest lodging: 17 miles away in Bend
Resort child care: Yes, 6 weeks and older
Adult ticket, per day: $32-$39 (98/99)

Dining:★★
Apres-ski/nightlife:★★
Other activities:★★★

Mt. Bachelor is not your typical mountain. At other resorts, the highest point often is difficult to distinguish from neighboring summits, which may be just a few feet higher or lower. But Mt. Bachelor, a stately volcanic cone that is part of the Cascades mountain range, rises from Oregon's high desert, visible for miles in every direction.

On the eastern side of the Cascades, where snow falls lighter and drier than at other northwestern resorts, Mt. Bachelor has become a popular destination for western skiers. Despite no on-mountain lodging and little nightlife, Mt. Bachelor attracts skiers with its dependable snowpack, clear dry air, average daytime winter temperatures of 26 degrees and fine skiing and snowboarding from early November to July.

Visitors should keep in mind that all that snow results from a lot of storms, and winds often close the Summit Express chair, a high-speed quad to the 9,065-foot treeless summit. An average stormy day brings winds of 60 to 70 miles per hour (the record is more than 200 mph), and those summit winds can kick up ground blizzards where the snow swirls into a whiteout six feet high. (Visibility is usually better lower on the mountain, where the ski trails are protected by trees.) But when the weather is clear and you're standing on top, you can see California's Mt. Shasta 180 miles to the south. That view, most commonly seen in spring, is fantastic.

Though the volcano is extinct, the innovative ideas of Mt. Bachelor's management are anything but. This is a resort that has been quick to embrace new concepts in the ski industry, such as electronic ticketing, a revolutionary ski school and high-speed quad chairs. It may be on the cutting edge of ski industry trends, but Mt. Bachelor manages to keep its atmosphere very untrendy. No one notices or cares whether your ski clothes match, or even how hot a skier or boarder you are.

Mountain layout

◆◆ **Expert** ◆ **Advanced:** Mt. Bachelor's Northwest Express Quad serves 400 acres of tree skiing and open-bowl terrain in an area called the Northwest Territory. When the Summit Express is open, experts should head for it. The steepest descent is through The Pinnacles, a jagged rock formation reached by a 150-foot hike from the top of the lift, then across the broad ungroomed expanse of Cirque Bowl. Next might be Cow's Face, far to the left of Summit Chair, steep but smooth. Because it's unknown to many skiers, it doesn't get carved into moguls, but wind packs it hard.

The longest continuous vertical on this mountain (3,365 feet) can be had by taking the Summit chair off the back side, occasionally traversing right and ending up at the bottom of the Northwest Express chair.

■ **Intermediate:** This mountain is best suited to intermediates. The Outback Express, with a 1,780-foot vertical rise, serves excellent intermediate runs. From this chair, Boomerang is the only run rated black, and it parallels the lift. One blue run, Down Under, often is left ungroomed for mogul enthusiasts.

Other popular chairs for intermediates are the Pine Marten Express and the Skyliner Express. Old Skyliner, off the Pine Marten chair, has some marvelous dips and rolls—far more fun than the usual freeway design of many intermediate trails.

Most of the lower mountain is sheltered by trees, but some runs, such as Flying Dutchman and Tippytoe, give the exuberance of upper-mountain skiing. You usually can find moguls on Grotto, Canyon and Coffee Run, all off the Pine Marten chair.

Intermediates can experience the heady sensation of being on the summit and still get down safely using the broad Healy Heights and Beverly Hills, which are always groomed. In fact, intermediates can't get into trouble at Mt. Bachelor: anything beyond their skill requires a knowledgeable decision to get into it—for example, the hike up to The Pinnacles.

●● **Beginner:** Green-circle trails descend from every lift except the Summit and Outback chairs. More difficult trails are on either side, funneling the faster skiers away from those still learning to control their turns.

● **Never-ever:** Never-evers get a rare treat at Mt. Bachelor: a high-speed quad chair, Sunshine Accelerator. High-speed quads move very slowly for loading and unloading, which makes them ideal to learn the tricks of riding chair lifts.

Note: Between the Outback and Red chairs is an unusual geologic feature, a lone cinder cone. It's not served by a lift, so powder lasts there until it's wind-packed. By getting up a head of steam from Leeway, skiers can swoop up nearly two-thirds of the way and climb the rest.

Mountain rating

Most of the terrain is ideal for intermediates and lower abilities. Experts probably will feel restless after a weekend—they'll have to discover the pleasures of the back side and Cinder Cone.

Cross-country (97/98 prices)

The **Mt. Bachelor Rossignol Cross-Country Center,** across the parking lot from the West Village base lodge, has 56 km. of machine-set trails. There are 12 loops, from the easy 1-km. First Time Around to the challenging 12-km. Oli's Alley. The 6-km. intermediate trail, called Zigzag, leads to a heated shelter with good views. The center has equipment rental, clothing and accessories, repairs, trail and lesson information and lunch. Most of the terrain is best suited for intermediate levels.

All-day passes are $10.50 for adults, $5 for children 7–12. Ages 65 and older pay $6.50. Children younger than 7 ski free.

Mt. Bachelor also operates 20 km. of groomed tracks at **Sunriver Resort,** about 14 miles from the downhill area. You can use all-day tickets bought here at the Mt. Bachelor Nordic facilities in the afternoon, and vice versa.

Snowboarding

The resort has an excellent and extensive program for snowboarders. A two-hour never-ever lesson is $40, including a full-day lift ticket and rental board. The resort has a halfpipe and a terrain park.

Lessons (98/99 prices)

Group lessons: Mt. Bachelor uses shaped skis to teach beginners through low intermediates. The program is based on positive reinforcement. Sessions for levels 6–9 (intermediate to expert) are $24, $20 with a dated performance card from your previous lesson. Levels 4–5 are $30 for a lesson only; $60 with lift ticket and rentals. Level 3 is $30 for a lesson; $56 adding lifts and rentals.

Never-ever package: Levels 1-2 are $30 for a lesson only; $40 for lesson, ski rental and lift pass.

Private lessons: $45 per hour; $10 for additional skiers. A private lesson with video analysis is $55. Half-day and full-day rates also are available.

Special programs: Too many to list here. We wish more resorts would offer the Women's Three-day Technical Equipment Clinic which explains how minor adjustments to your ski equipment can improve your skiing. This clinic is given by Jeanne Thoren, an expert in helping women ski better through equipment modification. Women who have attended claimed it was the best $250 they have ever spent.

Racing: The NASTAR course is off the Yellow Chair Wednesday, Friday, Saturday and Sunday; $5 for two runs. The course opens at 10 a.m. on Sundays; 1 p.m. otherwise. A coin-operated course runs daily for 50 cents per run. Buy tokens at the Perfect Turn Skier Development Center.

Children's programs: Learning groups are formed according to age, ability and maturity in the skiing environment. Rates are $65 for an all-day lesson, rentals, lifts and lunch for ages 7–12, $55 for ages 4–6. Half day rates are available, as are rates without rentals and lift tickets. You must register your child by 9:45 a.m. at either the West Village or Sunrise Skier Development Centers.

Child care (98/99 prices)

Ages: 6 weeks to 7 years.
Costs: $34 per day for ages 30 months and older; $36 for infants up to 30 months old. An introduction to skiing course for 3-year-olds costs $49.

Reservations: Highly recommended. Mt. Bachelor has child care facilities at West Village and Sunrise Lodges.

Call 382-2442 or (800) 829-2442.

Lift tickets (98/99 prices)

	Adult	Child (7-12)
One day	$39	$20
Three days	$108 ($36/day)	$46 ($15.33/day)
Five days	$160 ($32/day)	$72 ($14.40/day)

Who skis free: Ages 6 and younger.
Who skis at a discount: Ages 65 and older ski for $23 a day.

Note: If you usually ski fewer than ten runs per day, Mt. Bachelor's Flextime point ticket might be more economical. You pay for a certain number of points, which are electronically inserted into a credit-card-like ticket. Each lift has a different point value based on its length, so each time you board a lift, points are deducted from your total. You may use your leftover points the next day or even next season—they are fully transferable, and good for three years. The 200-point ticket is $41, while a 400-point ticket sells for $81. If you ski all day long, an all-day ticket is a better deal.

Accommodations

Mt. Bachelor's nearest accommodations are several miles away in or near Bend, population 34,000.

The most extensive lodging complex is **Sunriver** (800-547-3922 or 800-452-6874 in Oregon), a resort community 18 miles from Mt. Bachelor and 15 miles south of Bend. It has a private airport, restaurants, stores and many activities. Sunriver's transportation shuttles run throughout the expansive resort complex, and another shuttle goes between Sunriver and Mt. Bachelor (and costs $7, though this fee is included in some packages). But getting to Bend is tough without your own car. Winter rates run about $110 for rooms, $165 for suites and $174–299 for condos.

Inn of the Seventh Mountain (800-452-6810 in the U.S. or 800-874-9402 from Canada) is Mt. Bachelor's closest lodging, with restaurants, a grocery store that stocks nearly 99 brands of beer, a skating rink, hot tub, snowmobile and sleigh rides and a shuttle to the mountain. Economy rooms are $64, and three-bedroom condos are $262, with many offerings and ski packages in between.

Bend's most deluxe lodge is **Riverhouse** (800-547-3928 or 541-381-3111), nestled along the river close to restaurants and entertainment. Pool, indoor and outdoor spas and a Nautilus exercise room make this a mini-resort in the heart of town. Nightly rates range from $65 for two people to $185 for a river-view suite with three queen beds, two rooms and kitchen.

Bend has many other places to stay, including five RV parks, plus there is additional lodging in neighboring towns. Phone the **Bend Visitors' Information Center** for more information, 541-382-3221, or use the **Central Oregon Visitors Association** toll-free number, 800-800-8334, to book lodging, packages and transportation.

Dining

A team of three searched diligently for great food at this resort with little success. **The Skiers Palate** in the Pine Marten Lodge at Mt. Bachelor is quite good, as is the food at **Sunriver**. But in Bend the cooking at most of the 80-plus restaurants is basic and prices are based more on atmosphere than the chef's ability.

The elegant **Crossings at the Riverhouse** (389-8810), specializes in steak (and we always say, if you go to a steakhouse, order the steak). Good seafood is moderately priced at **McGrath's Fish House** (388-4555), which has several unusual entrées, especially those from Northwestern waters.

Pine Tavern Restaurant (382-5581), with the twin pine trees shooting out of the dining room roof, serves great steak, ribs, lamb and prime rib. **Rosette** (383-2780) rustles up a Mediterranean-Northwest cuisine with a strong hint of the Orient, and more lamb dishes than most restaurants. It's quiet and sophisticated.

Try **Chan's** (389-1725) for Szechwan, Hunan and Cantonese; **Mexicali Rose** (389-0149) for Mexican food; or **Giuseppe's** (389-8899), *Pacific Northwest* magazine's Best Ethnic Restaurant, for Italian. **Stuft Pizza** (382-4022) gets raves for its pizza, calzone and sandwiches.

Deschutes Brewery & Public House (382-9242), in downtown Bend, has four to six of its handcrafted brews on tap. The beer is great; the meals are so-so.

For breakfast, try **The West Side Bakery & Cafe** on Galveston for its eggs-and-pancake menu and its decor (amusing knickknacks on the walls and ceiling, and a model train that runs through its three dining rooms just below ceiling level), or **Café Paradiso** (385-5931) on Bond Street, which opens at 8 a.m. with the best smelling coffee in town and pastries, especially the cheesecake.

Après-ski/nightlife

Mt. Bachelor is not known for exciting après-ski, nor is Bend noted for dynamic nightlife, though both can be found. The **Castle Keep Lounge** in the lower level of the West Village lodge offers lively après-ski with occasional live music. Also check **The Riverhouse** and **E.L. Bender's** in town.

Later, you'll find dancing at **Willie D's, The Shilo Restaurant and Lounge, Pasha's** and **The Riverhouse,** all in Bend; **Owl's Nest Lounge** at the Sunriver Resort and **Josiah's** at Inn of the Seventh Mountain. Most of the live music is weekends only, but Willie D's rocks all week long. For quieter evenings, try **Café Paradiso** in Bend, a European-style coffee house with acoustic music. **Pine Tavern Restaurant** has a mature adult atmosphere overlooking Mirror Pond. **Legends** in Bend has comedy on Saturdays, and big-screen sports other nights.

Other activities

Shopping: **Bend Factory Outlets**, a 27-store outlet mall on Highway 97 south of Powers Road, has name brands such as Carter's Childrenswear, London Fog, Eddie Bauer and Bass Shoes. The real draw, though, is two **Columbia Outfitters** factory outlets, one downtown on Bond Street and the other at 55 N.W. Wall Street with bargain prices on Columbia's first-run, practical ski clothing component system with zip-in fleece jacket liners that can be worn separately. The stores, owned by a relative of the company's founder, also sell other brands.

Sunriver and Inn of the Seventh Mountain have **ice skating, horseback riding, sleigh rides** and **snowmobiling.**

The Oregon Trail of Dreams Training Camp offers **dogsled rides** by dogs that are training for Alaska's famed Iditarod race. Rates are $60 for adults; $30 for children less than 80 pounds. Call 382-2442 or (800) 829-2442.

The U.S. Forest Service, with a desk on the lower floor of Mt. Bachelor's West Village lodge has several interpretive programs, including a **snowshoe tour** with a USFS naturalist. Someone is available on weekends and daily during Christmas vacation.

Getting there and getting around

By air: United Express and Horizon Air have flights into Redmond/ Bend Airport (16 miles from Bend) from many West Coast cities. Portland is the nearest airport with major-airline service. The airport has a helpful website with information on ground transportation (www.flyrdm.com).

By train: Amtrak (800-872-7245, 800-USA-RAIL) provides service on the Coast Starlight, which runs from Los Angeles to Seattle. The closest stop is Chemult, 60 miles south of Bend. Arrange ahead for taxi pickup.

By car: Mt. Bachelor is 21 miles southwest of Bend, on the scenic Cascade Lakes Highway. Take Hwys. 26 and 97 from Portland, 162 miles away. State Hwy. 126 comes from Eugene (132 miles).

Getting around: A car is helpful. If you don't have one, be sure to stay in lodgings with shuttle service. Mt. Bachelor operates a free park-and-ride operation during the height of the season from its office on 14th Street in Bend, but you'll need a way to reach it.

Mt. Hood Region
Oregon

Timberline Facts

Summit elevation:	**8,540 feet**
Vertical drop:	**3,590 feet**
Base elevation:	**4,950 feet**

Address: Timberline Lodge
Timberline, OR 97028
✆ **Area code:** 503
Ski area phone: 272-3311
Snow report: 222-2211
Fax: 272-3710
ⓘ **Toll-free reservations:** (800) 547-1406
E-mail: timlodge@teleport.com
Internet: http://www.timberlinelodge.com

Expert:★★★ **Advanced:**★★★
Intermediate:★★★★★
Beginner:★★★★
Never-ever:★★★★★
Number and types of lifts: 6–2 high-speed quads, 1 triple, 3 doubles.
Skiable Acreage: 1,430 acres
Snowmaking: None
Uphill capacity: 5,585 skiers per hour
Snowboarding: Yes, unlimited
Bed Base: 71 rooms on mountain
Nearest lodging: slopeside, historic lodge
Resort child care: None
Adult ticket, per day: $28-$32 (97/98)
Dining:★★★★
Apres-ski/nightlife:★★★
Other activities:★★

Portland skiers jokingly call these "our little day areas," but the three ski areas within 15 miles of each other on the shanks of Mt. Hood, Oregon's most beautiful mountain, offer a fine range of experiences for destination skiers and snowboarders.

Most visitors come from Portland for the day or from Seattle for a night or two. Most of the lodging is in the resort town of Hood River, on the Columbia River, famed for windsurfing and about 35 miles north of Mt. Hood Meadows. Other lodging is closer, but limited. However, the skiing is quite varied and abundant. Best of all, it's within an hour's drive of a major airport, Portland International.

Too bad the region doesn't market interchangeable lift tickets, because it has promise as a no-frills winter destination. The terrain and conditions can keep up the enthusiasm of advanced skiers and snowboarders for days at a time, with naturally rugged terrain that hasn't been dynamited to a freeway finish. We found plenty of what we like to ski, as well as some great terrain for the lower ability levels at Timberline and Mt. Hood Meadows.

Timberline is known for its historic lodge and summer skiing. The lodge is a beauty; for more detail see the Accommodations section. Timberline was the continent's first ski area to offer lift-served summer skiing, and now more than 50,000 skiers come each summer. The Palmer Snowfield has a steady pitch at the advanced intermediate level. It's challenging enough for you to find World Cup ski racers from several countries practicing technique. A high-speed quad, Palmer Express, allows Timberline to keep the terrain open nearly the entire year, and gives the area the greatest vertical drop in the Northwest—3,590 feet. The deep snows of winter sometimes require cat drivers to dig out the lift, the upper terminal of which is inside the mountain. Spring skiing is incredible off this lift. In 1997, the Palmer Express ran until Sept. 7, when it was closed for 19 days for scheduled maintenance. Then the resort started running the lift again on Sept. 27 to start the the 97/98 ski season. Incredible.

Mountain layout

Half of Timberline skiing is still below tree line and the main lodge, but few experiences in the skiing world match a ride up the Magic Mile Super Express and the Palmer Express to the top of the Palmer Snowfield. The original Magic Mile lift was the second ski lift in the country, after Sun Valley's. Silcox Hut, which served as the original top terminus and warming hut, has been restored and is open to overnight groups. Below the Timberline Lodge are many blue and green runs, with a few short black diamonds. The webbed trail system between the trees makes each run feel like a wilderness excursion.

Snowboarding

Timberline has gone all-out for snowboarders. In winter the ski area has a terrain garden to challenge the best riders. The base of Paint Brush Glade has a halfpipe. Lessons and rentals are available. Timberline is known for its summer camps on the snowfield. The U.S. Snowboard Training Center is there during the summer. Call (800) 325-4430 for information.

Lessons (97/98 prices)

Timberline has the SKIwee program for kids ages 4–12, and charges $60 per day. Adult group lessons (9 and older) cost $24 for two hours of ski, snowboard or telemark instruction. Private lessons are $38 for an hour. A never-ever ski package (lesson, lift and rentals) is $30; for snowboarders, it's $45.

Lift tickets (97/98 prices)

Adults: $32 weekend and holiday, $28 midweek. Tickets valid any day are $27 (plus a handling fee) through Ticketmaster, (503) 224-4400. Children (7–12), $19. Children younger than 7 ski free with an adult. Tickets are valid 9 a.m. to closing. Timberline has night skiing until 10 p.m. that costs $11; however, it's included with a day ticket.

Mount Hood Meadows

Mountain layout

Mt. Hood Meadows has by far the most varied terrain of the Mt. Hood ski areas and is as big as many Western destination resorts. Heather Canyon has always been the favorite for experts, when it is open, but now three of its entry runs—Twilight, Pluto and Moon Bowl—are winchcat-groomed. That means advanced and upper-intermediate skiers can go where they before had feared to tread.

Mt. Hood Meadows

Summit elevation:	**7,300 feet**
Vertical drop:	**2,777 feet**
Base elevation:	**4,523 feet**

Address: 1975 SW 1st Ave., Suite M
Portland, OR 97201 (year-round office)
✆ **Area code:** 503
Ski area phone: 246-1810 (Portland);
337-2222 (mountain)
ⓘ **Toll-free reservations** (Hood River):
(800) 754-4663
Snow report: 227-7669
Fax: 337-2217
E-mail: info@skihood.com
Internet: http://www.skihood.com

Expert:★★★★ Advanced:★★★★
Intermediate:★★★★★
Beginner:★★★ Never-ever:★★
Number and types of lifts: 12–3 high-speed
quads, 1 quad, 6 doubles, 2 surface lifts
Skiable acreage: 2,150 acres
Snowmaking: None
Uphill capacity: 16,145 per hour
Snowboarding: Yes, unlimited
Bed Base: About 200 in Hood River
Nearest lodging: 11 miles at Cooper Spur;
35 miles at Hood River
Resort child care: none
Adult ticket, per day: $36 (97/98 price)
Dining:★★★
Apres-ski/nightlife:★★★ (Hood River)
Other activities:★★

The favorite intermediate area is under the Hood River Express chair, called "Hurry" (for its initials—HRE). Beginners have the runs under the Daisy, Buttercup and Red chairs. Mitchell Creek Boulevard, reached from the Red chair, is particularly great for kids. Night skiers are served by four chairlifts near the lodge, one of them a high-speed quad.

Snowboarding

Mt. Hood Meadows has a groomed halfpipe plus a few natural ones, plenty of freeriding terrain and jumps. Rentals and lessons are available. Breezeway is the terrain park. It's on the Park Place run east of the Hood River Express chair. Skiers are welcome in the park, too. The entrance sometimes has to have a line-up to avoid congestion. The "traffic guard" sends in 100 people every 15 minutes, just like the entrance ramps on urban freeways.

Lessons (97/98 prices)

Mt. Hood Meadows charges $27 for a 90-minute group lesson. Private lessons are $50 an hour, $30 for each additional person. Full-day programs for kids ages 4–12 cost $70, including lift ticket, lesson, rentals and lunch. Half-day children's lifts-lessons-rental package is $50. Adult never-ever packages (lifts, lessons, rentals) cost $35 for Alpine and $45 for snowboarding. Telemark group lessons cost $27. Alpine skiers and snowboarders who take never-ever lessons at night get a $5 discount.

Lift tickets (97/98 prices)

Tickets are $36 per shift for adults. (Shifts are 9 a.m.–4 p.m., 11 a.m.–7 p.m., and 1–10 p.m.) Ages 65 and older ski for $25 per shift, while ages 7-12 ski for $21 any time. Ages 6 and younger ski for $6. Night tickets (4–10 p.m.) cost $17 for any age. Half-day is $30. Nordic track fee is $9.

Mt. Hood SkiBowl

Summit elevation: 5,066 feet
Vertical drop: 1,500 feet
Base elevation: 3,566 feet

Address: P.O. Box 280,
Government Camp, OR 97028
✆ **Area code:** 503
ⓘ **Ski area phone:** 272-3206
Snow report: 222-2695
Toll-free reservations: None
E-mail: johnl@skibowl.com
Internet: http://www.skibowl.com

Expert:★★★ **Advanced:**★★★
Intermediate:★★
Beginner:★★★ **Never-ever:**★★
Number and types of lifts: 9–4 double chairs, 5 surface lifts
Skiable acreage: 960 acres
Snowmaking: 25 percent
Uphill capacity: 4,600 skiers per hour
Snowboarding: Yes, unlimited
Bed Base: Several lodges in Government Camp
Nearest lodging: Across highway
Resort child care: None
Adult ticket, per day: $20-$26 (97/98 prices)
Dining:★★
Apres-ski/nightlife:★
Other activities:★★

Mountain layout

Mt. Hood SkiBowl (that's not a typo; the ski area spells it that way) is gaining a reputation for challenging ski runs with the addition of its outback area and 1,500 feet of vertical reached from Upper Bowl. The mountain is now rated at 40 percent expert, but the 65 runs have enough variety for all skills. Though beginners have some nice terrain, SkiBowl's lift unloading ramps are sometimes black-diamond affairs, with steep pitches and some sharp turns.

Mt. Hood SkiBowl claims to be America's largest night-skiing area, with 34 of its runs lit at night, including some truly steep black-diamond runs. It also emphasizes ski racing, with programs for a variety of age groups.

Snowboarding

At SkiBowl, the Multorpor side and the Outback are favorites. The snowboard park, Surprise Run, is located off the Multorpor chair. It has a regulation 330-foot halfpipe and a full-on jib course. No skiers allowed.

Lessons (97/98 prices)

SkiBowl, with 100 ski instructors, has classes in racing, freestyle, cross-country and snowboarding. Group lessons cost $20 for 90 minutes, private lessons $35 for an hour and $20 for each additional hour. Ski Bowl also teaches lessons at night by appointment. The never-ever instruction package costs $25 for skiing and snowboarding, including all-day surface lift.

Lift tickets (97/98 prices)

Adults $26 ($15 nights), children (11 and younger) $18 ($11 nights). Like Mt. Hood Meadows, SkiBowl sells shift tickets: Opening to 4:30 p.m., 11

a.m. to 7 p.m., 1 p.m. to close. An adult day+night ticket is $31, $18 for children (same as the full-day price). Ages 6 and younger ski free with a ticketed adult. Ages 65 and older ski day shifts for $15; nights for $10. Buying tickets through Ticketmaster (503-224-4400) costs $24 plus handling fees for an adult day+night ticket. A surface tow-only ticket is $6.

Cross-country

Timberline has telemark lessons, weekends only, but no groomed cross-country trails. **Mt. Hood Meadows** has 15 km. of groomed Nordic track at the base of the Hood River Meadows lift, with rental equipment and instruction. Trail passes are $9, and the cross-country center is open Wednesdays through Sundays. Meadows also offers telemark instruction on weekends, $27 for a group lesson or $50 for a private.

The **Mt. Hood National Forest** has nearly 200 km. of cross-country trails. The Trillium Lake Trail is normally groomed and tracked weekly. Maps are available at any ranger station.

Accommodations

The only slopeside lodging in the region is **Timberline Lodge** (800-547-1406; 503-231-5400), 6,000 feet in the middle of the ski area and a National Historic Landmark. Built in 1937 by the Works Progress Administration, a Depression-era federal work program, it is filled with stunningly artistic details, such as carved stairway banisters, colored linoleum wall murals and wrought-iron fireplace decor made from old railroad tracks. Rates range from $95 to $180 for rooms with private baths. Eleven chalet rooms with a shared bathroom and shower across the hall go for $65. Though Christmas season is sold out 15 months in advance, try to book for early December when the decorations are in place.

Also at Timberline is a unique group lodging opportunity: **Silcox Hut** (503-295-1828 to make reservations). The 47-year-old structure, newly restored, was the terminus for the original Magic Mile chair lift. Now bunkrooms accommodate up to 24 guests (minimum 12, $80 per person, including dinner and breakfast).

Other lodging is in the town of Government Camp, across Highway 26 from SkiBowl. Our favorite is **Falcon's Crest Inn** (503-272-3403 or 800-624-7384), a delightful bed-and-breakfast run by Melody and Bob (BJ) Johnson. Its five rooms ($95 to $179) have private baths and varying decor (e.g. safari, 1920s). In December every room has a uniquely decorated Christmas tree. A $215 per person ski package includes two nights of lodging, two days and one night of skiing, shuttles to the ski areas and one gourmet dinner for two.

Those who prefer a little more privacy than a B&B gives can go across the street to the **Mt. Hood Inn** (503-272-3205 or 800-443-7777). This modern hotel has rooms with continental breakfast starting at $125 per night. Rooms with Jacuzzi tubs are $155. SkiBowl lift tickets are free to guests.

Other lodging at Government Camp includes **Huckleberry Inn** (503-272-3325) with rooms well under $100 and a dorm for $15 per person; or **Thunderhead Lodge Condominiums** (503-272-3368).

The Resort at the Mountain (503-622-3101 or 800-669-7666) is 20 minutes down-mountain from Timberline (and 45 minutes from the Portland airport). Here you can golf (27 holes) and ski in the same day. Rooms start at $94 per night; $134 with a kitchenette.

Eleven miles from Mt. Hood Meadows toward Hood River on Highway 35 is the **Inn at Cooper Spur** (800-929-2754; 503-352-6037). It has 1,200-square-foot log cabins that sleep seven and a group of hot tubs embedded in what may once have been a tennis court. Mt. Hood Meadows has several ski/lodging packages with Hood River B&Bs, inns and hotels, starting in the $50–$60 range per person, double occupancy.

A delightful B&B on the Washington side of the Columbia River is the **Inn of the White Salmon** (800-972-5226) loaded with local history and old-time charm. It offers packages with Mt. Hood Meadows.

Dining

Timberline Lodge has an elegant restaurant, the **Cascade Dining Room,** that serves meals at set times. The salmon and lamb are excellent. The **Blue Ox Deli** downstairs is sort of a theme bar of Paul Bunyan proportions, decorated with murals and original glass work by Virginia Vance. **Wy'East Lodge,** across the street, has several nice places for lunch.

Mt. Hood Meadows has two lodges, each with several eateries. North Lodge has the **Finish Line** for a great lunch, après-ski nibbles and drinks, and a view of the whole area. South Lodge has **Micro Pub & Sausage Haus,** with a good variety of microbrewed beer. You also can buy pizza cooked to order, espresso or latté, and pasta in the various restaurants.

SkiBowl has typical ski-cafeteria food in its two lodges, and at the mid-mountain warming hut. Beer and wine are available at the **T-Bar** in the East Lodge, and there's a full bar, the **Beerstube,** in the West Lodge.

In Government Camp, **Falcon's Crest Inn** (272-3403; reservations suggested) serves a fixed-price gourmet dinner for about $38. **Huckleberry Inn** has a coffee shop open 24 hours a day, and is the place for a hearty breakfast. **Mt. Hood Brew Pub,** next to the Mt. Hood Inn, has microbrewed beer, espresso bar, local wines and a pub menu.

In the town of Hood River are several good restaurants, among them **Big City Chicks** (1302 13th St.) for "healthy foods of the world" such as rum-soaked Bajan chicken and Veggie Enchiladas Mole in polenta tortillas.

Après-ski/nightlife

Generally, the choices are night skiing and sleeping. Exceptions are the **Ram's Head Bar** or **Blue Ox Bar** at Timberline and the **Finishline** and **Alpenstube** at Mt. Hood Meadows, all of which are relaxed as opposed to lively.

Other activities

Not much, at least up on the mountain. SkiBowl has **tubing** and a **bungee jump.** Hood River has some nice boutique **shopping.** Timberline Mountain Guides (800-464-7704 or 503-272-3699) in Government Camp, shows a lot of **ice climbing** beginners the ropes.

Getting there and getting around

By air: Portland has the nearest airport, 53 to 68 miles away, depending on the ski area.

By car: U.S. Highway 26 passes Mt. Hood SkiBowl, 53 miles east of Portland. For Timberline, turn left off the highway and continue for six miles. To get to Mt. Hood Meadows, go through Government Camp to Highway 35, then turn left. It's 68 miles from Portland. An alternate route to Meadows is to take I-84 east from Portland, following the Columbia River to the town of Hood River, where you turn south on Highway 35 for another 35 miles.

Getting around: A car is vital; however, if you rent you may find yourself in a Catch-22 situation. Tire chains are a necessity and you can get fined if you're caught without them (or four-wheel-drive) when "Traction Devices Required" signs are posted. The Portland airport has five rental-car agencies. All but National will permit chain installation as long as you pay for any damage to the car, but you must buy the chains. It's better to rent a four-wheel-drive car—most agencies have them.

All the Mt. Hood ski areas are in Sno-Parks, which require parking permits. They cost $2 per day, or $9.50 for the year and are available at the ski areas and at many stores on the way to the mountains.

Crystal Mountain

Washington

Summit elevation:	**7,012 feet**
Vertical drop:	**3,100 feet**
Base elevation:	**4,400 feet**

Address: One Crystal Mountain Blvd.,
Crystal Mountain WA 98022
✆ **Area code:** 360
Ski area phone: 663-2265
ⓘ **Reservations:** 663-2558, 663-2262 or
(888) 754-6400
Snow report: (206) 634-3771 (Seattle); (206)
922-1832 (Tacoma)
Fax: 663-0148
E-mail: crystalmountain@compuserve.com
Internet: http://www.crystalmt.com
Expert:★★★★★
Advanced:★★★★
Intermediate:★★★
Beginner:★★★★
Never-ever:★★★★★

Dining:★★★★
Apres-ski/nightlife:★★
Other activities:★
Number and types of lifts: 10—1 six-
passenger high-speed chair, 1 high-speed
quad, 1 quad, 2 triples, 4 doubles, 1 surface lift
Skiable Acreage: 2,300 (including 1,000
backcountry)
Snowmaking: 1.3 percent
Uphill capacity: 20,110 per hour
Snowboarding: Yes, unlimited
Bed Base: About 350 (176 rooms)
Nearest lodging: slopeside, cabins
Resort child care: Yes, 6 months and older
Adult ticket, per day: $35 (97/98 price)

When the weather is right, the snow is deep, and the avalanche danger is not too great, hardcore skiers from all over the West Coast beam themselves to Crystal for unparalleled skiing. The terrain is steep and thrilling, and there's enough of it to keep the adrenaline rushing all day. There's enough snow too, often 12 feet deep at the top. It snowed 65 inches one day during the 95/96 season.

It's Washington's only destination Alpine ski resort, just 90 minutes from Seattle. The on-mountain condos, lodges and restaurants delight local skiers who would otherwise have to leave the state for a ski vacation. It recently was purchased by Boyne USA, owners of Big Sky, MT; Brighton, UT; and two resorts in Michigan. Boyne installed the Forest Queen Express, Washington's only high-speed six-passenger lift, which replaced the old Chair 9. Future plans—subject to many approvals—call for an 80-passenger tram, midmountain restaurant, and the conversion of many of the fixed-grip chairs to high-speeds.

Crystal Mountain is a favorite vacation spot for some Canadian ski-hill employees. They don't want their names used, but whole groups of British Columbia liftees and front office personnel can't wait for their annual midwinter ski vacations to Crystal. Their reasoning: snow conditions at Crystal, near Mt. Rainier, are consistently drier and more stable than in British Columbia, and they prefer Crystal's ambiance, which is quite laid-back and low-key.

Mountain layout

◆◆ **Expert** ◆ **Advanced:** Black-diamond runs are a whopping 43 percent. That high expert percentage is partly because of the 1,000 skiable acres in the back country areas, both north and south. It's the kind of terrain that is out of bounds at most ski areas—woods, chutes and steep bowls.

■ **Intermediate:** Blue runs make up another 37 percent of Crystal's 2,300 acres. However, runs are fairly short, such as Lucky Shot, Little Shot and Gandy's Run, all from Summit House. For a longer run, ski Green Valley from the right of Summit House to the base of the Green Valley chair and continue to the base area on Kelly's Gap Road. The six-passenger chair also serves new intermediate slopes.

●● **Beginner:** Beginners can have fun on Broadway and Skid Road, both served by the base area lift, Midway Shuttle.

● **Never-ever:** Never-evers have their own Meadow and Fairway runs served by Discovery chair and the handle tow, both loading at the Children's Skiing Center.

Mountain rating

Crystal is best for expert and advanced (we reduce our five-star expert rating to four when the backcountry is closed), and for those starting out. Intermediate terrain is good, but we wish the trails were longer.

Cross-country

Crystal Mountain does not have nearby cross-country skiing, at least none of the organized, marked-trail variety.

Snowboarding

Crystal has woods, ridges and carving slopes that keep freeriders coming back. Boarder Zone, next to the Quicksilver Chair, has banks, rails, obstacles and a double halfpipe.

Lessons (97/98 prices)

Group lessons: Adult lessons for skiers and snowboarders cost $25 for a two-hour session, $35 for four hours.

Never-ever package: Skiers or snowboarders can take a two-hour lesson for $39 that includes a lift ticket and rental gear. The four-hour version is $10 more.

Private lessons: (one hour, one or two people) are $40 at 9 a.m. or 3:30 p.m., $50 at other times.

Racing: Crystal has a coin-operated course for $1 per run.

Children's lessons: The program is divided into ages 4–6 and 7–11. Rates include an all-day lift ticket. Cost is $30 half day, $52 full day. Rentals are an additional $10.

Child care (97/98 prices)

Ages: 6 months to 11 years.

Costs: Full-day care costs about $47 for ages 6 months to 2 years; $40 for ages 2 and older. A ski-lesson/day-care program for ages 3–4 is about $52, including lessons and equipment.

Reservations: Highly recommended. Call 663-0221.

Lift tickets (97/98 prices)

	Adult	Youth (11-17)
Single day	$35	$30
Three days	$105	$90
Five days	$175	$150

Who skis free: Ages 10 and younger (limit of two kids per paying adult; after that, $17.50 per child) and 70 and older.

Who skis at a discount: Noon-to-closing tickets cost $30 for adults. Beginner-only lift tickets are $18.

Accommodations

Lodging at Crystal is walking distance from the slopes. Three hotels and 96 condominiums vary widely in styles and prices, from $40 for two with a shower down the hall in the **Alpine Inn** to $363 for a **Crystal Chalet** condo on the weekends. The parking lot has 21 RV hookups, $15 per night each; $20 on holidays.

Two to five day packages are available. For the **Alpine Inn, Village Inn** and **Quicksilver Lodge**, call 663-2262 or (888) 754-6400. For all other lodging, call 663-2558.

Dining

Restaurants cater to both the white-linen and take-out crowds, with rustic dining, a cafeteria and après-ski lounges in between. A favorite of the play-hard crowd is the **Snorting Elk Cellar** in the Alpine Inn, known for its good microbrew selection.

Summit House, a rustic dining lodge at 6,872 feet, serves a passable version of the now-famous Northwest cuisine, but the main attraction is the view of Mount Rainier, so close it looks as if you can touch it.

Après-ski/nightlife

Sourdough Sal's (formerly Rafters) has live entertainment most Friday and Saturday evenings. The **Snorting Elk Cellar** is another gathering spot.

Other activities

A Crystal lift ticket entitles the bearer to enjoy the hot tub, sauna and showers for $4. In the Crystal Inn, these facilities are open seven days a week, 2–10 p.m. Massages are available but extra.

Getting there and getting around

By air: Seattle-Tacoma airport is served by most major airlines.

By car: Crystal is 76 miles southeast of Seattle. Drive south on I-5 from Seattle, take Exit 142 east to Auburn, Highway 164 to Enumclaw, and Highway 410 east to the Crystal Road.

By bus: Service from Puget Sound is available on the Crystal Mountain Express. Call (206) 455-5505.

Telephone area code: 360

Mt. Baker

Washington

Summit elevation:	**5,250 feet**
Vertical drop:	**1,500 feet**
Base elevation:	**3,750 feet**

Address: 1017 Iowa St.
Bellingham, WA 98226
✆ **Area code:** 360
Ski area phone: 734-6771 (This is the
number of the Bellingham office.
Mt. Baker only has cellular service,
used primarily for emergencies.)
Snow report: 671-0211
ⓘ **Toll-free reservations:**
(800) 487-2032 (Bellingham-Whatcom
Convention and Visitors Bureau)
Fax: 734-5332
Internet: http://www.mtbakerskiarea.com

Expert:★★★★★ **Advanced:**★★★★★
Intermediate:★★★ **Beginner:**★★
Never-ever:★★★
Number and types of lifts: 9 - 2 fixed-grip
quads, 6 double chairs, 1 rope tow
Skiable acreage: 1,000 acres
Snowmaking: none
Uphill capacity: 6,000 per hour
Snowboarding: Yes, unlimited
Bed Base: 300 in Glacier
Nearest lodging: 17 miles away in Glacier
Resort child care: Weekends/holidays only,
2 years (toilet-trained) and older
Adult ticket, per day: $18-$29.50 (97/98)
Dining:★ (on mountain) ★★★ (in Glacier)
Apres-ski/nightlife:★
Other activities:★

Tucked onto the side of a mountain in the northwest corner of Washington state is a resort with possibly the deepest snow of any ski hill in the country. At Mt. Baker, anything less than 100 inches at the lodge is considered slight. The ski area is not actually the 10,778-foot volcano of the same name. It's on an arm of 9,127-foot Mt. Shuksan, one of the most photographed mountains in the world, also one of the most listened to, since its careening chunks of steep glacial avalanche can be seen and heard for miles around (they're well out of the ski area, so no worries, mate). But imagine the thrill of witnessing one from a chair lift.

In an era when smaller ski hills and non-destination resort ski areas are disappearing— there are 35 percent fewer resorts than there were ten years ago—Mt. Baker's success is an exception. Location, location and location, between Seattle and Vancouver, B.C., has a lot to do with it, but the main ingredient is the average annual 600-inch snowfall.

World champion snowboarders practice regularly at Mt. Baker and live in the nearby town of Glacier. Aside from the abundant snow, a main attraction for snowboarders is the halfpipe, the only natural one in the region. Starting from the top of the Shuksan Chairs, it follows a creek bed for a few hundred yards and is normally buried under 20 feet of snow. The halfpipe is the site of the annual Mt. Baker Legendary Halfpipe Banked Slalom Snowboard Competition. The January event has earned a national reputation, attracting riders from all over the U.S., Canada and Europe.

Mt. Baker's award-winning day lodge, two quad lifts in three years and its expanded intermediate terrain are meeting snow sliders' hopes. Now, even on record days (more than 4,000 bodies is always a record) lift lines never top five minutes.

Its terrain helps, too. The mountain offers all-day possibilities to beginners, intermediates, and advanced skiers and snowboarders alike, with plenty of gentle groomed slopes, steeps, chutes, and woods that bring out the pioneer spirit. The slopeside White Salmon Day Lodge has spectacular views of Mt. Shuksan. It's three miles closer to Glacier, with full food service and espresso, beer and wine. The Cascadian architecture of the building is full of pleasant surprises, from the paw prints in the restrooms to salmon sculptures in the railings to hand-carved animal newel posts. Rental equipment and instruction are available only at the upper Heather Meadows Base Area.

One drawback to the low elevation of the ski area is that the freezing level can yo–yo, and marginally cold days can turn snow to rain without notice. Some ski patrollers keep a few sets of dry clothes for themselves; bringing a change of clothes is good insurance.

 ## Mountain layout

Newcomers sometimes have a tough time figuring how to get back to the Heather Meadows Base Area, because everywhere they go takes them farther away. With 1,000 acres to play with, that doesn't sound likely, but the ski area is laid out over two mountains, the Pan Dome side and the Shuksan (pronounced SHUCK-sun) side. Four chairs serve each side, but Shuksan is by far the more popular. It has the heaviest-duty terrain for snowboarders under the double Shuksan Chairs and the gentlest groomed slopes for beginners and intermediates.

◆◆ **Expert** ◆ **Advanced:** The Pan Dome side, served by Chairs 1, 2, 3 and 6, is for the mogul bashers and chute shooters. Hot skiers can play here endlessly challenging the steep and deep. Every time experts take one run, they are sure to find an other just as hairy. Shuksan has more wide-open, powder bowl type of terrain.

■ **Intermediate** ●● **Beginner:** Nearly three-fourths of Mt. Baker's terrain is labeled blue or green. Chairs 7 and 8 expand the Shuksan possibilities, but beginners may want to avoid Chair 8 for the time being—its terrain is mostly intermediate. The ride, however, rivals Blackcomb's Jersey Cream Express Chair for the majestic view of the mountain ridges past the area boundary at Rumble Gully.

On the Pan Dome side, beginners can easily get back to the lodge on the Austin and Blueberry runs. The signage is good, but don't follow tracks or other skiers if you don't know where they're going. You may end up on steep Pan Face or unmapped places called Rattrap and Gunbarrel. The ski patrol performs award-winning rescues on icy crags that are best avoided.

● **Never-ever:** The learning area is near the Heather Meadows base lodge (the only one of the two base lodges where you can get lessons and rentals at this point), served by Chair 2. The slope is long and gentle, not sectioned off, but not used by more accomplished sliders. Snowboard novices—some of whom feel immortal rather than timid—use this slope. Timid novices probably are better off learning elsewhere.

Mountain rating

"Of my 100 deepest powder days in the last 20 years, 80 of them have been at the Mt. Baker Ski Area," said a local powderhound and heli-skier. The challenge is to pick your days carefully and finish your skiing by 10:30 in the morning, when the runs are skied out.

Telephone area code: 360

Cross-country

Mt. Baker grooms a short Nordic trail loop to the north and west of the main upper parking lot. Elevation is about 4,000 feet and the trail is gentle. There is a $3 charge. The road ends at the ski area, so touring opportunities are all down-mountain on logging roads.

Snowboarding

In the old snowboarding days, snowboarders were carving turns here even where the ski patrol would rather not go. They opened new terrain within the boundaries and so helped skiers improve their skills. There were only a few boarders then; now they're a quarter of the mountain's business, at least.

"No chute too steep, no powder too deep," is the motto of the Mt. Baker Hardcore, a group of local snowboarding enthusiasts headed by extreme shredmaster Carter Turk. He co-produced "Baked," a 45-minute video of serious and not-so-serious snowboarding that challenges Warren Miller for astounding feats and offbeat humor. It's one of many videos that attract snowboarders to the Mt. Baker region.

The annual Mt. Baker Legendary Banked Slalom takes place in late January every year. Billed as not for the squeamish, the race is a luge-like run with 10- to 20-foot banked walls. The 29 gates are positioned on the walls. It's not hard to figure how a Mt. Baker snowboarder once won the extreme championship in Alaska.

Lessons (97/98 prices)

Lessons and rentals are offered only at the Heather Meadows day lodge. **Group lessons:** Adult ski and snowboard lessons start daily at 10:30 a.m. and 12:45 p.m. and cost $18 per person ($16 for age 15 and younger).

Never-ever package: A 90-minute lesson, ticket for the beginner lift and equipment is $36 for skiing adults; $33 for skiing youth (up to 15); for snowboarders, it's $43 and $41.

Private lessons: $50 for one hour.

Special programs: Mt. Baker's clinics focus on women, shaped ski techniques and the disabled (a SKIable Adaptive Program is for skiers who require adaptive equipment). Beginner telemark lessons are given on Sundays for $36 adult, $33 youth.

Racing: Mt. Baker has no public race course, but has racing for youth and other groups.

Children's lessons: The Komo Kulshan Ski Club is starting its 46th year of ski instruction at the Mt. Baker Ski Area. Komo Kids, as the learners are called, beef up their skills in what may be the best kids' ski program in the Northwest. It's an eight-week series of weekend lessons that runs in January and February every year. Lessons are given by PSIA-certified instructors of the Mt. Baker Instruction Programs. Cost is $125 for the season for ages 5–7 and $135 for ages 8–17; lift tickets extra. Call for children's lesson specifics.

Child care (97/98 prices)

Ages: Starts with toilet-trained 2-year-olds. Though no upper age is specified, normally kids older than 6 are on the mountain.

Costs: $25 all day, $13 half day.

Reservations: Advised; call Mt. Baker for information, 734-6771. Child care is offered weekends and holidays, but not all season.

Lift tickets (97/98 prices)

	Adult	Youth (7-15)
Weekend/holiday	$29.50	$22
Monday-Wednesday	$18	$13.50
Thursday & Friday	$20	$15

Who skis free: Ages 6 and younger.

Who skis at a discount: Ages 60–69 pay the youth price. Ages 70 and older pay $5.

Note: Midweek prices do not apply during holiday periods. Mt. Baker is open Fridays and weekends only during the month of April.

Accommodations

Self-contained campers are welcome to spend the night in the parking lot (no hook–ups, no charge), but the nearest accommodations are 17 miles away in Glacier.

Mt. Baker Lodging (800-709-7669 or 599-2453), in Glacier, rents vacation houses, from cedar cabins to large-group chalets, all with kitchens and fireplaces, from $85 to $275.

The **Mt. Baker Chalet** (800-258–2405 or 599-2405), at Mile Post 33 on the Mt. Baker Highway at the west end of Glacier, has 20 cabins and condos ranging in price from $60 to $225 per night.

The **Snowline Inn** (800-228-0119), sort of a two-story condo/hotel, rents studio units for two people for $65. Condo loft units for two to four people rent for $85.

Bellingham, 56 miles from the ski area on I-5, has a wider range of accommodations, including Best Westerns and B&Bs. **The Hampton Inn** (800-426-7866) near the Bellingham Airport, has fitness and business centers, free shuttles and tasteful rooms starting at $64 for two or more people. Those older than 50 pay $59–$64 for a room for up to four people (only the person signing for the room needs to be older than 50). Rates include a 21-item free continental breakfast. The **Bellingham-Whatcom Convention & Visitors Bureau** can be reached for more information at (800) 487-2032; http://www.bellingham.org.

Dining

The mountain's day lodge has a brown-bag room, a cafeteria-style restaurant and a taproom. Fast foods are available at the **Razor Hone Cafe**, at the foot of the Shuksan Chairs.

For dinner you can't beat **Milano's Cafe & Deli** (599-2863) at 9990 Mt. Baker Highway in Glacier. Milano's specialty is fresh-made pasta at very reasonable prices. The salmon ravioli and tomato sauces regularly draw raves, and the Caesar salad may be the best in the region. There's an excellent selection of Italian wines and regional microbrews. The atmosphere is excitedly post-ski, but most of the staff are snowboarders.

Après-ski/nightlife

All evening excitement takes place in the town of Glacier, 17 miles down the mountain. The **Chandelier Restaurant** has an active party lounge. Because of all the Canadians, you'll learn to say "give me a beers" and "eh" a lot.

Other activities

Anything you can do in a national forest you can do here, but you have to bring your own gear—snowmobiles, for example. Groomed trails leave Glacier in all directions, but no place rents the equipment. Ice skaters even hike up to Alpine lakes, and backcountry tourers go everywhere. The ski area rental shop has Redfeather snowshoes for pesky "deep stuff" days.

The **Air Bears Freestyle Ski Club** offers coaching in freestyle skills. One coach was in the 1992 Winter Olympics and the other spent three years as a circus aerialist. Contact Mt. Baker for more information.

Getting there and getting around

By air: Bellingham International Airport is served by Horizon and United Express. Rental cars are available at the airport. Seattle's airport is roughly 160 miles away from the ski area. Vancouver, British Columbia's airport is about 100 miles away, or 45 miles from Bellingham. If you fly into one of the major airports, it's your choice: A shorter drive, plus a customs check, or a longer drive without one.

By car: The Mt. Baker Ski Area is at the end of the Mt. Baker highway, 56 miles east of Bellingham, I-5, Exit 255. No public transportation serves the ski area. The drive from Bellingham takes 90 minutes; from Seattle, three hours; and from Vancouver, B.C., two hours.

Jackson Hole
Wyoming

Summit elevation: 10,450 feet
Vertical drop: 4,139 feet
Base elevation: 6,311 feet

Address: P.O. Box 290
Teton Village, WY 83025
✆ **Area code:** 307
Ski area phone: 733-2292
Toll-free snow report:
(888) 333-7766 (DEEP-SNO)
ⓘ **Toll-free reservations:**
(800) 443-6931 **Fax:** 733-2660
E-mail: info@jacksonhole.com
Internet: http://www.jacksonhole.com/ski
Expert: ★★★★★
Advanced: ★★★★★
Intermediate: ★★★★
Beginner: ★★
Never-ever: ★★★

Number and types of lifts: 11–1 aerial
tram, 1 eight-person gondola,
3 quads, 1 triple, 3 doubles,
and 2 surface lifts
Skiable acreage: 2,500 acres
Snowmaking: 7 percent
Uphill capacity: 8,624 per hour
Snowboarding: Yes, unlimited
Bed base: 10,000
Nearest lodging: slopeside
Resort child care: Yes, 2 months and older
Adult ticket, per day: $45-$51 (98/99 price)
Dining: ★★★
Apres-ski/nightlife: ★★★
Other activities: ★★★★

These are some of the contradictions you'll find on a winter vacation to Jackson Hole:

• This is one of the biggest ski areas in the United States: third-highest vertical at 4,139 feet (its vertical drop is served by one lift, giving it the longest continuous vertical drop in the U.S., if you're into those kind of statistics), more than 2,500 acres of terrain and 11 lifts. But when you look across the valley at the Tetons, you can't pick out the ski area. There are no telltale white ribbons cut through heavily forested terrain. The Tetons are largely treeless, but the trees that are there are nicely spread out, forming natural paths. From a distance, Jackson Hole's runs, chutes and bowls disappear, and all you see are some of the most rugged and beautiful mountain peaks in the world.

• Fat wallets and fancy ski clothes don't seem to impress anyone here. A duct-tape patch is a badge of honor, not a reason to buy new ski or snowboard clothes. This also is one of the few resorts in the world where ski-in lodging starts at $45 per person per night. And yet the town of Jackson has impressive shopping and art galleries where you can drop a thousand dollars in no time flat.

• Employees at the shops, restaurants and hotels in town are friendly and accommodating without being overbearing, with the relaxed, unflappable attitude you find in the off-season at other ski resorts. The attitude comes naturally, because winter *is* the off-season in Jackson. Every summer, this charming little town is overrun by tourists headed for two national parks, Grand Teton and Yellowstone. Jackson residents seem to feel that if they can survive four months of bumper-to-bumper RVs, then a few hundred thousand skiers and snowboarders are a piece of cake. Two wonderful things result from this backward calendar: hotel rooms are relatively cheap, and everyone is happy to see you. (The town of Jackson is 12 miles from the ski resort town, which is called Teton Village. And of course, winter is high season there.)

• You've probably heard about the Hole's menacing terrain, how it eats up skiers and boarders at the summit and spits them out at the base. Yes, it has gnarly slopes—they don't sell "I Survived the Tram" ski pins here for nothing. Yet it also has some excellent learning terrain—long, gentle, wide runs, where you might even catch a glimpse of a moose calf as he runs to join his mother.

 ## Mountain layout

♦♦ **Expert:** Fully half of Jackson Hole's 2,500 acres is marked with one or two black diamonds. It's no wonder the area has a reputation for steep, exciting skiing. Board the big red tram for the 12-minute rise to the top of Rendezvous Mountain. This is where the big boys and girls go to play. Jackson Hole used to charge a couple of bucks extra for tram access, but for the past couple of seasons, it's now part of the ticket. For convenience sake, we applaud the move. But having to buy that tram ticket gave you a few extra minutes to assess your skill level for that day, and provided a convenient excuse if you chickened out. ("Whoa...I'm a bit short on cash today, and I left my ATM card at the hotel. Meet you guys at lunch, okay?")

Once at the top, you have two choices. In one direction is the infamous Corbet's Couloir, a narrow, rocky passage that requires a 10- to 20-foot airborne entry. No thanks? Take the "easier" way down—Rendezvous Bowl, a huge face littered with gigantic moguls. Well, the bowl had waist-high bumps when we skied it—other times it's deep powder, another time it could be wind-packed crust. Point is, it's not groomed, so be prepared for anything.

Another face of the mountain is the Hobacks, a spacious area that offers some of the best lift-served powder skiing in America. Experts looking for a warmup should try Rendezvous' longest run, Gros Ventre, which starts out in Rendezvous Bowl, winds across the tops of Cheyenne and Laramie bowls, then mellows just enough the rest of the way down to earn a blue rating on the trail map. It may look bright blue on the map, but it's navy blue under your skis.

♦ **Advanced:** Advanced skiers and boarders can handle the tram runs, but before you jump aboard, test your skills on the dotted-blue-line runs in ungroomed Casper Bowl—shorter versions of the stuff you'll encounter off the tram.

■ **Intermediate:** Remember that 50 percent of that 2,500 acres is *not* black diamond. Even better, most of the tough stuff is completely separate from the easier runs—intermediates seldom have to worry about getting in over their heads. Intermediates will want to stay on Apres Vous Mountain, with 2,170 vertical feet of beginner and intermediate terrain, and Casper Bowl, with its wide intermediate runs, sprinkled with a few advanced. Follow the solid blue lines for groomed terrain and the broken blue lines for ungroomed powder or bumps. You'll run out of gas before you run out of terrain.

●● **Beginner:** Though Jackson Hole is a marvelous place for novices, it's tough for beginners trying to step up to the next level. It's a big step from those gently undulating green-circle slopes to Jackson Hole's blues. Although the upper parts of Apres Vous and all of Casper Bowl are wide and groomed, they have a much steeper pitch than blues at other resorts, enough to intimidate some lower-level skiers.

● **Never-ever:** One surprise at Jackson Hole is its excellent learning terrain. The base of Apres Vous mountain has a new fenced-in area, called Fort Wyoming, below the East's Rest Cutoff and the base area. It's served by a "magic carpet" moving sidewalk. Faster skiers and boarders can't get in, so those just learning won't get nervous.

Mountain rating

Color Rendezvous Mountain and the Hobacks jet black, with occasional slashes of navy-blue advanced intermediate. Casper Bowl is for intermediates to experts, depending on the grooming. Casper's groomed runs (a solid blue line on the trail map) are a cruising delight. The ungroomed blues (a dotted line) are just plain hard work, worthy of advanced skiers. Apres Vous is fantastic for advanced intermediates but so-so for advancing beginners. Never-evers will do fine the first couple of days, but beginner terrain is quite limited.

Snowboarding

A couple of natural halfpipes are Sundance Gully and Dick's Ditch, plus there's a groomed halfpipe on Lower Amphitheatre. Lessons and rentals also are available.

Nearby skiing

The **Snow King Ski Area**—half the cost of Jackson Hole—is in downtown Jackson, about 12 miles from Jackson Hole Ski Resort. Sixty percent of its 400 acres is rated advanced, thanks to a north-facing slope that plunges 1,571 feet. It doesn't have a lot of green-rated terrain, primarily a catwalk that traverses the mountain from the summit to the base. Because it is so steep, always shaded and often icy, locals call it "Eastern skiing out West." This small town area is a great practice hill with a steep consistent pitch. Lift tickets (all 97/98 prices) for adults are $28; for kids ages 14 and younger and seniors 60 and older, $18. The hill is open for night skiing Tuesday through Saturday. Tickets are $14 after 5:30 p.m., or you can buy an hourly ticket. Snow King's Web site is at http://www.snowking.com; e-mail is snowking@wyoming.com. SnowKing also has a long, multi-lane tubing park that is open weekdays from 4 to 8 p.m. and weekends noon to 8 p.m. The cost is $5.

Cross-country

Jackson Hole has some of the most beautiful natural surroundings in the United States. Nordic skiers can strike out for marked trails in Grand Teton or Yellowstone National Parks, or try one of the five touring centers near Jackson and Grand Targhee. Trail passes generally are less than $10 for adults, except at Cowboy Village at Togwotee, where trail use is by donation and you must bring your own equipment unless you're a guest there.

The **Jackson Hole Nordic Center** (739-2629 or 800-443-6139) serves as the hub of the Nordic systems in Teton Village with 17 km. of groomed track. Because it is next to the downhill ski area, it has telemark lessons as an option. Rentals, full-day beginner group lessons, half-day lessons for other levels and private instruction are available, as are guided excursions into the backcountry of Grand Teton National Park. Trail fee is $8 for adults, and $4 for children and seniors.

Other touring centers are **Spring Creek**, 20 km. with some fairly steep hills (733-8833 or 800-443-6139); **Teton Pines**, on a gentle golf course (733-1005 or 800-238-2223) and **Cowboy Village at Togwotee** (543-2847 or 800-543-2847).

Lessons (98/99 prices)

The ski/snowboard school is not only the place to get instruction (and that isn't a bad idea, given Jackson Hole's extreme terrain), but it is also the place to engage a knowledgeable mountain guide. Jackson Hole's nooks and crannies can best be enjoyed with someone who knows them.

Group lessons: $60 for a full day (morning and afternoon sessions) and $50 for morning or afternoon. Three-day morning group-lesson packages are $130, and other multiday discounts are available.

Never-ever package: Jackson Hole's Learn To Turn program is two days of lessons and lifts for $105, equipment rental extra.

Private lessons: Given most commonly in a two-hour morning lesson for $205 for one skier, $245 for two to three and $285 for four to six people. Afternoon private lessons are $185 for two hours.

Special programs: There are many, such as instruction for the disabled, the Mountain Experience for advanced to expert skiers that shows them the best terrain and snow conditions, and various camps for women, racing and teens offered at specified times of the season.

Racing: There's a NASTAR course off the Casper Bowl Triple Chair.

Children's lessons: The Explorer program for ages 6 to 13 is $67 for all day including lunch, $44 for half day. The resort also has ski lessons and day care for ages 3–5 as part of its day care program. This program costs $68 for all day and $53 for a half day.

You can make reservations for any ski school program including mountain guides by calling 739-2610 locally or (800) 450-0477.

Child care (98/99 prices)

Ages: 2 months to 5 years.

Costs: $65 for a full day; $50 a half day for ages 18 months to 5 years; $65 and $55, respectively, for ages 2–17 months. Parents must provide food for infants; toddlers get lunch and a snack in the price.

Reservations: Required, call 739-2691. Bring your child's immunization records.

Note: For babysitting at your hotel or condo, call **Babysitting Service of Jackson Hole**, 733-0685; (800) 253-9650, or **Childcare Services**, 733-5178. These services, members of the Jackson Hole Chamber of Commerce, have sitters trained in first aid and child CPR. **Baby's Away** (888-616-8495; 307-733-0387) rents and will deliver baby needs to your lodge, such as crib, stroller, car seat and toys.

Lift tickets (98/99 prices)

	Adult	Child (Up to 14)
One day	$51	$26
Three days	$150 ($50/day)	$75 ($25/day)
Five days	$225 ($45/day)	$113 ($22.60/day)

Who skis free: No one.

Who skis at a discount: Ages 65 and older ski at children's prices.

Note: Jackson Hole's lift ticket includes all lifts—chairs, tram, new gondola, and surface lifts, a policy that went into effect a couple of seasons ago.

You can buy a Jackson Hole Ski Three five-day voucher book for $220 ($44 per day). At Jackson Hole, it's valid for a lift ticket. At Snow King, it buys a lift ticket and dinner at Rafferty's Restaurant in Snow King Resort. At Grand Targhee, it's valid for a lift ticket and the round-trip bus transportation from Jackson.

 ## Accommodations

Choose from three locations: Teton Village at the base of the slopes, with fewer restaurants and nightlife options; the town of Jackson, with lots of eating, shopping and partying but 12 miles from skiing; or hotels, condos and two fine resorts between the two. Bus transportation between town and ski area is readily available. We haven't listed all of the available lodging, so call **Jackson Hole Central Reservations** (800-443-6931) for more information. This agency can book your entire trip, from airline tickets to activities. Other booking agencies are **Vacations Incorporated** (800-228-1025) or **Rocky Mountain Reservations** (800-322-5766).

Teton Village

The following lodging properties are all within steps of the slopes and each other, so the choice is on facilities or price rather than location. Most of these properties have ski packages. We list nightly room rates here.

Alpenhof (733-3242; 800-732-3244) is the most luxurious of the hotels. Built in peaked-roof Alpine style with lots of exposed and carved wood, it has an excellent restaurant and a large lounge that is a center of relaxed après-ski activity. Some of the 43 guest rooms have fireplaces. The hotel has a heated outdoor pool, Jacuzzi, sauna and game room. Room rates range from $88 to $398, depending on size of room and season; standard rooms in regular season are about $149.

The Best Western Inn at Jackson Hole (733-2311 or 800-842-7666) has spacious rooms. Many have kitchenettes, fireplaces and/or lofts. It has two restaurants, a heated outdoor pool and hot tub. One possible drawback: every time you leave your room, you step outside. That means bundling up to go to the hot tub or restaurant. Room rates are $75–$225; standard rooms in regular season are $125–$150.

Best Western Jackson Hole Resort (733-3657 or 800-445-4655), formerly the Sojourner Inn, plans to have a 63-suite wing ready for 98/99 complete with a heated walkway to the gondola. This property started out as a European lodge but additions have turned it into a rambling hotel with pool, sauna and Jacuzzi. The rooms in the original building don't have much space for ski luggage and paraphernalia, but the ones in the newer wing are larger and more modern. Room rates are about $100–$260; standard rooms in regular season are $125–$145.

The Hostel (733-3415) has some of the most inexpensive slopeside lodging in the United States—about $45–$57 per person. Rooms are spartan, but have private baths and maid service; amenities include a large lounge and game area and laundry facilities.

The Village Center Inn (733-3155 or 800-735-8342) has 16 one- and two-bedroom units, some with lofts, next to the tram. Not fancy, but inexpensive at about $110 a night. **Crystal Springs Inn** (733-4423) has 15 basic rooms for about $92 a night.

Condominiums and private homes are available through Teton Village Property Management (800-443-6840; 733-4610) and Jackson Hole Property Management (800-443-8613; 733-7945). Rates range about $100–$850 per night.

Jackson

Many of these accommodations also offer ski packages. All listed here are within a block of the public bus service to Teton Village unless noted.

One of the best, with a great location just off the main square, is the **Wort Hotel** (800-322-2727; 307-733-2190), an 1880s-style, four-diamond AAA-rated hotel just off the main square. Nightly rates are about $149–$295. Inside is the Silver Dollar Bar, with its curving bar inlaid with 2,032 uncirculated 1921 silver dollars.

Snow King Resort (800-522-5464; 307-733-5200) is a large hotel with a pool, indoor ice rink, game and fitness rooms and more. It is several long blocks from downtown, but right next to the Snow King Ski Area, which has night skiing. Rooms cost about $100–$170; suites and condos also are available for higher prices.

Two excellent B&Bs are **Rusty Parrot Lodge** (307-733-2000 or 800-458-2004) and **Davy Jackson Inn** (307-739-2294 or 800-584-0532). Both have inviting rooms (some with fireplaces) with down comforters. Rusty Parrot has more of a country lodgepole pine decor, while Davy Jackson leans toward Victorian, but you can't go wrong at either. Rates are about $119–$185 at Davy Jackson and approximately $180–$450 at Rusty Parrot. Rusty Parrot is about two blocks from downtown and half a block to the bus stop; Davy Jackson is three blocks to downtown and a block to the bus stop.

Between downtown and the ski area

The **Red Lion Wyoming Inn of Jackson** (800-844-0035; 307-734-0035) and **The Best Western Lodge at Jackson Hole** (800-458-3866; 307-739-9703) are practically next door to each other on Broadway (Highway 89) heading toward Teton Village from downtown. **Wyoming Inn** is decorated with antique reproduction furniture, but has no pool or hot tub (though some rooms have Jacuzzis). It serves a continental breakfast, but there is no restaurant. Rates at this trio range from $79–$219.

The Best Western Lodge at Jackson Hole (there also is a Jackson Hole Lodge, which is quite different) is a delight for children, because its exterior is decorated with carved painted bears and raccoons that hang from poles and peek from benches and mailboxes. Rates are about $109–$155. It has a swimming pool and hot tub, and the Gun Barrel Steak House is next door.

One of the best spots to see the rugged Grand Teton and its neighboring peaks is from the **Spring Creek Resort** (307-733-8833 or 800-443-6139), atop the East Gros Ventre Butte, which blocks the view of Grand Teton from most of Jackson. The resort has luxurious hotel rooms, condos and houses for rent, a marvelous gourmet restaurant and unsurpassed views of the Jackson Valley, Grand Teton and the ski area. Rates are about $120–$950 per night. Shuttles to town and skiing are provided.

On Teton Village Road a few miles from the ski area and town is **Teton Pines Resort** (307-733-1005 or 800-238-2223). Though it is better known for its summer activities, including a stunning 18-hole golf course, it is open in winter and has ski packages. The amenities list goes on and on: free pickup from the airport, free indoor tennis, use of a neighboring athletic club, daily continental breakfast, an excellent gourmet restaurant, 14 km. of cross-country trails, pool and hot tub. Rooms are spacious and beautiful and are about half the summer rates at $110-$625 per night.

 **Dining**

Jackson has more than 80 restaurants. All the best ones used to be in town, but now there are some outstanding ones in the outlying areas, as well. We'll start with the selection at the ski area, and work our way toward town. If you're staying in Teton Village, be sure to spend at least one evening in town, if only to see the lighted elk-horn arches in the town square.

Teton Village

At the elegant end of the spectrum are the **Alpenhof Hotel Restaurant** (733-3462), a quiet, genteel place that serves German and Austrian specialties, and **Jenny Leigh's** (733-7102) at the Inn at Jackson Hole, which specializes in wild game.

At the other extreme is the very funky **The Mangy Moose** (733-4913), beloved for its salad bar, down-home steak-and-seafood menu, and lively atmosphere (wash down a Giant Enchilada with the Moose Juice Stout local brew), or **Beaver Dick's** (733-7102), with a bar menu and enough stuffed animal heads to buy the local taxidermist a slopeside mansion. Somewhere between elegant and funky is **Dietrich's Bar & Bistro** (733-3242), in the Alpenhof Hotel, or the Best Western Resort's **Hennessey's** (733-3657), where pasta plates warm winter nights. Fondues are served each Friday.

The locals' breakfast favorite is at "the gas station," which is actually part of **Teton Village Market**, where the tasty breakfast burrito or scrambled eggs is $3.19 "out the door."

Jackson

For casual inexpensive dining, it's **Bubba's** featuring heaping plates of "bubbacued" ribs, chicken, beef and pork. No sense in giving you the phone number (it's at 515 W. Broadway), because Bubba's doesn't take reservations. Be prepared to wait, and while you do, send a member of your party across the street to the liquor store—Bubba's is BYOB.

Another casual place is **Mountain High Pizza Pie** (733-3646). **Nani's Genuine Pasta House** (733-3888) and **Anthony's** (733-3717) got raves from locals for their authentic Italian regional cooking. **Lame Duck** (733-4311) has the best reputation for Chinese cooking.

A good choice on the elegant end is **The Range** (733-5481), which gives classes on game cooking in addition to serving it. It serves a five-course, fixed-price, regional American cuisine dinner from an open-style kitchen, and also serves lunch and à la carte entrées. Other upper-scale choices are **Off Broadway Grille** (733-9777) for pastas, fresh seafood and meats; and **The Blue Lion** (733-3912), known for its roast rack of lamb.

The hearty-breakfast king is **Bubba's**. For tamer breakfast fare try **The Bunnery** (733-5474) with excellent omelets, whole-grain waffles and bakery items and **Jedediah's Original House of Sourdough** (733-5671) for superb sourjack pancakes. **Shades Cafe** (733-2015) is fine for gourmet coffees, espresso and lattes, but we found the breakfast somewhat lacking.

Between town and the ski area

For excellent dining, **the Granary** (733-8833) at Spring Creek Resort is hard to beat. Another top choice is **The Grille at the Pines** (733-1005) at the Teton Pines Resort, with a beautiful dining room and extensive wine list. **Stiegler's** (733-1071) has specialties from owner Peter Stiegler's home in Austria.

Gouloff's (733-1886), across the street from the Teton Pines, has game dishes such as pheasant-stuffed chicken and moose medallions (as well as pasta, beef and lamb). The Mexican restaurant with the best reputation is **Vista Grande** (733-6964). For casual dining, try the **Calico Italian Restaurant & Bar** (733-2460), halfway between Jackson and Teton Village at a bus stop on Village Road.

If you're headed to Grand Targhee, **Nora's Fish Creek Inn** in Wilson (733-8288) is a local favorite for any meal, especially breakfast.

For more ideas, pick up a copy of the Jackson Hole Dining Guide or browse through the rack of business-card-sized menus at your hotel (an excellent idea other resorts might well use). **Mountain Express** (734-0123) will deliver to your hotel from a dozen fine eateries.

 ## Après ski/nightlife

In Teton Village the rowdiest spot by far for après-ski and nightlife is **The Mangy Moose.** Close behind is **Beaver Dick's** at the Inn at Jackson Hole with its sports bar atmosphere. **Dietrich's** at the Alpenhof is much more sedate. **Sidewinders Tavern** features 26 televisions for Monday Night Football; Tuesdays is "Boogie Night" for dancing.

In town, **The Million Dollar Cowboy Bar** attracts tourists who love saddle bar stools, the silver dollars in the bar surface, and live Country & Western bands. Try it, corny as it sounds. **The Silver Dollar Bar** is similar, with more silver dollars in the bar. **The Shady Lady Saloon** at the Snow King Resort has live entertainment several nights a week. **Jackson Hole Pub & Brewery** has good microbrews and live entertainment.

 ## Other activities

Shopping here is what it should be at all resort towns—a selection of high-quality, moderately priced goods with friendly, helpful salespeople. Shopaholics should stay in town (the Wort Hotel is right at the center of the action). The covered wooden sidewalks encourage window shopping, even when it snows. There are far too many good shops to single out any of them, but you'll find art galleries, plenty of Western clothing and items made from elk antlers.

Several unusual activities center around Jackson's abundant wildlife. You can take a sleigh ride through the **National Elk Refuge** (733-0277). Between 7,000 and 9,000 elk winter in the valley, going calmly about their business as the sleigh passes. The cost is about $10 for adults and $6 for ages 6–12.

An outstanding educational tour is offered through the **Great Plains Wildlife Institute** (733-2623). On the institute's wildlife spotting tours, you ride with a biologist to help note the location and numbers of various birds and animals. A four-hour tour costs about $70 for adults and $40 for adult-accompanied children aged 3–12, with snacks provided. Full day and multiday tours also are offered. We spotted bison, elk, eagles, moose, deer, bighorn sheep, trumpeter swans and pronghorn. Everyone gets to use binoculars and a powerful spotting scope for up-close viewing.

The unique **National Museum of Wildlife Art** (733-5771) features the nation's premier collection of fine wildlife paintings, sculptures and other art, some dating back 170 years. Though the museum has been around since 1987, it moved into dramatic new quarters in 1994 across from the elk refuge.

Horse-drawn **dinner sleigh rides** are offered by Spring Creek Resort (733-8833) and Solitude Cabin (733-6657). Bar-T-Five (733-5386) has a **winter dinner show** with a barbecue dinner and "yarn-spinnin' " leading the entertainment.

Other activities include **dogsled rides, snowmobile excursions** to Granite Hot Springs, **helicopter touring and skiing,** and of course nearby **Grand Teton** and **Yellowstone National Parks.**

You can pick up a shopping, dining or vacation-planning guide at the Wyoming information center on the north edge of town, or call the Jackson Hole Chamber of Commerce (733-3316).

Getting there and getting around

By air: American, Delta, Skywest, United and United Express serve the Jackson Hole airport. Check with the resort central reservations (phone number is in the stat box) for air bargains. The airport gets direct or non-stop service from Chicago, Salt Lake City and Denver on jets (fewer small airplanes here).

By car: Jackson is on Hwys. 89/26/191 in western Wyoming. The town is 10 miles south of the airport, and Teton Village is 12 miles farther by Highways 89, 22 and 390.

Getting around: Whether to rent a car is a tossup. Skiers can get along fine without one, if they don't plan to do a lot of restaurant or nightlife hopping or skiing at Grand Targhee or Snow King. Unless you are used to driving steep Rocky Mountain passes, we recommend that you take the Targhee Express (733-3101) to Grand Targhee in snowy weather. It's $15 well spent.

Motorists, take note: Highway signs say little about the ski areas. From town, follow signs to Teton Village to get to Jackson Hole Mountain Resort, and to Wilson when driving to Grand Targhee.

Southern Teton Area Rapid Transit (START) buses run frequently between Jackson and Teton Village to 10 p.m. in ski season for a small fee. Four companies provide taxi services and airport shuttles: Jackson Hole Transportation (733-3135), Gray Line (733-4325), Buckboard Cab (733-1112) and All-Star Taxi (733-2888).

Grand Targhee

Wyoming

Summit elevation: 10,200 feet
Vertical drop: 2,200 feet
Base elevation: 8,000 feet

Address: P.O. Box SKI, Alta, WY 83422
✆ Area code: 307
Ski area phone: 353-2300
Fax: 353-8148
Toll-free snow report:
(800) TARGHEE (827-4433)
ⓘ **Toll-free reservations:**
(800) TARGHEE (827-4433)
E-mail: info@grandtarghee.com
Internet: http://www.grandtarghee.com
Expert:★★★★★ **Advanced:**★★★★★
Intermediate:★★★★ **Beginner:**★★
Never-ever:★★

Number of lifts: 4—1 high-speed quad,
1 quad, 1 double, 1 surface lift
Snowmaking: none
Skiable acreage: 1,500 lift-served acres
Snowboarding: Yes, unlimited
Bed Base: 432
Nearest lodging: slopeside, hotel and condos
Resort child care: Yes, 2 months and older
Adult ticket, per day: $34–$39 (97/98)

Dining:★★★
Apres-ski/nightlife:★
Other activities:★

If you like to ski or snowboard in powder but can't afford a heli-trip, Grand Targhee is the next best thing. About 500 inches of snow falls here each winter, and when it does, Targhee's groomers don't exactly work overtime. You gotta love a ski resort that designates beginner, intermediate and advanced *powder* areas on its trail map.

Did we scare away those of you who still flounder in fluff? Don't flip the page yet. This is one of the two best lift-served resorts in America for learning powder skiing (ironically, Alta, Utah, is the other; Grand Targhee's address is Alta, Wyoming). The trouble with powder at other resorts is you usually find it only on the steepest slopes, and it's tough to get a feel for loose snow when you're also struggling with the pitch. Grand Targhee leaves powder on some of its gentle rolling terrain, too, so anyone who wants to conquer powder will never have a better chance. If you are an intermediate, rent a pair of "fat skis" and cut loose. If you really don't want to deal with powder, Targhee grooms a few paths from the top of each lift.

The best part of this powder paradise is you won't have to share their fresh pillowy snow with the masses, because this resort is grandly isolated. Grand Targhee is in Wyoming, but the only way to get here is through Idaho. Its huge bowls of snow are on the western slope of the Tetons, which hug the border between the two states.

Targhee was the name of a local peacekeeping Indian chief who lived in the area more than 100 years ago (you'll see his portrait painted on one of the buildings). Grand comes from the 13,770-foot Grand Teton Peak. From here, you see the peak's less photographed but equally impressive west face.

When Averell Harriman was scouting for his dream resort in the 1930s, he narrowed the search to Targhee and the site that became Sun Valley. Local ranchers and farmers opened Targhee as a ski resort about 25 years ago. Targhee is close to ranch country, and many of its employees herd cattle or grow potatoes in the snowless months. A good number have never lived anywhere else. Though not talkative, they are quite friendly.

No ski area is perfect for everyone, however. If you go stir-crazy without a variety of restaurants and other things to do, we suggest you stay in Jackson and spend one day of your vacation here. But if you'd like to completely unwind, ski during the day, read a good book at night and head home new and invigorated, this is the place.

Mountain layout

◆◆ **Expert ◆ Advanced:** Targhee has two mountains: 1,500-acre Fred's Mountain, which is lift-served, and Peaked Mountain, which is another 1,500 acres of snowcat skiing. Experienced powderhounds will want to exercise this option. Ten skiers per snowcat, with two guides, head out to enjoy this snowy playground. The longest run is 3.2 miles and covers slightly more than 2,800 vertical feet.

■ **Intermediate:** As we said earlier, your best bet is to rent fat skis and head to the intermediate or beginner powder areas marked on the trail map. On Fred's Mountain, three chair lifts open high, broad descents mostly above treeline. Fred's has excellent cruiser runs and good bump slopes. Targhee doesn't have enough skiers per acre to make bumps, so the groomers make their own on the Big Thunder run. Widely spaced and perfectly symmetrical, they are excellent for beginning mogul skiers and those whose knees can't take the pounding of skier-made bumps. There is also tree skiing here and there. The resort grooms about 300 acres of runs; the rest—1,200 acres—is left to accumulate powder.

●● **Beginner ● Never-ever:** Targhee has a small area of groomed beginner runs at its base. But because this resort grooms so little of its terrain, and because there isn't much to do in the base area, we recommend you learn elsewhere, then come here after your confidence increases. This is not a difficult mountain, but it's definitely not for first-timers.

Mountain rating

Great for intermediates and above. Superb for learning powder skiing or snowboarding.

Snowboarding

The area has a gradual, groomed halfpipe. Snowboarding is allowed on all of Fred's Mountain. Phat Fred's is a new shop that has snowboard gear.

Cross-country

Grand Targhee Nordic Center has 15 km. of track groomed for touring and skating. The trails wind through varied terrain, offering beautiful vistas of the Greater Yellowstone area as well as meadows and aspen glades. Trail passes are $8 a day, $5 for a senior or child; children 5 and younger ski free.

The ski school teaches telemarking as well as touring and skating techniques. Group lessons are $27 and private lessons $55 an hour.

A snowshoe tour focuses on wildlife, with the guide pointing out tracks and explaining how animals survive the winter. This tour is $27, 2-person minimum.

Lessons (98/99 prices)

Many instructors have stayed on at the Ski Training Center since its first season in 1969. The training center is noted for its teaching of lessons with a coaching approach.

Group lessons: $27 for adults, at 10 a.m. and 1:15 p.m.

Never-ever package: Grand Targhee has a learner's lift-lesson-equipment package for skiing, but none for snowboarding. Call for rates.

Private lessons: $55 an hour, $20 for each additional person.

Special programs: Targhee runs a half-day powder skiing instructional trip for intermediate or better skiers for $170 each if three people go, $200 for two and $280 for one. Grand Targhee also has several special clinics such as Extreme Skiing and Women Ski The Tetons.

Children's lessons: Ages 6 and older are $27 for a half-day; $55 for a full day, with lessons and lunch, but not lift ticket. Programs for ages 3–5 are $65 for a full day, $45 a half day, with lessons, lifts, lunch and day care activities.

Child care (98/99 prices)

Ages: 2 months to 7 years.

Costs: 2 months to 2 years is $40 per day, $28 per half day. Ages 3 to 5, day care only, is $36 per day, $24 per half day. The program includes two snacks and lunch for the full day, a snack for half day.

Reservations: Required; call (800) TARGHEE (827-4433). Babysitting services are available outside of regular day care; ask at the front desk of your lodge.

Lift tickets

	Adult	Child (6-14)
One day (97/98)	$39	$25
Three days	$114 ($38/day)	$75 ($25/day)
Five days	$180 ($36/day)*	$125 ($25/day)

Who skis free: Ages 5 and younger.

Who skis at a discount: *Those who ski more than one day at Grand Targhee probably are staying there too. In those cases Targhee's lodging-lift packages are the most economical and practical. On all Targhee lodging packages, children ages 14 and younger stay and ski free, one child per paying adult. Ages 62 and older ski at children's prices.

Note: A full day of snowcat skiing, including lunch, snacks and beverages served in a Snowcat Skiing souvenir mug, is $225; $200 for Targhee package lodging guests. Half day is $160; $135 for Targhee lodging guests.

If you are staying in Jackson and coming here for a day, buy your ticket in advance at Grand Targhee ticket outlets in Jackson or Teton Village. You'll save $5. Call 733-3101 in Jackson to find the nearest ticket outlet. The Targhee Express is $51 for bus and lift ticket from Jackson Hole.

Or you can buy a Jackson Hole Ski Three book of five vouchers for $220, valid at Jackson Hole, Grand Targhee and Snow King (Jackson's in-town ski hill). When you use the voucher here, it includes the round-trip bus ride from Jackson, or a lesson (see the Jackson Hole chapter for more information on the vouchers).

Accommodations (97/98 prices)

The village sleeps 432 people at two hotel-type lodges and a 32-unit multistory condo building. All are within easy walking distance to lifts and base facilities. Nightly rates per room at the lodges run $59 to $172, at the condos $143 to $422.

Packages that include ski tickets and two group lessons are offered for seven nights and six days, five nights and four days, and three nights and three days.

For the hotel and motel rooms, regular season packages per person for two people range from $187 to $349 for three days, $271 to $533 for five nights and four days, and $384 to $744 for seven nights and six days.

For the Sioux Lodge condo lofts, regular season packages per person for two people range from $307 to $430 for three days and three nights, $467 to $665 for five nights and four days, and $652 to $926 for seven nights and six days.

Call (800) 827-4433 (800-TARGHEE) for information.

Dining

There's not much variety in this small village, but a lot of quality. Skadi's is Targhee's finest restaurant, with entrées such as rack of lamb, whiskey chicken, shrimp scampi and poached salmon, all in the $12–$24 price range. Skadi's also serves breakfast and lunch. **The Wizard of Za** is the spot for great gourmet pizza and pasta with fun and games for the family.

Wild Bill's Grille in the Rendezvous Lodge has pizza, a soup and salad bar, sandwiches and Mexican food for breakfast and lunch, while the **Trap Bar** serves a fine Idaho potato with all the trimmings, basic grilled sandwiches, burgers and chicken, plus après-ski snacks. Snorkel's has breakfast and lunch, featuring sinful pastries, espressos, deli-style sandwiches and desserts made fresh daily.

Après ski/nightlife/other activities

This is not Targhee's strong point. **Snorkel's** has après-ski with varietal wines by the glass, microbrew beers and upscale appetizers in a relaxed atmosphere. The **Trap Bar** is livelier, with live music.

Otherwise, there is an outdoor **heated swimming pool** and **hot tubs,** and **complimentary movies.** You can take a **sleigh ride** or go **snowmobiling. Souvenirs** can be found in Targhee's small general store or its ski clothing shop, High Country Colors. Mustang Sally's is a tiny boutique with some very fine clothing and jewelry made by Wyoming artisans. At the **Spa at Grand Targhee,** you can indulge in a massage, herbal or mud wrap, sauna or aromatherapy session.

If you need more than this, stay in Jackson, about an hour's drive away.

Getting there and getting around

By air: Targhee is served by airports in Jackson, Wyoming and Idaho Falls, Idaho. Jets fly into both airports and resort shuttles pick up guests by reservation. You can rent cars at either airport or at Grand Targhee.

By car: Targhee is just inside the Wyoming border on the west side of the Tetons, accessible only from Idaho. From Jackson, follow signs to Wilson on Highway 22, then go north on Highway 33 at Victor, Idaho. Turn east at the small town of Driggs (the sign is on the roof of a building), and drive 12 miles to the ski area. About eight miles from Driggs, you will start to suspect you're lost, but keep going—you can't make a wrong turn.

Coming from Idaho Falls, take Highway 20 to Rexburg, and turn east on Highway 33 to Driggs. Grand Targhee is 42 miles northwest of Jackson, 87 miles northeast of Idaho Falls and 297 miles north of Salt Lake City.

Getting around: If you are spending your entire vacation at Grand Targhee, don't rent a car—there's nowhere to drive. If you stay in Jackson, we recommend you ride the Targhee Express bus that picks up in Jackson and at Teton Village. It's $15 round trip; buy tickets at one of several locations (call 733-3101). The highway between Jackson and Grand Targhee is steep going over Teton Pass (up to 10 percent grade). We caution against staying at Targhee and driving to Jackson for the nightlife—if you want Jackson's nightlife, stay there.

Alyeska

Alaska

Summit elevation (lift–served): **2,750 feet**
Vertical drop: **2,500 feet**
Base elevation: **250 feet**

Address: P.O. Box 249
Girdwood, AK 99587
☏ **Area code:** 907
Ski area phone: 754-1111 or (800) 775-6656
Snow report: 754-7669 (SKI-SNOW)
Fax: 754-2200
ⓘ **Toll-free reservations:** (800) 880-3880
Internet: none at press time

Expert:★★★
Advanced:★★
Intermediate:★★★★
Beginner:★★★★
Never-ever:★★★

Number and types of lifts: 9–1 60-passenger
tram, 1 high-speed quad, 2 quads, 3 doubles,
and 2 surface lifts
Skiable acreage: 786 acres
Snowmaking: 12 percent
Uphill capacity: 10,355 per hour
Snowboarding: Yes, unlimited
Bed Base: 450
Nearest lodging: slopeside, hotel
Resort child care: babysitting services
Adult ticket, per day: $29-39 (98/99)
Dining:★★★★
Apres-ski/nightlife:★★
Other activities:★★★

Alyeska, 40 miles southeast of Anchorage, is an unusual resort: the base altitude is only 250 feet above sea level, the lowest of any major ski area in the world. Mt. Alyeska rises 3,939 feet, overlooking Turnagain Arm, a spectacularly beautiful extension that branches off Cook Inlet. The view from Alyeska is best savored from the Glacier Terminal at the top of the 60-passenger tram—mainly because if you see it for the first time while you're skiing, it will mesmerize you so that you're likely to run into something. Another thing about Alyeska that's unusual: in the early part of the ski season, the ski "day" is only about six hours long. Luckily, Alyeska has night skiing.

The lower half of the mountain is forested and the upper portion is above the tree line. Upper-mountain snow accumulations average 579 inches a season, with a high of 918 inches a couple of seasons ago. On a mid-April visit there can be 20 feet of snow on the upper mountain.

Images of Alaska tend toward ice, sled dogs, igloos and pipeline construction in subzero weather. Anchorage reality is much different. Warm Pacific currents keep winter temperatures at an average 10 to 30 degrees Fahrenheit. During our latest visit in February 1997, temperatures were a balmy 32 to 34 degrees, and we walked the streets of Anchorage during the day wearing fleece shirts and no jackets. Anchorage also is a bustling city with plenty to keep residents entertained through the long winter nights.

Alyeska has changed in a very big way during the past few years, growing from a rustic ski area to a luxurious resort. The resort now has a 60-passenger tram transporting skiers more than a mile from the base to midmountain, a high-speed quad, a new beginner quad chair lift, a day lodge and an on-mountain restaurant with gourmet evening dining accompanied by that great view. The final major component, the Westin Alyeska Prince Hotel, may be the only ski hotel in North America that has wake-up calls when the Northern Lights are flashing their mysterious, colorful beauty.

Anchorage and Alyeska are one time zone beyond the West Coast of the United States. So if it's 9 a.m. in Los Angeles and noon in New York City, it's 8 a.m. at Alyeska.

Alaska is one of the most spectacularly beautiful spots on Earth, winter or summer. When is the best time for a ski trip? We recommend late February during Fur Rendezvous, Anchorage's winter festival (more info in Other Activities). By that time of year, the temperatures start to rise (average high temperature is 26 degrees Fahrenheit; -3 degrees Centigrade), daylight hours increase (almost 11 hours), and "Fur Rondy," as it's called, is one big party for Alaskans, who converge from all over the state. You may need the diversion. When Alyeska's skies are clear, the skiing is great. But Alyeska's slopes sometimes are blanketed with severe whiteout or flat light conditions (we've checked with several ski journalists on this, and every one said this happened during part of their visit). Such conditions can be unnerving, especially above treeline, and can cause vertigo in susceptible skiers. Locals advise skiing at night (or late in the day) when visibility is better.

Mountain layout

◆◆ **Expert** ◆ **Advanced:** The high-speed quad Spirit of Alyeska carries skiers 1,411 vertical feet to the top of the lift-serviced terrain, which is at the base of the Alyeska Glacier. Up here it's wide-open, above-treeline skiing. The entire 2,500 feet of vertical is skiable in one continuous run, with intermediate to super-expert pitch depending on your choice of route.

Skiers and snowboarders also can hike to the 3,939-foot summit of Mt. Alyeska, where expert-level Glacier Bowl and the Headwall await.

From the quad, experts can go right and drop down Gail's Gully or Prospector and take a gully left or right of Eagle Rock, then back to the quad. Experts willing to work can take the High Traverse from the quad, arcing through The Shadows between Mt. Alyeska and Max's Mountain, dropping down through new snow and open steeps; or continue over the ridge to find good steeps and a short section of gladed skiing on Max's Mountain (when opened by the ski patrol).

Alyeska opened two new trails down the lower half of the steep North Face last season, making it possible to ski or board double-black terrain from the upper to the lower tram terminal. The expansion added about 306 skiing acres, all steep and tough, and you can scout it out while you ride up the tram. The upper part (called Tram Pocket) is above treeline; the lower part heavily forested with two trails—Jim's Branch and Last Chance. Skiers and boarders can descend Tram Pocket, then cut over to the rest of Alyeska's runs to avoid the gladed area below. The North Face is open when conditions permit.

■ **Intermediate:** Alyeska also has an unusual combination of open bowl skiing and trails through the trees directly under Chairs 1 and 4. Intermediates can take the new quad chair, drop into the bowl and ski whatever they can see. It doesn't take much judgment to figure out whether you are getting in over your head, and this bowl gives you plenty of room to traverse out of trouble. The bowl funnels into Waterfall and ends on Cabbage Patch before reaching the base area.

For intermediates taking the Spirit quad chair to the top of the resort, it's best to follow the Mitey Mite: swing left when you get off the chair. This takes you past the Glacier Express restaurant in the Glacier Tram Terminal, and back to the quad by three intermediate routes, or tip down South Face (very steep and ungroomed).

●● **Beginner:** Beginners will stick to the area served by Chairs 3 and 7. The area is pretty big, but unfortunately used by everyone on their way home.

● **Never-ever:** Don't make the long trip to Alyeska solely to learn to ski or snowboard. Not a huge amount of easy terrain, plus the flat light problem could put a serious crimp in those plans. If "the Alaska experience" (scenery, dogsledding in Iditarod country, being able to brag you "survived" Alaska in winter) is your main goal, then definitely make the trip. You can find some great things to do off the slopes while everyone else skis.

Mountain rating

Intermediates will have a field day, especially with the wide-open bowl skiing and spectacular views from the top of the Spirit quad. Experts have some good drops but the real challenge of Alyeska is the tremendous variety of terrain and snow conditions from top to bottom. Snow may be groomed, cut up or untouched. Often there is powder at the top, moistening to mashed potatoes at the bottom.

Cross-country

The 10-km. **Winner Creek trail** leaves from Alyeska's base and wanders through woods, across meadows and up and down gentle hills. The trail is not groomed, and locals recommend it for snowshoeing. Groomed and tracked trails are in the nearby **Moose Meadow** area—locals will point you there. It's groomed and tracked. Rental equipment is available at the Alyeska Prince Hotel's rental shop. In spring, you need to wait late enough in the morning for the ice cover to melt.

If you are a serious cross-country enthusiast, Anchorage is the place to go. About 115 km. of groomed cross-country trails are in **Kincaid, Russian Jack** and **Far North Bicentennial parks.** Kincaid Park is the best developed, with more than 1,500 acres covered by trails for all abilities. The Nordic Skiing Association of Anchorage (561-0949; grooming report, 248-6667) maintains the trails, all supported by donations and volunteer labor. (Hint: If you use the trails, please make a donation.) NSAA puts out a great map of the trails, printed on a water-resistant paper.

Snowboarding

Alyeska permits snowboarding on all trails and has several natural halfpipes in its main bowl area. Lessons and rentals are available.

Lessons (98/99 prices)

Group lessons: Alyeska packages its ski and snowboard lessons, a real benefit for those traveling from the Lower 48. For example, adult intermediate and advanced skiers can get a lesson, lift ticket and rentals for $58, a lesson and lift ticket for $48, or the lesson alone for $33. (The snowboard price is $68 in the first category, but the same in the latter two.)

Never-ever package: Never-evers pay $38 for a ski ticket-lesson-rental package, snowboard novices pay $43; for the lesson alone for both groups, it's $28. If you're not ready to ride Chairs 3 or 7 at the end of the lesson, the afternoon lesson is free.

Private lessons: Skiing, telemarking, Nordic skiing or snowboarding are $40 an hour, $20 for extra students. Telemarking and Nordic are not regularly scheduled, so make advance reservations with the ski school, 754-1111. If you're enrolled in a private lesson, you can get a lift ticket for $20 and rental packages for $10 for skiing and $15 for snowboarding.

Special programs: The Challenge Alaska Adaptive Ski School, a chapter of Disabled Sports USA, provides skiing for the disabled: all disabilities, all ages, by reservation only. A skier with a disability, and buddy, may buy discount lift tickets and rent adaptive ski equipment. Open Tuesday–Sunday, usually December 15 to April 15. The Alyeska Price Hotel and Tramway are fully wheelchair-accessible, and Challenge Alaska has material on other wheelchair-accessible accommodations and amenities. Challenge Alaska, Box 110065, Anchorage, AK 99511-0065; (907) 563-2658; fax (907) 561-6142.

Racing: A $1-per-run race course is open on weekends.

Children's lessons: First Tracks is offered for ages 6–13 at Christmas and Anchorage spring break for $45–$60 depending on ability level, rentals and lift tickets. At other times children's half-day lessons with rentals and lifts are $30 for beginners ($20 without rentals) and $40 with rentals and lifts for intermediate level and higher ($30 for lift and lessons; $25 for lesson alone). The children's programs are popular—try to make reservations (754-1111).

 ## Child care (98/99 prices)

Ages: 15 months to 10 years.
Costs: $33 full day, $19 half day for ages 15 months to 3 years; $31 and $18 for children 3 and older.

Reservations: A good idea; call 783-2116 or ask when you reserve lodging. The resort does not provide child care; this service is through Little Bear's Playhouse, Inc., a licensed child care facility in Girdwood, the town where Alyeska is located. Girdwood's public transportation is virtually nonexistent. You may need to transport your child to and from the center; ask about that when you call.

 ## Lift tickets (98/99 prices)

	Adult	Child (8-13)	Senior (60-69)
One day	$39	$17	
Three days*	$88 ($29.33/day)	$47 ($15.66/day)	

Who skis free: No one.

Who skis at a discount: Ages 7 and younger and 70 and older ski for $7. Students (14–17) with ID pay $25 for day tickets. Beginner lift tickets (Chairs 3 and 7) cost $18. Adult guests of the Alyeska Prince Hotel pay $33 per day.

Note: Keep in mind that Alaskan winter days are shorter than they are farther south. The lifts don't start running until mid-morning (about 10:30 a.m.), but the "ski day" ends about 5:30 p.m. (Daylight lingers for about 90 minutes after the sun sets in late February, and you can see very well.) Night skiing on 19 trails covering 2,000 vertical feet runs Fridays and Saturdays 4:30-9:30 from December through March: Adults $17, children and seniors $13.

*The best deal on multiday tickets comes with lodging-lift packages.

Accommodations

Because Alaska is quite a distance for most of *Skiing America*'s readers, air-lodging-lift packages are a good idea. **Daman-Nelson Travel** has a great deal from the West Coast with round-trip air on Alaska Airlines, four nights at the Westin Alyeska Prince Hotel, transfers and a three-day activity card good for lift tickets, cross country ski rentals or snowshoe rentals. The 97/98 per-person cost was $749 from California; about $100 less from the Pacific Northwest. Restrictions apply; call Daman-Nelson at (800) 343-2626 for details, or look at its Web site at http://www.d-n-travel.com.

The **Alyeska Prince Hotel** (800-880-3880, 907-754-1111) is a self-contained resort, and Alaska's only AAA four-diamond hotel. Packages are the way to go, and start at $348 per person for four nights of lodging and three days of skiing. Per-night rooms rates are about $160-$250, with suites more expensive. The hotel is part of the Westin chain, but its architecture is faintly reminiscent of the grand Canadian Pacific hotels, such as the Banff Springs Hotel and Chateau Lake Louise. Though the hotel has 307 spacious rooms, several restaurants, shops and other guest facilities, it has a very intimate feel. The Alyeska Tramway is right outside the door, or you can ride Chair 7 to the lower-elevation terrain at the ski area's base.

Other than the hotel, lodging is in condos or bed-and-breakfast inns. The **Alyeska Booking Company** (907-783-4386; fax, 907-783-2763; Internet: http://www.alaskawebsights.com/abc) can set you up, or try **Alyeska Accommodations** (888-783-2001 or 907-783-2000). B&Bs are generally $100 per night or less; condos range from about $125 to $250.

The larger bed base is in **Anchorage**, a 35- to 55-minute drive depending on weather. Major hotels include the **Regal Alaskan** (800-544-0553 or 907-243-2300), **Hilton** (800-HILTONS or 970-272-7411), **Holiday Inn** (800-HOLIDAY or 907-279-8671), **Sheraton** (907-276-8700) and **Westmark** (907-272-7561 or fax, 907-272-3879). The **Hotel Captain Cook** (907-276-6000 or fax, 907-258-4857) has a great downtown location, very convenient to the Fur Rendezvous festivities, shopping and restaurants. Another place we liked downtown was the historic **Anchorage Hotel** (800-544-0988 or 907-272-4553), very nice, quietly elegant, with 10 suites (each different), 16 standard rooms and complimentary continental breakfast.

We've listed a teensy portion of the lodging that's available. We expected lodging prices to be rock bottom in winter, but Anchorage does a steady convention business then. Prices aren't as high as they are in summer, but most are in the $100 to $200 per night range. More options are listed in the excellent free Visitors Guide, available by writing to the **Anchorage Convention & Visitors Bureau**, 524 W. Fourth Ave., Anchorage, AK 99501-2212. Phone: (907) 276-4118, fax 278-5559, e-mail: acvb@alaska.net.

Dining

These are some of our favorite restaurants; see the Visitors Guide for more selections.

In the Alyeska Prince Hotel the **Pond Cafe** serves breakfast, lunch and dinner with a California-Italian menu—try the caribou stew with a big sourdough cheese roll and lots of vegetables. Elegant dinners are the Prince's forté. We heartily recommend the **Katsura Teppanyaki Room**, open for dinner five nights a week. It seats about 20 diners around a U-shaped table facing the chefs who prepare the meals in front of you. We also dined at the **Seven Glaciers Restaurant and Lounge**—on the second level of the Glacier Terminal at 2,300 feet. The view is beyond belief and the gourmet meals are excellent. Call 754-2237 for reservations at all three.

Alyeska vicinity: Perhaps the best restaurant in the area is the **Double Musky Inn** (783-2822), a mile from the lifts on Crow Creek Road. It's mind-boggling to find great Cajun food in Alaska (go for the French Pepper Steak). We had heard it had spotty service, but that was not our experience. The decor is a delight—Mardi Gras beads everywhere and posters on the ceiling. Dress is casual—some Alaskans wear muddy boots to dinner. Busy nights may require a two-hour wait, but it's worth it. (They served 340 dinners on Valentine's Day, 1997—many to lovers who made the drive from Anchorage.) Entrées from $16 to $30. No reservations, opens at 5 p.m.; closed Mondays.

Chair Five (783-2500) is casual and big on burgers, but also offers prime rib, halibut and a tasty, very spicy chicken jalapeño. The Mediterranean pastas and sandwiches are good, too. It's in Girdwood business district next to the Post Office.

The Bake Shop in the ski area base lodge has killer soups, sandwiches, and energy-filled buttered sticky buns. Walk in, meals $4–$9. No soup refills if two people eat from the same bowl; otherwise, it's all you can slurp for $3.75. Lots of locals, ski instructors and patrollers here.

Turnagain House (653-7500), a white-tablecloth restaurant looking out on Turnagain Arm halfway to Anchorage, has a reputation for fine seafood and other dishes with excellent service. Entrées $15 to $30.

Anchorage: A special-occasion restaurant for locals is **Simon & Seafort's Saloon & Grill** (274-3502). It specializes in seafood and steak. Take a walk through the bar and try to find the on-purpose errors in the paintings. Ask for a table next to the large picture window, and get there before dark so you can admire the view across Knik Arm. Other choices for fine dining are the **Marx Brothers Cafe** (278-2133; reservations required) for inventive continental cuisine and impeccable service in a cozy frame-house setting which reminds us of a small New England inn, or the **Corsair** (278-4502), with continental cuisine offered by owner Hans Kruger. The style is elegant and the wine list is excellent—expect to spend the whole evening. Entrées at these restaurants are in the $18–$35 range.

For great views, especially at cocktail time, try the top-floor **Crow's Nest** (276-6000) at the Hotel Captain Cook, or **Top of the World** (265-7111) in the Hilton. **Josephine's** (276-8700) in the Sheraton also has a view, and is a good choice for Sunday brunch. Make reservations and bring $$$ if dining at any of these restaurants.

Many Japanese have settled in Anchorage, and good moderately priced restaurants such as **Akaihana** (276-2215) and **Tempura Kitchen** (277-2741) are among the Oriental eateries. They offer tempura, sukiyaki and other cooked dishes as well as sushi and sashimi. Anchorage also has Thai, Chinese and Korean restaurants.

For moderately priced, delicious food—and great beer—head to **The Glacier Brew House Restaurant** (274-2739) on Fifth Avenue.

Families should head to **Sourdough Mining Co.** (563-2272) for great ribs, corn fritters; **Gwennie's Old Alaska Restaurant** (243-2090) for big breakfasts, sandwiches, historic photos, costumed wait staff); **Hogg Brothers Cafe** (276-9649) for wow omelets), the **Royal Fork Buffet** (276-0089) or **Lucky Wishbone** (272-3454) for the best fried chicken.

Après-ski/nightlife

The **Aurora Bar and Lounge** in the Alyeska Prince Hotel has a moderately lively atmosphere in the bar, where skiers can watch sports on TV. Patrons may play the piano, sing and dance, and make the evening as lively as they want. The lounge is quieter, with a stone fireplace and comfortable sofas and chairs. For après-ski, head to the **Sitzmark Bar** at the base of Chair 3. The **Double Musky** and **Chair 5** also have taverns.

Anchorage has a highly developed nightlife and cultural scene, a legacy of pipeline days, long winter nights, and generous doses of oil patch money. The city reportedly had an orchestra before it had paved streets.

For theater, opera, drama and movies, buy the local newspaper (Daily News). There's a Friday morning entertainment tabloid that's very helpful. You may be surprised at the visiting artists and productions at the **Alaska Center for the Performing Arts** downtown. For recorded information, call (907) 263-2901.

We love wacky watering holes that have unique character. Anchorage has two great ones, but one is closed most of the winter, unfortunately. For loud rock and dancing try **Chilkoot Charlie's**, 2435 Spenard Rd., "where we cheat the other guy and pass the savings on to you." (They sell T-shirts with that slogan—it's a great souvenir.) Chilkoot's is huge—six bars with about 30 beers on tap, two stages (the night we were there during Fur Rondy, one stage had a rockin' band and the other had the Fur Bikini contest), pool tables and games, sports on TV (though it's impossible to hear the audio). Generally, the ratio of men to women is about seven to one, and any attire goes—one February night, we saw people dressed in gym shorts; others in business suits and cocktail dresses. The other unique nightclub is **Mr. Whitekeys' Fly By Night Club**, famed for its Spam appetizers and satirical, summertime Whale Fat Follies show. The club does a "Christmas in Spenard" show, but after that, it's closed for the winter, much to our disappointment. (We've seen the summer show; it's a hoot.)

Humpy's on Sixth Avenue has 36 beers on tap and occasional live entertainment. For quieter dancing and a slightly older clientele try **Legends** at the Sheraton or **Whale's Tail** at the Hotel Captain Cook, or the lounge at the Golden Lion Best Western. For country music, head to **Last Frontier Bar South.**

Other activities

The variety of winter activities is staggering. We have room to list just a sampling. We encourage you to get the excellent free Visitors Guide from the **Anchorage Convention & Visitors Bureau**, 524 W. Fourth Ave., Anchorage, AK 99501-2212. Telephone: (907) 276-4118; fax: 278-5559; e-mail: info@anchoragecvb.net

Think of Alaska in winter and you think of **dog sleds.** Call Chugach Express Dog Sled Tours in Girdwood near the ski area (907-783-0887 for reservations; last-minute calls don't work). If you're staying in Anchorage, drive about 20 minutes to the hamlet of Chugiak to Mush a Dog Team-Gold Rush Days (907-688-1391). As you travel the trail, you'll see a recreation of an Alaskan gold miner's camp. You'll be amazed at how cramped and cold those unheated tents must have been.

Dog sled races are a focal point of **Fur Rendezvous,** held annually in late February. The World Championship Sled Dog Race is the sprint (some sprint—25 miles a day for three days) counterpart to the more famous endurance race, **The Iditarod,** which follows Fur Rondy on the first Saturday in March. Fur Rondy also has fireworks, a snow sculpture contest, a small carnival, a snowshoe softball tournament (hilarious for spectators) and the World Championship Dog Weight Pull, a contest detailed in Jack London's book, *Call of the Wild*. Alaskan Natives come from all parts of the state for Fur Rondy, and many wear traditional fur parkas, stunning works of art with intricate patterns. By the way, if seeing people wearing fur offends you, don't come at this time. You'll only work yourself into a lather over something that has kept native Alaskans warm for centuries.

Several companies offer **flightseeing tours** via helicopter or fixed-wing planes. Though expensive, it is the best way to see Alaska's spectacular mountains and glaciers and well worth the money. We flew with Era Helicopters (800-843-1947, 907-266-8351 or fltsg@era-aviation.com) into the rugged Chugach Mountains that border Anchorage. On an overcast day, you'll gain an appreciation for the arduous conditions that 19th-century mushers endured to bring supplies over mountain passes from Seward to Anchorage. On a clear day, you'll see Mt. McKinley off in the distance, its broad hulk standing apart from surrounding mountains.

The **Anchorage Museum of History and Art** (343-4326) is a must-see, with excellent displays that show 10,000 years of Alaskan civilization, from ancient days through the Gold Rush and the great earthquake of 1964.

Closer to the Alyeska Resort, you can visit the **Alaska Sea Life Center** (907-224-3080), funded by Exxon Valdez oil spill restoration funds and dedicated to understanding and maintaining the integrity of Alaska's marine ecosystem. In Seward, Renown Charters and Tours (800-655-3806 or 907-224-3806) offers an exciting **wildlife cruise** that circumnavigates Resurrection Bay and touches briefly into the Gulf of Alaska.

Getting there and getting around

By air: Anchorage International Airport is served by many major airlines, including one of the best, Alaska Airlines.

By car: Alyeska Resort is 45 miles south of downtown Anchorage. Get on Gambell Street south, which becomes the Seward Highway, Route 1, along Turnagain Arm, which has one of the highest tides in the world. The drive is quite scenic; try to alternate drivers so everyone can admire the view.

Getting around: If you stay in downtown Anchorage or at the Alyeska Prince Hotel, you can get by without a car. Alaska Sightseeing can take you from the city to the resort with advance reservations. Ask at the hotel desk. Otherwise, you'll need a car. The Alyeska area (the town of Girdwood) doesn't have a local transportation system, so if you want to try some of the restaurants we listed, such as the Double Musky, rent a car.

Sugarloaf/USA

Maine

Summit elevation: **4,237 feet**
Vertical drop: **2,837 feet**
Base elevation: **1,400 feet**

Address: RR 1 Box 500,
Carrabassett Valley, ME 04947
✆ **Area code:** 207
Ski area phone: 237-2000
Snow report: 237-6808
ⓘ **Toll-free reservations:** (800) 843-5623 (THE-LOAF) or (800) 843-2732 (THE-AREA).
Fax: 237-2718
E-mail: info@sugarloaf.com
World Wide Web: http://www.sugarloaf.com/
Expert:★★★★★
Advanced:★★★★★
Intermediate:★★★★
Beginner:★★
Never-ever:★★

Number and types of lifts: 14—2 high-speed quads, 2 quads,1 triple, 8 doubles, 1 surface lift
Skiable acreage: 1,400 acres
Snowmaking: 92 percent
Uphill capacity: 21,805 per hour
Snowboarding: Yes, unlimited
Bed base: 7,800
Nearest lodging: slopeside, condos and hotel
Resort child care: Yes, 6 weeks and older
Adult ticket, per day: $49 (98/99 prices)

Dining:★★★★
Apres-ski/nightlife:★★
Other activities:★★

Nestled in the Carrabassett River Valley in western Maine, Sugarloaf/USA is a condo-studded ski resort near the small town of Kingfield. This is a major mountain, with more than 2,800 feet of continuous skiable vertical and the only above-treeline lift-serviced skiing in the East. The resort's slogan is "One Big Mother of a Mountain"—and according to our researchers, The Loaf lives up to it.

First-time visitors get a jaw-dropping first impression of Sugarloaf Mountain as they approach on Route 27 at "Omigosh!" corner. This unobstructed look shows a very big, very well utilized mountain. Runs snake down from the crown in every direction. Sugarloaf offers a variety of skiing that goes beyond its already impressive size—each of the mountain's many runs has its own unique twists and turns, and "boundary to boundary" skiing (off trail between the trees) means that the more adventurous have more to explore. As one guide put it, "Sugarloaf not only has good uphill capacity, it has exceptional downhill capacity, too."

Because it faces north toward the nearby Canadian border, Sugarloaf does not have an overabundance of sunshine. This, combined with its high latitude and elevation, means big natural snowfalls that come early and stay late—it claims to offer skiing during at least eight months of the year. When the sun peeks over the north side in March and April, Sugarloaf is a favorite spring skiing spot.

The great terrain is just one of the reasons many loyal skiers don't hesitate to drive that extra hour or so to get there. The resort recently received accolades for its guest service which some attribute to intensive customer service training for its employees, but more attribute to Sugarloaf's location—most of the employees are Maine natives who love the mountain and want others to love it, too.

Note: The United States has two ski/snowboard areas called Sugarloaf, one in Maine and the other in Michigan. The official name of this one is Sugarloaf/USA, but to save space and typing strokes, we will call it by its "first name," Sugarloaf.

New for 98/99: Snowmaking improvements and new grooming machines will allow the resort to begin its snowmaking process earlier in the season and recover faster from warm-weather spikes during the season. Among the new groomers are a winch-cat that will double the amount of steep terrain that is groomed nightly, and a new halfpipe groomer called The Grinder, which can better smooth a halfpipe during loose-snow and spring conditions. The Grand Summit Hotel will start the first phase of a two-phase expansion project, with 52 new units and a parking garage set for completion in 1999.

 ## Mountain layout

◆◆ **Expert:** This is a good all-around mountain for any level of skier, but what sets it apart is that it has enough steep and challenging runs to keep experts happily banging the boards all day. In addition to more than 500 acres of classic wooded New England ski trails, Sugarloaf also has 80 to 100 acres of treeless snowfields at the summit, where experts can experience Western-style, open-bowl skiing. The only downside to this is that only one lift, a fixed-grip quad, services the summit. Although it is much more reliable than the gondola it replaced, it still shuts down on occasion due to high winds.

Experts can easily figure out where to ski. Double-diamond on the trail map is the honest truth. Steep black runs beckon from the summit and most also can be accessed from the East Spillway double chair. The runs get more difficult the farther east you venture.

◆ **Advanced:** The blacks down to the King Pine quad are all sweet and steep, if a little short. Bump monkeys should head for Choker on this side of the mountain, or to Skidder on the west side; groomers are under orders not to touch these trails, or Ripsaw, Bubblecuffer and Winter's Way. Keep in mind that Choker, Ripsaw, Bubblecuffer and Winter's Way are natural snow trails. Avoid them if it's been a lean natural-snow season.

■ **Intermediate:** Advanced intermediates will find that they can handle most of the single-diamond blacks on this mountain. The Narrow Gauge run from the Spillway East chair is particularly worthy, and because it is officially rated for World Cup racing, in early season you may find yourself skiing next to the U.S. Ski Team.

With a few exceptions, the western half of the mountain is an intermediate playground. Tote Road and Timberwind are both long (Tote Road is three miles), wide cruisers that wind from the summit to the base village—skiers can be on these trails for a half hour, notes one Sugarloaf regular.

●● **Beginner:** At the base of the mountain, beginners will find the very broad and very gentle Boardwalk run, or try West Mountain run, under the chair by that name at the far right of the mountain looking up from the base. Those looking for a little more challenge graduate to the paths from the top of the Double Runner chairs and from there to the Wiffletree quad. Terrain off the Bucksaw chair offers even more challenge: a steeper pitch or narrower trails.

● **Never-ever:** First-timers start on the long, gentle Birches slope, served by two chair lifts, Snubber and Sawduster. This is a great learning slope with only one caveat: It also is the access slope for a lot of slopeside lodging, so we recommend that first-timers quit a little early.

Mountain rating

A giant in terms of vertical (a continuous 2,820 feet), Sugarloaf/USA is a favorite for Eastern experts and advanced skiers, with great tree, mogul and open bowl skiing. Traditional New England skiers will find those classic narrow winding trails they love, while intermediates and beginners will find plenty of wide open cruising. Though just one (albeit impressive) peak, Sugarloaf/USA offers as much variety as its once rival and now fellow American Skiing Co. resort, Sunday River.

Beginners and never-evers might be upset by the better skiers schussing through their learning area, which also serves as the trail back to the condos. However, on a good day, the more advanced skiers usually stay on the upper trails until long past lesson time.

Snowboarding

Allowed on the entire mountain. Sugarloaf is the home of a very large and long halfpipe—350 feet in length and with walls usually about 12 feet high. It also has a seven-acre snowboard park with 20- to 30-foot snow mounds, rails, staircases and barrels for bonking and sliding. The Ride On! snowboard shop, located in Village Center, has rentals; lessons are available through the ski school.

Cross-country (98/99 prices)

The **Sugarloaf/USA Outdoor Center** (237-6830) is the largest and most complete in Maine, with 101 km. of trails groomed with double tracks and lanes for skating. Most of the trails are well suited for beginners and intermediates. The center is off Rte. 27, south of the resort access road. Three trails reach it from the resort's lodging facilities and the village area. The center also has a lighted Olympic-sized outdoor skating rink and a 6,000-square-foot lodge with a giant fireplace, a south-facing deck, and food and drink at the Klister Kitchen, a locals' favorite.

Group and private lessons are available, as are equipment rentals. The all-day trail fee is $15 for adults, $10 for ages 13–18 and $10 for ages 6–12 and 65 and older. Multiday ticket holders may exchange a day of downhill for a day of cross-country including trail fee, lesson and equipment. Exchange tickets at the guest services desk in the base lodge.

Lessons (98/99 prices)

Group lessons: The ski school uses the Perfect Turn® program. It combines state-of-the-art ski technique with state-of-the-art educational theory (see Skiing for Everyone chapter).

Perfect Turn has 10 levels of clinics. For lower intermediates and above, the clinics normally last 90 minutes with a maximum of 11 clients. Enrollees watch a short video that demonstrates various ability levels. This eliminates the "ski-off," which can take up 40 minutes of a two-hour lesson. Clinics meet at three times each morning and cost $25.

Never-ever package: Perfect Turn levels for never-evers to beginners are 90 minutes to two hours. The $46 Level-1 package includes the clinic, shaped skis, boots and poles, a lift ticket for learning lifts. The resort guarantees Level 1 skiers that they will be able to ride a lift, turn and stop by the end of the clinic, or they can repeat it free or get their money back. Levels 2–3 cost $46 per clinic. New skiers start on shorter shaped skis on learning terrain, then "graduate" to longer skis on more challenging terrain.

Learn-to-Ride programs cost $55 and include coaching, equipment and a lift ticket.

Private lessons: $59 an hour.

Special programs: The Women's Turn program offers one-, two- and five-day programs with at least five instruction hours on the snow and after-ski activities. The 97/98 cost was $109 for one day, $215 for two, and $595 for five, which includes clinics, lift tickets, lunch on multiday clinicis and activities. Special 90-minute Women's Turn clinics are $25.

Racing: A NASTAR course is open.

Children's lessons: Perfect Kids programs are available for those ages 4–12 and ranging in price from $45 for half day to $58 for full day with lunch. Register at the Perfect Turn desk or in the Magic Mountain room in the base lodge. Moose Alley is a special kids-and-instructors-only section of the mountain where kids can do some controlled tree skiing.

Child care (98/99 prices)

Ages: 6 weeks to 5 years.

Costs: Full-day rates are $44 and half days are $28. Each additional day is $40; additional half days are $25.

Reservations: Required; call 1-800-THE-LOAF or (207) 237-6924.

Note: There are children's activities every night except Sunday in the Mountain Magic Room in the base lodge. Ages 5–12 have one type of activity, while teens do something else. Examples include games and movies for the young set, and skating, dances, Wallyball games (a volleyball-type game played on a racquetball court) and PG-13 movies for the teens.

Lift tickets (98/99 prices)

	Adult	Junior (6-12)
One day	$49	$31
Three days	$138 ($46/day)	$90 ($30/day)
Five days	$225 ($45/day)	$149 ($30/day)

Who skis free: Children ages 5 and younger; however, they must have a lift ticket, which can be obtained at a ticket window.

Who skis at a discount: Teen (called "young adult" here) prices (ages 13–18) are $44 for one day, $126 for three days and $205 for five. Ages 65 and older ski for the children's price. The College Edge program allows students with I.D. to purchase an Edge card for $45 which includes one day of skiing; subsequently, upon presentation of that card they ski/board for $34 a day on weekends and $29 a day midweek.

Sugarloaf/USA is one of the American Skiing Company resorts. For a description of discount programs that allow you to ski at all the resorts, see the Lift Ticket section in the Sunday River chapter.

Accommodations

Sugarloaf is a planned condominium community in the mold of Keystone or Copper Mountain. That said, it is one of the more tasteful layouts we've seen, the central village blending in well with the overall environment. Make reservations using the toll-free numbers listed in the stat box. Rates start at about $95 midweek and $110 weekends.

The Grand Summit Resort Hotel is the centerpiece of the Alpine village. The slightly more modest **Sugarloaf Inn** has a New England inn ambiance. The Sugarloaf Inn offers packages that include ski lessons and use of the Sugarloaf Sports & Fitness Club, with pool, spas, massage therapy, tanning beds, exercise equipment and indoor racquetball and squash courts.

More than 900 condo units are spread throughout the resort, all designed so skiers can ski back to their lodging. (Not all have lift access, but a shuttle runs from the lodging to the lifts.) Families like the **Gondola Village** units because they are close to the state-licensed child-care facility. The **Bigelow, Snowflower** and **Commons** units are more luxurious, and the **Sugartree** units offer easy access to the health club.

The resort has an RV parking area serviced by lifts.

Kingfield, 15 miles from the mountain, offers more affordable lodging. **Three Stanley Avenue** (265-5541) is a Victorian-style B&B that has rooms with either a private or shared bath. **The Herbert** (265-2000) is an old-fashioned country inn that welcomes dogs as well as their owners.

 ## Dining

Sugarloaf is compact, but has 18 eateries. **Gepetto's** (237-2192), Maine Restaurant Association's 1993 Restaurant of the Year, gets raves for its teriyaki steak. Our favorite for fine dining and atmosphere was **The Seasons** (237-6834) at the Sugarloaf Inn. For pizza or burgers in a homey, noisy atmosphere, try **The Bag and Kettle** (237-2451), locals call it The Bag. You can rate the local talent on Blues Monday while eating a Bag-burger and get the lore of Sugarloaf from the locals. For an English pub experience, try **Theo's Microbrewery & Pub** (237-2211), where the Sugarloaf Brewing Company peddles its wares. On Saturdays, and other nights during vacation weeks, take a snowcat to **Bullwinkle's**, (237-6939), Sugarloaf's on mountain restaurant, for a five-course, fixed-price candlelight dinner. Dress warmly, the restaurant can be chilly.

In the base village, for seafood, head to **Shucks**, (237-2040). **Dellie's** (237-2490), a small, mostly take-out restaurant underneath Shucks, has excellent homemade soups, sandwiches and salads. There's an express line for soups and drinks, but get sandwiches early and stash them away for later to avoid a long wait during peak lunch hours.

No trip to a Northeast ski area is complete without a visit to an authentic New England inn, and **The Inn on Winter's Hill** in Kingfield is worth the 15-mile drive. Sitting on the hill named after Sugarloaf's founder, Amos Winter, the inn has an excellent restaurant, **Julia's** (265-5421). Proprietors Richard and Carolyn Winnick will gladly conduct tours of this renovated inn. Without question, **One Stanley Avenue** (265-5541) is the best and most expensive restaurant in town. Chef Dan Davis serves a creative menu of regional cuisine prepared in classic ways. The **Herbert Hotel** (265-2000) is also worth a visit.

Hug's (237-2392), about two miles from the mountain's access road, is a good choice for traditional Italian food served family style at reasonable prices. Even more kid-friendly is **Tufulio's** (235-2010), located in Carrabassett Valley.

In Eustis, 11 minutes north of Sugarloaf, two restaurants are worth checking out: **The Trail's End** for steaks and the **Porter House** (246-7932) for home cooking with big portions.

 ## Après-ski/nightlife

On sunny days après-skiers crowd the decks of **The Beach** or **The Bag**. The hot spot for live music and dancing at night is the **Widowmaker Lounge**. For a more subdued atmosphere, try the **Sugarloaf**

Inn, home of the **Shipyard Brewhouse** or **The Double Diamond** in the Grand Summit Resort Hotel.

On Route 27 in the valley, you'll find the locals at **Carrabassett Yacht Club** or at **Judson's Motel,** the latter a favorite with UMaine and Colby College students.

Teenagers can head to **Avalanche,** an alcohol-free teen spot with a DJ and dance floor. Pre-teens have **Pinocchio's,** with video games, pinball and board games to keep them entertained.

Other activities

Shopping: The village has several shops, including Pat Buck's Emporium, a gift store that features handcrafted items by Maine artisans (including beautiful knitted sweaters); and Goldsmith Gallery, with gold and silver jewelry, photo frames, and similar items. In Kingfield you'll find Scent-sations, where you choose your favorite scent and the store will put it into lotions, shampoos and body oils. The Brick Castle carries a nice selection of regional art and upscale crafts. South of Kingfield, on Route 27 in New Portland, is Nowetah's Indian Store and Museum, with a good display of antique Native American crafts and a selection of current crafts for sale.

Dogsledding, horse-drawn sleigh rides, snowmobiling, snowshoeing, ice fishing and **skating** are among the activities that Sugarloaf Guest Services can arrange (237-2000).

Getting there and getting around

By air: The closest commercial airport is the Portland International Jetport. The Augusta airport is serviced by Continental Connection. Bangor International Airport also is serviced by major airlines. Guests who fly into Bangor or Portland and who reserve lodging & lift stays through Sugarloaf/USA reservations can reserve transportation at the time of booking. Reservation agents have listings of independent transportation partners and rental car services.

By car: Take I-95 north to Augusta, Rte. 27 through Farmington and Kingfield. Or take the Maine Turnpike to the Auburn exit, Rte. 4 to Farmington and Rte. 27 through Kingfield. The drive is about two-and-a-half hours from Portland.

Getting around: A car is optional—nearly everything in the resort is within walking distance. A free on-mountain shuttle runs on weekends and is on call during the week. To do anything away from the resort complex, you will need a car.

Sunday River

Maine

Summit elevation: 3,140 feet
Vertical drop: 2,340 feet
Base elevation: 800 feet

Address: P.O. Box 450
Bethel, ME 04217
 Area code: 207
Ski area phone: 824-3000
Fax: 824-5110
Snow report: (207) 824-5200;
(617) 625-8619; (508) 580-0667
ⓘ Toll-free reservations: (800) 543-2754
E-mail: snowtalk@sundayriver.com
Internet: http://www.sundayriver.com
Expert:★★
Advanced:★★★
Intermediate:★★★★
Beginner:★★★★★
Never-ever:★★★★★

Number of lifts: 18—4 high-speed quads,
5 quads, 4 triples, 2 doubles, 3 surface lifts
Snowmaking: 92 percent
Skiable acreage: 645 acres
Uphill capacity: 32,000 per hour
Snowboarding: Yes, unlimited
Bed base: 5,300 on mountain; 2,000 nearby
Nearest lodging: slopeside
Resort child care: Yes, 6 weeks and older
Adult ticket, per day: $49 (98/99 prices)

Dining:★★
Apres-ski/nightlife:★★
Other activities:★★

Sunday River, just outside of Bethel and tucked against the New Hampshire border, is a pleasant blend of old New England tradition with modern ski facilities. Bethel is a typically picturesque New England town, complete with white-steepled church and ivy-covered prep school. The main street is lined with historic buildings, and the village common is anchored by the 75-year-old Bethel Inn.

The Sunday River Ski Resort rises six miles to the north, a 90-minute drive from the Portland airport and about three-and-a-half hours from Boston. As you drive up the access road to the base area, you see condominium complexes, but they don't assault you; they blend with the trees and hills.

The resort doesn't have a main center. Three separate base lodges—South Ridge, Barker Mountain, and White Cap—provide basic cafeteria and sports shop facilities. South Ridge Lodge is the hub, housing the ski school, the corporate offices and a grocery store. The condo complexes are small centers to themselves, with most boasting an indoor or heated outdoor pool, hot tubs and saunas. A sense of quiet results: the bustle of people created by a town or central hub is dispersed into the condominiums.

It may be quiet, but Sunday River isn't dull. The high-powered snowmaking system pumps a mountain of snow and the high-speed lift system pumps skiers in prodigious numbers onto the slopes. Lift lines are never long, but the trails do get full. With the mountain laced with a warren of intersecting trails, prudent skiers always keep a watch uphill.

Something is always happening here—during the past few years, we've seen ski terrain expansions, new lifts, a new hotel, a new way of teaching skiing, and a new ski train from Portland. Off the mountain, its Bethel Station project now has a train station, a four-screen movie theater and a new restaurant.

Mountain layout

◆◆ Expert ◆ Advanced: Oz is a playground for high-level sliders. Served by a fixed-grip quad, it features a 500-yard-wide steep swath with tree islands and glades. You won't find the trails zig-zagging across the fall-line—Oz is a collection of straight fall-line tree-studded drops.

The Aurora area, served by a fixed quad chair and a triple chair, is still the spot to find tough skiing. Northern Lights, rated blue on the map, provides an easier way down the mountain, though it's no stroll through the park. Celestial, reached from Lights Out, is one of the nicest gladed trails. It starts out steep and wide, but mellows and narrows as you descend.

From the top of Barker Mountain a steep trio—Right Stuff, Top Gun and Agony—provide advanced skiers long sustained pitches. Agony and Top Gun are premier bump runs. Right Stuff is a cruiser early in the day after it's been groomed, but normally develops moguls by afternoon. Tree skiing fans will find a gladed area—Last Tango—between Right Stuff and Risky Business. This black-diamond natural slalom area is the gentlest and most spacious of the resort's seven mapped glades. Though it's not particularly steep, it's tight. A work road about two-thirds of the way down allows skiers to bail out onto Right Stuff. Those who continue through the trees will find the terrain getting steeper and narrower. If you're less than an expert, you won't have much fun on Last Tango's lower third.

From the top of Locke Mountain, T-2 plunges down the tracks of an old T-bar providing a spectacular view of Bethel, the valley and Mt. Washington.

The White Heat run is a wide swath straight down the mountain from the peak of White Cap. Double-diamond Shockwave, considered by many locals as tougher than White Heat, offers 975 vertical feet of big bumps and steep pitches. Two gladed areas called Hardball (skier right) and Chutzpah (skier left) start out deceptively mellow and open-spaced, but watch out. Technically, they are the most demanding on the mountain.

■ Intermediate: The top of North Peak has the largest concentration of blue runs, though there's an intermediate way down from the top of every peak. Jordan Bowl provides some of the best cruising in New England down Excalibur and Rogue Angel with some wide-open glades accessed by the mellow cruiser Lollapalooza. An advanced intermediate trail is Monday Mourning, which starts out steep and wide but mellows near the end, where the NASTAR course is located. Lower intermediates can head to the White Cap quad (far left on the map) and enjoy the relatively mellow Moonstruck, Starburst and Starlight runs.

●● Beginner: Once a skier is past the basic snowplow and into stem christies, much of Sunday River beckons. The North Peak triple chair opens long practice runs like Dream Maker. Lollapalooza, the green-circle trail in Jordan Bowl, is "like Dream Maker on steroids," as one frequent visitor said. It is long and wide with great views, but not a trail that beginners should start out on—the upper part can get bumped up on busy days, and probably should have a blue rating. Farther down it's quite mellow.

● Never-ever: First-timers start on Sundance and then have the entire South Ridge area to practice linking their turns. Twelve beginner runs in the South Ridge area are serviced by a high-speed quad, a triple, a double and a surface lift.

Mountain rating

Sunday River is perfect for beginners, with one of the most extensive lift-served novice areas in New England. Intermediates get a mountain full of terrain. Experts will find super steeps, glades and monster bumps on Oz, Jordan Bowl, Aurora Peak, Barker Mountain and White Cap. Sunday River's snowmaking system is one of the best and biggest anywhere.

Cross-country

Sunday River does not have a dedicated cross-country center. This part of Maine is known for some of the best Nordic skiing in New England. The **Bethel Inn Cross-Country Ski Center** (824-2175) behind the hotel links up with 40 km. of marked and groomed trials. They have rentals, lessons and evening sleigh rides. The Bethel Inn also has instruction in telemark. If you're a novice Nordic skier, this is a great place to learn—many of the trails are quite gentle.

Midweek, the trail fee is also good for entrance to the recreation center, with outdoor heated pool, sauna and fitness center, until 2 p.m.

The **Sunday River Ski Touring Center** (824-2410) is run by the Sunday River Inn on the Sunday River access road. It has 40 km. of groomed and tracked trails.

Carter's Cross-Country Ski Center (539-4848), off Rte. 26 in Oxford, provides another alternative for skinny skis, with 25 km. of tracks.

Forty-five minutes from Bethel is the **Jackson Ski Touring Center.** See the Mt. Washington Valley chapter for details of its ski touring programs.

Snowboarding (97/98 prices)

Sunday River has welcomed snowboarders for a long time, but has gone beyond the traditional resort practice of attracting boarders to one isolated snowboard park. Instead, snowboarders and skiers share terrain parks throughout the trail system, all of which have the usual features—hits, bumps, rolls, table tops, spines and more. Rentals and lessons are available. A Guaranteed Learn to Ride program, including board, boots, clinic and lifts, costs $44. Clinics are $25.

A 300-foot halfpipe is just above the White Cap base area on the Tempest trail. The Pipe is lighted at night and has an adjacent surface lift.

Lessons (98/99 prices)

Group lessons: The Sunday River Ski School created the innovative teaching program called Perfect Turn®. It combines state-of-the-art ski technique with state-of-the-art educational theory (see Skiing for Everyone chapter for a full description).

Perfect Turn has 10 levels. For lower intermediates and higher, the clinics normally last 75 minutes with a maximum of six skiers. Skiers watch a short video that demonstrates various levels of skiing ability. The video eliminates the "ski-off," which usually takes up about 40 minutes of a two-hour lesson. Clinics run about every half hour and cost $30.

Never-ever package: The package includes the clinic, shaped skis, boots and poles, a lift ticket for the South Ridge and North Peak. It costs $55 for Level 1. Sunday River guarantees Level 1 skiers that they will be able to ride a lift, turn and stop by the end of the clinic, or they can repeat it free or get their money back. The second and third learning experiences cost $65 apiece. A three-lesson package costs $134.

Private lessons: $60 an hour, $115 for two hours, $150 for half day, $270 for full day.

Racing: A course is on the Monday Mourning trail. It is available for private groups by appointment and open to the public on a limited basis.

Children's lessons: Sunday River's children's programs are among the best-organized and smoothest-running at any resort. The flow from equipment rental to classes is outstanding and all facilities are separate, which makes dealing with youngsters much easier.

Age 3 starts with Tiny Turns, an hour of private instruction with a half- or full-day session in day care. The private clinic is $30 if the child is registered in day care; otherwise, the clinic cost is the regular private rate.

Mogul Munchkins is for ages 4–6; Mogul Meisters is for those 7–12 years of age. Perfect Kids clinics cost $48 for a full day and $25 for a half day.

Child care (98/99 prices)

Ages: 6 weeks to 2 1/2 years.
Costs: The hourly rate is $7.75. Bring diapers, formula and food for infants. All-day programs are $48 including lunch, and half-day programs are $27 for older toddlers. Discounts apply for siblings.
Reservations: Advised midweek, required weekends. Call 824-3000.

Lift tickets (98/99 prices)

	Adult	Child (6-12)
One day	$49	$31
Three days	$138 ($46/day)	$87 ($29/day)
Five days	$230 ($46/day)	$145 ($29/day)

Who skis free: Children ages 5 and younger with parent.

Who skis at a discount: Ages 65 and older ski for half the adult price of the day. The College Edge program allows students with I.D. to purchase an Edge card for $45 which includes one day of skiing; subsequently upon presentation of that card, they ski for $33 a day on weekends and $29 a day midweek.

Multi-resort discounts: Sunday River is one of the nine American Skiing Company (ASC) resorts along with Sugarloaf/USA in Maine; Attitash Bear Peak in New Hampshire; Killington/Pico, Sugarbush and Mount Snow/Haystack in Vermont; The Canyons in Utah; Heavenly in California and Steamboat in Colorado.

The New England resorts, Steamboat, Heavenly and The Canyons share a Magnificent 7 ski pass that allows seven days of skiing at the participating resorts for $314.64 for adults, $293.65 for teens and $181.65 for children (6–12). Magnificent 7 cards are valid one year from the date of purchase and are non-transferable.

The Edge frequent skier program can be used to earn free lift tickets. Skiers and snowboarders can sign up at any of the ASC resorts. Program members will be credited with points every time they purchase a lift ticket, just like an airline frequent flyer program. The program also has features such as direct-to-lift ticketing (no more lines at the ticket window) and "cash-free" resort visits (purchases are charged to your credit card). Check with the resorts for more details.

Accommodations

The Summit Hotel and condominiums are the most convenient to the slopes. But Bethel also has a group of excellent B&Bs and old country inns. Call **central reservations** (800-543-2754), which will handle everything from air travel to day care.

The **Jordan Grand Hotel and Crown Club**, new to Sunday River last season, combines the best features of a first-class hotel and luxury condominiums, and it has ski-in/ski-out access. Amenities include a whirlpool spa, heated indoor/outdoor pool, full-service health club, gourmet restaurant, daily maid service, concierge and on-site licensed child care.

The **Summit Hotel and Conference Center** is trailside with a 25-meter heated outdoor pool, athletic club, and fine dining. Rates, which include lift tickets, start at $89 midweek and $129 weekend, per person for a double-occupancy unit. The **Snow Cap Inn** is a short walk from the slopes (rates per person, double occupancy, $69 midweek, $99 weekend, including lift tickets) and the **Ski Dorm** next door offers affordable digs ($23 midweek, $34 weekends and holidays, no lift tickets).

Locke Mountain Townhouses are the most upscale, but hard to get, with the ideally located **Merrill Brook** condominiums not far behind. Sunday River has nine condominium complexes throughout the resort, and all units are convenient to the slopes and all have trolley service. Rates include lift tickets and are per person, based on maximum occupancy for the unit. They start at $69 midweek, $89 weekends.

In Bethel, the **Bethel Inn** (207-824-2175) has old-style atmosphere and first-rate rooms. The rates include breakfast and dinner. Double rates run $60 to $125 per person. The inn also has a cross-country center and health club (see *Cross-country*).

The **Douglass Place** is Bethel's original B&B (207-824-2229). The proprietor has many tales to tell. **The Four Seasons** is in an old elegant building with excellent French cuisine (207-824-2755 or 800-227-7458). **The Sudbury Inn** (207-824-2174) has one of the best restaurants in town and is a favorite watering hole. **The Holidae House** (207-824-3400) in Bethel has drawn praise for its beautiful decor. These B&Bs cost about $45–$150 per night.

The Chapman House (824-2657) is a B&B in the heart of Bethel offering rooms and apartments as well as a ski dorm. There is a bountiful hot buffet breakfast and the guest kitchen, laundry, saunas and game room in the attached barn. Rates are $30–$95 per person.

Less than a mile from the base of the mountain, the **Sunday River Inn** (207-824-2410) offers a relaxed setting reminiscent of the great ski lodges of the '60s. It also operates the closest cross-country center. All rates include breakfast and dinner and range from about $40 for a dorm room where you bring your own sleeping bag to about $75 per person for a private-bath suite. Shared-bath rooms also are available.

Information about **other lodging** is available through Sunday River's central reservation line (800-543-2754) or the Bethel Area Chamber of Commerce (207-824-3585).

 ## Dining

Legends (824-3500, ext. 5858) in the Summit Hotel has a great menu and wine list. **Walsh and Hill Trading Company** restaurant (824-5067) in the Fall Line Condominiums is convenient and serves steaks and seafood. **Rosetto's Italian Restaurant** (824-6224) in the White Cap Lodge is open for dinner daily and for lunch on weekends and holidays.

Foggy Goggle in the South Ridge base is packed for lunch, with good reason. **The Peak Lodge and Skiing Center**, at the summit of North Peak, is a popular lunch spot with a giant deck. **BUMPS!** in the White Cap Lodge serves a pub menu which should be avoided unless you're starving.

In Bethel try the **Sudbury Inn** (824-6558) and the **Bethel Inn** (824-2175). The Sudbury recently renovated its dining room, making it even more attractive. Downstairs, **Sud's Pub** is popular for après-ski and pub food. For French cuisine head to **L'Auberge** (760-2774). **Mother's** (824-2589) on Upper Main Street is a favorite of students from the Gould Academy as well as skiers. The **Moose's Tale** (824-3541) in the **Sunday River Brewing Company** now serves food worthy of its excellent on-premise-brewed ales, locals tell us. **Skidders** (824-3696) makes great deli take-out.

The **Iron Horse** (824-0961) at Bethel Station, is housed in authentic railroad cars. Part of the experience includes the 7:45 p.m. freight train that rumbles by on the next track. The **Matterhorn** (824-6836) serves brick-oven-baked pizza and fresh pasta.

 Après-ski/nightlife

If you strike it rich you may find midweek action at Sunday River and in Bethel, but the real fun heats up on weekends.

Immediate après-ski is at the base of the slopes. **Foggy Goggle** in the South Ridge base area is the liveliest of the mountain spots. Try the **Shipyard Brew Haus** in the Barker Mountain base area or **BUMPS!** at the White Cap Base Lodge. In town head to the **Sunday River Brewery** or **Sud's Pub.**

At night, **BUMPS!** has bands on weekends and comedy nights planned for Tuesdays. The crowd leans toward young. The **Sunday River Brewery** has live music and excellent homemade brew. Downtown, the **Backstage** usually has karaoke during the week, with Country & Western and rock'n'roll bands on weekends. It also has the only pool tables in town. **Sud's Pub** has bands ranging from blues to bluegrass. A more sedate crowd fills **Legends** at the Summit Hotel for its acoustic music.

Other activities

Shopping: Bethel has some unusual shops, such as Bonnema Potters, with highly distinctive pottery depicting the Maine landscape; and Mt. Mann, a native gemstone shop. On Church Street, Samuel Timberlake produces fine reproductions of Shaker furniture.

At the resort, **swimming pools and saunas** are in virtually every condominium complex. Guests staying at the few condos that don't have them get privileges at nearby complexes. The ski dorm has video games and pool tables.

Other activities include **horse-drawn sleigh rides** (make reservations at the Guest Services Desk), **ice skating** or the **lighted halfpipe** at the White Cap Base Lodge. That lodge also is home to the **Teen Center and Arcade.**

Bethel Station, about four miles from Sunday River, has a four-screen **movie theater** and **video entertainment center** with interactive golf, batting cages and CD-ROM games, among other attractions. Rick's Deli or the Iron Horse Bar & Grill can satisfy your hunger pangs while you're at Bethel Station.

 Getting there and getting around

By air: The most convenient commercial airport is Portland International Jetport, 75 miles from Sunday River. Private pilots can land in Bethel. Bethel Express Corporation will pick up from either airport by reservation (824-4646).

By car: Sunday River is in western Maine an hour and a half from Portland and three-and-a-half hours from Boston. From I-95, take Exit 11 in Maine to Rte. 26 north, continue to Bethel, then take Rte. 2 six miles north to Sunday River.

RV parking, no hookups, is allowed in designated parking areas at the resort. An RV park is also at White Birch Camping, in Shelburne on Rte. 2.

By train: The Sunday River Silver Bullet Ski Express runs between Portland and Bethel. A bus takes skiers from Bethel to the slopes. Call the resort for schedules and fares.

Getting around: During the main part of the season, on-mountain transportation between the base areas is quite good on shuttlebuses that look like old trolley cars. The shuttle loop expands to include the condos at night. In shoulder season, the mountain shuttles are by request only. Several off-mountain properties, such as the Sunday River Inn and the Bethel Inn, have shuttle service to and from the slopes. Midwinter, you can get along without a car, but they're nice to have, especially if you want to go to Bethel. Early or late season, you'll need one.

Ski 93

New Hampshire

Waterville Valley, Loon, Cannon, Bretton Woods

Ski 93 Facts

✆ **Area code:** 603
Snow report: (800) 88-SKI-NH (887-5464)
ⓘ **Toll-free reservations:** (800) WE-SKI-93 (937-5493)
or (800) 227-4191 (Loon and Cannon areas)
Fax: (603) 745-3002 (Ski NH)
E-mail: info@skinh.com
Internet: http://www.skinh.com
Dining:★★★
Apres-ski/nightlife:★★★
Other activities:★★★

Waterville Valley, Loon Mountain, Cannon Mountain and Bretton Woods are all within 30 to 45 minutes of one another, accessible by I-93—hence their group marketing umbrella, Ski 93. Waterville is the most self-contained, while Loon has almost too much condo development; Cannon is the most historic and untamed; and Bretton Woods is tame but elegant.

You can ski them all with a five-day midweek, non-holiday lift ticket called the Family Pass, interchangeable at most New Hampshire resorts. It allows skiing at 17 areas, guaranteeing that a skier will never have to ski the same trail twice in one week or even two. The starting day is flexible, as long as you use it five consecutive midweek days. Call Ski New Hampshire (800-887-5464) or visit its Web site (www.skinh.com) for current prices.

Waterville Valley

Waterville Valley is one of the best known mountains in New England, largely because of the publicity from staging more than 30 World Cup ski races in the past quarter century (Waterville founder Tom Corcoran finished fourth in the 1960 Olympic giant slalom). Though the area is well suited for racing, it isn't what we would want for an entire week of skiing. For an extended weekend, though, it can be a lot of fun. Waterville Valley is sufficiently self-contained so that most visitors, once they enter, do not venture any farther than the slopes, just a short shuttlebus ride away from the lodging. There are a lot of other things to do, too, such as cross-country skiing, shopping or working out in a huge sports complex, with indoor and outdoor swimming pools, tennis, squash and racquetball courts, and indoor track. There is also an indoor skating rink. The "Winter Unlimited" package includes the use of all these activities for one price.

This year Waterville has focused its energy on developing its base lodge facilities. A new restaurant will open and additional space for seating will be constructed.

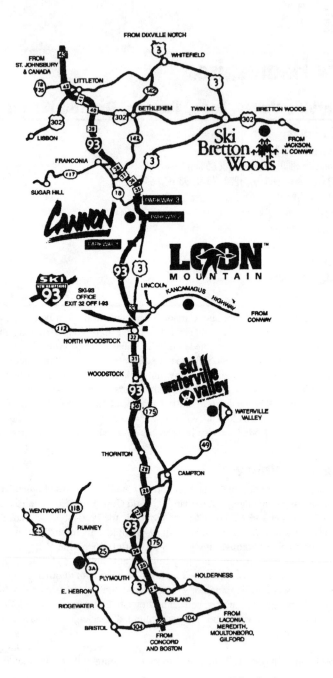

Telephone area code: 603

Waterville Valley Facts

Summit elevation:	4,004 feet
Vertical drop:	2,020 feet
Base elevation:	1,984 feet

Expert:★ Advanced:★★
Intermediate:★★★
Beginner:★★★★
Never-ever:★★★★
Address: One Ski Area Rd.,
Waterville Valley, NH 03215
✆ Area code: 603
Ski area phone: 236-8311
Snow report: 236-4144
Fax: 236-4344
ⓘ Toll-free reservations:
(800) GO-VALLEY (468-2553)
E-mail: info@waterville.com
Internet: http://www.waterville.com
Number and types of lifts: 11–
2 high-speed quad, 2 triples, 3 doubles,
4 surface lifts
Skiable acreage: 255 acres
Snowmaking: 100 percent
Uphill capacity: 14,867 per hour
Snowboarding: Yes, unlimited
Bed base: 2,500
Nearest lodging: quarter-mile
Resort child care: Yes, 6 months and older
Adult ticket, per day: $37-$44

Loon Mountain Facts

Summit elevation:	3,050 feet
Vertical drop:	2,100 feet
Base elevation:	950 feet

Expert:★ Advanced:★★
Intermediate:★★★★
Beginner:★★★★
Never-ever:★★★
Address: RR1, Box 41
Lincoln, NH 03251
✆ Area code: 603
Ski area phone: 745-8111
Snow report: 745-8100
Fax: 745-8214
ⓘ Toll-free reservations:
(800) 229-7829
E-mail: info@loonmtn.com
Internet: http://www.loonmtn.com
Number and types of lifts: 8–1 gondola,
1 high-speed quad, 2 triples, 3 doubles,
1 surface lift
Acreage: 250 trail acres
Snowmaking: 97 percent
Uphill capacity: 10,550 per hour
Snowboarding: Yes, unlimited
Bed base: 13,000
Nearest lodging: slopeside
Resort child care: Yes, 6 weeks and older
Adult ticket, per day: $38-$45

Waterville Valley now belongs to the Booth Creek resort family, which also includes Northstar-at-Tahoe, Sierra-at-Tahoe and Bear Mountain, all in California; Loon Mountain and Cranmore in New Hampshire; Grand Targhee in Wyoming; and four ski areas collectively called The Pass in Washington.

Mountain layout

◆◆ **Expert** ◆ **Advanced:** One of the toughest runs, True Grit, develops big moguls and drops down the Sunnyside face. Last season Waterville Valley added a tree skiing area at the left side of Valley Run, starting at the base of Lower Bobby's.

■ **Intermediate:** Waterville's trails were cut more recently than the Front Four at Stowe or the trails down Cannon, so they are not New England's typical steep and narrow—there's elbow room and a chance to check out the slope before committing to the fall line again.

Two former tough mogul runs, Ciao and Gema, now are groomed daily. Such trails as White Caps, Sel's Choice, Old Tecumseh and Tippecanoe are intermediate and advanced playthings.

Something more resorts should do: Waterville has a designated "easier mogul field." For those wanting to move to the next level, this is great practice.

●● **Beginner:** The Valley Run is a beginner/lower intermediate heaven with enough width to allow skiing for a couple of days down different sections. This run is now served by a new high-speed quad that takes skiers to the top of the run in only 4.5 minutes.

● **Never-ever:** Never-evers have a small area with a separate lift.

Snowboarding

Waterville has four terrain parks open to riders and skiers, among them a beginner's park and one for intermediates. The big kahuna is the Boneyard on the Lower Periphery trail (to the right of the trail map). It features terrain and objects for sliding, bonking and the other freestyle stunts. No skiers are allowed in Waterville Valley's Pipe Dragon-maintained halfpipe, which carries the superb name of Wicked Ditch of the East. New Hampshire law requires snowboarders to have a board leash or strap.

Cross-country

Waterville has 105 km. of trails, 70 of which are groomed and tracked for skating and gliding through the White Mountain National Forest. This cross-country center and the trail system is considered one of the best in New England by cross-country afficionandos. There are some lift-served cross-country trails as well.

Rentals and lessons are available, as are guided cross-country and snowshoe tours for all levels and ages. Call 236-4666 for more information. Cross-country trail fees are included as part of the Winter Unlimited lodging package; call for non-package pricing.

Lessons (98/99 prices)

Group lessons: $26 for 1.5 hours.
Never-ever package: Skiing or snowboarding, $57 for J-lift ticket, lesson and equipment.
Private lessons: $65 an hour for one skier.

Special programs: Several clinics that focus on bumps, powder or skiing for women, $32 each.

Racing: A recreational course, on Exhibition, is served by a surface lift.

Children's lessons: SKIwee costs $60 a day for ages 3–5, lunch extra. Programs for ages 6–8 and 9–12 cost $49 a day, including lift ticket, but lunch is extra.

Child care (98/99 prices)

Ages: 6 months to 4 years.
Costs: All-day is $40, with multiday discounts available. Half day is $30, hourly is $9. Lunch is an extra $5, or children may bring their own.

Reservations: Required if you want to ensure a space. Call 236-8311, Ext. 3196 or 3197. Waterville has two nurseries at the base area.

Lift tickets (98/99 prices)

Weekend Prices	Adult	Teen (13-18)	Child (6-12)
One day	$46	$41	$10
Three days	$113 ($37+/day)	$102 ($34/day)	$30 ($10/day)
Five days	$166 ($33+/day)	$142 ($28+/day)	$50 ($10/day)

Who skis free: Kids 5 and younger ski free anytime. Waterville often runs a Kids Ski Free promotion (for ages up to 12) when parents buy multiday lodging packages; ask about it.

Who skis at a discount: Ages 65 and older ski at children's rates. The one- and three-day prices are for weekends; midweek one-day prices are $40 for adults, $33 for teens, and $10 for children. Midweek three-day prices are $105 for adults, $86 for teens and $30 for children. Midweek five-day rates are $149 for adults, $120 for teens and $50 for children.

Accommodations at the resort

To make reservations at Waterville Valley, call (800) GO-VALLEY (468-2553). The "Winter Unlimited" package is all inclusive, offering all of Waterville's winter activities plus lodging for one price.

The **Golden Eagle Lodge** with condominium suites features a distinctive design reminiscent of the turn-of-the-century grand hotels at the White Mountain resorts.

Additionally, Waterville has four hotel properties and four groups of condominiums all located in the valley. **The Snowy Owl** is one of the most charming, a modern country inn with breakfast. The **Black Bear Lodge** is slightly larger and more hotel-like, and the **Valley Inn and Tavern** operates as a country inn with rates that can include meals. All are in the same price range with two-day lodging and lift weekend packages starting at around $130 (per person, double occupancy) and five-day midweek packages, starting at about $320. The new **Silver Fox** offers continental breakfast and is the most economical place to stay. **Condominiums** are also available.

Loon Mountain

Loon has some of the most convenient accommodations in New Hampshire. This resort is a behemoth—at least in lodging. It's one of the few resorts where the bed base is larger than the lift capacity, which has created crowded conditions at times. Fortunately, Loon has made a number of improvements during the past few years. Among these were trail improvements to relieve congestion in high-traffic stretches, new lifts to get people up the mountain faster, more snowmaking coverage and the creation of a dedicated learning area.

Loon Mountain limits lift ticket sales to keep the mountain experience positive. Continued improvements have meant the sold-out signs quit coming out every weekend; now it's about four days per season, with perhaps ten near-sellout days. The Unconditional Satisfaction Guarantee™ ensures you'll like the ski conditions or you'll ski free on your next visit.

Loon is owned by Booth Creek Ski Holdings which owns nearby Waterville Valley, Cranmore in the Mt. Washington Valley as well as resorts in the West. Check for interchangeable lift tickets and joint marketing programs

Mountain layout

◆◆ **Expert** ◆ **Advanced:** Advanced North Peak runs are challenging and well removed from lower intermediate traffic. The steeps are there, but half the bumps are groomed out.

■ **Intermediate:** The intermediate runs are good and solid, with no expert surprises around the next clump of trees. The upper trails are a bit twisted, narrow and seemingly undirected at the summit, but they open onto a series of wide intermediate pistes. A favorite is Flying Fox, a delightful cruise. Depending on snow conditions, skiers can link up with the West Basin via Upper Speakeasy, or they can drop down to the parking lot and take the 100-yard-long steam train ride to the adjacent base area. The West Basin area has a collection of intermediate trails.

●● **Beginner:** The center of the mountain, serviced by the Seven Brothers triple chair, has good intermediate trails that advanced beginners can handle.

● **Never-ever:** Never-evers have an improved learning area to the right of the West Basin.

Snowboarding

Snowboarding is allowed on the entire mountain except Blue Ox trail. Loon has a snowboard park on Lower Flying Fox covering 15 acres. It includes a 375-foot-long halfpipe and other terrain features. Riders can get easy access to the Loon Mountain Park by taking the Kanc Quad and the Seven Brothers lift. The park is regularly groomed with a Pipe Dragon and a new BR-400 groomer.

Cross-country

The **Loon Mountain Cross Country Center** (745-8111, Ext. 5568) has 35 km. of groomed and tracked trails. Children ages 5 and younger and seniors 70 and older ski free on Loon's cross-country trails.

Lessons (98/99 prices)

Group lessons: $27 for 90 minutes. Five sessions, $105.

Never-ever package: For skiers or snowboarders, this includes equipment, all-day lessons and a limited lift ticket for $59 per day. Enroll at either rental shop.

Private lessons are $55 an hour; $35 for additional hours.

Special programs: Specialty Ski Weeks are reserved for skiers who want to fine-tune their tactics on all terrain and in all conditions. The three-day midweek program is scheduled for various times throughout the season. Cost is $225.

Racing: A race course is served by the Seven Brothers lift.

Children's lessons: Full day for ages 3–4 including lunch and lifts is $69, half days $49. Full day for children ages 5–6 costs $69; $49 half day. An Adventure Ski Camp for ages 7–12 groups children by ability level. Price is $79 a day, including lunch.

All children's lessons are run out of the new Children's Center which also houses a rental shop for skiers and boarders to age 6.

Child care (98/99 prices)

Ages: 6 weeks to 8 years.
Costs: Half day, $35; full day, $49.
Reservations: Required; call 745-8111. Hours: 8 a.m. to 4:30 p.m. Loon has a spacious child care center near the Governor Adams Lodge, which replaces the center at Mountain Club.

Lift tickets (97/98 prices)

Weekend Prices	Adult	Child (6-12)
One day	$45	$28
Three days	$119 ($40)	$74 ($25)
Five days	$185 ($37/day)	$115 ($23)

Who skis free: Children ages 5 and younger.

Who skis at a discount: Ages 13–21 pay $32 midweek non-holiday, and $40 on weekends. Ages 70 and older pay $5 midweek and Sunday, but the regular adult price on Saturday. Loon has a popular Saturday-Sunday ticket for $79 for adults, $49 for children.

Midweek prices are $38 for adults; $25 for children.

Note: Ticket sales are cut off after approximately 6,000 have been sold. To reserve tickets or ski rentals in advance by major credit card, call (800)-229-LOON.

Accommodations at the resort

The Mountain Club on Loon (800-229-7829 or 603-745-8111) is a ski-in/ski-out property with everything under one roof—from parking to swimming pool, fitness club to restaurants. One problem: many of its rooms have a double Murphy bed with two small day beds along the windows. This arrangement is fine for couples, or for a family with young children, but it is awkward for two adults who don't want to sleep in the same bed. Package prices start at $79 per person, double occupancy. Loon also has condominiums. Make reservations through the Mountain Club.

Cannon Mountain

Cannon Mountain is state-owned and has long been known by experts as one of the most challenging mountains in the East. It has a 2,146-foot vertical served by an 80-passenger tram. When skiing here you see no signs of civilization except for the ski lodge. Though once known as a mountain where grooming consisted of shoveling some snow under the lifts now and then, Cannon now takes mountain preparation to heart. Of Cannon's 163 acres, 95 percent are covered by snowmaking. The trails are narrower in legend than they are in reality and the mountain can actually be skied by most intermediates. This is a place for advanced skiers to play and intermediates to push themselves.

A fixed-grip quad services the summit and exposes the skier to beautiful scenic vistas of the White Mountain National Forest. The Profile Trail presents the advanced intermediate with a well-groomed 2,400-foot thrill. The Upper Cannon, Tramway and Vista Way are all intermediate trails that are challenging but certainly negotiable, the steepest being Upper Cannon which offers New England-style steeps.

Cannon Facts

Summit elevation:	4,146 feet
Vertical drop:	2,146 feet
Base elevation:	2,000 feet

Expert:★★★ Advanced:★★★
Intermediate:★★★★
Beginner:★★★
Never-ever:★★★
Address: Franconia Notch
Franconia, NH 03580
✆ **Area code:** 603
Ski area phone: 823-5563
Fax: 823-8088
Snow report: (800) 823-7771
ⓘ **Toll-free reservations:** (800) 227-4191
E-mail: info@cannonmt.com
Internet: http://www.cannonmt.com
Number and types of lifts: 6–
1 80-person aerial tram, 1 quad, 1 triple,
2 doubles, 1 surface lift
Acreage: 163 trail acres
Snowmaking: 95 percent
Uphill capacity: 6,000 per hour
Snowboarding: Yes, unlimited
Bed base: 13,000 nearby
Nearest lodging: about 1/2 miles
Resort child care: Yes, 12 months and older
Adult ticket, per day: $28-$39 (98/99 prices)

Bretton Woods Facts

Summit elevation:	3,100 feet
Vertical drop:	1,500 feet
Base elevation:	1,600 feet

Expert:★ Advanced:★
Intermediate:★★★
Beginner:★★★★
Never-ever:★★★★
Address: Route 302,
Bretton Woods, NH 03575
✆ **Area code:** 603
Ski area phone: 278-5000
or (800) 232-2972
Snow report: 278-5051
ⓘ **Toll-free reservations:** (800) 258-0330
E-mail: skibw@brettonwoods.com
Internet: http://www.brettonwods.com
Number and types of lifts: 7–1 high-speed
quad, 1 triple, 3 doubles, 2 surface lift
Acreage: 175 trail acres
Snowmaking: 98 percent
Uphill capacity: 7,300 per hour
Snowboarding: Yes, unlimited
Bed base: 3,000+
Nearest lodging: slopeside
Resort child care: Yes, 2 months and older
Adult ticket, per day: $36-$44

The Front Five, as known to locals, are the intimidating trails seen from the highway. Three of them, Avalanche, Paulie's Folly and Zoomer, are marked black and rightfully so, especially Zoomer's bumps. The other two, Rocket and Gary's, have less pitch and no bumps.

Lessons (98/99 prices)

Group lessons: $20 per session.

Never-ever package: A special program includes up to three days of lift tickets, lessons and rental equipment for $40 per day for skiing; $45 for snowboarding. The first day includes two lessons, the last two days include all-mountain tickets.

Private lessons: $40 per hour.

Racing: NASTAR is offered weekends and holidays at 1 p.m. at $5 per run. Training sessions are at 10 a.m. and cost $20. A coin-op course is $1 per run.

Children's lessons: SKIwee costs $55 a day for ages 4 to 9, including lunch; and a similar program is available for children 10-12.

Telephone area code: 603

Child care (98/99 prices)

Ages: 12 months and older.
Costs: All-day care is $30 with lunch.
Reservations: Advised; call 823-5563.

Lift tickets (98/99 prices)

	Adult	Child (6–12)
One day	$39	$27
Two days	$73 ($36.50/day)	$49 ($24.50/day)
Three days	$94 ($31+/day)	$59 ($20/day)

Who skis free: Ages 5 and younger when with a ticketed adult.

Who skis at a discount: Ages 65 and older ski at children's rates, which are $27 on weekends and holidays and $19 midweek (New Hampshire residents aged 65 and older ski free midweek). Midweek prices across the board are lower—for adults they are $28 Monday, Wednesday and Friday. On Tuesdays and Thursdays, two people can ski for $28. A free Frequent Skier' Card is available that awards a free day of skiing with every six purchased. Prices listed are valid weekends and holidays.

Bretton Woods

Bretton Woods has been linked more with the grand old Mount Washington Hotel and international monetary meetings than with skiing, which is relatively new at the resort. This year, the hotel and the ski area are all under the same ownership and plans for expansion in the future are underway..

The skiing is mild and good for cruising. Bretton Woods ski resort also has a halfpipe for snowboarders. This mountain, like Waterville, is perfect for families and makes special efforts to ensure great family vacations.

Downhill variety is mixed with one of the best cross-country networks (outside of Jackson and Stowe) in New England, boasting 97 km. of prepared trails, most of which are best for beginner and intermediate levels. The Nordic area is centered on the grounds of the Mount Washington Hotel, which provides a spectacular setting.

At the downhill area, a beginner special costs $37 for skiing or snowboarding, including lift pass, lessons and equipment. Bretton Woods is noted for excellent children's ski programs. The Hobbit Ski and Snowboard School (ages 3–12) has ski lessons including lunch and rentals for $49; and snowboard lessons for $59 (snowboard learning ages are 8–12).

Bretton Woods' nursery takes children 2 months to 5 years, $20 a half day and $30 a full day including lunch. An evening care program provides dinner, night skiing and indoor play for $39 for ages 6–12 (no snowboarders or first-time skiers are in this program).

The Mount Washington Hotel is being winterized and the grand old hotel originally opened in 1902 will be opened for the first time for the winter season of 1999/2000. In addition, the ski area will expand to a new mountain peak adding 6 to 8 trails.

Lessons (98/99 prices)

Group lessons: $25 for 90 minutes.

Never-ever package: For skiers, this includes equipment, all-day lessons and a limited lift ticket for $39 per day. For snowboarders the cost is $44. Enroll at the rental shop.

Private lessons are $49 an hour.

Special programs: Intermediate programs for skiers that include shaped skis, lessons and lifts are $77. The snowboard program with rental, lifts and lessons is $79.

Children's lessons: Full day ski program for ages 4–12 including lunch and lifts is $55. Full day snowboard program for ages 8–12 including lunch and lifts is $65. Reservations are required for snowboard programs—all 800-232-2972.

Child care (98/99 prices)

Ages: 2 months to 5 years.

Costs: The Babes in the Woods program with stories, crafts and games is $39 for a full day (8 a.m.–4:30 p.m.) with lunch and $29 for a half day, a.m. or p.m.

Snow Play and Ski Readiness all-day care with a gentle introduction to skiing, for children ages 5 and younger, is $55 for a full day (8 a.m.–4:30 p.m.) with lunch or $45 for the morning only.

Reservations: Advised; call 800-232-2972.

Lift tickets (98/99 prices)

	Adult	Junior (6-15)	Seniors (62+)
One day (weekend)	$44	$29	$44
One day (weekday)	$36	$25	$29
Two days (weekend)	$80	$53	$80
Two day (weekday)	$65	$45	$52
Five days (weekday)	$135	$94	$109

Who skis free and at discount: Younger than 6 ski free; 70+ skiers ski for $10 dueing non-holiday midweeks.

Accommodations at the resort

The premier property here is the restored 1896 **Bretton Arms Country Inn**, a National Historic Landmark next to the cross-country area and one of the most elegant and romantic inns in the state. Rates are about $115 per night. The **Bretton Woods Motor Inn** features less expensive accommodations between the downhill and cross-country areas. Bretton Woods also has a grouping of townhouses. All Bretton Woods properties can be reached through (800) 258-0330 or 278-1000. In winter the ski area provides shuttlebuses to and from the slopes.

Ski 93 area accommodations

Reservations and information for many of the following properties can be obtained through the **Ski 93 Central Reservations Bureau** at (800) 937-5493 (phone number spells WE-SKI-93) or through Lincoln/Woodstock Central Reservations at (800) 227-4191.

Three motelish properties along Rte. 3 in Lincoln only minutes from Loon and Cannon join for advertising and have similar accommodation with mostly identical prices. Each has slightly different amenities. **Indian Head Motel Resort** off I-93, Exit 33 on Route 3 in Lincoln; (800-343-8000, 745-8000) is one of the centers of après-ski action with live bands and a great ice-skating pond and attached cross-country trails. Room rates start at $99. **The Beacon,** (800-258-8934, 745-8118) on the same road as Indian Head, also has indoor tennis and large indoor pools. Rates are $65–$150. **Woodward's Motor Inn** (800-635-8968, 745-8141) is the most family oriented. It has the area's only racquetball court and the best steaks in the region. Rates start at $40.

Just north of Franconia Notch and Cannon Mountain you'll find the **Red Coach Inn** (800-262-2493 (COACH-93), 823-7422), a modern hotel built behind a gabled cedar façade, a snowball's throw from the unspoiled New England town of Franconia (careful on the speed limit as you drive through). There is a large indoor pool and exercise room. Resorts most accessible from this hotel are Bretton Woods and Cannon, with Loon only a few minutes down I-93. Room rates are $70–$100.

The Woodstock Inn B&B (800-321-3985, 745-3951) is a typical quaint New England lodge. The main building is more than 100 years old with no two rooms alike. You'll find them tucked under the rafters, some with private bath, or shared bath, all with casual charm. The restaurant in the front of the inn is one of North Woodstock's most elegant; the one in the station at the rear is one of the town's liveliest. Rates per couple with breakfast: $69–$135. A room with a hot tub at the foot of your bed is a bit more.

Amber Lights Inn (726-4077) between Loon and Waterville has five relatively small rooms with big hospitality. Carola provides one of the area's breakfast experiences with secret egg-and-cheese creations, homemade muffins and breads slathered with home-preserved jellies and jams. Children younger than age 7 are discouraged. Room rates are $75–$96.

Wilderness Inn B&B (745-3890) is run by the Yarnells, a couple with small children, who make other families with youngsters welcome in their house. Parents note: this place has laundry facilities! The B&B is only steps from the center of North Woodstock, filled with shops and restaurants.

The Inn at Forest Hills (823-9550, fax 823-5555) has been beautifully restored by Joanne and Gordon Haym. The English Tudor-style B&B is built into a house which was once part of the grand Forest Hills Hotel. It provides a great New England tradition or a wonderful romantic setting with fine breakfasts just about a mile from the village of Franconia on Rte. 142 heading toward Bethlehem. Room rates start at $85 double occupancy.

The Mulburn Inn (869-3389) is another B&B in a great Tudor-style setting with oak staircase and stained glass windows. Located in Bethlehem, once considered one of the fresh-air centers of New England, this home provides hospitality in the midst of a tiny New Hampshire town at the northern edge of Ski 93 only about 10 minutes from Bretton Woods. Rooms are in the $70–$95 range.

Six miles north of the region at the crest of Sugar Hill you'll find the **Sunset Hill House** (800-786-4455 or 823-5522), a restored turn-of-the century inn built in 1882 in the era of Grand Hotels and Resorts. You can still stay in luxury and elegance with wonderful views of the Presidentials and the Green Mountains. This mountain resort also has 30 km. of cross-country tracks (free for guests, $6 trail fee for others). Double rooms are $75–$145 including breakfast. Call for ski-and-stay programs.

Among the least expensive places to stay are **Parker's Motel** (745-8341, 800-766-6835), which is about five miles from Cannon Mountain, or the **Riverbank Motel** (745-3374, 800-633-5624). Either has rooms starting at $45–$50 per night.

 ## Dining

The most elegant dining experiences in the southern Ski 93 region can be found at the **William Tell** (726-3618) on Rte. 49 just outside Waterville Valley or at the **Woodstock Inn's Clement Room** (745-3951), which gets high ratings from locals. The William Tell has a strong Swiss-German accent with excellent wines. The Clement Room is more eclectic with meals such as Beef Wellington and Veal Oscar. Both restaurants feature entrées in the $12–$19 range. The Woodstock Inn also serves great daily breakfasts as well as a fabulous weekend brunch; the William Tell is also known for its weekend brunch. For equally adventurous gourmet cuisine at the Bretton Woods end of Ski 93 try the **Bretton Arms Restaurant** (278-3000) in an elegant century-old atmosphere. Another spot recommended by locals for fine dining is **Sunset Hill House** (823-5522), which also has great views of the Franconia Range.

At Loon Mountain, try **Rachel's** (745-8111) or **The Granite Grille,** both at the Mountain Club. **The Common Man** (745-3463) offers good basic American dining with a roaring fireplace and rustic surroundings. For the place claimed by locals to have the best steaks, head to the **Open Hearth Steak House** at Woodward's Motor Inn. **Gordi's Fish and Steak House** (745-6635) is family-oriented and features Maine lobster and steaks. The **Tavern at the Mill** (745-3603) is set in a modernesque barn-like building, which is also one of the nightlife centers just outside the resort.

Truant's Tavern (745-2239) serves clever dinner entrées in a mock schoolhouse atmosphere—drinking in class was never so much fun. The bar hops on weekends. **Woodstock Station** (745-3951), in an old train station on Main Street, offers a creative menu of reasonable meals from meatloaf to Mexican, and is a local favorite. **G.H. Pizza** serves traditional and gourmet pizza, as well as hot and cold subs.

In Waterville Valley village **The Wild Coyote Grill** (236-4919) in the White Mountain Athletic Club serves American cuisine with a Southwestern flair. The calimari is a specialty. Or head to **Chili Peppers** (236-4646) which has the area's best Mexican food. For pizza call **Olde Waterville Valley Pizza Co.** (236-3663). **Valley Inn** (236-8336) offers good dining.

At Bretton Woods the **Top o' the Quad Restaurant** serves casual lunches and dinners Friday and Saturday with views of Mt. Washington's summit. Back down the mountain, try **Darby's Tavern** for hearty family dining, only a quarter-mile from the slopes. **Fabyans Station** is a good eatery in an old railroad station. In Franconia head to **Hillwinds**.

For breakfast try **Sunny Day Diner** or **Peg's Place** in North Woodstock. **The Millaway Cafe** in the Millfront Marketplace serves unusual fresh pastries—and gourmet coffee. In Waterville test the Belgian waffles and pastries at the tiny **Coffee Emporium** in Town Square.

 ## Après-ski/nightlife

After skiing at Loon, head to the **Granite Bar in the Mountain Club** for good weekend entertainment and a quiet après-ski spot. The **Paul Bunyan Lounge** at the Octagon base has a young rowdy crowd. Or head to **Babe's** at the Governor Adams Lodge.

Waterville now has a collection of bars in Town Square, each with slightly different après-ski. They are all within a few steps of each other. **Legends 1291** and **Chili Peppers** (which now is in Town Square) all serve up a good time, and later in the evening they stand in the same order, ranging from loud disco and rock to quieter music. The **World Cup Bar and Grill** at the mountain has the normal collection of skiers for après-ski until 5:30 p.m.

Just down the road from Waterville on the way back to the interstate try the **William Tell** for a cozy quiet après-ski or the **Mad River Tavern** for a more raucous setting. Both have popular dinner menus.

The North Woodstock area locals set up party camp at **Truant's Tavern** and **Woodstock Station. Gordi's Fish and Steak** in Lincoln serves up great munchies. **Indian Head Resort** in Lincoln offers good après-ski. From Wednesday through Sunday, live bands rock the joint. The **Tavern Sports Bar** is a low-key darts, video game and pool hall. Downstairs, the **Tavern at the Mill** has the area's best singles action with bands on weekends.

In Franconia (near Cannon), try **Village House**, a comfortable lounge with a lot of classic ski history and an evening entertainer who plays après-ski at the mountain's lounge; or **Hillwinds**, a large bar and lounge with live entertainment and a huge crowd on weekends.

Other activities

Shopping: Waterville Valley's Town Square has several specialty shops worth a look. Lincoln, home of Loon Mountain, has some factory outlet stores. The factory outlet bonanza of North Conway is 30 miles east of Bretton Woods. No sales tax makes buying all the sweeter.

Waterville Valley has **sleigh rides** and an **indoor fitness center**, as well as a refrigerated indoor ice arena for **skating.**

Loon Mountain has **skating, night tubing, children's theater** and a **wildlife theater.**

Cannon is home to the **New England Ski Museum,** a collection of ski memorabilia well worth a brief visit. Drive by **The Mount Washington Hotel & Resort** just east of the Bretton Woods ski area. Its setting against the towering Presidential Range makes a spectacular scene, especially at sunset when the snow-covered mountains turn pink. **Cannon's tram** is open for non-skiing sightseers for $9 a ride.

The **Rocks Estate** in Bethlehem, on a hilltop about 10 miles from Cannon, has **sleigh rides** and offers some forestry-related activities, being owned by the Society For The Protection of New Hampshire Forests. Call (800) 639-5373.

The **Sunset House** in Sugar Hill, about six miles north of the Old Man of the Mountain, has sleigh rides and ice skating. Call (800) 786-4455 or 823-5522.

Getting there and getting around

By air: Boston's Logan Airport is 130 miles away from the Ski 93 areas. Manchester Airport, 70 miles south, is serviced by Southwest, MetroJet, Comair, Continental Express, Delta's Business Express, USAir, and United. The airport phone nummber is 624-6556. Their Internet address is www.flymanchester.com.

By car: From I-93 heading north, Waterville Valley is 11 miles up Rte. 49 at Exit 28. Loon Mountain is on the Kancamagus Highway (Route 112) at Exit 32 in Lincoln. Cannon is visible from I-93 just north of Franconia Notch State Park, and Bretton Woods is on Rte. 302: take Exit 35 to Rte. 3, which meets Rte. 302 at Twin Mountain.

Getting around: A car is a necessity unless you stay close to the slopes at one resort and ski only there. Lincoln-Woodstock has a shuttle service and taxi, available anytime.

Mt. Washington Valley

New Hampshire

Wildcat, Cranmore, Attitash Bear Peak, Black Mountain, King Pine, Jackson Ski Touring and Shawnee Peak, Maine

Mt. Washington Valley Facts

Address: Chamber of Commerce & Visitors Bureau
P.O. Box 2300, N. Conway, NH 03860
ⓘ **Toll-free information:**
(800) 367-3364
Dining: ★★★★
Apres-ski/nightlife: ★★★
Other activities: ★★★★

✆ **Area code:** 603
Phone: 356-5701
Fax: 356-7069
E-mail: mwvcc@nxi.com
World Wide Web: http://
www.4seasonresort.com
Bed base: 16,000+

These six downhill ski areas, set into spectacular White Mountain terrain, combine with the Jackson Ski Touring Foundation (one of the world's best cross-country trail systems) and Great Glen, the wild skiing on Mt. Washington, and the year-round resort attractions of Mt. Washington Valley to make a multifaceted destination resort.

This was a destination resort long before anyone came here to ski. A quarter century before the Civil War, fashionable Northeasterners started coming here, first by stage line and then by railroad and carriage, for the summer to beat the heat to meet Hawthorne and Emerson, watch Bierstadt paint his mountain landscapes, and find suitable husbands for their daughters. Today, the few remaining grand old hotels they visited have been brought up to date to add their charm to the mix of condos, motels, country inns, and B&Bs. The Valley is still busier in the summer months than in the winter.

Legends of the early days of skiing—the late '30s—surround you. Ride up the Wildcat gondola and look back at the fantastic bulk of Mt. Washington with its huge scooped-out ravines. This is hallowed ground, where Toni Matt on his wooden boards schussed over the Tuckerman headwall in one long arc to win the 1939 Inferno race, summit to base in six and a half minutes—a record that still stands.

Most of all, what makes this area one of the pioneers of downhill skiing in America is the Eastern Slope Ski School, founded by Carroll Reed. This is where the Arlberg method of ski instruction was introduced to North America by Benno Rybizka and his Austrian teacher, the great Hannes Schneider, who was released by the Nazis in return for banking concessions.

If anyone wants skiing and a whole lot more, this is the place. The prime summer activities of hiking, climbing, and camping out are pursued in the snow-and-ice season by local and visiting fanatics. You can even practice your rock-climbing skills on an indoor wall.

Telephone area code: 603 (unless in Maine where 207 is noted)

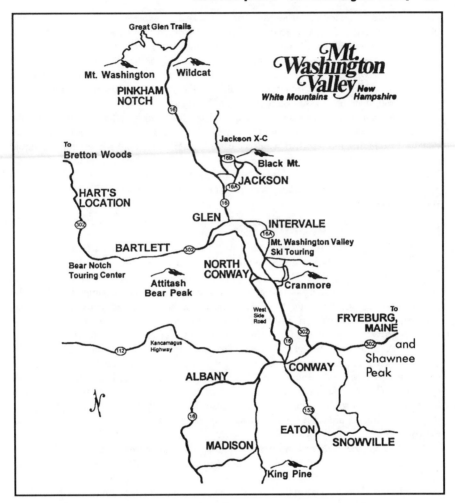

Restaurants, many of them tucked into the tiny country inns or restored barns in the Valley, are world class and have acknowledged gourmet reputations. In fact, this valley is home to one of the most famous cooking schools in the country.

Besides the skiing, picturesque inns and tempting restaurants, there are more tax-free factory outlet stores in Conway and North Conway than in any other area of the United States, making the region a top shopping destination.

One thing that would make it a bit more enticing would be some cooperation between the ski areas, hoteliers and merchants to make this valley a true regional resort. No single ski resort in the Valley is a worthy winter destination by itself, but as a group of resorts—combined with the Valley towns and the surrounding cross-country trails—Mt. Washington Valley becomes a formidable vacation force. Other winter resorts across the United States and

Canada would struggle to offer as complete and varied an experience. This is a wonderful place to come and ski, snowboard or cross-country. Wouldn't it be nice if a shuttlebus connected the resorts with the picturesque towns and the Valley offered a lift pass that would allow visitors to ski a different area each day? Unfortunately, rather than making it easier for visitors to discover the benefits of the Valley, the locals seem to march to different drums in different directions. Visitors are left to scramble for themselves to squeeze the essence from what is surely the most-blessed ski region in the Northeast.

A note about the fact boxes in this chapter: The Mt. Washington Valley facts are for the region. We also include fact boxes for the individual ski areas, including the bed base immediately surrounding the resort. If we don't list a Web site or e-mail address for individual resorts, it's because they didn't have one as of last summer, or were in the process of switching servers. The Mt. Washington Valley Web site has information on all of the ski areas. You also can get statewide information from Ski New Hampshire at info@skinh.com or http://www.skinh.com.

 ## Mountain layout

Wildcat: Wildcat has often been voted the ski area with the most spectacular scenery in the Northeast, with beautiful views across Pinkham Notch to towering Mt. Washington and Tuckerman Ravine. Wildcat is known as an untamed resort, but in the past few years it has smoothed some of the bumpy runs. Now the groomers roll all but two of the trails. Trails have also been widened and straightened extensively. However, this resort is still best for strong intermediate to expert skiers and snowboarders. Private Snowcat area for beginners with a triple chair with four trails.

The skiing is tempered by three factors: the cold, the wind and the pitch of the slopes. The cold, wind and capricious weather changes of nearby Mt. Washington are among the most extreme in North America, so Wildcat skiers need to be dressed properly for variable conditions. The plus side to inclement weather, of course, is a lot of natural snow; Wildcat often is the last New Hampshire ski area to close. Though Wildcat's slopes are wider than they used to be, the area still has a reputation for steep and narrow—in short, classic New England skiing.

Last season the resort has added a new high-speed quad cutting the time it took to reach the summit in half. New glade skiing will offer skilled skiers additional challenge. Intermediates should be able to handle Wildcat's groomed trails covered by snowmaking. For the best intermediate way down, head to the Polecat side of the gondola where you'll find the Valley's perennial favorite trail—the Lynx; for a descent where it is prudent to pay attention to the details of skiing, loop to the opposite side. Intermediate and beginner trails exist, but skiers at Wildcat are probably there for the challenge.

Attitash Bear Peak: This is a resort that has come of age. Without a doubt, this is the biggest and most extensive resort in the region. Just west of Glen on Rte. 302 in Bartlett, Attitash Bear Peak is an all-round mountain with a few expert touches. The Attitash side still features a warren of narrow New England trails filled with history and the newly cut Bear Peak trails provide wider and longer rolling, cruising terrain.

Attitash Bear Peak has a protected learning slope served by a triple chair, and there are several beginner trails around the Borvig lift. Ptarmigan is supposed to be one of the steepest trails in New England, but it is manageable for good intermediates because of the elbow room on the run. The rest of the mountain is enough to keep 80 percent of skiers perfectly satisfied,

Wildcat Facts

Summit elevation:	4,050 feet
Vertical drop:	2,100 feet
Base elevation:	1,950 feet

Expert:★★ Advanced:★★★
Intermediate:★★★★
Beginner:★★★
Never-ever:★★★
Address: Jackson, NH
✆ Ski area phone: 466-3326
Snow report: 1-888-SKI WILD
ⓘ Toll-free reservations: 1-888-4-WILDCAT
Number and types of lifts: 6–1 gondola, 1 high-speed quad, 3 triples, 1 double
Skiable acreage: 225 acres
Snowmaking: 100 percent
Uphill capacity: 8,540 per hour
Snowboarding: Yes, unlimited
Bed Base: None at the area
Nearest lodging: AMC about a quarter-mile
Resort child care: Yes, 18 months and older
Adult ticket, per day: $39-46

Attitash Bear Peak Facts

Summit elevation:	2,300 feet
Vertical drop:	1,750 feet
Base elevation:	550 feet

Expert:★★ Advanced:★★★
Intermediate:★★★★
Beginner:★★★★
Never-ever:★★★★★
Address: P.O. Box 308, Bartlett, NH 03812
✆ Ski area phone: 374-2368
Snow report: 374-0946
ⓘ Toll-free reservations: (800) 223-7669
E-mail: info@attitash.com
Internet: http://www.attitash.com
Number and types of lifts: 12–2 high-speed quad,1 quad, 3 triples, 4 doubles, 2 surface lifts
Skiable acreage: 273 acres
Snowmaking: 98 percent
Uphill capacity: 16,500 per hour
Snowboarding: Yes, unlimited
Bed base: 1,600 Nearest lodging: slopeside
Resort child care: Yes, 6 months and older
Adult ticket, per day: $35-$46

with Northwest Passage to Cathedral and Saco to Ammonoosuc serving up inspired cruising. Bear Peak features Illusion, Avenger, Kachina and Myth Maker, that provide a foursome of cruising delight (don't let the diamonds scare any intermediate away). It is hard to find four better side-to-side cruising trails all served by a high-speed quad anywhere in the country let along this valley.

Attitash Bear Peak is one of the few ski areas in the country that supplements its traditional all-day lift ticket with a computerized point ticket allowing skiers to pay by the vertical foot. Called the Smart Ticket®, it's transferable and is good for two years from purchase date. It's an excellent choice for those who only want to ski a few hours.

New for 98/99: A massive Adventure Center has been built to house all of the Learn to Ski and Ride programs and children's programs. Beginners will have a new "Snowbelt" lift and the rest of the skiers will enjoy a new high-speed quad that replaces Old Reliable.

Cranmore Mountain Resort: Cranmore is one of the oldest resorts in America, one that features good balanced terrain. If you arrive in North Conway in the evening, you can't miss it. You'll see the lights for top-to-bottom night skiing glow on Friday and Saturday nights and every night during holiday periods until 9 p.m. Tubing has become a major draw in the past season and it should continue to be a blast. Plans for 98/99 include improvements to the tubing hill, new lifts and in grooming.

Cranmore Facts

Summit elevation:	1,700 feet
Vertical drop:	1,200 feet
Base elevation:	500 feet

Expert:★ Advanced:★★
Intermediate:★★★★
Beginner:★★★★
Never-ever:★★★
Address: Skimobile Road,
N. Conway, NH 03860
✆ Ski area phone: 356-5544
Snow report: 356-7070
Toll-free reservations: 800-SUN N SKI (786-6754)
Internet: http://www.cranmore.com
Number and types of lifts: 6–1 high-speed quad, 1 triple, 3 doubles, 1 surface lift
Skiable acreage: 185 acres
Snowmaking: 100 percent
Uphill capacity: 7,500 skiers per hour
Snowboarding: Yes, unlimited
Bed base: 250
Nearest lodging: slopeside
Resort child care: Yes, 6 months and older
Adult ticket, per day: $29-$37

Black Mountain Facts

Summit elevation:	2,350 feet
Vertical drop:	1,100 feet
Base elevation:	1,250 feet

Expert:★ Advanced:★
Intermediate:★★★
Beginner:★★★★
Never-ever:★★★★
Address: P.O. Box B, Rte. 16B,
Jackson, NH 03846
✆ Ski area phone: 800-698-4490
Snow report: 800-475-4669
Number and types of lifts: 4–1 triple, 1 double, 2 surface lifts
Acreage: 130 trail acres
Percent snowmaking: 98 percent
Uphill capacity: 3,700 per hour
Snowboarding: Yes
Bed Base: 200
Nearest lodging: slopeside
Resort child care: Yes, 12 months and older
Adult ticket, per day: $20-$32

Black Mountain: This ski area on Rte. 16B may be the best place in the Valley for beginner lessons and family skiing. From the front side of the mountain, facing Whitneys' Inn, the area is reminiscent of a country club, but behind the ridge reached by the double chair are 38 sunny and sheltered south-facing trails ranging from beginner to advanced intermediate. Next to the Jackson Ski Touring area, Black Mountain has also become a center for cross-country skiers interested in trying out telemark skiing. Finally, Black Mountain's southern exposure provides a warmer place to ski when it's just too cold at other areas.

Shawnee Peak: Located about a 35- to 45-minute drive from North Conway in Bridgton, Maine, this family resort offers fantastic views across Maine flatlands and lakes to the White Mountains. It features excellent snowmaking and a twice-a-day grooming program that allows for "first tracks" twice a day if you're lucky.

The resort has challenging skiing on 34 trails that offer a bit of something for everyone. It is perfect for families, with the toughest runs at the top and left side of the mountain as you look at the trail map, and wide-open beginner slopes to the right (or west). Excellent, tight gladed areas are nestled between the two sides of the mountain. Most of the trails to the left are New England-narrow. Upper/Lower Appalachian is a great steep cruiser with fantastic

Shawnee Peak Facts

Summit elevation: 1,949 feet
Vertical drop: 1,300 feet
Base elevation: 649 feet
Expert:★★ **Advanced:**★★★
Intermediate:★★★
Beginner:★★★
Never-ever:★★
Address: Route 302, Bridgton, ME;
✆ **Ski area phone:** (207) 647-8444
Snow report: (207) 647-8444
E-mail: info@shawneepeak.com
Internet: http://www.shawneepeak.com
Number and types of lifts: 4–1 triple, 3 doubles
Acreage: 34 trails, 17 at night
Snowmaking: 99 percent
Uphill capacity: 4,600 per hour
Snowboarding: Yes, unlimited
Bed Base: 1,800
Nearest lodging: mountainside condos and lodges
Resort child care: Yes, 6 months and older
Adult ticket, per day: $35

King Pine Facts

Summit elevation: 850 feet
Vertical drop: 350 feet
Base elevation: 500 feet
Expert:★ **Advanced:**★
Intermediate:★★
Beginner:★★★
Never-ever:★★★
Address: Rte. 153, East Madison, NH 03849
✆ **Ski area phone:** 367-8896
Fax: 367-8664
Snow report: (800) 367-8897
ⓘ **Toll-free reservations:**
(800) FREE-SKI (373-3754)
E-mail: purity@moose.ncia.net
Internet: http://www.visitnh.gov
Number and types of lifts: 4–2 triple, 1 double; 1 J-bar
Skiable acreage: 35 acres
Snowmaking: 100 percent
Uphill capacity: 4,000 per hour
Snowboarding: Yes, unlimited
Bed Base: 200 **Nearest lodging:** slopeside
Resort child care: Yes, newborns and older
Adult ticket, per day: $21-$29

---

views that uses almost all the mountain's vertical. The lift system has no high-speed lifts, but with small crowds, skiers will get in plenty of runs.

Shawnee features the most extensive night-skiing facilities in New England with a lighted vertical drop of 1,300 feet covered by 17 trails.

Mt. Washington: If you like to get to the top the old-fashioned way (you *climb* it) try the famous spring skiing in Tuckerman Ravine; all winter, there's the Sherburne Trail and several other areas. Start from Pinkham Notch Camp (see Other Activities). Note: please heed all information about weather and avalanche conditions—Mt. Washington has some of the most vicious and quickly changing weather anywhere.

King Pine: This small area has a modest vertical drop, but for those just starting out and parents who want to keep an eye on young children, an unintimidating area is preferable. King Pine does have one short, steep trail—reportedly one of the steepest in the state—but top-level skiers are better off somewhere else. King Pine is adjacent to the Purity Spring Resort, which has slopeside lodging and ski packages.

Snowboarding

New Hampshire law requires snowboarders to have a leash or strap tethering the board to their leg. All these ski areas welcome boarders, and most have specific facilities for them.

Cross-country

Jackson Ski Touring Foundation (383-9355 or 800-927-6697; Box 216, Jackson, NH 03846), on Rte. 16A, is a mecca for Nordic skiers. It has more than 150 km. of groomed and backcountry trails (87 km. are groomed), suitable for all ability levels. Country inns are spaced throughout the region.

Mt. Washington Valley Ski Touring Association (800-282-5220; Box 646, Intervale NH 03845) has more than 60 km. of inn-to-inn trails, plus ski school and rentals.

The Appalachian Mountain Club (466-2721) maintains a network of ski touring trails radiating from the AMC Camp at Pinkham Notch; about 7 km. are rated Easiest or More Difficult (requiring skills up to a strong snowplow and step turn), but about 40 km. are rated Most Difficult, with long challenging hills and narrow trails. AMC also has unusual dining; see that section for more details.

The Nestlenook Inn (383-9443), also in Jackson, offers 35 km. of touring tracks that wind through its 65-acre farm.

Purity Spring Resort (800-373-3754 or 603-367-8896), home of King Pine ski area, has 25 km. of groomed and tracked trails near Madison. Rentals and lessons are available.

Great Glen Trails (466-2333) is a cross-country facility at the base of Mt. Washington. It has 10 km. of tracked and skate-groomed trails and another 6 km. that are skate-groomed. The lodge has retail, rentals (with Fischer Revolution short skis), food and instruction. One loop and the learning area have snowmaking. Telemarkers can take a snowcat partly up the Mt. Washington Auto Road, then ski down. Call Great Glen for more details on that program.

Lessons (98/99 prices)

All the areas have extensive ski schools. Shawnee Peak and Wildcat prices are from last season; as always, use them as a guideline.

Group lessons are $22 per session at Wildcat, $22 at Attitash Bear Peak, $20 at Cranmore, $25 at Black Mountain, $19 at King Pine and $18 at Shawnee Peak.

Never-ever packages (rentals, lifts and lessons) are $49 at Wildcat for skiing and $49 for snowboarding, juniors pay $49; $55 at Attitash Bear Peak; $37 for skiing and $40 for snowboarding at Cranmore; $30 for skiing and $40 for snowboarding at Black Mountain; $34 for skiing and $42 for snowboarding at King Pine; and $35 for skiing and $45 for snowboarding at Shawnee Peak.

Private lessons are $49 per hour for one student at Wildcat; $45 an hour at Attitash Bear Peak, $45 at Cranmore, $40 at Black Mountain, $35 an hour at King Pine, and $32 at Shawnee Peak with each additional skier costing $18.

Children's lessons (include lessons, lift ticket, and rentals; most full day programs include lunch; lower price is for half day): $59 at Wildcat on weekends, $49 on weekdays; $50 half day ($45 p.m.) at Attitash Bear Peak; $60 full day at Cranmore; $45 half-day at Black Mountain, $30 half day at King Pine, and at Shawnee Peak, $48/$35 for SKIwee ages 4–6, $58/$45 for Junior Mountaineers ages 7–12, and $22 for private lessons.

Child care (97/98)

Prices are $20–$40 per day; call for more information. Children's programs generally start at age 4 or 5 at these areas (call for specifics).

Attitash Bear Peak (98/99 prices) accepts children from 6 months to 5 years. Snow-play for ages 1–3 is designed to introduce children to skiing. Prices are $40 per day. Reservations recommended: 374-2368. Tiny Turns designed for kids ages 3–5 costs $45 an hour.

Cranmore (98/99 prices) accepts children aged 6 months to 5 years. Price is $40 for a full day or $6 per hour. The second child in the same family pays half price.

Wildcat's Kitten Club nursery has child care for 18 months–12 years (younger with advance notice). Prices are $39 for a weekend day, $29 for a weekend half day, $25 for a weekday full day and $15 for a weekday half day. Full-day programs include lunch.

Black Mountain also has nursery facilities for infants 6 months or older. Non-ski nursery is $40 full day and $20 half day. Hourly rates are $6.50.

King Pine takes infants to age 6, either hourly or at a day rate. The nursery is open 8:30 a.m.–4 p.m. Cost is $5 per hour with a two-hour minimum. Infants are charged an extra $2.

Shawnee Peak has a fully licensed day care facility for children aged 6 months to 6 years. It operates from 8:30 a.m.–5:30 p.m. on weekends and opens a half hour later on weekdays. Cost is $5 per hour up to a maximum of $30 a day.

Lift tickets (98/99 prices)

Attitash Bear Peak: Adults $46, weekends; $50, holidays ($42 midweek), children (6–12) $30 ($25 midweek). Attitash Bear Peak also sells an electronic ticket that allows skiers to pay by the run; a good choice for those who don't get full value from an all-day ticket. Attitash Bear Peak is one of the American Skiing Company resorts. For a description of corporate discount programs for all the resorts, see the Lift Ticket section in the Sunday River chapter.

Cranmore: Adults $37 weekends/holidays, $28 midweek. Children 6–12, $10 any day.

Wildcat: Adults, $46 weekends and holidays; teens (13-15), $39; juniors (5–12), $29. and seniors (65 and older), $39 weekends. Midweek for adults is $39, for teens and juniors, $25; and seniors, $25. Children age 4 and younger ski free with a ticket-holding parent. Two-day weekend tickets are $89 for adults ($45.50 per day) and $75 ($37.50 per day) for teens, $55 ($27.50 per day) for Juniors, $75 for seniors ($37.50 per day). Two-day weekday passes are $69 ($34.50 per day) for adults and $45 for teens and juniors. ($22.50 per day).

Black Mountain: $32 for adults weekends and $20 midweek. Juniors (18 or younger) pay $20 weekends and $15 weekdays. Ages 65+ pay the junior rate. Black Mountain sells a family weekend day ticket for $89 for two adults and two juniors.

King Pine: $29 for adults weekends, $21 weekdays. Kids (6–12) ski for $12 midweek, $19 weekends. Night skiing (Tuesday, Friday, Saturday and holidays): $14 adults, $10 children. Kids 5 and younger ski free.

Shawnee Peak: (97/98 prices) $38 on weekends and holidays and $29 midweek for adults; $24 on weekends/holidays and $21 weekdays for ages 7–12 and 65 and older. Children 6 and younger ski free when accompanied by a paying adult.

Night skiing (Fri.-Sat. 4–10 p.m.) is $23 for adults and $21 for juniors/seniors; $2 less midweek. Twilight (12:30–10 p.m.) tickets are $36 for adults and $23 for juniors/seniors on weekends; $25/$20 juniors on weekdays. A day/night lift ticket good from 8:30 a.m.–10 p.m.

is $39 for adults, $30 for juniors on weekends; $30/$22 weekdays. Riding the beginner lift is free during the week and every night.

 ## Accommodations

Accommodations in the Mt. Washington Valley are among the best in skidom if you like rustic, romantic, tiny country inns and bed-and-breakfast establishments. You won't find high-rises, but great old historic inns accommodate those who prefer the atmosphere of a large resort hotel. The Valley also has moderately priced motels suitable for families. Condominiums exist, but for the most part are concentrated at a few base areas. For lodging information (but no reservations), call the **Mt. Washington Valley Chamber of Commerce** at (800) 367-3364.

The Inn at Thorn Hill (800-289-8990 or 383-4242), in Jackson with views of Mt. Washington, is elegant without being stuffy. The carriage house oozes country touches and the cottages provide the most privacy. The dining is considered one of the best in the state. Rates are $180–$300 including breakfast and a three-course dinner.

The 1785 Inn (800-421-1785 or 356-9025) is an old-fashion country inn with what have been called the best views of the valley. Rates are $89–$99 for B&B per room.

Stonehurst Manor, North Conway NH; (356-3113 or 800-525-9100), was created from a turn-of-the-century mansion that belonged to the Bigelow family of carpet fame. It is still manorial—the setting, rooms and restaurant are absolutely elegant. A room is $86; master bedroom with balcony or the suite is $186 weekends with breakfast and dinner. Ask about the winter packages.

Four Points Hotel by Sheraton (800-648-4397; in New Hampshire 356-9300) at Settlers' Green in North Conway, with 200 rooms and suites, is handy to all the best outlet stores as well as the rest of North Conway. It has saunas, whirlpools, swimming pool, fitness center and ice skating. Children younger than 17 stay free. Rates are $79–$185.

White Mountain Hotel and Resort (356-7100 or 800-533-6301) at the foot of Cathedral Ledges (the enormous sculptured granite cliffs you see from all North Conway), is reached by taking River Road off Rte. 16, then West Side Road to Hale's Location. The views back across the Valley toward Cranmore are unmatched. Rates are $99–$159.

The Eastern Slope Inn Resort (356-6321 or 800-862-1600) in the heart of North Conway is a palatial New England Inn. This establishment has a bit of everything needed in a hotel. Rooms, suites and townhouses in winter cost $68–$242 a night per room.

The Eagle Mountain Resort, Jackson (383-9111; for reservations, 800-966-5779), is one of those lovingly restored classic 19th-century resort hotels. Rates during the weekend are $89–$159 per night; slightly lower midweek. Children age 15 and younger stay free if sleeping in existing beds; additional adults, $15 per person daily.

The Wentworth Resort Hotel, Jackson Village (383-9700 or 800-637-0013), is a grand old hotel in the elegant tradition. Rooms are spacious, furnished with antiques and equipped with period baths. Room rates are $89–$140 a night. Ask about the three- and five-day midweek cross-country packages that include lodging, breakfast and dinner.

The Christmas Farm Inn, Jackson Village (383-4313 or 800-443-5837), is a cluster of buildings around a larger house, each as quaint as the next. The main inn has 10 rooms, and the other buildings house larger rooms and small apartments. This is as convenient as it gets for the Jackson Ski Touring trails. All rates include breakfast and dinner. A 15 percent service charge and taxes will be added to your bill. Double-occupancy room rates are $136–$190, depending on location.

The **Wildcat Inn and Tavern**, Jackson Village (383-4245 or 800-228-4245), built a century ago and once the original Carroll Reed Ski Shop, is now old-shoe comfortable and delightful. Right across the street are the Jackson Ski Touring Foundation and Jack Frost Ski Shop. Double occupancy costs $69–$120. Numerous multiday packages available.

The **Green Granite Inn** (356-6901 or 800-468-3666) is on Rt. 16 at the beginning of "the strip." Last year, they added a new indoor pool and hot tub. The inn is comfortable, affordable and great for families. It's right in the heart of North Conway's shopping and is convenient to all of the Valley. There's a large open foyer with fireplace and stuffed moosehead. Continental breakfast is served every morning. Evening movies and children's programs are offered during weekends and vacation periods. Room rates are $59–$160.

For smaller, cozier bed-and-breakfast establishments, **The Buttonwood Inn**, North Conway (356-2625 or 800-258-2625), is tucked in the woods with cross-country skiing from the back door. Room rates are in the $80–$175 range.

The Eastman Inn (356-6707 or 800-626-5855) just south of the North Conway village on the main road, is a B&B with 14 rooms in one of the oldest houses in town, newly restored with antique charm. Rates per room are $75–$90. Breakfast with waffle irons practically at your table is superb.

The Cabernet Inn (356-4704 or 800-866-4704) is a charming 1842 Victorian cottage that now is a nine-bedroom B&B. Each room has a private bath, and the inn has a full country breakfast. It's on Rte. 16 just north of Conway Village, and the rates are $69–$169. Some rooms have whirlpools or fireplaces.

The Inn at Jackson (383-4321 or 800-289-8600), is located right through the covered bridge in Jackson. Situated on a knoll, the inn overlooks the village and offers guests a warm, grand foyer and hot tub to unwind in after a day on the slopes. All rooms have private baths and some feature romantic fireplaces and four-poster beds. The country breakfast will get you up in the morning and keep you going all day. Rates are $69 to $129.

The inn's sister property, **Whitneys' Inn** (383-8916 or 800-677-5737), is a restored 1840s farmhouse that sits at the base of Black Mountain in Jackson, allowing Alpine and cross-country skiing from the door. The Inn is perfect for families—children may eat early at the "kid's table" with supervised activities following, allowing the adults the opportunity to enjoy their meal and relax. Rates run midweek $38–$48 per person B&B, weekend & holiday $55–$65 per person B&B; meal plans are available.

Ellis River House in Jackson (383-9339 or 800-233-8309), overlooking the Ellis River, has 18 rooms, some with whirlpool tubs and/or fireplaces, and also has some of Jackson's most popular touring outside the door. Rates: $89–$199.

The Notchland Inn (374-6131 or 800-866-6131) on the "quiet side" of the Valley, Rte. 302 outside Bartlett, is a romantic setting with 11 rooms, all with fireplaces. It has hot tub, skating and cross-country skiing from the door. B&B rates are $130–$150 per couple per night; half-board rates are $170–$190, holidays excluded.

On the southern side of the Valley, the **Snowvillage Inn** (447-2818 or 800-447-4345), six miles south of Conway in Snowville, has 18 uniquely decorated guest rooms, some with fireplaces and sweeping views of the White Mountains. There's cross-country skiing and snowshoeing right from the front door, plus a very full country breakfast and large, comfortable living room and foyer with a fireplace. Rates are $139–$219 for two and include breakfast and dinner.

Riverside Country Inn (356-9060) has seven rooms and doesn't mind kids or dogs. It's on Rte. 16A in Intervale. Rates are $45–$95.

Red Jacket Mountain View (356-5411 or 800-752-2538), is a rambling, low, motel-like building with some loft rooms and bunk beds good for families. It has a panoramic view of the Moat Range and an indoor pool and hot tub. Rates: $89–$154.

Slopeside accommodation

The **Grand Summit Hotel at Attitash Bear Peak** (374-1900 or 800-223-7669) is brand-new, with 143 guest rooms, restaurant, lounge, health club, hot tub and a year-round heated outdoor pool that has an indoor entrance.

Attitash Mountain Village (374-6500 or 800-862-1600) has an indoor pool, hot tubs, sauna, a skating pond, exercise room, restaurant and lounge. Sample rates from a wide selection: one-bedroom unit sleeping four, $129–$149 midweek, $199–$219 weekend; three-bedroom unit sleeping 10–14, $265–$285 midweek, $345–$375 weekend.

For slopeside condos, **Mt. Cranmore Condominiums** (356-6851 or 800-223-7669) are right on the mountain and room rental includes guest privileges at the Cranmore Sports Center (see the Other Activities section). Representative winter rates start at: two bedrooms and loft, $175 weekday, $225 weekend, $1,025 per week (based on four people per unit); three bedrooms and loft, $255 weekday, $350 weekend, $1,625 weekly (based on eight). Add $15 for each additional adult per night.

To be really close to Mt. Washington, and to get a head start if you're climbing, skiing, or using its cross-country trails, there's the **Joe Dodge Lodge** (466-2727) at Pinkham Notch, run by the Appalachian Mountain Club, with room for 104. The two-, four- and five-bunk rooms are simple, and rates include either one or two meals. Lodging, dinner and breakfast on a weekend, for example, are $40–$47. The public room has a fireplace, library, board games, and a well-used piano.

For rock-bottom prices, head to **Hostelling International–White Mountains** in Conway (447-1001), where a bunk bed is $16 a night, with continental breakfast.

 # Dining

Mt. Washington Valley is home to some of the best restaurants in the nation. Competition between restaurants is so intense that locals call it the War of the Chefs. All of these noted in the next three paragraphs serve meals worth a special trip.

The Bernerhof (383-4414) has its own nationally famous cooking school. **Stonehurst** (356-3113) and **The 1785 Inn** in North Conway (356-9025) have excellent cusine. These three restaurants serve some of the best gourmet meals in the country, let alone the Valley.

In Jackson, **The Christmas Farm Inn** (383-4313), **The Inn at Thorn Hill** (383-4242), **Wentworth Resort Hotel** (383-9700), and **Wildcat Inn and Tavern** (383-4245) are all fairly expensive and serve gourmet meals.

If you're willing to travel to the outskirts of the Valley, you can get fine gourmet dining with great winter views at the **Notchland Inn** (374-6131) in Hart's Location, the **Snowvillage Inn** (447-2818) in Snowville, and the **Oxford House Inn** (207-935-3442) over the border in Fryeburg, Maine.

For more down-to-earth meals, try the **Scottish Lion** (356-6381) for a choice of British or Hawaiian meals on the menu, or the **Red Parka Pub** (383-4344) for great barbecued spare ribs and prime rib. It doesn't take reservations; expect up to a two-hour wait on Saturday nights. **Bellini's** (356-7000) and **Marcello's** (356-2313) are best for Italian food. **Horsefeathers** (356-2687) in North Conway, is perhaps the most popular spot in town, with everything from comfort food such as chicken pot pie to more the-chef's-gone-wild fare such as beef medallions with wild mushroom ravioli. **Delaney's Hole in the Wall** (356-7776) has a southwestern flair and head to the **Shannon Door Pub** (383-4211) for Irish entertainment and good thin-crust pizzas. Pizza, from thin-crust to deep-dish, is found at **Elvio's** (356-3307) on Main Street. New restaurants include **Decades Steak House** (356-7080) which serves hefty slabs of beef midst old-time memorabilia and, for casual meals, **Brandli's Pizza Pasta Grill** (356-7878) in Settler's Green that meets the test of good and cheap and lots to eat.

For breakfast head to **Peaches** (356-5860), upstairs to **Gunther's** with giant waffles and pancakes (356-5200) and the **Sugar House Eatery** (356-6295), all on the main drag in North Conway. In Jackson we recommend **Yesterday's** (383-4457).

The **Appalachian Mountain Club** (466-2727) at the base of Mt. Washington in Pinkham Notch gets rave reviews for a slightly different dining experience. Meals are served family-style—a great way to meet some new friends. Wednesdays are International Dinner Series, featuring a different country's cuisine and a slide show and talk from area residents who have traveled abroad. Available spots fill up days in advance, perhaps partly because of the price: adults $12, kids 12 and younger $8.

 ## Après-ski/nightlife

One of the best ski bars in the country is the **Red Parka Pub**, which offers lively après-ski and then nightlife activity into the wee hours. Something is happening every night, and its informal style runs to beer served in Mason jars, and vintage skis and creative license plates from all over covering the walls. On nights when there is no live music, live comedy or a movie is featured.

The place to be in Jackson is the **Wildcat Tavern** where folk rock is served up on weekends. On Friday and Saturday nights, **Horsefeathers** at North Conway hops, and the **Up Country Saloon** has live dance music. Locals hang out in **Hooligans, Horsefeathers** and **Delaney's Hole in the Wall** in North Conway.

The **Castle and Crown** is a new Irish pub in the building that used to house the Oxen Yoke near Cranmore. It has good pub grub and the normal range of Irish beers.

 ## Other activities

Shopping: Mt. Washington Valley has the best shopping of any ski resort in the nation—more than 150 factory outlets and no sales taxes. The area also has many unusual boutiques with creative gift items. Stop by the Chamber of Commerce in North Conway and pick up a Visitor Guide; there are far too many stores to list here.

The **Cranmore Sports Center,** 356-6301 at Cranmore base, is a huge all-season facility, with indoor and outdoor tennis courts, pool, aerobics classes, steamroom and sauna. It is also home to the largest (30 by 40 feet) indoor climbing wall in the Northeast. Classes are available through International Mountain Climbing School (356-6316).

Eastern Mountain Sports (356-5433) in the Eastern Slope Inn also has a range of winter climbing and hiking programs, including ice-climbing instruction, ascents of Mt. Washington, and traverses of the Presidential Range.

Serious climbers hang out at **International Mountain Equipment** (356-7013). Back-country skiers and telemarkers can buy anything they need and tune up their equipment. The owner, Rick Wilcox, has climbed Mt. Everest.

The **Appalachian Mountain Club** (466-2721) has an active schedule of courses and workshops on ski touring, snowshoeing, avalanches, and more. The club's maps and guidebooks to these mountains are an unrivaled source of indispensable information. Headquarters is at Pinkham Notch, across the road from Wildcat.

Take a **sleigh ride** in the Valley. Try Nestlenook's horse-drawn sleigh (383-0845) or The Farm off West Side Road (356-2694).

You can **ice skate** in Jackson, North Conway and Conway. Cranmore, Black Mountain and Shawnee Peak have very active **tubing** hills.

In Conway, the new **Ham Arena** (447-5886) for indoor ice skating is set to open in December 1998. It will have open skating, rentals and concessions. Two-hour skating lessons start at $4 for children and $5 for adults.

Getting there and getting around

By air: The closest airport is Portland, Maine, with major airline service from all over the country. It is about a 90-minute drive from North Conway. Manchester Airport, farther south in New Hampshire, is served by Southwest, US Air, MetroJet, United, Continental Express, ComAir and Business Express/Delta Connection, and is about a two-hour drive.

By car: The Mt. Washington Valley is 140 miles north of Boston. The best route from Boston is up I-95 to Rte. 16, then north on 16/302. An alternate route is to come north on I-93 and take Rte. 104 to Rte. 25 to Rte. 16, and on to North Conway. From Portland, follow Rte. 302.

North Conway has been notorious for its weekend traffic jams going through town. Most visitors approach from the south, and most of the ski areas are to the north. Conway and North Conway Village have added traffic cops at major lights on weekends and holidays, and locals tell us it has helped a bit. Even so, be patient if you're behind the wheel at 4 p.m. when the lifts close. Or, if you are driving from the Jackson/Wildcat/Attitash Bear Peak end of town to the south, take West Side Road to avoid most of the shopping traffic and the North Conway crowds.

Getting around: Bring a car.

Hunter Mountain
Ski Windham
New York

Hunter Mountain Facts

Summit elevation:	**3,200 feet**
Vertical drop:	**1,600 feet**
Base elevation:	**1,600 feet**

Address: P.O. Box 295, Hunter, NY 12442
✆ **Area code:** 518
Ski area phone: 263-4223
Snow report: 367-7669
ⓘ **Lodging reservations:** (518) 263-4641
E-mail: hunter@albany.net
Internet: http://www.huntermtn.com
Number of lifts: 12–1 high-speed quad, 2 quads, 2 triple chairs, 4 double chairs, 3 surface lifts
Snowmaking: 100 percent
Skiable acreage: 230 acres
Uphill capacity: 15,714 per hour
Snowboarding: Yes, unlimited
Expert:★ **Advanced:**★★★
Intermediate:★★★
Beginner:★★ **Never-ever:**★★
Nearest lodging: slopeside
Resort child care: Yes, 6 months and older
Adult ticket, per day: $37-$44
Dining:★★
Apres-ski/nightlife:★★★
Other activities:★

Ski Windham Facts

Summit elevation:	**3,100 feet**
Vertical drop:	**1,600 feet**
Base elevation:	**1,500 feet**

Address: P.O. Box 459, Windham, NY 12496
✆ **Area code:** 518
Ski area phone: 734-4300
Snow report: (800) 729-4766
ⓘ **Toll-free reservations:**
(800) SKI WINDHAM (754-9463) **Fax:** 734-5732
Internet: http://www.skiwindham.com
Number of lifts: 7–1 high-speed quad, 4 triples, 1 double, 1 surface lift
Snowmaking: 97 percent
Skiable acreage: 234 acres
Uphill capacity: 11,800 per hour
Snowboarding: Yes, unlimited
Expert:★ **Advanced:**★★
Intermediate:★★★
Beginner:★★ **Never-ever:**★★
Nearest lodging: walking distance
Resort child care: Yes, 12 months and older
Adult ticket, per day: $33-$42
Dining:★★
Apres-ski/nightlife:★
Other activities:★

These are the two closest large ski areas to New York City, only a two-and-a-half hours' drive north. These resorts are in the midst of the rocky Catskills—home to such legends as Rip Van Winkle. As far as skiing goes, the area woke with a vengeance almost thirty years ago. Trails were dynamited and bulldozed through rugged mountains, and snowmaking became an integral part of Eastern ski resorts.

The villages surrounding the mountains reflect the personality of their respective resort. Hunter and nearby Tannersville are basic one-street Adirondack towns with supermarkets, bars, pubs, discos, hotels and homes. Windham is the quieter sister with a more manicured look; delis rather than supermarkets, country inns instead of hotels. On the slopes, weekend crowds at Hunter reflect a singles Generation X heritage. Windham is a family resort and its skiers are far more sedate. In Hunter you may hear the bass throb of a disco beat and other sounds of merriment. The streets teem into the small hours. In Windham the loudest midnight sound may be the snow guns, a passing car or water gurgling downstream.

Hunter Mountain and Ski Windham are only ten miles apart. Both have the same amount of vertical but Hunter is a major leaguer, by far the bigger operation. It has become one of the snowmaking champions of the Northeast, shooting out mountains of snow and continually upgrading the system. When conditions are poor everywhere else in the region, this is where the skiers come expecting snow. Ski Windham offers good skiing but doesn't have the extent of its neighbor's snowmaking or as much difficult terrain. Each area has a high-speed quad pumping skiers up the mountain and keeping lines manageable.

Mountain layout

◆◆ **Expert** ◆ **Advanced:** Hunter's skiing is primarily solid intermediate with an advanced flair. Its toughest runs drop off the west side of the summit, bumpy and fast. At Ski Windham, turn right off the quad for advanced runs like Wheelchair and Wolverine. To the far left of the ski area are three fast blacks fed by their own triple chair. Although these trails are not as tough as those at Hunter, they will keep advanced skiers happy for a few days.

■ **Intermediate:** This is the strong point at both areas. The middle section at Hunter is where intermediates can run wild. Ski Windham, the perfect terrain for families of various abilities, has a strong intermediate flavor but without Hunter's twists and turns and changing scenery. Most of the blue runs are off the Whirlwind quad chair.

●● **Beginner** ● **Never-ever:** Hunter One, off to the left of the trail map, is a mellow beginner paradise, separate from the faster traffic. At Ski Windham, the Whiteway triple serves the beginner terrain. The area is adding a new "novice-to-intermediate" snowmaking-covered trail, 1.5 miles long, that descends from the east peak.

Note: Their proximity to New York and Long Island means that both resorts fill up on weekends. Many skiers drive up just for a day. But the quads go with the flow and lines rarely exceed fifteen minutes long. Midweek both mountains are practically empty, and a where-is-everybody atmosphere fills the slopes and lodges. Everything's a bigger bargain.

Mountain rating

Best for intermediates, good for advanced and beginner levels too.

Snowboarding

Snowboarding is allowed on the entire mountain at Hunter and Ski Windham. The former relocated its snowboard park last season and increased its size tenfold. Windham doubled the size of its park. Both have rentals and Learn-to-Snowboard packages for never-evers. Hunter also has a MINIrider program for youngsters 7–12. Both have Small Class Sessions that meet three times a day.

Lessons (98/99 prices)

Hunter: Group lessons are $20 for 90 minutes unless there are only one or two students, then it's an hour. With the Bring-A-Beginner package, one person buys a never-ever package and another skis for half price (all-area lift) midweek. The Learn-With-Me family lesson includes 90 minutes and focuses on the children while making it a family experience.

Never-ever packages (lift, lesson, shaped-ski rental) are $45.

Private lessons cost $45 per hour for one, with each additional skier paying $20. A three-hour private lesson costs $120. Early a.m. and late p.m. private lessons cost $35; additional skiers $15.

Children's lessons for ages 7–12 include lifts, lessons, rentals, box lunch and supervision. Weekend rates are $68 (including lunch and rentals); half day (rentals but no lunch), $48. Full weekday is $48, half $35. Open 9:30 a.m. to 3:30 p.m. There is SKIwee for ages 4–6 at the same prices.

Ski Windham: This resort has a full ski school program as well. **Private lessons** run $50 an hour for one person, $85 for two, $100 for three. **Group lessons** are $20 per 1.75-hour session, or $90 for a book of five sessions, $180 for a book of ten lessons. The resort also has a full range of **programs for children** ages 3–12.

Child care (98/99 prices)

Hunter: The day-care program, for children 6 months–6 years who have not yet begun to ski costs $25 for a full day, $15 for a half day. Just-For-Me-Because-I'm-Three combines day care with snowplay. It costs $30 for a full day (8:30 a.m. to 4 p.m.) and $20 for a half day. Lunch is not included, and is $3 per day per child.

Ski Windham: The Children's Learning Center (ages 1-7) offers non-skiers and skiers a variety of activities, and for those who like to sprawl out on the floor when they draw or read, the floors are heated. Full-day/half-day programs: $48/$33 for non-skiers; $64/$42 for skiers without rentals; and $78/54 with rentals.

Lift tickets (98/99 prices)

Hunter: Full-day weekend/holiday lift tickets cost $44 adult, $28 junior (12 and younger). Two days cost $82 for adults; $52 for kids; three days were $118/$75.

Midweek non-holiday lift tickets cost is $37 for adults and $22 for kids. A Frequent-Skier card gives more discounts the more you ski. Others who get discounts are seniors (65 and older), teens (13–18) and students with valid college IDs.

Ski Windham: A full-day ticket costs $42 adult/$34 junior (7–12) on weekends and holidays, and $33/$29 on weekdays. Tickets before mid-December and after mid-March cost $36 on weekends/holidays and $29 midweek for adults. Corresponding junior prices are $30 and $26.

On non-holiday weekdays, juniors ski free when accompanied by a paying adult (one child per adult). Children under age 6 ski free anytime when accompanied by a ticketed adult.

Accommodations

Hunter: This ski area pioneered a B&B program that now has about 30 country inns participating. These B&Bs have prices starting at about $100 per night. The program includes lift tickets and combined with the Kids Ski Free program is a money-saver.

Call (800) 775-4641 for lodging reservations. Try to stay at the actual resort villages. Palenville, considered nearby by reservation agents, is at the bottom of a steep grade. Condominiums are available for nightly, weekend or weekly rental. Weekend motel rates are $75–$95 per night. Budget accommodations are available 10 to 20 minutes away.

In the Hunter area our top three recommendations are the **Scribner Hollow Lodge,** with several luxury suites, **Villa Vosilla** and the **Deer Mountain Inn**. The **Liftside Condos** are very well appointed and convenient. The collection of excellent B&Bs includes the **Kennedy House** and **Washington Irving Lodge;** head to the **Hunter Village Inn** for more of a party atmosphere.

Ski Windham: Its reservation service (800-729-7549) has packages that include lifts, lodging and many discounts. The ski area owns the **Windham Arms Resort,** which has country inn hospitality with regular shuttles to the ski area. Four-day packages are available through Island Tours for the Windham Arms that include room, breakfast and dinner, skiing and transportation from New York City. Other accommodations within three miles of Ski Windham range from sprawling inns to B&Bs. **Evergreen at The Thompson House, Hotel Vienna, Point Lookout Mountain Inn** and **Christman's Windham House** are good hotels in roughly descending order of luxury. B&Bs to try include **Albergo Allegria, Danske Hus** and the **Country Suite.** Rates generally start at less than $100 per night, double occupancy, with weekend rates higher than weeknights.

Dining

There are scores of restaurants in this region. Around Hunter: **Mountain Brook Dining and Spirits** (263-5351) serves grilled fish, pasta, and so forth by a woodburning stove. The **Chateau Belleview** (589-5525) prepares fine continental cooking; **Swiss Chalet** (589-5445) has excellent cuisine; and **Deer Mountain Inn** (589-6268) is recommended by all the locals. For less expensive fare and great onion rings try **P.J. Larkins** (589-5568), **Fireside** (589-4216), and **Pete's Place** (589-9840), all favorites with virtually everyone. **Tequilla's Tex-Mex** (263-4863) satisfies the margarita craving. Try **Maggie's Crooked Cafe** (589-6101) in Tannersville for breakfast.

Near Windham try **Brandywine** (734-3838) for well-prepared, affordable meals (Wednesday's pasta special is a real bargain) and **The Frog's House** (734-9817). These two spots got the nod from most locals. **Theo's** (734-4455) has tasty Greek food and **Thetford's** (734-3322) has great steaks and seafood. **Temptations** at the Windham Arms Resort (734-3000) serves a '50s evening menu (tuna melt, grilled cheese, BLTs and clubs) in a pink-purple-chrome period decor. **Vesuvio** (734-3663) and **La Griglia** (734-4499) reputedly have the best Italian food in the area. **Chalet Fondue** (734-4650) has the best German menu in town. The best burger is charcoal-grilled at **Jimmy O'Connor's** (734-4270).

For breakfast try **Bagels-n-Buns** (734-4000) in Alpine Village or the **Four Stars** (734-4600) or **Starlight Cafe** (734-9862).

 ## Après-ski/nightlife

At Hunter, the end of the day hurrahs are the happy hours that transform the many rustic bars in town, and the imaginatively named **The Bar** in the base lodge, into throngs of ruddy faces and amplified jollity. Here and there a live band belts out tunes. After 7 p.m. the crowds disperse except for the hard core group, which congregates at **Slopes** and **Tanners** discos on the main drag.

Windham has no après-ski, unless you count the 3–7 p.m. weekend action in the **Legends' Lounge** in the base lodge. Even with live music and dancing, it won't set the slopes on fire. The **Dew Zone** is a club for ages 13 to 18. It has DJ music for dancing, video games, ping-pong and other events. Ski Windham also has **night skiing** on the C and D lifts Thursday through Saturday nights.

Other activities

Scant in both places. A little shopping, a little cross country skiing or snowmobiling and that's about it. Ski Windham also offers snowshoes, telemark skis and shorty skis in its Tech Center.

 ## Getting there and getting around

By car: The best access is up I-87, 120 miles north of New York City. For Hunter Mountain, take Exit 20 at Saugerties and follow Route 32 to Route 32A to the area. To reach Ski Windham turn north on Route 296 off of Route 23A or if coming on the N.Y. Thruway, take Exit 21 in Catskill and go west on Route 23 for 25 miles.

By bus: Both resorts provide buses from New York City, New Jersey, Long Island and Pennsylvania. From NYC, Hunter's bus leaves Mondays, Wednesdays, Fridays and Saturdays. Call (800) 552-6262 for information. Ski Windham's bus leaves Monday, Wednesday, Friday and Sunday. Call (516) 360-0369 or (718) 343-4444.

Getting around: At these resorts a car is virtually a must for getting around at night. Several local companies have 24-hour taxi service.

Lake Placid/Whiteface

New York

Summit elevation:	**4,416 feet**
Vertical drop:	**3,216 feet**
Base elevation:	**1,200 feet**

Address: Olympic Regional Development Authority (ORDA), Olympic Center, Lake Placid, NY 12946

✆ Area code: 518

Ski area phone: 523-1655 (ORDA)

Snow report: 946-7171

ⓘ **Toll-free information:** 800-462-6236

Fax: 523-9275

E-mail: info@orda.org

Toll-free reservations: (800) 447-5224 (800-44-PLACID)

Internet: http://www.orda.org (ORDA) or http://www.lakeplacid.com (Lake Placid Visitors Bureau)

Expert:★★★ **Advanced:**★★★
Intermediate:★★★
Beginner:★★ **Never-ever:**★★

Number and types of lifts: 10—1 quad, 2 triples, 6 doubles, 1 rope tow

Acreage: about 170 acres

Snowmaking: 93 percent

Uphill capacity: 10,385 skiers per hour

Snowboarding: Yes, unlimited

Bed base: 5,000

Nearest lodging: 1/2 mile in Wilmington about 9 miles in Lake Placid

Resort child care: Yes, 12 months and older

Adult ticket, per day: $39 (98/99 price)

Dining:★★★
Apres-ski/nightlife:★★★
Other activities:★★★★★

Its skiing alone would guarantee Lake Placid a spot somewhere in the middle of the pack of Northeast resorts. But add other activities and Lake Placid stands apart as a winter sports magnet. There's no doubt that the 1980 Winter Olympics were key in establishing that reputation, but, plenty of past Olympic sites have retreated into relative obscurity. At Lake Placid, the folks have picked up the flame and run with it. To fulfill the promise of Lake Placid so evident during the Olympics, they formed the Olympic Regional Development Authority (ORDA) to operate the multi-facility recreational area.

Because probably more world-class winter sports athletes still train and compete here than anywhere else in the free world (more than 8,000 a year), Lake Placid still has the atmosphere of an Olympic village. Groups of young athletes are everywhere, and there always seems to be one championship or another under way. Even the athletes themselves revel in watching the daring if demented souls who soar off the Olympic jumps.

Lake Placid urges you at every turn to participate. In addition to the bobsled run and one of the most extensive and well-prepared cross-country ski circuits anywhere, you can experience the luge run at the Mt. Van Hoevenberg Olympic sports complex about eight miles away.

For the uninitiated, bouncing off the walls of a luge track is not unlike being in a pinball game played by unseen Nordic giants, with you as the ball. Of course, no one in their right mind would *want* to experience firsthand the thrill of being launched off a 120-meter ski ramp, but you can get a breathtaking perspective on that madness by taking the glass elevator 26 stories to the top. The $7 ticket, thankfully, is round-trip.

Back on Main Street, the town itself is dominated by the arena where America watched its Cinderella hockey team enter the history books in 1980. Wonderfully situated on Mirror Lake, the town is full of charm, if just one standard motel away from being truly quaint. For a relaxing afternoon away from the slopes, take a dogsled ride across the lake. At night many visitors will find both relaxation and exercise on the Olympic Oval (where Eric Heiden won five gold medals), lulled into an easy rhythm by the sharp scrape of their skates in the crisp night air. A personal favorite, however, is the nighttime toboggan run. As many as six of your entourage can ride together, clutching and yelping, as you shoot down the lighted ramp and spill suddenly out onto the darkness of frozen Mirror Lake with a giddy sense of fear and elation. Lake Placid encourages you to "just do it."

Mountain layout

◆◆ **Expert** ◆ **Advanced:** With the greatest vertical drop of any mountain in the East (3,216 feet), Whiteface Mountain has some of the worthiest expert runs in the East. There's also a Medusa's head of excellent advanced and advanced-intermediate runs snaking down the forested slopes of Little Whiteface (a shoulder of this mountain). For experts The Slides is a real challenge. It is above treeline and is only open in good weather.

The most recent change to the trails is the widening of Ridge Runner, the summit trail that provides access to the men's and women's downhill trails, Cloudspin and Skyward. Experts will want to spend time on these runs at the top of Whiteface. These are sweethearts with plenty of pitch and moguls even for the hotdogs. Most of the runs down from Little Whiteface are also black, and they all have good grade.

Advanced skiers should also not miss the Empire and MacKenzie runs from the top of Little Whiteface. They're officially black, but under good conditions manageable.

■ **Intermediate:** Take the G-lift from the midstation up to the top of Little Whiteface. An observation platform just off to the left at the top of this double chair gives you an unparalleled view of the lakes and valley. Then try the snaking Excelsior run, which twists back down to the midstation. You can cut the rounded corners of this baby like a bobsled, choosing your own pace.

After that warmup, tackle Paron's Run or Follie's Trail from the tip-top of Whiteface (Lift F—Summit Triple). Before this run was added several years ago, intermediates had no way to enjoy either the awe-inspiring view or best-in-the-East vertical available from the top of the mountain.

●● **Beginner** ● **Never-ever:** These levels have a secluded area—off to the right looking up from the base, above Kids Kampus. The wide-open runs down to the bottom from the midstation are all suitable for lower intermediates, giving you a free run of half the mountain.

Note: Like many Eastern mountains, Whiteface stands unshielded, lording over a vast valley of forests and frozen lakes. Its position makes for some of the most spectacular views in the world, but winter winds do whip across that valley and up the walls of Whiteface with regularity. For many veteran Eastern skiers, the complaint about Whiteface has been that it's too often wind-blown, cold and icy. Having been there four times now, we would say that from our own experience, Whiteface is, well, frequently wind-blown, cold and icy. You can't fault any area for bad weather, and on an ideal day, Whiteface comes close to being as good as it gets in the East. To counter icy conditions the mountain has increased its snowmaking by 25 percent.

Mountain rating

Whiteface is one of those rare mountains that has more to offer experts and beginners, with less in the middle range for true intermediates. Experts will find much of the upper half of the mountain challenging, though anything below the midstation is generally a wide-open cruise with very gentle grade. Beginners will thus find anything below midstation much to their liking. Intermediates probably will feel bored by most of the lower half of the mountain, and stretched by much of the upper but can push themselves into the advanced stage on Little Whiteface.

Cross-country

Here again, the folks at Lake Placid have built strongly on the foundation laid by the 1980 Winter Olympics, and the Mt. Van Hoevenberg complex has cross-country skiing you are unlikely to find elsewhere—50 km. of marked trails that average 15 ft. wide, regularly groomed and patrolled; bridges built especially for cross-country skiers so you don't have to worry about traffic; snowmaking (5 km.), and emergency phones.

Within the complex are 10 marked loops offering one expert, six intermediate and three novice tours. Additional expert skiing is on the Porter Mountain racing loops. The start/finish stadium at the sports complex also features a ski shop, waxing room, small snack bar and warming room. Trail fees are $11 for adults and $10 for ages 6-12 and 62 and older. Children younger than 6 ski free.

Snowboarding

Snowboarding is permitted on all trails and lifts. Whiteface has lessons and rentals.

Lessons (98/99 prices)

Group lessons: $20 for two hours. Multiple lessons can be purchased at discounts. Ski week packages begin with a wine-and-cheese party, and end with a race and party.

Never-ever package: A group lesson with lower-mountain pass is $30; add equipment rental for $15. Or, do a private lesson with lower-mountain ticket for $65, and add equipment cost.

A five-day program called Parallel from the Start guarantees skiers will be skiing from the top of the moutain on the longest vertical in the East in just five days.

Private lessons: $50 an hour, with $30 for an extra person (limit of two). Discounts are offered on multi-hour lessons.

Racing: The resort has a coin-operated race course.

Children's programs: Lessons for ages 7–12 are $35 half day and $55 a full day, lunch included in full-day program.

SKIwee is for children ages 4–6. The drop-off area has adjacent parking. Half-day programs are $35. A full-day program costs $55 (including lunch). For more about the children's program, call 946-2223.

Child care (98/99 prices)

Ages: 1–6 years.
Costs: $20 per half day or $35 per day per child, with lunch included in full-day price.
Reservations: Recommended; call 946-2223.
Note: The Bunny Hutch is complete with a children's drop-off, adjacent parking for parents with children, a large nursery, children's rentals and an outdoor terrain garden.

Lift tickets (98/99 prices)

	Adult	Child (7-12)
One day	$39	$20
Three days	$106 ($35.33/day)	$60 ($20/day)
Five days	$159 ($31.80/day)	$100 ($20/day)

Who skis free: Children aged 6 and younger when accompanied by an adult, and ages 70 and older.

Who skis at a discount: Seniors 65–69 pay $20 any day. Discounts also apply in early ($29 for adults prior to Dec. 20) and spring season ($29 from March 30 until closing).

Accommodations

Lake Placid is one of the winter resorts that is using new technology to make life easier. Not only can you call the toll-free number in our stat box to make reservations, you also can make online reservations through the website (www.lakeplacid.com).

Some of the larger hotels centered around the town of Lake Placid tend to be of the more modern franchise variety. An important exception is the singular **Mirror Lake Inn** (523-2544), a traditional lodge right on the lake shore, and probably the finest overnight in the area (it's rated Four Diamond by AAA). The New England-style exterior continues inside with antiques, chandeliers and mahogany walls. The inn also offers such modern amenities as indoor pool, whirlpool, sauna, health spa, and game room. The two restaurants include one of the best in town, with candlelight dining overlooking the lake. Room rates are $95–$360, the latter for a suite.

The **Lake Placid Resort Holiday Inn** (523-2556 or 800-874-1980) in the town center is Lake Placid's largest hotel (209 rooms). It features great views of the lake and mountains, all rooms with refrigerators and microwaves, and some with Jacuzzi tub and fireplace. It has a large indoor pool, whirlpool, sauna, complete health club, 20 km. of cross-country trails and two restaurants, including The Veranda, one of the area's finest. Rooms are $59–$129 midweek and $89–189 on the weekends.

The **Best Western Golden Arrow** (523-3353 or 800-582-5540) is on the lake with spectacular views and has an indoor pool, Jacuzzi, sauna, weight room, and racquetball courts. Room-with-view rates are as low as $60 midweek, and $118–$148 per room on weekends. Also boasting similar amenities is the **Lake Placid Hilton** (523-4411 or 800-755-5598), with two indoor pools and private balconies for each room with a view of the lake. The hotel's bed-

and-breakfast package is quite popular, costing $88 for two, midweek. There is also a **Ramada Inn** (523-2587) and a **Howard Johnson** (523-9555) in town.

The **Lake Placid Lodge** (523-2573, formerly Lake Placid Manor), is a classic Adirondack lodge with rustic rooms, fireplaces and exceptional French-American cuisine. The restaurant is open to the public.

Skiers on a budget should try the **Edge of the Lake Motor Inn** (523-9430), **Town House Motor Inn** (523-2532), **Alpine Air Motel** (523-2180), the **Econo Lodge** (523-2750), and the **Wildwood** on the Lake (523-2750), all of which have rooms for less than $100, some as low as $50.

The nearest RV park is KOA in Wilmington, NY.

Dining

Considered the best restaurant in the area, **Lake Placid Lodge** (523-2573) serves continental cuisine. Also upscale and excellent is the **Hungry Trout** (946-2217), specializing in, you guessed it, fish (entrées $12.95 and up). **The Charcoal Pit** (523-3050), open for about 35 years, charbroils lots of steaks and chops.

Solid German fare is available at slightly more moderate prices at the **Alpine Cellar** (523-2180). A full menu of schnitzels, sauerbraten and rippchen (smoked pork) are available starting around $10.95 per entrée. A personal favorite is the **Artist's Café** (523-9493) which features a prime location overlooking Mirror Lake, as well as steak and fish at reasonable prices. After a chilly dogsled ride on the lake, take a break with a bowl of their excellent onion soup.

Nicola's Over Main (523-4430) and **The Great American Bagel Factory** (523-1874) are two other worthy choices, both on Main Street. The first has wood-fired pizza and a Mediterranean slant while the second is American-meal-on-the-fly with bagels, specialty coffees and sandwiches. And no ski town is complete without an inexpensive Italian restaurant featuring pizza—**Mr. Mike's Pizza** (523-9770) takes care of that craving.

Après-ski/nightlife

Lake Placid is large enough to generate its own heat as a nightlife center, drawing not only out-of-town vacationers but also the locals.

Because Whiteface lies separated from the town, however, most of the après-ski action is in the base lodge. **Steinhoff's** and **R.J. McDougall's**, just down the road from Whiteface are also good for an après-ski drink.

At night, the young and hot of foot head to **Mud Puddles**, on the side street next to the speed skating oval. High-tech disco gear is on full display around the dance floor. Most of the other nightlife action centers around the main hotels. **Cristy's** at the Holiday Inn features a large bar and even more generous dance floor, with music spun by a DJ (drink specials on Wednesday nights). **Roomers** at the Best Western also offers dancing to a DJ, or for a live band try **Dancing Bears Lounge** at the Hilton.

Anyone looking for a quieter nightspot should head for **The Cottage,** across the street from the Mirror Lake Inn. The fire's always going, and at sunset there's an excellent view of the lake and mountains.

Other activities (97/98 prices)

Lake Placid is nothing *but* other activities. The **bobsled rides** at Mt. Van Hoevenberg Olympic Sports Complex (seven miles from the village) include mile bobsled rides ($100 per person) and half-mile bobsled ($30 per person). The mile-long bobsled program is by reservation only (523 4436).

Luge rides (523-1655) are also offered Wednesday through Monday for $30 apiece. Tours of the **Olympic Jumping Complex,** with chair lift and elevator ride, cost $7 for adults, $4 for children and seniors. Hours are 9 a.m. to 4 p.m.

The **Olympic Speed Skating Oval** is open for public skating 7–9 p.m. daily and 1–3 p.m. on Saturdays and Sundays (523-1655) and the **Olympic Center Skating** is open from 1–3 p.m. on Mondays, Wednesdays and Thursdays. Cost for both is $5 for adults and $3 for juniors

Operating hours for the **toboggan run** on Mirror Lake are Wednesday, 7–9 p.m., Friday, 7–10 p.m., Saturday noon–4 p.m. and 7–10 p.m., and Sunday noon–4 p.m. The charge is $3 for adults, $2 for children, and $3 for the toboggan rental.

The **Kodak Gold Medal Total Winter Experience** costs $39. This includes a bobsled or luge ride, a day of cross-country skiing and admission to the jumping complex, museums and public skating.

The **Lake Placid Winter Olympic Museum,** with displays from the 1932 and 1980 Winter Olympics held at Lake Placid, is open daily. Admission is $3 for adults and $2 for juniors. Call 523-1655 ext. 263 for more information.

Getting there and getting around

By air: USAir commuter service serves Adirondack Airport, 16 miles away on Rte. 86 in Saranac Lake. Private planes can use Lake Placid Airport.

By train: Trains stop at Westport on the New York City–Montréal line. There has been a shuttle bus from the train station to the resort in the past, but at our press time, that was not certain for 98/99. If you plan to travel this way, ask the Lake Placid Visitors Bureau (phone number in the stat box). Amtrak has ski packages; call (800-872-7245; spells USA-RAIL) for more info.

By car: From the south, take Exit 24 (Albany) off the New York State Thruway (I-87). Take Northway (still I-87) to Exit 30, follow Route 9 north two miles to Route 73 and continue 28 miles to Lake Placid.

From the west, take I-90 (NY State Thruway) to Exit 36 (Syracuse) for I-81. Follow I-81 north to Watertown, then east on Route 3 to Saranac Lake. Then take Route 86 east to Lake Placid.

Getting around: It's about a ten-mile drive to both Whiteface (downhill) and Mt. Hoevenberg (cross-country) from the center of Lake Placid. Though scheduled buses exist, it's best to have a car.

Killington/Pico

Vermont

Summit elevation:	**4,241 feet**
Vertical drop:	**3,150 feet**
Base elevation:	**1,091 feet**

Address: Killington Road
Killington, VT 05751
☎ **Area code:** 802
Ski area phone: 422-3333
Snow report: 422-3261
ⓘ **Toll-free reservations:** (800) 621-6867
(621-MTNS)
E-mail: info@killington.com
Internet: http://www.killington.com
Expert:★★★
Advanced:★★★
Intermediate:★★★★
Beginner:★★★★
Never-ever:★★★★

Number and types of lifts: 33–3 gondolas,
6 high-speed quads, 6 quads,
6 triples, 4 doubles, 8 surface lifts
Acreage: 1,200 trail acres
Snowmaking: 72 percent
Uphill capacity: 53,288 per hour
Snowboarding: Yes, unlimited
Bed base: 5,500 (base),19,000 (region)
Nearest lodging: walking distance
Resort child care: Yes, 6 weeks and older
Adult ticket, per day: $50–$54.60 (98/99)
Dining:★★
Apres-ski/nightlife:★★★★
Other activities:★★

In the past few years, the "Beast in the East" has added considerably to its reputation as the biggest, highest, fastest, steepest, largest, simply *baddest* ski resort east of the Mississippi. Killington is in the process of adding the adjacent Pico area to its already vast domain with inter-connecting lifts, and the flashy Skyship gondola to whisk riders up to Killington Peak has greatly reduced sometimes agonizingly long lines in the morning at the base area. Because it lacks a true central village and most of the accomodations and nightlife are strung along the Killington access road, about the only superlative the area cannot claim is "quaintest." For rollicking good fun and skiing variety—spread across 7 mountains and 212 trails, from the meandering Juggernaut that at 10 miles is the longest (and one of the most gentle) in the country, to the infamous, gulp-inducing bumps Outer Limits—Killington stands among the top resorts in America.

Killington/Pico trumpets its size proudly. For example, it leads the East in vertical drop (3,150 feet), lift capacity (53,288 skiers per hour) and longest ski season (Killington strives to be the first ski area in the country to open — usually aiming for early October—and closes in June). But this resort also does so much so well. A vast snowmaking operation is why its season lasts eight months. All-inclusive packages offer some of the best deals in the country, with substantial savings over buying the components individually. It also has one of the best central reservations systems, which allows you to book everything from flights to car rental, lodging, child care and ski rental with one call: (800) 621-6867. And that trail map? One of the best, small enough to carry easily, but packed with info, including numbers to call if you lock your keys in your car.

The resort's shining star is its new eight-passenger heated gondola, K-1 Gondola to Killington Peak, which replaced the Killington double chair. Its other gondola, Skyeship, was added a few seasons ago. Riders can get on the Skyeship at a midstation near the base of the Needle's Eye Express quad chair, but they don't have to. They can board at the base station and get off 12 minutes later at the top of Skye Peak, a rise of 2,520 feet. A note of clarification on our stats: The Skyeship is actually separate lifts, connected by a computerized transfer station. Because the two stages can operate independently, Killington counts them as two lifts (just in case you were wondering where the third gondola is).

Two seasons ago, Killington acquired Pico, a ski/snowboard area about seven road miles away. Pico backs up to the Rams Head area of Killington, and plans call for lifts and trails that will connect the two resorts by the year 2000. Though we would prefer to give you separate stats for Killington and Pico, the resort's policy is to provide combined stats, as if it were already one resort, so that's what we list. We refer to "Killington/Pico" when we're talking about the whole enchilada (this introduction, primarily), and "Killington" or "Pico" when talking about each one individually. Lift tickets are valid at both areas. Public transportation between the two is via The Bus, which charges a nominal fee (less than $5) and stops at several locations along Killington Road. Catch it at the Snowshed Base Lodge.

Killington is part of the American Skiing Company (ASC), which owns several New England resorts and one each in Utah, California and Colorado.

Mountain layout

Killington's terrain is almost too sprawling to describe. We'd suggest that you take the Meet the Mountains Tour leaving at 9:45 a.m. from the tour sign in front of the Resort Center at Snowshed. The groups are assembled as much as possible by ability levels.

Killington has six separate base areas (the resort counts seven, but one of them is at Pico.) Three base areas are clustered within striking distance at the top of Killington Road. Snowshed and Rams Head are across the street from one another, and Killington base is just a bit up the road. Bear Mountain, home of the famed Outer Limits bump run, is on Bear Mountain Road off Rte. 4. The other two base areas are right off Rte. 4: the Skyeship Base Station, terminus for the long Juggernaut trail and the spot to catch Skyeship; and Sunrise Mountain, which is the closest when coming in from the East.

◆◆ **Expert** ◆ **Advanced:** Between Snowdon Mountain and Killington Peak is some of the toughest terrain. The Canyon quad chair services this area for access to double-diamond Cascade, Downdraft, Double Dipper and Big Dipper Glade.

Skye Peak, where Killington added new terrain two seasons ago, has proved to be one of the most popular sections of the mountain. Here you can play on Ovation, Superstar, Skye Lark and Bittersweet.

From the top of Skye Peak, advanced skiers can drop down Skye Burst by following the Skye Peak quad. This connection is not recommended for lower intermediates because it leads to the Bear Mountain quad, which services good advanced and expert terrain. From the top of the Bear Mountain quad, skiers can descend Devil's Fiddle or loop in the opposite direction down Wildfire. For bumpers the real thrill is to drop directly under the chair lift and challenge Outer Limits.

■ **Intermediate:** Needle's Eye drops beneath the second section of the Skyeship and is a nice wide cruiser. A trip back up the Needle's Eye chair will put skiers back on Bittersweet for a smooth cruise to the Killington Base Lodge or to Snowshed.

The Rams Head high-speed quad chair covers mainly beginner and intermediate terrain. Vagabond, off to the left of Rams Head chair, is an advanced run connecting with the Snowdon area. The Snowdon area is another cruiser's delight, and is served by two chairs from the base area and a Poma lift serving Bunny Buster, where the Alpine Park is located. Highline and Conclusion are good advanced cruising runs with excellent pitch. Bunny Buster and Chute are similar but with a more mellow slope.

●● **Beginner:** Green trails lead from all six interconnected peaks, which allows beginners the panoramic vistas and thrill of skiing from the summit, not possible at areas where the upper-mountain trails are reserved for seasoned skiers.

● **Never-ever:** Start at the Snowshed learning area, where four lifts serve a very long, very wide and nicely isolated slope with excellent pitch for those just starting out.

Note: Pico Mountain has trails for all abilities. Though part of Killington's operation, it is not interconnected. There are plans for an interconnect in the future.

Mountain rating

Overall, Killington rates as a very good choice for beginner and intermediate. Advanced skiers will have a lot of fun in select areas such as Skye Peak, Bear Mountain and Killington Peak. Though experts will find no extreme skiing, they can find trails that will test them.

Cross country

Mountain Meadows Ski Touring (775-7077) has 50 km. of trails meandering across Kent Lake and through surrounding forests. **Mountain Top Cross Country Ski Resort** (483-2311) in Chittenden has 110 km. of trails, 40 km. of dual-set tracks and 2.5 km. of trails with snowmaking.

Both areas have rentals, lessons, ski shop and warming hut, and Mountain Top offers sledding and horse-drawn sleigh rides.

Trailhead Ski Touring Center in Stockbridge (746-8038) has 60 km. of trails, with 35 km. groomed and 35 km. tracked. In Woodstock, the **Ski Touring Center** (457-2114) has 75 km. of trails, lessons and rentals.

Snowboarding

Lessons and rentals are available at Snowshed and Killington base lodges. Killington hosts a snowboard mogul contest on Outer Limits in the spring, and has three halfpipes and three snowboard parks.

Lessons (98/99 prices)

Group lessons: The Killington Skier Development Program uses the innovative teaching program called Perfect Turn®. It combines state-of-the-art ski technique with state-of-the-art educational theory (see the Skiing for Everyone chapter for more details). Perfect Turn has 10 levels. For lower intermediates and higher, the clinics normally last 90 minutes. Skiers watch a short video that demonstrates various levels of skiing ability. The video eliminates the "ski-off," which usually takes up about 40 minutes of a two-hour lesson. Clinics run about every half hour throughout the day and cost $29.

Never-ever package: The resort has added a new Perfect Turn Learn-to-Ski Center at Snowshed. Perfect Turn levels for never-evers to beginners are 90 minutes to two hours. The package includes the clinic, shaped skis, boots and poles, and a lift ticket for the beginner lifts. It costs $55 for Day 1. A three-day learn-to-ski package $134.

Private lessons: $70 an hour for one; additional skiers cost $40 apiece. Multihour discounts are available. A half day costs $190 and a full day is $335.

Special programs: Too many to list here. Among the topics are moguls, women's instruction, racing, adaptive instruction for the disabled and even instruction for instructors.

Racing: None for public participation

Children's lessons: Programs for ages 2–3 include lessons, lunch and equipment for $70 for a full day; $47 for a half day. Programs for older children, with lessons and lunch but no equipment, run $88 for a full day and $57 for a half day for ages 4–6, and $90 for a full day and $62 for a half day for ages 7–12.

Child care (98/99 prices)

Ages: Starts at 6 weeks. Killington doesn't specify an upper age limit.
Costs: $52 per day (with lunch) and $36 per half day (no lunch). Multiday discounts available.

Reservations: Required; call (800) 621-6867.

Note: All-day programs run from 8 a.m. to 4 p.m. Parents must supply food and beverage for children 23 months and younger. The Friendly Penguin Children's Center is located in the Rams Head Family Center.

Lift tickets (98/99 prices)

	Adult	Child (6-12)
One day*	$54.60	$34.65
Three days*	$151.20 ($50.40/day)	$91.35 ($30.45/day)
Five days*	$252 ($50.40/day)	$152.25 ($30.45/day)

Who skis free: Children 12 and younger ski free when accompanied by an adult who buys a Monday-Friday five-day pass. Children 5 and younger ski free when with a parent.

Who skis at a discount: Ages 65 and older, same price as kids. Ages 13–18 ski for $49.35 for one day and $90.30 for two days. Last season the College Edge program allowed students with I.D. to purchase an Edge card for $45 which includes one day of skiing; subsequently upon presentation of that card they ski for $33 a day on weekends and $29 a day midweek, expect the prices to be a few bucks more this season.

*Note: Killington does not include the Vermont sales tax of five percent in its advertised prices. (An aside for our European and Australian readers: If an American ski resort is required to pay a sales tax on lift tickets, it is the common practice to include it in the ticket price.) Because this is such an unusual policy, we have included the five percent tax in the prices we list here.

A lodging-lift package provides the best deal. Also, take a look at the Lift Ticket section of the Sunday River chapter, where we have listed discount ticket programs that allow you to visit any of the American Skiing Company resorts in the Northeast, California, Colorado and Utah. For the multi-resort ticket programs, sales tax is included in the price.

 ## Accommodations

Killington is working to create a pedestrian village at its main base area. The **Killington Grand Resort Hotel** opened in March 1998 and will be in full swing this season. The hotel is high-end luxury, with conference facilities, 200 units from hotel rooms to penthouses, a full-service restaurant, swimming pool, health club and slopeside location. The hotel is one of five Grand Resort hotels operated by the American Skiing Company. The units are sold on a quarter-year ownership basis, where the owner can use the unit up to 13 weeks per year. At other times, the units are available for nightly rentals or for members of the Resorts Condominiums International time-share organization. Rates for this winter were not available at our press time; but expect them to be on the high end, befitting the luxury designation.

You may make reservations for the Grand Hotel and all of the following properties by calling the **Killington Travel Service** (800-621-6867). Killington's lodging has a wide price range, with much of it reasonable. Call for specific rate information.

The top hotel on the mountain road at Killington is **The Inn of the Six Mountains** (800-228-4676 or 422-4302), with a 65-foot indoor lap pool, exercise room and frequent shuttles to the slopes. Rates are based on double occupancy, breakfast included.

Killington Village has good values and the best location, with nearby athletic club facilities, some nightlife and an excellent shuttlebus system. Of the Village condominiums, the **Highridge** units are by far the most desirable. Other good choices are the **Sunrise** condos at the base of Bear Mountain and **The Woods at Killington**, which boasts Jacuzzis and saunas, and a complete spa.

Both the **Mountain Inn** and the **Cascades Lodge** are very convenient but they are also basic. The Cascades has a nice indoor pool and the Mountain Inn has some of the best nightlife when the bar is hopping.

The **Cortina Inn** (3333 or 800-451-6108 or cortina1@aol.com), on Rte. 4 just past the Pico ski area, is very good. It has a health club, pool, spa, two restaurants, children's activities on holiday weekends, and many large suites. (Web site: http://www.cortinainn.com)

The **Vermont Inn** (775-0708 or 800-541-7795 or vtinn@aol.com), with 18 rooms and fireside dining, everything homemade, is a charming New England country inn. Breakfast and dinner are included in the rates. Costs for two people are about $250–$370 for two nights, and $600–$900 for five nights. Fireplace rooms are available.

The **Red Clover Inn** (775-2290 or 800-752-0571) is five miles from Killington Road on 13 acres. This farmhouse estate has private baths, country decor and handmade quilts in each room. Room rates, including breakfast and dinner for two, are about $175–$250 on winter weekends, less during the week.

Another favorite is **The Summit Lodge** (422-3535 or 800-635-6343). The casual and friendly atmosphere is infectious and the staff is helpful.

Of the other properties on Killington Road, **The Red Rob**, **Killington Village Inn** and **Chalet Killington** rate in that order. The food is reportedly best at the Red Rob, and both the Killington Village Inn and the Chalet have a casual atmosphere. Rates include breakfast at the Red Rob and Chalet, and breakfast and dinner at the Killington Village Inn.

Near the base of the Killington Road is the **North Star Lodge** (422-4040), which has a pool and shuttle service and is surrounded by good restaurants. Rates per person, double occupancy, no meals, are about $160 for three nights, $200 for five nights.

The Grey Bonnet (775-2537) on Rte. 100 north received numerous recommendations. There is a nice indoor pool, sauna and pub. Room with breakfast and dinner costs about $290 per person for five nights. You will need your car to get to the ski area.

A favorite luxury spot of ours is the **Woodstock Inn and Resort**, about 17 miles east of Killington. Rooms are cozy and beautifully decorated, with hand-stitched quilts on each bed. The dining room wine list has 184 selections, both foreign and domestic. Midweek, the inn has a very attractive package with downhill skiing at nearby Suicide Six or cross-country skiing at the Woodstock Ski Touring Center. Call (800) 448-7900.

 ## Dining

The Killington area has more than 60 restaurants. The best in the area—ranked among the top in the nation by *Food and Wine* and *Condé Nast Traveler*—is **Hemingway's** (422-3886). We have not eaten at the new restaurant, **Ovations**, at the Killington Grand Resort Hotel, but its chef was lured away from The Balsams Resort in New Hampshire.

Our favorites are **The Summit** (422-3535, reservations suggested), an award-winning restaurant with a menu that changes nightly and a great wine list; **Jason's** (422-3303, reservations suggested) in the Red Rob for excellent Northern Italian food; the **Cortina** (773-3333) with excellent New England fare; and the top-rated **The Vermont Inn** (800-541-7795 or 775-0708), with fine formal dining. We haven't tried it personally, but the **Red Clover Inn's** (775-2290) gourmet menu changes nightly and sounds delicious. It received the 1995 Award of Excellence from *Wine Spectator*. **Churchill's House of Beef and Seafood** on Rte. 4 between Killington and Rutland is worth the drive for great food and an extensive wine list.

At **Charity's** the bar is cozy and welcoming, the portions healthy and the menu of steaks, BBQ, and Italian dishes like Tortellini Siciliano and Shrimp Diavlo can appease virtually any hungry skier's appetite (entrées from $10 to $16).

Claude's and **Choices** (422-4030) on the Killington Road are recommended by lots of locals. Both are in the same building and owned by the same chef. Claude's is the more elegant of the two with entrées that include escargots, scallops and beef Wellington.

For restaurants a bit kinder to the budget: the **Wobbly Barn** is known for steaks and a great salad bar (no reservations); **Mrs. Brady's** and **The Grist Mill** are consistent; **Charity's** has specials every night for those hanging out after happy hour; and **The Back Behind Saloon** is inexpensive and getting more popular every year. All except the Back Behind Saloon are on the Killington Road—you'll find the saloon at the junction of Rtes. 4 and 100 at the foot of the Northeast Passage.

 ## Après-ski/nightlife

Killington deserves a reputation for one of the best après-ski scenes in the nation, with the atmosphere generally raucous and young, and the festivities often driven by excellent East Coast bar bands. Immediate après-ski action can be found in **Charity's**. **Outback Pizza** comes highly recommended for its happy hour(s) as well. It is a favorite locals' hangout on weekdays, with entertainment and dancing extending into the evening on weekends. Après-ski at the mountain includes the **Killington Base Lodge** and the **Long Trail Pub** at Snowshed.

The Pickle Barrel has a lively happy hour with dancing later in the evening and is frequented by a young college crowd. **Casey's Caboose** is a favorite locals' haunt with killer spicy buffalo wings. An older, quieter set meets at the **Summit** for happy hour.

For rowdy après-ski and then dancing to loud music, head to the **Wobbly Barn Steakhouse.** When the bar at the **Mountain Inn** has live entertainment, it's great fun.

Those over the age of 30 may want to opt out of the mosh pits at Wobbly Barn and the Pickle Barrel, and head down the road to **The Grist Mill.** The crowd is slightly older but very lively, and the weekend DJ plays lots of that good ol' time rock and roll.

Other activities

Shopping: New last season was Shops at the Shack, several outlet-style shops at the intersection of Rte. 4 and Killington Road. In Killington, stop at the Greenbrier Gift Shop for handcrafted items and gourmet ware. Woodstock, about 17 miles east of Killington on Rte. 4, is one of Vermont's most beautiful villages and packed with art galleries and shops. Nearby Bridgewater has an outlet mall with about 60 stores.

Ground Zero Fun Park has snow tubing, a luge track, ice skating, a restaurant and other activities at the top of the K-1 gondola Wednesday through Saturday nights. An **outdoor skating rink** is below the Summit Lodge on the Killington Road. For **snowmobiling information** call the Cortina Inn, 773-3333, or Killington Snowmobile Tours, 422-2121.

Getting there and getting around

By air: Green Mountain Limousine Service (773-1313) runs transfers from the Burlington airport for about $50 per person round-trip, and meets most flights. Thrifty Rental Cars has an office at the Inn of the Six Mountains. Other airports with commercial service are at Rutland (Continental Connection and Colgan Air) and West Lebanon, NH (Delta).

By car: Killington is at the intersection of Rtes. 4 and 100 in central Vermont near the city of Rutland, about three hours from Boston and about 90 minutes south of Burlington.

By train: Amtrak serves Rutland through Whitehall, NY. Connections from New York City to Killington take about five hours. Train-lodging-lift packages are available. Call (800) USA-RAIL (872-7245) for train info, or Killington Travel Service (800-621-6867) for package info.

Getting around: Bring or rent a car. Though you may not use it between your lodging and the slopes, Killington is very spread out, and you may want to visit the attractions nearby.

Manchester region
Stratton Mountain Resort
Bromley

Vermont

Stratton Facts

Summit elevation: 3,875 feet
Vertical drop: 2,003 feet
Base elevation: 1,872 feet
Address: RR1 Box 145,
Stratton Mountain, VT 05155
✆ **Area code:** 802
Ski area phone: 297-2200
Snow report: 297-4211
ⓘ **Toll-free reservations:**
(800) STRATTON (782-8866)
Fax: 297-4300
E-mail: skistratton@intrawest.com
Internet: http://www.stratton.com
Number and types of lifts: 12–
1 twelve-passenger gondola, 1 six-passenger
high-speed chair, 4 quads, 1 triple,
3 doubles, 2 surface lifts
Skiable acreage: 565 acres
Snowmaking: 80 percent
Uphill capacity: 21,078 per hour
Snowboarding: Yes, unlimited
Bed base: 8,000 in region
Nearest lodging: slopeside
Resort child care: Yes, 6 weeks and older
Adult ticket, per day: $48-$52 (98/99 prices)

Bromley Facts

Summit elevation: 3,284 feet
Vertical drop: 1,334 feet
Base elevation: 1,950 feet
Address: P.O. Box 1130,
Manchester Center, VT 05255
✆ **Area code:** 802
Ski area phone: 824-5522
Snow report: 824-5522
ⓘ **Toll-free reservations:** (800) 865-4786
Internet: http://www.bromley.com
Number and types of lifts: 9–1 quad,
5 doubles, 3 surface lifts
Skiable acreage: 300 acres
Snowmaking: 84 percent
Uphill capacity: 9,045 per hour
Snowboarding: Yes, unlimited
Resort child care: Yes, 6 weeks and older
Adult ticket, per day: $25-$46 (98/99 prices)

The Region's Ratings
Expert:★★ **Advanced:**★★
Intermediate:★★★★
Beginner:★★★★
Never-ever:★★★★

Dining (in region):★★★★★
Apres-ski/nightlife (in region):★★★
Other activities (in region):★★★

Manchester is the quintessential Vermont town with a tourist touch. While a true-blue Vermont farmer would consider it a Disney re-creation of what Vermont should be, visitors love it. It has factory outlets, gift shops, craft shops, antique shops, Orvis fly fishing on the Battenkill River, white-spired churches, manorial hotels, gourmet dining. And it's all very upscale for the most part. Accommodations run the gamut from quaint country inns for the well-heeled to plenty of motelish lodging or condos for families. At the wrong times of day weekend traffic can be atrocious. The Manchester area serves two mountains—Stratton and Bromley.

Stratton, 20 miles from Manchester, is in the midst of major changes: the resort has been acquired by Intrawest, parent company of Whistler/Blackcomb and Panorama in British Columbia, Tremblant in Québec, and Snowshoe in West Virginia, among others. Intrawest has won several awards for its ski-resort design.

Bromley, six miles east of Manchester, can be called the shy sister. Its slopeside village is a scatter of condos and private homes, no stores. Offering fewer than half the trails of Stratton, it pushes uncrowded runs, a sunny southern exposure and great value in the absence of bigger-better-faster skiing superlatives. Bromley will double the size of its base lodge for 98/99, which will expand seating, the children's center, rental facilities and more.

Mountain layout

Stratton: For the more challenging terrain, head straight to the Starship XII and the summit. Polar Bear, Grizzly Bear and Upper Tamarack—all served by the Grizzly double chair—are narrow runs in fine New England tradition with good vertical. Upper Kidderbrook to Freefall provides another good advanced cruiser. Upper Standard starts steep but mellows at the bottom. The double-diamond trails are steep, with bumps that short skiers may have a hard time seeing over. Upper Spruce is the easiest of the double-diamond trails. Stratton has more than 50 acres of woods and glades.

Stratton is a cruising mountain. The upper mountain has some steeps for advanced intermediates. Upper Lift Line to Lower Lift Line is made for big giant-slalom turns. The lower mountain and Sun Bowl are strictly for those who want to look good—very good. Stratton has a wonderful feature for beginners: a Ski Learning Park with 10 gentle trails. It includes a terrain garden, where bumps and rolls are sculpted by the mountain staff, so beginners can practice their balance and independent leg action.

Bromley: Most of Bromley's 41 trails come down blue from the summit leading into gentle cruising greens, perfect practice runs for intermediates and beginners, but hardly deserving of names like Shincracker. A few seasons ago, Bromley added a few blacks to the mountain's steeper east side. Short and sharp, the longest of these challenging runs—Stargazer, Havoc and Blue Ribbon—bring you down to the Blue Ribbon Quad. There is limited tree skiing between Pabst Peril and Avalanche.

Mountain rating

Stratton is one of America's best ego-inflating ski areas. Excellent grooming on the mostly intermediate terrain makes it even easier. Experts can find some good challenges, but don't expect to be pushed—come here to feel good about your skiing.

Intimate in atmosphere and size, Bromley is perfect for those who prefer not to sweat when skiing. Best for families looking for a day in the sun, it is varied enough for groups of different abilities. Intermediates and below stay right, leaving the better skiers to play on the east side.

Cross-country

The Manchester area offers an excellent series of trails through the surrounding hills.

Hildene (362-1788) is in Manchester Village with 15 km. of trails winding through the pine-covered estate of Robert Todd Lincoln. There is a warming hut in the carriage barn, with rentals, trail tickets and light refreshments.

Nordic Inn (824-6444), just east of Peru, has trails that wander into the Green Mountain National Forest.

The Stratton Ski Touring Center (297-4114) is located at the Sun Bowl and has 20 km. of tracked cross-country trails and 50 km. of backcountry skiing. Lessons and guided tours are available. Beginner terrain and great views are available at the Stratton Mountain Country Club, which now is connected to the touring center. Stratton offers snowshoe rentals here and at its mountain summit, backcountry Nordic skiing, "Skinny Sticks Picnics" and moonlight tours; call for prices and details.

Viking Ski Touring Center (824-3933) in Londonderry provides 30 km. of groomed trails through woods and open fields, best suited for intermediates, but with some advanced trails, too. This is one of the oldest cross-country centers in North America.

Porc Trails (824-3933) are a series of ungroomed trails maintained by the West River Outing Club of Londonderry. If you intend to use them, make sure someone knows where you are and when you intend to return: the trails are not patrolled daily. Call for directions and parking locations.

Snowboarding

Stratton was one of the pioneers in this high-growth branch of the ski industry and one of the first major areas to allow the sport. Jake Burton Carpenter, grew up skiing there. Stratton has three terrain parks, a 380-foot halfpipe and ever-changing obstacles, including rails, spines, tabletops and quarterpipes. One terrain park allows beginning riders thrills suitable to their skill level. The top of the halfpipe now is lighted.

Bromley has its own terrain park, called Snowboard Heaven, on the Lord's Prayer run. The park has all the features—pipe, rolls, jumps, its own T-bar and loud music. Each year it holds the "VEW-DO" fest. For never-evers there is a Snowboard Starter class.

Lessons (98/99 prices)

Stratton

Stratton has a new on-mountain Adventure Center where you can try telemark skis, snowshoes, a snowboard or skiboards, mini-skis designed for fun and tricks, especially in the halfpipe and other places frequented by snowboarders.

Group lessons: $25 for 1.75 hours. Ten sessions cost $210; 20 sessions, $340. The multi-lesson books are transferable, making them perfect for families. Anyone purchasing a Stratton vacation package gets a two for one lesson deal.

Never-ever package: Package includes two 1.75-hour lessons, a beginner lift ticket and equipment for $55 for skiers, $65 for snowboarders.

Private lessons: $65 an hour, additional skiers $30. Extra hours are discounted.

Special programs: For disabled skiers, and a multi-day program for women.

Racing: NASTAR racing is $5 for two runs. A self-timed course costs $1 a run.

Children's lessons: All day (two lessons) with lunch (no lift ticket needed) is $69 for ages 4–6. All day with lunch and lift ticket is $84 for ages 7–12 ($69 without lifts).

Bromley (98/99 prices)

Group lessons: $24 for two hours.

Never-ever package: Called The Beginners Circle, this program is for ages 15 and older. The $47 cost includes a 1.75-hour lesson, equipment and a beginners-lift ticket. Snowboard Starter has the same features, but costs $55.

Private lessons: $47 for one hour, $22 each additional person. Multiple-hour discounts available.

Children's lessons: The Mighty Moose Club (3–5 years) includes playtime, skiing sessions and equipment for $37, half day; $63 full day. Mountain Club (6–12 years) includes lift tickets, lessons and lunch, but no day care and no rental equipment for $57 per day.

Child care (98/99 prices)

Stratton: The Childcare Center in the base lodge takes children from ages 6 weeks through 5 years; $69 includes lunch and a snack. Half-day costs $45. Reservations required; call (800) 787-2886 (800-STRATTON).

Bromley: The Bromley Kids' Center accepts children aged 6 weeks to 6 years. Half day $20, full day $40. Call 824-5522 for reservations and information.

Stratton lift tickets (98/99 prices)

(weekend/weekday)	Adult	Child (7-12)
One day	$52/$48	$37/$35
Three days	$138/$112 ($46+-37+/day)	$89/$85 ($30-28+/day)
Five days	$207/$162 ($41+-32+/day)	$132-127 ($26+-25+/day)

Who skis free: Children younger than age 7.

Who skis at a discount: Ages 65–69 and 13–17 ski for $46/$42 for one day, $125/$106 for three days. Those 70 and older ski for children's prices.

Stratton and Okemo have joined forces on a multiday lift ticket plan that permits skiing or boarding at either resort. For details, call either resort.

Bromley lift tickets (98/99 prices)

(weekend)	Adult	Child (7-14)
One day	$46	$30
Two days	$75 ($37.50/day)	$50 ($25/day)

Holiday rates are approximately $5 more per day.

Who skis free: Children ages 6 and younger ski free everyday; ages 70 and older ski free on weekends and holidays.

Who skis at a discount: Ages 65–69 ski for $30; ages 13–17 ski for $39 for one day, $62 for two and $84 for three. Those who want to use only the terrain park lift pay $15.

Note: These are weekend rates—holiday rates (Christmas/New Year's, Martin Luther King in mid-January, and President's Weekend in mid-February) are a little higher. Midweek rates are $25 for everyone from opening to mid-January and from mid-March to the end of the season. From January 19th through March 15th costs are adults, $35; teens, $30; Juniors and Seniors, $25 with multiday discounts.

Accommodations

Stratton

The **Village Lodge** (297-2500) is smack in the middle of Stratton and is the premier property for location—walk out your door and you are a hundred yards from the gondola. The Village Lodge, with rooms decorated in subdued colors, has no amenities such as pool, dining room, or lounge; for those, take the shuttle to its larger sister hotel, the **Stratton Mountain Inn** (297-2500) in the center of the village with a spa, dining areas, lounges and a variety of rooms. These hotels offer superb locations, excellent facilities and wonderful restaurants.

The **Birkenhaus** (297-2000) still has its old-world flavor with excellent service and European-style attention. This is a small inn with some of the best food on the mountain. The **Liftline Lodge** (297-2600) provides Stratton's most economical lodging on the mountain.

The **Mountain Villas** are a collection of condos suitable for families. Stratton Reservations has plenty of condos all within easy reach of the slopes. Note: The prices on these properties are significantly lower when you buy a Stratton Mountain package. Children younger than age 6 stay and ski free anytime. Children 12 and younger stay free in the same room with their parents.

Bromley

All accommodations are in condos and private homes (up to 4 bedrooms), either slopeside or fed by a shuttle to the base lodge. Best deal: three-day midweek special of $75 per person per day including lift ticket and lessons (based on four people in a two-bedroom condo). No pets. There is also a special midweek deal at the **Sun Lodge** providing non-holiday rates of $49 a night for room, lifts and breakfast. A new family package (with a two-night minimum) will offer a room for two adults and two kids for $110 a night including lifts. Call (800) 865-4786 or (802) 824-5458.

Manchester/Manchester Center

For **Manchester and the Mountains** information and lodging referrals call the Chamber of Commerce at (802) 362-2100; otherwise, call lodging individually. Manchester is filled with many tiny B&B establishments and New England hotels in the Currier and Ives tradition. Most discourage children, and indeed keeping tabs on kids in these antique-filled houses would not make for a relaxing vacation.

Some of the best properties in the region are the **Wilberton Inn** (802-362-2500 or 800-648-4944) which is a classic, fashionable address; the **Equinox** (802-362-4700 or 800-362-4747, reservations only) grand, impressive, aloof and expensive (but surprisingly reasonable if you get a package deal); **The Inn at Manchester** (802-362-1793) a quaint smaller country inn with 19 rooms; **1811 House** (800-432-1811) has six rooms filled with antiques and a nice British Pub featuring single-malt whiskeys and imported beers; and **The Palmer House** (802-362-3600), an unpretentious AAA 4-Diamond hotel in Manchester Center with comfortable spacious country decor, four-poster beds, hot tub and sauna, built around a courtyard. **The Manchester View Motel** (800-548-4141) with fabulous views, and the **Weathervane Motel** (800-362-2444) called by many a "great secret," are both AAA 4-Diamond motels with heated pools and great locations.

A few miles out of Manchester Center, **Barrows House** in Dorset (802-867-4455, 800-639-1620) is a restored 200-year-old country inn on expansive grounds, away from the bustle but still close to Manchester Center's shopping and dining.

Families will like the **Aspen Motel** (802-362-2450), **Johnny Seesaws** in Peru (802-824-5533), and **The Red Sled** (802-362-2161).

These property management companies deal with condos throughout the area: **Alpine Rentals** (800-817-4562, 802-824-4562), **Bondville Real Estate** (800-856-8388; 802-297-3316), or **Winhill Real Estate** (800-214-5648, 802-297-1550).

The cheapest lodging is the **Vagabond** (802-874-4096), a hostel on the way to Jamaica (a nearby town, not the island in the Caribbean).

 ## Dining

In Manchester try these for fine dining—**The Black Swan** (362-3807) which gets two thumbs up from everyone; **The Chantecleer** (362-1616) which is gourmet dining and no children allowed; **Reluctant Panther** (362-2568), with a romantic setting and no children allowed; and **Bistro Henrys** (362-4982) for French bistro cuisine in an 18th-century farmhouse.

For family fare in Manchester strike out for the **Sirloin Saloon** (362-2600) with a steakhouse ambiance and a great salad bar. Kids are readily welcomed and it is mobbed on weekends. **Mulligan's** (362-3663 Manchester; 297-9293 Stratton) serves moderately-priced, basic, bland, American fare with a good kids' menu in a loud, TV-in-every-corner atmosphere. It has two locations—in Manchester and at Stratton. **Laney's Restaurant** (362-4456) has an open kitchen where you can see items being grilled.

For Mexican, head to **Canoeceros** (362-0836) in Manchester. For Italian/American meals and pasta try **Garlic John's** (362-9843) which attracts big crowds.

The **Little Rooster Cafe** (362-3496) is a great breakfast spot with good lunches as well in Manchester on Rte. 7 (closed Wednesdays). **Zoey's Deli & Bakery** (362-0005) is a good spot to pick up pastries, breads and sandwiches, but seating is very limited.

The best food at Stratton Mountain is at the **Birkenhaus** (297-2000), which receives rave reviews from virtually everyone. **Sage Hill Restaurant** (297-2500) has great views and a good kitchen—though a more creative Vermont breakfast might be in order. The lunch and dinner menus are creative, extremely well prepared and wonderfully presented. **Mulberry Street** (297-3065) offers pizza, pasta and a cigar-and-martini bar with a ventilation system that draws out the cigar smoke. The **Liftline Lodge** (297-2600) has great deals during the week—when even liftline attendants say it's a deal, check it out. Two new eateries here are **Cafe on the Corner,** for gourmet breakfast and lunch; and **Portabello's,** with fine Mediterrean cuisine for lunch and dinner. **Outback at Winhall River** (297-3663), just south of the access road, has phenomenal lobster bisque together with other casual fare. Tell the kitchen to go slow on the salt and order red wine by the bottle rather than by the glass.

A small restaurant is **Brush Hill** (896-6100) in West Wardsboro on Rte. 100, eight miles away from Stratton Mountain Village. Ask a local how to find the back road to Mount Snow and take it. When you hit Rte. 100, turn right and it's a couple of hundred yards on your right. Reservations only; closed Mondays and Tuesdays.

Other top gourmet spots in the vicinity are **The Three O'Clock Inn** (824-6327) in an old restored farmhouse in South Londonderry; **Mistral's at Old Toll Gate** (362-1779) in the center of Manchester; **Barrows House** on Rte. 30 in Dorset and **The Dorset Inn** (867-5500), also on Rte. 30 and the oldest continuously operating inn in Vermont. Jackets are preferred in these. Most entrées will run $15 to $20. The two Dorset restaurants are about a 15-minute drive from Manchester Center in the opposite direction from the ski areas.

For more down-to-earth, out-of-Manchester fare try the **River Cafe** (297-1010) in Bondville, with the best ribs in the area. The Italian food served upstairs at **The Red Fox** (297-2488) in Bondville was recommended by about every local.

Après-ski/nightlife

In Manchester, the scene is at **Park Bench Café** with pitchers of margaritas, or **Mulligans Bar** in Manchester Village. Once you get started just wander through town, bar to bar, until you find the spot with the evening's action. A Saturday night must-do for blues fans is a stop at the **North Grill** in Manchester Center.

At Stratton, après-ski is on the deck of **Grizzly's** with entertainment almost every weekend, in **Mulligans** with its 50 different types of beer or **The Tavern** in the Stratton Mountain Inn. In the evenings the action on the mountain continues in **Mulligans** (with live entertainment on weekends) and **The Roost** with live music. Off the mountain, try the locals' hangout, **Red Fox** in Bondville, for live music Fridays and dancing. If you're into the cigar and martini crazes, head to **Mulberry Street**. You can select from a long list of martinis, and enjoy a smoke, thanks to a special ventilation system that keeps the bar from being enveloped in a gray haze.

Other activities

Shopping: This is a major non-ski activity here. About 40 factory outlet stores are spread among five shopping centers and several stand-alone stores in Manchester and Manchester Center. These towns also have boutiques and shops that stock handcrafted regional gift items, unusual clothing and other things.

The **Stratton Sports Center** has indoor tennis, racquetball, indoor pool, hot tubs, saunas, fitness center, tanning salons, and massages. The **Stratton Mountain Resort Activities Center** (297-4315) can hook you up with everything from museums to sleigh rides.

Getting there and getting around

By air: Manchester is about 90 minutes from the Albany airport and requires a car for easy access.

By car: Manchester Center is at the intersection of Rtes. 7A and 30 in southwestern Vermont, about 140 miles from Boston and 235 miles from New York City. Stratton is on Rte. 30 about 20 miles east of Manchester. Look for the Stratton Mountain Road from Rte. 30. If you're heading straight for Stratton from I-91, take Exit 2 at Brattleboro, follow signs to Rte. 30, then drive 38 miles to Bondville and the Stratton Mountain Road.

Bromley is six miles from Manchester traveling on Rte. 11, eight miles west of Londonderry.

Getting around: Bring a car.

Mount Snow

Haystack

Vermont

Summit elevation: 3,600 feet
Vertical drop: 1,700 feet
Base elevation: 1,900 feet

Address: 105 Mountain Road,
Mount Snow, VT 05356
☎ Area code: 802
Ski area phone: 464-3333
Snow report: 464-2151
ⓘ **Toll-free reservations:**
(800) 245-7669 (245-SNOW)
E-mail: info@mountsnow.com
World Wide Web: http://www.mountsnow.com
Expert: ★
Advanced: ★
Intermediate: ★ ★ ★
Beginner: ★ ★ ★
Never-ever: ★ ★

Number of lifts: 26–3 high-speed quads,
1 quad, 10 triples, 6 doubles, 4 surface lifts,
2 magic carpets
Snowmaking: 85 percent
Trail acreage: 768 acres
Uphill capacity: 36,425 per hour
Snowboarding: Yes, unlimited
Bed Base: 12,000
Nearest lodging: Base area, condos, hotel
Resort child care: Yes, 6 weeks to 5 years old
Adult ticket, per day: $48-$51.45 (98/99)

Dining: ★ ★ ★
Apres-ski/nightlife: ★ ★
Other activities: ★ ★

Mount Snow/Haystack has the snowmaking efficiency of Killington, is closer to major cities than Stratton, and has just as careful grooming, but somehow it has remained down-home and unpretentious. West Dover and Wilmington are true Vermont villages, slightly rustic without boutique-filled commercialism.

Mount Snow and Haystack have 134 trails and 26 lifts. The two mountains are not interconnected by lifts, but a five-minute shuttlebus ride connects the bases.

Mount Snow works as perfectly as any area in the country at making snow and moving skiers around on the mountain. On its own it has 90 trails, ranging from narrow tree-lined ribbons to broad swathes such as Sundance, 100 yards wide. As you look up at the mountain the terrain is almost perfectly divided from right to left into expert, intermediate and beginner sections. Snowmaking blankets more than 80 percent of the mountain, providing snow from November through early May. Haystack has 1,400 vertical feet with 44 trails and six lifts.

Accommodations are in condos and lodges clustered at the mountain, with more lodging within 10 miles of the resort. Though the mountain base has no village complex, West Dover (three miles) and Wilmington (nine miles) are traditional quaint Vermont towns.

New for 98/99: Children's Learning Center terrain increases by 2,000 feet to the bottom of the Snowdance trail. The new slope will create a separate learning area for adults, too. The expansion will be served by a new triple chairlift. The building of the Grand Summit Resort Hotel last season had created a new hub at the base area, so this season, a new restaurant, a welcome center and two delis will be added.

Mountain layout

◆◆ **Expert** ◆ **Advanced:** Aggressive skiers and snowboarders looking to stir the adrenaline should head straight for the North Face area, a grouping of isolated steeper runs, some of which are left to bump up. The Sunbrook area, which catches the sun, has mostly cruisers, but Beartrap—the one advanced run—is a haven for bump skiers, in part because of its sunny face and snowmaking coverage. Beartrap has its own double lift, and the resort pumps out all loud music from 900-watt speakers to get you in the spirit.

At Haystack, advanced skiers and snowboarders should head for the Witches, a separate area like the North Face. The trails sometimes have bumps but aren't a huge challenge, so restless advanced skiers and riders shouldn't leave the North Face to come here. True experts may find satisfaction in the 12 designated tree skiing areas (you'll see the orange lines on the map), which are open somewhat sporadically when powder conditions allow. For daredevils, Un Blanco Gulch Snowboard Park has enormous side hits, spines, and jumps and, unlike many other parks, allows skiers.

■ **Intermediate:** Other than the North Face, the rest is tailored to long GS turns between snow-encrusted stands of fir, with a whole range of steep falling off the summit, dropping to the village area as great cruisers. The names give you an idea of what to expect—Ego Alley, Sundance and Snowdance. This is the perfect place to dance on the snow. The Sunbrook area, which catches the sun, is an ideal spot for lower intermediates.

At Haystack, stick to the lower Hayfever lift (for time reasons if nothing else—the peak chairs are long). Last Chance usually has some good bumps to warm up on, and after a little practice the intermediate skier or snowboarder will probably be ready to try his hand at Witches.

●● **Beginner** ● **Never-ever:** To the far south of the resort is Carinthia, which offers long mellow runs for advanced beginners, lower intermediates and anyone else who wants to have a playful cruise. There are enough zigs, zags and small drops to keep a skier awake.

The Carinthia area has been much improved with its own high-speed quad and has its own parking lot, for people who like to stay away from the hustle and bustle of the main base area. Lower Nitro sometimes has bumps at the beginning, so beginners might want to shy away at first. From the peak, Deer Run is a long, winding trail that keep a beginner more than occupied. There are also a few long, winding trails from the peak, like the 2.5 mi. Deer Run.

At Haystack, the lower mountain, segregated from the upper, is for beginners. The upper mountain also has a few great beginner/advanced beginner trails, like Last Chance and the sprawling Outcast.

Mountain rating

The emphasis is definitely on the intermediate. Advanced skiers and boarders can try some of the relatively tough runs on the North Face, but if you are an expert, don't come out of your way to ski them—they're not that tough. Beginners and never-evers, get ready to improve—this mountain has just your kind of terrain.

One added spice thrown into an otherwise basic recipe—Mount Snow's Greatest Hits—a series of marked jumps and side hits built fresh each morning. They appear often at random on some of the easiest trails to satisfy those snowboarders and skiers itching for a little air.

Snowboarding

Snowboarding is allowed on both mountains, and there are some great trails for boarders of all levels. Mount Snow's Greatest Hits—a series of spines, side hits, and jumps that are built fresh each day on various trails—will be especially enticing for those who like to get airborne. There are also a few excellent snowboard parks. Un Blanco Gulch, located on the Canyon Trail, has a quarterpipe, spines and plenty of jumps. The Gut, over in the Carinthia area, is Vermont's longest halfpipe and the only one lit for night riding. It now has its own surface lift, Belly-up. El Diablo is a small park located on the Exhibition trail. At Haystack, the new Palmercross Park on the Needle Trail has enormous banks, rollers, drops, and hits.

Cross-country

Four major ski touring centers are near Mount Snow. The largest is **Hermitage Cross-Country Touring Center** (464-3511) on Coldbrook Road in Wilmington with 40 km. of trails that form a circle from the warming hut to Mount Snow and back. **Sitzmark Ski Touring Center** (464-3384), **Timber Creek** (464-0999) and the **White House Touring Center** (464-2135) offer more than 60 km. of trails skewed toward the intermediate Nordic skier. Advanced cross-country skiers can ski the 2.5-mile Ridge Trail connecting the Haystack and Mount Snow summits. The one-way Ridge Trail fee is $10.

Lessons (98/99 prices)

Group lessons: Instruction here is the innovative teaching program called Perfect Turn® (see Everybody Skis chapter for a description).

Perfect Turn has several levels of clinics. For lower intermediates and higher, the clinics normally last two hours with a maximum of six people. Skiers and riders watch a short video that demonstrates various levels of ability, then place themselves into the proper clinic. Clinics run about every half hour and cost $30.

Never-ever package: Beginners will have their own Discovery Center, a separate lodge with everything from ski and snowboard rentals to lessons and videos. Learn to Ski or Snowboard for first-timers is a half day program. The package includes the clinic, shaped skis, boots and poles, and a lift ticket for beginner lifts. It costs $52 for Level 1. The resort guarantees Level 1 skiers or riders that they will be able to ride a lift, turn and stop by the end of the clinic, or they can repeat it free or get their money back. Packages for levels 2–3 (those who still are using green-circle trails) cost $62.

Private lessons: $62 an hour.

Special Programs: Women's Programs, Telemarking Programs, and Senior Programs are available. There are also separate clinics available for advanced skiers and snowboarders. Call the resort.

Children's lessons: Perfect Kids programs are available for those 4–12. Ages 4–6 enroll in Snow Camp. The full-day cost is $74, including lessons and lunch, but no equipment. Ages 7–12 enroll in Mountain Camp or Mountain Riders. The full-day cost is $64, for lessons, lunch but no equipment. Lifts are covered while kids are in lessons, but half-day enrollees will need to buy a lift ticket if they want to continue on their own. Half-day costs are $35 for Snow Camp and $30 for Mountain Camp or Mountain Riders.

Child care (98/99 prices)

Ages: 6 weeks to 6 years.
Costs: $60 for a full day with lunch; $260 for five days.
Reservations: Required; call 464-8501 or (800) 245-7669.

A pre-ski program will cost an additional $18 with rentals.

Note: The fully-licensed Mount Snow Child Care Center has expanded this season with new age-appropriate rooms and additional play space. Kids also can play in a brand-new indoor playground on the second floor of the Clock Tower Building (Main Base Area), next to the child care center. The area features a ball crawl, climbing tubes and slides, video games, basketball games, air hockey, parents lounge and concessions.

Lift tickets (98/99 prices unless noted)

	Adult	Junior (6-12)
One day (97/98)*	$51.45 (97/98)	$32.55 (97/98)
Three days*	$153 ($51/day)	$96 ($32/day)
Five days*	$256 ($51/day)	$159 ($32/day)

*Note: Mount Snow's advertised ticket prices no longer include the Vermont sales tax of five percent. If tax is required for American lift tickets, it usually is included in the advertised price. We try very hard to eliminate price surprises, so we have included the tax here, and rounded the price to the nearest dollar.

Who skis free: Children ages 5 and younger. Children 12 and younger ski free when their parent buys a five-day midweek lift ticket.

Who skis at a discount: Ages 65 and older ski for junior prices; ages 13–18 pay $128 for three days; $212 for five days (the one-day price was not available). Prices listed here are for weekends and holidays. Midweek prices are lower. Though this season's single-day prices were not set at our press time, the 97/98 midweek prices were $45 for adults, $39 for teens and $29 for children and seniors.

Mount Snow tickets also are valid at Haystack. Tickets to ski Haystack alone (97/98 prices) are: Adults, $39 weekend/holiday and $25 midweek; for children and seniors, $25 on weekend/holiday and $18 midweek.

Mount Snow/Haystack is one of the American Skiing Company resorts, most of which are in the Northeast. For a description of discount programs that give benefits at all the resorts, see the Lift Ticket section in the Sunday River chapter.

Accommodations

At the base area are a group of condo projects and a lodge that have shuttle service to the slopes. Most of the other lodging lines Rte. 100 between the slopes and the town of Wilmington, with some tucked on side roads back into the foothills.

Rates vary, depending on season and the size of the unit. Per-person rates start at about $110 for two-day weekend packages; five-day midweek packages (Sunday through Thursday nights) are a bargain—some as low as $35 per person per day. For a **vacation planner** with descriptions of most area properties, write: Mount Snow, 105 Mountain Road, Mount Snow, Vermont 05356, or call (800) 245-7669 (245-SNOW).

The **Grand Summit Resort Hotel & Conference Center** (464-6600 or 800-290-1823) is Mount Snow's new pride and joy, a ski in/ski out luxury resort hotel with over 200 rooms in the Main Base Area. It features valet parking, restaurant, an outdoor heated swimming pool, a health club, conference facilities and day care. Two-day weekend, $199; five-day ski week, $360.

The Inn at Sawmill Farm (802-464-8131), on Rte. 100 in West Dover, is one of the nation's top country inns, and in a class by itself. Entry is through a portion of the former barn. This inn is quite formal, with men required to wear jackets in the public areas and restaurant after 6 p.m. Children younger than 10 are not allowed. The inn does not take credit cards.

Snow Lake Lodge (800-451-4211 or 802-464-7788) is a sprawling 92-room mountain lodge at the base of the main skiing area. While still fairly basic, the lodge does have a fitness center, sauna, indoor hot tub, outdoor Jacuzzi, and après-ski entertainment each evening. The Sundance lift is 300 yards away or skiers can ride the free shuttle. The Snow Lake Lodge is excellent with children as well. Rates include breakfast and dinner.

Andirons Lodge (800-445-7669 or 802-464-2114) on Rte. 100 in West Dover is just two miles from the lifts. These are simple paneled rooms with double beds; some have additional twin beds. There is an indoor pool, a sauna and game room. The attached Dover Forge restaurant serves affordable meals.

Nordic Hills Lodge (800-326-5130 or 802-464-5130), 179 Coldbrook Road, Wilmington. All rooms have cable TV. Rates include breakfast and dinner.

Gray Ghost Inn (800-745-3615 or 802-464-2474), on Rte. 100, West Dover, is a large country inn operated by a British couple. Many rooms have smaller beds or bunk beds for children. Rates include breakfast.

Trail's End (800-859-2585 or 802-464-2727), Smith Road, Wilmington. This inn has 15 country-style rooms. Meals are served family style at three round tables, so visitors probably will return home with new friends.

Old Red Mill (800-843-8483 or 802-464-3700), Rte. 100 in Wilmington about 15 minutes from the slopes. This inn, created from a former sawmill, is one of the bargains in the region. Rooms are small, only about 7 by 12 feet with a double bed, but all have TV. Larger rooms are available for families. The common areas are rustic.

Horizon Inn (800-336-5513 or 802-464-2131), Rte. 9 in Wilmington, has an indoor heated pool, whirlpool, sauna and game room.

Best Western—The Lodge at Mount Snow (800-451-4289 or 802-464-5112), at the base of Mount Snow, has midweek packages that include free lodging for kids 12 and younger.

Bed & Breakfasts

Mount Snow also has a group of charming and elegant bed and breakfast establishments with rates starting at about $125 per night on weekends and $70 midweek. These B&Bs are smaller, most with fewer than 15 rooms.

The Doveberry Inn (800-722-3204 or 464-5652) on Rte. 100, West Dover. This house is run by Michael and Christine Fayette, both culinary-school-trained chefs. No children younger than age 8 permitted.

West Dover Inn (800-732-0745 or 464-5207), Rte. 100, West Dover, is an historic country inn built in 1846 with 12 elegant rooms furnished with antiques, hand-sewn quilts, and color TVs. There are also two suites with fireplaces and whirlpool tubs.

Deerhill Inn (800-464-3100), Valley View Rd. in West Dover, is a romantic hillside inn with panoramic views of Mount Snow and Haystack.

The Red Shutter Inn (800-845-7548 or 464-3768), Rte. 9, Wilmington. This 1894 country home has been converted into an elegant country inn. There are nine guest rooms.

The **Nutmeg Inn** (464-3351), Rte. 9W, Wilmington. Built in a 1770s home and decorated with country accents and quilts, this B&B has ten rooms and three fireplace suites.

The **White House of Wilmington** (464-2135), Rte. 9, Wilmington, is an upscale 23-room inn serving breakfast and dinner.

Condominiums

Rates are based on the size of the unit and number of bathrooms. They start at about $250 on the weekends; half that midweek.

The **Mount Snow Condominiums** (800-451-4211 or 464-7788) are at the base of the lifts; only the Seasons complex is actually ski-in/ski-out and is the most highly recommended with an athletic center, indoor pools, saunas and hot tubs. The Seasons complex prices are slightly higher.

Timber Creek Townhomes (800-982-8922 or 464-1222) are luxury condos across Rte. 100 from the ski area. They have a fitness center and 18 km. of cross-country trails just outside. Shuttlebuses run between the complex and the ski area.

Greenspring at Mount Snow (800-247-7833 or 464-7111) are upscale condos a mile from the slopes. This complex has the best athletic center in the area.

 ## Dining

The top dining experience (and the most expensive) is the **Inn at Sawmill Farm** (464-1130). Jackets are required on all male guests (they have a selection of blazers to borrow). No credit cards accepted.

The Hermitage (464-3511) serves excellent meals at less stratospheric prices. A very large dining room with the world's largest collection of hanging Delacroix prints. The wine cellar claims 40,000 bottles of 2,000 different labels. All game birds and venison are raised on the premises and the jams, jellies and maple syrup are homemade.

The Summit Hotel will feature **Harriman's Restaurant & Pub** (464-6600) with breakfast and Vermont country dinners. The pub will serve bistro lunches. **The Route 66 Café** will be in retro mode with creative breakfasts and lunch with wraps, sandwiches and smoothies.

For other fine dining try **Betty Hillman's Le Petit Chef** (464-8437), **Two Tannery Road** (464-2707), and **Gregory's** (464-5207), next to the West Dover Inn. **Doveberry Restaurant** (464-5652) is small and intimate with husband-and-wife chefs, culinary school graduates who have worked in Nantucket and San Francisco. The menu is Northern Italian.

The Deerhill Inn and Restaurant (800) 626-5674 or 464-3100, on Valley View Road in West Dover, features American cuisine.

Fennessey's Parlor (464-9361) serves up consistently good food at reasonable prices according to locals. Decor is turn of the century. At Mount Snow, a new 125-seat **Steakhouse,** built during the summer of 1998 between the Main Base Lodge and the Grand Summit Hotel, serves dinner.

Dot's of Dover (464-6476) serves breakfast and lunch daily and dinner on Thursday, Friday and Saturday, plus an excellent Sunday brunch. The chili has won awards and they give you your O.J. in a jar. The ownership also serves dinner daily at **Dot's Restaurant** on Rte. 9 in Wilmington (464-7284).

The **Shipyard Brew Haus**, on 4th floor of the Main Base Lodge, has pub food and Shipyard beers on tap. Although the prices aren't much different, it's a welcome change from the snack bars that usually dominate base lodges. It's open select weekdays and weekends.

For economical eats, try **Poncho's Wreck** (464-9320), a local institution with an eclectic dining room serving Mexican food, steaks, lobsters and fresh fish. **B.A.'s Red Anchor** (464-5616), under the same ownership, serves its famous ribs and seafood specialties.

The Vermont House (464-9360) on Wilmington's main street, serves good food for cheap prices and is one of the locals' favorites. **Deacon's Den** (464-9361) is a good place for pizza, burgers and sandwiches right after skiing. **TC's Tavern** (464-9316) serves up good Italian food.

Après-ski/nightlife

The **Snow Barn** features live music most nights Thursday-Sunday. Both Snow Barn and Deacon's Den usually have cover charges.

Snow Barn has a separate area for pool and other games, with a central stone fireplace and a pizza-window. At **Cuzzins** you can get a monstrous 24 oz. can of Fosters. **Walt's Pub** at the Snow Lake Lodge has a quiet, family-style atmosphere with "unplugged" music on Saturday nights and Otter Creek Night on Mondays, featuring Otter Creek beer on tap and 10 cent wings.

Only in West Dover would you find that one of the most popular new nightspots, the **Silo**, is actually in a converted grain Silo (in the Silo Family Restaurant on Rt. 100). It caters to a young crowd and has practically a monopoly on nightlife for the snowboarding set. Downstairs, there's also a smoke-filled cigar bar for aficionados. Locals mostly head to **Dover Bar & Grille** (464-2689).

Other activities

Shopping: Though Wilmington has a few quaint shops, this is not a major activity at Mount Snow.

For **snowmobiling**, try High Country Snowmobile Tours (464-2108 or 800-627-7533), Snowmotion Snowmobile Tours (464-5504), or Rock Maple Snowmobile Tours (800-479-3284), all in Wilmington.

Winter walks are available in the Green Mountain National Forest. Naturalist Lynn Levine will teach you about wildlife on 2.5-hour animal tracking and "owl moon" walks.

There is a **movie theater** on Rt. 100 in West Dover showing first-run movies. **Planet 9 Adventure Center** (464-4191), at the Carinthia slopes, has nightime ice skating, sledding and night riding for snowboarders at The Gut halfpipe. Sled rentals are available, though you may bring your own or use inner tubes and toboggans, Wednesday to Saturday, 5–10 pm.

Getting there and getting around

By air: The closest airports are in Albany and Hartford's Bradley International, both less than a two-hour drive.

By car: Mount Snow is the closest major Vermont ski resort to New York and Boston. It is on Rte. 100, nine miles north of Wilmington.

Getting Around: A car isn't completely necessary, but it is pretty helpful, especially at night. During the day, take shuttlebuses to and from the lifts; at night, take the MOOver, a free shuttle that makes about 30 stops along Rte. 100 from West Dover to Wilmington. It runs late on weekends. Can't miss it—the buses are painted like Holstein cows.

Okemo Mountain

Vermont

Summit elevation:	**3,344 feet**
Vertical drop:	**2,150 feet**
Base elevation:	**1,194 feet**

Address: 77 Okemo Ridge Road
Ludlow, VT 05149-9708
✆ **Area code:** 802
Ski area phone: 228-4041
Snow report: 228-5222
Fax: 228-4558
ⓘ **Toll-free reservations:**
(800) 786-5366 (800-78-OKEMO)
E-mail: okemo@ludl.tds.net
Internet: http://www.okemo.com

Expert:★
Advanced:★
Intermediate:★★★★
Beginner:★★★
Never-ever:★★

Number of lifts: 13–3 high-speed quads,
4 quads, 3 triple chairs, 3 surface lifts
Snowmaking: 95 percent
Skiable acreage: 470 acres
Uphill capacity: 23,200 per hour
Snowboarding: Yes, unlimited
Bed Base: 10,000
Nearest lodging: Slopeside, condos
Resort child care: Yes, 6 weeks and older
Adult ticket, per day: $48-$52 (98/99 prices)

Dining:★★★
Apres-ski/nightlife:★★
Other activities:★★

Intermediate skiers arriving at Okemo will think they have arrived in skiers' heaven when ride up the Nor'easter high-speed lift, then begin their descent down virtually any trail stretching down 2,150 feet of vertical. This is a place where the skiing experience seems effortless. Ribbons of trails stream from the peak with amazing consistency in width and pitch. Strategically placed high-speed lifts power skiers uphill and keep lift lines to a minimum. Everything is smooth, from the excellent grooming and snowmaking to the slopeside accommodations and ski school.

Beneath the hulking shoulders of Okemo Mountain, the small town of Ludlow provides quaint Vermont touches to the high-tech enhancements on the slopes. Skiers who decide to stay on the mountain in one of the condominium units never really have to descend back into this small village. But Ludlow and nearby Proctorville certainly add favorably to the overall vacation setting, especially for shopping in a handful of stores and enjoying different après-ski and dining at a handful of excellent restaurants.

This is also an excellent snowboarding mountain with perfect slopes for boarders as well as a halfpipe, a snowboard park and a lift dedicated to taking snowboarders to the entrance of the halfpipe and park. Cross-country enthusiasts have 20 km. of groomed tracked trails at nearby Fox Run.

Mountain layout

The mellow skiing and most of the beginning ski school action takes place on the gentle rise served by two quads, South Ridge Quads A and B. These two quads also provide access to several clusters of condos and townhouses slopeside as well as serving as the gateway to the rest of Okemo's lift system from the Base Lodge. There can be a slight logjam at these two lifts, but once up on the mountain you can ski to a triple chair a fixed quad or a high-speed quad that takes skiers to the upper trails.

The Northstar Express high-speed quad draws the biggest crowd but moves skiers up-mountain in a hurry, unloading at a cluster of black trails on the left, blues on the right. A less crowded option is to ski down another 100 yards to the seldom used Sachem quad, which serves a good batch of intermediate tune-up runs or take the Glades Peak quad that allows skiers to access the South Face area with its cruisers, bumps and glades.

♦♦ **Expert** ♦ **Advanced:** There are no true double-black trails on the mountain. Outrage and Double Black Diamond are both gladed and not particularly precipitous, but enjoyable and challenging with proper snow conditions. The best challenges for seasoned experts are the glades that have been opened recently to skiers. Forest Bump is 16 acres of tree skiing off the Rimrock trail. Loose Spruce and Stump Jumper provide tight and not-so-tight glades just to the right of the South Face high-speed quad. The other way that Okemo created above average skiing conditions is with bumps. Wild Thing, Blind Faith and Punch Line are often left to bump up, but when they are groomed with the bumps cut down, they are delightful cruising runs. If the challenge you seek is from bumps, ask a ski patroller where to head.

■ **Intermediate:** Overall, the pitch on this mountain is so consistent and the trails are so similarly cut, a skier would be hard pressed to describe the difference between Dream Weaver at one side of the mountain and Heaven's Gate on the opposite side. This is not a negative, just a fact of life on this mountain. At Okemo, intermediates should choose their trails based on crowds. Our experience has been that while a cruise down groomed Punch Line and Blind Faith may be crowded, wide arching turns can be made down Upper and Lower Tomahawk and Screamin' Demon without another skier in sight.

●● **Beginner:** Upper (and Lower) Mountain Road is the easiest route from the top. Or take Easy Rider or Sunburst, the next trails over. The Green Ridge triple and the Solitude Peak high-speed quad have many runs for beginners. Beginners can ski virtually anywhere on this mountain that is marked as intermediate. The trails are wide enough to allow traverses and the pitch is mellow enough for them to maintain control.

● **Never-ever:** Okemo has a learning area near the base lodge, served by two quads and two surface lifts. Riding the surface lifts is free. Unfortunately, the never-ever lessons take place in an area that is criss-crossed by more advanced skiers moving between lifts and condos. The child-care area is tucked away from other skiers.

Mountain rating

If you're an expert or advanced skier, Okemo won't offer enough of a challenge unless you yearn for bumps or glades. But beginners and intermediate skiers and snowboarders will think they've died and gone to heaven. Never-evers might want to look for another resort with a separate learning area, but Okemo is designed to bring never-evers up onto the mountain very quickly. This mountain can be a great ego boost to every skier.

Snowboarding (98/99 prices)

Okemo has a large snowboarding community not confined to the young and restless. Gray-haired ski patrollers and instructors foster a pro-boarding attitude.

They have two halfpipes and a quarterpipe as well as a half-mile-long snowboard park. A boardercross track is featured in Okemo's second terrain park on Chief. A sound system cranks out tunes at 600 watts. Rentals are available on the mountain, at the board center in Ludlow at Sport Odyssey and at Northern Ski Works.

A First Tracks (never-ever) snowboarding package (lesson, rentals, beginner lift ticket) is $50 for adults, $45 for young adults (13–18) and $40 for juniors (7–12). Adults can take a three-day snowboard camp designed for their needs for $339 at select times during the season, and teens aged 13–18 have TEENriders lessons on weekends and holidays.

Cross-country

Fox Run Resort, set along the Black River, only a half-mile from Okemo Mountain, has fine facilities with 26 km. of trails and a rental and repair shop. They also offer snowshoeing. Call 228-8871 for information.

Lessons (98/99 prices)

Group lessons: $27 for a 1.75-hour lesson. Seniors pay half. You can take a free run with an Okemo ski or snowboard instructor on weekends from 10–11 a.m. and 1:15–2:15 p.m. The station is off the Sachem Quad chair lift, which services the three basic levels of terrain.

Never-ever package: For skiing or snowboarding, packages include lesson, rental equipment and beginner lifts, and cost $40 for ages 7–12, $45 for ages 13–18 and $50 for adults.

Private lessons: $60 per hour with additional hours costing $50 and each additional skier charged $40 per hour.

Special programs: Upper-level groups concentrate on various subjects, such as moguls, black diamonds, parallel turns or learning how to use shaped skis. Three-day adult snowboard camps cost $369.

Women's Ski Spree is a multiday indulgence for women of all abilities. Cost is $499 for the five-day program, $369 for the three-days, and $199 for six Sundays (includes lift ticket).

Racing: NASTAR and an electronically timed dual course sponsored by Mountain Dew are on the same course on the Blackout run. Cost for NASTAR is $4 per run ($3 for kids) and $1 per run after that; the Mountain Dew course is $1 per run.

Children's lessons: Children aged 4–7 enroll in SKIwee, a national program. SKIwee is $65 for a full day with lunch, $40 for a half day, with multiday discounts. Okemo has Snow Star riders at the same prices as SKIwee for ages 5–7 who want to snowboard. Small-sized boards are available for rent at an extra cost.

Young Mountain Explorers and Young Riders, ages 7–12, have supervised lesson programs for $91 a day or $119 for two days (lift ticket included in cost) with discounts for additional days. Teens have their own lessons, Get Altitude, $69 for a full-day and $126 for two days.

Prices are about $2–$3 higher on holidays for children's lessons.

A one-hour Parent & Tot program allows kids to learn with Mom and Dad for $80. The instructor will leave parents with tips on helping their child improve on the slopes.

Child care (98/99 prices)

Ages: 6 weeks to 8 years.
Costs: $45 for a full day with lunch, Monday–Friday; $50 on weekends and holidays. Half days are $28 midweek; $30 weekends and holidays.

Reservations: Recommended; call 228-4041 and ask for the Penguin Playground DayCare Center.

Note: Every Saturday evening from January through March, Okemo has Kids Night Out, an evening child care program. It costs $10 per hour per child, or $30 for the four-hour session per child, or $40 for two to four children. Okemo also sells an unlimited season child-care pass for $1,195 or $1,395 with introduction to skiing lessons as well.

Lift tickets (98/99 prices)

	Adult	Young Adult (13-18)	Junior (7-12)
One day	$52 (weekend)	$44 (weekend)	$33 (weekend)
	$48 (midweek)	$42 (midweek)	$21 (midweek)
Three days*	$133 ($44/day)	$115 ($38.33/day)	$85 ($28.33/day)
Five days*	$215 ($43/day)	$185 ($37/day)	$135 ($27/day)

Who skis free: Children ages 6 and younger, or those riding beginner surface lifts.
Who skis at a discount: Ages 65 and older ski for Junior rates.

Note: *These are weekend "regular" prices. Multiday prices during holiday periods are a little higher. The single-day rate listed is valid weekends and holidays.

All listed prices include Vermont sales tax.

Accommodations

Okemo has many **slopeside condos and townhouses** (800-786-5366). Per-person rates vary widely depending on proximity to the slopes and size, but a range would be $115–$200 off-mountain to $245–$445 slopeside for a five-night ski week including breakfast and dinner. Kids ages 12 and younger stay free at Okemo Mountain Resort condos.

The Okemo/Ludlow area, including Chester, Springfield, Weston, Plymouth and Proctorsville, has more than 50 country inns, B&Bs and motels.

The **Castle Inn** (226-7222) on Rte. 131 in Proctorsville served as the Governor's mansion in days gone by. Weekend daily rate per room, double occupancy, breakfast and dinner, is about $190–$245. The dining is truly gourmet and the 11 rooms are quite elegant.

The **Echo Lake Inn** (824-6700 or 800-356-6844), north on Rte. 100, is a charming New England inn with weekend rates of $110–$168 with breakfast and dinner, $90–$120 with breakfast. Presidents Coolidge and McKinley slept here.

The **Black River Inn** (228-5585) in Ludlow has a 1794 walnut four-poster bed in which Lincoln rested his 6-foot-4-inch frame. Weekend rates start at $125 with breakfast and dinner, and $95 with breakfast.

The **Cavendish Pointe Hotel** (226-7688) offers the full service of a 70-room country-style hotel, restaurant, indoor pool, lounge and game room. Daily weekend rate is $65–$85 per room, no meals. The hotel is on Rte. 103, two miles from Okemo.

The **Hawk Inn and Mountain Resort** (672-3811 or 800-685-4295) has luxury country inn and townhouse facilities. This complex features indoor/outdoor pool, sauna, Jacuzzis, sleigh rides and fine dining. Bed and breakfast rates are $95–$175 midweek and $125–$200 on weekends.

The **Best Western Colonial Motel** (228-8188) offers very affordable lodging within walking distance of Ludlow's shopping, nightlife and dining.

Happy Trails Motel (228-9984) in Ludlow offers great bargains with a good hot tub.

The **Shoestring Lodge** (228-6217) offers a quiet, No Smoking environment for $20 per night per person. It is both on the Okemo shuttle bus route and walking distance to town .

 **Dining**

Echo Lake Inn (228-5585) in Ludlow. The chef, Kevin Barnes, has been creating gourmet delicacies for over a decade. Meals created here have been featured in Bon Appetit and Vermont magazines.

The **River Tavern Restarant** at the Hawk Inn and Mountain Resort (672-3811) serves delicious meals. The Tortilla crusted Lamb Chops with tart cherry chipotle sauce are wonderful and reminiscent of a European gourmet platter.

The **Castle** (226-7222), in Proctorsville, is also open to diners and the owners serve cuisine fit for royalty. Try the Atlantic Poached Salmon served with Caviar.

Michael's Seafood & Steak Tavern (228-5622) on Rte. 103 just east of Ludlow is in a ramshackle sort of place that belies its true character. Many specials and the excellent cuts of steak bring back patrons for good dining at moderate prices. Try the Broiled Artichoke Hearts, created by combining a garlic cream sauce with Vermont cheddar cheese, and the Perfect Poulet, a mix of chicken, artichokes and plum tomatoes topped with Romano cheese.

The **Governor's Inn** (228-8830) on Main Street in Ludlow, serves a gourmet fixed-price menu starting at 6 p.m. with hors d'oeuvres and cocktails. Dinner follows at 7 p.m.

The following restaurants are not as upper crust, but serve excellent affordable meals perfect for families.

Priority's (228-2800) in the Village Center is the most convenient spot if you're staying on the mountain. Its affordable meals are superb. The Shrimp Puttanesca with capers and olives in a red sauce is excellent.

Nikki's (228-7797) at the foot of the Okemo Mountain access road has a very good reputation as well. Nikki's is moderately expensive, but its Osso Bucco con Orechiette or steamed whole Maine lobster are favorites of the loyal repeat clientele.

D.J.'s Restaurant (228-5374) gets high marks from locals for its prime rib, steak, seafood, pasta and fabulous salad bar. **Cappuccino's** (228-7566) also gets raves for chicken and pasta specials as well as beef, pork, veal and vegetarian meals. The interior is nicely decorated—you'd swear you just walked into a Laura Ashley showroom.

The **Combes Family Inn** (800-822-8799) serves a single-entrée dinner at 7 p.m. each evening. Call for the day's menu and to make reservations.

The **Ludlow Cooking Company** (226-7251) in town also has sandwiches, deli items, rich desserts, and something handy for condo dwellers—meals to go, mostly of the Italian variety, but also great Homestyle Stuffed Cabbage for any homesick Polish skiers.

A State of Bean (228-2326) at the base of the access road has overstuffed chairs and couches, and serves fresh-baked muffins and pastries, homemade soups, sandwiches, salads, desserts and of course, a variety of coffee drinks.

North of Ludlow on Route 103 is **Harry's** (259-2996), an understated place that has a high repeat business because of its moderate prices ($9–$13) and international cuisine.

In nearby Chester stop and have a meal at **Raspberries and Thyme** (875-4486) On the Green. Breakfast and lunch is always good. Dinner is served Wednesday to Sunday.

For the best breakfast values head to Main Street in Ludlow to **Cafe at deLight** (adjacent to the restored mill at the town's only stoplight), or to **Mr. B's** (in the Grand Union shopping mall, and finally to **The Hatchery** across the street from Cafe at deLight.

For pizza try **Christopher's** (228-7822) or **Wicked Good Pizza** (228-4131).

Après-ski/nightlife

For après-ski on the mountain, try **Sitting Bull Lounge,** with a wide-screen TV, après-ski parties, $1 draft beer day on non-holiday Wednesdays and live music on weekends; **Priority's,** also with wide-screen TV and ski flicks; or **The Loft** (here, be ready for sticker shock and bring cash—lots of it).

Later in the evening, **The Pot Belly** has country rock, '60s and '70s classics with a great bar and a big TV. Watch out when ordering their wines by the glass—they simply recork any leftover bottles each night and save them for the next day, so only order the wine if you can see them open a new bottle. **Charaktors** at the bottom of the access road has live entertainment and comedy on weekends—be prepared for a cover charge, even if the bar is empty and ready to close. **The Black River Brewing Company** is one of the best deals in town. The home-brew is good and other local microbrews are available.

Other activities

Shopping: Ludlow also has a wide array of specialty shops with clothing, antiques and gifts. One of the best browsing stores in the Northeast, the **Vermont Country Store,** is in nearby Weston on Route 100. It's full of useful little items that are hard to find elsewhere, such as pant stretchers (wire frames that help natural-fiber pants dry without wrinkles) and Vermont Bag Balm, which helps heal sore cow udders and chapped hands. The store is open every day except Sunday from 9 a.m. to 5 p.m. A similar store is located in Chester On the Green. **The Green Mountain Sugarhouse** is three miles from Ludlow on Rte. 100, the spot to get those Vermont maple syrup gifts.

Ice skating is free under the lights at Dorsey Park, but you need your own skates. **Snowmobiling** is available by calling 226-7529.

For **hot tubs and spas** head to Knight Tubs (228-2260) in Ludlow, open from 3–11 p.m.

Getting there and getting around

By air: Rutland, a 25-minute drive, is served by Colgan Air with direct connections to Newark and Lebanon, NH, has Delta and USAir Express service; however, the nearest major airports are Burlington, VT, Manchester, NH, or Hartford, CT, all about two hours away.

By car: Okemo is in south-central Vermont on Route 103 in Ludlow, about two hours from Albany, NY; three hours from Boston; and 4.5 hours from New York City.

By train: Amtrak has service from New York's Penn Station to Rutland, 25 miles to Okemo. Thrifty has a car rental office at the train station in Rutland.

Getting around: We recommend a car. Though the immediate resort area is compact and easily walkable, you will want to try some restaurants, nightlife or activities nearby. However, Okemo has a free shuttle through Ludlow and Proctorsville on weekends, Christmas vacation and President's holiday weekend.

Telephone area code: 802

Smugglers' Notch

Vermont

Summit elevation: 3,640 feet
Vertical drop: 2,610 feet
Base elevation: 1,030 feet

Address: 4323 Vermont Rte. 108 South
Smugglers' Notch, VT 05464-9537
(Area code: 802
Ski area phone: 644-8851
Snow report: 644-1111
**(i) Toll-free reservations and
information:** (800) 451-8752
Toll-free from the United Kingdom:
0800-89-7159
E-mail: smuggs@smuggs.com
Internet: http://www.smuggs.com/
Expert:★★★★
Advanced:★★★
Intermediate:★★★
Beginner:★★★★
Never-ever:★★★★★

Number and types of lifts: 8–5 double
chairs, 3 surface lifts
Acreage: 254 acres marked trails; access to
750 acres of woods
Snowmaking: 61 percent
Uphill capacity: 6,600 per hour
Snowboarding: Yes, unlimited
Bed base: 2,000
Nearest lodging: walking distance, condos
Resort child care: Yes, 6 weeks and older
Adult ticket, per day: $42-$46 (98/99)

Dining:★★
Apres-ski/nightlife:★
Other activities:★★★

Family vacations are the specialty of Smugglers' Notch. While other ski resorts were hyping faster lifts, extreme terrain and more snowmaking, this small resort decided to concentrate on service to the family niche of the ski and snowboard market. That has been their focus for the past decade and the dividends have been exceptional. *Family Circle, SKI, Snow Country, Travel & Leisure, FamilyFun* and *Better Homes and Gardens* magazines and AOL's Family Travel Network have all given Smugglers' #1 rankings for family vacations.

The commitment to families is total—pedestrian-friendly village with stores, restaurants, an outdoor ice rink, sledding hill, indoor pool, saunas, steam baths, indoor and outdoor tennis, massage, crafts classes, sleigh rides, movies, parties for kids and adults and the largest licensed day-care facility in New England.

Vacation packages can be crafted to include lodging, lift tickets, ski school and day care in any combination. Once families arrive and pick up their welcome packets, most will never have to deal with additional payments except meals.

Many parents who come with their children will be surprised to find big mountain skiing as well. Its 2,610 vertical feet places second behind Killington for Vermont's longest vertical descent. Smugglers' has three mountains, one of which, Madonna Mountain, gives a 2,100-foot drop off one chair.

For those not focused on family vacationing, Smugglers' is a well-kept secret. When there is good snow, this is as good as skiing and boarding gets in New England. Granted, the lift system is old and seems to creep up the mountain, but the time on the flanks of Madonna Mountain is worth every minute of lift time. You normally will have the mountain almost to yourself.

Incidentally, the area was named for the smugglers and bootleggers who brought in forbidden English goods in the War of 1812 and booze during Prohibition, storing the contraband in a cave between Madonna Mountain and Spruce Peak, the latter one of the peaks at Stowe. Though Route 108 passes Smugglers' and continues through the notch to Stowe, it is closed in winter.

Mountain layout

◆◆ **Expert** ◆ **Advanced:** If you are a day visitor of intermediate skiing ability or better, don't turn in to the main village. Continue up the hill to the top parking lot. Here you'll find fewer cars and a short walk to a point where you can ski right to the Sterling lift. This lift reaches 20 intermediate and advanced trails. Best of all, you can ski back to your car at day's end.

When you are sufficiently warmed up, seek out some real challenge from the top of Madonna Mountain. Smugglers' lays claim to the East's only triple-black diamond trail, The Black Hole, which is in the woods next to Freefall. We've never known Smugglers' to overhype its skiing, so we have to believe the run is as tough as advertised. For a slightly tamer experience on Madonna, three legitimate double-black-diamond trails beckon the true expert. Freefall is just that. The turns come quickly and you drop 10 to 15 feet with each turn. The F.I.S. trail sports a 41 percent gradient, and with the addition of top-to-bottom snowmaking has become a tad more civilized than in the past. Smugglers' grooms nightly, but some of the natural snow trails are left untouched and the trails are posted as such. Management swears that many Mad River types ski Smugglers' for that very reason.

If you're hooked on glades, it's tough to find a better glade run than Doc Dempsey's. We just wish it were longer. Madonna has several other glade areas that aren't specified trails. The best bump runs are F.I.S., the middle portion of Upper Liftline, Smugglers' Alley, and Exhibition on Sterling Mountain. There's also a new black run on Sterling, Bootlegger, that has a clean fall line—tons of fun, we're told.

If you are staying in the village, you'll need to ride to the top of Morse and ski down the green-circle Midway trail to get to the upper-mountain lifts. Return to the village is by the easy Meadowlark Trail or intermediate Northwest Passage. A shuttle also is available.

■ **Intermediate:** Fifty-six percent of the trails are rated intermediate, and many are well suited to recent ski-school grads. Intermediate runs are concentrated on Madonna and Sterling peaks. Smugglers' and Stowe cooperate on a Smugglers' Notch/Stowe Connection. Club Smugglers' guests of two days or more may ski or snowboard at Stowe one day at no additional charge. No need to drive, either. They take an intermediate trail, Snuffy's, between Smugglers' Sterling Mountain and Stowe's Spruce Peak, a short 10-minute link.

●● **Beginner** ● **Never-ever:** The third mountain at Smugglers' is Morse, with five trails ranging from beginner to expert. It is the ski schooler's mountain. You won't find any hot-shots.

Morse also is home to Mogul Mouse's Magic Lift, a half-speed double chair especially kind to beginners and young children. From the top of the lift winds the Magic Learning

Trail, with nature stations, exploration paths and ski-through "caves." The resort plans a new double chairlift and learning center in the Morse Mountain Bowl for 98/99 called The Highlands Lift and Learning Center.

Smugglers' has no high-speed quads or triple chairs, which sometimes contributes to moderate waits at the lift loading area on weekends and holidays. The tradeoff is that the trails are not congested.

Mountain rating

Smugglers' is good for all types of skiers and boarders. Kids swarm over Morse Mountain—center of ski school classes, après-ski marshmallow roasts and hot chocolate—a magnet for skiers who revel in a family atmosphere. Experts and advanced skiers/boarders should head to Madonna Mountain and intermediates can cruise down Sterling. There's terrain for everyone.

Snowboarding

The resort's Prohibition Park has a halfpipe, multiple hits, spines and rolls, and piped-in music. This season, Smugglers' will add a beginner terrain park with a learner halfpipe on Sterling Mountain's Birch Run, offer clinics on performing tricks, install a handle tow next to the halfpipe in Prohibition Park, and sell a "hikers' ticket" and/or Madonna II-only ticket, so that those who want to spend their time in the park don't have to buy the full-mountain ticket. Smugglers' also has the Night School of Boarding three nights a week at Sir Henry's Learning & Fun Park at the base of Morse Mountain. The three-hour sessions are open to novices aged 6 and older.

Cross-country

More than 23 km. (about 14 miles) of scenic cross-country skiing on groomed and tracked trails is accessible from the main Smugglers' area. The Nordic Ski Center offers rentals, lessons, skate skiing, backcountry and night tours, and snowshoe rentals and tours. New for 98/99 will be a ski & snowshoe combo backcountry tour.

Lessons (98/99 prices)

Snow Sport University (Smugglers' ski school) Director Peter Ingvoldstad has been acclaimed as one of the most innovative teachers in the country. Lessons are included with most Ski/Snowboard Week packages at Smugglers'.

Group lessons: Just short of two hours, $24.

Never-ever package: $49 for a three-hour coaching session, rentals and lift ticket valid on Morse Mountain on Saturdays and Sundays.

Private lessons: $55 per hour.

Special programs: Classes on style, terrain tactics, halfpipe tricks, family tours, night snowboarding lessons and programs for skiers 55 and older.

Racing: A race course is located in the Volvo Carving Arena on Lower Liftline on Wednesdays, Thursdays and weekends. Two runs are $4.

Children's programs: Kids and teens are divided into the following age groups: 3–5, 6–12 and 13–18. The teen program allows that age group to meet new friends with whom they can hang out at the supervised evening teen activities.

Though lesson registration now is done when you make your initial reservations, getting rental equipment is probably the only remaining hassle you will encounter after resort registration. Anyone with kids can imagine—it's a zoo. If possible, try to pick up rental equipment the afternoon before lessons start. Once kids are assigned to a class, forms are filled out, clothes tucked away and ski boots are pulled on, the instructors get the kids busy with coloring books and games, and young children are given their own trail map and journal in which they can record their ski or snowboard progression. That's a good time for parents to get lost.

Smugglers' has a "Mom & Me/Dad & Me" program that teaches parents how to teach their youngsters to ski. These lessons, essentially specialized private lessons, are for children aged 2 or older and a parent of at least intermediate skiing ability. Parents are taught games to make learning fun, and safety tips such as how to ride the lift with kids.

Child care (98/99 prices)

Ages: 6 weeks to 6 years old.
Costs: $49 per day or $215 for five days.
Reservations: Make them when you book your vacation, either with your travel agent or by calling the toll-free number listed in the fact box.

Note: Alice's Wonderland Child Care is a major reason why *Family Circle* magazine chose Smugglers' as the top family resort for three years running. The facility is staffed with professional caregivers who may also be hired for evening babysitting.

Every night except Monday, Friday and Sunday, the center has Parents' Night Out, with dinner and activities for ages 3–12 so Mom and Dad can have some fun on their own.

Lift tickets (98/99 prices)

	Adult	Youth (7-17)
Weekend day	$46	$30
Midweek day	$42	$30
Multiday	**	**

Who skis free: Ages 6 and younger and 70 and older.
Who skis at a discount: Those 65–69 ski for $30.
Note: **If you're staying for more than one day here, the wise move is to buy a lodging package that includes tickets and lessons.

Accommodations (98/99 prices)

At Smugglers' the primary and desirable place to stay is in the Resort Village. More than 2,000 beds are within walking distance of the lifts. Prices start at $445 per adult and $375 for youth for a five-day Club Smugglers' package, including lifts and lessons (packages for fewer days can be arranged). Children aged 6 and younger ski and stay free. Packages include a welcome party, use of the pool and hot tub, family game nights, outdoor ice skating, family sledding parties, a weekly torchlight parade with fireworks finale and a farewell party. There is also Snowtime Theatre, nightly teen activities and adult entertainment (don't get overwrought—it's clean adult fun).

Condos at Smugglers' are spacious, clean and family-furnished—the furniture is sturdy and comfortable, without expensive bric-a-brac items at risk of being knocked over accidentally. Our condo was well stocked with family-style board games.

Smugglers' central check-in area is designed around the concept that once you check in, you have everything you need—lift tickets, instruction vouchers, rentals and day care. Computers at the front desk are tied to key areas such as the rental shop to make the resort very guest-friendly. We give Smugglers' credit for continuing to improve the check-in system, but the check-in area can get a bit backed up—sometimes a lot backed up. Plan to have one parent stand in line while the other takes fidgety kids for a walk in the Resort Village (if you check in at night, one parent can take the kids sledding or swimming, a resort spokeswoman said). Remember, the payoff comes later—once you check in, you won't have to wait in line again for tickets or lessons.

 ## Dining

You never have to leave the Village to eat. For home-baked breakfast treats and giant cookies, try **The Green Mountain Cafe and Bakery** with fresh-roasted coffee, espresso or cappuccino. Lunch favorites include chili in a bread bowl, spinach salads and made-to-order deli sandwiches. The **Riga-Bello's Italian Eatery** offers daily specials, pizza, salads, calzones and stuffed breads with meat and vegetable fillings—for eating there, taking out or delivery to your condo. The **Mountain Grille,** with a view of the slopes, is open continuously for breakfast, lunch and dinner, including light fare entrées. Kids on the FamilyFest® Package get free kids' meals from a special buffet of family favorites like hot dogs and macaroni and cheese at the Mountain Grille when parents order a meal.

The **Hearth and Candle** is a privately operated restaurant in the Village with a friendly, though more formal, atmosphere. Families are served in the cozy Hearth Room, and couples desiring a quiet atmosphere are escorted upstairs to the adults-only Birch Room. Entrées range from steak and pasta to exotic preparations of fish and game.

A new entertainment and dining feature is **Smugglers' Adventure Dinner.** Snowcat transportation to the top of Sterling Mountain brings guests to The Top of The Notch, a mountain hut lit only by candles. The renowned Hearth and Candle serves a gourmet venison stew appetizer, a choice of three entrees, and its famous apple crips. Snowshoeing on Sterling Pond under a starlit sky settles the hearty meal.

Restaurants dot the route between the resort and Jeffersonville, five miles away. Some examples:

Across from the entrance to the Village Center is the ever funky **Cafe Banditos** with low-cost Mexican food, hickory-smoked chicken and ribs and a children's menu. Down the road is the **Three Mountain Lodge**, eclectic dining in a classic log-lodge atmosphere. Steaks, seafood, veal, lamb, Vermont turkey and light meals are moderately priced.

The Hungry Lion, three miles away, is a popular family restaurant that offers daily specials, vegetarian dishes, homemade breads and desserts, and a "cubs" menu. For parents on a restaurant date while their children enjoy the Parents' Night Out program at the resort, **The Windridge Inn** in Jeffersonville is a fine place to dine on grilled salmon, rack of lamb, roast duck or pork tenderloin. It has been lovingly restored to its 18th century charm with numerous rabbit-ear and Windsor chairs under original-hewn timbers.

Après-ski/nightlife

Smugglers' has great nightlife, but it's family oriented. Even our child-less staffers who have visited here end up having more fun than they initially imagined. Activities provide fun for all ages; for example, a family sledding party on lighted Sir Henry's Hill; a Pictionary Family Tournament, featuring the popular draw-and-guess game; and a pizza-and-ice-cream-sundae party.

For more traditional fun, try **The Club Cafe** for après-ski and nighttime entertainment such as karaoke on Wednesdays and dancing to DJ music on Saturdays. Saturday is also comedy night. **Banditos Cantina** turns into the liveliest weekend spot at Smugglers', with large-screen sports and music videos, pool table or live bands. Teens have the nightly **Outer Limits Teen Center** with music videos, snacks, and dance parties. "Learn to Be a Magician," for kids ages 7–12, is a new apres-ski program.

Other activities

Shopping: The Village Center has a few shops, stocked with necessities and typical T-shirt/hat/pin souvenirs. But if you want handmade Vermont crafts, you can make your own! Smugglers' has an unusual activity, **Artists in the Mountains**. Local artisans teach classes in traditional New England crafts, such as tin punching, basket weaving, stenciling and dried flower arranging. The classes include materials and cost $35–$40.

As noted, there are kids' parties, karaoke, sleigh rides, sledding, a swimming pool, hot tubs, and ice skating.

Getting there and getting around

By air: Burlington International Airport is 40 minutes away. Shuttles are available (24-hour notice required; book it when you book lodging).

By car: Smugglers' Notch is on Route 108 near Jeffersonville in northwest Vermont.

Getting around: Everything is within walking distance at the resort. If you want to visit some of the restaurants in or on the way to Jeffersonville, you'll need a car.

Stowe

Vermont

Summit elevation: 3,640 feet
Vertical drop: 2,360 feet
Base elevation: 1,280 feet

Address: 5781 Mountain Rd.
Stowe, VT 05672
☎ Area code: 802
Ski area phone: 253-3000
Snow report: 253-3600
ⓘ Toll-free reservations:
(800) 247-8693 (24-STOWE);
for slopeside lodging only, (800) 253-4754
Advance Ticket Sales: 888-253-4TIX
Fax: 253-2159
E-mail: skistowe@sover.net
Internet: http://www.stowe.com
Expert:★★★★
Advanced:★★★★
Intermediate:★★★★
Beginner:★★★★
Never-ever:★★

Number and types of lifts: 11—1 high-speed
quad, 1 eight-passenger gondola, 1 triple,
6 doubles, and 2 surface lifts
Skiable acreage: 480 acres
Snowmaking: 73 percent
Uphill capacity: 12,326 per hour
Snowboarding: Yes, unlimited
Bed base: 5,000+
Nearest lodging: Slopeside, hotel
Resort child care: Yes, 6 weeks and older
Adult ticket, per day: $38-$50 (97/98 prices)

Dining:★★★★
Apres-ski/nightlife:★★
Other activities:★★★

Stowe has an undeniable blue-blood lineage as one of the oldest and most distinguished Eastern ski resorts. Its ski patrol, founded in 1934, is the oldest in the United States, and its winter carnival is the longest running such event in the nation. In its early days, it was a definite "in" spot during the winter. For a period of time in the 1980s, however, Stowe let its slopeside facilities cross that invisible line separating quaint from antiquated. But management has kept up a steady stream of improvements for the past several years, with the idea of smoothing out some of the wrinkles of age without sacrificing the regal bearing and atmosphere—a job well done.

Those improvements have included more snowmaking, better lifts and updated skier base facilities. However, Stowe retained its long, narrow, twisting runs cut close into the surrounding forests—runs that are an important part of making Stowe a classic New England ski experience.

Though marketing efforts seem to have this town with its charming white steepled church and main street lined with historic buildings nestled at the foot of the large ski mountain. Reality is that the skiing is about seven miles away. To truly enjoy all this area has to offer, you need a car.

Mountain layout

◆◆ **Expert:** Part of the legend of Stowe revolves around its Front Face, and the fact that it features some of the steepest and most difficult runs in skidom. Having descended the Front Four is a badge of honor for Northeast skiers, and deservedly so, given the nature of Goat, Starr, Liftline and National. Besides being steep, the headwalls are frequently draped with vintage New England ice and the trails are liberally moguled.

Experts who are gunning for all four should begin with National and Liftline. The resort's winch cats allow groomers to prepare these two from time to time, so this is a good place to get used to the considerable steepness of the Front Four.

Starr is not groomed, and the view from the top of this run, as it disappears in a steep dive toward the base lodge area far below, is one you won't forget. If you haven't met your match by this time, then you're ready for Goat, a moguled gut-sucker no more than three to five bumps wide.

Another suggestion is a short but lovely little moguled path through tight trees called Centerline, just to the right of Hayride. Centerline was one of the runs that was widened and smoothed to remove the double fall line. Snowmaking also was added here, making it one of the early-season options for high-level skiers. Experts also can try Waterfall, which runs under the gondola line and is a small waterfall during the summer. To ski it, you have to be aggressive and be able to jump.

◆ **Advanced:** A very nice section of glade skiing through well-spaced trees is just off the top section of Nosedive. Chin Clip from the top of the gondola is long, moguled, and moderately narrow, but it does not have quite the steep grade that the Front Four boast.

■ **Intermediate:** This group can enjoy nearly 60 percent of the trails, including much of Spruce Peak. At Mt. Mansfield, ski to the right or left of the Front Four. Advanced intermediates will probably want to chance the tricky top part of Nosedive for the pleasure of skiing the long, sweeping cruiser that beckons further down. Going left from the top of the FourRunner Quad, take Upper Lord until it leads you to a handful of long excellent intermediate runs all the way to the bottom in Lower Lord, North Slope, Standard and Gulch.

From the quad, reaching the intermediate skiing under the gondola presents a problem. The connection between these two parts of the mountain is not convenient unless you are willing to take a run down Nosedive, rated double-black at its top. (Yes, it's narrow with big moguls, but there's enough room to pick your way down. We got our advanced intermediate staff member down it before she realized its rating.) If you don't want to chance Nosedive, it's a hike from the quad area over to the gondola, or you can take the green-circle Crossover trail toward the bottom of the mountain, which allows skiers to traverse directly across the Front Four to the gondola base. If you want to work your way back from the gondola to the quad, take the Cliff Trail, which eventually hooks up with Lower Nosedive and dumps you at the base of the high-speed chair.

If you feel as though you need a little elbow room after too many tight New England trails, try Perry Merrill or Gondolier from the gondola, or cut turns about as wide as you want down Main Street on Spruce Peak, across the base parking lot.

Upper Spruce Peak is like skiing was in the old days, which means "no snow from heaven, no skiing." The Big Spruce double may be the coldest lift on the mountain, and certainly the oldest. When the snow is good and the wind isn't blowing, though, the mountain is a cruiser's delight, and powder days are a real treat. From the top of Spruce Peak, skiers can cross over to Smuggler's Notch (see that chapter for more details on the interchangeable ticket).

Intermediates may also enjoy Stowe's night skiing. The upper portion of Perry Merrill and all of Gondolier are lit Wednesday through Sunday (seven nights during holidays) until 10 p.m. The ride up is in the warm gondola.

●● **Beginners:** One route we would recommend to all levels is the four-mile-long, green-circle Toll Road, which starts at the top of the FourRunner quad. This is a marvelous trail for lower-level skiers, but the more proficient probably will enjoy it too—less for its challenge than for its beauty. You will pass through a canopy of trees, where you can hear only quiet sounds, such as birds chirping or snow plopping from the branches. A little later you'll find the small wood-and-stone Mountain Chapel, where on Sundays at 1 p.m. you can attend an informal church service. You just won't find this type of intimate ski trail out West.

● **Never-evers:** First-timers should start at Spruce Peak base area, then work up to the runs off the Toll House chair (Chair 5), then advance to Chair 4.

Snowboarding

A new quarterpipe and a hew halfpipe have been added to the resort's four terrain parks (making a total of three halfpipes), aimed at beginner (Easy Street), intermediate (Lower Lord, Midway) and advanced levels (Jungle on Lower Standard). Stow has a lighted 300-foot halfpipe at Midway.

On the mountain trails, beginners should focus on Lower Spruce, then Mansfield, Gondolier, Perry Merrill and Sunrise for long carving runs. As the day progresses, advanced boarders should move from Liftline and Nosedive to Hayride and Centerline, then North Slope.

Cross-country (96/97 prices)

Stowe has one of the best cross-country networks in the country. Four touring areas all interconnect to provide roughly 150 groomed km. of trails, and an additional 110 km. in the backcountry.

The **Trapp Family Lodge** (253-5719; 800-826-7000) organized America's first touring center and has 55 km. groomed and machine-tracked trails that connect to another 80 km. in the Mt. Mansfield and Topnotch Resort networks. The fee is $12 a day for adults, $2 for children, free for those younger than 6. Rentals and instruction are available. See Accommodations and Dining for more information.

The **Edson Hill Touring Center** (253-7371) has about 50 km. of trails with 35 km. trails groomed. Elevation varies from 1,400 to 2,100 feet. The fee is $10 a day for adults, $5 for children, ages 6 and younger are free.

Stowe Mountain Resort (253-3000) has 75 km. of trails, 35 km. of which are groomed. The daily fee is $10 for adults and $6 for children.

The **Topnotch Resort** (253-8585) has 25 km. of trails, most of which are groomed and tracked. Trail fee is $10 for adults, $6 for children.

Lessons (98/99 prices)

Group lessons: $29 for 90 minutes.
Never-ever package: The Stowe for Starters program, skiing or snowboarding, is $60 with lesson and lift ticket.
Private lessons: $60 an hour, with multihour and multiperson discounts.

Special programs: Need a little guidance getting down the Front Four? A clinic concentrates on Goat, Starr, National and Liftline and costs $29 for 90 minutes. Other clinics are Equipment Makover, a guided session for $75 that matches skier abilities to the equipment best suited for them (includes demo equipment fees), Breakthrough To Carving workshop for advanced intermediates for $29 and a Mountain Experience Week that works on mastering varying snow conditions and terrain while getting to know the mountain. Call for prices on the latter program.

Snowboard clinics concentrate on halfpipe maneuvers, carving and pushing the outer limits.

Children's lessons: Headquartered at Spruce Peak. Full-day Adventure Center ski programs with lunch are $75 for those ages 3–12 years. Snowboarding programs are the same price but limited to children ages 6–12.

Note: Telephone extension for the ski school is 3683 or 3682.

Lift tickets (98/99 prices)

	Adult	Child (6-12)
One day (97/98 rates)	$50	$30
Three days	$125 ($42/day)	$74 ($25/day)
Five days	$190 ($38/day)	$112 ($22+/day)

Who skis free: Children ages 5 and younger with paid parent or guardian.

Who skis at a discount: Ages 65 and older ski for the same price as children. Multiday, non-holiday tickets can be bought by phone, three days in advance at a 10 percent discount.

The Stowe Vacation Card is free to all who purchase a multiday lift ticket and fill out the application. The card offers freebies and discounts.

Note: These prices are valid January through March. Early and late season prices are lower, and holiday prices are a little higher. Night skiing is $20 for adults and $16 for children. A twilight ticket, valid from 1 to 10 p.m., is $38 for adults, $22 for children. All prices include Vermont sales tax.

Child care (98/99 prices)

Ages: 6 weeks through 6 years.

Costs: Full day with lunch is $55 ($50 for each additional day). Half day with snack is $42.

Reservations: Required; call 253-3000, Ext. 2262. The children's center is at the Spruce Peak area.

Accommodations

Stowe features Added Value packages for downhill and cross-country skiing. Extras include night skiing, extra half days, lessons, etc. If you're staying at least three days, ask about these packages. Call (800) 247-8693 (24-STOWE). Lodging ranges from small country inns and large resorts to hotels in the old New England tradition.

Ye Olde England Inne (253-7558; 800-477-3771, toll-free in the U.S. and Canada; 0-800-962-684 toll-free from the U.K.), is on the Mountain Road. This is bigger than a country inn and smaller than a full-fledged hotel. It has an English country motif and lavish Laura Ashley touches. Every room is decorated differently. A new addition perched on the hill behind the inn, aptly named The Bluff House, features luxury suites with unobstructed views over the valley. Room rates include breakfast. Rates: About $116–$215 per room, double occupancy.

Stowe Inn at Little River (253-4836 or 800-227-1108), right in the middle of town, has expanded beyond its 1814-era colonial roots with more modern units across the parking lot and River's Edge—giving a total of 43 rooms. For atmosphere opt for the old Main Inn with its wide-planked floors and four-poster beds. The restaurant is an excellent place from which to watch the village light up at night. Rates per room are $140–$350.

Green Mountain Inn (253-7301 or 800-253-7302) on Main Street is a charming old inn with a super location in the middle of town. The wide-planked floors are pine, as is the furniture, with many old four-poster canopied beds. Rooms that front on the street are a little too noisy for light sleepers; delivery trucks start to rev their engines at the nearby stop light at about 6 a.m. The hotel has an annex that is not quite so quaint but is off the main road. Room rates with breakfast are $110 to $185.

Butternut Inn (253-4277 or 800-328-8837) on Mountain Road ia country inn in the classic sense. Of those we visited, the Butternut was our favorite in Stowe. It reflects the eccentricities of the owners, transplanted from Texas. The inn is No Smoking and no children are allowed. Every aspect of the inn is done nicely: its rooms are all different, guests are pampered, dinners are prepared only for the inn guests and include Angus beef and Tex-Mex, which alternate with more traditional New England fare. Anyone who wants everything done beautifully will appreciate the Butternut. Room rates: $95–$160 double occupancy with breakfast and après-ski snacks.

Ten Acres Lodge (253-7638 or 800-327-7357) is on Luce Hill Road. This country inn was converted from an 1840s farm house. As with all country inns, rooms vary in size; those in the main lodge are relatively simple, but the common areas on the first floor are beautiful. Ten Acres Lodge also has a group of eight modern units, called the Hill House, tucked into the woods behind the old farmhouse. These all have fireplaces in the rooms and share an outdoor hot tub. Rates including breakfast: $100–$140 per room double occupancy.

The Gables Inn (253-7730 or 800-422-5371), on Mountain Road, is what all friendly country inns should be. Not a quiet, stuffy place with antiques and Mozart playing, where you're afraid of breaking something, this is a real lived-in house, which helps everyone have a good time. The breakfasts are among the best in Stowe and guests wouldn't think of eating anywhere else—for dinner either. Room rates, based on double occupancy: $85–$140 per person with two meals.

The Resorts

When the Trapp Family's life was dramatized in *The Sound of Music,* their everlasting fame was guaranteed. **The Trapp Family Lodge** (253-8511 or 800-826-7000), which they established near Stowe upon arriving in the United States, is a legend in its own right. Unfortunately, the original building burned down in the late 1970s, and was completely rebuilt from 1980 to 1983. It is still the most popular and upscale place to stay in the area, and is still in the family—it's now run by a son.

This is a self-contained resort with an excellent cross-country center. The collection of restaurants is among the best in the area, and a modern pool and fitness center provide excellent amenities. Make reservations early because this lodge is normally full throughout the season (Christmas reservations should be made about a year in advance). Rates with breakfast and dinner: $110–$200 per person, double occupancy.

Not as famous as the Trapp Family Lodge, but much closer to the lifts and the town, **Topnotch at Stowe Resort & Spa** (253-8585 or 800-451-8686; in Canada 800-228-8686) boasts the most extensive fitness center and spa in the area. Topnotch has rooms and condos, along with excellent meeting facilities. It also has the only four covered tennis courts in Stowe. Room rates: $190–$240 per person. Condos run about $280–$560.

The Inn at the Mountain (800-253-4754 or 253-3000), part of the Stowe Mountain Resort, is four-diamond rated by AAA, and we have no argument. This beautiful inn and the surrounding condominiums (available through the same telephone number) comprise the only ski-in/ski-out facility in Stowe. The flavor is old-world New England warmth. The name of the Broken Ski Tavern in the Inn commemorates the founding of the first steel ski, which was introduced here. An early prototype is hanging, in pieces, above the fireplace.

While the ambiance in the Inn may be old-world, the Fitness Center (free to all guests) across the parking lot is modern. Room and condo unit rates based on double occupancy and including breakfast and dinner are $205–$385.

The best family accommodations in Stowe are at the **Golden Eagle Resort** (253-4811 or 800-626-1010). This sprawling complex has more than a dozen buildings and facilities, from motel rooms with kitchenettes to apartments. Along with an excellent restaurant, The Alpine, the complex has one of the best fitness centers in town, which includes an indoor pool. It is all unpretentious and affordable. Because there are dozens of pricing options, the best bet is to contact the property and explain what you are looking for, but in general, room rates are $110–$170.

The Stoweflake (253-7355 or 800-253-2232), down the road a bit from the Golden Eagle, is more upscale and has a pool and fitness center. Rates with breakfast and dinner based on double occupancy are $138–$198 a night, (without meals, $78–$145). The Stoweflake manages a nice group of townhouse condominiums with studios to three-bedroom units for $165–$470.

The Vermont State Ski Dorm (800-866-8749 or 253-4010), at the foot of Mount Mansfield, offers bunk-style sleeping with shared bathroom facilities. Rates are about $35 a night with breakfast and dinner. Non-meal rates are available. Another dorm that specializes in youth groups is **The Round Hearth at Stowe** (253-7223), with prices similar to the Vermont State Ski Dorm.

 **Dining**

Stowe has long been famous for its cuisine. **Ten Acres** (253-7638) and **Ile de France** (253-7751) are considered by most to be the top gourmet spots in the area. Entrées at both restaurants range from $17 to $24. An up-and-coming restaurant is the **Blue Moon Café** (253-7006) with innovative fine dining.

The **Trapp Family Lodge** (253-8511) puts on an excellent Austrian-style meal for a fixed price of about $34. There normally is a choice of about a dozen entrées.

For a total dining experience, try the **Cliff House Restaurant** (253-3000) at the top of Stowe's gondola. A gourmet four-course meal awaits at about $35 per person, plus tax and tip.

For alternatives that aren't budget-busters, try **Miguel's Stowe-Away** (253-7574) or the **Cactus Café** (253-7770) for Mexican food, **Restaurant Swisspot** (253-4622) for fondues and decadent Swiss chocolate pie, and **Gracie's** (253-8741) for great burgers and meat loaf. **The Shed** (253-4364) has a microbrewery and is a great spot for steaks and prime rib. **Foxfire** (253-4887) has good Italian food, as does **Trattoria La Festa** (253-8480). **The Whip** (253-

7301), in the basement of the Green Mountain Inn, is a good place for a light dinner or sandwiches. **Mr. Pickwicks Polo Pub** in the Olde England Inne (253-7558) serves excellent game.

H.H. Bingham's (253-3000) in the Inn at the Mountain at the base of the Toll House lift, serves moderate continental cuisine with entrées in the $12 to $18 range; hearty lunches, too.

On-mountain, there are several choices for lunch and snacks. The **Midway Café** in the Midway Lodge has fresh-baked pastries and muffins and gourmet coffee, the **Cliff House Café** at the gondola top has a nice upscale atmosphere with meals for about $39 per person, and the **Broken Ski Tavern** at the Inn near the Toll House lift is quite relaxing and a little more upscale.

A breakfast favorite is **McCarthy's,** next to the movie theater, adjacent to the Baggy Knees complex. Also the breakfast at **The Gables** shouldn't be missed, especially on weekends.

Après-ski/nightlife

The ingredients that make the perfect après-ski spot are all there in just the right measure at the **Matterhorn Bar**. On the mountain road, this raucous little roadhouse is packed and rollicking after the slopes close. There's a dance floor, a disc jockey, loud music, a rectangular bar that makes for easy circulation, pool tables, big-screen TV. More low-key après-ski at the mountain is in the **Broken Ski Tavern** at the Inn at the Mountain.

You can count the hot spots on one hand, and still have fingers left over. Stowe's college-crowd hangout is **The Rusty Nail**, the in spot for dancing and live music.

Mr. Pickwick's at the Olde England Inne gets a good pub crowd with its 100-plus different beers, and the bar at **Miguel's Stowe-Away** seems to be a singles meeting place.

Other activities

Shopping: Stowe has over a hundred shops and art galleries for browsing, most in town. Shaw's General Store is a century old and was the town's first ski shop. Other unusual shops are Moriarty Hats & Sweaters for knitted goods, and Exclusively Vermont, for Vermont-made products.

Indoor tennis can be played at the Topnotch Racquet Club on the Mountain Road. Four Deco Turf courts are available as well as lessons for hourly fees. In the Village, Jackson arena has an Olympic-size **ice skating** rink. Call 253-6148.

Swimming open to the public, can be found at the Golden Eagle Resort (253-4811), Mountaineer Inn (253-7525), Salzburg Inn (253-8541), Topnotch Resort & Spa (253-9649) and the Town & Country Motor Lodge (253-7595).

Rent **Snowmobiles** at Nichols Snowmobiles (253-7239) or from Farm Resort (888-3525). Get **Snowshoe** rentals and guided tours from Umiak Outdoor Outfitters (253-2317).

Horse-drawn sleigh rides take place at Edson Hill Manor (253-7371), Stowehof Inn (253-9722), Pristine Meadows (253-9901), Charlie Horse (253-2215), Stoweflake (253-7355), the Trapp Family Lodge (253-8511) and Topnotch (253-8585).

Ben and Jerry's ice cream factory (244-5641) is just down the road in Waterbury and has tours that include samples. Winter is not nearly as busy as summer, so it's a good time to visit. **The Cabot Cheese Factory** (563-2231) is also open.

Stowe also has **horseback riding** at Edson Hill Manor (253-7371) and Ryder Brook (888-7916).

Special events include the Stowe Winter Carnival in January, the country's oldest winter party; the Stowe Challenge Cross-Country Races in February; and a Sugar Slalom race with maple-sugar-on-snow at the finish line and the Stowe Snow Beach Party, both in April.

Getting there and getting around

By air: Numerous flights arrive at the Burlington International Airport, which is 45 minutes from Stowe. Most hotels have a transfer service; you can also rent a car. The Stowe Area Association will give you discounts on flights and rental cars when you make your hotel reservations.

By train: A romantic trip aboard Amtrak's Montrealer offers private berths, cocktail-bearing attendants, and the incomparable sensation of watching the moonlit landscape of New England whirl past your window to the lonely call of the train whistle. You arrive in Waterbury, 15 miles from Stowe, early in the morning (the Stowe trolley meets each daily arrival and departure). Reservations required. The Stowe Area Association offers 10 percent off Amtrak tickets with no date restrictions.

By car: Distance from Boston is about 205 miles; from New York, 325 miles. The resort is a few miles north of Waterbury Exit 10 on I-89.

Getting around: You can manage without a car, but we recommend one. We realize that this will only contribute to increased street congestion, but the alternative is the Town Trolley, which runs between the village of Stowe and Mt. Mansfield. It provides, in the words of a British journalist who begged a ride back into town with us, "an epic voyage." The trolley. Makes. A lot. Of stops. Between town. And. The. Mountain. It costs $1 per single ride and $5 for a week-long pass. It is fine for *short* jaunts and operates until 11 p.m.

Sugarbush
Mad River Glen

Vermont

Sugarbush

Summit elevation:	**4,135 feet**
Vertical drop:	**2,650 feet**
Base elevation:	**1,485 feet**

Expert: ★★★
Advanced: ★★★
Intermediate:★★★★
Beginner: ★★★★
Never-ever:★★★★
Address: RR1, Box 350
Warren, VT 05674-2381
✆ **Area code:** 802
Ski area phone: 583-2381
Snow report: 583-SNOW
ⓘ **Toll-free reservations:** (800) 53-SUGAR
Fax: 583-6303
Internet: http://www.sugarbush.com
Number and types of lifts: 18—4 high-speed quads, 3 quad chairs, 3 triples, 4 double chairs, 4 surface lifts
Skiable Acreage: 432
Snowmaking: 68 percent
Uphill capacity: 24,363 per hour
Snowboarding: Yes, unlimited
Bed Base: 6,600 (2,200 on mountain)
Nearest lodging: slopeside
Resort child care: Yes, 6 weeks and older
Adult ticket, per day: $44-$49.35 (98/99)

Mad River Glen

Summit elevation:	**3,637 feet**
Vertical drop:	**2,000 feet**
Base elevation:	**1,637 feet**

Expert: ★★★★★
Advanced: ★★★★
Intermediate:★★★
Beginner: ★★★
Never-ever: ★
Address: PO Box 1089
Waitsfield, VT 05673
✆ **Area code:** 802
Ski area phone: 496-3551
Snow report: 496-3551
ⓘ **Toll-free information:** (800) 828-4748
Fax: 496-3562
E-mail: ski@madriver.com
Internet: http://www.madriverglen.com
Number and types of lifts: 4—3 double chairs, 1 single chair
Skiable Acreage: about 115
Snowmaking: 15 percent
Uphill capacity: 3,000 per hour
Snowboarding: No
Bed Base: 6,600
Nearest lodging: about a quarter-mile
Resort child care: Yes, 6 weeks and older
Adult ticket, per day: $29-$38 (98/99)

If Vermont is quintessential New England, then the Mad River Valley is a pretty fair candidate for quintessential Vermont. Its two main towns, Waitsfield and Warren, meet the visual requirements of anyone looking for the classic New England country town. Beautiful white and pastel clapboard houses fill the streets, historic buildings have been lovingly restored, and the narrow white-ribbon ski trails of Sugarbush stand out on the pine-green wooded slopes of 3,975-foot Lincoln Peak. Country inns and charming excellent restaurants abound, yet condos and hearty-fare eating establishments meet the needs of skiers on a budget.

This region is anchored by one big two-mountain resort and one smaller traditional resort—Sugarbush and Mad River Glen respectively. This pair could not be more different in their approach to the sport. Sugarbush is modern with high-speed lifts and potent snowmaking, surrounded by condos; Mad River Glen is the way skiing used to be claiming one of the few single chairs left in the country to takes skiers up to a warren of narrow trails cut through thickly wooded mountains with almost no snowmaking and no condos. Sugarbush is part of one of America's largest ski corporations. Mad River is America's only ski cooperative. For co-op purchase information, call the resort.

Mountain Layout

The skiing is on three separate mountains. Sugarbush Resort has two of them—Lincoln Peak Area and Mount Ellen Area (formerly called Sugarbush South and Sugarbush North, respectively). Mad River Glen on Route 17 is the third.

Each area provides a different experience. Heading the list of positives is the terrain, which goes from super gentle to super steep, and is well maintained. (Notice we did not say "groomed." Generally, both areas groom what needs to be groomed and leave alone what should be left alone.)

◆◆ **Expert** ◆ **Advanced:** At Lincoln Peak, the runs served by Castlerock lifts are very black and no place for the timid. The entire Castlerock area offers narrow New England-style steeps, and if you are lucky the Castlerock run will occasionally be groomed, making for a heavenly smooth steep. The Castlerock lift is popular with those in this ability level, so be aware that sometimes there is a wait; usually not more than eight to 10 minutes. However, the benefit is that these narrow trails do not fill up with yahoo skiers. You have to want to be there to end up at Castlerock.

From the top of the Heaven's Gate triple, experts can drop down a trio of short steeps directly below the lift or descend Organ Grinder with its tricky double fall line. To the left, also accessible by the Super Bravo Express, is the legendary Stein's Run with its steep moguled face and a trio of slightly less challenging expert runs.

Mount Ellen is primarily an intermediate playground, though the double blacks at the top—F.I.S., Black Diamond, Exterminator and Bravo (the latter a single-diamond)—are among the toughest in New England.

Mad River Glen is a throwback to earlier ski days. Mad River Glen prides itself on being tough (even the beginner trails here might be graded intermediate elsewhere), traditional (it's one of two areas in the nation with a chair lift for solo riders), natural (little snowmaking, combined with plenty of tight tree skiing), daring (can't imagine any other ski area with so much "out-of-bounds" skiing) and homey (skiers with serious tracks to carve have got to love a cafeteria with peanut-butter-and-jelly sandwiches to go).

This season, the resort has a new CTEC double chair. This chair has the same capacity of the chair it is replacing, so there will not be any more skiers on the mountain.

Telephone area code: 802

Mad River Glen is unique among ski areas in the country. It is the only mountain owned by a cooperative of skiers. They are determined to maintain a natural mountain experience.

True experts have one goal: the top of the single chair. The lines do get long—very long. Meanwhile, the real experts happily wait—this is what skiing in the East is all about. And when they get up there, they have it almost to themselves.

From the top of the single chair, experts can immediately drop down the Chute or the Fall Line, or if they are with a guide or local madman they can venture into the area called Paradise, entered by dropping down an eight-foot waterfall. Ask around for Octopus's Garden and the 19th and 20th Holes. If you look like you know how to ski, a local may direct you there.

At the single chair midstation, tree skiing beckons through the Glades on one side of the lift line and Lynx on the other. More timid souls can traverse on Porcupine and drop down wide-open Grand Canyon or thread through the Bunny Run.

■ **Intermediate:** At Lincoln Peak, a good start for an intermediate would be to take the Super Bravo chair, then traverse to the Heaven's Gate triple and the top of the mountain. From here take Upper Jester, rated blue (but barely more than a green), then choose from Down-spout, Domino, Snowball, Murphy's Glades or Lower Jester. The most fun for intermediates on this part of the mountain is the terrain reached by the Super Bravo lift. Warning: there is a long runout at the bottom of Jester. The North Lynx triple, reached by the Gatehouse Express chair, takes skiers higher on the mountain. Here intermediates will have relatively wide runs and good cruising. Also, the snowboard park has been moved to this area to take advantage if the higher altitude and better early-season snow.

An intermediate tree-skiing region at Lincoln Peak, called Eden, is between Spring Fling and Lower Snowball. .

Mount Ellen has wide-open cruising runs that a skier won't find at Lincoln Peak or at Mad River Glen. On the map, the intermediate runs from the top of the Summit quad chair seem relatively short, but the map is misleading. The Rim Run connecting to Northway and then to either Which Way, Cruiser or North Star comprises one of the classic cruising runs in the United States. The other intermediate section is Inverness, served by a quad chair and offering a good training area.

The single chair at Mad River Glen also has plenty of well groomed terrain for the solid intermediate. And guess what? It's not icy—Mad River Glen ex-owner Betsy Pratt let her groomers know that this was her mountain, she wanted to ski it, and she didn't want to skate it. They found a way to scoop and buff the snow, when the weather cooperates it is surprisingly easy to ski. Antelope and Catamount are relatively moderate routes down the mountain.

At the top of the section served by the Sunnyside double chair, intermediates can turn to the left and drop down Quacky to Porcupine, Grand Canyon and Bunny, or they can go below the lift and to the right down a short series of expert trails, Panther, Partridge, Slalom Hill and Gazelle, most of which empty into Birdland.

●● **Beginner:** The far right side of the Lincoln Peak area is served by the Gatehouse Express chair. Beginners will want to stick to this section of the mountain, practicing on Pushover and Easy Rider and then graduating to Slowpoke and Sleeper.

At Mount Ellen, Walt's Trail is a long green run from the top of the Inverness chair. The Green Mountain quad also serves gentle terrain.

At Mad River Glen, Birdland is ostensibly the beginner area. Granted, there are Duck, Lark, Robin, Wren and Loon for beginners, but there are also lower intermediate tight runs like Snail and Periwinkle. Even though there are green circles at every fork in the trail, intermediates can have plenty of fun here too. Learn to ski here and little will daunt you elsewhere.

● **Never-ever:** Lincoln Peak has Easy Rider, a gentle slope served by a double chair. Mount Ellen has Easy Street, off to one side and also served by a double chair. Mad River Glen is no place for a first-timer to start.

Mountain rating

Experts should head to Mad River Glen; the Castlerock and Paradise sections of Lincoln Peak; and the short-but-steep Black Diamond, Upper F.I.S. as well as Exterminator and Bravo at Mt. Ellen.

Intermediates and cruise hounds will have the most fun at Mount Ellen. If you're looking for day-long challenge, strike out for Mad River Glen and if you are just entering the intermediate ranks, test Jester and the Gate House area of Lincoln Peak.

Beginners have their best area at Mount Ellen, and acceptable sections of Lincoln Peak near Gate House. Never-evers should stick to Mount Ellen first, Lincoln Peak's novice terrain second, but stay clear of Mad River Glen—take at least a week's lessons first.

Cross-country

The Inn at the Round Barn Farm cross-country area has 30 km. of groomed trails, instruction, and ski and snowshoe rentals ($10 trail fee, free for inn guests). This area is associated with The Sugarbush Center—inn guests ski free there as well. The **Blueberry Lake** with 30 km. of trails and **Ole's** (near the airport) with 35 km. are under the same management. Trail fee is $9. If you head to Ole's get ready for some bushwacking.

Snowboarding

Boarding is allowed everywhere at Sugarbush. The Sugarbush snowboard park has been moved to the North Lynx triple chair area of Lincoln Peak/ Sugarbush South. The area features a custom-designed snowboard park and a precision-cut halfpipe built by a Pipe Dragon.

Snowboarding has been banned at Mad River Glen since the 93/94 season, when some impolite boarders ticked off the owner. That policy is unchanged. The co-op membership vote on allowing snowboarding failed with eighty-six percent voting against sharing the mountain with snowboarders.

Lessons (98/99 prices)

Sugarbush is part of the American Skiing Company and uses the Perfect Turn® program (see Skiing for Everyone chapter for an explanation). **Group clinics** are $28 for all levels except never-evers. There are multi-clinic discounts—two clinics cost $52, three clinics cost $72, and five clinics cost $500. **Guaranteed Learn to Ski,** which includes lesson, lifts and rentals, is $55 for level 1 skiers and snowboarders (never-evers); adding level 2 is plus $24; level 2–3 alone is $65. **Private lessons** are $62 an hour. A half-day private lesson for one is $156/142 (a.m./p.m.); for two skiers, $216/$162; for three skiers, $276/$182.

Children are divided into age groups for instruction. The Microbears program is for ages 2 1/2 to 3, with a little bit of skiing and day care for $62 full day, $42 half day. The Minibears program takes kids ages 4–6 years old for a combination of ski school and play activities for $65 full day, $46 half day. The Sugarbears program is for those ages 7–12 and costs $77 for a full day and $55 for half day, and the Catamounts program is for ages 13–16 and costs $82 for a full day. Children's programs include lunch and lift tickets, plus equipment for the age 6-and-younger crowd.

Mad River Glen has a ski school that, like the area, marches to its own drummer. **Private lessons** cost $40 per hour with each additional person $15; a half-day (three hours) private lesson is $100 with each additional skier paying $25; and a full day (six hours) $170 with each additional skier paying $40. **Group lessons** cost $30 for the first two hours and $20 for the next session. Group lessons are only avaible on weekends and holidays. The **never-ever package** including lifts, lessons and rentals is $35 for the first two hours and $20 for the next session. Mad River offers **clinics** covering moguls, telemarking, shaped skis and so on for $30 per two-hour session.

Mad River Glen also has programs for children aged 6–12 at the same prices as adults. Two runs through the NASTAR race course cost $5, with a dollar for each additional run.

Child care (98/99 prices)

The **Sugarbush Day School and Nursery** was the first child-care facility ever established at a Vermont ski resort. It takes children aged 6 weeks to 3 years. Two emergency medical technicians and a registered pediatric nurse are in residence. Toddlers, Day Cubs (6 weeks–6 years) get a program that uses games on and off the snow to introduce skiing. Full-day program with lunch is $52; half day is $36.

Mad River Glen has the Cricket Club Nursery (496-2123) for kids ages 6 weeks to 6 years. Infant care to 18 months on $40 for a full day and $25 for a half day. Child care for ages 18 months–6 years is $35 for a full day and $21 for a half day. Ski and Play programs are $50 for a full day with lunch and $28 for a half day. No reservations.

Sugarbush lift tickets (98/99 prices)

	Adult	Child (6-13)
One day* (97/98)	$49.35	$29.40
Three days*	$138.60 ($46.20/day)	$72.45 ($24.15/day)
Five days*	$231 ($46.20/day)	$120.75 ($24.15/day)

Who skis free: Children ages 5 and younger.

Who skis at a discount: Sugarbush lowers ticket prices for adults in its Value Season, opening through mid-December and in April. Ages 65 and older ski for the child's price.

Sugarbush is one of the American Skiing Company resorts, most of which are in the Northeast. For a description of the Magnificent 7 Card and Edge Card discount programs that give benefits at all the resorts, see the Lift Ticket section in the Sunday River chapter. Sales tax is included if you buy either of these cards in Vermont.

*Note: Sugarbush has an unusual ticket pricing policy. Prices no longer include the Vermont sales tax of five percent. (An aside for our European and Australian readers: If an American ski resort is required to pay a sales tax on lift tickets, it is the common practice to include it in the anounced ticket price.) Because this is such an unusual policy, we have included the tax in the prices we list here.

Mad River Glen lift tickets (98/99 prices)

	Adult	Junior (6-15)
One day, midweek	$29	$20
One day, weekend	$36	$24
One day, holiday	$38	$28

Who skis free: Ages 70 and older. Children 5 and younger are issued a free ticket when skiing with a paying adult.

Who skis at a discount: Ages 65–69 ski at junior prices. Multiday pricing works like this: If you buy a two-day ticket, you get $2 off the price each day. For example, a Friday-Saturday ticket costs $59—$2 off the midweek price for Friday and $2 off the weekend price for Saturday. For a three-day or longer ticket, you get $3 off the daily price.

 ## Accommodations

This area has some of Vermont's finest country inns and B&Bs, all of which can be booked through **Sugarbush Central Reservations** (800-537-8427; spells 53-SUGAR), **Sugarbush/Mad River Chamber of Commerce** (800-828-4748; spells 82-VISIT), or call the inns directly.

Topping the list is **The Inn at the Round Barn Farm** (496-2276) a mile from Route 100 across the wooden bridge on East Warren Road (indeed, this rates with the best B&Bs we've seen anywhere in ski country). The farmhouse has been made into an elegant, spacious, 11-room bed-and-breakfast. It is peaceful and quiet, strictly No Smoking, with children discouraged. Lodging/ski packages for two people including breakfast range from about $180 for a small room with shower and private bath to about $290 for the stunning Richardson Room with Vermont-made canopied king bed, skylights, gas fireplace, oversized Jacuzzi and steam shower. There are 30 km. of cross-country tracks outside the door.

Tucker Hill Lodge (496-3983 or 800-543-7841), two miles from Sugarbush's lifts, has 22 rooms, each with a choice of breakfast, or breakfast and a four-course dinner. Prices per day per person are about $65–$85 for the room-and-meals deal.

If you like history, you'll adore **The Waitsfield Inn** (496-3979 or 800-758-3801) in the center of Waitsfield Village. It started life in the 1820s as a parsonage, was a sleeping-bag dorm for young skiers in the '60s and '70s, and is now a quaintly elegant 14-bedroom B&B. Each of the rooms is named for someone who lived in the house during the 19th century, and a booklet gives short biographies. A highlight is the inn's common area, a charming room built in what was once the stable. The inn is run by Steve and Ruth Lacey; he a droll Brit and she a bouncy Californian. Prices start at $140 for a lodging/lift package for two.

Lareau Farm Country Inn (496-4949) is a roomy 14-bedroom farm house with beautiful views. Every room is unique. The American Flatbread Kitchen which makes pizza-like flatbread in a stone and mud oven, is housed in the attached barn. On weekends the workers clear the barn floor of equipment, throw plaid tablecloths over work tables and open as a flatbread restaurant.

West Hill House B&B (496-7162) has seven bedrooms (all with private bath) and has ski-stay packages starting at $80 per person per night, double occupancy.

Beaver Pond Farm Inn (583-2861) is right on the cross-country trails of the Sugarbush golf course. Ski-stay packages start at about $85 per person per night.

The most luxurious full-service hotel property is the **Sugarbush Inn** located on the access road. Ski-and-stay packages start at about $80 per person based on double occupancy. The inn and its 46 rooms are well-kept but nondescript. The inn has 25-km. of cross-country trails, indoor pool, and fitness center.

The **Weathertop Lodge** (496-4909) on Rte. 17 between Waitsfield and Mad River Glen has packages starting at about $88 per person. Closer to Sugarbush resort you'll find **Sugar Lodge** at Sugarbush (800-982-3465), only a half mile from Lincoln Peak, with a massive fieldstone fireplace. Rates at both are reasonable; call for current information.

The **Inn At The Mad River Barn** (496-3310) has very rustic spacious rooms and some of the best lodging food in the valley (both in quantity and quality). To stay here is a step into a wonderful 1940s ski lodge.

Families will want to check into the **Madbush Falls Country Lodge** on Rte. 100 (496-5557) or the **Hyde Away** (496-2322). Both are great spots for children and close to the slopes. The Hyde Away has become the favorite locals' hangout for shooting pool.

Of the condominiums in the Village at Sugarbush, the most luxurious are the **Southface Condominiums** with hot tubs in each unit and a shuttlebus ride from the slopes. **The Snow Creek** condos are ski-in/ski-out, but you have the noise of snow guns at your back window during snowmaking operations. The **Paradise** condos are newer but a good walk from the slopes; however, they have good shuttle service. **The Summit** units are roomy and **Castle Rock** condos are close to the slopes. **Unihab** looks like boxes stacked on one another, and **Middle Earth** condos are 10 minutes from the lifts and small.

Rates range from $145 for a one-bedroom in value season to $635 for a four-bedroom during holidays. Guests may use the indoor pool, tennis, racquetball, squash courts, aerobics, Jacuzzi, steam room and Nautilus equipment at the Sugarbush Sports Center for an additional fee. These condos are close to the children's center.

Almost as close to the lifts as Sugarbush Village units is the **The Bridges Resort and Racquet Club** (583-2922 or 800-453-2922). This complex has tennis courts and an indoor pool. These units are quieter than the mountain units and have wonderful amenities as well as a regular shuttle.

Skiers heading for Mad River Glen should check into the **Battleground** condos (496-2288 or 800-248-2102).

 **Dining**

With more than 40 eating establishments, the valley boasts a very high excellent-restaurant-per-skier ratio. The only other competition in New England is the Mt. Washington Valley in New Hampshire.

The top of the line is **Chez Henri** (583-2600) in Sugarbush Village at the base area of Lincoln Peak. The restaurant manages to capture a true French bistro feeling—it is romantic and cozy, with low ceilings and a flickering fire. The owner, Henri Borel, personally greets guests and makes them feel at home. He also supervises the excellent wine selection. Chez Henri features lunch, fondue in the late afternoon, then dinner until 10 p.m. Entrées range from $13.50 to $22.

Sam Rupert's (583-2421), down a driveway to the left as you approach the Sugarbush parking lot, has developed lots of fans and offers an eclectic menu rivaling any in the area, along with a good reasonable wine list. Magician Bill Brunelle performs twice a week.

The Common Man (583-2800) has attracted an excellent clientele and has a reputation for good food, but for our money it's just a bit too big. The atmosphere is great—the dining area is in what might be called a New England Baroque barn with crystal chandeliers. Entrées generally are $12–$18.

The **Bass Restaurant** (583-3100) on the access road serves tasty heart-healthy creative meals ($10–$16) around a giant fireplace. This spot has been getting rave reviews from locals and visitors alike.

John Egan's Big World Pub & Grill (496-3033) serves excellent food. John has teamed up wth the former chef from the Tucker Hill Lodge, Jerry Noony. They have created a casual dining experience with flavorful food. It is closed Mondays.

Giorgio's Cafe (496-3983) in the Tucker Hill Lodge on Rte. 17 between Waitsfield and Mad River Glen serves good Italian meals.

The Grill (583-2301) is a casual dining spot in the Sugarbush Inn and **Knickers** in the clubhouse at the Sugarbush Cross Country Center is enjoyable.

Mad River Barn Restaurant has a popular Saturday buffet, and dinners Sunday through Friday from 6:30 to 8 p.m. Meals are prepared by Chef Cris McGandy and the owner herself, Betsy Pratt, founder with her husband of Mad River Glen. A Sugarbush tradition worth the effort is the **American Flatbread Kitchen** (496-8856) open only on weekends at the Lareau Farm Country Inn.

For families out to stretch the budget and still get good wholesome food at reasonable prices, number one is the **Hyde Away** (496-2322) on Rte. 17. For simple quick food, try **The Den** (496-8880) on Waitsfield's main street, or **D.W. Pearl's** (496-8858).

Good spots for breakfast are **D.W. Pearl's**, the **Hyde Away** and **Pepper's Restaurant** (583-2202) at Pepper's Lodge. The Mad River Barn lays out excellent homemade muffins and jams and serves only real maple syrup.

Après-ski/nightlife

Après-ski starts at the base lodges, which do booming business at the bar as the lifts close. Or head to **Chez Henri** where the bar fills up with people quietly drinking beer or wine. The **Hyde Away** is where you will find the locals; the **Blue Tooth** is most popular with tourists. One or the other of Sugarbush's base lodges will usually have a live band for après-ski. On weekends try the **Sugarbush Inn** for a slightly more upscale crowd.

For the Mad River Glen crowd, the base area bar, **General Stark's Pub,** follows the retro atmosphere of the area with plenty of fun in an old-time bar. After leaving Mad River Glen the next place to stop is the **Mad River Barn**. The bar there looks like an old Vermont bar should look: moose head hanging over the fireplace, hunting scenes on every wall, big couches and stuffed chairs, wood paneling and bumper pool or shuffleboard.

In the evenings, **Gallagher's** has dancing with a mix of music from rock to country-rock and an interesting crowd. **Mad Mountain Tavern,** across from Gallagher's, is popular with the dancin' crowd because of live music on weekends. **Chez Henri's** disco attracts a quieter slightly older group.

Other activities

Shopping: Waitsfield and Warren have art galleries, country stores and antique and collectible shops that are fun for browsing and buying. Most shops in tiny Warren Village are within easy walking-distance of each other.

The **Sugarbush Sports Center** and the **Bridges Resort and Racquet Club** have various sports and exercise facilities.

Snowshoe treks (583-0381) are available from the summit of Sugarbush's Mount Ellen to Lincoln Peak.

Sleighrides and skijoring (496-7141) can be arranged at the Vermont Icelandic Horse Farm in Waitsfield. (Skijoring involves being pulled behind a horse or snowmobile while on skis.) Other farms offering sleighrides are the Lareau Farm Country Inn (496-4949) and Whispering Winds Farm in Moretown (496-2819).

Ice skating rinks are at Tucker Hill Lodge, Sugarbush Inn or the Skatium next to Grand Union in Waitsfield.

Mad River Flick (426-4200) has first-run movies, plus something at the concession stand most movie theaters don't offer—beer and wine.

Getting there and around

Getting there: Sugarbush is off Rte. 100, about 20 miles south of Waterbury. Burlington airport is about an hour away. Amtrak offers train-ski-lodging packages, with daily service from New York, Philadelphia and Washington, D.C. For information, call (800) 237-7547 for packages; (800) 872-7245 for train only.

Getting around: Sugarbush has three free shuttles: the Village shuttle, which connects several lodging properties with Lincoln Peak; the Parking Lot Jitney, which circles each area's parking lot; and the Fun Shuttle, which connects lodging at Sugarbush Village with Waitsfield's downtown. The first two work fine. The nightly Fun Shuttle runs once an hour from 6 p.m. to 12:30 a.m. For a one-time visit to town it's okay, but for more frequent visits, bring or rent a car.

You will need a car to get to Mad River Glen.

Marmot Basin/Jasper
Whistler/Blackcomb
Banff Region
Vancouver
Lake Louise
Red Mountain
Banff Mt. Norquay
Sunshine
Tremblant
Québec
Montréal

Canadian
Resorts

Canada is a great destination for a ski vacation. Generally, the giant mountains and vast snow-fields are in the West, while the narrow trails and quaint ski towns are in the East, just as they are in the U.S.; however a Canadian ski vacation also has some very attractive differences. Some examples:

• Some of Canada's leading ski areas are in national parks. Banff and Jasper National Parks have four ski areas within their boundaries. The scenery is magnificent and wild animal sightings are common.

• You can stay in an opulent, historic hotel, even if you're on a budget. The Canadian Pacific chain includes several grand hotels built to accommodate late 19th- and early 20th-century luxury rail travel. Some call them winter Snow Castles. In summer they are jammed with tourists willing to pay premium rates, but in winter, prices plummet.

Prices are in Canadian dollars, which, at press time, was about $1.45 Canadian dollars for each U.S. dollar. Whenever possible, we list prices so they include the G.S.T., Canada's Goods and Services Tax of 7 percent. Many resorts like to list their prices without the G.S.T., so if our prices are "higher" than others you've seen advertised, that's probably why. Foreign tourists can get a G.S.T. refund for goods they take out of the country and on hotel rooms they pay for themselves (but not on rooms prepaid through a travel agent). You can't get refunds for meals or services such as transportation or lift tickets. Most hotels have refund forms.

Canada can be as cold as you've heard, or warmer than you imagined. We've skied in windbreakers in January, and huddled in fleece neck-warmers during a sudden April snowstorm. Our advice is to plan for everything.

United States citizens should bring a passport if they have one. If not, U.S. citizens must have citizenship and residency proof, particularly if traveling by air. A birth or baptismal certificate, or voter card is sufficient. A driver's license alone is not. And by the way, these requirements are more for return to the U.S. than for entry into Canada.

Single and divorced parents, take note: In an effort to prevent child stealing, Canadian immigration requires that any parent entering Canada alone with their child present proof of custody, such as a notarized letter from the other parent. Anyone traveling with someone else's child (grandparents, uncles and aunts, friends) must present a notarized letter signed by both of the child's parents. If you're driving with friends in separate cars, be sure kids are matched with parents when crossing the border. Sometimes you'll breeze through without being asked for proof, but it's best to be prepared.

Banff, Canada

Sunshine Village
Banff Mount Norquay

Dining:★★★★	E-mail: through Web site
Apres-ski/nightlife:★★★★	Internet: http://www.skibanfflakelouise.com
Other activities:★★★★★	Bed Base: 10,000 in Banff

Some places on Earth are so beautiful that they must be seen—words are inadequate to describe what unfolds before your eyes. Banff National Park is one such place.

The Canadian Rockies are among the world's most spectacular mountain ranges, and Banff National Park is the best known of the four national parks that stretch along the spiny border between Alberta and British Columbia. The Canadian government established Banff—the country's first national park—in 1885. Nearly 100 years later, the United Nations declared the four national parks—Banff, Jasper, Yoho and Kootenay—World Heritage Sites.

Today national parks are areas to be preserved; strict regulations govern land use within their boundaries. But a hundred years ago, when Banff was newly established, the philosophy was that a national park needed such improvements as tourist facilities so that everyone could enjoy the spectacular scenery. Before such thinking changed, four ski areas and some stunning hotels were established within these parks. This chapter profiles the areas nearest Banff, and chapters on Lake Louise and Jasper follow.

Skiers and snowboarders owe it to themselves to take a trip here. Winter provides stunning vistas but few crowds. Winter sports of all varieties are abundant. The summer tourist stampede has long subsided, residents are relaxed and friendly, and lodging prices are at rock-bottom, even in the most luxurious hotels.

For the first-time visitor, Banff is a good place to headquarter. The townsite—that's the word locals use, not town—is compact, yet filled with excellent restaurants, shopping and nightclubs. The two ski areas, one that overlooks the townsite and the other a few miles away, are quite good. We recommend that destination visitors also spend a day or two at Lake Louise, the largest ski area in this region, about 45 minutes away.

Mountain layout—Sunshine Village

You can explore three mountain peaks in two provinces at Sunshine Village. It's the larger of the two Banff areas, ten miles from the townsite. Much of the skiing at Sunshine Village is wide-open, with an infinite number of ways down, some smooth, others moguled, all exhilarating.

Sunshine has the longest ski season in the region, sometimes even into June, and the most snow (360 inches as opposed to 120 and 140 at the other areas). It has spectacular views—if the weather's clear.

Visitors arrive here by an unusual route: up a narrow canyon in a six-person gondola from the parking lot, then around a sharp left turn. After 10 minutes, you can get off at mid-

Sunshine Village Facts

Summit elevation: 9,200 feet
Vertical drop: 3,757 feet
Base elevation: 5,440 feet
Address: Box 1510, Banff, Alberta,
Canada T0L 0C0
☎ Area code: 403
Ski area phone: 762-6500
Snow report: 760-7669
ⓘ Toll-free reservations: (800) 661-1676
Fax: 762-6513
Internet: http://www.skibanff.com
Number of lifts: 12–1 gondola, 3 high-speed
quads, 1 triple chair, 3 double chairs, 4 surface lifts
Snowmaking: none
Skiable acreage: 3,168
Uphill capacity: 17,000 per hour
Snowboarding: Yes, unlimited
Nearest lodging: slopeside, hotel
Resort child care: Yes, 19 months and older
Adult ticket, per day: $46 (97/98 prices)
Expert:★★★★ Advanced:★★★★
Intermediate:★★★★
Beginner:★★★★
Never-ever:★★★★

Banff Mount Norquay Facts

Summit elevation: 7,000 feet
Vertical drop: 1,650 feet
Base elevation: 5,350 feet
Address: P.O. Box 219, Suite 7000, Banff,
Alberta, Canada T0L 0C0
☎ Area code: 403
ⓘ Ski area phone and snow report: 762-4421
Fax: 762-8133
Number of lifts: 5–1 high-speed quad,
1 quad chair, 2 double chairs, 1 surface lifts
Snowmaking: 90 percent
Skiable Acreage: 162 acres
Uphill capacity: 6,300 per hour
Snowboarding: Yes, unlimited
Nearest lodging: about 2 miles
Resort child care: Yes, 19 months and older
Adult ticket, per day: $35 (97/98 prices)
Expert:★★★★
Advanced:★★★★
Intermediate:★★★
Beginner:★★
Never-ever:★★

Regional Tri-Area Lift Passes (98/99 prices including GST)

The Banff/Lake Louise Region has an interchangeable lift ticket. It allows unlimited skiing at Sunshine, Banff Mt. Norquay and Lake Louise and a free shuttle between Banff/Lake Louise hotels and the ski areas. It is available for those skiing at least three days. It also includes a scratch-and-win coupon for when used at Banff Mount Norquay to make up the price difference.

	Adults	Children (6-12)
three days	$152	$57
five days	$253	$95
seven days	$354	$133

station to head to the Goat's Eye area, or continue on the gondola for another 10 minutes to the "base area" village at 7,082 feet. (A clarification: The base-elevation stat we list is for the gondola base; this book uses the term "base area" to mean the greatest concentration of shops and services.) Though there's a new rental shop at the gondola base, it's after you get off the gondola that the play really starts, around a lodge, rental shop, general store, restaurant and the only slopeside lodging in the national parks. From here a half dozen lifts and tows take off in all directions. Most people never head all the way down until the end of the day, some not until the end of their vacation.

◆◆ **Expert** ◆ **Advanced:** Goat's Eye Mountain, which opened in 1995, features 1,900 vertical feet of black and double-black routes with a couple of view-strewn cruiser blues, heading all the way to the village from the 9,200-foot summit. Accessed by a high-speed quad, Goat's Eye has opened a large area of above-treeline acreage and gut-sucking chutes.

You'll find equally exhilarating descents from the Continental Divide High-Speed Quad, which rises 1,450 feet to the nearly 9,000-foot summit of Lookout Mountain. (Take either the Strawberry Chair or Angel High-Speed Quad to reach it.) At the top, you cross the Continental Divide from Alberta into British Columbia.

If it's your first time here, try the run down the face of Angel, called Ecstasy—just to get ready for the high country. From the top of Angel High-Speed Quad, it's wide-open above-treeline terrain, with spectacular views of the Continental Divide.

The most challenging route from the Continental Divide Chair is far to the right as you head down, toward the Tee-Pee Town chair. Keep in mind that there's a cliff. The appeal in getting as far out along the cliff edge as you dare is virgin snow. If you stay on the edge, you have to dip down a drop innocuously called The Shoulder. It's the only thing on the mountain labeled black which should be double black. To avoid it, turn left and you'll negotiate single blacks and find some great tree shots.

You'll find some mogul runs off the Tee-Pee Town Chair. If that's mild for you, take the WaWa T-bar on the opposite side of the Village up to a ridge with a left-hand dropoff called Paris Basin. It doesn't even look like a run, but they ski it. If you get there and decide against it, you can take an easy cat trail back down.

■ **Intermediate:** There's terrain from every lift for skiers and snowboarders at this level; however, be sure you are confident at this ability level if you try the runs on Goat's Eye or the peak of Lookout Mountain. (Think twice if the weather's socked in, too.) If you're ready to try a few blacks, you'll find some short ones off the Wheeler double chair and the Fireweed T-bar, both down-mountain from the other lifts. Enjoy this area any time of the day, then ride the gondola to the top from its midstation, but most people play here in the afternoon on their way back down.

●● **Beginner:** The Strawberry Park triple chair and the Wheeler chair have gentle wide slopes good for those still perfecting their technique.

● **Never-ever:** Never-evers learn near the base village, where a tow rope pulls them to the top of a short gentle slope that is off to one side.

Note: The three-mile run at the end of the day from the Village down to the parking lot is a long luscious trip for beginners, but it will seem tame for many intermediates. Advanced skiers can play on drops to the left, but they're short and eventually rejoin the trail.

To find powder after a storm, head immediately to ByeBye Bowl (left, facing down off the Divide), but it gets blown off quickly. The day after a storm, try Paris Basin. To stay in the sun, ski Standish Face in the morning and Lookout Mountain (Continental Divide) in the afternoon. Ski tours depart from the upper gondola terminal at 9:50 a.m. and 12:50 p.m. daily.

Mountain rating

Sunshine has a deserved reputation as a cruiser's mountain. The percentage of expert terrain increased with the addition of Goat's Eye, but this still remains a well-balanced mountain with fun for all levels.

Snowboarding

Rentals and lessons are available. Dell Valley is a natural halfpipe near the Strawberry Triple Chair.

Lessons (98/99 prices in Cdn$)

Group lessons: $25 per session.
Never-ever package: A 2.5-hour lesson, rentals and lift ticket is $59.
Private lessons: $65 an hour (no charge for an additional person).
Multihour discounts are available.

Special programs: Sunshine Village encourages the traditional Ski Week, a week-long stay at the slopeside Sunshine Inn, by providing packages including classes with the same instructor. Groups can be divided by ability level or by family, and includes evening activities. Because prices vary by season and size of room, call for prices. Performance Seminars are $30 afternoon clinics that focus on moguls, steeps, powder, video or racing.

Sunshine Village participates in Club Ski, a three-day program featuring lessons with the same instructor and group, but skiing one day each at three resorts (see the Lift Ticket section in the Lake Louise chapter for details).

Children's programs: Ages 3–6 just venturing onto the slopes can get a combo ski-and-play program for $28 for the full day (lunch is $5 extra) or $25 for half day. Equipment is included. Kids in that age group who already know how to ski can get a private one-hour lesson for $30, equipment and lift ticket extra. Young Devils is for kids aged 6–12 just starting or well on their way. The price is $45 for full day with lunch, $25 half day.

Child care (98/99 prices in Cdn$)

Ages: 19 months to 6 years.
Costs: Full day is $23, half day is $15, lunch is $5 extra.
Reservations: Recommended; call 762-6560.

Lift tickets (97/98 prices in Cdn$ including GST)

	Adult	Child (6-12)
One day	$46	$15
Three days	$128 ($42.83/day)	$45 ($15/day)
Five days	$208 ($41.79/day)	$75 ($15/day)

Who skis free: Children 5 and younger.

Who skis at a discount: Students 13–25 and those 65 and older ski for $38. Students need ID to qualify for the discount.

Note: A Sunshine Card is available for $49.95 that includes two free days of skiing (the first and the third), plus holders can purchase midweek lift tickets for $31 a day and weekend day tickets for $36. Do your homework—six days of skiing only costs $174–$184 depending on when you purchase your card.

Check out Tri-Pass if staying in Banff. It is valid at Sunshine Village, Banff Mount Norquay and Lake Louise, and includes bus rides from hotels to the ski areas. The bus ride alone is about $15 round-trip between Banff and here, so the Tri-Area Pass can be a good deal depending on whether you need to take a bus or have a car and how much you want to ski at Lake Louise versus Sunshine and Banff Mount Norquay all factor in to your decision.

Mountain Layout—Banff Mount Norquay

Just a 10-minute drive from Banff, this small ski area with the big name boasts some of the best grooming in Western Canada, and has a money-back guarantee: If you don't like the conditions within an hour of buying your ticket, turn it in and get a refund.

The Cascade Lodge at the base was built in 1996 after the previous lodge burned down. It houses a restaurant, bar, three large stone fireplaces and the usual services.

◆◆ **Expert** ◆ **Advanced:** The view of Banff and the Bow Valley from the North American chair is spectacular. This is the lift that takes you to those bump ribbons. Be postively sure you want to be there: you used to be able to ride back down if you didn't like what you saw, but no longer. This is very tough stuff, with no blue or green ways down.

Lone Pine is the name of that double-black mogul belt that plunges down a 35 percent gradient. There's a daily contest (when the lift is open) called Club 35,000 to see who can make the most consecutive runs in seven hours on this 1,360-foot, skeleton-jarring wall. It takes 27 runs to make the club, and many have done it, which says a lot for local physical fitness.

Another appeal for the adventure seeker is a chute on Norquay called Valley of the Ten, a narrow drainage perfect for thrills. To get to it, skiers at the top of North American chair drop off (correct terminology) to the left into a drop-out (accurate again) called Gun Run, the steepest thing on the mountain. The easiest way down from the Norquay side, still a tough black, is Memorial Bowl.

■ **Intermediate:** From the first look, Norquay looks like a haven for mogul maniacs, but the terrain unseen from the base on the Mystic Express Quad is mainly groomed intermediate. Intermediates should stick to the two quads, Mystic Express and Spirit.

Intermediates wanting to stay in the sun all day have a challenge. Since at midday none of Mystic gets sun except the front two runs, Black Magic and Ka-Poof, both blacks, they'd better learn to ski bumps.

● **Beginner:** One tow and a short double chair serve a little bit of terrain at the base. Adult beginners may get bored after a few runs. The step up to the Mystic Chair runs is big.

Mountain rating

Levels intermediate to expert will find plenty of challenge here, especially since even the blues here are far more difficult than those found in most U.S. resorts. Beginners are better off at Sunshine Village.

Snowboarding

Banff Mount Norquay is a great supporter of the sport. A snowboard park with two halfpipes, quarter pipe and Canada's first turbo pipe grinder is near the base and served by the Cascade Chair.

Lessons (98/99 prices in Cdn$)

Group lessons: $28 for two hours.

Never-ever package: $35 for a two-hour group lesson, lift ticket on the Cascade chair and rental equipment. A first-time snowboard package is also available, prices may be different.

Private lessons: $55 per hour, each additional person $15. Before 10 a.m. a private lesson is $45.

Banff Mount Norquay participates in Club Ski, a three-day program of lessons with the same instructor and group, but skiing one day each at three resorts (see the Lift Ticket section in the Lake Louise chapter for details).

Children's lessons: Full day is $35; two hours, $28. Lunch is extra.

Child care (97/98 prices in Cdn$)

Ages: 19 months to 6 years.

Cost: Full day, without lunch, is $22. Half day, either morning or afternoon, is $15. Add a ski lesson, and the costs are $30 and $25, respectively. Lunch is $5.

Reservations: Recommended; call 760-7709.

Lift tickets (97/98 prices in Cdn$ including GST)

	Adult	Child (6-12)
One day	$35	$15
Three days	$95 ($31.66/day)	$41 ($13.66/day)
Five days	$140 ($28/day)	$60 ($12/day)

Who skis free: Children 5 and younger ski free when an adult buys a lift ticket.

Who skis at a discount: Students 13–25 with student ID and seniors 55 and older ski for $29. Banff Mount Norquay has night skiing on Fridays and Saturdays for $19 (the only night skiing in Banff).

Banff Mount Norquay also sells a flex-time ticket for $19, good for two hours Monday–Friday except the two weeks surrounding Christmas and New Year's Day. If we were here for a week of skiing, we'd use the Tri-Area Lift Pass at Lake Louise and Sunshine Village, and buy a flex-time pass to use here. If you want to ski here again after two hours (and you may—it's a fun place, yet small), *then* use a day on your Tri-Area Pass. When you use it here, you also get a free coupon for night skiing and a "Scratch-N-Win" coupon good for food items.

Cross-country—Banff area

There are some lovely easy loops along the Bow River. Take Banff Avenue to the end of Spray Avenue, or turn left and cross the river. Trails wind through the whole area. **Parks Canada** puts out a very informative booklet on Nordic skiing in Banff National Park; you can get a copy for a small fee at the Banff Information Center, 224 Banff Ave., 9 a.m. to 5 p.m.

Banff Springs Golf Course Clubhouse offers ski and skate rentals, plus group and private lessons. Maps and information on trails are available at the Clubhouse.

Accommodations (prices in Cdn$ plus GST)

Rooms can be found for as little as $50, and even the premier locations are within most budgets.

The Sunshine Inn (762-6500; 800-661-1676) on the Sunshine Village mountain at the top of the gondola is the only lodging in Banff National Park with ski-in/ski-out convenience. Rooms start at less than $100 per person in low season, then rise to about $200 for larger rooms in regular season. All nightly rates include lift tickets, and the hotel runs a Ski Week program.

Banff Mount Norquay now owns the cozy, spiffed-up, 1960s-era **Timberline Inn** and Big Horn Steakhouse (762-2281; www.banfftimberline.com) at the bottom of its access road. Technically it's Banff's only ski-in hotel (you can ski in along an ungroomed 1.5-kilometer trail, but you'll need the inn's shuttle to take you to the lifts). Rates range from $78–$132, including Norquay lift tickets. The shuttle also will run guests into town in the evening.

Other lodging is in Banff. We strongly recommend the experience of staying at the **Banff Springs Hotel** (800-441-1414 in the U.S. and Canada, 762-2211), the wine-colored, Scottish-influenced castle perched on a small hill, a short walk from downtown. You have seen this classic rundle-rock monolith in many photos, its pointed, green-copper roofs rising from the nine-story walls, framed by evergreens and craggy peaks. Its public areas are expansive, designed for turn-of-the-century mingling—we're talking a ballroom for 16,000. Rates during the winter are a bargain compared to summer. The hotel has ski-lodging packages and a full-service spa. Ski-and-spa packages also are available.

Banff Park Lodge and Conference Center (800-661-9266; 762-4433) which hosts many cultural activities, is an expanse of cedar buildings in a wooded area two blocks from downtown. Rates are in the $100–$150 range.

The Mount Royal Hotel (800-267-3035 Western Canada only; 762-3331) has a great location in downtown Banff, an excellent choice for those who enjoy nightlife. It gets a fair amount of street noise from Banff Avenue but has an exceptionally good restaurant. Rates are in the $70–$100 range.

The Inns of Banff (800-661-1272; 762-4581) a modern, multi-level lodge with balconies in most rooms, is a 15-minute walk from downtown. The rooms are fairly large and rates are $80–$100.

High Country Inn (800-661-1244; 762-2236) on Banff Avenue is one of the least expensive at $70–$100 per night.

Banff International Hostel (762-4122) on Tunnel Mountain Road just added a 66-bed wing with 2- and 4-bed rooms with private bathrooms. Showers are shared. Facilities include a laundry, kitchen and cafe. Beds start at $19 per night.

For other lodging information, contact **Banff/Lake Louise Central Reservations,** (800-661-1676) a reservations service that books lodging in Banff, Lake Louise and Jasper.

Dining

For those staying at Sunshine Village, the **Eagle's Nest Dining Room** in the Sunshine Inn offers fine dining with lobster and filet mignon. **The Chimney Corner**, the inn's fireplace lounge, serves a sit-down lunch of croissants, soups, salads, pastas, ribs and steak sandwiches.

In the townsite of Banff, diners have a tremendous variety and number of restaurants to choose from. You will find almost every variety of ethnic food, as well as the familiar steak-

and-seafood restaurants. Restaurants here, especially those on Banff Avenue, often are on the second floor above the shops. Sometimes the entrances are obvious, sometimes not.

The Banff Springs Hotel alone has 11 restaurants, including **The Samurai** (762-6860), which serves Japanese cuisine. **The Pavilion** (762-6860) serves Italian dinners, while the **Alhambra Dining Room** (762-2211, Ext. 6841) offers Spanish cuisine. **Waldhaus** (762-6860) serves fondue and other German, Austrian and Swiss fare at long tables that seat a dozen people. **Grapes** (762-2211, Ext. 6660) is the 26-seat wine bar, but it also serves light meals. **Solace** (762-1772), the restaurant at the hotel spa, serves healthy, low-fat fare.

Le **Beaujolais** (on Banff Avenue at Buffalo Street, 762-2712) received high praise for its French cuisine. Meals can be ordered à la carte, but the restaurant specializes in fixed-price three- or five-course meals. You are likely to see diners in coats and ties, though neither is required. **The Bistro** (on the corner of Wolf and Bear streets, 762-8900) is owned by the same restauranteurs but is considerably more casual and cozy. It serves a variety of pastas, salads and meat and poultry meals; open for lunch and dinner.

For gourmet Italian, you can try **Giorgio's Trattoria** (219 Banff Ave. 762-5114) for Northern Italian pastas and pizzas, or **Guido's** (116 Banff Ave. above McDonald's, 762-4002) for American Italian food, such as spaghetti, lasagna and chicken parmigiana. **Ticino** (415 Banff Ave., 762-3848) specializes in dishes from the Italian part of Switzerland.

Coyotes Deli & Grill (206 Caribou St., 762-3963) serves breakfast, lunch and dinner at reasonable prices, with Southwestern, vegetarian and pasta dishes on the menu (also fresh-squeezed juices). **Grizzly House** (207 Banff Ave., 762-4055) specializes in fondue and steaks, both beef and wild game. **Earls** (229 Banff Ave. at Wolf Street, 762-4414) got rave reviews for moderately priced Canadian beef steak, fresh salmon, pasta and thin-crust pizza.

One of the most fun places to eat breakfast, lunch or an informal supper is **Joe Btfsplk's Diner** (221 Banff Ave. 762-5529). Set in a 1950s-style diner decor complete with jukebox and Elvis posters, this restaurant serves huge portions.

For gourmet coffees and light snacks, try **Evelyn's Coffee Bar** on Banff Avenue, **Banff Coffee Company** on Bear Street, or **Jump Start Coffee and Sandwich Place** on Buffalo Street near the post office.

Après-ski/nightlife

Après-ski is more quiet than rip-roaring in Banff, at least in our experience, but things really get going at night. Younger crowds probably will enjoy Banff nightspots, while older skiers might be happier at the Banff Springs Hotel's many bars and lounges. The Happy Bus shuttles skiers to night spots around Banff until midnight for $1, or you can walk between most lodging and town.

Aprés-ski, head to the bar at **The Mt. Royal Hotel.** Crowds also start to gather at **The Rose and Crown**, an English-style pub with draught ale, a pool table, darts and an occasional live band.

At night, **Bumper's Loft Lounge** has a casual crowd, with live entertainment and ski movies. **High Noon Saloon** has a pool table, cigars and Calgary's Big Rock ale on tap. **Wild Bill's** on Banff Avenue has Country & Western bands and a huge dance floor. **Barbary Coast** on Banff Avenue is billed as a sports bar, but the night we were there, it had a blues/soft rock band so excellent that we stopped our bar-hopping research. **Magpie & Stump** serves up great nachos and some of Banff's best après-ski. **Outabounds** on Banff Avenue (but the entrance is on Caribou Street), with DJ dancing and occasional live bands, attracts visitors in their 20s, as does **Silver City.**

In the Banff Springs Hotel, the **Rob Roy Room** has dining and dancing and the **Rundle Lounge** has quiet music for hotel guests. At the **Waldhaus** by the Banff Springs Golf Course, Happy Hans and Lauren, on accordion and trumpet, get everybody singing.

Other activities

Shopping: The Banff Springs Hotel has nearly 50 shops, many of which have unusual items, such as regional handicrafts. Our favorite in the hotel was The Canadian Pacific Store, with items that reflect the bygone elegance of luxury train travel.

In the townsite, shopping is almost an athletic activity, with hundreds of shops lining Banff Avenue and its side streets. Most shops are clustered in little malls where you can enter the store from the inside on crummy days, or from the outside in good weather. Worth a drop-in: The Hudson's Bay Company, a department store famed for its blankets and Canada's oldest company, founded in 1670; and Roots Canada, for fine leather-and-cloth backpacks and handbags, and casual clothing.

For non-kitschy Canadian souvenirs: Orca Canada or Great Northern Trading Company (clothing, jewelry, knickknacks), Rocks and Gems (for inexpensive jewelry made from native Western Canadian gemstones), Bear Country Shirts (where we found the nicest quality T-shirts and sweatshirts) or A Taste of the Rockies (for gifts such as smoked salmon, jams and honeys).

Banff has much to do. Winter sports are numerous with **skating** (at Banff High School or the Banff Springs Hotel), **snowshoeing** (check with sports shops), **dog sledding** (Mountain Mushers, 762-3647), **ice fishing** (Fishing Unlimited, 762-4936) and **sleigh rides** (Warner Guiding and Outfitting, 762-4551). Yamnuska (678-4164) offers introduction courses to **ice climbing** and **ski mountaineering.** One of the most famous **heli-skiing** companies, Canadian Mountain Holidays, is headquartered here (762-7100). You also can go **helicopter sightseeing** with Alpine Helicopters (678-4802) to view the magnificent mountain peaks. On a clear day, take the **Sulphur Mountain Gondola** (762-2523) for a beautiful vista of the Bow Valley. Adults $12, children $6.

Four **museums** of note: Banff Park Museum for the story of early tourism and wildlife management; Whyte Museum of the Canadian Rockies, for historic and contemporary art and historic homes; the Luxton Museum, for Plains Indians history and the Natural History Museum for local geology.

Getting there and getting around

By air: Calgary Airport is served by major airlines. Either Brewster Transportation (762-6700) or Laidlaw Transportation (762-9102) will get you from the airport to Banff.

By car: Banff is 85 miles west of Calgary on the Trans-Canada Highway, an hour-and-a-half drive. The Sunshine Village exit is five miles west of Banff; it's five more miles to the gondola base parking area. Banff Mount Norquay is on Norquay Road, one exit past the Banff townsite. Free shuttles pick up skiers at eleven Banff hotels and the bus depot.

Getting around: It is possible to ski Banff and Lake Louise without a rental car by using free shuttlebuses to the ski areas or Happy Bus ($1 a ride) within the town and region. (Taxis are available, too.) For exploring, it's best to have a car.

Telephone area code: 403

Lake Louise Ski Area

Banff Region, Canada

Summit elevation: 8,765 feet
Vertical drop: 3,365 feet
Base elevation: 5,400 feet

Address: P.O. Box 5, Lake Louise
Alberta, Canada T0L 1E0
☎ Area code: 403
Ski area phone: 522-3555
Snow report: 762-4766 (Banff)
ⓘ Toll-free reservations: (800) 258-7669
Fax: 522-2095
E-mail: vertical@skilouise.com
Internet: http://www.skilouise.com
Expert:★★★★
Advanced:★★★★
Intermediate:★★★★
Beginner:★★★★
Never-ever:★★★★

Number and types of lifts: 11–2 high-speed
quads, 1 quad, 2 triples,
3 doubles, 3 surface lifts
Skiable acreage: 4,200
Snowmaking: 40 percent
Uphill capacity: 15,499 per hour
Snowboarding: Yes, unlimited
Bed base: 2,500 within 10 minutes
Nearest lodging: About two miles away
Resort child care: Yes, 6 days and older
Adult ticket, per day: $46 (97/98 price)
Dining:★★★
Apres-ski/nightlife:★★
Other activities (including the Banff region):
★★★★★

Lake Louise, Canada's second largest ski area, has always been a world-class mountain with rather shabby, second-class facilities. But with the 1998 opening of a 36,000-square-foot Lodge of the Ten Peaks and a remodel of the original lodge, Lake Louise now has classy facilities to match its mountain. The lodge was built from 2,500 fir, pine and spruce logs, most of them thinned from the Ptarmigan slope to open glade skiing and riding. Its three-story stone fireplace is "ranch rock" from owner Charlie Locke's nearby cattle ranch. The lodge floor was made from recycled tires (very boot-friendly).

Mountain layout

Lake Louise has three distinct areas: the Front Face, the Back Bowls and the Larch Area. The Lake Louise trail map has an excellent synopsis of where different ability levels should head, so be sure to grab one.

◆◆ **Expert** ◆ **Advanced:** On the Front Face, advanced skiers can give the Men's Downhill or Ladies' Downhill trails a try to get an idea of what the big boys and girls ski when Lake Louise hosts World Cup races.

When you're ready to head for the Back Bowls, which is where this level skier or boarder will want to spend a lot of time, you can take Top of the World high-speed quad, or ride the Olympic Chair from the base to the Summit Platter.

About the Platter: first off, realize that it used to be a T-bar until they decided the steepness demanded concentration, not conversation, so it's one up at a time now. The terrain is nicely moguled, wide and above treeline—almost all black diamonds with a touch of blue.

Though experts will like all the Back Bowls, Paradise Bowl holds special attractions such as cornices, chutes and gladed areas. Just keep riding the Paradise Chair and you'll find them all. You'll find more glades under the Ptarmigan Chair, across the valley floor from the Larch Chair.

In the Larch area, there's great tree skiing directly under the lift between Larch and Bobcat runs. From the top of the Larch Chair, you'll see that some powder freaks have hiked up to the 8,900-foot summit to leave tracks down Elevator Shaft Chute, between two rock outcroppings. The chute is within the ski area boundaries.

For a more modest thrill in a less traveled area, exit left off Larch Chair, then stay right and high on a gladed traverse until you find a deep powder bowl under Elevator Shaft. Called Rock Garden, it's not labeled on the map but it's in bounds, a hidden playground of loops, swoops, moguls and Cadillac-sized rocks.

■ **Intermediate:** On the Front Face, don't miss Meadowlark, reached by the Eagle Chair, or Gully, reached from Top of the World. Intermediates can reach the Back Bowls via the Top of the World quad or the Summit Platter, which will take you a little higher on the back side to a run called Boomerang, an immensely fun cruiser that seems to go on forever. If the weather is socked in, however, skip Boomerang.

The Larch Area has the best intermediate skiing, as shown by the long lines at the only chair that serves it. However, the line moves fairly fast, and it's worth the wait. Wolverine, Larch and Bobcat are all long cruisers.

●● **Beginner:** Those with a little experience can ride the Friendly Giant quad chair and head down Wiwaxy, a 2.5-mile cruiser. Next step is Eagle Chair to try Deer Run and Eagle Meadows.

If you're getting pretty confident and would like to try the Back Bowls, ride the Eagle Chair and take Pika down the back. You also can descend from the Top of the World chair on Saddleback, but don't try Saddleback on a low-visibility day. There are no trees to guide you, and a couple of narrow spots you must negotiate. Beginners have a couple of nice runs in the Larch area, Marmot and Lookout.

● **Never-ever:** First-timers enrolled in lessons will start on the Sunny T-Bar.

Note: If you want sun all day and want to ski the whole area, go to the Back Bowls in the morning, ski Larch midday and end up on the Front Face. Take a free guided tour by Friends of Louise, a volunteer group, three times daily starting at Whiskyjack Lodge.

Mountain rating

A key factor in Louise's 60 years of skiing history is that skiers of all abilities have terrain suited to their skill level from all lifts except the Summit Platter. This makes it nice for groups of varying levels who want to ride together on the lifts.

Cross-country

Chateau Lake Louise (522-3511) has about 150 km. of groomed trails and access to hundreds of miles of backcountry trails, with stunning views of the lake and mountains. The ungroomed, well-marked trail to Skoki Lodge, a rustic log cabin (meaning no electricity, no plumbing, wood-burning stove), begins just above Temple Lodge at the ski area and heads up the valley and over Boulder Pass, seven miles one way. If you're not up for skiing so far into the wilderness, follow the gentle Shoreline Trail starting in front of Chateau Lake Louise, an easy mile and a half one way. Skiing *on* Lake Louise is not recommended.

A complex 20-km. network called **Pipestone Loops** starts four miles west of the Lake Louise Overpass on the Trans-Canada Highway. Although all are marked beginner, some are suitable for the intermediate.

About 25 miles from Lake Louise, just over the border into British Columbia, is **Emerald Lake Lodge** (343-6321 or 800-663-6336). It has a 40-km. network of groomed trails with views of the Presidential Range, lodging in comfortable cabins and activities such as skating, snowshoeing and a games room. The lodge has a shuttle to the Lake Louise ski area.

About half a dozen other trails in the area cover roughly 90 km. of groomed touring. Rental shops, especially the one in Chateau Lake Louise that also rents clothing, can furnish trail maps.

Before setting out on any of the trails, check trail conditions at a park warden's office. Be aware that trail classification is done by healthy Canadians in good shape.

Snowboarding

Yes, everywhere on the mountain. There's a boarding park off Wiwaxy, reached by the Olympic Chair. Snowboard rentals and lessons are available.

Lessons (97/98 prices in Cdn$)

Group lessons: $25 for 1.75 hours for skiers or snowboarders.
Never-ever package: $39 ($49 for snowboarders) includes a 1.75-hour lesson, equipment rental and beginner lift ticket. If you aren't getting the hang of it at the end of the lesson, you can take an afternoon lesson free. Arrive well before the lesson to pick up equipment.

 Private lessons: $65 per hour, reduced to $45 if taken after 3 p.m.; extra skiers, $15 each. Private snowboard lessons cost $55; $45 after 3 p.m.

Special programs: The Club Ski Program operates at Lake Louise, Sunshine Village and Banff Mount Norquay. Groups of similar interest and expertise ski together with the same instructor for four hours a day at each of the three areas, then dine at an optional closing-night dinner with prizes. The program starts Mondays and Thursdays, and one benefit is lift-line priority. The three-day program costs $144. Club Snowboard is similar, but costs $134.

Racing: Lake Louise has a dual-slalom NASTAR course on Wiwaxy, $1 per run.

Children's lessons: The Kinderski program, ages 3–4, provides supervised day care, one ski lesson and indoor and outdoor play at the beginning and end of day. Cost is $27, or $31 for two one-hour lessons. In the Kids Ski program, children aged 5–12 are guided around the mountain with instruction along the way for $28 for the morning or afternoon; $45 for full day. The program includes a lift ticket. Optional lunch is $5.

Child care (98/99 prices in Cdn$)

Ages: 6 days to 3 years. Toddlers have their own play area. Children ages 3–6 get a combination of day care and one to two hours of ski lessons.

Costs: The program includes a hot lunch. Babies' care (younger than 19 months) is $25 per day or $4 per hour. Toddler care (19 months–3 years) is $4 per hour. Day care for kids ages 3–6 is $3.50 per hour, with three-hour minimums.

Reservations: Infants younger than 19 months require reservations; reservations are recommended for other ages. Call 522-3555.

 ## Lift tickets (97/98 prices in Cdn$ including GST)

	Adult	Student/Senior
One day	$46	$36
Three days	$132 ($44/day)	$102 ($34/day)
Five days	$215 ($43/day)	$165 ($33/day)

Who skis free: Children younger than 6.

Who skis at a discount: In the chart above, students are ages 13–25 with student ID and seniors are 65 or older. Children pay $15 per day. Skiers interested in the Banff areas should buy the Tri-Area Pass (see the Banff chapter for details and prices).

 ## Accommodations (Prices Cdn$)

The **Chateau Lake Louise** (800-441-1414; 522-3511) nests on the shore of Lake Louise, with the spectacular Victoria Glacier in the distance. This hotel dates back to a log chalet built in 1890. Winter rates are a fraction of the summer prices: $125–$175 for most rooms, but the rates vary depending on occupancy. It has nearly 500 guest rooms, several restaurants, shops, Nordic ski center, masseuse, and free ski shuttles.

The **Post Hotel** (800-661-1586; 522-3989) is a cozy, beautifully furnished 93-room log lodge with great views on all sides and fireplaces in 38 of the rooms, two of which are lovely riverside cabins with heated slate floors. It's personal and quiet, with the warmth and elegance provided by Swiss innkeepers. The buffet breakfast is a board of tasty delights. Except for Christmas, rates are in the $145–$340 range. There is a free ski shuttle.

Lake Louise Inn (800-661-9237; 522-3791) is a moderately priced family hotel with a noisy bar; $77–$141; with kitchens, $143–$232.

Deer Lodge (800-661-1595; 522-3747) is the Chateau's antithesis, though they are located quite close to each other. Deer Lodge has no television, for example, but it has a great rooftop hot tub. It's old and rustic, but well kept up; $95–$210.

The **Canadian Alpine Centre & International Hostel** (522-2200), on Village Road, is a very modern facility with two-, four- and six-bed rooms with private bathrooms and showers, laundry, kitchen and cafe. Nightly bed rates start at $18.

Banff/Lake Louise Central Reservations (800-661-1676) is a central reservations service that books lodging in Banff, Lake Louise and Jasper. **Resorts of the Rockies** (800-258-7669) books ski packages and lodging for these Western Canada resorts: Lake Louise, Nakiska, Fortress, Wintergreen, Fernie and Kimberley.

Dining

On-mountain lunch options are: **The Powder Keg**, with nachos, sandwiches and pizza; **The Sitzmark**, with more substantial fare like burgers and salads; and the **Northface Dining Room**, with two luncheon buffets—soup and sandwiches for $8.50, and hot entrees for $11.95.

For dinner in the **Chateau** (call 522-3511 for all), the most elegant dining room is the **Edelweiss**, serving such entrées as salmon and duckling. The **Walliser Stube Wine Bar** serves Swiss cuisine such as raclette and fondue. **The Poppy Room** is a family restaurant, the only one open for breakfast in winter, aside from the 24-hour deli. **Glacier Saloon** has steak sandwiches, finger food and salads. It's a little dark, so ask for a seat near the windows.

   The Post Hotel (522-3989) is generally recognized as serving the finest Continental cuisine in Lake Louise. For a special occasion, this is a wonderful place.

   Deer Lodge (522-3747) has homemade breads, patés, fish, veal and beef dishes as well as innovative specials and pastries.

   Lake Louise Station (522-2600) is a restored railway station with views of the mountains and freight trains that rumble past. The menu is quite extensive, with pastas, lamb, Alberta steaks and fresh salmon, among other dishes. Couples might like a table in the Killarney car, which was the private railroad car of a Canadian Railroad president.

Après-ski/nightlife

The **Sitzmark Lounge** is the après-ski spot at the mountain. It's on the third floor of the Whiskyjack Lodge at the base area and has an open fireplace.

   Après-ski and nightlife center in the hotels. At the Chateau, **The Glacier Saloon** has a lively atmosphere and dancing, while the **Walliser Stube** is serene. Quiet conversation is possible at **The Saddleback Lounge** in the Lake Louise Inn and The Post Hotel's **Outpost**.

   On Saturday evenings, the **Brewster Cowboys Barbeque & Dance Barn** near the Chateau provides hearty cowboy food and Western entertainment from mid-December to early April. Tickets run about $32 for adults; less for kids. It includes a sleigh ride to the barn. On Mondays (and Fridays from February through April) is the **Lake Louise torchlight dinner and ski**. Be on the Friendly Giant Express to Whitehorn Lodge by 4 p.m. or you'll miss all the fun—après-ski appetizers, buffet, participatory entertainment, dancing and a guided torchlight ski down the mountain where buses take you back to Lake Louise lodging. Adults, $41.12, children, $18.70; beer and wine extra.

Other activities

The Banff/Lake Louise area has many opportunities for other winter sports such as skating, snowshoeing, tobogganing and fishing; see the Banff chapter for phone numbers.

Getting there and getting around

By air: See the Banff chapter for information.
By car: Lake Louise Village is 115 miles west of Calgary and 36 miles from Banff.

   Getting around: Bus service is available from the airport direct to most hotels. The Lake Louise shuttlebus is free and operates from most hotels to the base of the ski lifts. Buy the Tri-Area ski pass and your bus transportation is included. We recommend a car for extensive sightseeing.

Marmot Basin

Jasper, Alberta
Canada

Summit elevation: 7,940 feet
Vertical drop: 2,300 feet
Base elevation: 5,640 feet

Address: P.O. Box 1300
Jasper, AB, Canada T0E 1E0
✆ **Area code:** 403
Ski area phone: 852-3816
Snow report: 488-5909 (Edmonton)
Fax: 852-3533
ⓘ **Toll-free reservations:** no central
reservations system
E-mail: skimarmo@telusplanet.net
Internet: http://www.skimarmot.com
Expert:★★★★
Advanced:★★★★
Intermediate:★★★
Beginner:★★★ **Never-ever:**★★★

Number and types of lifts: 6–1 high-speed
quad, 1 triple chair, 3 double chairs,
2 surface lifts.
Skiable acreage: 1,000 acres
Snowmaking: 1 percent
Uphill capacity: 10,787 skiers per hour
Snowboarding: Yes, unlimited
Bed base: 5,500
Nearest lodging: About 11 miles away in
Jasper
Resort child care: Yes, 19 months and older
Adult ticket, per day: $39 (97/98 price)
Dining:★★★
Apres-ski/nightlife:★★★
Other activities:★★★

The largest of the Canadian Rockies National Parks, Jasper is studded with lakes, threaded by cross-country trails, and decorated with spectacular drives such as the Icefields Parkway. Overloaded with tourists in the summer, it's delightfully uncrowded in the winter.

Far into the northland and separated from the hustle of Banff by a three-hour drive, Jasper is far enough north, and far enough from a major airport (Edmonton: three hours) that people aren't here by mistake or on a whim. They come for the scenery, the remoteness, the wonder of a herd of elk outside their chalet and the call of Canadian geese swooping over Lac Beauvert in the spring while the ski area still has winter snow.

The townsite of Jasper sprang up from a tent city in 1911, when the Grand Trunk Pacific Railway was laying steel up the Athabasca River Valley toward Yellowhead Pass, and its growth was rather helter-skelter. Hugging the Athabasca River and nestled against the train station, the town is relatively nondescript, consisting of clapboard cottages, a steepled Lutheran church, stone houses and lodgings with no single architectural scheme.

Mountain layout

◆◆ **Expert** ◆ **Advanced:** Marmot has tree-lined runs toward the bottom and wide-open bowls at the top. Generally, the higher you go, the tougher the skiing gets.

There's excellent glade skiing off the Triple Chair and Kiefer T-bar, both of which serve Caribou Ridge. Below are mogul runs, negotiable by an intermediate when groomed (about once a week). Off to the right, facing downhill, advanced skiers have trees in a black area misnamed Milk Run.

By staying high to the right above Milk Run and Gun Sight, you can take Knob Chair, up another 900 vertical feet. From the top of that lift, hardy Canadians hike the last 600 feet up to Marmot Peak. It's all Alpine bowls up here. Experts will want to drop into the fine powder in outrageously large Dupres Bowl, with Dupres Chute dividing it from Charlie's Bowl, that's even steeper and stays untracked longer. It should be a double black. The most horrendous bump runs are just to the right of the Knob Chair—Knob Bowl and Knob Hill.

Stay high and even farther to the right (facing down the mountain) from The Knob. Experts have different playgrounds all to themselves—treeless Thunder Bowl or gladed Chalet Slope. Powder lasts the longest here—it takes three lifts to arrive.

■ **Intermediate:** Every lift has an intermediate way down, even The Knob. On blustery days, stay low on the mountain, where trees provide shelter from winds that sometimes block visibility on the naked summit.

●● **Beginner** ● **Never-ever:** The three lifts at the base serve most of the lower-level terrain. Beginners have expansive mountain access, with 1,100 vertical feet on Eagle Express after they master terrain from the Red T-bar. They can even head up to Caribou Ridge for an above-treeline thrill where a wide trail, Basin Run, takes them safely back to the lower slopes.

Note: Free Mountain Magic Tours at 10:30 a.m. and 1:30 p.m. leave from Lower Chalet.

The area's one high-speed quad, Eagle Express, serves as the primary chair to the upper-mountain lifts. It can get crowded sometimes; don't come back to the base during peak loading times, such as mornings before 9:30. Instead, try Caribou Chair on the lower mountain far to the right where there's rarely a wait. It has terrain for all abilities and also will get you to the upper-mountain lifts. You can reach it directly by driving past the main lodge and heading for the farthest parking lot.

Mountain rating

Skiers of different levels can ride the same lifts, a factor which makes Marmot good for group skiing. The terrain is evenly divided between ability levels.

Cross-country

This is prime ski touring country, and even if you've never tried it, the scenery is guaranteed to draw you into the sport.

Jasper Park Lodge trails, about 19 km., are unparalleled for beauty and variety—lake shores, Alpine meadows and forests. They're gentle, groomed and easily accessible. The easiest is Cavell, a 5 km. lope with the elk. The perimeter loop samples a little of everything the Jasper Park Lodge trails offer.

Near Jasper Townsite, a good beginner trail is **Whistlers Campground Loop,** 4.5 km., level and lit for night skiing. **Pyramid Bench Trail,** 4.7 km. rated intermediate overlooking the Athabasca River Valley. **Patricia Lake Circle,** 5.9 km. and rated intermediate (the recommendation is to follow the trail clockwise), provides stunning views of Mt. Edith Cavell, the region's most prominent and dramatically sloped peak. Most lodges have trail maps. For **guided tours,** contact Edge Control, 852-4945; Beyond the Beaten Path, 852-5650; Maligne Tours, 852-3370; or Alpine Art, 852-3709. Ask about rentals and/or instruction, too.

A full day's ski over Maccarib Pass from the Marmot Basin Road on the north shore of Amethyst Lake leads to Tonquin Valley Lodge and hearty home-cooked meals and welcome beds. Contact Tonquin Valley Ski Tours, Box 550, Jasper, Alberta T0L 1E0; 852-3909.

Snowboarding

Snowboarders have full access here. The New Ground Snowboard Cup is held in the spring and the area has a snowboard park. Lessons and rentals are available.

Lessons (98/99 prices in Cdn$ including GST)

Group lessons (age 13 and older): $25 for two hours ski or snowboard.
Never-ever package: Includes lift pass, lesson and equipment for $42 for ages 6 and older ($50 for snowboarding).
Private lessons: $45 an hour, $150 all day; additional skiers $18 each an hour.
Special programs (moguls, racing, powder): $25 per person with a minimum group of three. Ski Improvement Weeks include five two-hour sessions, Monday to Friday; video, a fun race and a Jasper Night Out. Cost for adults is $100; for children ages 6–12, $72.
Racing: The Diet Coke Star Series is a dual slalom course, electronically timed, where your time is compared with a pacesetter's to determine if you qualify for a gold, silver, bronze or participant medal. Cost for two runs is $4.
Children's lessons: $16 for a two-hour group lesson.

Child care (98/99 prices in Cdn$ including GST)

Ages: 19 months through 5 years.
Cost: $5 an hour, with supervision during the lunch hour, but lunch is an extra $5. All-day care is $24.
Reservations: 852-3816.

Lift tickets (98/99 prices in Cdn$ including GST)

	Adult	Junior (6-12)
One day	$42	$17
Three days	$122 ($40.66/day)	$51 ($17/day)
Five days	$202 ($40.40/day)	$85 ($17/day)

Who skis free: Children younger than 6.
Who skis at a discount: Youth/student prices (ages 13–25) ski for $33 for a full day, but college-age students must be full time and present a valid student ID. Seniors aged 65 and older ski for $29 per day.
During the Jasper in January festival, everyone 13 and older skis for $29 per day.

Accommodations

Jasper Tourism and Commerce, (Box 98, Jasper, Alberta, T0E 1E0; call 403-852-3858) will provide information on activities or send a ski vacation planner that includes rates. The region has no central reservations service.
Although **Jasper Park Lodge** (852-3301 or 800-441-1414) is one of the Canadian Pacific Hotels, it's not in the grand style of the Chateau Lake Louise and Banff Springs. Set on 1,000 acres, it's a grouping of traditional log cabins from the 1920s and new cedar chalets with spacious modern suites. (The older buildings have all been renovated and are thoroughly

modern in the areas that count, such as bathrooms.) The lodging buildings are linked by pathways along Lac Beauvert to the main building which is built like a hunting lodge and houses all the restaurants, night spots and shops.

The lodge suggests all the best qualities you remember from kids' summer camp, combined with the amenities you expect from a fine resort. Rates start under $100 before Christmas, and reach $315 for large suites during peak periods. Nordic and downhill ski packages are available. On the grounds, **Milligan Manor** is a restored eight-bedroom deluxe cabin overlooking the fairway and its resident elk herd.

Other lodging is in Jasper Townsite, and many room rates are Cdn$100 or less a night. **The Astoria** (852-3351; 800-661-7343) is a small hotel of character with elegantly renovated guest rooms. **Chateau Jasper** (852-5644; 800-661-9323) has indoor pool and whirlpool, dining room, cocktail lounge and heated underground parking. **The Athabasca Hotel** (852-3386; 800-563-9859) one of Jasper's original lodgings, is close to the bus and VIA RAIL station. **Marmot Lodge** (852-4471; 888-852-7737) has rooms with kitchens and fireplaces; indoor pool, sauna and whirlpool on the premises. No charge for children under age 12. **Pyramid Lake Resort** (852-4900) has skating and cross-country trails at your doorstep. Five miles from the townsite, it has a lovely view, private whirlpools, kitchenettes and fireplaces.

 ## Dining

At Jasper Park Lodge, the **Beauvert Dining Room** overlooks the Lac Beauvert, is expansive and seats 550, but the **Edith Cavell** is the flagship restaurant, with white-glove tableside service. French veal and shrimp in a pastry are specialties. For breakfast, **The Meadows** serves wholesome food in a country setting; service continues all day.

In town, **Tonquin Prime Rib Village** (852-4966) serves steaks, prime rib, barbecued ribs, seafood and Italian dishes. It has a bar and a beautiful view; make reservations. **Fiddle River Seafood Company** (852-3032) gets raves for creative fresh fish cooking. **Embers Steakhouse** (852-4471) serves light and healthy cuisine (beef, local fish) in a casually elegant restaurant. A lovely buffet brunch on Sunday can be had at the Chateau Jasper's **Beauvallon Dining Room** (852-5644). Make reservations.

Athabasca Restaurant (852-3386) in the Athabasca Hotel has been recommended for good hearty meals. **Miss Italia** (852-4002) is the spot for Italian cooking.

Mountain Foods Cafe (852-4050), a sit-down or take-out restaurant, has affordable prices for its deli items. Pizza is at **Jasper Pizza Place** (852-3225), Greek cuisine at **L&W Restaurant** (852-4114), Japanese entrées and sushi bar at **Tokyo Tom's** (852-3780).

For great breakfasts and other meals, try **Papa George's Restaurant** in the Astoria Hotel (852-3351) or **Coco's Cafe** (852-4550), with fresh baked goods and gourmet coffees.

On the slopes, Marmot Basin has two food service areas. Upstairs in the Lower Chalet, **Caribou Dining Lounge** features a hearty three-cheese pizza, sandwich bar and the local tradition, Marmot Basin Edible Soup Bowl—a delicious, hearty novelty. **Paradise Chalet**, midmountain, has cafe and lounge. On busy days, lunch before 11:45 or after 1:15.

 ## Après-ski/nightlife

Jasper is not known for rocking nightlife, but it's not dead, either. The **Atha-B Club** in Athabasca Hotel has the liveliest dancing in town. The hotel also has **O'Shea's**, an Irish pub. **Whistle Stop** at Whistlers Inn is a good pub-type night spot with darts, pool and big-screen sports; and **De'd Dog Sa-**

loon in the Astoria Hotel is a locals' hangout. **Fireside Lounge** in Marmot Lodge has nightly entertainment.

At Jasper Park Lodge, the **Emerald Lounge** has hearty après-ski snacks, and **Tent City Sports Lounge** recalls the history of the lodge and has lively entertainment.

Other activities

Heliskiing in Valemount, British Columbia, 56 miles away along a scenic drive, is available mid-February to mid-April. Contact Robson HeliMagic at 566-4700 for information.

Ice skating, snowshoeing and **sleigh rides** operate from Jasper Park Lodge. **Snowmobiling** is not allowed within the national park, but a company offers guided tours about 70 miles from the townsite; call 852-6052.

Sightseeing companies run bus tours to the more scenic vistas, including the Icefields Parkway, which has ragged peaks, frozen waterfalls and glaciers as attractions. Call Brewster Transportation, 852-3332 or Mountain Meadow Tours, 852-5595 for details. Plan to take one day to drive along the Icefields Parkway (Highway 93)—you won't be sorry.

Canyon Crawls are guided tours through Maligne Canyon where visitors walk (and crawl) 1.2 miles through a 6- to 20-foot-wide gorge on the frozen river past ice caves, frozen waterfalls, towering canyon walls and colors frozen into the ice. You should be in reasonable physical shape to crawl up some head-high waterfalls and squeeze through narrow spots. This is usually available from December through March. Call Maligne Tours at 852-3370; Beyond the Beaten Path, 852-5650; or Jasper Adventure Center at 852-5595. The tour is about $25 for adults, $13 for children. The Jasper Adventure Center conducts canyon tours at 7 p.m. (as well as daytime), where crawlers wear headlamps and can hear the wolves howl.

If you fly into Edmonton, tour the **West Edmonton Mall**. Part shopping center, part amusement park, it covers 48 city blocks, has more than 800 stores, and includes (among other attractions) an indoor amusement park with a triple-loop roller coaster called Mindbender, a dolphin show, and an indoor water park with enormous water slides and 85-degree temperatures. If you can swing the bucks, stay at the adjoining **Fantasyland Hotel,** where every floor is decorated in a theme such as Hollywood, Canadian Pacific Railway, Roman, Polynesian, and so forth. It's an experience.

Getting there and getting around

By air: Edmonton has the closest airport. Air Canada and Canadian Airlines have the most frequent flights from most North American cities, but U.S. carriers such as Delta, American, Alaska and Northwest also fly here. If you don't rent a car, Greyhound operates daily service from Edmonton and Vancouver; call 421-4211.

By car: From Edmonton, Jasper is 270 miles west on Highway 16. The ski area is 12 miles south of Jasper via Highway 93, 93A and Marmot Basin Road.

By train: VIA RAIL operates service to Jasper from Edmonton and Vancouver on its newly restored '50s-style art deco train, the Canadian. U.S. travel agents have more information.

Getting around: A car is best here. The ski area is a few miles from the town and lodging. Brewster Transportation operates the Banff-Jasper Ski Bus and the Marmot Basin Bus Service from Jasper; call 852-3332.

Red Mountain

British Columbia, Canada

Summit elevation: 6,800 feet
Vertical drop: 2,900 feet
Base elevation: 3,900 feet

Address: P.O. Box 670
Rossland, B.C., Canada V0G 1Y0
✆ **Area code:** 250
Ski area phone: 362-7384
Snow report: 362-5500
ⓘ **Toll-free information and reservations:**
(800) 663-0105 **Fax:** 362-5833
E-mail: redmtn@wkpowerlink.com
Internet: http://www.ski-red.com
Expert:★★★★
Advanced:★★★★
Intermediate:★★★ **Beginner:**★★
Never-ever:★

Number and types of lifts: 5–3 triple
chairs, 1 double chair, 1 T-bar
Acreage:1,800-plus
Snowmaking: None
Uphill capacity: 7,000 skiers per hour
Snowboarding: Yes, unlimited
Bed base: 300 rooms within 6 miles
Nearest lodging: slopeside, mountain inn
Resort child care: Yes, 18 months and older
Adult ticket, per day: $35-$40 (98/99 price)
Dining:★★★
Apres-ski/nightlife:★★
Other activities: ★★

The charming town of Rossland and its surrounding mountains were settled by gold miners in 1897. Today it still has a gold mine feel thanks to an unpretentious, friendly ski resort called Red Mountain. This resort epitomizes how skiing used to be—inexpensive, with friendly locals, low-frills and a pure adrenaline rush from top to bottom.

Nancy Greene trained on Red, and won Olympic gold in 1968. Kerrin Lee-Gartner, also from Rossland, did the same in 1992. In fact, Red Mountain has contributed more skiers (27) to Olympic and World Cup competition than any other mountain in North America.

Until 1989, the mountain was owned and operated by a community ski club. Its casualness is appealing. Even today, maps don't show boundaries. This is the kind of place you come to if you want to ski or board all day long, have something to eat, washed down by a cold beer, flop into bed at night, then do it all again the next day.

Mountain layout

◆◆ **Expert** ◆ **Advanced:** Red Mountain consists of two distinct mountains, Red and Granite. Red is reached by a fast yet somewhat outdated double chair that carries you to advanced intermediate and expert terrain.

A sign at the bottom of the lift warns skiers that there are absolutely no beginner runs serviced by the Red Mountain chair.

If your ability level can handle Red's terrain, you will be rewarded with steep pitches on Upper War Eagle, The Cliff, Stilhang and the precipitous run on the Face Of Red, 1,420 feet of leg-burning, black-diamond vertical.

Tree skiing is a big draw here. No point in choosing a favorite run through the woods, because you may never find it again—skiers who have worked here for years still find new routes. Skiers are advised to double up in the woods. A free Snow Host service is available to newcomers, and it's smart to take the tour.

Red's sister peak, Granite, also has a lot to offer the upper-end skier or boarder, such as tree skiing, chutes, glades, steeps and cliff bands. The Orchards, Chutes of Pale Face, Cambodia, Needles and the Slides are just some of the runs where experts will shine and advanced skiers may be humbled. Bump enthusiasts can test their skills on Sluice and Centre Star, while powder hounds will find secret stashes in Papoose Bowl, Sara's Chute and Beer Belly.

■ **Intermediate:** On Granite, try the Paradise Triple chair. Nicely groomed runs here are hemmed in by sweet-smelling Dutch elm trees. On Red, the T-bar serves gentler terrain. (This is also where you'll find the snowboard park.)

● **Beginner:** On Red, Dale's Trail winds gently around like a logging road, and Little Red Run is served by the T-bar. On Granite, South Side Road winds from the Paradise side to the base. Long Squaw/Easy Street run is five miles long and rated green. Some say you're a beginner when you start on this trail and an intermediate by the time you finish. The beautifully cut Silver Sheep run is another option.

● ● **Never-ever:** Red Mountain has some new slopes for the lower-ability levels; nevertheless unless you are extremely athletic, we recommend you try another resort for your virgin ski or snowboard experience.

Mountain rating

Red Mountain is exceptional for advanced intermediate to expert skiers. Trees and rock ledges make it a snowboarder's dream. Lower intermediates and beginners may be discouraged by the lack of gentle slopes.

Cross-country

Blackjack Cross Country Ski Club across the road, has 55 km. of trails, both double-tracked and skating. Trails wind past hemlock stands, frozen beaver ponds and abandoned orchards.

Free cross-country skiing on tracks set after every snowfall is available 25 km. north of Rossland (on Hwy. 3B) in the **Nancy Greene Provincial Park.** Trails are maintained by the Castlegar Nordic Ski Club.

A one-use-only lift ticket gives access to 30 square miles of backcountry skiing on **Granite Mountain.** Check first with the ski patrol for snow conditions.

Snowboarding

The woods here appeal to freeriders. Beginners should stay on the open slopes or practice off the T-bar. There is a snowboard park with quarter- and half-pipes and jumps. Le Rois Sport Shop rents equipment.

Lessons (98/99 prices in Cdn$ including GST)

Group lessons: $25 for a two-hour session on skis or snowboard.
Never-ever package (lifts, lesson and rentals): For skiing, it's $40 a day for adults; $34 for ages 7–15. For snowboard lessons, $46 for ages 9–15 and $51 for ages 16 and older.

Private lessons: One hour, $45; $20 for each additional person. A personal guide is $55 for one or two skiers for 2.5 hours of guiding through expert terrain; additional skiers cost $10 apiece. Participants must be age 16 or older and experts.

Special programs: Women's Day is every Wednesday with a two-hour lesson, discounted lift tickets and an après-ski party. The ski school also conducts weekly ski and snowboard camps.

Racing: No public racing.

Children's lessons: Ages 3 1/2–6. A two-hour lesson with hot cocoa break is $30; an all-day program with lessons and day care is $42 per day (lunch $3 extra). Reservations for the full-day program are required.

Child care (98/99 prices in Cdn$ inlcuding GST)

Ages: 18 months to 6 years.

Costs: $4 per hour, $2.50 for each additional child; most children bring a lunch.

Reservations: Not required, but appreciated. Call 362-7114. The child-care center also can provide a list of babysitters.

Lift tickets (98/99 prices in Cdn$ including GST)

	Adult	Child (7-12)
One day	$40	$21
Three days	$102 ($34/day)	$51 ($17/day)
Five days	$175 ($35/day)	$88 ($17.60/day)

Who skis free: Children ages 6 and younger and seniors ages 75 and older.

Who skis at a discount: Skiers age 65–74 pay $21. Students aged 13–18 ski for $33 a day, $88 for three days and $148 for five days. A beginner-lifts-only ticket is $10 (for T-bar and Silverload lifts).

Note: The five-day price we list is for a book of five transferable tickets that need not be used on consecutive days.

Accommodations

Red Mountain Central Reservations can book all travel, lodging and ski packages. Its toll-free number is (800) 663-0105, or call (250) 362-7700 if you are calling from another continent and can't access the toll-free number. We list a few choices, but there are others. Prices at Red Mountain are very reasonable, generally less than $100 per night, though the Ram's Head is a little more expensive.

The **Ram's Head Inn** (362-9577) has ski-in/walk-out access. This comfortable country inn is No Smoking with 13 units, hot tub, sauna, bountiful breakfast, recreation and ski wax room in a cozy setting.

The **Red Shutter Inn** (362-5131) has ski-in/ski-out access. **Red Mountain Cabins & Motel** have cabins equipped with small kitchenettes. The 67-room **Uplander Hotel** (362-7375) in Rossland sets the standards for lodging and dining.

Dining

Rossland's main street is Columbia Avenue. Here you find the friendliest staff and terrific food at the **Sunshine Cafe** (362-7630), a local favorite.

A special date deserves an elegant meal at the Uplander Hotel's **Louis Blues Restaurant** (362-7375), with excellent wine list, specials and decadent desserts.

The corner of Washington and 2nd Avenue harbors three eclectic restaurants—**Mountain Gypsy Cafe** (362-3342) for moderately priced pizzas and calzones; **Elmer's Corner Cafe**, a funky spot for vegetarian food and fresh baguettes; and **Flying Steamshovel** (362-7323), a fun and lively neighborhood pub with great views.

Après-ski/nightlife

For immediate après-ski, head to the **Rafter's Lounge** upstairs in the base lodge. By 5 p.m., the action has headed to Rossland. The Uplander Hotel's **Powder Keg Pub** has terrific jazz every Wednesday and Saturday evening. The **Flying Steamshovel** is another gathering spot, but the action is mostly where you and your friends get together.

The biggest party of the year is the **Winter Carnival** for three days near the end of January with a snow sculpture contest, dances and other festivities. Call 362-5399.

Other activities

Shopping: Rossland has a small collection of unusual shops, such as Tree House Gallery, GoldRush Books and Espresso and Feather Your Nest.

The Rossland Arena has **hockey games, curling matches** and public ice skating. **Paragliding** in tandem with a pro patroller is offered off the top of Red ($60).

Getting there and getting around

By air: The airport in Castlegar, 20 miles north, is served by Air B.C. or Time Air from Vancouver, Edmonton and Calgary. Hotel pickup and rental cars are available, or call Castlegar Taxi, 365-7222. The nearest airport with U.S.-carrier service is Spokane, 125 miles south.

By car: Red Mountain is ten miles from the Canada-U.S. border on Hwy. 3B. From Spokane, take Hwys. 395 and 25 north to Rossland.

Getting around: We recommend a car for off-slope exploring.

Tremblant

Québec, Canada

Summit elevation: 3,001 feet
Vertical drop: 2,131 feet
Base elevation: 870 feet

Address: 3005, Chemin Principal
Mont-Tremblant, Quebec, Canada J0T 1Z0
☎ **Area code:** 819
Ski area phone: 681-2000
Snow report: (514) 333-8936 (Montreal)
ⓘ **Toll-free information and reservations:**
(800) 461-8711 or (819) 681-2000
Fax: (819) 681-5990
E-mail: mtr@tremblant.com (reservations)
Internet: http://www.tremblant.ca (ski area) or
http://www.tremblant.com (reservations)
Expert:★★★ **Advanced:**★★★★
Intermediate:★★★★ **Beginner:**★★★★
Never-ever:★★★

Number and types of lifts: 11–1 six-person
gondola, 5 high-speed quads, 1 quad, 3 triples,
1 surface lift
Acreage: 502
Snowmaking: 80 percent
Uphill capacity: 22,750 skiers per hour
Snowboarding: Yes, unlimited
Bed base: 3,000-plus at resort base
Nearest lodging: slopeside, hotel & condos
Resort child care: Yes, 12 months and older
Adult ticket, per day: $48–$52 (98/99)

Dining:★★★★
Apres-ski/nightlife:★★★
Other activities: ★★★

Tremblant is one of the historic peaks in North American skiing. It began in the 1930s—in 1932, if you count Tremblant's founding from its inaugural Kandahar downhill ski race; or in 1938, the hectic year that Philadelphia businessman Joe Ryan hiked to the top of Mont Tremblant, purchased it, and opened North America's second true winter resort (Sun Valley was the first, two years earlier). Tremblant virtually invented the ski week concept—lessons, lodging and parties all packaged as one fun vacation—and a nearby ski area, Gray Rocks, helps to keep the concept alive and kicking today.

In its early days, Mont Tremblant (as the resort was then known; resort management recently dropped the "Mont") was an attraction for East Coast socialites. But in recent decades, Tremblant was simply a ski mountain. Folk would come from Montreal and Ontario for a day or two of skiing and then head home. Several years ago the mountain was purchased by Intrawest and the area underwent a complete makeover with the addition of modern high-speed lifts, state-of-the-art snowmaking, new trails and mountain facilities. But what returned Tremblant to its former standing as a *resort*, not just a ski area, was the development of a mountain village based on the narrow streets, old buildings, cozy restaurants and quaint shops of Old Quebec. It was designed and built by Intrawest Corporation, a Canadian company that specializes in developing ski-resort base villages. The change is phenomenal to anyone visiting Tremblant after an absence of a few years.

Tremblant's new center is a collection of condominiums, restaurants and shops built in the old Quebec style. A Canadian Pacific "snow castle" hotel rises at the top of the resort and a Marriott Residence Inn dominates the lower end of the base village. Between these two hotels is a series of interconnected condominiums with underground parking, providing convenient accommodations for vacationers at most price and all comfort levels. The "Cabriolet," a stand-up, six-person gondola, takes skiers and boarders from the lower levels of the village and the public parking areas to the base of the main lifts, plus it serves the novice learning slope. You will find everything you need right at the base area, but don't stop there. The complete resort experience includes the old village of Mont Tremblant and the picturesque town of St. Jovite.

This experience also includes the Québecois culture and the French language. Though the employees speak English, the native language here is French, and you will earn big smiles from locals if you give it a try. For many skiers and boarders, Québec is green-circle foreign travel—you get all the fun and excitement of trying out a foreign language with none of the frustration of not being understood. Plus, there's little or no jet lag for North Americans (depending on if you come from the West or East Coast).

Note: In its marketing materials, Tremblant lists most of its prices—lift tickets, lessons, lodging and the like—without taxes added. We have done the math for the lift ticket section, but in most other sections, you'll need to calculate the 7 percent federal Goods and Services Tax (GST) *and* the 6.5 percent Québec provincial tax.

 ## Mountain layout

Tremblant is a hulk of a mountain with extensive skiing on two sides. The trail map proclaims "north" and "south" sides, but these sides would be more accurately portrayed with designations "east" and "west." Using those designations makes it easy for skiers to follow the sun—simply ski on the "north side" in the mornings to catch the rising sun and the move to the "south side" for the afternoons.

Most skiers and boarders start from the south side where the base village is. However, on crowded days many savvy locals make the 25-minute drive to the parking lot on the north side of the mountain where they can avoid the crowds and get the first crack at skiing in the morning sun.

◆◆ **Expert:** The most challenging sections of the mountain are in the sector called The Edge that is off to the far skier's right looking uphill on the North Side. It is reached by the Letendre trail that starts halfway down the North Side and brings skiers to the base of the Edge fixed-quad chair. This chair rises over 1,000 vertical feet and serves only expert and advanced terrain. Only one trail, Action, is cut; the other descents are through the trees. This gladed skiing in Reaction and Sensation is cut wide enough for strong intermediates, but the glades dropping to the right down Emotion will push experts to their limits. Also on the North Side are Tremblant's major bump runs and super steeps. If you want to drop down steep bumps try Dynamite, the steepest; and Expo, beneath the lift and wide enough for big wipeouts. The drop down Devil's River and into the woods at Boiling Kettle is also a rush.

◆ **Advanced:** For the most part, the single blacks are excellent choices for advanced skiers and boarders, especially those who are just moving up a category from intermediate. However, we found quite a range among Tremblant's single-black diamond trails—some a challenge worthy of the rating, such as Banzai and Le Tunnel; others that could have been rated blue-square cruisers, such as Géant; and at least one black-diamond, Dernier cri, that we thought barely deserved a blue rating, at least the day we skied it.

Double-blacks deserve their rating, and if you're relying on the trail map to guide you, beware: Tremblant uses an overlapping double-black-diamond symbol that doesn't look that much different than the single black symbol. It looks more like a fat single diamond, or as if the printer didn't quite get things lined up on the second run through the press. Anyway, if you aren't careful, you may end up on something above your ability.

Among the tougher descents on the South Side are the steep drops off the catwalk down Vertige (a double diamond) and Dunzee. These harrowing steeps and bumps are easily avoided, if you prefer. To the skier's left (trail-map right), Ryan is one of the mountain's original trails, narrow and twisting down the mountain with short, very manageable stretches of steeps that earn its lower section a double diamond on the trail map. It's nothing compared to Dynamite—consider it a narrow advanced cruiser. But if you think Ryan is challenging at the top, you can bail out on blue-square Charron before you get to the narrow part.

On the North Side, the tougher blacks are down the middle, and the easier blacks are to skier's right (trail-map left), Géant and Duncan.

■ **Intermediate:** On the South Side, Grand Prix, Beauvallon and Alpine are great wide-open cruising runs. If intermediates hang to the skier's right side of the mountain they will have a cruising blast. The Curé Deslauriers trail, toward the lower part of the mountain, has been contoured to form snow waves—it's a blast, kind of a skier's terrain park. Kandahar, though rated black, is groomed. It has one fairly steep section, but is a good choice for an upper-intermediate skier or boarder. At the end of the day, Johannsen—a short blue stretch at the base—gets moguled and/or mushy, depending on temperatures. To avoid blowing out your knees, head directly across the top of Johannsen and scoot down green-circle Roy Scott.

The North Side appears tough on the trail map, but in reality is more intermediate than advanced. Stick to the far right or far left and you can't go wrong. Géant, Coyote, and Duncan Haut are all fine for confident intermediates, and in some respects, are better than Beauchemin and Lowell Thomas, which are rated blue and get a lot more traffic.

●● **Beginner:** Though the North Side has a couple of acceptable beginner runs, skiers and boarders at this level will have a scary experience getting to them via the ski route over the summit. Therefore, just about all will stick to the South Side. From the top of the Flying Mile lift, beginners head left to La Passe and Nansen bas or they can head right down Standard and Bière-en-bas (named after a shortcut secretly bushwacked by a racer when the mountain staff would race down the mountain at the end of the day for beers—first man down got to drink for free). Finally, beginners can make the big step to the top of the mountain and make wedge turns and stem-christies down La Crête and all of Nansen. All in all this is a fantastic area to start, but stick to Nansen or Roy Scott at the end of the day to avoid the crowds.

● **Never-ever:** Novices start at the rope tow near the bell (the ski school meeting place). The Onésime run served by the Cabriolet lift is very gentle and out of the main traffic pattern most of the day, though it's a mushy mess by late March. After never-evers master the terrain served by the rope tow, they advance to the short Escargot triple chair.

Mountain rating

Tremblant is good for experts, great for advanced and intermediate skiers (though we're still a bit puzzled over some of the trail ratings), very good for beginners and acceptable for never-evers. (Our visit was in late spring, so our judgment of the never-ever terrain was a bit skewed by the fact it was the consistency of Malt-O-Meal.)

The weather and snow conditions couldn't have been nicer during our spring visit; however, we heard many stories of days when the mercury drops well below zero (and that's Fahrenheit we're talking about). Bring warm clothes.

Nearby skiing

Gray Rocks is a mouse compared to Tremblant—it has 620 feet of vertical and four chair lifts. When you stand at Tremblant's summit, you can see Gray Rocks' 22 compact runs a few miles in the distance. It may look small, but Gray Rocks is a mouse that roars. Good trail planning and maintenance makes Gray Rocks ski like a much bigger mountain. Trails wrap around the mountain, rather than plunge straight down, and they incorporate the natural features of the terrain.

This is one of the best learning mountains in North America, and Gray Rocks has capitalized on that strength by carving out a big slice of the student skier market. The success of its Learn-to-Ski Week is overwhelming, with thousands of North Americans taking lessons every season. Lessons are not only for timid never-evers. Skiers of every level are faced with a challenging week of perfecting technique. Ski Weeks have been offered since 1951 and include everything—lodging, meals, instruction, video analysis, lift tickets, access to Le Spa fitness center and indoor pool, gratuities, a souvenir pin and photo, and full social calendar and activities.

Part of the success is creating group camaraderie, on and off the slopes. Since people learn best when they are relaxed and having fun, Gray Rocks considers its off-slope program as important as the lessons on the hill. Nightly entertainment, *oui*. But après-ski also has such creative alternatives as a cooking course, French lessons, wine-and-cheese get-togethers, classical guitar concerts, sleigh rides, a spa and fitness center—the list goes on. Gray Rocks has a day care and "Ski'N'Play" program for children, and even has a pet kennel.

Gray Rocks also offers an all-inclusive "ski getaway" (room, meals, entertainment, gratuities, skiing, fitness center), with the option to add lessons and clinics.

The best deal here is a package, in which lift tickets valid at Gray Rocks and its sister resort, Mont Blanc, are included (call 800-567-6767 for reservations, or check the website at http://www.grayrocks.com). Ski Week prices range from $1,030 to $1,620 (Cdn$; 98/99 prices) per person double occupancy, depending on the time of year. (Single occupancy is available for $1,180–$1,690.) Weekend and "vacation" (non-skiing) packages also are available.

Cross-country

Canadians have serious winters so they definitely take all of their winter sports seriously. Case in point: the abundant and varied cross-country choices available to visitors to the Tremblant region. If you can tear yourself away from the downhill slopes, a day or more on the cross-country trails here will give you a true flavor of the region.

More than 140 km. of cross-country trails are scattered through the region, most of which are found in **Parc du Mont-Tremblant** (688-2281 or e-mail, meftremblant@cil.qc.ca). A ski pass is $15 at Parc du Mont Tremblant. Trails wind through maple and birch forests and provide views of wildlife and lakes.

A coalition of land- and business-owners, the Centre de ski de fond Mont-Tremblant Saint-Jovite Inc. offers a network of 110 km. of trails, with 50 km. double-tracked and 12 km. skate groomed. The undulating trails are known for their magnificent vistas, but, alas for the novice skier, the majority of these vantage points are located on diamond and double-diamond trails.

There are two networks of marked, patrolled and groomed trails. The La Diable network has nine trails totalling 56 km. with six heated huts along the way. The La Pimbina network has seven trails, 30 km. all together, with two heated huts. Trail fees are $6 for adults, and $4 for children younger than 12, those ages 65 and older, and anyone in a group of 20 or more. Snowshoeing trail passes are $4. Skis and snowshoes are available for rent, and you can also arrange a trip on marked but ungroomed trails to backcountry bunkhouses.

Choose in-village, inn-to-inn trails in the Mont Tremblant/St. Jovite region, a wilderness trek in the nearby Parc du Mont-Tremblant or experience the longest linear park in North America, the 200-kilometer "Le P'tit Train du Nord," that runs from Saint-Jerome through Mont Tremblant to Mont-Laurier.

Popular choices for the average cross country skier, who will still get his or her share of magnificent views and occasional sightings of wildlife, include the winding Domaine St. Bernard, the Jack Rabbit and skiing on the Gray Rocks golf course. A portion of Le P'tit Train du Nord linear park is also incorporated into these trails.

To get away from all civilization, except for a few strategically located heated huts, head to the Parc de Mont-Tremblant and plan to make a day of it (or two days if winter camping and "an intense encounter with our Quebec winter," as they put it, appeals to you).

This vast nature reserve offers two reception centers, complete with ski and snowshoe rentals and 86 km of marked, and groomed trails. Pack a lunch and ski out to one of the heated huts — trail loops of varying degrees of difficulty and length may be chosen. If you're lucky, trail guides will stop by a hut to tell you more about the history and the wildlife of the region.

Snowboarding

"Le surf des neiges," which English speakers know as snowboarding, is welcome on all trails, and rentals and lessons are available. Tremblant has a snowboard park on the South Side. The area is groomed by the state-of-the-art Scorpion snowpark grooming machine.

Lessons (98/99 prices in Cdn$, taxes not included)

Group lessons: $36 for a morning 90-minute session; $32 for afternoon. **Never-ever package (lifts, lesson and rentals):** For Discover Skiing, it's $49; for Discover Snowboarding, it's $57.

Private lessons: One morning hour, $81; afternoons, $65.

Special programs: Ski Week is 14 hours of skiing or snowboarding with the same instructor for $175 for skiing and $200 for snowboarding.

All instruction private or group can be taken on normal skis, shaped skis, snowboard or snowblades.

Racing: The Chrono-Course is open every day.

Children's lessons: Ages 3–12 pay $65 for a full day, including lunch. Tremblant offers Kids Ski Weekends for $136 (7 hours over two days) and Ski Weeks (four days with lunch included) for $210 on skis or $235 on snowboard.

Child care (98/99 prices in Cdn$, taxes not included)

Ages: 12 months to 6 years.
Costs: $46 a day, including lunch. Day care, snowplay and ski programs for ages 3–6 are $61 and up. A 14-day program costs about $150.

Reservations: Call (888) ECOLE-SKI (326-5375). Or, check with the conciérge at your hotel or condo for babysitting services that come to your room.

The Kidz Club is at the base of the new gondola lift. It features a new beginner hill as well as a "Magic Carpet" to take children back to the top of the hill.

Lift tickets (98/99 prices in Cdn$ including taxes)

	Adult	Child (6-12)
One day	$52	$25
Three days	$150 ($50/day)	$69 ($23/day)
Five days	$240 ($48/day)	$105 ($21/day)

Who skis free: Children 5 and younger.
Who skis at a discount: Skiers 65 and older pay $39. Students aged 13–17 ski for $39.
Note: These are prices rounded to the nearest Canadian dollar. These prices include the 7 percent federal GST and the 7.5 percent provincial tax in this section; however, remember to add these taxes to prices in other sections.

Accommodations

(98/99 prices in Cdn$ without taxes, unless noted)

Mont Tremblant Reservations can book all lodging and has some good travel, lodging and ski packages. Its toll-free number is (800) 567-6760, or call 425-8681 if you are calling from another continent and can't access the toll-free number. (MTR's fax number, e-mail address and website also are listed in our stat box.) We list lodging choices in the base-area village, but there are less expensive alternatives nearby. Five-day fly-stay-and-ski packages from the East Coast, double occupancy, start at about $563 per person (U.S. funds, 97/98 prices) from Boston and around $728 from Florida. The least expensive times are early December and after the first week in April, but you also can get some deals from January to mid-February and again in late March.

The lodging-lift package prices we list with each hotel or condo are five-day, per-person, based on double occupancy and do not include taxes. (Two- and three-day packages also are available.) We list a range, based on season and size of unit, from the smallest unit in value-plus season (early December and mid-April) to the largest unit at holiday season (Christmas-New Year).

Staying in the base village is the way to go. At the upper end of the village, the full-service Canadian Pacific hotel, **Chateau Mont Tremblant** (800-441-1414 or 681-7000), has ski-in/walk-out access, conference facilities, shops, restaurants, the works. Quite popular, too. We were unable to tour any of the 316 rooms on our visit last year because the hotel was booked solid, we were told. If the rooms are as nice as the common facilities and if they live up to the Canadian Pacific standard (good bet on both), we can assume you'll be quite comfortable. Packages range from $354 to $743.

The **Marriott Residence Inn, Manoir Labelle** (888-272-4000 or 681-4000) is at the lower end of the village, near Vieux Tremblant (see Dining chapter for more on that). Built in

1995, it has 127 units ranging from studios to two-bedroom penthouses, indoor parking, laundry facilities, a concierge and a complimentary "deluxe" continental breakfast, among other amenities. Packages including five nights and six days of skiing cost $309 to $717.

The **Kandahar Resort Hotel** has rooms, suites, one- and two-bedrooms units. Packages including five nights lodging and six days of skiing cost $239 to $818.

Lining the cobblestoned street that leads from the Chateau to the Marriott are three- to four-story buildings that house restaurants and shops on the ground floor and condominiums above. The **Saint Bernard, Johannsen** and **Deslauriers** condos (800-461-8711) are very roomy and beautifully furnished. It's great fun to peek out of the windows (some units have small balconies) at the activity on the street below. If you're worried about nightclub noise, don't. The village planners concentrated those in Vieux Tremblant, a mini-village of cottages between the Marriott and the condos. Packages range from $239 to $818.

Other condo complexes are within two miles and have shuttle service to the slopes. **Pinoteau Village** (800-667-2200) and **Condotels du Village** (800-567-6724) have kitchens, balconies and fireplaces. Pinoteau Village has cross-country trails outside its doors, while the Condotels have a clubhouse with a sauna, hot tub, small exercise room and pool table. Package prices at the Condotels range from $229 to $499; at the Pinoteau, $465-$1,015 (this is based on three people in a one-bedroom condo).

Mont Tremblant Reservations also can book the **Club Tremblant** (800-567-8341), where rates include breakfast and dinner, as well as lodging and lifts; **Gray Rocks** (800-567-6767), which has its own small ski area and specializes in the all-inclusive, heavy-on-socializing Ski Week; the luxurious **Intrawest Resort Club** (800-799-3258) or several condos, cozy inns, inexpensive motels and historic lodges in the villages of Mont Tremblant and St. Jovite.

New in 98/99: Hotel packages at the resort include a *passeport* in the value season. This will include four hours of snow toy trials, one ovbernight ski tuneup, 90 minutes of ski tips with an instructor and free Kidz Club for children ages 6 and younger. Advanced reservations are required.

 ## Dining

Tremblant Village consists of a narrow, somewhat steep, cobblestoned pedestrian street lined with three- to four-story buildings that have shops and restaurants on the ground floor and lodging above. At the top of the street is a large plaza called Place St. Bernard, which is ringed by another multi-story, lodging-and-shops building. In back of that is the Chateau Mont Tremblant.

At the other end of the street is Le Vieux Tremblant, a mini-village of cottages that include some of the original buildings constructed at Tremblant in the 1930s. These cottages house many of the villages' restaurants and most of its bars. Farther down the street is the Marriott and Kandahar hotels, and the base of the Cabriolet lift, which takes passengers to the top of the village near Place St. Bernard.

Packing tip: Bring shoes with good traction. The cobblestone street is fairly steep. Though it has shallow steps built along each side, most people walk in the street (no vehicles are allowed). It can be slippery late at night and early in the morning when melted snow has frozen again.

Most of the restaurants have moderately priced food, and you can have lunch-type foods for supper, if you like. At the foot of the Mont Tremblant Express High Speed Quad in the pedestrian village, there are a number of outdoor BBQ venues. At their daily outside grills you can get a hot dog with chips, hamburgers or grilled chicken for less than $5. Most restaurants on the Place St. Bernard have an outdoor grill blazing on a sunny day with additional snacks and soft drinks.

When the sun is shining, you can also enjoy live bands performing in the Place St. Bernard. Other light meals are available nearly around the clock.

Near the Place St. Bernard: Inside the **Cafe Johannsen at Mt. Tremblant** you can get self-serve soups, bagels, salads, beers, coffee and muffins. **Les Delices du St. Bernard** (681-4555) is a European-style deli offering a variety of cheeses, patés and cold cuts, sandwiches, freshly baked breads and other deli dishes. Great picnic supplies. There's a liquor store right next door.

For the best coffee in town, visit **Au Grain de Café** (681-4567), which also serves European pastries. It's a bit out of the way, but not far off the plaza.

The atmosphere at **Mexicali Rosa's** (681-2439) is cozy-ethnic, but the food is fair, especially for those who live in the Southwest. The restaurant's big draw is its location for outdoor sunshine dining right on the plaza.

Le Shack Resto-bar (681-4700) serves a daily breakfast buffet and is *the* spot for people-watching during lunch or an after-ski beer or two. It is best known for nightlife, but more about that later.

In Vieux-Tremblant: **Cafe Bistro Ryan** (681-4994) is the place to go when you get the late-night munchies, because it's open from 7 a.m. to 4 a.m! It's a rather scruffy spot but the menu offers breakfast, sandwiches (hot and cold), salads, soups, quiches, desserts, coffees with spirits as well as a menu of non-alcoholic beverages. At **TremBagel** (681-4456) you can get real Montréal-style bagels with a variety of spreads and fillings. The bakers use a 300-year-old recipe and make everything from scratch. This style bagel is flavored and the texture is achieved by putting honey in the boiling water and baking the batch in a wood-fired oven. It is not as chewy, but sweeter than New York bagels.

The three owners of **Creperie Catherine** (681-4888) used to cook aboard ships. Now, they offer Bretonne-style crepes with any kind of filling you could possibly dream up in a delightful indoor/outdoor building. This style of crepe is made from a thin batter similar to pancake batter but without baking powder. Batter is spread on an 18-inch hot plate for less than a minute, then flipped, browned and folded in quarters. Next come the ingredients—from smoked salmon to asparagus, escargot to ice cream, chocolate and maple syrup. It's a great stop for breakfast and desserts. The Chocolate Blast is a favorite sweet crepe.

Microbrasserie La Diable (681-4546), or "Microbrewery of the She-devil," serves light meals of European sausages alongside their six unique craft beers, brewed right on the premises. Be sure to note alcohol percentages listed on the menu as well and order accordingly. Don't mistake a 4 percent Diable for an 8.5 percent Extreme Onction!

La Savoie (681-4573) serves traditional French Alps fare in a cozy French Alpine setting. Everything on their menu is "all-you-can-eat" and prices are per person. Specialties include savoy cheese raclette—heated and scraped cheese with cold meats, salad, potatoes and pickles; fondues served with a variety of meat, seafood, vegetables and breads; and *pierrades,* or hot-stone grilling, with choices of beef, duck, chicken and seafood. You cannot get a hamburger and fries here! Strictly for an elegant yet relaxed lunch and dinner. The communal dining experience is great for larger parties.

The **Pizzatéria** (681-4522) has such enticing garlicky, spicy flavors floating from their doors, you'd be hard-pressed not to stop in. As the name suggests, their speciality is pizza with every topping imaginable. You can order to take out or be seen on their strategically placed outdoor deck, perfect people-watching territory.

More drop-dead pastries grace the cases at **La Chouquetterie** (681-4508), which translates as sugar tree. Their specialty is the cream puff, Tropez style. The shop is immaculate and offers morsels which look as though they were made by artists. One can hardly bring one's self to bite into such beautiful works of art. It has freshly baked breads as well.

Queues de Castor (681-4678), also known as Beavertails, is a tiny take-out spot just a few doors down from the plaza on the Le Deslauriers side. Through the walk-up window that opens onto the street you can order the traditional Canadian pastry called a Beavertail (because that's what it looks like). It's an oblong flat piece of fried dough topped with sweets. This has been so popular the owners have graduated to adding tomato sauce, cheese and meats to make Beavertail pizza.

The **Coco Pazzo Deli** (681-4774) is an Italian gourmet deli that sells cheeses, salamis, prosciutto and many kinds of dry pastas. It's known for its three or four daily take-out specialties—different varieties of pasta combinations prepared by their restaraunt's owner-chef, Luigi Clementi. A dish called Gigi is most in demand—a blend of pasta, capicolli and mushrooms. It's around the corner from their restaurant, also called **Coco Pazzo**. A friendly waitstaff serves gourmet Italian fare in a light, airy, high-ceilinged room with a large fresco on one wall. An ambitious menu includes braised veal shank, baked French-cut rack of lamb, and an interesting variety of pastas, pizzas, salads and antipasti. *Snow Country* awarded the restaraunt one of the top ten new resort eateries in 1996. An elegant yet low-key dining experience.

Le Gascon (681-4606) serves traditional French-style bistro food. Sample offerings at their wine bar or sit outside on their corner terrace overlooking Lake Miroir.

 ## Après-ski/nightlife

We list these in order from the quieter, mellow spots to the noisy party places. Since many of the hot spots also are restaurants, see the Dining section for more information.

On sunny days, the best après-ski is in the **Place St. Bernard**, where a stage often is set up with a live band cranking out the tunes. People sit in chairs with a brew and enjoy the sun, listen to the music and watch everyone looking for their friends.

Microbrasserie La Diable has canned music, good sausages for late-night snacks and six beers brewed on the premises. A good place to have a conversation with friends or a quiet spot for couples. If you nurse your beer long enough, friends are sure to show up.

Le Shack is a bit louder and often has a live band on the weekends. Selected the "wildest après-ski" by *Ski Canada* in 1996, the dancing never stops. Shooters are served in the traditional Québec glass ski boot.

Cafe de l'Epoque in Vieux Tremblant sports strobe lights, loud live music (also CDs) and lots of bodies pressed together on the crowded rustic wood dance floor. OK at night, but a bit of a pit when exposed to daylight. No decor, but a great place to party after dinner. Animation, wild contests, pool and pizza bar.

P'tit Caribou is also in Vieux Tremblant and gets high ratings from *Ski Canada*. Great, live, loud music, bar-top dancing and a wild après-ski hot tub on the deck. The room is small and drab but the people and the noise create the party ambience.

Bizztrado, located in the old Inn which also has a kid center, is a teen bar, a dark, grungy, cavernous room with a painted fridge, video games, pool tables and all the other things teenagers consider cool.

424 • Tremblant — Canada

Other activities

Shopping: The village has about 25 shops. Some of the fanciest are in the Chateau Mont Tremblant. Several of our female staffers were doing independent research on the same trip, and all came up with the same favorite shop: **Galerie Soutana.** Most things in the stylish, comfortable shop look like museum pieces. The owners, Susan Solowey and Denis Wanamaker do all their own buying, mostly in the Southwestern United States, South America and Canadian interior and are extremely knowledgable about the aboriginal pieces they have gathered. Look for stunning native jewelry, leather boots and garments, carvings and other authentic art and crafts.

The village also has a two-screen **movie theater.** One screen shows a French film, the other a recent Hollywood release. Next door is a video shop, which supplies rentals for the many condos with VCRs. You also can take a **sleigh ride,** go **ice skating** on Lac Miroir, go for a **dogsled ride** or **snowmobile ride.** The Chateau Mont Tremblant has a **spa** with facials, manicures, massages and the like. More information is available from the Tremblant Resort Association, 681-3000, Ext. 6642 between 11 a.m. and 5 p.m.

A new **AquaClub,** billed as "A Lake in the Laurentians," includes an exercise room, spa, and a lake created to evoke the Laurentian outdoors complete with beach and waterfall.

If you visit between mid-February and April, when the maple sap is running, you can sample a bit of Québecois culture known as the **sugar shack (cabane à sucre).** These restaurants are open only for about five weeks a year (though some operate year-round now) and usually have been run by the same families for several generations. We sat at long tables and were served family-style a meal of ham, bacon, potato and an omelette-like dish. We poured maple syrup over everything (tasted great, but we're sure it had a bit to do with the music, singing, great company and a pre-meal dose of "caribou," a very strong Québecois liqueur served in a glass-ski-boot shot glass). If you're the adventurous type who likes to experience local culture, ask your concierge about it, or the Tourist Association of the Laurentians (514-436-8532) can provide a list.

Getting there and getting around

By air: Montréal has the nearest major airport, 75 miles away. Air Canada has many direct or non-stop flights from the United States.

By car: From Montréal, take autoroute 15 north to Sainte-Agathe, where the 15 merges with 117. Continue on autoroute 117 north past St. Jovite. About two kilometers (a little more than a mile) past the town, at the second flashing yellow light, turn right on Montée Ryan (there's a Sunoco gas station on the left). Follow signs to Tremblant.

Getting around: Most visitors arrive by car, so rent one if you fly into Montréal. We weren't too impressed with the ground transportation to the airport. And then to get some use from the car, we suggest side trips to Mont Tremblant Village and St. Jovite, or even some of the smaller ski areas in the surrounding area.

Whistler/Blackcomb

British Columbia, Canada

Whistler Resort Facts

Address: 4010 Whistler Way, Whistler, BC, Canada V0N 1B4
✆ **Area code:** 604 ⓘ **Toll-free reservations:** (800) 944-7853 (800-WHISTLER)
Fax: 932-7231 **Internet:** http://www.whistler-resort.com
Bed Base: 5,000+ **Nearest lodging:** slopeside, hotel, condos
Resort child care: Yes, 18 months and older **Snowboarding:** Yes, unlimited
Adult ticket, per day: $55-$61 (98/99 prices, including G.S.T. tax)
Dining:★★★★ **Apres-ski/nightlife:**★★★★★ **Other activities:**★★★★★

Whistler Mountain Facts

Ski area phone: 932-3434
Snow report: 932-4211
Base elevation: 2,140 feet
Summit elevation: 7,160 feet
Vertical drop: 5,020 feet
Number of lifts: 15–1 10-person gondola,
1 6-person gondola, 4 high-speed quads,
3 triples, 1 double, 5 surface lifts
Snowmaking: 4 percent
Skiable acreage: 3,657 acres
Uphill capacity: 23,495 per hour
Expert:★★★★★
Advanced:★★★★★
Intermediate:★★★★★
Beginner:★★★
Never-ever:★★★

Blackcomb Facts

Ski area phone: 932-3434
Snow report: 932-4211
Base elevation: 2,214 feet
Summit elevation: 7,494 feet
Vertical drop: 5,280 feet
Number of lifts: 17–1 eight-person gondola,
6 high-speed quads, 3 triples,
7 surface lifts
Snowmaking: 11 percent
Acreage: 3,414 skiable trail acres
Uphill capacity: 29,112 per hour
Expert:★★★★★
Advanced:★★★★★
Intermediate:★★★★★
Beginner:★★★
Never-ever:★★

Whistler/Blackcomb has emerged as one of the most popular resorts in North America; in most ski magazine surveys, it ranks Number One (or darn close). There are several reasons for this: two mountains with the largest vertical drop on the continent (over 5,000 feet for each), tremendous bowl skiing, runs that wind down the mountain seemingly forever—and to top it off, a marvelous three-village base area with lodging, restaurants and nightclubs, all within walking distance (cars are banned from Whistler Village center). Both mountains are now operated by Intrawest Corporation, which has operated Blackcomb Mountain for many years and developed the beautiful pedestrian village at its base. Finally, both mountains belong to the same family, and are now the one great resort that most tourists always thought they were.

Generally, Whistler (the name most folks use for this two-mountain resort) gets rave reviews, but two drawbacks that come up most often by word of mouth sound worse than they really are. One is Whistler's weather. Located somewhat close to the Pacific Ocean at a low base altitude just over 2,000 feet, Whistler can get heavy rain or dense fog at times. But, the weather at the bottom isn't always what's at the top—it may be raining in Whistler Village, but snowing (or even sunny) on the summit. Crystal-clear, sunny days happen frequently, especially later in the season, and on those days skiing conditions are just awesome. Skiers will sometimes cite horrendous lift lines (primarily at base areas early in the morning) as the other problem, but in reality the few lines that develop look longer than the actual wait, thanks to high-speed lifts at the five base areas.

Plenty of skiers and snowboarders adore Whistler/Blackcomb. This is one of the most international ski resorts, attracting skiers from Australia, Asia, Europe and Latin America as well as North Americans.

Whistler Village is European-style, built to house, feed and amuse tourists. Whistler has more than100 restaurants and bars, and more than 180 shops. More than 4,000 rooms are in condos, B&Bs, lodges and hotels, and more are being built.

There are now officially three designated villages in the valley: Whistler Village, Marketplace (formerly known as Whistler North) and Upper Village (the Blackcomb base). Town Plaza connects Whistler Village and Marketplace, and is lined with hotels, restaurants and shops. Each village is about a five-minute walk from the others.

New for 98/99: Lots of improvements at Whistler Mountain, some of which are an express lift to the Peak, plus some tamer ways down from there; and expansion of the Roundhouse Lodge, which will feature several intimate eating areas along with an IBM business center for those who actually enjoy mixing business with pleasure.

 ## Mountain layout

Ski both mountains. Part of the appeal is to stand on one mountain and look across the steep Fitzsimmons Valley at the runs of the other—to chart out where to go or gloat over where you've been. Both mountains offer complimentary tours for all abilities, which may be the best way for those new to this resort to learn their way around. Tours meet outside the Roundhouse Lodge on Whistler and the Rendezvous on Blackcomb at 10:30 a.m. and 1 p.m.

◆◆ **Expert** ◆ **Advanced:** At Whistler, it's a good idea to start at the ten-person Whistler Village Gondola and take a speedy ride up 3,800 vertical feet to Roundhouse Lodge. Ascending over so much terrain, you'll think you're at the summit, but one glance out the gondola building reveals a series of five giant bowls above the treeline. These spread out from left to right: Symphony Bowl, Harmony Bowl, Glacier Bowl, Whistler Bowl and West Bowl (plus the unseen Bagel Bowl, far to the right edge of the ski boundary), all served by the Harmony Express.

Experts will pause just long enough to enjoy the view and then take Peak Chair to the 7,160-foot summit, turning left along the ridge to drop into Glacier Bowl. Or they'll do the wide mogul apron, Shale Slope, in upper Whistler Bowl, rest awhile at the ridge and then have another go below Whistler Glacier. There are no marked runs here—it's wide open. Be creative and let fly. Double-diamond skiing off this summit is in West Bowl.

Though most of the expert playground is above treeline, the lower mountain has a few advanced challenges, most notably the Dave Murray Downhill, which starts at the top of the Orange Chair and drops more than 2,000 feet to the Whistler Creekside base.

Don't forget there's another whole mountain. Blackcomb's gondola, Excalibur, is just to the left of Whistler Mountain's 10-passenger lift. A high-speed quad, Excelerator, at the top of the gondola, connects skiers to another high-speed quad, Glacier Express, which unloads at Blackcomb's glacier skiing at the summit.

Another fast way up Blackcomb Mountain is on the speedy Wizard Express, a sleek quad with an aerodynamic Plexiglas windscreen that also keeps out the rain, which can be a menace at the 2,200-foot base area. At the top of the lift, 2,230 feet higher, you're still not halfway up the mountain. Hop on Solar Coaster, next to Wizard Express unloading area, for another 2,000 feet. Here at Rendezvous Restaurant are routes for all abilities.

To get into the wide-open territory from Rendezvous, take Expressway, a lazy beginner's traverse, to 7th Heaven Express. That lift takes you to Mile High summit, where a free guided exploration of this upper terrain for intermediate and advanced skiers is available daily at 11 a.m.

From the Mile High summit, the routes off the back side into Horstman and Blackcomb Glaciers give the feeling of being hundreds of miles into the wilderness. (You can also reach these glaciers by taking the Glacier Express, which you reach from Rendezvous by heading to the bottom of the Jersey Cream Express chair.)

While going down the spine off the back of Horstman, keep to the left and peer over the cornice into the double-black-diamond chutes. Just seeing the abyss—or seeing someone hurl himself into it—gives quite a rush.

The best known of these severe narrow chutes is Couloir Extreme. The entry requires a leap of faith and skill. Nearby is Cougar Chute, also a double black. One of the most difficult chutes on the mountain is Pakalolo, which is very narrow and steep with rock walls on either side. "You don't want to miss a turn," a local says. Another, called Blowhole, drops from the trail leading to the Blackcomb Glacier from the Horstman Glacier.

■ **Intermediate:** Resort work crews had plans to construct some easier descents from the top of the Peak Chair during the summer of 1998. Before that improvement, there were two intermediate ways down. One, Highway 86, is to the right of West Bowl, keeping to the ridge around Bagel Bowl instead of dropping in. The other is Burnt Stew, arguably the most scenic on the mountain. It goes high and wide off to the left of Harmony Bowl, sometimes flattening into a bit of a trudge. Reached by a long cat track that loops behind the bowls, its views are dominated by the imposing Black Tusk peak. Of the bowls at the top, Symphony is the mildest.

If you want to know what skiing a distance of five miles feels like, take the Alpine T-bar near Roundhouse Station and turn right to find the bronze plaque identifying Franz's Run, one of the longest ski trails in North America. It turns and pitches and rolls and goes forever, ending up at the Whistler Creek base.

At Blackcomb, intermediates will especially love the trails off the Jersey Cream Express. They are wide and as smooth as the name implies. The runs under the Solar Coaster chair also are good blues.

Don't let the summit intimidate, especially in sunny weather. Intermediates can easily handle runs in the 7th Heaven area and on the two glaciers. In fact, the long run down the Blackcomb Glacier on a bluebird day is a memory you will cherish.

●● **Beginner:** At Whistler, beginners won't be able to experience the upper bowls, but will find green-circle routes down from the Roundhouse, which is, after all, more than 3,800 feet above the village. Pay attention to signs. Once you're on an intermediate trail, there's usually no escape.

A surprise for Blackcomb beginners is a sinuous run called Green Line. This takes off from the upper terminal of 7th Heaven Express and follows the natural contours of the mountain from top to bottom on trails that are groomed daily. It's a thrilling way for beginners to do big-mountain skiing, but getting down, down, down may take all day. Another easy descent from the Hut is the Crystal Traverse run. It winds below the glaciers, becomes the Crystal Road and passes the Glacier Creek Lodge before joining Green Line two-thirds down the mountain.

● **Never-ever:** At Blackcomb, the three learning areas are at the base. At Whistler, the never-ever area is at the Whistler Village Gondola's midstation, about 1,000 feet higher than the base. Both learning areas are covered by snowmaking and are fairly isolated from high skier traffic (Blackcomb's is sectioned off).

Mountain rating

When you ask locals which mountain they prefer, you get mixed responses. Even super experts have reasons for enjoying both, and intermediates will have a field day on either set of slopes. Beginners can have a good time, especially because they can get down from the summit (and it's always fun to get to the top).

This is one of the best resorts for nonskiers, because of the many enjoyable activities off the mountain, and because nonskiers can ride the Whistler gondola to admire the view.

Cross-country

Nordic skiing is available on the municipal **Lost Lake Trail,** 28 km. of double-tracked trails with a skating lane. Trails are well marked, and start a quarter-mile from the village. Trail passes are Cdn$10, but skiing is free after 8:30 p.m. At night, a 4-km. stretch of trail is lit until 11 p.m. The Chateau Whistler Clubhouse, on the golf course, is a great rest stop, as is the log hut at Lost Lake. Call 932-6436 for conditions or information.

Most avid cross-country skiers take **BC Rail** to the Cariboo region and the 100 Mile House, with more than 150 km. of groomed tracks. For information, contact BC Rail Passenger Services, Box 8770, Vancouver, B.C. V6B 4X6, or call 984-5426 or Great Escape Vacations at (800) 663-2515.

Snowboarding

Whistler Mountain grooms its competition-grade halfpipe nightly. It's accessible from the top of the Green Express chair, and just below it is the terrain park on the Green Acres trail. Two-day adult camps (average age getting closer to 40) are about $160, which includes camp, a Fresh Tracks Breakfast on the hill, T-shirt and après activities.

Blackcomb Mountain, home of five-time world champion Craig Kelly's summer snowboard camps, has a big halfpipe at the top of Solar Coaster and a terrain park on Catskinner. The mountain attracts mostly freeriders.

Lessons (98/99 prices in Cdn$ without GST)

Group lessons: $59 for half day; $79 for full day; however, prices "vary depending on the time you visit," says our resort contact. It's best to call ahead for information and to reserve a space in a class, (800) 766-0449, or locally, 932-3434.

Never-ever package: Packages including lift, lesson and rental start at $95 for a full day, for skiers or snowboarders.

Private lessons: $265 for a half day; $415 for a full day.

Special programs: Both mountains offer adult workshops in parallel skiing, bumps, powder and racing, as well as multi-day camps aimed at women, advanced skiers wanting to reach a higher level, and other topics. Call for details and prices.

Racing: Whistler has a NASTAR course under the Green Express chair. Blackcomb has two NASTAR courses, one on Springboard under the Solar Coaster Express, and the other on Cougar Milk in the Jersey Cream area.

Children's programs: Full-day lessons for ages 18 months–12 years (in various programs separated by age and ability) cost $69. Lunch is included, but rental equipment and lift tickets are extra. One popular program for ages 3–12 is a five-day camp that starts each Monday. Children's rental package includes a helmet. Teen programs are offered daily for $69 for a full day including lunch.

Child care (98/99 prices in Cdn$ not including GST)

Ages: 18 months to 3 years.
Cost: Full day is $69, which includes lunch.
Reservations: (800) 766-0449 or (604) 932-3434.

Note: An introduction to skiing lesson is included in this program, if the kids want to ski. If not, they play in the snow or inside, a spokesman said. The program also includes crafts, story time and other activities. Whistler/Blackcomb's child-care centers are at the Whistler Village Gondola base building, the Creekside Gondola and the base of the Wizard Express (Upper Village Blackcomb base).

Other options: The **Chateau Whistler** and **Delta Whistler Resort** offer babysitting to their guests, and **Tiny Tots** (938-9699) and **Nanny Network** (938-2823) provide babysitting services. The Whistler Activity Center (932-2394) also can refer you to babysitting services. **Baby's Away** (932-4844) rents and will deliver baby needs to your lodge, such as crib, stroller, car seat and toys.

Lift tickets (98/99 prices in Cdn$ including GST)

	Adult	Child (7-12)
One day	$61	$30
Three days	$180 ($60/day)	$88 ($29/day)
Five days	$294 ($59/day)	$144 ($29/day)

Who skis free: Children 6 and younger.

Who skis at a discount: Teens (13–18) and seniors 65 and older ski for $153 for three days, $250 for five.

Note: Prices are rounded to the nearest dollar, and include Canada's Goods and Services Tax (G.S.T.). For more on G.S.T., see the Canada introductory chapter. Tickets are good at either mountain, and prices are a little higher during the week between Christmas and New Year's Day.

Those who drive to Whistler can save about $5 per lift ticket by purchasing them at 7-Eleven stores in Squamish, a town about 25 miles south of the resort.

 ## Accommodations (Prices in Cdn$ without tax)

Lodging runs from dorm bunks to European-style B&Bs to luxury hotels. Most guests stay in the village condominiums. Price ranges are wide, and so are choices. Lift-and-lodging packages also are tempting. (Chateau Whistler even offers a Weekend Spa Package.) The best starting point is **Whistler Central Reservations**, (800) WHISTLER (944-7853). Remember, there will be 17 percent taxes added to lodging bills—10 percent hotel and the seven percent Canadian Goods and Services Tax (GST). During holiday periods (generally late December), seven-night minimum stays are given priority, as a general guideline.

Chateau Whistler (800-441-1414) is part of the Canadian Pacific Hotels (owners of Chateau Lake Louise and Banff Springs Hotel) with 563 rooms in 13 stories, an expansive sun deck stretching below the high turrets, two restaurants, night club and extensive health club. Rates: $319–$1,099.

Other than the Chateau, the largest deluxe lodging is **Delta Whistler Resort** (800-268-1133 from the U.S. and Canada, or 604-932-1982) with 300 rooms, 30 percent of which are kitchen-equipped suites. Hotel rooms are $99–$349, studios are $129–$399, and a one-bedroom suite is $249–$499.

The **Pan Pacific Lodge** (888-905-9995; 604-905-2999; www.panpac.com/hotels) is a new high-end hotel just a few paces from the Blackcomb Excalibur and Whistler Village gondola bases. It has 121 suites with gas fireplaces.

The **Residence Inn by Marriott-Whistler/Blackcomb** (800-331-3131 or 604-905-3400), is secluded, up at the end of Painted Cliff Road on the Blackcomb side. Prices range from $220 to $595. **Pinnacle International Resort** (604-938-3218), on Main Street in Village Centre, bills itself as Whistler's first "boutique/romance hotel." It has suites with a queen bed and double Jacuzzi close to the fireplace. Prices range from $120–$350.

The **Glacier Lodge** (800-777-0185 or 604-938-3455) is decorated in pale plush. One-bedroom condominiums are $150–$385; two-bedroom, $309–$565. Lodge rooms are $130–$195. The **Crystal Lodge** (800-667-3363 or 604-932-2221) has 140 rooms from $87–$330. Cozy common areas around the fireplaces give a European atmosphere. Families who don't mind a slightly longer walk to the village center may find the **Tantalus Lodge** (800-268-1133 from the U.S. and Canada or 604-932-4146) suitable for $169–$379. All 76 units have two bedrooms, two baths, full kitchen, fireplace and balcony.

The **Hearthstone Lodge** (800-663-7711 or 604-932-4161) rates range from $129 to $450 (the latter for a two-bedroom condo in high season). Rooms in the **Listel Whistler Hotel** (800-663-5472 or 604-932-1133) start at $199. Medium-priced units are available at **Blackcomb Lodge** (800-667-2855 or 604-932-4155); mini-kitchenette studios rent for $145–$345.

The **Holiday Inn SunSpree Resort** (800-229-3188) is in Whistler Village Centre. Its suite design is very imaginative, and maids are not allowed to use sprays in certain "allergy-free" rooms. Rates are from $99–$399.

The **Whistler Fairways Hotel** (604-932-2522; 800-663-5644) is well-placed, just off the hubbub of the central core, but with nice views of the Whistler Golf Course. Rates range from $100–$750.

The **Edgewater Lodge** (604-932-0688) is on a peninsula of Green Lake, bordering a golf course and the River of Golden Dreams. Great for those who want luxury and no village hubbub. Prices range from $105–$255.

The least expensive accommodations are outside the village at **Shoestring Lodge** (604-932-3338) offering dorm beds for $20–$25 per night and twin or queen rooms from $60 to $100. **Whistler Resort and Club** (604-932-2343) has rooms for $80–$120 a night, depending on the season. Three dormitory lodges and a youth hostel have beds at about $20 a night—**Coast Mountain Lodge** (604-938-1280), **Fireside Lodge** (604-932-4545), **UBC Lodge** (604-932-6604) and **Whistler Hostel** (604-932-5492).

Whistler also has upscale B&Bs, owned by families and sharing a central living area. These are located in residential areas and usually have no more than six rooms. Most have private baths. Rates are $75–$220 and include breakfast. Ask for those with BC Accommodations approval.

Durlacher Hof (800-891-1137 or 604-932-1924) is the genuine B&B article for skiers wanting an Austrian lodging experience. At the door, you swap your boots for boiled-wool slippers. Each of the seven rooms has its own bath and extra-long beds. Visiting celebrity chefs prepare dinner on the weekends. Room rates are $150–$275, which include full breakfast and afternoon tea.

 ## Dining

Having so many restaurants in town keeps the pride factor high among Whistler chefs. Consequently, this resort has some fantastic meals.

For years locals have said the **Rimrock Cafe and Oyster Bar** (932-5565) in Highland Lodge is the best restaurant in town. It is at Whistler Creek, a short ride away. Well-prepared seafood is complemented by an extensive wine list. **Les Deux Gros** (932-4611) is another favorite for the best in French fare. It's about a mile south in Twin Lakes Village.

Val d'Isère (932-4666) in the heart of Whistler Village features fine French cuisine. Umberto Menghi, a flamboyant Italian chef whose TV cooking show is popular in Canada, is well known for his restaurants in Vancouver and two in Whistler—**Trattoria Di Umberto** (932-5858) and **Il Caminetto Di Umberto** (932-4442). Continental cuisine is featured. Umberto's main man for 16 years, Mario Enero, now owns **La Rua** (932-5011). **Araxi** (932-4540), on the village square, serves Mediterranean dinners, imaginative pastas and pizza.

Bear Foot Bistro (932-1133), in the Listel Whistler Hotel, has an accomplished menu that begins with 225 wines. Go for it with appetizers such as crisp-baked Asian shrimp and crab cakes, entrées such as the hunter's pot of rabbit, duck, and Arctic musk ox, and desserts such as phyllo crusted bananas with hot buttered rum and French vanilla ice cream. This unusual restaurant also features working artists in the dining room and a small dining room for cigar lovers.

The Old Spaghetti Factory (932-1081) in the Crystal Lodge has moderate prices as does **Evergreens** (932-7346) in the Delta Whistler Resort. Evergreens has a fine buffet breakfast for $10.25. Right next door along the same promenade, the **Cinnamon Bear Sports Bar** (932-1982) serves off the same menu from 11 a.m. to 11 p.m. **Ingrid's Deli** (932-7000), in Village Square, is a German-style deli that has a locals' favorite: a giant veggie burger. **The Keg** (932-5151) has good steaks and basic American-type food.

Auntie Em's Kitchen (932-1163), in the Village North Market Place, is a way-above-average deli with a deep menu featuring monster vegetarian sandwiches, matzo-ball soup and good breads and sweets, especially the cranberry-date bar. **The Bagel Street Cafe** (932-3131) produces an incredible variety of bagels, $6.25 per dozen. The Breakfast Bagel with scrambled eggs is $3.25 and for $4 you can get the Skier's Package lunch to go, with a bagel, cream cheese, cookie and a beverage.

Caramba (938-1879), in Town Plaza, is the new favorite of our staff Whistler experts, who travel here each season. It is "Mediterreaneanish," with a great putanesca pasta, wood-fired pizzas, and a Caramba salad (chicken, butter lettuce, peanut sauce), all at very reasonable prices.

On the Blackcomb side, top dining spots are the **Wildflower** (938-8000) in the Chateau Whistler for fresh seafood and innovative Northern Italian pasta, **Portobello** (938-2040) and **Monk's Grill** (932-9677).

At the streetside entrance to the Le Chamois building is a Thai restaurant, **Thai One On** (932-4822). The Pak Tua Gai, peanut sauce on a bed of spinach with chicken, is a fine entrée for $10.95. Pad Thai Jay is a great-tasting vegetarian alternative for $6.95, especially washed down with Whistler Mother's (as it's spelled on the label) Pale Ale, on tap. **Zeuski's Taverna** (932-6009), in the Whistler Town Plaza, has moderately priced Greek food.

Lots of visiting Japanese means excellent Japanese restaurants: **Sushi Village** (932-3330) and **Tokyo Tom's** (923-2221). For steaks cooked Japanese steakhouse-style, it's **Teppan Village** (932-2223) or **Sushi Ya** (905-0155) in the Marketplace area.

Moderate-priced dining is also available. **The Crab Shack** (932-4451) across from the conference center has affordable steaks, chicken and pasta. **Moe's Deli and Bar** (905-7772) has a huge family and casual-style menu.

Good food is served on the mountains, too. The best on each are **The Roundhouse Lodge**, at the almost-top of Whistler Mountain, and **Christine's** (938-7353) in the back of the Rendezvous Lodge on Blackcomb. Reservations are a good idea here. Eager skiers can board the Whistler Village Gondola at 7:30 a.m. for an $11.95 (or for light eaters, $6.95) buffet breakfast (lift ticket extra) and first rights to the runs. Whistler also offers **Moonlight Dine & Ski** four times per season, on full-moon nights only. Call 932-3434 for dates and cost. On the Blackcomb side, the Glacier Creek Lodge has the **River Rock Grill** with potato bar, oriental noodle bar and a great array of pastas and pizzas. In the same lodge, the **Glacier Bite** has hearty soups and salads, with bistro-style counter service.

Condo renters: **The Galloping Grocer** will deliver groceries to your condo for your arrival. Prices are higher than your local grocery store, but reasonable; for example, about $5 (Cdn) for Classico four-cheese pasta sauce. Call 604-932-6222 to get a grocery list.

 ## Après-ski/nightlife

Après-ski spills out onto the snow from **Longhorn Saloon & Grill** at Whistler Village Gondola base and **Merlin's** at Blackcomb. Both are beer-and-nachos spots with lively music. **Citta** in the center of Whistler Village is also a good après-ski site. **Dubh Linn Gate**, an Irish pub in the new Pan Pacific Lodge, also is catching on for immediate fun when the lifts close.

For a quieter environment at the Whistler base, **Crystal's Lounge** from 3 to 6:30 p.m. hosts specialty coffees and guitar and piano music to help create a warm, gentle atmosphere. On the Blackcomb side, **The Mallard Bar** in the Chateau Whistler provides quiet piano music après-ski. **Cinnamon Bear Bar** in the Delta Mountain Inn hotel has live music.

Later in the evening, the reggae and rock at **The Longhorn** start at 9 p.m. Another disco is the **Savage Beagle,** and behind the Savage Beagle you'll find **Tommy Africa's** with a young crowd at the pool tables. The locals seem to congregate at **Garfinkle's** which has beer by the pitcher, TVs on almost every wall and a well-used dance floor. It's now in a larger location in the Town Plaza area. **Maxx Fish** is the newest hot spot—a trendy disco with a wild interior paint job, next to Aviano in Village Square.

 ## Other activities

Shopping is plentiful. We don't mention T-shirt shops as a general rule, but Shirtprint, 1030 Miller Creek Road near Village Square, stocks shirts of high quality and the prints can be personalized. Canadian-made gifts are at Skitch Knicknacks and Paddywacks, 4222 Village Square. And finally, Expressions provides a great rainy day activity: You Paint It Ceramics. You pick a pattern, or do a freehand paint job and pick up your mug, bowl or whatever after the glaze is fired. It's in the Stone Lodge, unit 125 at 4338 Main Street, Marketplace. While you're at that address, you can **check your e-mail** at nearby Mail Boxes Etc. for $2.75 for 15 minutes.

Ski school staff give presentations about the mountains, ski movies and refreshments at **Whistler Welcome Night**, every Sunday and Thursday evening at 6:30 p.m. at the Whistler Conference Centre.

Heli-skiing is offered by Tyax Heli-Skiing (932-7007), Whistler Heli-Skiing (932-4105), Western Canada Heli-Sports (938-1700) or Mountain Heli-Sports (932-2070). The same companies have **scenic flights,** as does Whistler Air (932-6615), which also features the option of landing on a glacier.

Hundreds of miles of logging roads are accessible for **snowmobiling**. Whistler Snowmobile Guided Tours (932-4086) and Blackcomb Snowmobiling (932-8484) have tours several times a day, and evening rides. Canadian Snowmobile Adventures (938-1616) offers luxury evening tours up Blackcomb Mountain.

Covered **tennis** courts are at the Delta Mountain Inn, **ice skating** and drop-in **hockey** take place at Meadow Park Arena (938-3133) a few miles north of the village and **snowshoe** treks are offered by Canadian Snowshoeing Adventures (932-0647) at the midstation of the Whistler Village Gondola. **Sleigh rides** are offered by Blackcomb Sleighrides (932-7631).

The **Whistler Activity and Information Centre** (932-2394) provides information and reservations for these or other activities.

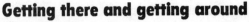

Getting there and getting around

By air: Most major airlines fly to Vancouver. Perimeter Transportation connects the Vancouver Airport to Whistler five times a day (seven times on weekends), with the last bus leaving at 5:30 p.m. on weekdays and 9:30 p.m. on weekends. Fare is about $45 one way. Reservations are required. Call 261-2299.

Note on ground transportation: The Perimeter bus pickup is only at certain hotels. If you are staying somewhere that isn't on the list, you must get yourself and your bags to a pickup point on time. So keep that in mind as you make lodging reservations.

Allow plenty of time in the Vancouver Airport, both arriving and leaving, for customs declarations and currency exchange.

By train: The most scenic way to travel is to board BC Rail's passenger trains. Trains leave North Vancouver at 7 a.m. daily, arriving at 9:34 a.m. They depart Whistler at 6:10 p.m. and arrive at North Vancouver at 8:45 p.m. Advance reservations are required. Roundtrip fare is about $54 for adults, $34 for children ages 2–12. Taxis go from the airport to the train station and a bus picks up train passengers at several downtown locations. Call (800) 663-8238 or (604) 984-5246.

By bus: Maverick Coach Lines operates from the downtown Vancouver bus depot at the corner of Dunsmuir and Georgia, and charges about $17 one way (call 662-8051). Vancouver Airporter shuttle will get you to the bus depot; call 244-9888.

Getting around: Forget renting a car. You'll never use it while you're staying at Whistler Village.

Regional Getaways

Resorts in this chapter are best for weekend or, better yet, short midweek visits. They have enough activity and trails for two to three days, but not quite enough for an extended holiday.

These ski areas all have the following common features, *unless otherwise noted:*
- lodging within a 20-mile radius (Note: Some of the phone numbers listed for lodging are reservations services; others just provide information about lodging in the area. If no phone number is listed for lodging, call the ski area.)
- snowboarding, usually with lessons, rentals and snowboard parks
- a day lodge with food service
- adult and child lessons (children usually start at age 4)
- equipment rentals
- weekend lift ticket prices from 1997/98. Children's prices are usually valid for ages 6–12; we've tried to identify when age ranges differ from that norm. Children ski free with an adult if they are younger than the ages listed in the child rate. (Discounts for midweek, seniors, teens and others may be available; please call the resort.)

We list toll-free phone numbers where available, plus the resort's recorded information line and website address. If you can't get a live voice from the info line, try the ski area's office number. (The toll-free numbers may not be applicable nationwide, since these resorts draw visitors primarily from the nearest urban areas.) Where we say, "None found," for Web site, that means we couldn't find an official site from the resort as of summer, 1998.

We list these extras where they apply: child care for tots younger than ski-school age, night skiing, and approximate distance from the nearest metropolitan area with a major airport.

Where two or more ski areas are close enough to be explored on the same weekend trip, they are presented together, but with separate contact information. Such ski areas are owned by different companies and do not have interchangeable lift tickets unless that is specifically noted.

Western U.S.

California/Nevada

Mt. Rose, Reno, NV; (702) 849-0704; (800) SKI-ROSE (754-7673)
Internet: http://www.skirose.com
5 lifts; 900 skiable acres; 1,440 vertical feet

Mt. Rose has the highest base elevation in the Tahoe area at 8,260 feet, which means it gets snow earlier than other areas (and gets snow when it's raining at lower elevations). It has two base areas, the result of Mt. Rose incorporating a neighboring ski area, Slide Mountain, several years ago. The Slide base area has primarily intermediate terrain with some advanced pitches, while the Rose side has very gentle beginner slopes, good intermediate trails and some long advanced runs.

Lift ticket prices: Adults, $38; Children (12 and younger), $14.
Distance from Reno: About 22 miles on Hwy. 431.
Lodging information: (800) 367-7366 (FOR-RENO) or (800) 824-6348 (TAHOE-4-U).
Note: Mt. Rose's area code is due to change to 775 in December of 1998.

Ski Homewood, Homewood, CA; (530) 525-2992

Internet: http://www.skihomewood.com
10 lifts; 1,200 skiable acres; 1,650 vertical feet

Ski Homewood, on the west shore of Lake Tahoe, is one of three Tahoe ski areas that can qualify for Best View Of The Lake honors. (The others are Diamond Peak and Heavenly, detailed in the *Lake Tahoe* chapters.) This area, though smallish by Tahoe standards, has more than 1,200 skiable acres accessible from either of two base areas called North Side and South Side. Child care starts at age 2 and is at the South Side Lodge.

Lift ticket prices: Adults, $35; Children (9–13), $11.
Distance from Reno: About 50 miles from Reno via I-80 west and Hwy. 89 south.
Distance from Sacramento: About 120 miles via I-80 east and Hwy. 89 south.
Lodging information: (800) 824-6348 (TAHOE-4-U).

Boreal, Truckee, CA; (530) 426-3666

Internet: http://www.borealski.com
9 lifts; 380 skiable acres; 600 vertical feet

You can't miss Boreal when you're driving toward Tahoe from Sacramento. It is a wide ridge of fairly short ski trails right off I-80 on the Donner Pass. Boreal, purchased in 1995 by the company that owns Alpine Meadows, is very popular with riders, who like the short, straight runs off the summit and "Jibassic Park," the resort's snowboard terrain park. Boreal also has runs down its back side.

Boreal has night skiing and is the home of the Western Ski Sport Museum, run by the Auburn Ski Club and generally open during Boreal's ski hours.

Lift ticket prices: Adults, $28; Children (5–12), $10.
Distance from Reno: About 45 miles west on I-80.
Distance from Sacramento: About 80 miles east on I-80.
Lodging information: (800) 824-6348 (TAHOE-4-U) or (530) 426-3666, ext. 123.

Bear Valley, Bear Valley, CA; (209) 753-2308

Internet: http://www.bearvalley.com
11 lifts; 1,280 skiable acres; 1,900 vertical feet

Bear Valley is one of those word-of-mouth ski areas beloved by those who know it's at the winter terminus of Highway 4. This area has many things to like: 450 inches of snow annually; a town just big enough to provide lodging, food and alternate activities (cross-country skiing, ice skating and most snow sports); and an enticing advanced and expert area called Grizzly Bowl that makes up about 30 percent of the terrain. The Grizz is below the base area, and that's its drawback. With no snowmaking coverage and an elevation of 6,600–7,750 feet, Grizzly Bowl isn't always open. However, the upper mountain is covered by snowmaking and has a few black-diamond runs amid its great beginner and intermediate terrain.

Bear Valley has child care starting at age 2, and also has a program for skiers with physical disabilities.

Lift ticket prices: Adults, $35; Children (7-12), $13.

Distance from San Francisco: About 190 miles east on I-580 and I-205, north on I-99, then east on Hwy. 4. Bear Valley is on the west slope of the Sierra Nevada and not accessible from Tahoe or Mammoth.

Lodging information: Press 5 after calling the recorded information line to get phone numbers for various hotels and condos. Two recommendations: The Lodge at Bear Valley (800-794-3866) is three miles from the slopes (as close as you can get) and smack in the center of the little town. About 25 miles down Hwy. 4 is The Dorrington Hotel & Restaurant, a charming shared-bath B&B in a historic house. The restaurant is worth a stop on the drive home.

Badger Pass, Yosemite National Park, CA; (209) 372-1000

Internet: http://www.yosemitepark.com/activities/badger/

5 lifts; 9 trails; 800 vertical feet

This is a tiny 62-year-old ski area best suited for beginners, patient intermediates and families with young children. Though the ski area is charming (and the employees are wonderful), what makes Badger Pass a great winter weekend destination is not the downhill skiing. It's special because it's inside Yosemite National Park. The park's legendary crowds disappear in the winter, so you'll share the majesty of the Yosemite Valley with a comfortable number of humans. Activities include ranger-naturalist snowshoe walks, ice skating, sightseeing tours and lots more.

Yosemite has a renowned cross-country ski center headquartered at Badger Pass with lessons, 40 km. of machine-groomed track and another 150 km. of marked trails, including a 17-km. skating lane on the rim of the Yosemite Valley to Glacier Point.

Lift ticket prices: Adults, $28; Children (12 and younger), $13.

Distance from San Francisco: About 230 miles east on I-580, I-205 and Hwy. 120.

Distance from Los Angeles: About 290 miles north on I-5 and I-99, then east on Hwy. 41. Note: Hwy. 120 between Yosemite and Lee Vining is closed in winter, making Badger Pass inaccessible from Mammoth.

Lodging information: (209) 252-4848.

Snow Summit, Big Bear Lake, CA; (909) 866-5766

Internet: http://www.snowsummit.com

12 lifts; 230 skiable acres; 1,200 vertical feet

Bear Mountain, Big Bear Lake, CA; (909) 585-2519

Internet: http://www.bearmtn.com

11 lifts; 195 skiable acres; 1,665 vertical feet

Southern Californians just don't know how good they have it. On a sunny winter day, it is entirely possible to spend the morning skiing at Big Bear (as the locals call it) and the afternoon playing a round of golf in Palm Springs or surfing in the Pacific Ocean. These neighboring ski areas, in the mountain town of Big Bear Lake, are less than a two-hour drive from the fabled desert resort in one direction and the beach in the other.

The Big Bear areas, though at an altitude of between 7,000 and 8,800 feet, rely heavily on snowmaking to cover the runs. Both are snowmaking experts and have a reliable water supply from Big Bear Lake. Even if the season has been dry, you'll find surprisingly good snow on the runs. And if the winter has been a wet one, the conditions can be quite good.

The terrain is largely intermediate-level, with a couple of runs at each that qualify as advanced, not expert. Snowboarding is hugely popular here, with boarders constituting about a third of the business. The town has many lodging and restaurant options and a charming, walkable downtown.

Snow Summit has child care starting at age 2 and night skiing. Bear Mountain is one of many ski areas owned nationwide by Booth Creek.

Lift tickets: Snow Summit: Adults, $32; Children (7-12), $10. Bear Mountain: Adults, $42; Children, $10. Bear Mountain's tickets for ages 13–22 are $32.

Distance from Los Angeles: About 110 miles east on I-10, I-215, Hwy. 30, Hwy. 330 and Hwy. 18.

Distance from Ontario (nearest commercial airport): About 60 miles by I-10, I-215, Hwy. 30, Hwy. 330 and Hwy. 18.

Lodging information: Big Bear Lake Resort Association's Lodging Referral Service, (909) 866-7000.

Colorado

Arapahoe Basin, Arapahoe Basin, CO; 888-ARAPAHO (272-7246)

Internet: http://www.arapahoebasin.com

5 lifts; 490 acres; 2,270 vertical feet

A-Basin, as the locals call it, is the highest lift-served skiing in North America, with a high point of 13,050 feet. Its above-timberline terrain is subjected to howling winds, plummeting temperatures, and white-out conditions. This is the closest thing Colorado has to skiing the high Alps.

The "Pali" side of A-Basin was created for the strong, hardy skier or snowboarder who braves bumps, weather, wind and super-steep terrain to push his or her envelope of experience. The entire east wall has chutes, gullies and steeps regularly searched out by experts, and dozens of expert runs drop from the top of the Palivacinni Lift. When all is said and done, the heart of A-Basin for experts is the Pali, a legendary avalanche chute, a steep stamped in nature.

For all its gnarly reputation, A-Basin has excellent beginner terrain. Never-evers start on their own lift, Molly Hogan, and the flat, nearly separate terrain beneath it. Wrangler is a very wide flat trail on the far left side of the map. Chisolm and Sundance are the next steps up the ability ladder. All three wind down from the top of the Exhibition chair lift. Intermediates can test themselves from the top of either the Lenawee or Norway chairs and enjoy above-timberline bowl skiing. Thanks to its elevation, A-Basin doesn't hit its stride until late January when the gullies fill in and the rocks have sufficient cover. It's skiable until June, sometimes into early July.

Lift tickets: Adults $39, Children $12.

Distance from Denver: About 100 miles west via I-70, Exit 205 at Dillon. Drive east for about 12 miles on Hwy. 6. You'll pass Keystone about halfway up Hwy. 6.

Lodging information: The nearest lodging is at Keystone; see that chapter or the Summit County chapter.

Loveland, Georgetown, CO; (303) 569-3203

Internet: http://www.skiloveland.com

10 lifts; 836 acres; 1,680 vertical feet

Have you ever gone into the Eisenhower Tunnel along I-70 west from Denver and wondered about the ski area you can see as you disappear into the darkness?

This is Loveland, a ski area in two parts, connected by a lift and a shuttle service. Loveland Valley, the area you see on the left as you approach the tunnel, is great for beginners, intermediates and anyone who wants to hide from the stiff winds that sometimes plague Loveland Basin, which has terrain for all abilities, most of which you can't see from I-70. Advanced and expert skiers should head for Chair 1 for bumps and chutes, Chair 8 for the powder bowl of The Plunge and Chair 4 for trees and more chutes. Intermediates can handle everything else, particularly Chairs 2, 4 and 6.

Child care starts at 12 months. Lodging can be found in Georgetown, Idaho Springs or Dillon, each within 15 miles.

Lift tickets: Adults $35, Children (ages 6–14), $17.

Distance from Denver: 56 miles west via I-70 (about 80 miles from Denver International Airport).

Lodging information: (800) 225-LOVE (5683).

Monarch, Monarch, CO; (888) 996-7669, (719) 539-3573

Internet: none found
4 lifts; 670 acres; 1,160 vertical feet

Monarch, located on the Continental Divide, is known for powder, powder and more powder. It gets about 350 inches of snow a year, but only about 170,000 skier visits a year (many Colorado destination resorts get that many in just a couple of weeks). That means a lot more untracked snow to play in.

The resort caters to families, and has groomed beginner and intermediate terrain for those who don't like the steep and deep. Nonskiers can take scenic rides in the covered gondola, but this area is fairly isolated and without many off-slope activities. Child care starts at 2 months.

Lift tickets: Adults, $32; Children (7-12), $18.

Distance from Denver: About 160 miles southwest via Hwys. 285 and 50. **Distance from Gunnison** (closest airport): About 35 miles east on Hwy. 50.

Lodging information: (800) 332-3668. Monarch has an overnight lodge three miles away; other lodging is in Salida, 18 miles east.

SilverCreek, SilverCreek, CO; (970) 887-3384

Internet: http://www.skisilvercreek.com
5 lifts; 251 acres; 1,000 vertical feet

SilverCreek advertises itself as "Colorado's Smallest Destination Resort." With 64 percent of its business coming from out of state, the description is accurate. The resort caters to families, and indeed is well suited for them, with ski-in/ski-out condos, a hotel, child care starting at 6 months, free weekend ski races for children and many off-slope activities. The average stay, according to resort officials, is four days.

SilverCreek has two mountains. East is the easier terrain, while West has slopes rated for intermediate to advanced skiers.

Lift tickets: Adults, $32; Children, $15.

Distance from Denver: About 80 miles west via I-70 and Hwy. 40.

Lodging information: (800) 827-9226.

Sunlight Mountain Resort, Glenwood Springs, CO; (800) 445-7931

Internet: http://www.sunlightmtn.com

4 lifts; 440 acres; 2,010 vertical feet

Not only is this a less pricey ski option if you're headed to nearby Aspen, but Glenwood Springs is the home of the world's largest hot springs pool, two blocks long and kept at a toasty 90 degrees.

Most of Ski Sunlight is intermediate terrain, though the double black diamond Sunlight Extreme provides steep and gladed challenges.

Lift tickets: Adults, $28; Children, $19.

Distance from Denver: About 175 miles west on I-70 and Hwy. 82. The closest airport is Vail/Eagle, about 30 miles east of Sunlight Mountain.

Lodging information: (800) 445-7931, option 3.

Utah

Brian Head, Brian Head, UT; (800) 27-BRIAN (2-7426); (435) 677-2035

Internet: http://www.brianhead.com

6 lifts; 500 acres; 1,320 vertical feet

Brian Head, in Utah's southwest corner, holds two distinctions among Utah resorts: it is one of very few *not* within an hour of Salt Lake City airport, and it draws virtually all its customers from Southern California and Southern Nevada. For these skiers, Brian Head is very accessible (all freeway until the last 12 miles) and has an excellent variety of terrain covered by that famous dry Utah powder.

Brian Head has skiing on two peaks. Navajo Peak has some of the best beginner and lower intermediate terrain to be found anywhere, while Giant Steps Peak has solid intermediate terrain with a few advanced pitches. In midwinter, the resort offers snowcat skiing from Brian Head Peak's summit, which overlooks Giant Steps.

Child care starts at 12 months, and the town has several condo complexes, restaurants and a hotel. There is night skiing every Friday and Saturday, plus during holiday periods.

Lift tickets: Adults, $35; Children, $20.

Distance from Las Vegas: About 200 miles north by I-15 and Hwy. 143.

Lodging information: (800) 272-7426.

Snowbasin, Huntsville, UT; (801) 399-1135

Internet: http://www.snowbasin.com

9 lifts; 3,200 acres; 2,400 vertical feet

This area had very big growth plans for the summer of 1998. If all was completed on schedule, it nearly doubled its lifts and terrain, from five lifts serving 1,800 acres to nine lifts serving 3,200 acres. The four new lifts are two eight-passenger gondolas, a high-speed quad and a jigback tram. The 2002 Olympic committee chose Snowbasin to host the men's and women's downhill, Super G and Alpine combined races, because of its very long runs within sight of the day lodge.

All other lifts except the one serving the beginner slope are triples that rise 1,100 vertical feet or more. That's a lot of skiing from one lift ride. Right now, Snowbasin is visited mostly by skiers and boarders who have heard good things from their friends. By the turn of the century, though, the secret will be out.

Snowbasin is rimmed by jagged mountain peaks; Mt. Ogden Bowl is easily reached from the Porcupine chair, but other bowls require a traverse.

Snowbasin is owned by the same company that owns the Sun Valley resort in Idaho and the Little America hotel chain.

Lift tickets: Adults, $29; Children (11 and younger), $20.

Distance from Salt Lake City: About 55 miles north via I-15, east on I-84 and north on Hwy. 167 (Trapper's Loop).

Lodging information: Most lodging is in Ogden City, about 17 miles west, or Ogden Valley, about nine miles west. (800) 554-2741.

Sundance, Sundance, UT; (801) 225-4100

Internet: http://www.sundance-utah.com

4 lifts; 450 acres; 2,150 vertical feet

Though this ski area has been owned by actor-director Robert Redford for nearly 30 years, it has never been highly marketed—on purpose. Redford has achieved a balance between skiing, the arts and an intimate environment. The ski area limits lift tickets to 1,200 per day. Lift tickets and a full breakfast are included in lodging rates.

Snowboarding is not allowed, but the area has Nordic skiing, snowshoeing, two excellent restaurants and screenings of award-winning films from past and present Sundance Film Festivals. (This annual event, held in larger Park City, celebrates the achievements of independent film makers.)

Lift tickets: Adults, $35; Children (12 and younger), $22.

Distance from Salt Lake City: About 50 miles south via I-15, east on Hwy. 52, north on Hwy. 189, then a short hop west on Hwy. 92. You also can take Hwy. 92 east from I-15, which is a little longer but more scenic.

Lodging information: (800) 892-1600.

Idaho

Bogus Basin, Boise ID; (208) 332-5100; (800) 367-4397

Internet: http://www.bogusbasin.com

8 lifts; 2,600 skiable acres; 1,800 vertical feet

Bogus Basin, 16 miles from Boise, is much more than a day hill you might expect so close to a city. Like Colorado's Winter Park, Bogus is a big, community-owned, full-service destination resort. The mountain also has two restaurants, Nordic skiing and the 70-unit, mid-mountain Pioneer Inn. Child care starts at 6 months.

Bogus has night skiing every day until 10 p.m. on 1,500 vertical feet. That's the most extensive night skiing in the Northwest. It also has 360-degree skiing around its highest peak. The Superior Lift services 7,590-foot Shafer Butte on the front side and the Pine Creek lift serves the back side. Don't miss the back side. It's like the front on steroids.

And the name? Legend says that "fool's gold"—iron pyrite—was mined there and marketed to gullible city folks as the real thing. Real gold also was mined in the area however, and all the ski runs are named after legitimate mines.

Lift tickets (98/99 prices): Adults, $31; Children (7–11), $8.

Distance from Boise: About 16 miles north. Coming east or west on I-84, take the City Center Connector to the River Street exit, then 15th Street to Hill Road to Bogus Basin Road.

Lodging information: The number for the on-site Pioneer Inn is (800) 367-4397. In Boise, the Grove Hotel (a Westcoast 5-star hotel) is central to downtown: (800) 426-0670.

Brundage Mountain, McCall, ID; (800) 888-7544, (208) 634-7462
Internet: http://www.brundage.com
6 lifts; 1,300 acres; 1,800 foot vertical

Payette Lake, which Brundage overlooks, is beautiful and sparsely populated, with many outdoor activities including good intermediate downhill skiing. From the top of the mountain you can see the Salmon River Mountains, Payette Lakes, Oregon's Eagle Cap Wilderness and the Seven Devils towering over Hells Canyon, America's deepest river gorge. The skiing is pleasant and uncrowded, with occasional challenging drops, but mostly cruisers.

Brundage has a reputation for some of the lightest powder in the Pacific Northwest, and the mountain offers guided skiing via snowcat in a permit area of over 19,000 acres in the Payette National Forest. Child care starts at 6 weeks.

Lift tickets: Adults, $29; Children (7–12), $17. Brundage also has a teen price, which is $24.
Distance from Boise: About 100 miles north via Hwy. 55.
Lodging information: (800) 888-7544.

Montana

Bridger Bowl, Bozeman, MT; (406) 587-2111
Internet: http://www.bridgerbowl.com
6 lifts; 1,200 acres; 2,000 vertical feet

Bridger Bowl is a funky, friendly ski area that offers some of the best steeps, narrows and radical chutes in Montana. Its non-profit status means it can offer some great skiing at a low price. Experts can enjoy the upper mountain and hike the perilous Ridge, while families ski groomed intermediate and beginner cruisers on the lower mountain.

Bridger has yet to install a high-speed quad, but the existing lift system adequately handles weekend traffic from the nearby Montana State University town of Bozeman. Child care starts at 3 months.

Lift tickets: Adults, $29; Children (12 and younger), $12.
Distance from Bozeman: About 16 miles north by Hwy. 86.
Lodging information: Bridger Bowl Vacations, (800) 223-9609.

Red Lodge Mountain Resort, Red Lodge, MT; (406) 446-2610
Internet: http://www.montana.net/rlmresort
6 lifts; 500 acres; 2,016 vertical feet

Tucked in a valley in the Beartooth mountain range lies the quaint old mining town of Red Lodge. Red Lodge Mountain's Grizzly Peak, located four miles west of town, caters to families and intermediate skiers. The mountain recently doubled its skiable terrain with the opening of much needed advanced and expert trails in the Cole Creek Drainage area.

Lift tickets: Adults, $32; Children, $12.
Distance from Billings: About 65 miles west on I-90 and south on Hwy. 212.
Lodging information: (800) 444-8977.

Montana Snowbowl, Missoula, MT; (406) 549-9777
Internet: http://travel.mt.gov/winter/dhski/ms.htm
4 lifts; 900 skiable acres; 2,600 vertical feet

This virtually unknown Montana hangout has been called The Un-resort—untamed, ungroomed, unpretentious and undiscovered. It also had a reputation of being unforgiving and not easily mastered by the faint of heart. Beginners and intermediates may find much of the terrain beyond their abilities. This unusual area is a local favorite and attracts the college crowd from the University of Montana. The ski area is open every day except Tuesdays.

Lift tickets: Adults, $26; Children, $13.

Distance from Missoula: About 12 miles.

Lodging information: Missoula Chamber of Commerce, (406) 543-6623.

New Mexico/Arizona

Angel Fire, Angel Fire, NM; (800) 633-7463

Internet: http://www.angelfireresort.com

6 lifts; 375 skiable acres; 2,050 vertical feet

This four-season resort 22 miles east of Taos is well suited for beginners and intermediates. Its relatively gentle terrain attracts many multi-generational families, who cruise down the green-circle Headin' Home run from the summit to the base as if they had been skiing all their lives. Angel Fire has challenging runs too, but it will make lower-level skiers feel like champs. Child care starts with infants. If you are planning to spend the night, check into the 157-room Legends Hotel right at the base of the ski area.

Lift tickets: Adults, $36; Children (12 and younger), $20.

Distance from Albuquerque: About 165 miles north on I-25, Hwys. 285 and 68 to Taos, then east on Hwy. 64.

Lodging information: (800) 633-7463.

Red River, Red River, NM; (505) 754-2223

Internet: http://www.taoswebb.com/redriver

7 lifts; 242 skiable acres; 1,600 vertical feet

Another family-oriented area, 37 miles northeast of Taos. Terrain leans toward beginner and intermediate. The ski area is smack in the town's center, which means 90 percent of the town's 6,400 beds—cabins to condos—are within a mile of the slopes. A Nordic ski area is three miles away. Day care is available.

Lift tickets: Adults, $37; Children (12 and younger), $23.

Distance from Albuquerque: About 170 miles, north on I-25, Hwys. 285 and 68 to Taos, then north on Hwy. 522 and east on Hwy. 38.

Lodging information: (800) 331-7669.

Sandia Peak Ski Area, Albuquerque, NM; (505) 242-9133

Internet: None found.

6 lifts plus a 55-person tram; 200 skiable acres; 1,700 vertical feet

Sandia Peak is Albuquerque's playground. Just east of New Mexico's largest city, it has runs for all levels. Take the Sandia Peak Aerial Tramway, touted as the world's longest, or you can drive to the 10,378-foot summit.

Lift tickets: Adults, $30; Children (12 and younger), $21.

Distance from Albuquerque: About 20 miles from the airport to the tram base.

Lodging information: (800) 473-1000.

Ski Apache, Ruidoso, NM; (505) 336-4356

Internet: http://www.skiapache.com

11 lifts; 750 skiable acres; 1,900 vertical feet

Located in south-central New Mexico, 200 miles from Albuquerque, this resort is owned and operated by the Mescalero Apache Indian tribe. The ski area has no lodging, but there is plenty in Ruidoso, 16 miles away. Ski Apache's terrain is 45 percent advanced, but the beginner and intermediate trails have a good reputation for being well groomed. Some steep runs are winch-groomed. The view from the 11,500-foot peak is reportedly spectacular. Ski Apache also has the state's largest and oldest program for disabled skiers.

Lift tickets: Adults, $39 ($42 holiday); Children (12 and younger), $24 ($27 holidays).

Distance from El Paso, TX: About 125 miles north via Hwys. 54 and 70. Ski Apache is about 190 miles south of Albuquerque, so El Paso is the nearer major airport.

Lodging information: (800) 253-2255. StoryBook Cabins (505-257-2115) or the Best Western Swiss Chalet Inn (505-258-3333 or 800-477-9477) are recommended. For condo accommodations, call (800) 457-4666. Tribal-owned Inn of the Mountain Gods (800-545-9011) has ski packages and shuttles to the resort 20 miles away.

Ski Rio, Costilla, NM: (505) 758-7707

6 lifts; 800 skiable acres; 2,150 vertical feet

The most northerly of New Mexico's ski areas, Ski Rio re-opened a couple of seasons ago after an area-wide facelift, including an improved base lodge and extended snowmaking. With its remote location (close to the Colorado border off Hwy. 196), skiers usually have the mountain to themselves.

Ski Rio has a very unusual attraction, a snow skate/snowboard park with obstacles and terrain specific to snow skates, which look like ski boots with slick bottoms. The terrain is mostly wide and good for cruising, and a great place to learn. Ski Rio uses the Perfect Turn® instructional program, which emphasizes total positive reinforcement. Ski Rio also has child care starting at 12 months.

Lift tickets: Adults, $31; Children, $21.

Distance from Albuquerque: About 180 miles north via I-25, Hwys. 285 and 68 to Taos, then north on Hwy. 522 and east on Hwy. 196.

Lodging information: (800) 227-5746.

Sunrise Park Resort, McNary AZ: (520) 735-7600; (888) 804-2779; (800) 772-7669 (snow report)

Internet: http://www.aminews.com/sunrise

12 lifts; 800 skiable acres, 1,800 vertical feet

The White Mountain Apache Tribe owns and operates Sunrise Park, Arizona's largest ski area. Three mountains feature wide-open runs, with a base of 9,200 feet rising to an 11,000-foot summit. Much of the terrain is intermediate, with a few challenging advanced drops and two isolated base area beginner areas. Weather this far south is often good, and snowfall averages 250 inches a year.

Child care is offered at both base areas. The area has night skiing. The 100-room Sunrise Park Hotel is about three miles away.

Lift ticket prices: Adults, $32; Children (12 and younger), $18.

Distance from Phoenix: About 215 miles east on Hwy. 60, Hwy. 260 and Hwy. 273.

Lodging information: (800) 554-6835.

Arizona Snowbowl, Flagstaff AZ: (520) 779-1951

Internet: http://www.azsnowbowl.com

4 lifts; 131 skiable acres; 2,300 vertical feet

The San Francisco Mountains rise abruptly above Flagstaff, 140 miles north of Phoenix. They provide the most challenging skiing in Arizona and some of the best views anywhere.

The altitude is surprising for a state known for its deserts and canyons—the base area is 9,200 feet and climbs to 11,500 feet. From the top of Mount Agassiz the view includes the

Grand Canyon slash, the red rocks of Sedona, and mountains outside Kingman. Snowbowl's 50-acre beginner slope is separate from the rest of the ski area and has a modern day lodge with room for 300 people. The Agassiz Lodge, at the base of the higher lifts, is nearly four decades old and tight on space.

Lift ticket prices: Adults, $33; Children (8–12), $18. (Children 7 and younger ski free.)

Distance from Phoenix: About 150 miles north via I-17 and Hwy. 180. (The area is seven miles north of Flagstaff.)

Lodging information: (800) 828-7285.

Washington

The Summit, Snoqualmie Pass, WA; (206) 236-7277; (206) 236-1600 (info line)

Internet: http://www.summit-at-snoqualmie.com

30 lifts; 1,916 acres; 2,200 vertical feet

The Summit comprises four separate ski areas, all within a mile of each other on Snoqualmie Pass. Three are connected by trails, and the fourth, Alpental, is a mile away on another face. The four areas—Alpental, Summit West, Summit Central and Summit East— share an interchangeable lift ticket and offer a free shuttle so skiers can get from one to the others. Our stats reflect the combined lifts and acreage, while the vertical listed is for Alpental. The vertical drop at the other three areas varies from 900 to 1,080 feet.

Alpental (closed on non-holiday Mondays) has the most rugged reputation, Summit West (closed non-holiday Mondays and Tuesdays) features gentle green and blue runs, Summit Central (closed non-holiday Wednesdays and Thursdays) has mostly gentle terrain with a few serious black-diamond drops off the ridge, and Summit East (open weekends only) has some great tree runs and a snowboard halfpipe among its attractions. A Nordic ski area offers 55 km. of trails. Child care starts at 12 months and is offered at Summit West and Summit Central. Night skiing operates until 10:30 p.m. (9 p.m. Sundays) on any mountain open that day. Night child care is available by reservation.

Midweek prices are quite a bit lower than weekend prices, which are listed here.

Lift tickets: Adults, $32; Children (7–11), $22. (Children 6 and younger ski for $8.)

Distance from Seattle: About 50 miles east on I-90.

Lodging information: Summit Inn, (800) 557-7829.

Stevens Pass, Skykomish, WA; (360) 973-2441

Internet: http://www.stevenspass.com

11 lifts; 1,125 acres; 1,979 vertical feet

Stevens Pass began in 1937 with a rope tow powered by a V-8 engine. Now with 11 lifts, it is a favorite of Seattle-area skiers and snowboarders. Good spots for venturesome skiers are Mill Valley, with its black-diamond Borealis run, and the chutes reached by the 7th Heaven Chair. The Southern Cross Chair is 1,000 feet shy of a mile long, but if you swerve back and forth between the trees, you can easily double the distance back down to the bottom. Southern Cross and Jupiter lines are the shortest during lunch.

The Way Back trail, above Mill Valley's Corona bowl, is part of the gentle intermediate route to the valley floor. It's called the Way Back because beginners and intermediates can turn right onto Skid Road and descend gracefully to the base area. The Double Diamond run leading to the base area is in fact a double diamond. Adjacent woods make for some good off-piste skiing when the snow is fresh. Stevens Pass has night skiing until 10 p.m. There are 25 km. of groomed cross-country trails five miles east of the resort on Hwy. 2.

Child care for toilet-trained tots starts at age 2 1/2.

Lift tickets: Adults, $35; Children (7–12), $24. (Midweek prices are lower.)

Distance from Seattle: About 80 miles east on Hwy. 2.

Lodging information: SkyRiver Inn in Skykomish, (360) 677-2261. Leavenworth, a tourist town with an Alpine theme, is 37 miles east of Stevens Pass. For lodging information there, call Bavarian Bedfinders at (800) 323-2920.

New England

Maine

Saddleback, Rangeley, ME; (207) 864-5671

Internet: http://home.earthlink.net/~nortonc/ski/me/sdlbk/index.html

5 lifts; 41 trails; 110 acres; 1,860 vertical feet

If you're looking for a New England ski area the way they used to be, Saddleback is the place to go. The Appalachian Trail crosses its summit ridge, and litigation to keep the "view-shed" of the trail pristine has prevented Saddleback's owner from investing much in the mountain. Thus, underdeveloped, uncrowded, untamed are the words most often used to describe this area located in prime snowmobiling territory—skiers have to compete with snowmobilers for lodging in Rangeley, located 7 miles from the base.

Skiers will also find a real Maine experience in the town of Rangeley, which has at least a dozen restaurants. Saddleback's wide-open, gentle learning slope with its own chairlift, Gold Rush, attracts those wishing to learn the sport far from prying eyes, i.e. before they head to Sugarloaf. Plus, experts can have fun in the Nightmare Glades, on Bronco Buster or on Mule Skinner, which is consistently picked one of the East's top 10 extreme ski trails. Although known as a great family area, the word is out for single women to head to Saddleback after a snowfall—guys looking for powder flock there to ski the 30 percent of the mountain's terrain that never sees a groomer.

Lift tickets: Adults, $38; Teen (14-18), $34, Children (7-13), $26.

Distance from Boston: About 5+ hours. Take 95 North to the Maine Turnpike, get off at Exit 12 and follow Route 4 north through Farmington to Rangeley.

Lodging information: For the limited number of condos on the mountain (400 trailside), call the ski area number, (207) 864-5671. To reach the Rangeley Chamber of Commerce, call (800) 685-2537.

Massachusetts

Jiminy Peak, Hancock, MA; (413) 738-5500; (888) 454-6469

Internet: http://www.jiminypeak.com

8 lifts; 30 trails; 1,140 vertical feet

Jiminy Peak caters to families and intermediates with its terrain that isn't too steep and isn't too flat. Its instructional programs include some of the most popular national programs, SKIwee for kids and Perfect Turn for adults. Night skiing includes New England's longest lighted trail, Left Bank, and its day-care center takes infants as young as six months.

Lift tickets: Adults, $39; Children (ages 7-12), $28. (Midweek is less expensive.)

Distance from Albany, NY: About 40 miles via I-90, Rte. 43 and Brodie Mountain Rd.

Lodging information: (800) 882-8859.

Wachusett Mountain, Princeton, MA; (978) 464-2300; (800) 754-1234
Internet: http://wachusett.com
5 lifts; 18 trails; 1,000 vertical feet

Wachusett is the highest mountain in central Massachusetts. It has some decent advanced trails dropping from the summit, but all are groomed several times a day, taking the bite out of anything that may have been tough. If you want fast cruisers, this is the place to strap on your boards. Try Conifer Connection or Balance Rock for intermediate cruising. Head to 10th Mountain for bumps. Beginners stick to the cluster of Easy Rider, Sundowner and Indian Summer. Night skiing is open from 4–10 p.m.

Lift tickets: Adults (8 a.m.–4 p.m.) $35 weekend, $29 weekday; Junior (10 and younger)/Seniors (65 and older) $27 weekend; $24 weekday; Kids 5 years old and younger are $5 anytime. Call for night skiing rates.
Distance from Boston: About 50 miles via Rtes. 2 and 140.
Lodging information: You're on your own, or call the resort for a referral.

New Hampshire

The Balsams Wilderness, Dixville Notch, NH; (603) 255-3400; (800) 255-0800, NH; (800) 255-0600 U.S. and Canada
Internet: http://www.thebalsams.com
3 lifts; 13 trails; 85 acres; 1,000 vertical feet

This is a small, hassle-free, friendly ski area that on its own might not warrant a write-up, but coupled with The Balsams, a four-star, four-diamond destination resort located deep in the northern wilds of New Hampshire, this is almost a don't-miss for skiers of all levels. However, even its public relations director acknowledges that while an expert skier will enjoy his first day there, he or she might be a little bored on the second day.

But who cares! The Balsams Wilderness has award-winning chefs who prepare a full breakfast buffet (or you can order from the menu) and five-course dinner daily. It's said you can put your car keys away once you check in and you don't even need to carry your wallet. Children's programs, which even include mealtimes as well as skiing, keep the youngsters occupied so the parents can relax. And when the kids are in bed, the hotel offers movies, dancing and entertainment nightly. Oh, yeah, we shouldn't forget the skiing. The alpine trails are varied, the people are very friendly (they are really up in the woods!) and the area gets lots of snow. The Balsams also offers 64 km. of cross-country trails with one circuit that has a vertical drop of 500 feet more than the ski area (for the less daring, there's also lots of cross-country on the golf course).

Lift tickets: Adults, $25; Children, $18. (Skiing is complimentary for hotel guests.)
Distance from Boston: About 220 miles north via I-93 (to Exit 35) then Rte. 3 to Colebrook and Rte. 26 to Dixville Notch.
Lodging information: (800) 255-0800, NH; (800) 255-0600, U.S. and Canada.

Gunstock, Gilford, NH; (800) GUNSTOCK or (603) 293-4341
Internet: http://www.gunstock.com
7 lifts; 47 trails; 1,400 vertical feet

Gunstock is primarily a resort for skiers who like to cruise. Advanced skiers can ski through glades on Middle Trigger and find bumps on Tiger. Intermediate cruisers will stick to Recoil, Ramrod and Gunsmoke trails with their views of Lake Winnipesaukee. There are some intermediate glades on Lower Recall and Musket. Night skiing is open on fifteen trails served by five lifts. Beginners have their own separate area, called Gunshy. Snowboarders will find a 600-foot halfpipe. Cross-country skiers can enjoy 42 km. of trails for skating and gliding. The surrounding NH lakes region has thousands of rooms and plenty of restaurants as well as other activities such as ice fishing and snowmobiling.

Lift tickets: Adults, $39 weekend, $28 weekday; Junior (6–12) and Senior (65-69) $24 weekend, $20 weekday. Night skiing is $19; $15 for kids and seniors. Skiers ages 5 and younger and 70 and older ski free.

Distance from Boston: About 90 miles via I-93 and Rtes. 3 and 11A.

Lodging information: (603) 293-4341 or (800) GUNSTOCK (486-7862).

Mt. Sunapee, Mt. Sunapee, NH; (603) 763-2356

Internet: None found.

8 lifts; 41 trails; 1,510 vertical feet, 200 skiable acres

Mt. Sunapee is being reborn under the managment of the owners of Okemo Mountain. A new high-speed quad will power skiers to the summit in less than six minutes and new snowmaking will produce better coverage and a longer season. A new fixed quad chair lift will double lift capacity in the Sun Bowl section of the mountain. New grooming machines will comb the mountain and a new Pipe Dragon groomer will create an enhanced snowboard experience. Mt. Sunapee is a family mountain attracting a loyal following of skiers who like its New England feel and its close proximity (less than two hours) to Boston. Mt. Sunapee skis a lot bigger than it is, with two different base areas and a separate beginner area. Sunapee offers one of the best ski-area views in New England—eight ski areas, from Mt. Mansfield to Stratton, *and* Lake Sunapee—and one of New Hampshire's finest summit lodges, complete with fireplace and balconies, to enjoy it all from.

Lift tickets: (98/99 prices) Adults, $41 weekend, $36 weekday; Young Adult (13–19), $36 weekend, $31 weekday; Junior (7–12) and Senior (65+) $30 weekend, $26 weekday. Skiers ages 6 and younger ski free.

Distance from Boston: About 100 miles via I-93, I-89 and Rte. 103.

Lodging information: Lake Sunapee Business Association, (800) 258-3530.

Ragged Mountain, Danbury, NH; (603) 768-3475

Internet: http://www.ragged-mt.com

6 lifts; 34 trails; 1,250 vertical feet; 150 skiable acres

Popular with Boston day-trippers, Ragged planned to add 15,000 square feet to Elmwood Lodge, a new triple chair in its learning area and two new trails. Situated in the middle of New Hampshire, it provides excellent learning terrain at very affordable prices.

Lift tickets: Adults, $30 weekends and holidays, $15 midweek; Children, $25 weekends and holidays, $15 midweek. Skiers ages 5 and younger ski free.

Distance from Boston: About 105 miles via I-93 to Rte. 4 West to 104 East.

Lodging information: (800) 887-5464

Vermont

Ascutney Mountain Resort, Brownsville, VT; (802) 484-7711; (800) 243-0011
Internet: http://www.ascutney.com
4 lifts; 46 trails; 1,530 vertical feet

Ascutney presides over the Connecticut River Valley right on I-91 tracing the New Hampshire/Vermont border. Ascutney has trails cut the old-fashion way (translate that as having wonderful character) that roll with the natural contours of the mountain. There is a good mix for advanced and intermediate skiers as well as a separate beginner area perfect for learning. The base area is anchored by a 240-room ski-in/ski-out suite hotel. The resort has focused on family activities with a tubing hill, ice skating, pizza parties, torchlight parades and a good children's ski school.

Lift tickets: Adults, $39 weekend/holiday, $34 weekday; Juniors (7–16) and Seniors (65–69) $26 daily. Those 6 and younger and 70 and older ski free.

Distance from Burlington: About 105 miles south I-89, I-91, Rte. 5 and Rte. 44. Ascutney is about 130 miles from Albany, NY, and about 135 miles from Boston or Hartford, CT.

Lodging information/reservations: (800) 243-0011.

Bolton Valley, Bolton, VT; (802) 434-2131
Internet: http://www.boltonvalley.com
6 lifts; 50 trails; 1,625 vertical feet

Bolton Valley is an uncrowded family-owned resort with a focus on family skiing. Bolton is one of the best areas for combining downhill and cross-country in Vermont. The downhill skiing includes a backcountry area for telemark skiers as well as abundant tree skiing. The Nordic Center at 2,100-foot elevation is one of New England's highest, providing some of the best early season conditions. There are 100 km. of cross-country trails. The Bolton Mountain Lodge and surrounding condominiums are ski-in/ski-out and have an excellent sports center with pool, sauna, spa, weight room and tennis.

Lift tickets: Adults (15+), $38; Children (7–12), $30. Ages 6 and younger ride lifts for $10. Vermont residents get a hefty discount. Night skiing (until 10 p.m.): Adult $18, Children $10.

Distance from Burlington: About 20 miles via I-89.

Lodging information: (800) 451-3220.

Burke Mountain, East Burke, VT; (802) 626-3305, snow phone (800) 922-2875
Internet: http://www.burkemountain.com
4 lifts; 30 trails; 2,000 vertical feet

Burke Mountain is a free-standing mountain tucked in the far northeast part of Vermont with fantastic panoramas from its summit; it is neither part of the Green Mountains nor part of the White Mountains. This relatively undiscovered resort caters to intermediates and beginners, but has some good gladed skiing for higher ability levels. Burke Mountain is the home of Burke Mountain Academy, a private high school dedicated to ski racing. This mountain was home to Olympian Diane Roffe-Steinrotter during her high school days. There is ski-in/ski-out lodging perfect for families, and a SKIwee program for young children.

Lift tickets: Adults, $38 weekend/holiday; $15 weekday; Teens (13–19) and Seniors (60–69), $33 weekend/holiday; $15 weekday; Juniors (6–12), $23 weekend, $15 weekday. Skiers 5 and younger and 70 and older ski free.

Distance from Burlington: About 95 miles via I-89, Rte. 2, I-91 and Rte. 114.

Lodging information: (800) 541-5480.

Jay Peak, Jay, VT; (802) 988-2611, snow phone (802) 988-9601
Internet: http://www.jaypeakresort.com
7 lifts; 325 trail acres; 64 trails and glades; 2,153 vertical feet

Jay is a big mountain by Eastern standards, almost 4,000 feet high with a vertical drop of 2,150 feet. Jay gets lots of snow—an average of more than 300 inches per year. Jay Peak has Vermont's only tram, a 60-passenger vehicle that whisks skiers from the base to the summit. If you are staying at the Hotel Jay, the tram is just outside your room.

Because of Jay's proximity to French-speaking Québec, 52 percent of its skiers hail from Canada and about half of those speak French. Jay is a day tripper's resort, with late-arriving crowds on weekends. Be smart and arrive early; try to catch the 8:30 a.m. tram to the summit. Enjoy the views of four states and Canada (don't forget your camera) and head over to Stateside area on the blue Vermonter trail. At Stateside you can ski some of Jay's most popular trails without any congestion or lift lines. Lines do form at the tram when all the late arrivals queue up, but Jay's trails are spread out and seldom congested.

Experts will like the 100-plus acres of glades. Jay is proud of its tree-skiing opportunities and even posts bilingual warning signs that explain the dangers and rules of skiing in the woods. For beginners still in the wedge, the green trails are quite good, though not abundant. This mountain is not suited for the lower intermediate skier, except those willing to take on a challenge, because of the extreme variations in the difficulty level of the blue terrain.

Lift tickets: Adults, $42; Juniors (7–14), $30. Ages 6 and younger and 65+ ski for $5.
Distance from Burlington: About 65 miles on Rte. 242.
Lodging information: (800) 451-4449, outside Vermont.

Suicide Six, Woodstock, VT; (802) 457-6661, Ski Reports (802) 457-6666
Internet: http://www.woodstockinn.com/skiatinn.html
3 lifts; 21 trails; 650 vertical feet

Suicide Six is part of the Woodstock Inn and Resort. Though small, it has limited terrain for every ability level. This season it has focused on expert trails and glades to compliment the intermediate and beginner areas. Recently the resort added a halfpipe for snowboarders. The Woodstock Inn also has one of the better cross-country skiing trail systems in the state as well as an excellent indoor sports facility.

Lift tickets: Adults, about $34 weekends; $19 weekdays; Children, $22 weekends; $15 weekdays. Lodging and lift packages are the way to go here; call the inn for more information.
Distance from Burlington: About 100 miles via I-89 and Rte. 4. Suicide Six is about 125 miles from Albany and about 150 miles from Boston.
Lodging information: Woodstock Inn, (800) 448-7900 or (802) 457-1100.

Midwest

The biggest Midwestern ski areas may not have the great verticals of mountains to the east and west, but they have enough terrain, fine facilities, and uphill capacity to tune anyone up for bigger adventures. The following are the best Midwestern ski destinations. Expect lift tickets to be between $25 and $35 except Michigan's Lower Peninsula, where weekend tickets midseason will be in the high-$30s to low-$40s. All the resorts offer midweek price incentives and stay-and-ski packages.

Michigan's Lower Peninsula:

Boyne Highlands and Boyne Mountain,
Harbor Springs and Boyne Falls, MI; (800) 462-6963 (GO-BOYNE)
Internet: http://www.boyne.com
22 lifts, 82 trails, 520 vertical feet

The Mountain and Highlands, situated about 30 minutes apart, are near Petoskey and Harbor Springs, two towns that are New England lookalikes and have been a Midwest winter vacation area since the 1920s. The Mountain's steep chutes and mogul fields are legendary among flatlanders. In an effort to soften its tough image, a large new beginner area and tow were added in '95. This is a Midwest classic with sweeping bowls and Eastern-style trails that slice through the hilly hardwoods. An intermediate mountain by reputation, it recently added some tougher terrain. If advanced skiing is what you seek, head for the Mountain.

Both areas feature a high-speed lift, unusual in the Great Lakes states. Each resort has an uphill capacity approaching 22,000 skiers per hour—tops in the Midwest. Boyne's snowmaking capabilities are well known among Midwestern skiers. The Mountain routinely stays open on weekends through April, and has extended into May on a couple of occasions—most recently in 1996. The Mountain opened 12 new runs during the past couple of seasons along Disciple's Ridge, and is creating a new village area at the base.

Plenty of lodging and amenities exist at the resorts and in the area. Many skiers choose to stay in town and day-trip to the ski areas. Call Boyne Country CVB at (800) 845-2828.

Nubs Nob is just across the valley from the Highlands. Nubs offers the best trio of advanced slopes in the Lower Peninsula. Recent additions of 12 runs and a quad lift help round out the variety. It's the locals' choice. Most skiers up for an extended weekend will add a day of skiing at Nubs.

Lift tickets at Boyne: Adults, $40 weekends; $33 weekdays; Children (9–12), $28 weekends; $22 weekdays. Teens ski for $37; 8 and younger ski free.

Distance from Detroit: About 250 miles via I-75 to the Gaylord exit, then M-32 west to U.S. 131. Distance from Chicago: About 250 miles via I-94 to I-196 north to Grand Rapids, to U.S. 131.

Lodging information: (800) GO-BOYNE (Boyne USA) or (800) 845-2828 (Boyne Country Convention and Visitors Bureau.

Sugar Loaf, Cedar, MI: (616) 228-5461; (800) 748-0117
Internet: http://www.theloaf.com
7 lifts, 20 trails, 500 vertical feet

With the backdrop of Lake Michigan's ice-blue waters, sand dunes and the Manitou Islands just off the coast, Sugar Loaf offers one of the best combinations of views and skiing in the Lower Peninsula. In addition to great cruising runs such as Devil's Elbow and The Wall, it has two of the steepest slopes around the Great Lakes—Awful-Awful and Manitou Extreme (the latter is the only FIS-sanctioned race hill on the Lower Peninsula). The Loaf has condo and hotel accommodations and a variety of restaurants.

Lift tickets: Not available; call the resort.

Distance from Detroit: About 250 miles via I-75 to the Grayling exit, then M-72 through Traverse City and follow signs. Distance from Chicago: About 230 miles via I-94 to I-196 north, then follow U.S. 31 north to Traverse City, pick up M-72 west and follow signs.

Lodging information: (800) 952-6390.

Crystal Mountain, Thompsonville, MI: (616) 378-2911

Internet: http://www.crystalmtn.com
7 lifts, 22 trails, 375 vertical feet

Crystal Mountain skis much bigger than its 375-foot vertical. It's a great family area that offers solid intermediate slopes and lots of lower-level trails. As evidence of its appeal, Crystal ranks annually among the top 10 resorts for overall NASTAR participants. It has a variety of lodging and a fitness center with a pool. It is adding a new area off the backside of the mountain, featuring half a dozen runs and a new lift.

Lift tickets: Adults, $37; children (7-12), $23; teens (13-18), $30. Discounts midweek.
Distance from Detroit: About 240 miles via I-75 to U.S. 10 to M-115, which leads to the resort. **Distance from Chicago:** About 230 miles via I-94 to I-196 north to Grand Rapids, to U.S. 131 to M-115.
Lodging information: (800) 968-7686.

Shanty Creek/Schuss Mountain, Bellaire, MI: (616) 533-8621; (800) 348-4440

Internet: http://www.shantycreek.com
9 lifts, 30 trails, 450 vertical feet

These two resorts offer a nice weekend retreat. They are about five miles apart but are now operated as one with an interchangeable lift ticket. Shanty has the nicest lodging, but Schuss has the better skiing—a good skier will get bored quickly at Shanty. The Schuss Mountain slopes got 12 new runs last season and upgraded chairlifts.

Lift tickets: Adults, $39; children $25; teens and ages 55–69, $32. Midweek prices are less. Night skiing is $15 for adults; $10 for kids.
Distance from Detroit: About 225 miles via I-75 to the Grayling exit, then M-72 west to Kalkaska, north on U.S. 131 to Mancelona and follow the signs. **Distance from Chicago:** About 225 miles via I-94 to I-196 north to U.S. 131 to Mancelona and follow the signs.
Lodging information: (800) 678-4111.

Michigan Upper Peninsula—Big Snow Country:

This is a rugged land of dense forests, long winters, deep snows and a collection of ski areas called Big Snow Country, comprised of these four ski areas, plus Whitecap Mountain in Wisconsin. The region receives over 200 inches of snowfall annually. Resorts listed here are all located near Ironwood and Hurley, about a seven-hour drive from Chicago or four hours from the Twin Cities, and are close enough together to be visited during the same trip.

Indianhead Mountain, Wakefield, MI: (906) 229-5181; (800) 346-3426

Internet: http://www.indianheadmtn.com
9 lifts, 22 trails, 638 vertical feet

Blackjack, Bessemer, MI: (906) 229-5117; (800) 848-1125

Internet: http://www.skiblackjack.com
6 lifts, 20 trails, 465 vertical feet

Big Powderhorn Mountain, Bessemer, MI: (906) 932-4838; (800) 222-3131

Internet: http://www.bpla.com
9 lifts, 24 trails, 600 vertical feet

Porcupine Mountain, Silver City, MI: (906) 885-5275

Internet: None found.
4 lifts, 14 trails, 647 vertical feet

Whitecap Mountain, Montreal, WI; (715) 561-2227

Internet: None found.

8 lifts, 32 trails, 400 vertical feet

These five ski areas markets themselves together as Big Snow Country, though each operates independently. Here's a rundown on each:

Indianhead runs are wide boulevards. It's an intermediate's dream—long, smooth runs—but they all look the same. The skier who likes a good challenge may get bored here, but it is a great family area. The lodge and compact ski area sit atop the mountain. Runs fan out into the deep forests below, but all the lifts funnel back to the lodge on top. The main lodge was originally a dairy barn, part of a hilltop farm dating from the turn of the century. It's quite rustic and charming. A new pool and fitness center were added in recent years.

Blackjack appeals to intermediate and advanced skiers, befitting its brawny lumberjack image. They will enjoy busting down some of the wide bump runs or exploring the many narrow chutes and trails that fork off the boulevards. The Black River meanders through the valley—very picturesque.

Big Powderhorn Mountain offers a good variety of trails and the most uphill capacity in the immediate area (9,600 per hour). It has tree-lined trails, open bowls, rambling runs and narrow chutes to explore, plus the most slopeside lodging, restaurants and après-ski activity in the area.

About 45 minutes north of the Ironwood/Hurley area, **Porcupine** offers stunning Lake Superior views. Perched on the shoreline, the lake is clearly visible from every run. It's a great family area with a wide variety of runs that caters to all ability levels. Most skiers daytrip from the other ski areas, but limited lodging is available. Outstanding cross-country skiing and snowmobiling opportunities are available in the vast Porcupine Mountain State Park, which is designed as a wilderness area.

Whitecap has had a facelift in recent years. Several new shops and a conference center have been added to the day lodge, but the expansion still preserves the Old-World charm. The most interesting mix of trails in the area drops down three peaks in every direction. It's the one place in the Midwest where a trail map comes in handy. Located in the Pekonee Mountains, it's in sight of Lake Superior on a clear day.

Lift tickets (Adults, one day): Indianhead, $33; Big Powderhorn Mountain, $28; Blackjack, $27; Porcupine, $25; Whitecap, $33. Discounts offered midweek and to seniors and teens.

Lift tickets (Children, one day): Indianhead, $20; Big Powderhorn Mountain, $16; Blackjack, free, ages 8 and younger; Porcupine, free; Whitecap, $20. Discounts offered midweek.

Distance from Minneapolis: About 300 miles via U.S. 8 to U.S. 51 in Wisconsin, then head north to Hurley where you follow signs to the individual resorts. **Distance from Chicago:** About 350 miles via I-94 or I-90 to Madison, then U.S. 51 north to Hurley.

Lodging information: Western Upper Peninsula Con/Vis Bureau, (906) 932-4850.

Minnesota

Blessed with superb ski terrain and consistently cold temperatures, northern Minnesota has some of the best snow conditions east of the Rockies, and the northwoods scenery is spectacular. What's here? Three excellent ski areas with big vertical drops (for the Midwest)—Giants Ridge, 550 feet; Spirit Mountain, 700 feet; and Lutsen, 800 feet. They are located around Duluth and within an hour or so of each other.

Lutsen, Lutsen, MN; (218) 663-7281, (800) 360-7666
Internet: None found.
8 lifts, 48 trails, 800 vertical feet

About an hour north of Duluth on Hwy. 61 (immortalized by Bob Dylan in the 1960s), Lutsen is the closest thing to true mountain skiing in the Great Lakes area. It has the only gondola in the Midwest and the skiing is off of four peaks (à la Killington). It will remind you of a New England ski area—long rock-ribbed trails flanked by birch and pine, and tight short headwalls. Moose Mountain offers the best cruisers between the Appalachians and the Rockies. The many Lake Superior views are magnificent. A variety of accommodations exist at Lutsen Mountain and along the north shore—rustic to plush, simple to gourmet. Cross-country skiing also is plentiful throughout the area.

Lift tickets: Adults, $42; Children, $29. Midweek, prices are $39 and $29, respectively.
Distance from Minneapolis: About 180 miles via I-35 north to Duluth, then pick up U.S. 61, which leads right to the resort.
Lodging information: (800) 360-7666.

Spirit Mountain, Duluth, MN; (218) 628-2891;(800) 642-6377
Internet: None found.
8 lifts, 21 trails, 700 vertical feet

Spirit Mountain has good vertical, long runs, snowy winters and great views of Duluth and the harbor perched on the Superior shoreline. The skiing is long on intermediate and beginner runs, without much variation in pitch and few twists and turns. A high-speed covered quad services the beginner trails—nice on cold days. An expert won't find much challenge here.

Lift tickets: Not available; call the resort.
Distance from Minneapolis: About 90 miles via I-35 north, which passes by the ski area.
Lodging information: (800) 642-6377

Giant's Ridge, Biwabik, MN; (218) 865-4143
Internet: None found.
5 lifts, 19 trails, 500 vertical feet

About an hour's drive northwest of Duluth, this area is not as crowded as the other two. The trails soar off the crest and are varied in pitch, with a headwall here, a bowl there. The day lodge is first class, and so is the cross-country skiing. The resort added a beautiful new lodging facility in 1998.

Lift tickets: Not available; call the resort.
Distance from Duluth: About 60 miles via U.S. 53 north, then follow the signs.
Lodging information: Not available.

Wisconsin

The skiing here has a certain ruggedness that you won't find in Michigan's Lower Peninsula. It doesn't receive the natural lake-effect snow that Michigan gets, but the areas do an adequate job of snowmaking.

Devil's Head, Merrimac, WI; (800) 338-4579 (DEVILSX)
Internet: None found.
15 lifts and tows, 21 trails, 500 vertical feet

The beautiful Baraboo Bluffs overlooking the Wisconsin River Valley have excellent beginner and intermediate skiing. One of the beginner runs is nearly two miles long. Devil's Head's drawbacks are limited advanced terrain and not much variation. It is a full-service resort with a country-club atmosphere. Weekend crowds can be huge.

Located just down the road is **Cascade,** with 460 vertical feet and a wide variety of skiing. It's straightforward skiing, with solid cruising and hefty faces for the bumps. It has more uphill capacity than Devil's Head (14,000 per hour), but weekend lines can still be long. These two resorts, just three hours from Chicago, are together consistently rated the top day-trip destinations in the Midwest.

Lift tickets: Not available; call the resort.

Distance from Chicago: About 180 miles via I-94 or I-90 to Portage, WI exit, then follow signs.

Lodging information: (800) 472-6770.

Mid-Atlantic:

Pennsylvania: The Poconos

Romantic hideaways, major highways and big-city convenience have made the hills of Northeastern Pennsylvania a weekend retreat for some of America's largest metropolitan areas. The region has long had a honeymoon reputation with lodges offering heart-shaped beds and in-room spas. Beds of all shapes are in plentiful supply—80,000 within an hour of the hills.

A few notes about this region: Weekends tend to be very crowded. Most areas have 100 percent snowmaking and state-of-the-art grooming. All the areas now permit snowboarding, and most have added terrain parks and/or halfpipes. Most of the terrain is intermediate, with a few short-but-sweet black diamonds, and plenty of isolated beginner areas. Each mountain maintains a hill specifically for never-evers.

But the new trend is toward tubing. Families who enjoy winter but don't ski or board can ride single or family tubes at areas adjacent to the ski slopes, and meet up with family members who do ski or snowboard. Many state parks and some resorts have cross-country areas. The Poconos Mountain Tourist Bureau at (717) 424-6050 provides a cross-country report.

Blue Mountain, Palmerton, PA; (610) 826-7700; Snow report (877) 754-2583

Internet: http://www.aminews.com/bluemountain

7 lifts; 75 acres; 1,082 vertical feet

This area is the closest to Philadelphia, and offers the Poconos' highest vertical, 1082 feet on Challenge. The pitch is steep and steady with moguls and a headwall near the bottom. With ideal conditions, you might think you were skiing Vermont. The area features night skiing seven nights a week and tickets are sold according to the hours you want to ski. Blue Mountain has a halfpipe for snowboarders and a tubing hill with two lifts and 11 chutes.

Lift tickets: Weekday adult tickets range from $27–$33; children's tickets $20. Weekend adult tickets range from $33–$40; children $25.

Distance from New York or Philadelphia: About 100 miles. Skiers heading to Blue Mountain should take the Northeast Extension of the Pennsylvania Turnpike to Exit 33 or 35 then follow the signs.

Lodging information: (800) 762-6667; (800) POCONOS.

Jack Frost/Big Boulder, Blakeslee, PA; (717) 443-8433 or (717) 722-0100

Internet: http://www.big2resorts.com

14 lifts (combined); 155 skiable acres (combined); 600 vertical feet (Jack Frost)

These two areas, marketed as the Big Two Resorts with an interchangeable lift ticket, are on opposite sides of Rte. 940 and a few miles from each other.

Big Boulder was one of the first Poconos ski areas and one of the first to cover its trails with machine-made snow. Today beginners and intermediates practice their skills day and night on its 2,900-foot-long, 475-foot-high hill. Friday nights, you can ski until 10 p.m.

The Jack Frost lodge is at the top of the mountain. The 21 slopes and trails are straight, top to bottom, with variety in pitch.

Each mountain has a snowboard terrain park and halfpipe. Both mountains have tubing hills, with a combined 20 chutes served by seven lifts.

Big Boulder offers a 3-km. cross-country trail at the top of the Edelweiss lift. The trail winds its way through Hickory Run State Park. Adjoining Jack Frost is a 15-km. trail winding through the open land surrounding the ski area.

Lift tickets: Lift tickets are interchangeable at both areas. Night skiing is offered at Big Boulder only. Weekday prices: adults, $36; weekends, $42. Children (6–15) ski anytime for $22.

Distance from New York: About 100 miles. To reach Jack Frost/Big Boulder from New York, take Exit 43 from I-80. Jack Frost is five miles north by Route 115 then west on Route 940. Big Boulder is south of the interstate via Routes 115 and 903. **Distance from D.C.:** About 60 miles by I-10, I-215, Hwy. 30, Hwy. 330 and Hwy. 18.

Lodging information: (800) 468-2442.

Camelback, Tannersville, PA; (717) 629-1661; snow report (800) 233-8100.

Internet: http://skicamelback.com

12 lifts; 139 skiable acres; 811 vertical feet.

This area is the closest to metropolitan New York, and only about 20 minutes farther from Philadelphia than Blue Mountain. It is an intermediate cruising heaven with 33 trails and two fairly new high-speed quads.

Although Margies and the Hump are rated expert, they tend to get slick early. The best skiing is on the intermediate/advanced-beginner trails, such as Mark Anthony, Pharaoh and Nile Mile (125 feet wide and a mile long). These trails and Cliffhanger, a 5,000-foot double-black-diamond, can be reached via the Stevenson high-speed quad.

Night skiing is offered on 26 of the 33 trails every night. A learning center with its own lift offers adult never-evers special packages using shaped skis. Children aged 4–6 can enroll in the Sugar Bear ski program (lifts, lessons, lunch and equipment) for $65 midweek and $70 weekends. Ages 7–12 pay $70 midweek and $80 weekends for the same program, but can opt for snowboarding instead of skiing.

Lift tickets: Midweek for adults is $34; children (12 and younger), $28. Children shorter than 46 inches ski free with an adult. Weekend prices are adults $41, children, $33.

Distance from New York: About 100 miles. To reach Camelback, take Exit 45 from I-80, then follow signs.

Lodging information: (800) 762-6667; (800) POCONOS.

Other Pennsylvania areas:

Whitetail, Mercersburg, PA; (717) 328-9400

Internet: http://www.skiwhitetail.com

6 lifts; 108 skiable acres; 935 vertical feet

Whitetail concentrates on giving Eastern skiers an upscale ski experience with its beautiful, modern base facility, 100 percent snowmaking, a child-care center and 11,200 person-per-hour lift capacity. Night skiing is available.

Lift tickets: Adults, $42; Children (7–12), $35. Midweek and senior discounts available.

Distance from Baltimore or Washington D.C.: About 90 miles via I-70 west.

Lodging information: (717) 328-9400.

Elk Mountain Ski Area, Union Dale, PA; (717) 679-2611

Internet: http://www.elkskier.com

6 lifts; 25 trails; 1,000 vertical feet

By Pennsylvania standards, this is a tough mountain. The slopes are good for advanced skiers and solid intermediates who want some practice. The beginner trails can be difficult on an icy day. There is no real resort area, but the region has about 50 hotels. Elk is in the northeast corner of Pennsylvania near Scranton. Night skiing and child care are available.

Lift tickets: Adults, $39; Children, $31.

Distance from Scranton: About 26 miles via I-81.

Lodging information: Special packages are offered at nearby motels. Best accommodations are at Nicholas Village in Clarks Summit.

Seven Springs, Champion, PA; (814) 352-7777

Internet: http://www.7springs.com

11 lifts and 7 tows; 30 trails; 750 vertical feet

Hidden Valley, Hidden Valley, PA; (814) 443-2600; (800) 458-0175

Internet: http://www.hiddenvalleyresort.com

6 lifts and 2 tows; 17 trails; 610 vertical feet

These resorts are about three-and-a-half hours from Baltimore and Washington and an hour from Pittsburgh. Seven Springs has the best base facilities and more difficult trails; however Hidden Valley offers quieter surroundings. Trails will keep beginners and intermediates happy for a day or two. Both areas have child care (starting at "walking age" for Seven Springs; 18 months and older at Hidden Valley) and night skiing.

Lift tickets: In the high $30s for adults; low $30s for kids. For specifics, call the resorts.

Distance from Pittsburgh: About 55 miles east via the Pennsylvania Turnpike.

Lodging information: Hidden Valley, (800) 458-0175; Seven Springs, (800) 452-2223.

Doe Mountain Ski Area, Macungie, PA; (610) 682-7100; 1-800-ISKI-DOE

Internet: http://www.doemountain.com

7 lifts; 15 trails; 500 vertical feet. 100 percent snowmaking coverage.

This is a small mountain but one of the closest to Philadelphia near Allentown. The 1,300-foot summit offers beautiful views of the Lehigh Valley. A good place to learn to ski or snowboard and get some turns in before heading to the big resorts. Night skiing is also available. Resort has cafeteria, grill and bar, lockers, ski school, active ski patrol and free midweek babysitting.

Lift tickets: Adults, $27 weekdays, $35 weekends; children (6–12) and seniors (62–69), $18 midweek, $24 weekend; skiers 5 and younger and 70 and older ski free.

Location: 54 miles NW of Philadelphia and 85 miles west of New York City.

West Virginia
Snowshoe/Silver Creek, Snowshoe, WV; (304) 572-1000
Internet: http://www.snowshoemtn.com
11 lifts; 53 trails; 1,500 vertical feet (Snowshoe)

Snowshoe sits atop Cheat Mountain, topping off an inverted resort: the facilities are at the summit. The area often gets 200 inches of snow and has extensive snowmaking. This is the most elaborate and extensive resort in the South. Nearby Silver Creek Resort is a terrific family area. Though the two areas are separate, a shuttle transports skiers the short distance. One lift ticket is good at both areas. Silver Creek is less crowded, and the slopes are wider and better designed than at Snowshoe. The downside is the skiing is less challenging. Child care is available starting at age 2; call for reservations.

Lift tickets: In the low $40s for adults; high $20s for kids. For specifics, call the resort.
Distance from Lewisburg, WV (Greenbriar Valley Airport): On Rte.219 north 60 miles.
Lodging information: (304) 572-5252.

Canaan Valley, Davis, WV; (304) 866-4121
Internet: None found.
3 lifts; 34 trails; 850 vertical feet
Timberline Four Seasons Resort, Davis, WV; (304) 866-4801
Internet: http://www.timberlineresort.com
3 lifts; 35 trails; 1,000 vertical feet

A long-time favorite ski area for D.C.-area skiers, Canaan (pronounced Kuh-NANE) Valley ski area is located in a pristine wilderness area. Deer stroll in front of the park hotel. Terrific cross-country skiing is nearby. The downhill skiing is good for all levels.

Timberline was one of the first in the country to welcome snowboarders. It is a small family area, boasting a two-mile long beginner's run. It's usually uncrowded compared to next-door Canaan, and many of the skiers are resort property owners.

Lift tickets: Adults in the mid-$30s; children in the high $20s. For specifics, call the resort.
Distance from Pittsburgh: About 145 miles southeast.
Lodging information: Canaan Valley, (304) 866-4121; Timberline, (800) 766-9464.

Virginia/Maryland
Wintergreen, Wintergreen, VA; (804) 325-2200
Internet: http://www.wintergreenresort.com
5 lifts; 17 slopes and trails; 1,003 vertical feet

Wintergreen is less than an hour south of Charlottesville along the famed Skyline Drive. While natural snow is limited, the manmade variety is religiously pumped out day and night. The lodge is rather upscale with boutiques and antiques. Most skiing is mellow, but The Highlands offers a thousand feet of bumps with limited crowds. Night skiing and child care are available.

Lift tickets: Adults $39, Children $32.
Distance from Charlottesville, VA: About 45 miles southwest.
Lodging information: (800) 325-2200.

Wisp, McHenry, MD; (301) 387-4911
Internet: http://www.gcnet.net/wisp

7 lifts; 23 trails; 610 vertical feet

Located above scenic Deep Creek Lake, Wisp is the closest thing below the Mason-Dixon Line to skiing Lake Tahoe. A solid family ski area with terrain for all levels; intermediates will especially enjoy cruising on the back side of the mountain. Night skiing is available, but no child care for children younger than age 4.

Lift tickets (98/99 prices): Adults $42, Children $29.

Distance from Pittsburgh: About 125 miles southeast via I-79, I-68 and Rte. 219.

Lodging information: (301) 387-4911.

Western Canada

Silver Star, Silver Star Mountain, BC; (800) 663-4431; (250) 542-0224

Internet: http://www.silverstarmtn.com

8 lifts; 1,200 acres; 2,500 vertical feet

First-time visitors to Silver Star love the frontier ambiance of the 1890s Victorian Gaslight village. With a street full of wooden buildings and no cars, Silver Star has a compact touch of elegance, even with 1,000 beds, restaurants, lots of shopping and an aquatic center.

Silver Star claims to be the second largest downhill ski resort (after Whistler/Blackcomb) in British Columbia, with 81 runs on two mountain faces. However, Big White also claims that distinction. It really doesn't matter. Silver Star, Big White and Sun Peaks are all close enough together to include on one trip, and all three are very good-sized, so you'll keep busy the better part of a week.

At Silver Star, the challenging Putnam Creek Basin is called the "Valley of Adventure." It's served by a long high-speed quad and has plenty of expert and intermediate runs. An expansion a few years ago doubled Silver Star's terrain.

The trails on the Vance Creek side are a mix of mostly beginner and intermediate. Five chair lifts serve this section, and night skiing goes until 10 p.m. Silver Star has enough variety to satisfy skiers for several days, with few ropes, fences or "restricted" signs for a very open feeling.

The Silver Star Nordic Center has 35 km. of trails at the base of the village, connected to 49 km. more in adjacent Silver Star Provincial Park. The resort trails are groomed and 4 km. are lighted for night skiing.

Lift tickets (Cdn$): Adults $45, Children $23.

Distance from Vernon, B.C.: About 12 miles. Scheduled flights are met by limousine.

Distance from Vancouver: The nearest major airport is here, about 260 miles away.

Lodging information: (800) 663-4431. Silver Star Village has six inns and hotels, plus a 47-site RV park at the ski area. Skican offers air-lodging-lift packages from many U.S. metro areas; call (800) 268-8880 for information.

Sun Peaks, Kamloops, BC; (250) 578-7842; (800) 807-3257

Internet: http://www.sunpeaks.com

6 lifts; 1,100 acres; 2,953 vertical feet

Sun Peaks is Japanese-owned, but run by Al Raines and his ski-race-champion wife, Nancy Greene Raines, who helped to build Whistler into the destination resort it is today. Word on the street is "enjoy it before it gets too big." Sun Peaks got *Snow Country*'s 1995 award for Best Trail Design. Other recent improvements have been two quads, two new lodges, an 80-acre intermediate family area, a snowboard park and a snowmaking system.

One of those quads, the 1.5-mile Sunburst Express, serves a six-pack of black-diamond steeps. Really advanced runs are off the higher chairs and T-bar in the form of chutes, bowls and headwalls. Beginners shouldn't fret, for they have their own area near the Village Day Lodge. Snowboarders have a couple of halfpipes and an obstacle course off to the side of the intermediate runs served by the Sundance Express. Just a warning: If you use lifts as meeting places, be aware that Sun*dance* and Sun*burst* chairs unload at different points.

Sun Peaks is known locally by its former name, Tod Mountain. The resort was named for a fur trader, John Tod. However, *Tod* in German means "Death." Because they hope to attract an international clientele, the managers decided that Sun Peaks sounded better.

Lift tickets (Cdn$): Adults in the low $40s; children in the low $20s.

Distance from Kamloops, B.C.: About 37 miles. The Kamloops airport is served by regional airlines. Drive north on Hwy. 5 to Heffley Creek, then go east for 13 miles. **Distance from Vancouver:** About 220 miles by Highways 1 and 5.

Lodging information: (800) 807-3257 for accommodations at the resort or in Kamloops.

Big White, Kelowna, BC; (250) 765-3101; (800) 663-2772

Internet: http://www.bigwhite.com

9 lifts; 2,075 acres; 2,550 vertical feet

Big White overlooks the Okanagan Valley and its 100-mile-long lake. Though it's been around for nearly 40 years, it has been only in the last decade that it has grown into resort status. About $30 million was invested during the summer of 1997 to build two hotels and expand two others. The Okanagan Valley is the hot winter destination in the West at the moment, and many advise getting here soon while it's still pretty affordable.

The mountain is big, with plenty of terrain to explore. Trails are mixed by ability level on almost every lift, so groups of all ability levels can ride together and meet at the bottom. A few lifts serve primarily one ability level—the Powder Chair serves mostly black runs, while Ridge Rocket Express has mostly blue runs under its path. Big White has a separate learning area at is base. You'll find the toughest stuff off the Alpine T-bar at the summit.

Lift tickets (Cdn$): Adults, $46; Children, $24, Goods and Services Tax (GST) included.

Distance from Kelowna, B.C.: About 34 miles east/southeast from Kelowna, which is served by regional airlines. Take Hwys. 97 and 33, and Big White Road to the Village Centre.

Distance from Vancouver: About 273 miles by Highways 97C.

Lodging information: (800) 663-2772; (250) 765-8888.

Panorama, Invermere, BC; (250) 342-6941; (800) 663-2929

Internet: http://www.panoramaresort.com

8 lifts; 2,000 acres; 4,000 vertical feet

Panorama was bought a few years ago by Intrawest Corporation, owners of several North American ski resorts, including Blackcomb. In 1997, the resort added more than than 400 acres of new skiing terrain and two new multiuse lodges in the Ski Tip Village development. Panorama is known for its high percentage of intermediate and expert runs, and, since everything is below treeline, it has an abundance of glade skiing.

One of the lifts, Quadzilla, travels nearly a mile from the base area. Continue up the Horizon chair nearly another mile to get to most of the black diamond runs. Two T-bar rides will get you to the very top. The beginner area, with a platter and a chair, is in the lowlands, away from the hubbub. First-time visitors can learn their way around with a free guide service. Nearly half the area is covered by snowmaking, and there are 22 km. of groomed cross-country trails. Sleigh rides are free.

The resort has its own village with ski-in lodging and eight restaurants.
Lift tickets (Cdn$): Adults $42, Children $21.50; Goods and Services Tax (GST) extra..
Distance from Cranbrook, B.C.: About 75 miles north on Hwy. 93. Cranbrook is served by regional air carriers. **Distance from Calgary:** The nearest major airport is about 185 miles via the Trans-Canada Highway and Hwy. 93 through Banff and Kootenay national parks. The resort is 11 miles from Invermere on Hwy. 93.
Lodging information: (250) 342-6941; (800) 663-2929 from Western Canada only. Panorama has condos and a 102-unit hotel.

Kananaskis Country, Alberta

Kananaskis Country, a 4,000-square-kilometer spread of spectacular natural countryside, is just 56 miles (90 kilometers) west of Calgary, and in the same direction as the mountain resorts of Banff and Lake Louise. The nearby Nakiska ski hill was built for the 1988 Olympic downhill ski races, and the Village at Kananaskis was added as the adjacent venue for lodging. Nearby day trips include Fortress Mountain and Nakiska for downhill skiing and the Canmore Nordic Centre.

Lodging includes the Kananaskis Hotel (251 rooms) and the Lodge at Kananaskis (68 rooms). There are a few shops, a post office, small grocery and some good restaurants. Outdoor recreation in Kananaskis Country includes downhill and cross-country skiing, sleigh rides, ice skating, tobogganing, dog sledding, snowshoeing, snowmobiling and ice fishing.

The restaurants are gourmet surprises out in the middle of a wild countryside teeming with roaming bears, elk and sheep. L'Escapade dining room at the Lodge at Kananaskis is candle-lit and semi-formal, and serves dishes such as monkfish tails, duck, lamb, venison, free-range pheasant and fork-tender Alberta beef. The Fireside Pasta Bar in the lobby of the Lodge at Kananaskis is an elegant but informal venue for light, early evening dining with pasta and salads as specialties. For a casual lunch or dinner, try Brady's Market downstairs in the shopping mall, where steamed mussels and Mediterranean pizzas are big on the menu. At Obsessions, an excellent sandwich deli in the same shopping mall, you can design your own generous sandwich from a lengthy list of ingredients. If you just can't say no to karaoke, head out after dinner to the Big Horn Lounge, which also serves appetizers and light snacks such as soups, salads, burgers, sandwiches, chips and pasta.

Canmore Nordic Centre, Canmore, Alberta

The Canmore Nordic Centre was the site of the 1988 Olympic Nordic events, and it continues to host regional, national, and international races. Just a few miles up the hill from the town of Canmore, it has 35 miles of trails. They're designed on the stacked loop system, with rest points. New trails include a 15-km. novice trail. The trails are groomed daily. There is night skiing on 2.5 km. of lit trail until 9 p.m., and lessons and rentals are available.
Trail fees: $5 for adults; $4 for ages 55+ and 12–17; $3 for ages 6–11; free younger than 6.

Fortress Mountain, Kananaskis Country, Alberta; (403) 264-5825

Internet: http://www.skifortress.com
6 lifts; 328 acres; 1,082 vertical feet

Fortress Mountain has the unusual combination of three-quarters beginner/intermediate terrain within the boundary and advanced snowcat-served skiing outside the boundary. It has the highest (6,800 feet) base elevation in the Canadian Rockies, and sits on the eastern side of the Continental Divide.

Primarily a day hill for Calgarians, a one-hour drive away, Fortress has three sides—front, back and another front beyond the back (very similar to its big-sister resort, Ski Louise). To reach the bulk of the black-diamond terrain, take the lift up from the base lodge, ski straight ahead and down from the top, and from the valley floor ride the double chair up the opposite side.

Fortress has no night skiing, but it's still very popular with families and school ski clubs. Fortress gets 180 inches of snow annually, benefitting from its peak elevation of 7,775 feet. Forty per cent of the area has snowmaking. Cat skiing (February until mid- April) costs $195 for the day, or $100 for a half day. Heliskiing is sometimes available.

If you're staying in Kananaskis Village, a smart choice since there are two deluxe Canadian Pacific hotels there, shuttle service to Fortress is complimentary and takes only 20 minutes.

Lift tickets: Adults, $32; Youth, $25; Children, $12

Distance from Calgary: 71 miles. Take Hwy. 1, drive 41 miles west of Calgary, go south on Hwy. 40 for 25 miles and take the Fortress Mountain Road for five miles.

Lodging information: (403) 591-7108. This is the number for the Fortress Mountain Lodge, which is ski in/ski out. Overnight RVs are welcome, with a charge for electric hookups. Hotel Kananaskis & the Lodge at Kananaskis: (800) 258-7669; (403) 591-7711; Fax, (403) 591-7770.

Nakiska, Kananaskis Country, Alberta, (403) 591-7777

Internet: http://www.skinakiska.com
5 lifts; 250 acres; 2,412 vertical feet

Nakiska, home of the 1988 Olympic downhill events, is 50 miles south of Banff, and is a day hill for the skiers of Calgary. The Men's Downhill run starts at 8,000 feet and is very popular with snowboarders.

Nakiska and Fortress are a 30-minute drive from each other, and since the lift tickets are interchangeable, it's easy to ski both in the same day. Shuttles from Kananaskis Village to Nakiska run on the hour.

For Nordic skiers, Nakiska offers half-day guided tours of the Ribbon Creek basin for groups of five or more.

Lift tickets: Adults, $36; Youth/Student/Senior, $29; Children $15

Distance from Calgary: 54 miles. Head west on Hwy. 1 until you can see the ski trails.

Lodging information: Hotel Kananaskis & the Lodge at Kananaskis: (800) 258-7669; (403) 591-7711; Fax, (403) 591-7770.

Eastern Canada

Mont-Sainte-Anne, Beaupré, Québec; (418) 827-4561; (800) 463-1568

Internet: http://www.mont-sainte-anne.com
12 lifts, 51 trails (400 skiable acres), 2,050 vertical feet

Mont-Sainte-Anne is just 25 miles east of Québec City, one of the most beautiful cities in North America. The resort has trails covering 38 miles rising above the St. Lawrence River. The mountain has some of the most advanced lift and ski pass systems in North America. The capacity of this lift system is nearly 18,000 skiers per hour, so it's rare to find lift lines even on weekends, when Québec seems to come en masse to ski. The lift system includes two high-speed quads (one bubble-topped) and an eight-person gondola.

The views down to the river are spectacular. The skiing is perfect for virtually every level except an expert looking for chutes and wide powder bowls. Snowmaking blankets 85 percent of the terrain.

The Children's Center offers day care for children aged 6 months and older. A Kinderski school takes learners from 3 to 6 years of age.

Dining here includes some of the finest restaurants in the province. Close to the mountain are restaurants such as La Camarine, rated among the top 10 in Québec for its progressive French cuisine; L'Alpina and Chez Baker for elegant French cuisine and Chez Albert and L'Aventure for Italian dining (L'Aventure also serves Mexican food).

Finally, Mont-Sainte-Anne has a splendid variety of off-mountain activities. Its nearby cross-country center is the largest in Canada. Dogsledding, ice skating, snowshoeing, snowmobiling and paragliding are also options.

Lift ticket prices (Cdn$): Adults, $37.38; children (7–13), $23.47. Mont-Sainte-Anne also has discounts for teens and seniors, as well as a computerized lift system that lets you pay for skiing by the run. These prices do not include taxes.

Distance from Québec City: About 25 miles by Rte. 138 to Beaupré and Rte. 360 to the resort. Mont-Sainte-Anne is about three hours east of Montréal.

Lodging information: (800) 463-1568. Mont-Sainte-Anne has many fine accommodations within steps of the lifts, plus there's a huge variety of lodging in Québec City.